A Systemic Perspective to Managing Complexity with Enterprise Architecture

Pallab Saha
National University of Singapore, Singapore

A volume in the Advances in Business
Information Systems and Analytics
(ABISA) Book Series

BUSINESS SCIENCE
Reference
An Imprint of IGI Global

Managing Director:	Lindsay Johnston
Production Manager:	Jennifer Yoder
Publishing Systems Analyst:	Adrienne Freeland
Development Editor:	Christine Smith
Acquisitions Editor:	Kayla Wolfe
Typesetter:	Lisandro Gonzalez
Cover Design:	Jason Mull

Published in the United States of America by
Business Science Reference (an imprint of IGI Global)
701 E. Chocolate Avenue
Hershey PA 17033
Tel: 717-533-8845
Fax: 717-533-8661
E-mail: cust@igi-global.com
Web site: http://www.igi-global.com

Library of Congress Cataloging-in-Publication Data

A systemic perspective to managing complexity with enterprise architecture / Pallab Saha, editor.
     pages cm
  Includes bibliographical references and index.
  Summary: "This book highlights the current advances in utilizing enterprise architecture for managing organizational complexity by demonstrating its value and usefulness"-- Provided by publisher.
  ISBN 978-1-4666-4518-9 (hardcover) -- ISBN 978-1-4666-4519-6 (ebook) -- ISBN 978-1-4666-4520-2 (print & perpetual access) 1. Information technology--Management. 2. Management information systems. 3. Computer architecture. 4. System design. 5. System theory. I. Saha, Pallab, 1970-
  HD30.2.S95175 2014
  658.4'038011--dc23

                                        2013020605

This book is published in the IGI Global book series Advances in Business Information Systems and Analytics (ABISA) (ISSN: 2327-3275; eISSN: 2327-3283)

British Cataloguing in Publication Data
A Cataloguing in Publication record for this book is available from the British Library.

For electronic access to this publication, please contact: eresources@igi-global.com.

Advances in Business Information Systems and Analytics (ABISA) Book Series

Madjid Tavana
La Salle University, USA

ISSN: 2327-3275
EISSN: 2327-3283

MISSION

The successful development and management of information systems and business analytics is crucial to the success of an organization. New technological developments and methods for data analysis have allowed organizations to not only improve their processes and allow for greater productivity, but have also provided businesses with a venue through which to cut costs, plan for the future, and maintain competitive advantage in the information age.

The **Advances in Business Information Systems and Analytics (ABISA) Book Series** aims to present diverse and timely research in the development, deployment, and management of business information systems and business analytics for continued organizational development and improved business value.

COVERAGE

- Big Data
- Business Decision Making
- Business Information Security
- Business Process Management
- Business Systems Engineering
- Data Analytics
- Data Management
- Decision Support Systems
- Management Information Systems
- Performance Metrics

IGI Global is currently accepting manuscripts for publication within this series. To submit a proposal for a volume in this series, please contact our Acquisition Editors at Acquisitions@igi-global.com or visit: http://www.igi-global.com/publish/.

Titles in this Series

For a list of additional titles in this series, please visit: www.igi-global.com

A Systemic Perspective to Managing Complexity with Enterprise Architecture
Pallab Saha (National University of Singapore, Singapore)
Business Science Reference • copyright 2014 • 554pp • H/C (ISBN: 9781466645189) • US $185.00 (our price)

Frameworks of IT Prosumption for Business Development
Małgorzata Pańkowska (University of Economics in Katowice, Poland)
Business Science Reference • copyright 2014 • 347pp • H/C (ISBN: 9781466643130) • US $185.00 (our price)

Handbook of Research on Enterprise 2.0 Technological, Social, and Organizational Dimensions
Maria Manuela Cruz-Cunha (Polytechnic Insitute of Cavado and Ave, Portugal) Fernando Moreira (Portucalense University, Portugal) and João Varajão (Universidade de Trás-os-Montes e Alto Douro, Braga, Portugal)
Information Science Reference • copyright 2014 • 943pp • H/C (ISBN: 9781466643734) • US $325.00 (our price)

Managing Enterprise Information Technology Acquisitions Assessing Organizational Preparedness
Harekrishna Misra (Institute of Rural Management Anand, India) and Hakikur Rahman (University of Minho, Portugal)
Business Science Reference • copyright 2013 • 344pp • H/C (ISBN: 9781466642010) • US $185.00 (our price)

Information Systems and Technology for Organizations in a Networked Society
Tomayess Issa (Curtin University, Australia) Pedro Isaías (Universidade Aberta, Portugal) and Piet Kommers (University of Twente, The Netherlands)
Business Science Reference • copyright 2013 • 432pp • H/C (ISBN: 9781466640627) • US $185.00 (our price)

Cases on Enterprise Information Systems and Implementation Stages Learning from the Gulf Region
Fayez Albadri (ADMO-OPCO, UAE)
Information Science Reference • copyright 2013 • 370pp • H/C (ISBN: 9781466622203) • US $185.00 (our price)

Business Intelligence and Agile Methodologies for Knowledge-Based Organizations Cross-Disciplinary Applications
Asim Abdel Rahman El Sheikh (The Arab Academy for Banking and Financial Sciences, Jordan) and Mouhib Alnoukari (Arab International University, Syria)
Business Science Reference • copyright 2012 • 370pp • H/C (ISBN: 9781613500507) • US $185.00 (our price)

IGI GLOBAL
DISSEMINATOR OF KNOWLEDGE

www.igi-global.com

701 E. Chocolate Ave., Hershey, PA 17033
Order online at www.igi-global.com or call 717-533-8845 x100
To place a standing order for titles released in this series, contact: cust@igi-global.com
Mon-Fri 8:00 am - 5:00 pm (est) or fax 24 hours a day 717-533-8661

Editorial Advisory Board

Table of Contents

Section 3
The New Science of Practice: Experiments, Cases, and Examples

Detailed Table of Contents

Section 1
Shaping Enterprise Architecture: The Next Frontier

Chapter 1

Pallab Saha, National University of Singapore, Singapore

Governments are changing by design, necessity, and compulsion. This change is being exacerbated and shaped by megaforces that interact in a complex labyrinth of evolving nodes and connections. As a result, today's government leaders and policy makers operate in a realm of confounding uncertainties and astounding complexities. These lead to incomplete and often non-actionable information that make decisions increasingly speculative. To unlock the grid and move forward, it is acknowledged that governments of the future have to be connected. Connected government is no utopia. It is simply a pragmatic approach to capitalize on complexity. Enterprise Architecture (EA) as a meta-discipline provides governments and leaders the means to address the twin challenges of dynamism and complexity. As governments become increasingly hyper-connected, they ought to be examined as systems, where holism, causality, heterarchy, and interrelationships are crucial to ensuring overall coherence in a state of omnipresent flux. This contrasts with the traditional fixation on efficiency and cost. Going beyond the rhetoric, this chapter demonstrates the value of amalgamating the systems approach within the EA methodology to address a national priority in Singapore, and provides insights to amplify the impact of EA by integrating creative thinking to tackle complex problems.

Section 2
Creating Ecologies of Innovations: Developments and Convergence

Chapter 2

Hadi Kandjani, Griffith University, Australia
Peter Bernus, Griffith University, Australia
Lian Wen, Griffith University, Australia

The concept of self-evolving/self-designing systems is defined using the notion of life cycle relationships. The authors propose that to design complex enterprises as systems of systems on each level of hierarchy one should maintain a self-designing property, that is, the designers should be part of the system. It is explained that by so distributing the design authority, under certain circumstances the "apparent complexity" of the system visible to any one designer can be reduced. To ensure the success of organised self-design, the approach uses their extension of Suh's axiomatic design theory with the "axiom of recursion." The authors quantitatively demonstrate through two examples the benefits of applying these design axioms in enterprise engineering to reduce the complexity of a system of interest, as well as the complexity of a system which designs the system of interest.

Chapter 3

Marc Rabaey, Open-Raxit, Belgium

Complex systems interact with an environment where a high degree of uncertainty exists. To reduce uncertainty, enterprises (should) create intelligence. This chapter shows that intelligence has two purposes: first, to increase and to assess (thus to correct) existing knowledge, and second, to support decision making by reducing uncertainty. The chapter discusses complex adaptive systems. Enterprises are not only complex systems; they are also most of the time dynamic because they have to adapt their goals, means, and structure to survive in the fast evolving (and thus unstable) environment. Crucial for enterprises is to know the context/ecology in which they act and operate. The Cynefin framework makes the organization and/or its parts aware of the possible contexts of the organization and/or its parts: simple, complicated, complex, chaotic, or disordered. It is crucial for the success of implementing and using EA that EA is adapted to function in an environment of perpetual change. To realize this, the chapter proposes and elaborates a new concept of EA, namely Complex Adaptive Systems Thinking – Enterprise Architecture (CAST-EA).

Chapter 4

In this chapter, the authors pose a theory for the governance of enterprise coherence. The proposed theory consists of three key ingredients: an Enterprise Coherence-governance Assessment (ECA), an Enterprise Coherence Framework (ECF), and an Enterprise Coherence Governance (ECG) approach. The ECA provides an explicit indication of the degree at which an organisation governs its coherence, while also providing a base to achieve a shared understanding of the level of coherence, and actions needed to improve it. The ECF is a practice-based framework that enables enterprises to make the coherence between key aspects, such as business, finance, culture, IT, etc. explicit. The ECG approach offers the instruments to guard/improve the level of coherence in enterprises during transformations. An important trigger to develop this new theory was the observation that many transformation projects fail. These failures even included projects that used an explicit enterprise architecture to steer the transformation. The theory was developed as part of the GEA (General Enterprise Architecting) research programme, involving twenty client organizations. Based on a survey of the possible causes for the project failures, the requirements for the research programme are identified. In developing the theory on enterprise coherence, the following hypothesis is used as a starting point: the overall performance of an enterprise is positively influenced by a strong coherence among the key aspects of the enterprise, including business processes, organizational culture, product portfolio, human resources, information systems, IT support, etc. The research programme uses a combination of design science-based iterations and case study-based research to develop and iterate the theory for enterprise coherence governance. In this chapter, the authors also discuss one of the conducted (real world) case studies, showing the application of the enterprise coherence theory.

Gone are the days when organizations were concerned with increasing efficiency by mastering repetitive tasks. The competitive, boundary-less world of today has dramatically altered the primary challenges of an organization: fluidity, coherence, and connectedness are the hallmarks of successful organizations. Concomitant with this epochal transformation is the emergence of information systems as the backbone for conducting any business. Today, one cannot find any enterprise or government that is not permeated by information systems at all levels. That the role of information systems is so central to any organization is evident from the prescient words of management legend, Peter Drucker, that the future CEO may be the CIO. With extended enterprises so very common, how do we not lose sight at the bigger picture while making decisions? Systems thinking advocates cultivation of viewing the "whole" and seeing the parts (of the whole) in the context of dependence with other parts (of the whole) and their interactions. Architecture should help create necessary artifacts to understand and manage the complexities. Developing insights on how things work together and the influence of one part over the other is at the heart of architectural conversations. There is thus a natural connect between leadership, architecture, and systems thinking. This chapter explores the nature of evolving enterprises and the increasing relevance of systems thinking in architectural activities. The author discusses the importance of systems thinking to enterprise architecture and illustrate, with TOGAF as an example, how to apply the principles of systems thinking. A conceptual case study is presented to illustrate the application of systems thinking in architectural governance.

Enterprise Architecture (EA) is a consulting practice and discipline intended to improve the management and functioning of complex organizations. The various approaches to EA can be classified by how they define what is to be architected and what, as a result, is the relevant environment. Traditionally, management has been understood as "Planning, Organizing, Command, Coordinating, and Controlling" (POCCC), that is, the role is bounded within the organization. The corresponding EA approach suggests architecting IT systems to support management, with the implicit environment being members of the organization as well as partner organizations. As the objective of EA practice expands to include organizational members, technical systems, and a wider set of stakeholders, so too does the complexity it must address. This results in an enlarged domain of issues and concerns. Finally, if the objective of EA is a sustainable enterprise, then physical, societal, and ecological environments radically increase the complexity of actualizing this goal. Corresponding to this increase in scope is a parallel shift in the scope of management concerns. With the goal of pushing EA towards concerns regarding enterprise sustainability, an open socio-technical system design perspective of EA, which we have named Enterprise-in-Environment Adaptation (EiEA), is discussed. EiEA offers a comprehensive approach to respond to the demands for complexity management that arise when working towards enterprise sustainability; yet, it requires that organisations also embrace deep culture changes, such as participative design, worker empowerment, as well as shared accountability and responsibility, to name a few.

Multiple approaches for Enterprise Architecture (EA) management are discussed in literature, many of them differing regarding the understanding of the EA as well as of the performed management activities. Applying a cybernetic point of view, the differences between these approaches can be mitigated, a more embracing perspective can be established, and fields for future research that lack support in current EA management approaches can be identified. In this work, the authors apply the Viable System Model (VSM) as reference for elaborating an overarching conceptualization of the EA management function. In comparison to the VSM reference, they discover that system five of the VSM—the identity system—is underrepresented in prevalent EA management approaches. Using a building block-based approach that makes reuse of existing best practices for EA management, the authors outline a development method that addresses the challenge of identity of an EA management function by enabling an organization-specific design thereof. The development method can be used to govern the EA management function by providing means and techniques to configure and adapt, that is, to design and to re-design an EA management function tailored to the specific situation of an organization.

Section 3
The New Science of Practice: Experiments, Cases, and Examples

The Outcome Document of the recent international diplomatic conference on sustainable development, Rio+20, portrays it as a multi-stakeholder process aimed at increasing the wellbeing of present and future generations in a dynamic, inclusive, equitable, safe, lasting, and environmentally balanced fashion, emphasizing that it should lead to poverty eradication, social development, the protection of all human rights and the elimination of human-provoked damage to the natural environment and resource-base. This reflects a highly complex process. Whereas the wording of its features and purposes exhibits considerable progress in the international policy dialogue, it appears that, among analysts, policy-makers, and practitioners around the world, there could be still large dispersion in the precise understanding of many underlying notions, the main issues, and their interrelationships. Consequently, there is not yet enough clarity among all stakeholders as to how to proceed on the implementation of coherent and coordinated strategies and policies for sustainable development. This chapter presents an analytical framework to look at these matters from a systemic perspective, with the intention of inspiring non-specialists to consider the advantages of the Enterprise Architecture approach to generate more clarity, facilitate communication, enhance policy coherence, and foster cooperation and partnerships for improving sustainable development. Some practical uses of the systems approach to enhance strategy, organization, and management for sustainable development are suggested.

This chapter augments current Enterprise Architecture (EA) frameworks to become pattern-based. The main motivation behind pattern-based EA is the support for strategic decisions based on the patterns prioritized in a country or industry. Thus, to validate the need for pattern-based EA, it is essential to show how different patterns gain priority under different contexts, such as industries. To this end, this chapter also reveals the value of alternative managerial strategies across different industries and business functions in a specific market, namely Turkey. Value perceptions for alternative managerial strategies were collected via survey, and the values for strategies were analyzed through the rigorous application of statistical techniques. Then, evidence was searched and obtained from business literature that support or refute the statistically supported hypothesis. The results obtained through statistical analysis are typically confirmed with reports of real world cases in the business literature. Results suggest that Turkish firms differ significantly in the way they value different managerial strategies. There also exist differences based on industries and business functions. The study provides guidelines to managers in Turkey, an emerging country, on which strategies are valued most in their industries. This way, managers can have a better understanding of their competitors and business environment and can develop the appropriate pattern-based EA to cope with complexity and succeed in the market.

Chapter 10

Edward M. Newman, National Defense University, USA

The purpose of the chapter is to provide clarity on what a Federated Enterprise Architecture (FEA) is and what the benefits as well as risks are in contrast to a non-federated enterprise architecture. The chapter draws upon organizational theory, federalist theory, and case studies to explicate what constitutes a federated model and the expected federated EA benefits. There are a number of challenges with the concept of a FEA. Two are focused on in this chapter: the meaning of federated EA and associated benefits and risks. The first is the use of the term "federated," which occurs rather frequently in ICT literature, such as "federated search" or "federated database design," and in the context of IT governance, "federal model" in Drs. Weill and Ross's book IT Governance. The term also appears in the non-ICT context such as "federated insurance." However, the term "federated" is frequently not defined and when defined speaks to a decentralization concept. This distinction is relevant to the understanding and success of a federated EA implementation. In reviewing federalist theory, there is a clear difference between decentralization and federalism. It is argued that the so-called federal or federated "model," as described, is not federated but is a form of decentralization. The second challenge within the EA discipline is the lack of benefits attributed to a FEA. In the few sources that exist for FEA benefits are either not stated or the stated benefits could equally apply to a non-FEA. It is argued that scalability is the singular key benefit that FEA provides over a non-FEA, and the following non-FEA benefits are enhanced: 1) agility and IT innovation, 2) process consolidation and business process standardization and discipline, and 3) interoperability. However, while there are clear benefits to FEA, there are inherent risks.

Chapter 11

Torben Tambo, Aarhus University, Denmark
Lars Bækgaard, Aarhus University, Denmark

Services are fundamental to the provisioning of business activities. Enterprise Architecture (EA) is maintaining the relationship between strategy, business, and technology. A clear definition and agreed understanding of services is critical to realising information technology artefacts. Services, however, tend to be more complex than the mere act of interaction or working processes, and should be seen out of the cultural, organisational, and managerial factors surrounding them. This chapter uses a service model consisting of execution, context, and intention with an underlying claim that all three elements must be present to make services meaningful. EA must be seen in the light of this. This chapter addresses the issues related to combined transformation of organisations, service systems, and consequently, EA. The transformation changes loosely coupled, distributed organisations into Shared Service Centres (SSCs). A case study of a far-reaching SSC transformation from Denmark is presented where eGovernment services are moved from local government level into a national SSC structure referred to as Udbetaling Danmark (lit. PayDK). Major findings include: (1) When eGovernment reaches a certain level of maturity, it dissolves its original reason and no longer follows a progressive maturity model. Instead, it leads to a more radical reorganisation emphasising operational efficiency. (2) Development and management of complexities and uncertainties in governmental administrative services are closely associated with the development of eGovernment through ongoing refinement of EA and service frameworks. (3) The policy-driven reshaping of governmental services, originally themselves being SSCs, can lead to iterative SSC formations, each seeking to establish a professional logic of its own. (4) The systemic perception connected to EA and service science provides valuable insight into service transformation before, during, and after the transformation. This chapter aims at a deeper understanding and discussion of services in developing eGovernment policies and architectures, but findings are readily applicable in general business environments.

Enterprises are like living creatures in the ecosystem – there are vast varieties of species; each individual in any species is unique, complex, dynamic, and constantly interacting with its ever-changing environment. Also, like living creatures, enterprises have many commonalities. These commonalities exist in all enterprises, regardless of their business, size, environment, culture, lifecycle stage, or any other factor. Enterprise Architecture (EA) management helps enterprises discover their commonalities, adopt best practices to manage the commonalities, and apply holistic and systemic approaches to tackling unique complexity encountered by enterprises. This chapter extracts thinking from many thought leaders in the EA discipline and consolidates a dynamic and multi-dimensional alignment approach to managing an enterprise's architecture as a living system. This integrated approach utilizes the "Fractal" concept in Chaos Theory and identifies six common alignment dimensions in enterprises. This approach includes dynamic alignment mechanisms to help enterprises navigate the increasingly complex and ever-changing world. This approach bridges individual alignments with enterprise optimization. A fictional example of a disaster relief operation is used to illustrate how the EA approach could help a relief enterprise navigate through the complexity and dynamics of the disaster relief operation to achieve life-saving results.

This chapter outlines the rational foundations of the enterprise architecture discipline to date and describes ways and situations in which the traditional approaches of enterprise architecture fail to account for a number of contemporary market and economic situations and organizational behaviors. It characterizes new methods and approaches loosely based on systems thinking, with examples from the Australian e-government experience, and argues that the discipline must re-invent itself to incorporate a post-rational perspective to stay relevant. The chapter concludes with narratives of how the new enterprise architecture must engage with business to stay relevant over the next decade and beyond.

Enterprise Architecture (EA) can be thought of as a powerful tool to transform electricity (distribution) utilities into more service-oriented and also economically viable enterprises, if not sustainable enterprises (spanning the so-called triple-bottom-line, viz., profits, people, planet). Developing regions (such as India) face even greater challenges than global concerns about electricity. Developing regions' utilities are often loss making and have numerous operational challenges (including high theft and a weak/unstable grid). They also face a populace with limited means to pay (putting pressures on pricing) but also a large swath of potential consumers whom they have not yet reached. The rise of Information and Communications Technology (ICT) offers the ability to know what (and how much) is going where, with high time and geographic precision, covering not merely flows of electricity but also money, information, control, manpower, etc. More than converting data into information, it can lead to improved decision-making ("knowledge" and "wisdom"). Ultimately, harnessing ICT not only speeds up processes, but also transforms the enterprise. The widest-reaching form of EA transformation has been called a Smart Grid, an ongoing transformation of utilities worldwide. EA done right is complex, but so is electricity distribution. Instead of hiding or ignoring complexities, EA internalizes them into the decision-making process. While decision-makers cannot ignore issues of political economy, an Enterprise Architecture lens focuses on incentives, operations, and planning important for all enterprises independent of public versus private ownership.

Foreword

The English verb "to manage" was originally derived from the Italian maneggiare, meaning to handle and train horses.... The emphasis is on learning with, abiding with, adapting to, respecting, and working with another complex entity: the horse and rider as co-evolving brambles in a wider thicket of social traditions surrounding beauty and form. Around the early 18th century, this original meaning merged with the French term ménage, or household, making it easier to adapt the meaning of the combined term manage to the metaphor of the obedient machine, to the corridors of power, and to the actions of controlling and directing. (Williams, 1983)

This book comes at a timely moment in the development of enterprise architecture as a discipline. The levels of uncertainty, interconnectivity, and speed of change facing all organisations can seem overwhelming. This has too often resulted in an attempt to eliminate complexity by creating controllable and manageable structures. Enterprise architecture has been defined by Gartner (n.d.) as "a discipline for proactively and holistically leading enterprise responses to disruptive forces by identifying and analyzing the execution of change toward desired business vision and outcomes." Under this definition, the role is less that of the architect and more of the draughtsman. The vision and the outcomes are given; the role of the architect is to create the frameworks, models, and processes to realise that vision.

This represents a linear model of causality, even considered systematically. As commonly practiced, in particular in its manifestation in process engineering and six-sigma, the assumption of a knowable future state, a desirable and measurable set of outcomes, has become a dominant belief system. Management in this context is about controlling and directing the imposition of order in a vain attempt to eliminate uncertainty. The dominant metaphor is one of a machine that can be engineered. The assertion is that complexity can be eliminated by good management.

The reality is very different. We have a growing set of insights from complex adaptive systems theory that indicate a large part of this complexity is inherent to the nature of interactions and constraints within the system. If it cannot be eliminated it has to be absorbed. A complex system is non-linear in nature; it has dispositions, but is not causal in the conventional sense of that word; the same thing only happens again the same way twice by accident. Such systems are modulated by constraints and interventions as a result of which patterns of meaning emerge over time. The metaphor is that of ecology not a machine.

The role of the systems architect is radically changed by the application of complex adaptive systems theory. The old responsibilities and methods are not abandoned, but their use is now confined to those aspects of a system that have sufficient sustainable constraints in play to create a level of predictability.

It is now about creating a structure in which applications can emerge from multiple interactions over time. It requires the business equivalent of planting grass in an open space and seeing where people walk before investing in building paths. Of course, the direction can be influenced, but it cannot be controlled.

Social computing provides a model for this. Multiple applications operate within a general set of constraints that enable interaction. A modern desktop or smart phone carries with it a fragmented, messily coherent set of applications that can be substituted as needed and tailored for individual use. Standards often emerge based on practice; safe-to-fail experiments are the order of the day. The result is a resilient, flexible system able to handle the unanticipated.

Learning that lesson is key for systems architecture. We cannot afford the high level of constraint that has characterized the last few decades, but neither can we descend into anarchy. We need to think of management and by implication design in the context of the original *maneggiare* not the command and control capabilities of a machine.

David John Snowden
Cognitive Edge, UK
2013

REFERENCES

Gartner. (n.d.). *Enterprise architecture*. Retrieved from http://www.gartner.com/it-glossary/enterprise-architecture-ea/

Williams, R. (1983). *Keywords: A vocabulary of culture and society*. London: Fontanta Press.

David John Snowden *is a Welsh academic, consultant and researcher in the field of knowledge management. He is the founder and chief scientific officer of Cognitive Edge, a research network focusing on complexity theory in sensemaking. Snowden, an authority on the application of complexity theory to organisations, tacit knowledge, and an observer in the way knowledge is used in organisations, has written articles and scholarly works on leadership, knowledge management, strategic thinking, strategic planning, conflict resolution, weak signal detection, decision support, and organisational development. He holds an MBA from Middlesex University, and a BA in Philosophy from Lancaster University; and started his active career life with Data Sciences Ltd (formerly Thorn EMI software), acquired by IBM in 1996. He was the Director of IBM's Institute for Knowledge Management and the founder of the Cynefin Center for Organizational Complexity. Snowden developed the Cynefin framework, a practical application of complexity theory to management science. Snowden joined as a visiting professor at the University of Pretoria in 2007. He is currently an adjunct at the Hong Kong Polytechnic University and a visiting fellow at Warwick University, Nanyang University, the Università Cattolica, and the Singapore Management University. He has held visiting positions at the universities of Canberra and Surrey.*

Preface

The mainstreaming of enterprise architecture as a management discipline is well underway. This is a far cry from the earlier notion of it being used as an IT planning methodology. In other words, enterprise architecture is being re-architected, re-shaped, and re-configured. A *Harvard Business Review* paper in June 2012 identifies architecture as one of the pre-requisites to effective leadership. Much has been discussed, debated, and written about how the traditional avatar of enterprise architecture tends to be highly IT-centric and IT-driven. While IT itself is becoming more ubiquitous and democratized, the role of the IT department in the context of enterprise architecture has never been openly contested. Most of today's enterprise architects are not able to convincingly articulate the value they bring to enterprises. As a result, they are marginalized, and their opinions and views are not sought during critical business decisions. In addition, being tucked away inside IT departments exacerbates the situation even further. Most current enterprise architects are primarily Senior IT Managers with glorified job titles of "enterprise architects." They lack the influence to architect enterprises in the truest sense. Lack of influence makes enterprise architects inward-oriented and isolated, thereby amplifying this vicious circle.

Enterprises are no longer grappling to have access to the latest technologies; harnessing technology to enable business outcomes is a given. Emergence and confluence of several mega-trends are exposing enterprises to unprecedented levels of complexities. Therefore, it is only natural that when enterprises are exposed to complexities they become complex themselves. In today's world, no one enterprise (organizations, governments, and even nations) can hope to thrive in total isolation completely insulated from the ensuing complexities. This then elevates the importance of tackling complexities as a critical success factor in ensuring sustained growth, long-term impact, and effective leadership. The role of enterprise architecture in making this happen cannot be overstated.

As a supra-departmental activity, enterprise architecture is on the cusp of change. It is increasingly being viewed as a method to comprehend enterprise complexities and suggest interventions to tackle such complexities. In other words, enterprise architecture is being adopted with the intent and aim of managing enterprise complexity. This thinking resonates well with the senior leadership as managing complexity has indeed surfaced as the single most important management priority. The fact that enterprise architecture (and enterprise architects) provides the potential to demonstrate the ability to address this priority takes them to some sort of rarefied strata in terms of impact and influence. This is hugely different from traditional enterprise architects, who in most cases have difficulty in gaining access to true enterprise level architecture and getting appropriate and continued management attention.

While using enterprise architecture as the method to tackle complexity makes sense, it is also crucial to understand that such an approach has to be anchored around compelling business priorities. This enables enterprise architects to focus and direct their energy to something that the enterprise sees as important. This book represents the first formal work of literature in this seminal area. The aim is to elevate the level of maturity of enterprise architecture discipline and practice. It is achieved through a compilation of chapters covering theory, concepts, examples, and case studies in a balanced manner. The chapters were selected carefully and reviewed for consistency to the book's overall message. Beyond advocacy, this book aims to encourage original thinking, demonstrate current advancements, and even highlight gaps or areas requiring further work.

This book is structured into three sections, consisting of fourteen chapters in all. The chapters were carefully selected after being subjected to a rigorous review process spearheaded by the Editorial Advisory Board (EAB). In addition to rigor, relevance, and applicability, I have also attempted to make the book representative of the different regions in the world. This selection is deliberate as it allows readers insights into a multitude of country-specific challenges, peculiarities, and nuances. It is obvious such initiatives would be ongoing activities, thus the chapters represent snapshots in time, representing the current state of practice. The following paragraphs provide an overview and summary of book sections and chapters:

SECTION 1: SHAPING ENTERPRISE ARCHITECTURE: THE NEXT FRONTIER

This first section, consisting of one chapter, aims to provide the genesis to the entire book. Chapter 1, "Systemic Enterprise Architecture as Future: Tackling Complexity in Governments in the Cusp of Change," introduces the concept of a strategic systems-based approach to enterprise architecture, discusses enterprise complexity and how this impacts enterprises, and elaborates how systemic enterprise architecture provides the mechanism for enterprises to tackle such complexities. This is accomplished through a detailed case study from the healthcare sector in Singapore. The primary motivation for this chapter is to position systemic enterprise architecture as a more pragmatic approach to effective and impactful business outcomes. The chapter goes into detail with elaborate descriptions taking enterprise architecture to the next level of maturity. To establish the framework for greater adoption and capability development, this chapter culminates with ten broad principles of systemic enterprise architecture. This is deliberate because the subsequent chapters have been logically sequenced to demonstrate the realization of these principles by way of new theories, concepts, and case studies.

SECTION 2: CREATING ECOLOGIES OF INNOVATIONS: DEVELOPMENTS AND CONVERGENCE

Consisting of six chapters, this section aims to establish the theoretical foundations of systemic enterprise architecture. Chapter 2 "Enterprise as Complex Systems: Extended Axiomatic Design Theory and its Application in Enterprise Architecture Practice," builds on the primary notion introduced in Chapter 1 (i.e. enterprises are complex adaptive systems). Typically, leaders and architects tend to detest this concept of enterprises being both complex and dynamic, wherein ambiguity, interdependence, diversity, and flux are the norms. Current management theories and practices prefer to ignore these fundamental traits found in all enterprises. Enterprises are approximated as complicated yet predictable entities and architected and operated accordingly. Chapter 2 demonstrates why enterprises are (and should be) considered as system-of-systems, and their design should be part of this system. Using an extension of Suh's axiomatic design theory, Chapter 2 shows how complexity is tackled by adopting self-design at each level of hierarchy.

Chapter 3, "Complex Adaptive Systems Thinking Approach to Enterprise Architecture," corroborates the ten principles of systemic enterprise architecture from Chapter 1, by proposing a *Complex Adaptive Systems Thinking – Enterprise Architecture* approach. The efficacy of this approach is evidenced in its ability to comprehend and reduce uncertainty by creating intelligence. This is critical, as uncertainty is a source of risk. The proposed approach in this chapter successfully weaves in the Cynefin framework and makes an effort to explicitly differentiate complicated and complex systems (usually used interchangeably and incorrectly). The CAST-EA approach successfully leads to double and triple loop learning in enterprises.

As is evident from the definition of enterprise architecture in Chapter 1, creating and sustaining coherent enterprises is the preeminent goal, Chapter 4, "A Theory for Enterprise Coherence Governance," presents and discusses an approach to govern enterprise coherence. This is actualized using three essential steps; firstly, by evaluating the degree to which enterprises govern their coherence; secondly, by explicitly establishing coherence between different elements such as business, finance, and culture, among others; and finally by gauging and improving enterprise coherence during major transformation initiatives. The theory proposed in this chapter was created with the involvement of twenty organizations and, therefore, is validated for practical applicability.

Chapter 5, "Architecture Leadership and Systems Thinking," reiterates the centrality to systems thinking in the context of enterprise architecture. It is critical for leaders to embrace *holistic* perspectives and propagate this throughout the enterprise. Too often business leaders and management are busy within their own silo of the enterprise, mostly at the cost of completely ignoring how their *silo* is inter-connected to the rest of the enterprise. They exhibit the classic trait of being *micro-smart* and *macro-dumb*, which time and again creates conflicting requirements and competition for resources and management attention. Chapter 5 demystifies systemic enterprise architecture using TOGAF as an example coupled with a conceptual case study. The choice of TOGAF is deliberate, as it is by far the most popular of the current enterprise architecture framework that is also vendor agnostic. The chapter demonstrates the realization of *boundary-less enterprise* through the adoption of systemic enterprise architecture.

The scope and nature enterprise architecture typically varies, usually depending on the desired goal. This means that the environment or the ecosystem that is relevant to the enterprise also varies. When enterprise architecture initiatives move above and beyond IT to include other critical aspects, it creates a larger set of stakeholders, conflicting interests, and radical increases in the overall complexity to be tackled. It increases the number and nature of business and management concerns that enterprise architecture needs to contend with. Chapter 6, "Enterprise-in-Environment Adaptation: Enterprise Architecture and Complexity Management," posits the EiEA approach to respond to the increased demand for complexity management and elaborates the cultural changes enterprises need to embrace in order to effectively steer architecture initiatives with larger footprints.

Chapter 7, "A Systemic View on Enterprise Architecture Management: State of the Art and Outline of a Building Block-Based Approach to Design Specific Enterprise Architecture Management Functions," looks into the issue of multiple approaches to enterprise architecture management that exists in the literature today. A plethora of such practices leads to inconsistency and absence of convergence. Obviously, each approach may have their own group of enthusiasts who proclaim its superiority (over others). This chapter presents a building block-based approach making use of some of the current best practices in enterprise architecture. Building blocks enable modularization and allow enterprises to choose, configure, and adapt their architecture management to suit specific requirements and expectations. This way of tailoring assumes there is no one-size-fits-all when it comes to architecture management and that the enterprises need to be given the flexibility and capability to shape architecture management practices according to their requirements.

SECTION 3: THE NEW SCIENCE OF PRACTICE: EXPERIMENTS, CASES, AND EXAMPLES

Building on from the theories and concepts in the previous section, this section presents cases and examples to give insights into the current state of practice. The cases and examples covered in this section span multiple industries and sectors. This is deliberate, as it provides a better grasp of the finer nuances of the discipline to all readers. Consisting of the next seven chapters, this section starts with Chapter 8, "Enterprise Architecture of Sustainable Development: An Analytical Framework," which uses sustainable development as the use case to demonstrate the benefits of enterprise architecture. This example is particularly useful because the notion of sustainability brings forth a multitude of stakeholders, their conflicting (and vested) interests, existence of diversity, inter-dependence, ambiguity and flux, operations that work in an heterarchical mode, little direct authority, and emergence. In other words, almost all characteristic traits described in Chapter 1 are seen in action in this example. This chapter shows the use of enterprise architecture as the means to bring in more clarity, facilitate communication, foster cooperation and partnerships, and ultimately enhance policy coherence. Policy coherence is an important building block towards enterprise coherence.

Chapter 9, "Competitive Pattern-Based Strategies under Complexity: The Case of Turkish Managers," demonstrates how current enterprise architecture frameworks and practices can be strengthened and made more effective by becoming more pattern-based. The objective of incorporating patterns is to create conditions to make better strategic decisions. This chapter discusses the pattern-based enterprise architecture approach in Turkey. Derived from primary data collected through a survey and subjected to rigorous statistical analysis, the chapter provides guidelines for business managers, with the purpose being a better understanding of the competition, the overall business landscape, and more effective strategies. In short, this chapter facilitates better strategic thinking crucial to management of business complexity.

Over the years, it has been seen that *dictatorial* or a purely *compliance-based approach* to enterprise architecture seldom sustains. This can primarily be attributed to its misfit with organizational realities and its difficulty in inclusion of emerging complexities. In other words, such approaches tend to be more suited to *simple* enterprises that operate in a strictly hierarchical manner. In the same context, federated approaches are gaining ground because of the advantages they bring to the table and their suitability to deal with business complexities. However, current literature seems to be equating federation with decentralization, which the chapter dispels. This is where the Chapter 10, "Federated Enterprise Architecture: Meaning, Benefits, and Risks," comes in. The chapter clearly explains federation is a model of governance and contrasts it with decentralization. The chapter then elaborates the rationale of, benefits derived from, implications of, and risks introduced by adopting the federated approach to enterprise architecture. It argues why the federated approach is potentially the most effective mechanism to deal with scalability issues when enterprises factored in are large and by right complex.

Chapter 11, "Transitioning to Government Shared Service Centers: A Systems View," is a transformation case study from Denmark. Usually government enterprise architectures overly focus on government processes and how efficiently they can be automated, making the entire business architecture very operational and transactional in nature. Moving away from processes to services is easier said than done, as it entails a complete change of mindset. A service includes other soft and often subjective, yet critical factors like culture, organization, and management. It goes beyond mere transaction and looks into citizen or customer engagement. Therefore, an aggregation of several factors raises complexity. This chapter elaborates on all of these issues and goes further in recommending changes that need to be brought in the way policies are crafted and implemented. This is where embracing a systems view brings in advantages and benefits and makes government transformation more desirable and outcome-based.

Disaster-relief presents a unique set of characteristics. By its very nature, it is a time-sensitive, highly intense activity that demands well-orchestrated actions and has the potential to impact people and their lives. Coordination and ability to *think-outside-the-box* play a critical role because of the inherent unpredictability. At times, it may seem as though the whole operation is very chaotic, wherefore agility is crucial. Chapter 12, "Navigating Complexity with Enterprise Architecture Management," shows why adopting a holistic and systemic approach during disaster-relief can make a very significant difference. This chapter uses the *fractal* concept in chaos theory to identify six common alignment dimensions in enterprises. The chapter demonstrates how enterprises can then utilize these alignment dimensions to anchor the architecture management activities. All of these unique interesting aspects are explained with an illustration of disaster-relief.

Chapter 13, "Enterprise Architecture's Identity Crisis: New Approaches to Complexity for a Maturing Discipline," argues that even though enterprise architecture as a discipline has traditionally emerged from IT, and has been used to build and manage better IT systems, it is time for enterprise architecture to grow and spread its wings to the entire enterprise. This is consistent with the first of the ten guidelines of systemic enterprise architecture presented in Chapter 1. Chapter 13 presents the case of the criticality of managing complexity as the biggest reason for enterprise architecture. The chapter lists activities like design, synthesis, design-thinking, perspective, and problem negotiation as primary capabilities for enterprises to be able to manage complexity. It then elaborates these ideas with examples from Australia's electronic government experience. The chapter concludes with a list of to-dos that enterprise architecture must include as a discipline to continue to stay relevant for the next decade and beyond. This chapter is a unique blend of several aspects of the journey of enterprise architecture as a discipline and reiterates key points from earlier chapters.

Chapter 14, "Growing Complexity and Transformations of the Power Sector: India as an Example of Developing Regions using Enterprise Architecture and Smart Grids," the final chapter of the book, expands the scope of the *enterprise* to an entire sector, not limited to a single organization. Chapter 14 is an in-depth case study of the use of enterprise architecture as a means to transform power distribution in India. The uniqueness of this case study comes from the fact that large emerging economies exhibit very distinctive characteristics. The entire production (generation), transmission, and distribution activities are often not economically viable. Their operations and profitability are constrained by the consumers' limited ability to pay for services; yet given the social dimension involved, they cannot be denied electricity (like healthcare presented in Chapter 1 and disaster-relief in Chapter 12). The chapter presents *Smart Grid* as one of the promising solutions to address some (if not all) of problems and constraints plaguing the power distribution companies. That said, adoption of Smart Grid demands changes and deep reforms in how the power is distributed. The entire value network needs an overhaul. Balancing distributor and consumer priorities is paramount, and Smart Grids is plausibly the most pragmatic solution to this complex problem.

In being the first book that views management of complexity as the rationale to embrace a systemic perspective to enterprise architecture, this is a seminal work. The compilation, besides balancing theory and practice, reveals the current state of art in this area. As the chief editor, I view this book as a beginning to a new era in the life of enterprise architecture. My vision is shared and supported by the authors, who contributed their high-quality chapters. I hope and sincerely expect that this book will spur further work by sparking curiosity.

Pallab Saha
National University of Singapore, Singapore
2013

Acknowledgment

These are exciting times for enterprise architecture and enterprise architects. The discipline is on a cusp of change, and this is being reflected in the way old (traditional) mental models are being challenged and reshaped. I have had the privilege of interacting with some of the finest in the business and polishing my thinking and skills, which in some ways led me to conceive this book in the first place. In certain ways, I used the social media channels to propose new ideas, to which I received feedback and criticism. The realization that a book like this is necessary and will make the required impact and contribution to current literature came about when a discussion I posted on *LinkedIn* went viral. That said, the book had to be a team effort, and my intent was to bring top academics, serious practitioners, and inspirational creators into this single platform as a coherent team.

First, I would like to thank IGI Global for (again) giving me the opportunity to continue my wonderful collaboration with them. This is my fourth book with them, and it has been a great partnership so far.

Secondly, I would like to thank all the contributing chapter authors. Their contributions have been invaluable. They are all well experienced and respected experts representing both academia and practice.

Last but not the least, the contribution of the Editorial Advisory Board (EAB) cannot be overstated. These are globally recognized experts who took time off their busy schedules to review chapters, provide constructive feedback, and improve the overall quality of chapters. The EAB played a crucial role in enhancing the quality of the book. Interacting with them over the years has enriched my understanding in many ways.

The authors and the members of the EAB had to deal with my often-aggressive deadlines and nagging reminders. They have been wonderful partners in this journey with an outstanding spirit of cooperation and a shared vision of success of this book.

This book would not have become a reality without the blessings of my mother, Shrimati Anima Saha, and my father, Late Shri Jagatbandhu Saha. I thank Neeta, my wife, for her love, support, and patience while this was being written. A special word of love goes to our most adorable daughter, Anushka. Neeta and I were blessed with Anushka when I started working on my first book, and with this fifth book, she is now in Primary 2.

Pallab Saha
National University of Singapore, Singapore

Section 1

Shaping Enterprise Architecture:
The Next Frontier

Chapter 1
Systemic Enterprise Architecture as Future:
Tackling Complexity in Governments in the Cusp of Change

Pallab Saha
National University of Singapore, Singapore

ABSTRACT

Governments are changing by design, necessity, and compulsion. This change is being exacerbated and shaped by megaforces that interact in a complex labyrinth of evolving nodes and connections. As a result, today's government leaders and policy makers operate in a realm of confounding uncertainties and astounding complexities. These lead to incomplete and often non-actionable information that make decisions increasingly speculative. To unlock the grid and move forward, it is acknowledged that governments of the future have to be connected. Connected government is no utopia. It is simply a pragmatic approach to capitalize on complexity. Enterprise Architecture (EA) as a meta-discipline provides governments and leaders the means to address the twin challenges of dynamism and complexity. As governments become increasingly hyper-connected, they ought to be examined as systems, where holism, causality, heterarchy, and interrelationships are crucial to ensuring overall coherence in a state of omnipresent flux. This contrasts with the traditional fixation on efficiency and cost. Going beyond the rhetoric, this chapter demonstrates the value of amalgamating the systems approach within the EA methodology to address a national priority in Singapore, and provides insights to amplify the impact of EA by integrating creative thinking to tackle complex problems.

INTRODUCTION

The interior department is in charge of salmon while they're in fresh water, but the commerce department handles them when they're in saltwater. And I hear, it gets even more complicated once they're smoked. - President Barack Obama, 2012

DOI: 10.4018/978-1-4666-4518-9.ch001

Governments around the world are faced with new demands, expectations and challenges in delicately balancing often conflicting requirements. These are further being exacerbated by nearly uncontrolled information flows enabled by massive advances in information technology (APCICT, 2011). Many countries are in the midst of unprecedented economic and political changes, at times even bordering on crisis situations. These provide the ideal fodder for ballooning trust deficit between governments and their citizenries. The governments' ability to provide clean, transparent and development-oriented governance is being questioned like never before. The perception of the inability of governments to provide better governance is dominant, particularly in key areas like – crime, education, healthcare, sustainable economic growth, transportation, wellness and welfare. The delicate nexus between governments, citizens, civil society, businesses and other stakeholders is being subjected to tremendous pressures and tensions, often contributing to the role of the government itself being redefined and even reinvented (Chapman, 2004). This labyrinth of factors is leading to growing disillusionment and approaching the danger point. Additionally, the people and civil services are becoming increasingly vocal in their objection to government policies, ever-increasing administrative loads and the plummeting quality of government services. In the United Nations (UN) e-government survey of 2012, the need for a holistic approach to governance, which integrates factors pertaining to the efficiency and distributional aspects of sectoral policies, has been identified (UNDESA, 2012). The holistic approach to government and government services are acquiescent to and consistent with the expectations from greater adoption of ICT (APDIP, 2007a, 2007b). The survey brings forth three crucial strategies to achieve the holistic perspective:

- Recognize the opportunity for synergy among institutions that deliver government services.
- Reengineer the enabling ecosystem of government services to actualize inter-institutional linkages within the government.
- Advance coordination and connectivity between ecosystems and development outcomes.

Though this has been a common thread across the UN e-government surveys in 2008 and 2010, the 2012 survey clearly identifies the mega-trends in e-government, which include the increasing acceptance of whole-of government (W-O-G) paradigm in architecting and delivering government services, the importance of embracing multi-channel service delivery perspective, factoring in the prevalence of digital divide in certain countries, fulfilling ever increasing demands from citizens and pushing for an inclusive approach (UNDESA, 2008, 2010, 2012). To move forward, the recommendations from the survey include recognizing the transformative nature of e-government when embracing a W-O-G perspective, shifting from structurally disintegrated forms of government to one that is more connected, collaborative, and coherent, to ensure that the digital divide does not remain an insurmountable obstacle and fulfil the need to reach out to all citizens, particularly the disadvantaged and vulnerable groups (CISCO IBSG, 2004).

THE FUTURE OF GOVERNMENT

The World Economic Forum (WEF) in its report in 2011 provided ample insights into how governments of the future would be (WEF, 2011a, 2011b). Interestingly, the recommendations are closely aligned and consistent with the strategies shown in the UN e-government survey of 2012, which were briefly mentioned earlier in this chapter. According to WEF, governments will necessarily have to be:

- Networked that connects governments, businesses, citizens, NGOs and the civil society at multiple scales and levels; hence for governments it is crucial to build the capacity to operate effectively in complex, interdependent networks of enterprises and systems across the public, private and non-profit sectors to operate effectively in order to co-produce value.

- Collaborative by design, as effective sharing of best practices will be needed to enable public sector innovation; the cornerstone of governments will be networked governance, transparency, collaboration, participation and co-innovation.
- Operationalized by transformed civil services resulting from modernization initiatives that will change the way in which the civil services are perceived; the modernized civil service will embrace technology and will be closely interconnected with the citizens in matters of policy implementation.
- Measured and evaluated by the various stakeholders in terms of their ability to operate in a holistic and coherent manner with multi-stakeholder partnerships as the new normal, which cares of citizens from all economic and social classes and is inclusive by default.

Unlike governments today, the governments in the future will be forced to adopt a service centric view and organize themselves around critical service themes (WEF, 2011a, 2011b). The concept of service themes will facilitate the increasing focus on networked form of operations that is common both to the WEF and UN e-government survey findings. Figure 1 depicts an indicative list of service themes.

The service themes will necessitate deep collaboration, information sharing, efficient processes, co-innovation, co-production, transparency and holistic operating models both, within and between governments (CISCO IBSG, 2009). This will happen because governments will be evaluated using quality of life metrics, as also shown in Figure 1. The massive transformational change sweeping across many countries is the shift from traditional form of government (called Government 1.0) to a more networked form of government (metaphorically called Government 2.0). Figure 2 depicts the major characteristics of the evolution of governments (Halstead et al.,

Figure 1. Indicative service themes and performance areas for governments

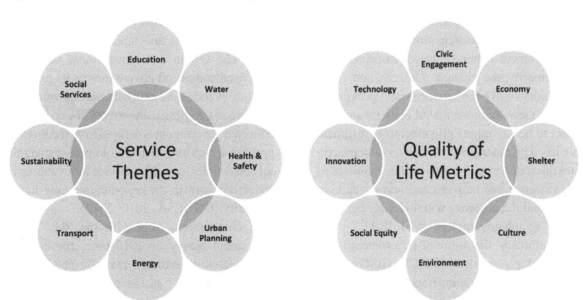

Figure 2. Governments in the cusp of change

Dimension	Government 1.0	Government 2.0
Operating model	• Hierarchical • Rigid	• Networked • Collaborative • Flexible
New models of service delivery	• One-size-fits-all • Monopoly • Single channel	• Personalized • Choice-based • Multi-channel
Performance-driven	• Input-oriented • Closed	• Outcome-driven • Transparent
Decision-making	• Spectator	• Participate

2009). In most countries, some elements of evolution have taken place, some are in the process of transformation. Given the complexities involved due to the scale of change, this is an ongoing journey.

This shift in the business of government is also evident in the nature of the findings and recommendations provided by the UN e-government surveys across 2008, 2010, and 2012 (UNDESA, 2008, 2010, 2012). The principal reason through which this shift is being manifested and realized is in the intensity of participation (in governments and government matters) by the various stakeholders, primarily the citizens. Citizens and other stakeholders will become more vocal in expressing their views on government matters, and will expect to be key inputs providers to government policies. The emergence of social media exacerbates this transformation even further. Interactions and conversations between and across the civil society and the citizenry will no longer be "controlled" by the government (WEF, 2011).

In summary, the future of government is the connected government (CISCO IBSG, 2004; WEF, 2011) Of paramount importance is that this shift will be expected and demanded by various stakeholders. However as a caveat, governments will face several challenges in making this gradual but inevitable shift to connected government, which are discussed in subsequent sections.

CONNECTED GOVERNMENT: THE GENESIS

Connected government enables governments to connect seamlessly across functions, agencies and jurisdictions to deliver effective and efficient services to citizens and businesses (UNDESA, 2008). The UN in its e-government survey of 2008, used connected governance as its primary criteria to evaluate and rank national e-government programs. According to the survey, the concept of connected government is derived from the W-O-G approach which utilizes technology as a strategic tool and enabler for public service innovation and productivity growth, the key outcome being digital prosperity (UNDESA, 2010, 2012).

In continuation of this theme, the UN e-government survey of 2010 takes the concept of connected government even further, adding, "citizen centricity" as the primary watchword (UNDESA, 2010). This approach to government service delivery requires countries to shift from a model of providing government services via traditional modes to integrate electronic modes wherein the value to the citizens and businesses gets enhanced. According to the UN, such IT-enabled services (e-services) can actually improve the rate and quality of public service delivery in times of economic crises (APDIP, 2007b).

Therefore, connected government, where e-services are a crucial component, leads to several benefits, both internally to the provider agencies and governments, and externally to the consuming citizens and businesses. Figure 3 lists the typical benefits of transformation to connected government.

Government transformation is a long term endeavor that is seldom impacted by any short term technology trends. In their transition toward connected government, all governments typically traverse through the four primary stages of e-government capability and maturity, each stage representing a progressively higher level in the government transformation continuum. The four widely used stages of e-government capability and maturity are; Web presence, interaction, transaction and transformation (UNDESA, 2008, 2010). Furthermore, connected government is the desired state that countries strive to reach as part of their transformation journey of e-government

maturity. However, there is no straightforward way to describe what exactly connected government means and its implications for countries (Microsoft, 2010, 2012).

Based on the current state of the practice and available literature, connected government is expected to entail certain characteristics and capabilities. These characteristics and capabilities, described below, are clearly stated to be the key contributors to e-government development according to the UN e-government survey of 2010, and in turn contribute to national development. These characteristics and capabilities, structured as dimensions, allow connected government to be viewed as a multi-dimensional construct. The dimensions of connected government are:

- **Citizen Centricity:** This refers to viewing governments from the outside-in, i.e. understanding the requirements and expectations of citizens become the pre-eminent guiding principle for all government policies, programs and services (AGIMO, 2010). In short, this represents the service-dominant logic which requires governments to operate as one enterprise and organize themselves around citizen demands and requirements. Aside for the citizens

Figure 3. Typical benefits from connected government

Benefits from Connected Government	
Internal **(To Provider Agencies and Governments)**	**External** **(To Consumer Citizens and Businesses)**
1. Avoidance of duplication 2. Reduction in transaction costs 3. Simplified bureaucratic procedures 4. Greater efficiencies 5. Richer communication & coordination 6. Enhanced transparency 7. Greater information sharing 8. Secure information management	1. Faster service delivery 2. Greater efficacy 3. Increased flexibility of service use 4. Innovation in service delivery 5. Greater participation and inclusion 6. Greater citizen empowerment 7. Greater openness and transparency

per se, other government constituents, such as businesses and civil organizations, are captured in the social inclusion dimension described later.

- **Common Infrastructure and Interoperability:** This refers to the use of standards and best practices across governments to encourage and enable the sharing of information in a seamless manner. Interoperability is the ability of enterprises to share information and knowledge within and across enterprise boundaries (Saha, 2010). The underlying foundation for effective interoperability comes from standardized common infrastructure.

- **Collaborative Services and Business Operations**: Connected government requires ministries and agencies to collaborate. It is not difficult to uncover success stories about integration and interoperability at the technology level. However, to collaborate at the level of business services and functions requires political will. This is because collaboration at this level is disruptive leading to shallower stovepipes, elimination of redundant or overlapping services and discovery of common and shared services, which in turn result in redistribution of authority and control for some segments of the government.

- **Public Sector (Networked) Governance:** This refers to the decision rights, and the accountability framework required for implementing all the other strategies for connected government. Good governance is a non-negotiable factor in the success of connected government, more so in countries that have multiple levels of governments (i.e. federal / central; state / provincial; and town / city) where various levels could be administered by different political parties.

- **Networked Organizational Model:** As Theresa Pardo and Brian Burke discuss in their work on government interoperability, this refers to the need to accommodate new organizational models wherein the enterprise (in the context of the W-O-G) is a network of relatively autonomous ministries and agencies working in a coherent manner to deliver value to both citizens and businesses (Pardo and Burke, 2008). This makes the whole-of-government a Networked Virtual Organization (NVO) that operates seamlessly toward a common mission.

- **Social Inclusion:** This refers to the ability of governments to move beyond horizontal and vertical integration of government service delivery to engaging the citizens and businesses at relevant points in the policy and decision-making processes. E-democracy and social inclusion ensure that delivery of government services is not a one-way exchange (OMB, 2012). Innovative ways of using technology to facilitate constituent participation and building a consultative approach are imperative for the success of connected government.

- **Transparency and Open Government:** This refers to the political doctrine which holds that the business of government and state administration should be opened at all levels to effective public scrutiny and oversight (Nordfors et al., 2009). In its broader construction, it opposes reason of state and national-security considerations, which have tended to legitimize extensive state secrecy.

The levers that contribute to performance along the dimensions are presented later in this chapter. In addition, connected government is expanded to include four evolutionary stages, described in a subsequent section of this chapter. Together, they allow much greater clarity and granularity in the description, role, structure and implications of connected government that so many countries seek to achieve (Saha, 2007).

According to the UN, moving to connected government requires a holistic and coherent framework, which cannot be achieved by piecemeal approaches and mechanisms. Such a framework recognizes the integrated presence of e-government both as an internal driver of transformation within the public sector and an external driver of better governance (Saha, 2008). Typically, governments are the largest enterprises. They are further characterized by complex federated structures where individual government organizations work in their respective silos. This often leads to fragmented business processes and duplicated systems and technologies, creating obstacles in cross-agency interoperability (APDIP, 2007b). Government-wide architecture allows end-to-end business processes, standard technologies, rationalized data structure and modularized e-services that can be assembled as required to deliver e-services (Pardo & Burke, 2008). As part of an earlier research, several governments were assessed for their maturity on connected government. This was used to derive the evolutionary stages of connected government, which are (Saha, 2012):

- **Intra-Governmental:** Connectedness among and between government ministries and agencies that usually lead to the W-O-G perspective and being viewed as a single virtual and networked enterprise. This also includes interactions and coherency at multiple layers of government (national, state, province, district, city). Notwithstanding the richness of interactions, the extent of connectedness is limited within the boundaries of government.
- **Inter-Governmental:** This is connectedness between sovereign countries driven by common and shared goals and objectives on issues that have multi country or global repercussions (examples include law enforcement, customs, counter-terrorism, health, intellectual property, free trade agreements, etc.).

- **Extra-Governmental:** This refers to the connectedness between government and associated business enterprises and partners outside of the government. This type of connectedness allows the creation of services that may be planned and delivered in collaboration with non-governmental entities, seamlessly integrated and usually leading to service ecosystems. Co-production of government is the outcome.
- **Ubiquitous:** This refers to connectedness that facilitates multi-dimensional multi-channel all pervasive communications between all stakeholders (but focusing more on citizens) by way of participation, engagement, openness, government transparency and accountability. This is the stage wherein government itself acts as a platform and coherency is imperative as connectedness is fully diffused, comprehensive and encompasses the emotional aspects as well.

Figure 4 shows the four evolutionary stages of connected government derived by expanding the connected stage in the approach used by the UN (UNDESA, 2008). Figure 5 portrays their key characteristics, and the relationship between government connectedness and performance. The indicative performance areas have been shown earlier in Figure 1.

It is crucial to view the four evolutionary stages of connected government in the context of intensity and richness of participation needed to make it happen. Greater engagement leads to better outcomes at lower cost, more innovative solutions and services, acceptability of greater diversity, better use of resources and higher compliance to decisions (Muehlfeit, 2006). Therefore, an important enabler of connected government is participation, as discussed earlier. Participation 2.0 requires a paradigm shift in the way interactions between governments and other entities take place.

Figure 4. Evolutionary stages of connected government

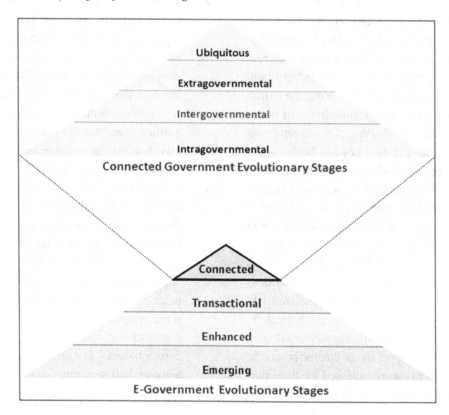

THE EMERGING COMPLEXITY PARADIGM

The underlying premise that future governments will be increasingly connected has already been established. The key points in the context of connected government, which impact the way enterprise architecture is planned, designed and adopted, includes the following:

- The connected government represents the highest level of e-government maturity; therefore, countries must first traverse the preceding maturity levels, before they can embrace the vision of connected government. Moving up e-government maturity levels increases the underlying complexity of the government and governance (Saha, 2012).

- There are various degrees and scope of "connectedness" that impacts the stages of connected government, as portrayed in Figures 4 and 5. As the scope of connected government shifts from "intra-governmental" to "ubiquitous," there is an exponential increase in complexity.

- Connected government implies and demands networked operating models, that is characterized by a collaborative approach to decision making, delivery government services via multiple channels, performance that is outcome-driven and deep participation by the citizens in government matters.

- The current approach to public-policy making, based on reduction of complex issues into separate, rationally manageable components is no longer appropriate to the

Figure 5. Stages of connected government and government performance

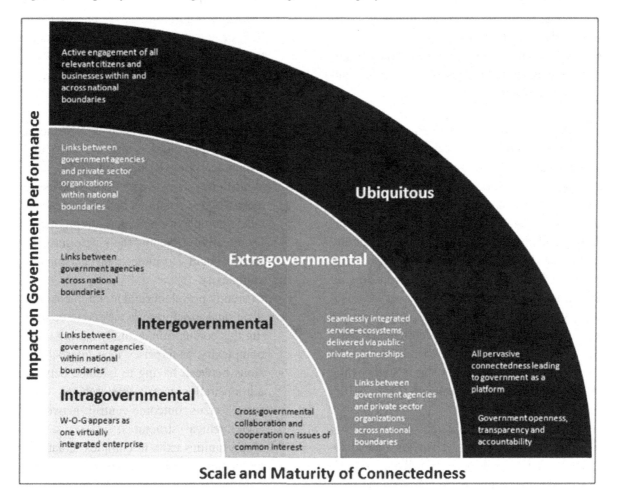

challenges faced by governments; in the connected paradigm, the interactions (linkages) play a dominant role in influencing the behavior of the enterprise; furthermore, complexity is often rooted in patterns of interactions among the elements.

• Embracing a systemic perspective in the context of connected government is supported by: (1) the ubiquity of information flows, within and outside the government; (2) the pressure on social policy to be more inclusive and holistic; (3) the inherent connectedness between government entities, bringing new opportunities and vulnerabilities; (4) globalization and the ways in which this integrates previously disparate

systems; (5) the increasing demands to cope with ambiguity, uncertainty, non-linearity, and pervasiveness; (6) explosion of unintended consequences of government actions (Birkinshaw and Heywood, 2010).

Without doubt, governments are becoming increasingly complex. Generally speaking, the four main causes of rapid escalation of enterprise complexity are:

• **Diversity:** The differences and diversity in perspective and action.
• **Interdependence:** The number and nature of relationships in the enterprise.

- **Ambiguity:** The extent to which organizational factors are unclear, difficult to comprehend and act upon.
- **Flux:** The extent to which variation and experimentation coexist with order and standardization.

The three most common consequences of increasing complexity are, firstly; the interdependence and connections between the variables become wider and deeper making them harder to comprehend. Secondly, the lack of understanding of the underlying causal relationships make forecasting and planning very difficult and generally inaccurate. Finally, as time gets compressed, it creates a feeling of several things happening all at once leading to inadequate responses and unacceptable latency (KPMG, 2011). Below are the key findings from the enterprise complexity study by the Economist Intelligence Unit, KPMG and the Global Chief Executive Officer Study by the IBM Institute for Business Value (IBM, 2010a; KPMG, 2011; EIU, 2011).

- The global financial crisis and globalization have significantly contributed to businesses becoming more complex and most enterprises are not prepared for this inevitable shift. Business leaders should be willing to conceive multiple futures and embrace uncertainty.
- Enterprises are finding it increasingly difficult to understand the complexity and design appropriate interventions to tackle complexity. Rapid escalation of enterprise complexity is the single biggest source of anxiety for business leaders and more than half of the CEOs doubt their ability to manage it.
- Increasing customer expectations and demands is the single biggest contributing factor of enterprise complexity, followed by increasing regulatory requirements and

rapid organic growth. The acceleration of change is as unsettling as the change itself.
- Rise of enterprise complexity is exposing firms to undesirable risks and making them increasingly more vulnerable, leading to reduced agility and responsiveness and increased cost of doing business. Executives fear that deficiency in their understanding of the complexities is making them take wrong decisions (Richardson, 2008).
- Whilst enterprises are exploring the use of technological solutions and approaches to tackle complexity and increase productivity; creativity remains the single most effective quality to understand and manage complexity.
- Currently prevalent rigid hierarchical organizational structures are viewed to be feeding this conundrum, actually adding to the complexity. Enterprises face internal tensions between having to balance between administration-centric hierarchical structures versus outcome-centric networked (heterarchical) structures.
- Opportunities exist in complex situations; leveraging it allows enterprises to gain competitive advantage, create new and better strategies, expand into new markets and improve efficiencies.

These findings, undoubtedly applicable to governments, provide adequate evidence about the criticality of complexity as a primary factor in shaping EA programs and their outcomes. There are four types of complexity that enterprises (and government leaders) have to typically grapple with. Laws, regulations and other extraneous interventions can be classified as imposed complexity. Complexity as a result of the business being naturally complex is called inherent complexity. In contrast, resulting from choices and selections about how the business operates, what it produces and sells, to whom and how, leads to designed complexity. Finally, unnecessary complexity emerges from growing disconnect between the needs of the enterprises and the elements (policies, processes, procedures, systems) supporting it (Sargut and Mcgrath, 2011). Enterprises are addressing complexity in a myriad of ways, which include improvements to information management, reorganizing all parts of the business, significantly changed approach to human resources among others (Gharajedaghi, 2011). Thus, tackling complexity provides an excellent anchor to architect the enterprise and contributes to enterprise coherence.

Nowhere is the complexity more evident, than in the World Economic Forum's Global Risks Report 2012 (WEF, 2012). The report identifies fifty global risks, categories them into five areas (economic, environmental, geo-political, societal and technological). The most crucial factor in tackling these risks are that the risks are connected via a system-of-systems and cannot be investigated in isolation. This connectedness brings in all elements of complexities described earlier.

Therefore, complexity in governments in the midst of transformation creates conditions for "dystopia" – i.e. attempts at building better governments unintentionally lead to negative consequences. The vulnerabilities and consequently, the inefficiencies brought in by complexties that are not fully understood, cannot be overstated (WEF, 2012). As the world gets more connected by the day (governments included), the ineffectiveness of the traditional siloed approach gets amplified – with economists now estimating USD 15 trillion in waste and lost resources, globally. These complex systemic inefficiencies are interwoven, and the primary obstacle in tackling these remains the mindset – i.e. moving from short-sighted siloed approach to long-term system-of-systems leadership and decision making (IBM, 2010b). The world is a complex system-of-systems, with each system being a union of public and private sector entities that span multiple industry sectors, explained in Figures 4 and 5. At the fundamental

level, the core systems include: infrastructure, finance, food, government, healthcare, leisure, transportation, communication, education and power. There are inefficiencies embedded in all of these core systems. However, healthcare and government exhibit the highest amount of bloat. The Healthcare system has the potential for the largest amount of efficiency gains, with economists estimating that the current level of inefficiency could be reduced by nearly thirty-five percent (IBM, 2010b). An illustration from the healthcare sector is elaborated in the later sections.

NETWORKED GOVERNANCE AND COMPLEXITY LEADERSHIP

As countries move up the connected government ladder, portrayed in Figures 4 and 5, the nature of governance essential to support the demands and expectations at each level becomes more "networked" and less "hierarchical." Connected governments are far more complex, exhibiting all the characteristics discussed earlier. Enterprises of higher complexity require governance networks that are more heterogeneous (Dooley, 2002). However, heterogeneity has implications for efficiency, as such networks comprise of participants with disparate views, interests, motivations, relationships and rationale (Hamel, 2007). This shift by itself brings in new levels of complexity, as it necessitates participation, active involvement, transparency, experimentation and adaptivity, preemption of long-term consequences, interactivity, congruency, self-regulation, and social capital (Heywood, Spungin and Turnbull, 2007). Therefore, the move to connected government requires a fundamental reorientation of governance. In the connected government paradigm, governments become part of a larger network of organizational entities, that come together driven by a common goal, and often bringing complimentary capabilities to fulfill service delivery (CISCO IBSG, 2009). Therefore, governance networks, which play a crucial role in the success of connected government, are defined as a relatively stable horizontal articulation of independent, but operationally autonomous actors who interact through negotiations, which take place within a regulative, normative and cognitive framework that, to a certain extent, is self-regulating, contributing to the production of public purpose within and across policy segments (Hoogerworst, 2009). By factoring in the allocation of decision rights and inter organizational mechanisms, the suitability of networked governance for connected government can be gauged from the significant advantages it contributes, which include: (1) ability to foster constructive and more effective solutions; (2) greater legitimacy to the decision-making process and the decision outcomes; (3) ability to link across different tiers of the government; and (4) ability to facilitate knowledge exchange and capacity-building.

It is clear that for the connected government to succeed embracing the networked form of governance is imperative. However, networked governance, even with its huge advantages, needs to be adopted with certain guidelines. These include:

- Political-administrative leadership and direction are necessary.
- Democratic accountability is essential to ensure effectiveness.
- Adequate autonomy to work independently.
- Responsibilities of network configurations should be made explicit, and clearly distinguished from those of the hierarchical aspects.
- Need for cooperation and collaboration with a sense of urgency.
- Trust is the underlying foundation of collaboration and participation in the network should be based on reputation and credibility.
- Networks should have their identity and face.

Implicit in networked governance is the efficiency paradox. To address the complexity of sustainable development challenges, governments are required to open up (Morecroft, 2007). But the very act of opening up brings in new complexities; aspects that were previously considered externalities now become complex interdependent factors and trade-offs that must now be considered and negotiated (Reed, 2006). This process more often than not leads to protracted discussions and introduces some delay in decision-making and implementation. Network features such as centralization, density, nature and strength of relationships and leadership are thus essential elements that contribute to the effectiveness of networked governance (Rouse, 2000; Snowden and Boone, 2007).

Based on the review of current literature, there are three typical forms of network governance. These are self-governance, lead organization and network administrative organization as shown in Figure 6. The key characteristics of these three forms of networked governance are depicted in Figure 7.

As governments advance to the connected paradigm enabled by networked form of governance aiming to tackle complexity these bring in, the critical role of leadership in actualizing this cannot be overstated. The Law of Requisite Complexity states that it takes complexity to tackle complexity – a system must possess complexity equal or more than of its environment in order to function effectively (Armson, 2011). Despite the needs of the connected government era, much of the leadership paradigms and approaches remain largely grounded in a bureaucratic framework that is characterized by top-down, hierarchical, efficiency and control oriented. For the connected government perspective to function effectively and deliver results the model of leadership must be grounded in complexity, not bureaucracy (Jackson, 2011). The leadership approach must enable emergence, non-linearity, holism, adapt-

Figure 6. Three forms of network governance

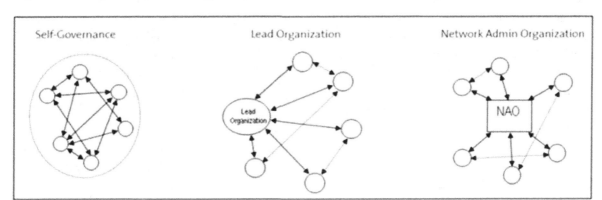

Figure 7. Key characteristics of the forms of networked governance

Governance Forms	Trust Required	Number of Participants	Shared Goal Consensus	Network Level Competencies
Self Governance	High density	Few	High	Low
Lead Organization	Low density, highly decentralized	Moderate	Moderately low	Moderate
Network Administrative Organization	Moderate density, NAO monitored by members	Moderate to many	Moderately high	High

ability, asymmetry and learning among other things. To fulfill the demands of connected government, potentially there are three types of leadership approaches:

- **Administrative Leadership:** Is about individuals in formal managerial roles who plan, coordinate and control organizational activities. This is a top-down approach based on the notions of authority, position and control;
- **Adaptive Leadership:** Is an emergent, interactive approach designed to produce adaptive outcomes in a social system. This approach requires a high degree of social capital and is based on the fundamental notions of complexity and asymmetry.

Adaptive leadership has been found to be suitable to link different enterprise levels; and

- **Enabling Leadership:** Refers to the ability of leaders to create the conditions that actualize adaptive leadership and allow for emergence. This approach advances networks by: (1) encouraging interaction; (2) creating interdependency; and (3) motivating creativity and learning.

This then begs the question – what does it take for managers to become leaders? In his article *How Managers Become Leaders* published in the Harvard Business Review in June 2012; author Michael Watkins presents the seven seismic shifts needed to effectuate into leadership roles (Watkins,

2012). Managers must learn to move from specialist to generalist, analyst to integrator, tactician to strategist, bricklayer to architect, problem solver to agenda setter, warrior to diplomat and supporting cast member to lead role. While it is not expected that managers negotiate these shifts all at once, nonetheless, these represent a demanding set of capabilities needed (Wilson, 1990).

GOVERNMENTS AS SYSTEMS

A system is defined as a set of interrelated things encompassed by a permeable boundary, interacting with one, another and an external environment, forming a complex but unitary whole and working toward a common overall goal. Section 4 discussed the existence of complexity in governments, more so when the connected government becomes the overriding vision and goal. In short, governments are complex and at times paradoxical. This stems from the fact that governments are by far the largest enterprises and with size comes complexity. Complexities in governments are of both types—combinatorial complexity and dynamic complexity (Jackson, 2011).

Complexity arising due to the sheer number of components and elements that are interconnected refers to combinatorial complexity. Dynamic complexity, on the other hand, arises due to the velocity of change and the quantum of interactions between the components and elements. In addition, unpredictable delays between decisions and their effects (and counter-effects) completes the picture of what constitute, according to Gartner,

"wicked problems." Governments are excellent examples of complex adaptive systems. Complex systems are characterized by: (1) large number of interacting components; (2) non-linear interactions leading to disproportionately major consequences; (3) dynamic behaviors where solutions cannot be imposed, rather they arise from circumstances (emergent); (4) existence of history that influence the present and the future; (5) substantial unknown unknowns; and (6) inability to predict the future. Governments around the world are facing several challenges (wicked problems) and are under pressure to address these challenges in more open, accountable and transparent ways from active and vocal citizens and businesses alike (Gall, 2010).

From a leader's point of view, it is hence imperative to probe, sense and respond; create environments that allow for patterns to emerge; encourage interactions and diversity to deal with such complexities. The emergence of pattern-based leadership provides the necessary impetus and direction. In order for governments to perform and transform, it is critical that the characteristics of complex adaptive systems and their implications are understood (see Figure 8).

Enterprises (in this case government) characterized by the above, require much more than conventional thinking in order to understand the system, and the challenges that the system faces. The success of government transformation programs thus becomes dependent on comprehending the entire system. Ambiguity in understanding the system is one of the primary reasons for public sector transformation showing less than satisfactory results and success rates. It is amply evi-

Figure 8. Generic characteristics of complex adaptive systems

Generic Characteristics of Complex Adaptive Systems	
1. Constantly changing	6. Self-organizing
2. Tightly coupled	7. Adaptive
3. Governed by feedback	8. Counterintuitive
4. Non-linear	9. Policy resistant
5. History dependent	10. Trade-off dependent

dent that countries are adopting a whole-of-government enterprise architecture (W-O-G EA) as the meta-discipline to trigger, design and realize connected government, and taking a systemic perspective is the most logical way to move forward. Despite all these seemingly impressive efforts, the adoption of W-O-G EA has been less than impressive. This is evidenced by Gartner's *Hype Cycle for Government Transformation 2011*, wherein W-O-G EA would require another ten (10) years before reaching full maturity and delivering benefits justifying its immense potential (Burton and Allega, 2010, 2011).

On the upside, however, Gartner's *Hype Cycle for Enterprise Architecture 2011* does state that W-O-G EA is past the bottom of the trough of disillusionment. There is no dearth of literature and other enabling resources for countries to build their enterprise architectures. However, after the initial enthusiasm, things are difficult to sustain with questions often being raised regarding the efficacy of government EA efforts. This is not surprising at all. EA efforts in the past decade or so have concentrated on building what could be termed as solutions to the EA problems. As it is evident from this research, nearly all EA efforts currently focus on building frameworks, methodologies, guidelines, principles, best practices and tool support (Burton and Allega, 2010; Burton and Allega, 2011).

Without fully understanding the underlying system, the success achieved through the above has been limited. This leads to two logically explainable reactions: (1) frantic efforts to improve the frameworks, methodologies, guidelines, principles, best-practices and tool support; and (2) discontinuance of the W-O-G EA altogether by terming it as "too difficult" and "too complex." The need of the moment is not better solutions, but better thinking about the problems. Gary Hamel in his book *The Future of Management* states that solving a systemic problem requires

understanding its systemic roots. This is the first of the ten (10) rules for management innovation. It is in this context that conventional open-loop thinking to solving business problems needs to be replaced with systems (closed-loop) holistic thinking (Hamel, 2007). A systemic perspective is used to understand how the numerous components of the governments act, react and interact with one another with the intent of improving the adoption of W-O-G EA for connected government.

This provides a comprehensive, holistic and a more coherent way of anticipating synergies and mitigating negative emergent behaviors, which would facilitate the development of policies and other relevant intervention mechanisms (Perdiculis, 2010). Using systemic perspective encourages strategic thinking. Figure 9 compares systems thinking with conventional thinking.

The primary purpose of building causal loop diagrams is to gain insight into the underlying structure of a messy, complex situation. A system model (output from the causal loop diagramming) depicts how the variables interrelate, and where there are opportunities to intervene in the modeled system to influence its behavior (Garcia-Lorenzo et al., 2003). A causal loop diagram is an intellectual device that forces deep thinking, and one of the most effective mechanisms to visualize, understand and communicate complexity (WEF, 2012). The conventions of causal-loop diagrams are not described here, as excellent literature is already available in this area. Unfortunately, the same cannot be said about the reasons for less than optimal adoption of W-O-G EA by many countries. Gartner's *Hype Cycle for Enterprise Architecture 2011* clearly states that W-O-G EA is currently immature and is still about ten (10) years from attaining full maturity and adoption. It does not provide the reasons for the current state and what needs to be done to address this "wicked problem" that connected government is (Burton and Allega, 2010, 2011).

Figure 9. Comparing conventional and systemic thinking

Conventional (Open-Loop) Thinking	Systemic (Closed-Loop) Thinking
Static thinking Focusing on particular events.	**Dynamic thinking** Framing a problem in terms a pattern of behavior over time.
Systems-as-effect Viewing behavior generated by a system as driven by external forces.	**System-as-cause** Placing responsibility for a behavior on internal factors and actors.
Fragmented Believing that really knowing something means focusing on the details.	**Holistic** Believing that to know something requires understanding the context of relationships.
Factors thinking Listing factors that influence or correlate with some results.	Operational thinking Concentrating on causality and understanding how a behavior is generated.
Straight-line thinking Viewing causality as running in one direction, ignoring the interdependence and interaction between and among the causes.	**Loop thinking** Viewing causality as an ongoing process, with effect feeding back to influence the causes and the causes affecting one another.

The steps used to develop system models used extensively in this chapter are as follows (McGarvey and Hannon, 2004; Jackson, 2011):

1. **Systemic Understanding:** Complex adaptive systems consist of several interacting components, which need to be understood "spatially," "dynamically" and "historically." This first step triggers the initial understanding of systems and situations within the limits of uncertainties. This involves factoring in formal and informal structures, broad environmental scanning, and stakeholder perspectives. Clarity in scope and agreement on the boundaries are the primary outcomes of this step;

2. **Systems Synthesis and Modeling:** With inputs gained from understanding the scope and boundaries of the system, this step then aims to develop conceptual models that capture the key factors (variables) and the interrelationships between them. It is im-

perative that all factors (variables) depicted in the models are validated with supporting data. The aim at this juncture is to obtain a true representation of the situation.

3. **Systemic Analysis and Selection:** Having system models provide the necessary inputs for a deeper investigation of the variables, their behaviors and the interdependencies. The process of discovery is the cornerstone in this step. The purpose is to understand "why" the system behaves in the manner it does. The investigative analysis facilitates discovery of any patterns lurking underneath, which are usually not visible externally but only manifest as symptoms, at most times defying effective explanations.

4. **Systemic Transformation**: This step is to identify interventions that provide the means to steer the system to the future state. The transformation step creates a relationship between the future and the present for designing a successful change program.

5. **Systemic Action**: While the previous phase is where the "strategic thinking" happens via identification of interventions, this step looks at ways and means to actualize the change by operationalizing the interventions. Typically, these happen through a series of action items, which refine the interventions as "focused initiatives," "amplifiers" and "enablers." It is important that these three work coherently to make the required changes successful.

With the primary aim of advancing the adoption of W-O-G EA for connected government, there is a clear need to: (1) uncover the critical influencing factors; (2) identify the relationships between and among the factors; (3) recognize the underlying dynamics; (4) propose plausible inter-

vention strategies to address the situation. It can be mentioned with a high degree of confidence that the systems thinking approach presents the highest potential to view W-O-G EA adoption from a holistic perspective, which also happens to be a major gap in the current literature.

Figures 4 and 5 portrayed the four evolutionary stages of connected government. At each level, the concept of "system" is clearly evident. However, moving from "intra-governmental" to "ubiquitous" stages bring forth the concept of "system of systems" as the ecosystem comprising of the whole extends and expands beyond single agencies and government entities, to entire governments that are multi-level, includes businesses, citizens, civil societies and other non-governmental organizations (IBM, 2010b).

Figure 10. Strategic success factors to connected government

Connected Government Dimensions	Strategic Success Factors
1. **Citizen Centricity**	A. Citizen requirements & expectations B. The government appears and operates as one C. Multiple channels of engagement D. Adaptability of government services
2. **Common Infrastructure & Interoperability**	A. Technology standards B. Government-wide applications & systems C. Data exchange standards D. ICT & infrastructure management
3. **Collaborative Services & Business Operations**	A. Collaborative business functions B. Shared services C. Shared information D. Service innovation & back office reorganization
4. **Public Sector (Networked) Governance**	A. Complex adaptive leadership B. Business outcome accountability C. Governance structures, policies and practices D. Institutionalization of governance
5. **Networked Organization Model**	A. Multi-stakeholder cooperation B. Ministry / agency and government level autonomy C. Cluster based approach & common mission D. Public value network
6. **Social Inclusion**	A. Citizen engagement at various levels B. Citizen outreach C. Responsive government D. Social Capital
7. **Transparent & Open Government**	A. Public scrutiny & oversight B. Data discovery, availability & accessibility C. Performance management & accountability D. Legal Framework(s)

Figure 10 lists the dimensions of connected government introduced in the earlier section, along with their strategic success factors.

Therefore, as seen from Figure 10, connected government is an interplay between a large group of variables and determinants, set within a social, cultural, economic, technological and environmental landscape. These lead to a massive explosion in complexity of the scale that is nearly impossible to fathom. Inability to comprehend and manage complexity on this scale makes it extremely challenging for countries to move up the connected government ladder. The factors contributing to and the consequences of enterprise complexity have been discussed earlier. Complexity, ambiguity and uncertainty have the capacity to absorb large amounts of resources, and have the ability to render any actions ineffective.

A PRIMER TO ENTERPRISE ARCHITECTURE

Traditionally, EA has been used to drive business transformation efforts. However, the strongest drivers for EA is to gather insights into the current enterprise and provide foresight for the future enterprise. The principal challenge faced by Chief Enterprise Architects today is to institute an EA program that can orchestrate sustainable changes throughout the enterprise, while simultaneously providing direction and leadership to transformation planning that is needed to support the enterprise's mission. In summary, EA is a robust planning activity which helps enterprises understand the process by which business strategies translate into operational reality in a coherent manner. EA is an ongoing process necessitating a structured and systematic method for architecture planning and implementation. Metaphorically, an EA is to an enterprise's strategy, operations and systems as a set of blueprints is to a city and its buildings (Saha, 2007, 2008, 2012). However, EA comes with additional challenges given that the primary

frame of reference, the enterprise, is a complex adaptive system. Even as architecture teams are "architecting," the enterprises being architected continue to function and as a result remain dynamic and ever changing. By following an architecture-based approach, enterprises usually aim to address issues pertaining to: (1) strategic alignment and execution; (2) information accuracy and integrity; (3) infrastructure management; (4) security; (5) technology acquisition and compatibility; (6) business value of IT; (7) corporate governance; (8) business collaboration; and (9) procurement among others (Saha, 2008). Though EA is often assumed to take the strategy as input with the aim of achieving business to IT alignment, increasingly, evidence of the reverse is also surfacing. In other words, enterprise strategies are being influenced by technological capabilities, resulting from the ubiquity of IT in today's enterprises.

Conventionally, EA consists of a collection of interconnected architectural domains (also called viewpoints or perspectives). These are:

- **Policy and Strategy Architecture:** Which establishes principles, rules and guidelines aimed at providing direction to the entire enterprise.
- **Business Architecture:** Which defines enterprise business outcomes, functions, capabilities and end-to-end business processes, and their relationships with external entities required to execute business strategies.
- **Data / Information Architecture:** Which deals with the structure and utility of information within the enterprise, and its alignment with its strategic, tactical and operational needs.
- **Application Architecture:** Which specifies the structure of individual systems based on defined technology.
- **Technical Architecture:** Which defines the technology environment and infrastructure in which all IT systems operate.

The above five domains largely represent the current state of practice in the discipline of EA. In their book *Coherency Management–Architecting the Enterprise for Alignment, Agility and Assurance*, authors Doucet, Gotze, Saha and Bernard present and discuss the extended and embedded modes of EA in addition to the traditional mode (Doucet et al., 2010). They assert that as enterprises start embracing the more advanced extended and embedded modes, the need for synergy and consistency amplifies, thus facilitating the attainment of coherence, the ultimate goal of EA. Successful EA not only captures the five domains, but also the relationships between them. Having linkages between the five domains provide line-of-sight (or traceability) to the relevant stakeholders of the EA. Figure 11 depicts the key domains of EA, with a special focus on government EA.

EA effectively supports the business, enables information sharing across departments / divisions / enterprises, enhances the management's ability to deliver effective and timely services and improves operational efficiencies. Committing to an ongoing EA practice within an enterprise enables a business-aligned and technology-adaptive enterprise that is effective efficient and agile (Doucet et al., 2010). With this background and emerging trends, therefore:

Enterprise Architecture is defined as the ongoing process of building the ability to tackle complexity, with the pivotal goal of creating and sustaining coherent enterprises.

Most governments worldwide are in the midst of substantial public sector transformation activi-

Figure 11. Components of government enterprise architecture

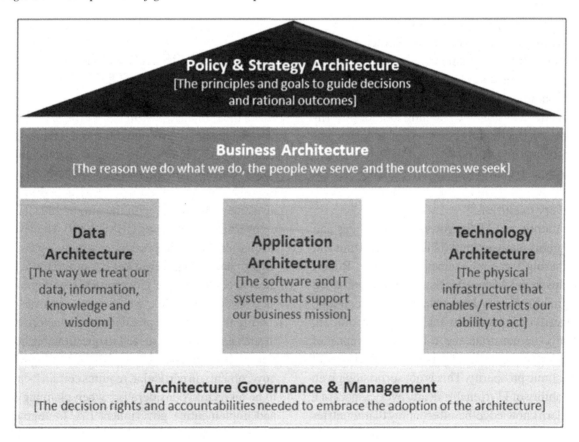

ties. A majority of these initiatives is triggered by the need to have better, and seamless government services delivered online. The focus on automating government services often is largely limited to specific ministries and agencies (OMB, 2007). However, such initiatives lack the cross-ministry / agency viewpoint and coordination. This creates challenges in embracing a W-O-G approach with its associated benefits, which are much more than the benefits derived by merely taking agency-centric viewpoints. These shortcomings are clearly evident in the findings of the UN Global E-Government Survey 2010 (UNDESA, 2010). According to the UN, the value of e-government will be increasingly defined by its contribution to national development. Lack of coherent strategy is often cited as the primary reason for under-development of e-government. Moving forward, more and more countries are adopting national e-government strategies and multi-year action plans, and EA is the strategy that governments are increasingly looking toward.

According to Haiyan Qian, Director of the Division for Public Administration and Development Management, United Nations Department of Economic and Social Affairs (UNDESA), "EA is an effective strategic planning tool for governments by [facilitating] creation of linkages and improving interoperability among government agencies, benefiting both internal operational processes as well as improved public service delivery to citizens."

Adoption of IT for government services and programs plays an important role in crafting and furthering the e-government initiatives. Robert Atkinson and Andrew Mackay, in their report titled Digital Prosperity-Understanding the Economic Benefits of Information Technology Revolution, clearly demonstrate the role and influence of IT adoption to national productivity and overall economic prosperity. This is not surprising given the ability of IT to enable nearly every aspect of a modern knowledge-based economy that countries increasingly aspire to be. The ubiquity of the IT

makes it even more compelling to embrace and derive benefits out of. Figure 12 depicts the systemic view of this phenomenon that is dominated by several reinforcing loops, allowing countries to leverage on information technology to power their national economies (Atkinson and McKay, 2007).

An ICT based economy tends to be less resource intensive; it finds favour in many countries (Zenghelis, 2010). This is evident from the quantum of money being spent by countries towards their respective electronic government activities and programs. Mega-trends like big data, analytics, cloud based services and social media are disrupting long-held assumptions and operating models (Dutta and Mia, 2010, 2011). Technology by itself is becoming more ubiquitous and accessible, and cheaper too. Governments are becoming increasing technology enabled, and this coupled with an overall rise in tech-savvyness of government leaders and decision makers (Fishenden et al., 2006).

FRONTIERS OF GOVERNMENT ENTERPRISE ARCHITECTURE

Given the immense potential EA brings, over the past decade or so governments around the world have embraced EA as the means to enable public sector transformation, catalyze modernization, improve strategic alignment, and actualize IT investment discipline with the aim of advancing e-government initiatives (IBM, 2009). However, despite all of these impressive efforts and massive investments into government EA programs, a lot more needs to be done. Government EA programs face several obstacles, which force countries to modify their program profiles and characteristics in such a way that these lead to questionable benefits and effectiveness (Saha, 2012). Dealing with governments, in particular, requires certain factors to be taken into consideration when planning for and implementing government EA, to augment its effectiveness and results (Liimatainen et al.,

Figure 12. ICT enabled economic growth and digital prosperity

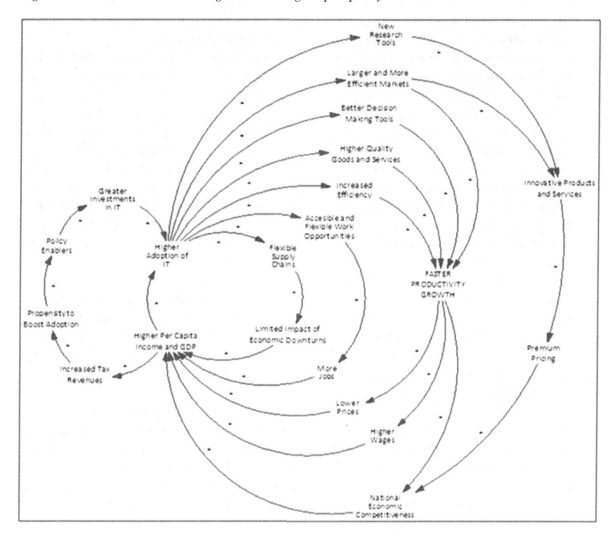

2007). These factors, representing a culmination of emerging trends and a multitude of lessons learnt over the past decade demand a complete rethink in the way government EA is approached, developed, implemented and practiced (Hjort-Madsen, 2009). Their collective impact is widespread and fundamental, are therefore essential guidelines for any enterprise architecture focused connected government initiative. These factors are:

- **Architecting for Emergence and Flux:** Edward Deming has asserted that organizations need to be viewed and managed as

systems. Integrating the systemic approach to EA provides the capability to tackle complexity and build enterprise coherence. Contrary to conventional wisdom, EA must be architecting for emergence and flux, rather than architecting for stability and constancy.

- **The Architecture of the Enterprise:** The transition from EA being equated to Enterprise IT Architecture to its literal meaning of "architecture of enterprise" demands that it be viewed as a complete holistic meta-discipline that has the potential to link other management disciplines and bring in public sector innovation. The next generation of EA will have to form the backbone of all successful enterprises, and the misconception that enterprises do not have architecture until they initiate a formal project, and a team tasked with managing the project will start to fade. The underlying principle that every functioning enterprise has architecture will take hold.

- **The Primacy of Interconnections:** The emphasis of architecture development will have to shift from designing the various architectural views and viewpoints to designing the interconnections between various views and viewpoints so as to achieve enterprise coherence. Doucet et al. have identified the dimensions of enterprise coherence, which are: (a) designed; (b) organized; (c) consistent; (d) connected; and (e) institutionalized.

- **Governments as Systems:** Governments are complex adaptive systems, wherein the assumptions of separability, linearity, correlation and predictability will no longer be valid. Capitalizing on complexity will become the primary reason for embracing a formal approach like EA.

- **Networked Governance:** Sustainable development incorporating complex interactions, unanticipated conditions will require a fundamental rethink in way governance is practiced. Networked forms of governance will take hold to deal with the changes, and shifts described earlier. The process of designing and implementing policies will have to be based on facilitation and influence rather than control and compliance.

- **Benefits from Priorities:** Benefits realization from government EA initiatives will accrue as a result of EA addressing specific national or public sector priorities. The emphasis would be on improving the entire system, rather than piecemeal results.

Strategies for improvements will have to accommodate for emergence in addition to deliberate approaches.

- **Heterarchical Structure:** Current EA frameworks and methodologies consider enterprises as functional hierarchies, which employ the command and control paradigm, as top-down, separated from work, target and budget driven by an ethos of central control and reaction. This is the starting point; the rest of the architecture activity embeds and even amplifies this mindset, thus creating a biased and often incorrect view of the enterprise, leading to ineffective architecture. This is because they: (1) are non-linear, dynamic and oftentimes manifested via random chaotic behaviors; (2) are composed of independent entities, at times exhibiting conflicting behaviors; and (3) demonstrate behavioral patterns that are emergent in nature.

Figure 13 shows a summary of influencing factors shaping the EA discipline and practice. These advances and frontiers of government EA are essential inputs in establishing the contours of connected government presented in the subsequent sections. These factors all also influencing the way in which EA is positioned within the enterprise. This is discussed subsequently.

Up to this point the following have been discussed and elaborated:

1. What is connected government? Why is it important for the future of governments? How is it positioned in the context of e-government?
2. What factors influence the shift to connected government? What makes connected government more complex? What are the implications of this increased complexity?
3. What are the strategies to deal with complexity? How can EA be utilized as a platform

Figure 13. Factors influencing connected government with enterprise architecture

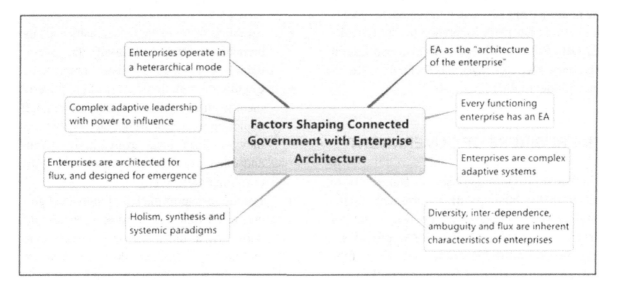

to deal with the complexity that connected government brings in?

4. What factors shape EA within the context of actualizing the potential of connected government?

With these theoretical and conceptual underpinnings established, the next three sections demonstrate with an illustration the approach to realize connected government using EA as the primary platform. The narrative is a result of the author's direct first hand experience.

STRUCTURING THE CONNECTED GOVERNMENT

The first step in architecting the connected government is to develop the structural perspective. This is crucial because it allows delineation of the government business and key IT enablers. This portion consists of a set of interrelated reference models. The primary purpose of the reference models is to:

- Structure the business and technology aspects of the government, with a whole-of-government perspective.
- Facilitate collaboration across boundaries (across agencies and government layers).
- Identify duplications and redundancies, and prioritize opportunities for closing such gaps.
- Craft a common taxonomy to describe the government from an outside-in viewpoint.

The purpose of this chapter is not to develop and prescribe the reference models, as these differ from country to country. The next two subsections, briefly describe the general process for developing reference models. This is then followed by short descriptions of the "uses" or "application scenarios," which also form an integral part of the development process. Reference models are developed with a purpose. The description later, demonstrates how the reference models are put to use in the context of connected government. Consistent with Figure 11, typically there are four reference models, each corresponding to the business, data, application and technology architecture components of the EA. The policy and strategy architecture is covered separately, and linked to the reference models. The four reference models are the: (1) Business Reference Model (BRM); (2) Data Reference Model (DRM), Application Reference Model (ARM), and Technology Reference Model (TRM) (Saha, 2012).

THE BUSINESS OF GOVERNMENT

The BRM provides a consistent framework to structure the business of government, facilitating a W-O-G outside-in functional view of the entire government. The BRM provides a framework facilitating a functional view of the government's Lines of Business (LOBs) and Business Functions, irrespective of the actual government entities performing the specific business functions. By taking a functional (and not an organizational) view of the government business, the BRM enables collaboration, sharing and reuse. The BRM is not the same as the hierarchical organizational structure. The organization structure serves an administrative purpose, at times capturing the reporting lines. The BRM serves as the foundation for connected government. The BRM usually covers the first three levels of the government business architecture. Individual government entities (e.g. ministries, agencies and departments) fill in the lower granular levels of the government business architecture, linking back to the BRM. Figure 14 shows the suggested hierarchical structure of business architecture. While a prescribed approach to structuring the business of government is a sovereign issue, the important factor is that countries and their governments need to be consistent and transparent with this. Establishing and enforcing a BRM typically has serious and deep political ramifications. Therefore, this is where the biggest mindset changes are needed.

BRMs

- Establish a common mechanism and approach to structure and classify the government business from a holistic perspective.
- Capture the functional view of the government from an outside-in perspective; i.e. It depicts government functions in the way they would be made available to citizens and other external stakeholders, from the consumer viewpoint.
- Lead to disintermediation of individual government entities (ministries, agencies, departments) as functional view, captured in an end-to-end perspective, does not make explicit the specific provider entity. The rationale being, as long as the service is available, and delivered within the acceptable performance standards, it should not matter to the consumers (citizens and other external stakeholders) as to who provides the service. From a practical perspective, it is entirely possible that a portion of the service may be provided by an entity in the private sector, but this fact is not visible to the consumers.
- Make possible the identification of common and shared business functions, clarity in governance by providing the input to assign accountability and authority, and government transformation and digitization.
- Embody collaboration, co-creation, and networked operating models and allow for the governments to appear as one single integrated entity to citizens and other external stakeholders. This integrated view realizes the vision of connected government.

BRM usually follows a functional hierarchical approach (OMB, 2007). The suggested meta-structure for the development of the BRM is depicted in Figure 15. Later in the chapter, an example of BRM Level 1 view, depicting the business areas and the LOBs is shown. The next level of the BRM enveloping the entire set of busi-

Figure 14. Hierarchical structure of the business architecture

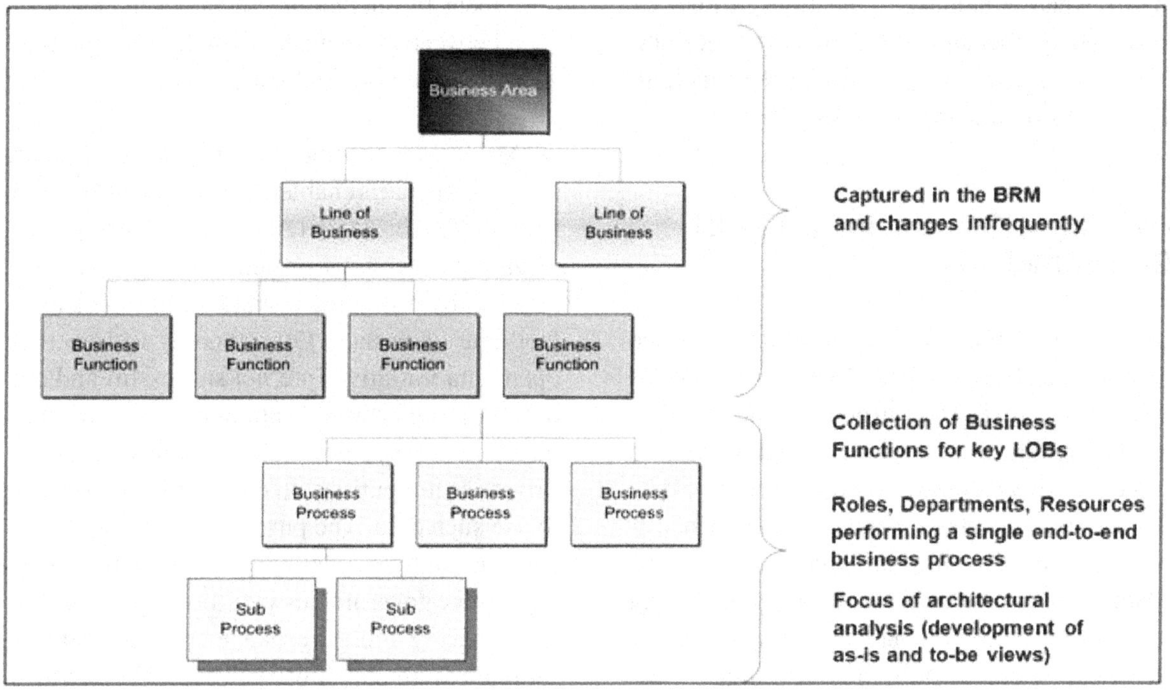

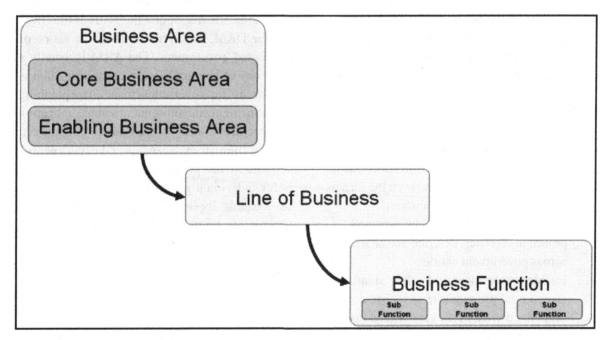

Figure 15. Suggested meta-structure for business reference model

ness functions is captured as a two-dimensional matrix, wherein the business functions are mapped to the governmental organizational entities and functions tasked with performing the function. This is shown later in Figure 33.

INFORMATION TECHNOLOGY IN GOVERNMENT

In support of the BRM, three other reference models must be developed. These are the DRM, ARM and TRM. The purpose of the DRM is to capture the high-level data architecture, to promote government-wide data discovery, data description, data sharing and data governance & management. The DRM provides the underlying (data) foundation to realize collaboration, sharing and reuse, the three crucial outcomes targeted by the BRM. In other words, the DRM supports the goals of the BRM, and in turn enables the vision of connected government. The DRM consists of conceptual and logical overview of key data that is used across the government to facilitate planning and prioritizing the subsequent actual data architecture efforts in individual government entities (ministries, agencies, and departments).

DRMs

- Harmonize data across the government to set the platform for standardization, classification, sharing, reuse and even the formation of common areas of interest.
- Establish a common mechanism and approach to discover, describe and share data across government entities.
- Enable government-wide data standards; an essential pre-requisite to realize collaboration, co-creation and networked operating models. It allows the manifestation of the "government-appears-and-operates-as-one" vision.

- Support the functional view of the government by facilitating seamless interactions between government entities, with the sole aim of end-to-end integration.

DRMs provide the underlying foundation to the digitization that is enabled by IT applications and systems (OMB, 2007). DRMs also catalyze public private partnerships in delivering government services by providing a standard mechanism to facilitate open data. Oftentimes it is seen that open data initiatives are not successful and are not able to enhance innovations because either the data that is made available is not usable, or the private sector entities do not have the capability to use such data. The purpose of the ARM is to capture the high-level application architecture, to promote government-wide discovery, description, sharing and governance and management of application capabilities. The ARM provides the underlying (application) foundation to realize collaboration, sharing and reuse, the three crucial outcomes targeted by the BRM. In other words, the ARM supports the goals of the BRM and the DRM, and in turn enables the vision of connected government. The ARM is usually a directory of key application capabilities that is used across the government to facilitate planning and prioritizing the subsequent actual application architecture efforts in individual government entities (ministries, agencies and departments). As part of the governance process, the intent is for individual government to refer to ARM for reusable application capabilities, before attempting to build one. This decision process is depicted in Figure 16.

ARMs

- Facilitate identification of common and shared application and application components, and therefore set the stage for reuse and assembly based approach to application development.

Figure 16. Decision process to use the application reference model

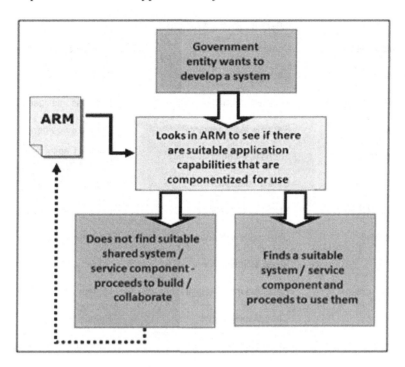

- Institute a mechanism to reorganize applications along application capabilities, to reduce overlaps and redundancies, bring forth application gaps and to advance reusability at a W-O-G scale.
- Enable W-O-G application standards; an essential co-requisite to realize collaboration, co-creation and networked operating models. It allows the manifestation of the "government-appears-and-operates-as-one" vision.
- Support digitization of the functional view of the government by facilitating seamless interactions between government entities, with the sole aim of end-to-end interoperability.

As an illustration, Figure 17 shows an indicative list of potential application capabilities. The list, by no means, is exhaustive and is intended to provide a starting point for further discovery and refinements. The caveat is that ARMs do not go into the actual solution (application) architectures, but only provide the inputs to such activities when needed.

The Technology Reference Model (TRM) provides guidance in the design, development and implementation of IT to improve the efficiency, effectiveness and interoperability of IT resources across the W-O-G. The TRM describes the infrastructure technologies and their respective technical standards that are logically grouped into domains. Typically, each domain has a set of principles, technology categories, technology components, architecture design considerations, policies, technical standards, general standards, best practices and technology watch. Figure 18 shows the typical technology domains that constitute the TRM. The domains are indicative, and can be modified based on specific requirements. As a caveat, the TRM solely deals with the physical technology infrastructure. TRMs:

Figure 17. Suggested list of application capabilities

Application Capabilities		
Business Rules Management	Content Management	Online Help & Tutorials
Directory Services	Document Management	Digital Rights Management
Administration & Reports	Knowledge Management	Business Intelligence
Search & Retrieval	Records Management	Data Management
Collections & Payments	Forms Management	Human Capital & Workforce Management
Grants Management	Data Visualization	Assets & Materials Management
Scanning / Indexing / OCR	Statistics & Analytics	Financial Management
Correspondence & Mail	Subscriptions Management	Communication
Workflow	Alerts & Notifications	Systems Management
Collaboration & Workgroups	Reservations & Registrations	Preferences
Audits & Logging	Case Management	Portal
Identity Management	Catalog Management	Routing & Scheduling
Security Management	Conferences & Virtual Meetings	Call Center Management
User Profiles, Personalization & Preferences	Dashboards	

Figure 18. Suggested domains in the technology reference model

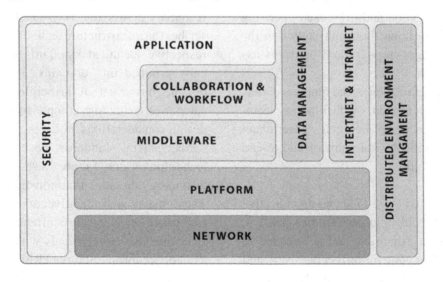

- Provide a mechanism to establish and enforce technology standards, which allow governments to take benefit of economies of scale.
- Provide a relatively easy point of entry to many government EA initiatives due to their ease of development, enforcement and adoption.

As a general guideline, governments are encouraged to take benefit of external and open standards when developing TRM (e.g. TOGAF TRM or several interoperability frameworks available). In other words, given that technologies available and used are fairly standard, it is more productive not to spend time reinventing the wheel with TRM, and instead expend more time and resources towards BRM, DRM and ARM.

THE CONNECTED PERSPECTIVE

The previous two sub-sections presented the structure, purpose and intended outcomes of four reference models, namely, the BRM, DRM,

ARM, and TRM. To provide a collective and comparative view of the four, Figure 19 portrays their key distinguishing characteristics. As is evident from Figure 19, there has to be a very strong business rationale to develop TRMs from scratch. Additionally, widespread technology ubiquity, maturity, tech-savvyness and the advent of cloud based service delivery models further exacerbate the need to de-focus from complete in-house development of TRMs and even some elements of ARMs. This is a welcome development, as it allows governments to focus on the real issues and priorities, rather than technology infrastructure.

For EA to be the foundation for connected government, it is imperative that the four reference models are viewed in a holistic integrated manner. In other words, individual reference models can provide some benefits on their own. However, to accrue the full benefit of EA, it is essential that the reference models are linked (connected) and analyses are performed in the context of such linkages. In the absence of the linkages (connections), the architectural line-of-sight (or traceability) is impossible to achieve, leading to lack of synthesized view. The follow-

Figure 19. Distinguishing characteristics of architecture reference models

	Business Reference Model	Data Reference Model	Application Reference Model	Technology Reference Model
Ease of Development	Low	Moderate	Moderate	High
Internalization & Adoption Difficulty	High	High	Moderate	Low
Multi-Stakeholder Interest & Involvement	High	Moderate	Moderate	Low
Amenability to Industry (External) Standards	Low	Moderate	High	High
Complexity & Influence	High	Moderate	Low	Low
Frequency of Change	Low	Moderate	Moderate	High
Impact of Change (on the Organization)	High	High	Moderate	Low
Contribution to Connected Government	High	High	Moderate	Low
Visibility & Public Scrutiny	High	Low	Moderate	Low
Overall Derived Benefits	High	Moderate	Moderate	Low

ing paragraphs briefly explain the analyses that can potentially be performed with and on the reference models:

1. BRMs must be mapped to:
    a. DRMs in order to identify business functions and business processes that have no corresponding data support and enablement.
    b. DRMs in order to identify business functions and business processes that have multiple data entities supporting them.
    c. Key internal and external stakeholders (roles) involved in the realization of the business functions and business processes as a RACI (Responsible, Accountable, Consulted, and Informed) chart.
    d. Key organizational entities (agencies, departments, groups, teams) to establish the network of participants in the business functions and business processes.
    e. ARMs in order to identify business functions and business processes that have no corresponding automation (application) support and enablement.
    f. ARMs in order to identify business functions and business processes that have multiple applications / application modules supporting them.
2. DRMs must be:
    a. Mapped to ARMs in order to identify data entities that have no corresponding automation (application) support and enablement.
    b. Mapped to ARMs in order to identify data entities that have multiple applications / application modules supporting them.
    c. Mapped to key stakeholders to clarify the issues pertaining to data ownership, data custodianship, data privileges and

the like. This is critical from a data governance perspective.
    d. Assessed for aggregation requirements to fulfill business requirements for management reporting and decision making.
    e. Augmented with the inclusion of standard structured processes and policies for future discovery, description and usage.
3. ARMs must be:
    a. Mapped to TRMs to uncover instances and extent of technology homogeneity / diversity;
    b. Enhanced by mapping applications to applications in order to comprehend the interactions between them, the nature of interactions and the extent of dependency; and
    c. Mapped to applications to uncover the degree of reuse and its impact on business function and business process support.

The above, collectively, provide a connected perspective, which is holistic. This view is usually termed as the Enterprise Connected View (ECV), and in this context the enterprise is the W-O-G. This is shown in Figure 20, which provides vertical, horizontal and lateral line of sight, across the entire government.

The development of the reference models, followed by the creation of the ECV is an outcome of both "forward" and "reverse" engineering. The use of "forward" engineering is logical and natural. The use and value of "reverse" engineering cannot be ignored because:

- Most governments already have invested substantial resources to build and deploy IT to automate portions of the government services. Given the spread and the ubiquity of IT in government / public sector, it is highly unlikely that discovery of elements

Figure 20. Enterprise connected view for line of sight

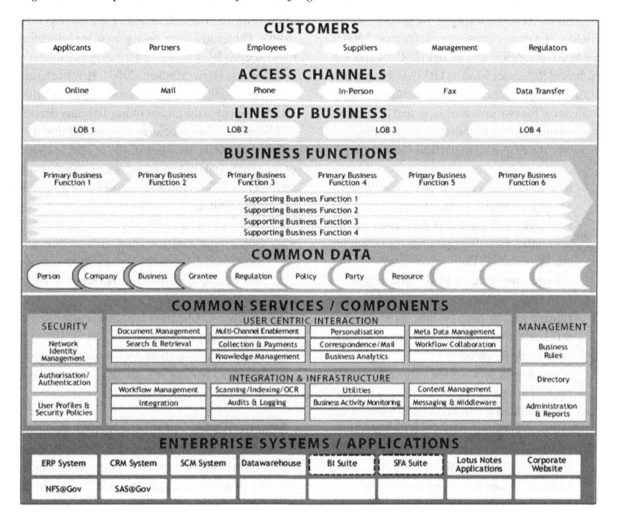

that go on to make the DRMs, ARMs, and TRMs will start from scratch.

- The existing IT systems may not be efficient, may be fragmented, and yet could contain very useful information for further leverage.
- Finally, in reality, at times it is politically not feasible to completely sidetrack existing IT systems.

Another phenomenon that materializes from the foundation provided by the reference models and the ECV is the emergence of shared services. The overlaps and redundancies between the various government entities (ministries, agencies and departments) provide excellent fodder to be abstracted out as common and shared services, wherein the benefits of economies of scale can be quintessentially derived. This nature of "outsourcing" makes government entities more efficient, focused toward their core areas of operations and responsive to their stakeholders. In this context, the benefits of standardization are unmistakably clear and visible.

The Federal Enterprise Architecture (FEA) is a good example of reference models and the benefits they bring into the W-O-G paradigm (OMB, 2007; NIA, 2008). The FEA, consisting of five reference models, namely, the Performance Reference Model (PRM), Business Reference Model (BRM), Service component Reference Model (SRM), Data Reference Model (DRM), and the Technical Reference Model (TRM), is designed to facilitate cross-agency analysis, identification of duplicative investments and gaps, and derivation of opportunities for collaboration across agencies. However, the FEA has two critical shortcomings:

1. It is overly IT-centric. The cross-agency analysis, identification of duplicative investments and gaps, and derivation of opportunities for collaboration across agencies are IT oriented. The primary purpose is to optimize investments in IT. This makes the FEA framework an enterprise IT architecture framework. In other words, its scope and influence are limited to only the IT aspects of the federal agencies.
2. The linkages between the various reference models are weak or non-existent. The FEA Consolidated Reference Model Version 2.3 released in October 2007 has no guidelines on how the reference models are to be cross-linked for deeper analysis. Absence of the linkages makes it difficult to craft the ECV and uncover the traceability.

ACTUALIZING THE CONNECTED GOVERNMENT

Developing reference models, as described in the previous section, create an understanding about the structure of the business, data, application and technology domains (or perspectives). They provide the methodological infrastructure needed to realize the vision of connected government. In other words, reference models are necessary but not sufficient to connected government.

As stated earlier, the development of reference models does require analyses, identification of gaps and high-level opportunities. Addressing such gaps often lead to initial or foundational improvements to the structure of the various domains. Therefore, even on its own, architecture reference models provide benefits to governments (Janssen and Hjort-Madsen, 2007). However, the reference models, in some sense, represent the "static" aspect of the architecture. To really derive full benefits of architecture, it is critical that the reference models are used in the context of one or more national (business) priorities. Anchoring architecture efforts towards one or more national priorities result in:

- Converging and focusing architecture efforts towards something viewed as important by the government and other numerous stakeholders.
- Quicker justification of architecture efforts and resources required.
- Better quantification and monetization of benefits, leading to greater effectiveness and visibility.

For the purposes of this chapter, an example of Singapore's healthcare sector is elaborated. The example deals with the approach to tackle chronic disease management, which is a high priority national issue in Singapore. As management of chronic diseases is a major issue in many developed economies, there are lessons to be learnt from the below example by many countries and governments.

As mentioned earlier in this chapter, the healthcare domain is high-priority in many regions around the world. The urgency to study and understand this domain gains momentum given the massive demographic shifts taking place. Healthcare (especially in the government) has the highest potential for efficiency gains (about 35%) if it is analyzed with a systemic mindset. Economists estimate that the annual global savings potential from improvements to the healthcare systems is about USD 4 trillion (IBM, 2010b). Therefore, healthcare is an area that has the strategic, operational, social and economic rationale to being a national (business) priority.

THE HEALTHCARE CONUNDRUM

Health care is a complex adaptive system with a strong social focus (Rouse, 2008). Figure 21 shows the key stakeholders in the health care ecosystem as identified by the World Health Organization (WHO). WHO also highlights the interconnectedness that is both existing and desirable to ensure high-quality health care at affordable costs (WHO, 2005). Hierarchical decomposition does not work for complex adaptive systems. Health care systems operate in a heterogeneous environment of public and private services, with numerous business operating models that make a coherent design, implementation and operation of integrated health care systems challenging (WEF, 2013).

In general, health care systems around the world are on a troublesome and dangerous path with a combination of high costs, uneven quality,

frequent errors, and limited access to care. The situation is further exacerbated by changing demographics that bring forth issues that have hitherto never been analyzed in totality. Michael Porter and Elizabeth Teisberg in their book Redefining Health Care-Creating Value Based Competition on Results list out key causes of the ills that afflict the health care industry. Broadly, these are: (1) prevalence of the commodity mindset; (2) focus on reducing short-term costs; (3) variation in quality and costs based on geographical location; (4) incentives to the health care providers to blend in and follow standard procedures; (5) continued practice of academic specialties replicated in health care providers; (6) questionable patient attitudes and motivations; (7) patient care centered on medical conditions; and (8) incentives to health plan and health care providers to aim for short-term goals and performance metrics (Porter and Teisberg, 2006).

Furthermore, the overall health care systems get even more muddled with the advent of new and emerging issues that get amplified due to the ever-changing demographics. The disease profile of the

Figure 21. Stakeholders in the health care ecosystem

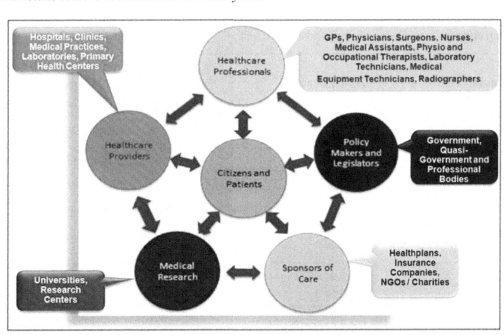

world is changing ever so rapidly, and long held notions about health care systems are no longer true and at most times even misleading (Rouse, 2007). A health care phenomenon that is confounding governments across the world is the ever growing issue of management of long term conditions (or chronic disease management). Chronic diseases have emerged as the largest cause of death and source of health care costs in developed countries. In many countries, deaths from chronic diseases now outstrip mortality for traditional health concerns such as injuries and communicable diseases. While the primary purpose of this chapter is not to present a detailed review of chronic diseases and their management (Savigny and Adam, 2009). The next section discusses the trends and information pertaining to chronic diseases. These trends and information are presented as they are critical to understanding the business domain with the aim of providing critical inputs to the systems models

presented in the subsequent sections. The quantum of background information on chronic diseases provided is deemed to set the context and fulfill the objective of this chapter – i.e., to demonstrate the use and value of strategic (systems) thinking as an integral element of the EA discipline, thereby making EA more forward-thinking and business effectiveness oriented rather than focusing on operational efficiencies. This change in the way EA itself is viewed is necessitated to support the massive shifts that are being observed.

CHRONIC DISEASES: THE SCALE OF THE PROBLEM

To set the context for the rest of the chapter, Figure 22 shows a comparison of chronic and acute illnesses. As it is evident, the characteristics of chronic conditions are all too different when

Figure 22. Comparing acute and chronic illness

		Acute Disease	**Chronic Illness**
1.	Onset	Abrupt	Usually gradual; long latency period
2.	Duration	Limited and time bound	Lengthy and indefinite
3.	Cause	Usually single	Usually multiple (co-morbidities); changing in nature over time; may cause functional impairment
4.	Diagnosis & Prognosis	Usually accurate	Often uncertain
5.	Medical Intervention	Usually effective and precise	Often indecisive; adverse effects common
6.	Outcome	Cure	Long term management
7.	Uncertainty	Minimal	Pervasive
8.	Patient Involvement	Passive; only as recipients of the treatment	Active; sometimes for administration of medication
9.	Strategy	Treatment efficacy	Prevention or delay in onset; disease management

compared to acute illnesses. In fact, they are a study in contrast and is the primary root cause of a majority of the health care challenges that countries today face.

It is clearly evident from Figure 22 that policies, procedures, processes, systems and other supporting mechanisms established for acute illnesses would be grossly inadequate and even incorrect when applied to chronic illnesses. The WHO lists heart disease, stroke, cancer, asthma and chronic obstructive pulmonary diseases and diabetes as the major ones. This chapter does not examine any specific chronic disease (WHO, 2005). Instead, it views chronic diseases in a collective aggregated manner. It is sufficient for the objective of the chapter as the lessons learnt and other findings can be generalized. The rising prevalence of chronic diseases is a major disturbing issue for governments around the world. Before effective interventions can be designed, several critical questions have to be confronted:

1. What leads to chronic diseases? Are there any medium and long term patterns emerging?
2. Why has the prevalence risen so sharply globally to become a public health priority? How many people will be afflicted with one or more chronic diseases?
3. Are certain parts of the society more vulnerable to chronic diseases? Why?
4. Are there effective ways to deal with this emerging healthcare pandemic? How can we prevent or delay this pandemic?

It quickly becomes apparent that tackling chronic diseases require a holistic, systemic and interdisciplinary perspective that fuses many viewpoints (UK Government Office of Science, 2010). Crafting effective interventions necessitate: (1) the need to gain a deep understanding of current systems and procedures, their behavior over time and plausible futures; (2) the synthesis of different stakeholder perspectives and their interdependence in the system, which can affect and be affected by the system; and (3) the need to comprehend the impact of formal and informal networks and procedures, which can be in favor or in conflict with the other systems. With the above information as context, the following are the mega-trends in chronic diseases that are currently underway. They are examined since they provide a rich source of factors and variables to be used as inputs for the systems models elaborated in subsequent sections. It is to be noted that the purpose of these mega-trends is to understand and gain adequate insights into the phenomenon to derive sufficient information to effectuate strategic (systems) thinking. The intent is not to provide a detailed discourse about chronic disease management per se. These facts and figures are largely taken from relevant literature made available by the WHO (WHO, 2005; La Trobe University, 2008).

1. An estimated 388 million people will die from chronic diseases in the next decade. With increased investment in the prevention or delay of chronic disease onset, it will be possible to prevent 36 million premature deaths in the same time horizon. Without action to address the causes, deaths from chronic diseases will increase by 17% between 2005 and 2015.
2. The macroeconomic impact of chronic diseases will be substantial. Large countries will likely forego in excess of USD 1 trillion in national income over the next decade. Averted deaths with better management of chronic diseases would translate into substantial gains in the national economic growth.
3. Globally, a misconception that chronic diseases mainly affects high-income countries is widely prevalent. Furthermore, there is also a belief that lower and middle-income countries must focus on infectious diseases before chronic diseases. These misconcep-

tions are contrasted by the fact that 80% of all chronic disease deaths occur in low and middle-income countries.

4. Globally, there has been an unprecedennted rise in the cost of healthcare. This is attributed to factors both in the "demand" and the "supply" sides of the healthcare systems. The demand-side factors include – higher patient expectations and growing burden of diseases, while the supply-side factors are rising unit cost of care and sub-optimal allocation of resources. In addition, factors like lack of incentives for patients to minimize cost, increase in capacity artificially inducing demand, lack of performance transparency and higher survival rates leading to more years of treatment, directly contribute to healthcare costs rising much faster than general inflation.

5. Globalization, urbanization and population ageing are the key underlying socioeconomic, cultural, political and environmental determinants contributing to modifiable and non-modifiable risk factors. The most common modifiable risk factors leading to chronic diseases include unhealthy diet, physical inactivity and tobacco use. The non-modifiable risk factors include age and genetics.

6. Chronic diseases and poverty are interconnected in a vicious cycle. On one hand, poor people are more vulnerable for several reasons, including increased exposure to risks and limited access to health services. While, on the other hand, chronic diseases can lead to poverty in individuals and their families. Together, these two have the potential to lead to a downward spiral of worsening disease and poverty. This phenomenon directly brings down the individual and national productivities.

7. In general, health care services and systems are primarily designed for acute care. Services and systems for chronic care are usually carved out by "tweaking" them from the acute care. This, despite the fact that chronic diseases constitute 70% of the disease burden, thus creating a massive mismatch between supply and demand.

8. Different chronic diseases themselves have some degree of inter-connectedness, that is, the incidences of co-morbidities, which usually worsens with age, plays an important role in complicating treatments and interventions. This is depicted in Figure 23.

9. The total number of people aged 70 years and above worldwide is expected to increase from 269 million in 2000 to 1 billion by 2050. Age is an important factor in the accumulation of modifiable risks for chronic diseases; that is the impact of risk factors increases over the life course. The demographic transition currently underway is truly dramatic. That said, it is important to note that most developed countries have a rapidly ageing population, primarily due to the dual effects of increasing life expectancy and dangerously low birth rates. For example, countries in East Asia have a total fertility rate of under 1.2. This compares very unfavorably, given that a country requires a total fertility rate of 2.1 just replace its population. From 1975, through to present, Singapore's TFR has never been above the replacement level. Singapore's current fertility rate stands at 1.29 in 2012. In other words, Singapore faces a prolonged reproductive recession.

10. Sub replacement level birth rates, if unchecked, have devastating on the working-age population. In 2012, Singapore has two citizens entering the workforce for every citizen retiring. In 2030, there will be 0.7 citizens entering the workforce for every citizen retiring. In other words, Singapore's citizen workforce is slated to shrink unless efforts are made now to reverse the trend.

11. Another negative impact of an ageing population is that it leads to a shrinking pool of

Figure 23. Potential co-morbidities associated with major chronic diseases

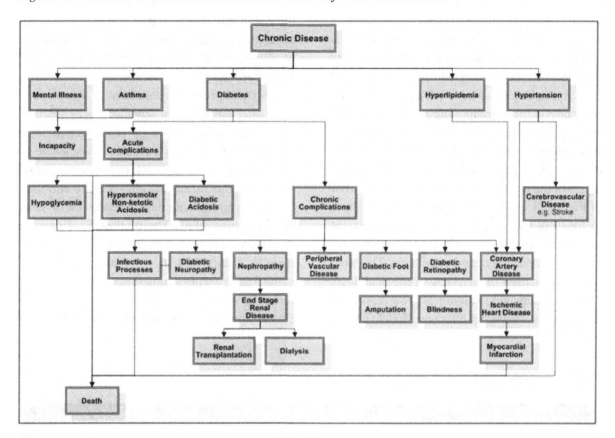

potential caregivers, thus affecting the very quality of chronic care, pushing the whole health system to a further downward spiral. At current projections, Singapore's old-age support ratio (i.e. number of young people available to support people over the age of 65) will plunge from 5.9 to 2.1 by 2030.

All the above facts and figures, in some sense, capture the symptoms ailing the management of chronic diseases. The most natural reaction would be to address these symptoms through short term quick-fix type of solutions. Such an approach would be conventional (open-loop) thinking demonstrating the characteristics are shown in Figure 9 earlier. There is substantial literature elaborating the dangers of open-loop thinking. In contrast, bringing in the closed-loop thinking provides the ability to "look at the big picture" in a unified collective manner, understand the inter-

connectedness and interdependencies between the various elements and parameters involved. In other words, in the context of the chronic diseases, all the above facts and figures would have to be looked at collectively in a systemic perspective (Joffe and Mindell, 2006; Leischow et al., 2008). No doubt management of chronic diseases is a "wicked problem" that requires deeper holistic thinking. It is to be noted that the megatrends above look at chronic diseases collectively in a generic manner, and do not granularize it in terms of individual disease types or patterns (Abegunde and Stanciole, 2006).

STRATEGIC (SYSTEMS) THINKING

According to Edward Deming, an over-whelming majority (94%) of all organizational issues are systemic in nature. Usually, leaders and managers do not fully understand the systemic issues. This is absolutely true with regard to management of chronic diseases. The work presented in this chapter was carried out for a healthcare cluster in Singapore. The cluster consists of a group of polyclinics, large hospitals, specialist centers and other provider entities looking at community and home-care services. The cluster is also supported by a group of enlisted general practitioners and other business partners. In summary, all the elements of the health care ecosystem shown earlier in Figure 21 exist in this cluster. Some of these elements of the ecosystem are in their own right large and complex enterprises, having their own strategy, management and operations. The business areas within the purview of the healthcare cluster are depicted in Figure 24. This represents the cluster's Business Reference Model (BRM).

The BRM depicts the outside-in perspective of the health care cluster. It only shows the business areas and business functions without depicting which provider entity (enterprise) within the cluster provides the service.

This perspective is important as it organizes the cluster business in a way that makes sense to the service recipients (i.e. citizens and patients). The service recipients do not need to be aware of the health care cluster's internal administrative structure. This makes the cluster more end-user (patient) centric without cluttering them with administrative details. The implication of viewing the business from a patient centric perspective includes disintermediation of individual provider entities and assumes seamless integration between them. In short, to the patients and citizens, the cluster appears as one, the manifestation of the

Figure 24. Health care cluster business reference model (level 0 view)

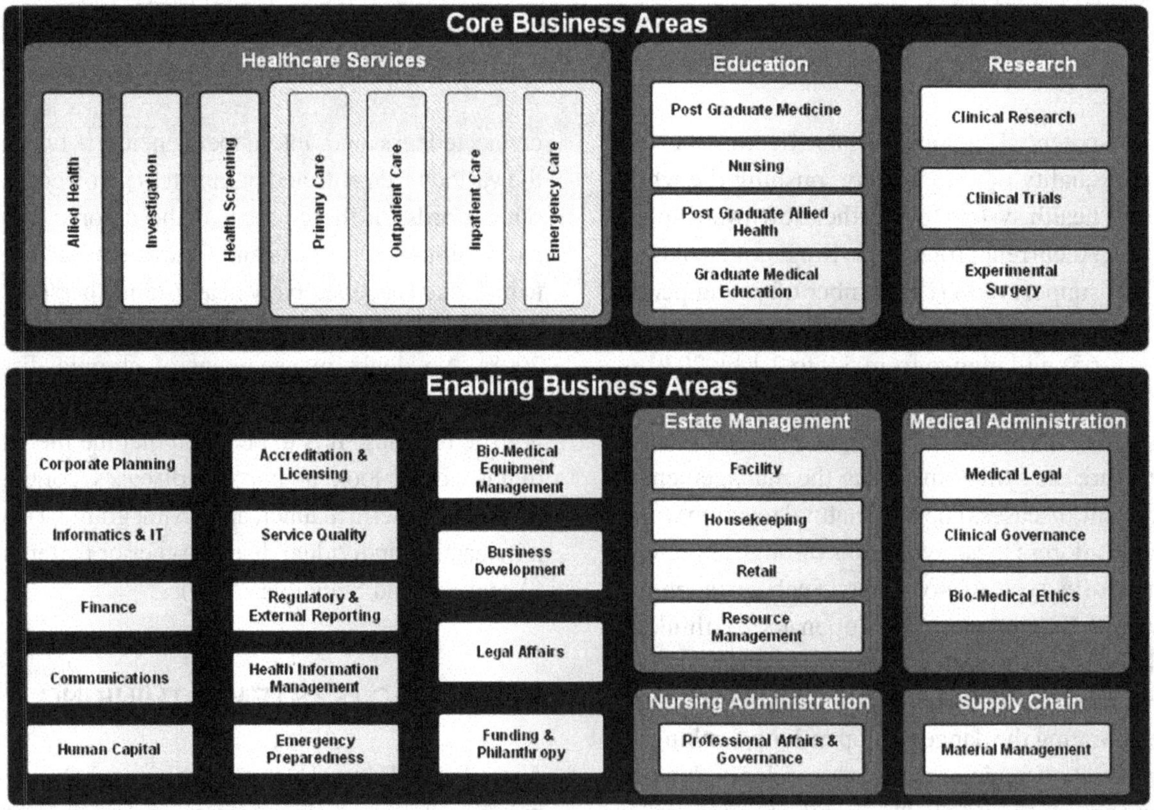

connected health paradigm. This is essential for countries aiming to reform their public health sector. Though not central to this chapter, an interesting side note is that such a connected paradigm in the health care sector is an essential precursor to the success of Electronic Health Record (EHR) programs that many countries have enthusiastically initiated.

Purely, from a technology perspective, the BRM needs to be supported and enabled by other reference models (e.g. the DRM, ARM, and TRM, as explained earlier. Despite each individual provider entity tasked with different aspects of the care delivery value chain, it was very clear upfront that tackling chronic disease management required a holistic and integrated approach, because it had both cluster-wide and nationwide ramifications. Chronic disease management "touched" every business area shown in Figure 24, thus the integrated approach is an imperative.

The Care Delivery Value Chain (CDVC) proposed by Michael Porter and Elizabeth Teisberg in their book *Redefining Healthcare-Creating Value Based Competition on Results*, is a powerful technique to capture the integrated view. The CDVC provides an excellent technique to identify and sequence the care functions and sub-functions in an integrated manner working through the "care journey" that a patient traverses via the different stages. The CDVC also depicts the various participating provider entities in the delivery of the care (Porter and Teisberg, 2006). This highlights the collaborative aspects of the care delivery which is essential for better and effective care. However, in order for us to understand and dissect a complex problem, not only is it important to understand the interactions between the various provider entities and the functions they perform, but also to capture and fully understand the interactions between the various factors and variables that form the core and contribute to the complexity and dynamism. This is achieved through adopting strategic (systems) thinking. The subsequent paragraphs elaborate the adoption of strategic (systems) thinking fac-

toring in the mega-trends that have already been presented earlier. This contrasts very well with the usual approach, wherein the approach would be to identify a few key business functions from the BRM, sometimes called "hotspots," prioritize them and analyze them to address the issues in consideration.

This analytical approach characterized by its "divide-and-rule" mindset is reductionist in nature and put forth all the ingredients that usually tend to make enterprises "micro-smart" and "macro-dumb." The underlying rationale for the adoption of strategic (systems) thinking is that "any assumption that the effectiveness of the whole will be achieved automatically, as long as the parts are optimal, can no longer be sustained with the systemic paradigm." Strategic (systems) thinking is able to capture the wisdom of diverse stakeholders. This notion is strengthened by the WHO World Health Report which states that "the responses of many health systems so far have been generally considered inadequate and naïve. Inadequate, insofar as they not only fail to anticipate, but also to respond appropriately – too often with too little, too late or too much in the wrong place. Naïve insofar as a system's failure requires a system's solution – not a temporary remedy" (WHO, 2005). That said, strategic (systems) thinking is not a silver bullet. Its adoption does not automatically mean that addressing complex business issues becomes easier without changing the mindset that caused the problem to start and aggravate.

A COMPLEX SYSTEM

There is an underlying complexity to chronic diseases, which means that any approach to tackling it must take a multi-faceted perspective. The complexity is accentuated by the interplay between a wide variety of variables and influencing factors related to individual habits and preferences, physiology, food consumption, individual psychology and social psychology (Homer and Hirsch, 2006). This chapter uses the system mapping approach consisting of several causal loops (Senge, 1990; Sterman, 2000). The next few sections progressively construct the complete system map by adding causal loops. The purpose is to show how the different seemingly independent variables co-exist and influence each other. This allows for deep insights and facilitates the identification of impactful interventions.

Taking the chronic disease facts and figures presented earlier, the problem framing process starts with the common modifiable risk factors (like unhealthy diet, physical inactivity and use of tobacco) triggered by the underlying determinants of globalization, urbanization and ageing population; this increases the overall risk of chronic diseases, which leads to the eventual onset of chronic diseases. The onset of the disease requires financial resources to provide for adequate care and treatments, thus increasing the overall economic burden for the individual. The situation is further exacerbated by the fact that the populations with

chronic diseases are likely to be less productive (as compared to healthy population), leading to foregone income (WHO, 2005).

This leads to a drop in resources and financial capability to afford proper care, further increasing the negative impact of the chronic diseases. This is depicted in Figure 25, and collectively termed as the avoidable burden loop. This is a positive loop as it represents a downward spiral and clearly demonstrates the long-term negative consequences of chronic diseases both on the individuals and countries. The loop is deliberately named so because it implicitly captures a phenomenon that is largely avoidable if individuals and countries focus on reducing the common modifiable risks. This thinking is in line with the WHO recommendations. The avoidable burden loop thus becomes the central core of the problem frame, the nodal loop, around which other chronic disease factors and variables are progressively added in the form of more loops. This process is elaborated in the subsequent paragraphs of this section.

Figure 25. Underlying factors and the chronic disease onset

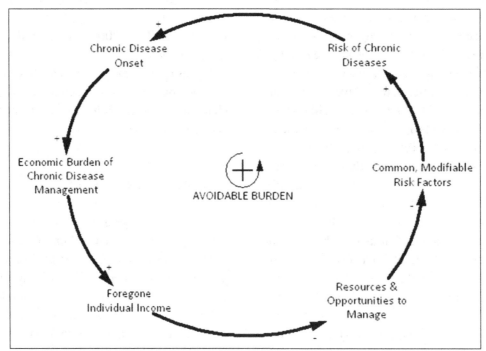

As the incidences of chronic disease care become more prevalent and expensive due to the downward spiral shown in Figure 25, there is increased pressure by the citizens and the civil society on the government to subsidize disease care. Being a political hotbed, most governments provide subsidy en-mass, i.e. there is a great likelihood that the section of the society that not need the subsidy are also subsidized. To address this, the concept of "means testing" is rightly being introduced in Singapore.

This subsidy is realized through various means, for instance, the patient can directly be subsidized, or the healthcare providers can be compensated for treating patients with chronic diseases. Usually governments adopt a multi-pronged approach to deliver the subsidies as it provides them greater leverage. Irrespective of the means of providing the subsidy, the impact on the national income and the economy is inevitable. This is the shown in the subsidy response loop. This leads to further negative impact on the resources available for the

healthcare sector in general (and chronic disease management in specific). Hence, the subsidy has the potential to become a national burden, if it is not carefully targeted as shown in the national cost loop.

These two loops together work in tandem and have the potential to create serious shortcomings in the healthcare ecosystem by constraining the availability of resources and opportunities to manage chronic diseases. This then feeds into the core downward spiral depicted by the previously described avoidable burden loop. The foregone national income has a direct negative impact on the available resources and leads to the deterioration of overall quality of life, eventually leading to higher risks of chronic diseases. In other words, individual and national poverty aggravate the problem of chronic diseases even further.

On top of this, increasing life expectancy actually worsens the problem even further. This is depicted in the life expectancy matters loop. Figure 26 shows the three new loops and also

Figure 26. Role of subsidies, foregone national income, and life expectancy

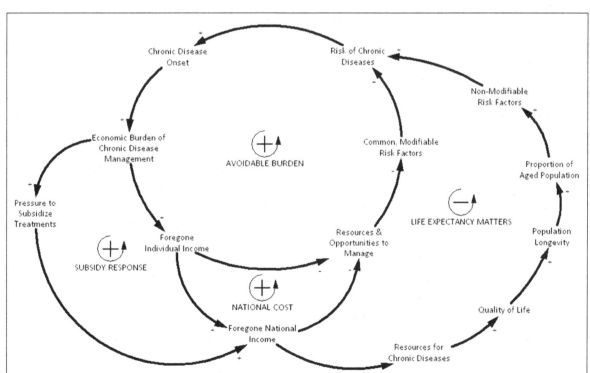

amply demonstrates how these three loops actually worsen the downward spiral. This is an interesting phenomenon wherein one downward spiral is strengthened by a series of other interconnected loops, via common factors and variables. Strategic (systems) thinking makes this behavior explicit and apparent. This is precisely how whole systems thinking propagates and makes the approach more amenable to effective interventions by anticipating and yet formally structuring.

Long term evidence proves that with timely and effective interventions and proper medication management, most patients with chronic diseases can actually lead near-normal lives with minimal interruptions. This is further made possible by recent advancements made in the medical sciences. This means most patients can actually drastically reduce their visits to specialists. In other words, in most situations general practitioners and polyclinics are sufficient to continue with treatments and keep the diseases at bay. Reducing interactions with specialists directly leads to lower costs for payers and also ensures that specialists, who are always in short supply, do not become the bottleneck in the whole ecosystem. Escalation in healthcare costs in general, and cost of treating patients with chronic conditions is largely due to incomplete knowledge of the delivering patient care. Provider charges are not a good surrogate for provider costs, and this is supported by empirical evidence. Furthermore, the muddle is aggravated because the providers have structured the crucial components of their costing around the way they are reimbursed.

With the previous notions in mind, there is also empirical evidence to prove that as subsidy is increased (by the government), it becomes more attractive to refer a specialist and the usual inclination is to refer a specialist as the first-level intervention, irrespective of whether it is needed or not. This demonstrates normal human behavior, which is driven by incomplete and misconceived mental models on the part of the patients. This behavior is the evidence of questionable patient attitudes

and motivations that *Michael Porter* and *Elizabeth Teisberg* have identified and highlighted in their book (Porter and Teisberg, 2006). This behavior leads to crowded hospitals and specialist centers, elongating queues and waiting times. This has an impact on the national productivity and eventually the gross national income. This phenomenon is captured in the involving specialists loop.

Building up from the life expectancy matters loop, and ageing population leads to a drop in working (and productive) adults, which have a negative impact on the gross national income; an eventual drop in investments available for healthcare occurs as it erodes the tax base over time. Typically, governments respond to this by increasing the retirement age limits, as is currently being seen in many countries. However, the downside is an older working population would also be more prone to chronic diseases. An erosion of the tax base results in governments earning lower revenues through taxes and other levies. In other words, as the proportion of working adults drop; there are less people to contribute into the country's financial system, and an increasing number who require financial assistance during their non-productive years. In addition, a dropping birthrate also ensures that not an adequate number of working adults come into the system in the decades to come, further eroding future tax base (DeVol et al., 2007).

This effectively has long-term negative implications on the national economy and resources available for healthcare, thereby increasing the chronic disease morbidity and mortality, further strengthening avoidable burden loop described earlier. This behavior is captured in the chronic disease deaths loop. This affects the quality of life and eventually leads to greater risks of chronic disease onset. There is evidence that as gross national income falls, the proportion of the population in the lower-income category bulges and usually tends to be most badly affected. In other words, the poorer sections of the society become even poorer, thus enlarging the chasm between the rich and the poor, primarily because of unequal distribution of wealth. The inequality (measured as the GINI index) increases the intensity and the spread of poverty. This, without doubt, leads to increases in chronic disease morbidity and mortality as shown in the poverty hurts loop. The WHO has clearly demonstrated the existence of a downward spiral between chronic diseases and poverty. Figure 27 depicts the involving specialists, chronic disease deaths, healthcare investments and poverty hurts loops. Chronic diseases constitute 70% of the disease burden. The supply-demand mismatch between acute and chronic care is already an observed phenomenon. Wrong patient attitudes and motivations leading to crowded hospitals is a result of the involving specialists loop, examined earlier. This is further worsened by the fact that crowded hospitals have a greater tendency to focus on the wrong priorities (i.e. focus on immediate priorities) at times even hurting the long-term effectiveness.

According to a study by the Harvard Law School, medical bankruptcy is a clear and present possibility. In the United States, 62% of all bankruptcies have a medical cause. Most medical debtors are well-educated, middle class and nearly three-quarters have medical insurance (Himmelstein et al., 2009). It is amply evident that current systems, policies, procedures, and processes are not designed to handle chronic care.

Given the immediacy of needs and other operational pressures, healthcare providers usually tend to spend a greater proportion of their time and resources in providing acute care and treating patients with infectious diseases. This is captured in the unclear priorities and priority for acute-care loops in Figure 28.

According to a survey done by the WHO, the cost of chronic disease care is by far the most significant challenge for both individuals and governments. In general, the escalation in the cost of healthcare far outstrips the broader inflation

Figure 27. Macroeconomic consequences of chronic diseases

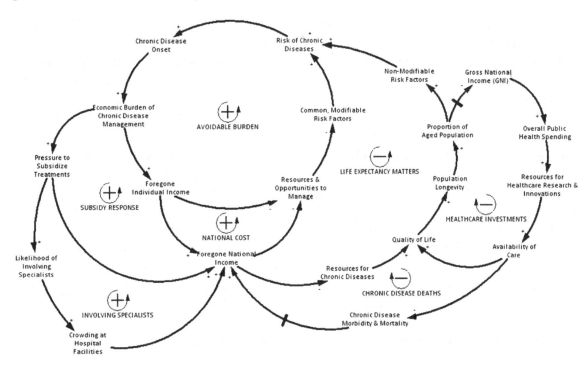

Figure 28. Amplification of the supply-demand mismatch and unclear priorities

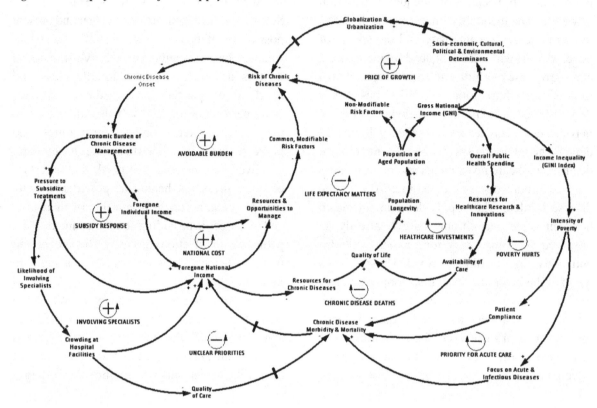

(WHO, 2005). The situation is even more acute when viewed from the chronic disease perspective. As the cost of chronic care treatments escalates, people attempt to cover through insurance (wherever possible). With wrong patient attitudes and motivations, the typical behavior is for patients to prefer specialists over general practitioners (already discussed earlier). This inflates the overall costs in the whole of the healthcare ecosystem. As costs rise, insurance firms are forced to become more stringent in their checks and approvals. Given that insurance firms have a profit-making motive, this worsens the situation even further. This increases the incidence of non-coverage for existing customers and lengthens the list of exclusions for potential new customer, leading to insurance becoming less attractive. As insurance becomes less attractive, the insured tend to opt out of the programs and potential new customers not

finding insurance attractive are not inclined to insure themselves or their families. This creates twin headwinds for the insurance sector as existing customers opt-out and new customer base expansion slows down. The overall collective insurance base gets severely restricted. For the population that stays back as part of the insurance programs, the premiums go up because there are not enough healthy people to pay for the programs and plans. All of these happen, even as the whole ecosystem is plagued by increasing life expectancies and falling birth rates. The paradox is in the fact that insurance firms want to insure the healthy, whereas the healthy do not want to get insured because of the overall unattractiveness of the programs and plans. This death spiral is depicted in Figure 29, through the costs of treatment, questionable insurance effectiveness and gaps in quality of healthcare loops. The loops in Figure

Figure 29. The health insurance death spiral

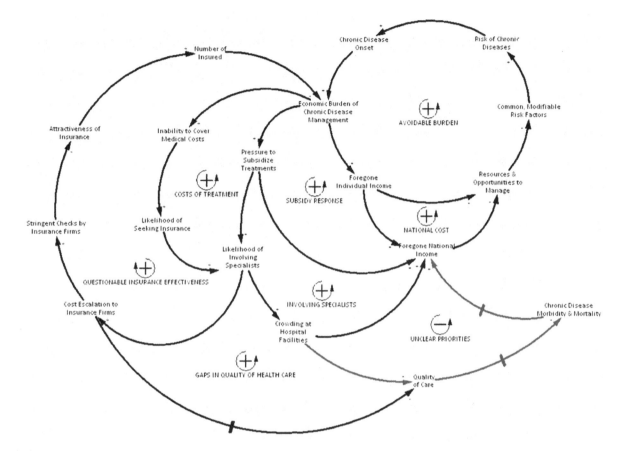

29 also amplify the mismatch between supply and demand. The current insurance plans and programs are designed for acute care, and then "tweaked" to work for chronic care. In addition, the upward trend in the GNI provides the fodder for socio-economic, cultural, political and environmental determinants, magnifying the globalization and urbanization pre-factors that lead to increase in risks of chronic diseases.

Figures 25 through to 29 examined the various factors relevant in the context of chronic diseases. The various loops that were discussed aimed to link these factors in a series of causal connections. Figure 30 depicts the complete business systems model for chronic disease management. The synthesized view:

1. Enables capturing and understanding the "forest" before digging into the "trees." This is an essential perspective that allows for discovery and understanding of both combinatorial and dynamic complexities. According to the IBM Global CEO Study 2010, public sector leaders believe the escalation of complexity is the most important issue confronting enterprises. Strategic (systems) thinking facilitates creative thinking that is essential to address the challenges of complexity (IBM, 2010a).

2. Does not clutter the holistic perspective as the individual organizational entities (in this case provider entities like general practitioners, polyclinics, hospitals, specialist centers,

Figure 30. Chronic disease management systems map

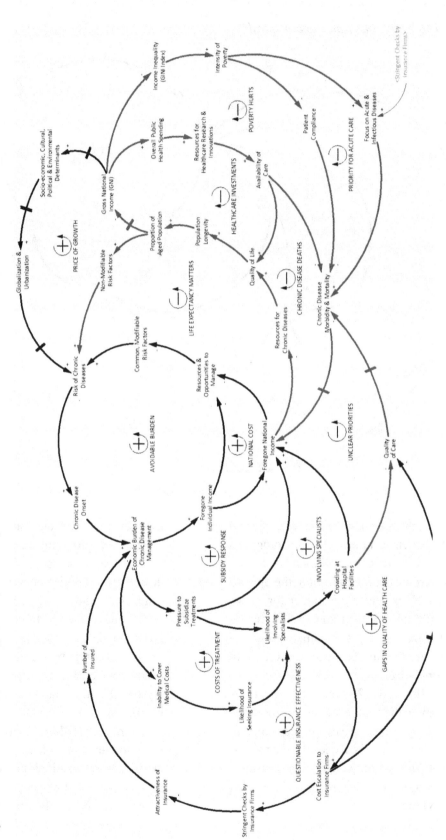

community and home care providers) take the backseat, and instead the focus on the common underlying concern or issue that is being examined. This enables the connected view. In other words, the focus is on the interactions rather than the entities involved. This is essential for architects to become designers of coherence rather than designers of components and layers.

3. Frames the problem space in a way that allows for organizational leaders to design strategic interventions and to envision the impact of these interventions both upstream and downstream. The strategic interventions can then be examined, prioritized and effectuated through smaller more tactical action items. This creates a culture of and a capability for operating dexterity, providing both insight and foresight.

4. Encourages collaboration and co-creation as the key stakeholders are now able to view the problem in an integrated manner and also realize that addressing the issue requires these stakeholders to think collectively and holistically. It also discourages piecemeal and stovepipe approach. Multidisciplinary and multi-stakeholder involvement is an essential success factor for effective enterprise architecture and leadership.

5. Catalyzes business design and innovation by taking benefit of all the above current and emergent perspectives, thereby providing a relatively sustained advantage. This is supported by a survey done by the Boston Consulting Group (BCG).

From the complete system map as shown in Figure 30, it is evident that all four sources of complexity, i.e. diversity, interdependence, ambiguity and flux come into play. The existence of imposed, inherent, designed and unnecessary complexity cannot be overstated (Schwaninger, 2006). Acknowledging this is important, as it allows us to understand the systemic complexity and accordingly design the rights interventions to tackle the same (Trochim et al., 2006).

Following are some illustrations of the different types of complexity that exist:

- **Imposed Complexity:** The health care sector as a whole is a complex maze of rules, regulations and policies. As in almost all countries, these tend to be mandatory that need to be complied with. There is very little that a single health cluster or a hospital can do about this;

- **Inherent Complexity:** The nature of health care, intrinsically, is complex. Delivering health services is not just a matter of diagnosis and medication. The social, cultural, economic, political, technological issues are tightly intertwined and complex labyrinth;

- **Designed Complexity:** From a holistic perspective, there are many entities that have to come together and collaborate to provide health services. This is more so in case of chronic diseases, because the patient's interaction with the health service provider cannot be treated as episodic. The entities is this value network (polyclinics, hospitals, specialist centers, home-care centers, communicate care centers and insurance firms) are different enterprises, jurisdictionally, that form the ecosystem (system map) shown in Figure 30. This map is characterized by change in existing nodes and connectors, disappearance of existing nodes and connectors and appearance of new nodes and connectors, making it difficult to apply "predictive reasoning"; and

- **Unnecessary Complexity:** These arise from misalignment between the needs and priorities, and the processes supporting it. For example, while the systemic priority would be to deal with patients with chronic diseases, the actual hospital policies and processes are designed to optimize acute care. The supply-demand misalignment becomes the source of complexity that is largely avoidable.

Complexity can be held at various levels of the enterprise. In case of chronic disease management, complexity resides in the entire system (i.e. the entire enterprise). It is to be noted that the entire enterprise in this context includes the entire SingHealth cluster, which by itself is a complex labyrinth of individual polyclinics, hospitals, specialist centers among others. In such an architecture, ability to manage complexity is a source of competitive advantage – as the underlying complex system is very difficult to replicate and master. This demands highly creative and adaptive leadership and operational dexterity (KPMG, 2012a, 2012b). The next section describes the design of appropriate interventions with the above background in consideration.

STRATEGIC INTERVENTIONS

Peter Senge in *The Fifth Discipline* argues that to solve difficult problems one needs to understand the "interrelationships rather than things, for seeing patterns of change rather than static snapshots" (Senge, 1990). To design effective intervention strategies, it is critical to "diagnose" the issues correctly and frame the problem space. Insight and foresight are both crucial. Figure 31 depicts problem space in a synthesized view. It captures several factors and connects them via a series of loops, all of which have been discussed earlier. It is important to note that the factors, and the loops are specific to the local conditions in Singapore. They need to be suitably adapted prior to use in other situations. Needless to mention, the specific interventions would depend on the

context of specific nuances. Designing the right interventions are as important as the location these interventions would be applied. However, part of the strategic intervention design should also include uncovering and understanding the inherent delays in the system, for the system with long-term delay cannot respond to short-term changes. In a complex system, there are places where a small shift in one "thing" can produce large changes in (almost) everything. The places are termed "leverage points–the points of power." Donella Meadows in her article Leverage Points–Places to Intervene in a System identifies and elaborates generic leverage points where interventions are most likely to be impactful and results bearing (Meadows, 1999). The intervention framework used here consist of the following levels (levels depicting the impact on the system):

- **Level 5 – Paradigm**: Deepest held beliefs driving the system.
- **Level 4 – Goals**: Objectives the system is trying to achieve.
- **Level 3 – Structure**: Strengthening linkages between various actors / stakeholders involved in the system.
- **Level 2 – Feedback and Delays**: Inclusion of self-regulation, self-reinforcement and adaptation.
- **Level 1 – Structural Elements**: Optimizing the subsystems and the physical structure of the system.

Moving forward, the next logical step from an architectural perspective is to propose steps that could be taken to address the chronic disease pandemic. These "steps" are called strategic interventions, as they tend to be long-term in nature and often require series of action items to be executed and operationalized. The WHO recommends ten steps to applying systems perspective in the design and evaluation of strategic interventions (WHO, 2005).

Figure 31. Chronic disease management system map with suggested interventions

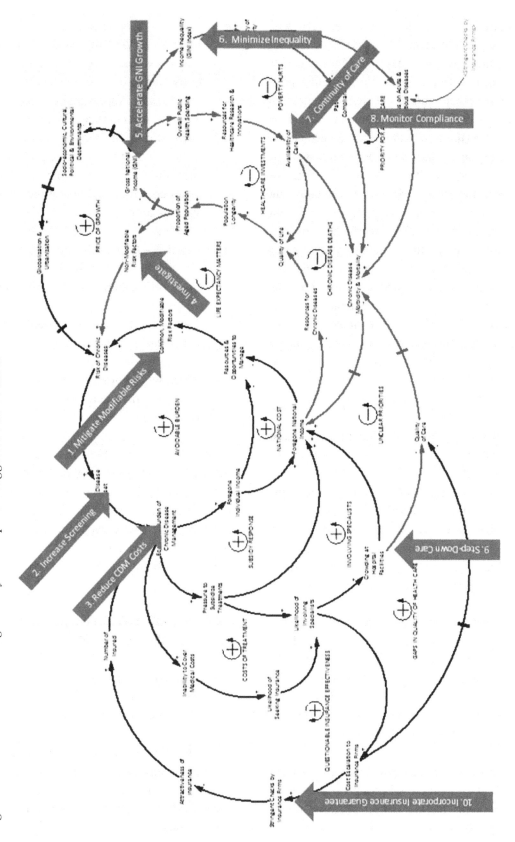

Figure 31 depicts the synthesized view with the strategic interventions (as arrows), and the significant delays are also shown. Management of chronic diseases is a national priority in Singapore, as in many other countries. This is evidenced by the fact that the Singapore Government has always been viewing this from a long-term perspective and designing policies and programs to suit current and emerging needs. Healthcare services in Singapore are one of the most advanced and arguably, one of the best in the world. With regard to chronic diseases, the government clearly demonstrates long-term vision, which is achieved by a series of small yet focused and progressive action items.

In the national budget announcement for 2011, made in March 2011, the government announced a series of action items that are intended to tackle this gigantic public health issue of chronic disease management. The action items announced include:

1. Establishing the Geriatric Education and Research Institute.
2. Expanding the Home Nursing Foundation.
3. Scaling up operations of the Agency for Integrated Care.
4. Contributing to the Community Silver Trust.
5. Expanding the Medifund budget.
6. Extending the Medication Assistance Scheme.
7. Encouraging step-down care with the expanded Primary Care Partnership Scheme.

The actual implementation of these action items is not within the scope of this chapter. However, the ten interventions (shown in Figure 31) and the seven action items, collectively actualize the intervention framework presented earlier. The five-level framework and its various elements are realized as follows (Meadows, 1999):

- **Level 5 – Paradigm:** Viewing management of chronic diseases as a complex problem, that is a national priority requiring a systemic approach.

- **Level 4 – Goals:** Reducing the prevalence of and delaying the onset of chronic diseases by encouraging physical activity, early screening, healthier dietary habits and healthier food supply.

- **Level 3 – Structure:** Enhancing seamless chronic disease care services by enabling greater coherence and connectivity, information sharing and increased trust for cross-enterprise collaboration between the various entities in the care delivery value network.

- **Level 2 – Feedback and Delays:** Strengthening the reinforcing loops, while tackling (or weakening) the balancing loops wherever feasible.

- **Level 1 – Structural Elements:** Reducing the cost of healthcare in general, encouraging telemedicine, quality regular physical education, affordable healthy foods, accessible treatment options, and wider government financial support.

By demonstrating the ability to adapt to change, influence and shape the environment it operates in, reconfigure itself to suit the changing needs and make a net positive contribution to the viability and development of the larger healthcare ecosystem in Singapore, SingHealth clearly demonstrates the evidence of being a learning enterprise.

POWER OF STRATEGIC (SYSTEMS) THINKING

It is obviously clear from the above that the action items are targeted to meet specific needs and address some of the strategic interventions depicted in Figure 31 earlier. Comparing the strategic interventions and the action items shows that the strategic interventions are more long-term in nature, while the action items tend to be more tactical and executable in nature. The strategic interventions are excellent inputs for governments to develop policy enablers. Furthermore, strategic thinking also facilitates deeper understanding of policy resistance that is often displayed by "stubborn" problems (Williams and Hummelbrunner, 2009). Figure 32 shows the author's own assessment of the strategic interventions covered by the announced action items. It is clearly seen that the action items put forth reflect the pre-emptive anticipatory thinking on the part of the government (Zokaei, Seddon and O'Donovan, 2011). The problem at hand, chronic disease management, is a complex and stubborn one. Hence the action items demonstrate the progressive series of tasks that are being planned and performed to tackle it. It is to be noted that the Singapore government already has existing plans and schemes for management

of long term conditions, example policies and programs pertaining to: (1) ageing workforce; (2) chronic disease care costs; (3) programs mitigating modifiable risk factors; (4) pre-emptive screening; and (5) GNI / GDP growth and economic well-being. In Figure 32, the action items are limited to the ones specifically announced in the March 2011 national budget. In summary, a very promising start has been made towards fruition, and it is comforting to see that progress is being made in the right direction. This is the essence of effective strategic (systems) thinking. It is imperative that the complex effects, synergies and emergent behavior of system interventions are fully understood in order to take the benefit. Additionally, any intervention with system-wide

Figure 32. Mapping strategic interventions to the announced action items

Strategic Interventions Identified	1. Establish the Geriatric Education and Research Institute	2. Expand the Home Nursing Foundation	3. Scale up Operations of the Agency for Integrated Care	4. Contribute to the Community Silver Trust	5. Expand the Medifund Budget	6. Extend the Medication Assistance Scheme	7. Step-Down Care with the Primary Care Partnership Scheme
1. Mitigate Modifiable Risks							
2. Increase Screening							
3. Reduce CDM Costs	√	√√	√	√√	√√	√√	√
4. Investigate Non-Modifiable Risk Factors	√√						
5. Accelerate GNI Growth							
6. Minimize Inequality							
7. Continuity of Care	√	√√	√√	√			
8. Monitor Medication Compliance		√	√				
9. Step-Down Care		√√	√	√			√√
10. Incorporate Insurance Guarantee							

Figure 33. Discovering collaboration opportunities across boundaries

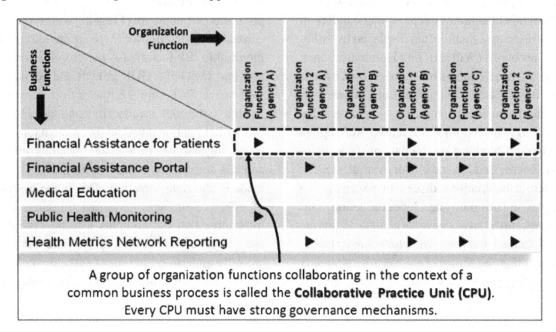

implications cannot be considered "simple" and allows enterprises to capitalize on complexity (Ritchley, 1991).

Strategic thinking establishes the vision, while action items enable the actualization of that vision. This is an essential element for enhancing the effectiveness of the EA, as often EA is perceived of being overly skewed towards "housekeeping" type of activities, rather than facilitating the enterprises to think forward and enable the "visioning" process. The perception is not entirely incorrect and current EA frameworks reinforce this even further. Current EA frameworks take a top-down, centralized planning approach to EA. They attempt to establish a "target" architecture and set a roadmap to achieve the target. While this planned deliberate approach does provide some directions, the notion of "emergence" is virtually non-existent. Unlike traditional architecture methods (e.g. in civil / construction setting), enterprises are inherently dynamic and always in a state of flux. Hence, these crucial differences demand that the existence of flux is factored in. With the missing notion of "emergence," current EA frameworks try to ar-

chitect for stability, which is an unnatural state for enterprises. This mismatch between reality and existing methods creates substantial shortcomings in the benefits enterprises derive out of EA. This leads to cynicism and at times complete rejection of EA because the systemic complexity does not get the attention it ought to.

Enterprises find the current frameworks onerous and intimidating as they tend to quickly take them into a journey of deep and granular analysis, without spending adequate time for future thinking. Enterprises overly focus on improving the operational enablers at the cost of strategic wisdom and direction. Ignorance, complexity and capability gaps are cited most frequently as the primary reasons. Operational enablers mean: (1) frameworks; (2) methodologies; (3) reference architectures and models; (4) tool capabilities; (5) competency building activities; (6) guidelines and standards; (7) best practices and the like. The skewness in favor of operational enablers is hard to miss. Though operational enablers are important, they, by no means have the ability to supplant the strategic perspective. Their role is primarily in supplementing strategic wisdom and direction. In the absence of the strategic perspective, the EA program virtually navigates part-blind leading to cynicism, lack of persistence, erosion of confidence and loss of attention by the organization leaders. It almost takes a crisis to make deep changes. And when it is time to address the crisis, the focus is on symptoms, not causes.

Embracing strategic (systems) thinking as part of the EA process not only addresses the perception, but also elevates the role of EA as a management and leadership discipline. It ups the innovation stakes, moving up from operational innovation to business model innovation, which goes to the very core of business design (Johnson, 2010; . This factors in and influences the value proposition and the operating model of the enterprise. Because this involves a multi-dimensional and coherent set of activities, innovation at this level is both challenging to execute and difficult to imitate. There is empirical evidence that profit outperformers focus on business model innovation by a substantial margin (Lindgradt, 2009). The author has personally been involved in guiding such a mindset change, hence being able to vouch for it. That said, it would be a while or current EA frameworks to make strategic (systems) thinking as an integral part of their methodologies and approaches.

In the current state of practice, EA programs and initiatives are often conceived and driven by the IT department. In this context, there already are substantial literature and other supporting evidence that the IT department, more often than not, finds it challenging to deeply engage the business or the domain side of the enterprise. According to the IBM Global CIO study, realizing business innovation has been identified as the first and foremost activity as being increasingly expected from CIOs (IBM, 2009). Questionable credibility on part of the IT department exacerbates the lack of communication, leading to disengagement and eventual loss of momentum and interest in EA. It

gets relegated as an "IT project." Embracing strategic (systems) thinking allows for: (1) a business understanding of business concerns / problems; (2) synthesis to take precedence over analysis, which is essential to manifest the "enterprise-wide" view of the architecture; (3) triangulation of emergent strategy development with the more traditional top-down strategic planning; (4) identification of leverage points wherein the interventions tend to be most impactful; (5) framing the problem space in a way that is comprehensible by the senior executive leadership in the enterprise; (6) de-emphasizing on the siloed mindset; (7) establishment of collective strategic priorities; and (8) designing for coherence (consistent, collaborative, connected).

Figure 31 shows the ten strategic interventions and how they are most likely to be prioritized by the various action items. As it is evident, in the near term, the priority is to manage the costs related to chronic disease care. This is seen from the level of coverage that interventions like reduce CDM costs; continuity of care and step-down care receive through the action plan. Measuring and managing healthcare costs in general, remains a challenge for every country. This is so because of the inherent complexity of healthcare delivery, well-entrenched fragmentation in the healthcare delivery, lack of and difficult to enforce standardization and politically sensitive nature of the service itself. As an example, in order to reduce CDM costs, the six-step process recommended by Kaplan and Porter can be adopted (Kaplan and Porter, 2011). The six steps, which provide a plausible approach to adopt a cost measurement system are:

1. Select a medical condition (a chronic disease) and / or a patient population to be evaluated.
2. Develop the care delivery value chain for the selected medical condition.
3. Develop the process maps, involved resources for the care functions and activities derived from the care delivery value chain.

4. Obtain time estimates for each process and estimate the cost of supplying patient-care resources.
5. Estimate the practical throughput and capacity of each resource provider and compute the capacity cost rate.
6. Compute the total costs for each patient's cycle of care.

ACTING ON THE STRATEGIC INTERVENTIONS

Figure 31 shows all the ten identified interventions, while Figure 32 shows them mapped to the budgetary action items. From Figure 32, as an example, intervention "Reduce Chronic Disease Management (CDM) Costs" comes up as a high priority, given the number of active items targeted to tackle the costs of treatment. At this juncture, it is crucial to refer to the BRM (see Figure 24), as:

1. The mapping of business functions to organizational entities clearly identifies the organizational entities involved during the implementation (execution) of the business function.
2. The RACI chart clearly spells out the nature of involvement of the organizational entities.
3. The elements of networked governance (see Figures 6 and 7) are identified. In case of the healthcare cluster, the identified form of governance was "lead organization."

The enterprise connected view (see Figure 20) provides the architectural capability to link strategic interventions to business functions, data entities, application capabilities and technology infrastructure essential to support and implement the interventions. The approach to the utility of architecture reference models for the implementation of strategic interventions is shown Figure 34.

The above provides the mechanism not only to establish strategic interventions, but also to ensure that the underlying architectural framework is crafted and available to implement the interventions (systemic action) (Butland et al., 2007). To summarize:

- In the systems mapping work, a qualitative, causal loop model has been developed in order to:
  - Help understand the complex systemic structure.
  - Contribute to developing a tool that helps policy makers in the generation, definition and testing of possible policy options to respond to emerging challenges.
- In a complex system, there may be several candidate nodal variables. The selection of a nodal variable is based on:
  - **Scientific Relevance:** To what extent does it cohere with observable facts?
  - **Decision-Making Relevance:** To what extent does it reflect relevant "key performance indicators" which govern decision-making?
  - **Heuristic Power:** To what extent does it help us make sense of the complexity?
- A causal loop model is a device to describe the systemic structure of a complex problem. As such it serves three very essential purposes of:
  - Making sense of complexity.
  - Communicating complexity.
  - Enabling development of strategy to intervene in a complex system.

The system model shown in Figure 31 can be extended and enriched by adding goals and objectives. These goals and objectives render the system model as a performance management tool, which

Figure 34. Architecture reference models for systemic action

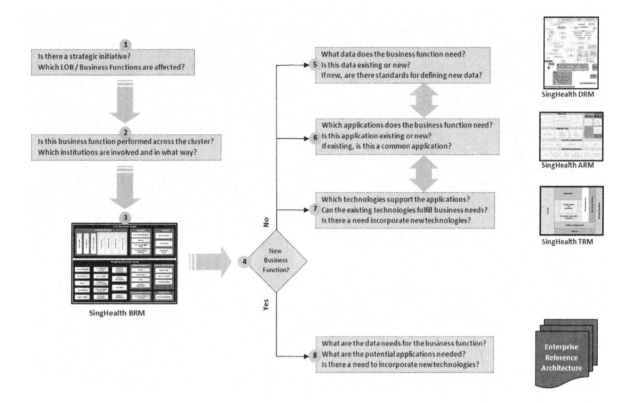

can be used for monitoring of the interventions, their impact on the factors and variables and to pre-empt any kind of unintended consequences (dystopia) (Stroh, 2000). Figure 35 shows the extended system model with the indicative goals and objectives.

CONNECTING THE DOTS

In the same manner, other strategic interventions can be elaborated and actualized in a more granular and measurable fashion. Once the above is achieved, identifying the most relevant business services, business functions and processes to execute the action items becomes the next logical step, followed by the other downstream steps in the development of the IT architecture (Leechul, 2010; Ross, Weill and Robertson, 2006). This would ensure that the business functions and pro-

cesses are adequately IT enabled, and investments are ploughed into the right activities (Microsoft, 2009b). This chapter does not attempt to elaborate the downstream IT architecture steps as there is already a plethora of literature available that covers the topic. Figure 36 summarizes the phases and steps that are typically required to effectuate connected government driven by EA. The phases, steps, sequence and the other elements depicted in Figure 36 are indicative in nature.

Implementing strategic interventions using the methodology require government entities to develop their own specific EAs. In the process of developing their EAs, these government entities usually discover data, application and technology architecture components that: (1) are highly relevant to specific local requirements of the government entity in question; and (2) provide candidates for building / contributing to the W-O-G reference models discussed earlier. This approach ensures

Figure 35. Managing performance of systemic actions

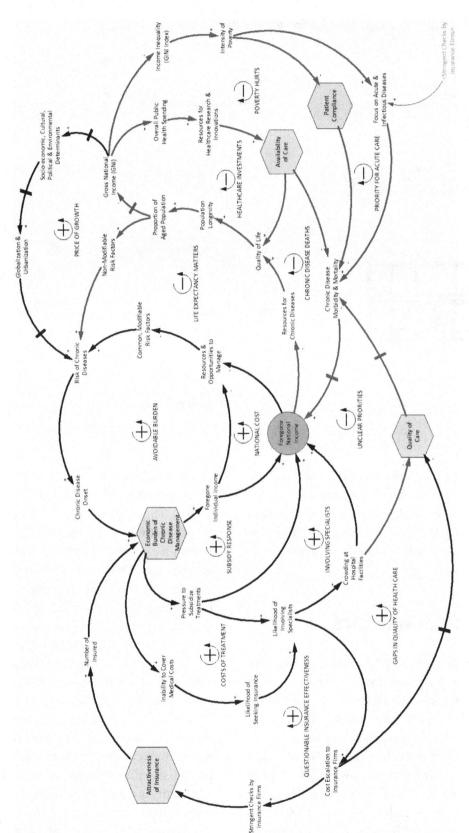

Figure 36. High-level integrated methodology for connected government

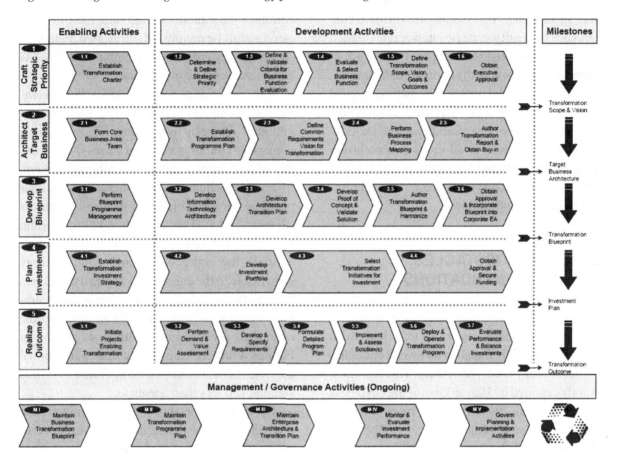

that reference models are always relevant, updated and reflects the current requirements of the individual government entities. Such candidate components may or may not eventually make it into the reference models for inclusion, but the important point is to ensure that such a feedback process to continually update the reference models exists and there are agreed upon criteria to make the assessment for inclusion or otherwise.

The current approach to policy-making, relying on reduction of complex issues into separate, rationally manageable components, is not appropriate for the challenges faced by governments all over the world (Stroh, 2000). The approach in Figure 36 tightly blends systems thinking into EA, is different from the traditional "command-and-control" based EA approaches in that:

- Interventions are ongoing and based on learning that is effective, rather than specifying targets to be met.
- The priority is to improve the overall system performance, factoring in the needs of the various stakeholders.
- The policy-making and the strategy development focus on the processes of improvement, rather than control of the organizational entities involved.
- Implementation deliberately encourages innovation, and crucially includes evaluation and reflection as part of the overall design.

As Mintzberg has pointed out, there is no such thing as a gap between strategy and implementation; there are only policies whose poor design fails to take into account the realities of implementation. In summary, this section demonstrated the approach to identify strategic interventions needed to address a selected national priority. The use of reference models actualizes these interventions. The reference models provide the methodological discipline and supporting infrastructure, while the system models provide visibility to the underlying structure, which is all cases is a collusion of several factors and variables. It is critical to understand the eco-system before interventions can be created and executed.

ENABLERS, OBSTACLES, AND RECOMMENDATIONS

Achieving the vision and full potential of connected government is easier said than done. Such efforts are typically fraught with several obstacles, and technology is not one of them. This sentiment is aptly captured by Haiyan Qian of the UNDESA when she said "W-O-G EA is more a reform process of the government sector, rather than streamlining of the government ICT structure." This is evident from Figures 31 and 32 wherein all the strategic interventions are "business" interventions and action items, which have the potential to impact future policies. Implementation of these interventions may or may not require IT systems, however, ascertaining that would be downstream IT architecture activity (as seen from Figure 36). In most (if not all cases) technology itself can be taken for granted. Failures in connected government initiatives can very seldom be attributed to technology. Connected government initiatives are influenced by a labyrinth of factors, that work together to create a complex set of enablers and inhibitors. It is up to the governments and their respective leadership to understand the complexities and expend efforts in ensuring that the collective impacts of the inhibitors do not exceed the collective impacts of the enablers. In reality, given the enormity of connected govern-

ment initiatives, it is practically impossible to eliminate the inhibitors. That said, their impacts can certainly be minimized and tackled. Figure 37 shows the key enablers and inhibitors to W-O-G EA for connected government.

It is important to note that connected government is a complex paradigm. All enablers and inhibitors, as seen from Figure 37, exist in all scenarios. The only factor that varies is the intensity of their impact and interplay between them. In complex situations like these, it is neither practical nor desirable to eliminate all inhibitors (Reisner, 2011). This is because, up to a certain point the inhibitors act to inject checks and balances to the entire system and avoid runaway growth due to the enablers. Complexity, enablers and inhibitors and their collective impacts amplify manifold as countries aim to move up the connected government maturity stages (as in Figures 4 and 5). Complexity makes traditional approach of deliberate planning, while useful, less suitable and less than adequate.

Given all of the above, the following are ten recommendations that can be used by governments as guidelines, in the quest to connected government:

1. Anchor all connected government initiatives and activities to one or more national (or government priorities). Lack of this, invites unnecessary cynicism and perception of a "paper exercise" with little practical relevance. Priorities can be derived from the service themes shown in Figure 1. Operational concerns like technology standardization, open data, IT planning, application consolidation, government service automation, infrastructure management, application landscape planning are at best, tertiary.

2. Utilize enterprise architecture as a means to the vision of connected government, and position the team in the right place with adequate authority to get things done.

Figure 37. Enablers and inhibitors to connected government

W-O-G EA Adoption for Connected Government			
Impacting Enablers and Inhibitors	**Intensity of Impact [H, HM, M, L]**	**Likelihood of Occurrence [H, HM, M, L]**	**Composite Rating [H, HM, M, L]**
Enablers Complexity Triggered Transformation			
Capability Multiplier			
IT Industry in Motion			
Technology Adoption & Usage Maturity			
Government as an Enterprise			
First Movers			
Bandwagon			
Success Breeds Success			
Facilitated Diffusion			
Architecting the Enterprise			
Inhibitors Diverging Agendas			
Technology Empires			
Business Empires			
Program Costs			
Burden of Stretch Targets			
Complacency			
Political Landmines			
Not Invented Here			
Legend: H → High; HM → High-Medium; M → Medium; L → Low			

Oftentimes, the EA team that is put in place has the capability, but not the authority to even influence to make massive transformations connected government brings into the governments. Figure 38 lists why EA should not be assigned to the IT ministry or department. In the government context, Ministries of Finance, Public Administration or the Prime Minister's Office are potential alternatives. In addition to "responsibility," even the "ownership" of government EA should be at the appropriate level. This shift (of EA to outside the IT department) is further intensified with the enormous technology maturation, innovation, trans-

formation of technology service delivery models and growing strategic importance of IT. These inevitably lead to the marginalization of the traditional IT departments and Chief Information Officers (CIOs). Figure 39 shows the four archetypes pertaining to IT involvement in the EA, while Figure 40 presents the consequences of the archetypes. According to current estimates less than five (5) percent of current government organizations fall into Quadrant D.

3. Extend the role of the government audit department(s) to include architecture. This ensures continuity for the architecture efforts, and enables standardization in the audit and

Figure 38. Six reasons why EA should not be assigned to the IT department

Responsibility for and Ownership of Enterprise Architecture
6. Enterprise Architecture > Enterprise IT Architecture; hence the scope and footprint of EA is the enterprise in its entirety.
5. True EA leads to redistribution of authority and reallocation of accountability, both beyond CIO jurisdiction.
4. Focus and orientation of the EA is a business decision, and benefits are solely business derivable.
3. The primary goal of EA is to build coherent enterprises, not better IT systems.
2. Enterprises are complex adaptive systems; therefore holistic synthesis takes precedence over fractional analysis.
1. EA failure is an enterprise failure, not an IT failure; therefore resistance to EA is a consequence of failure, not the cause for it.

Figure 39. Role and influence of the IT department on enterprise architecture

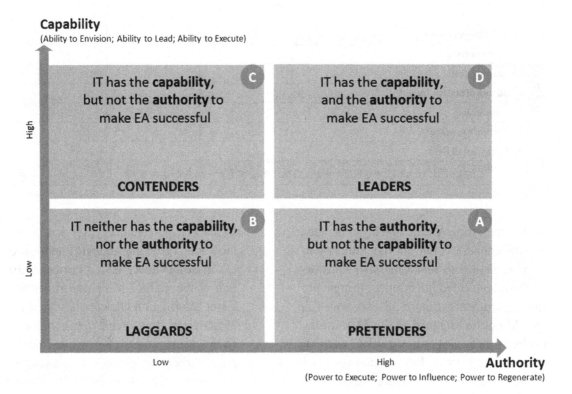

assessment. This, in turn, leads to more realistic comparison and progress assessment.

4. Select the desired connected government stage (see Figure 4) and the preferred entry point to W-O-G EA based on requirements and other influencing factors. It is possible to be at different stages of the connected government maturity for different government

Figure 40. Consequences of the IT involvement archetypes

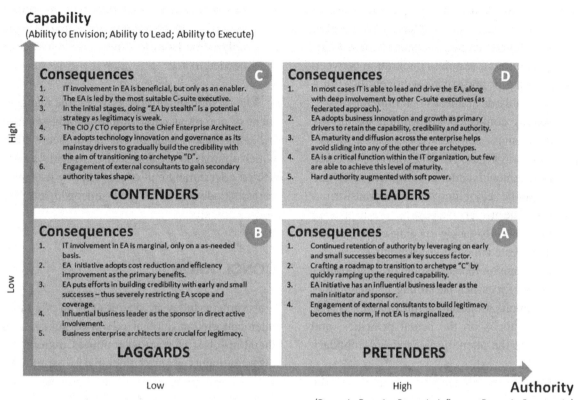

priorities. Countries, traditionally, commit of the folly of using technology architecture as the most frequent entry point to W-O-G EA. However, due to lack of adequate authority and very limited jurisdiction, never move beyond. This approach provides some initial benefits, which over time trickles down to insignificant levels. This leads to erosion of interest towards connected government vision and activities.

5. Ensure all resources and efforts expended contribute to the greater goal of digital prosperity and economic upliftment. In summary, connected government needs to contribute to the larger national ecosystem, and in doing this, especially in the developing countries, take cognizance of the digital divide.

6. Question deeply entrenched mental models, often based on assumptions and beliefs that do not exist or are presently irrelevant. Some such mental models are:

a. Government is the absolute of all public data. Except in cases of data pertaining to national security, the emerging mental model is one of government being the custodian of all public data.

b. Government is the creator and regulator of all government services. Except in cases where government involvement is needed in an exclusive basis, it is highly advisable to explore private sector participation in delivering government services. The primary criteria should always be service quality, and not the entity that delivers the service. This is also in line with the stages in connected government. At the higher levels (extra-governmental and ubiquitous), seamless integration between public and private sector entities is not only desirable, but an imperative.

7. Assess connected government using the dimensions and strategic success factors shown in Figure 10. The goal of connected government is better government, catalyzed by public sector innovation and transformation. The primary purpose is EA is to provide the means to tackle ensuing complexities, and create coherent governments.

8. Leverage on industry standards and frameworks for issues pertaining to technology and application architecture domains. These allow focus on the actual priorities, and reduce the attention needed on secondary issues.

9. Manage the complexity by embracing the following soft-rules:

   a. Create a platform to enhance the understanding of what other entities do and how they perform.

   b. Elevate and reinforce the role of "integrators." In a connected environment, the entities, teams or individuals that link the various participating elements are crucial. In Figure 7, these are usually the "lead organizations" or the "NAOs."

   c. Expand the jurisdiction and authority levels of the integrators. In a traditional setting, it is usually the nodes, not the connectors that carry the jurisdiction.

   d. Exploit the power of reciprocity to foster productive cooperation between different participants in the connected environment.

10. Prioritize on using the potential of enterprise architecture in providing foresight. Too many of the current EA approaches are overly fixated on "housekeeping" type of activities. While, these may provide some initial benefits to governments, sustained benefits only come from foresight and innovations needed to act.

The recommendations above enable management of complexity not by prescribing specific behaviors, but by creating an environment within which optimal behaviors required to achieve connected government can occur. This by itself is a colossal undertaking for governments of any size and complexity.

CONCLUSION

Governments today are operating in an ever more interconnected and globalized world. Linkages and their impacts stretch across countries, regions and even continents and are vulnerable to disruptions. Inter-governmental treaties and agreements are more than not held hostage to conflicting interests. In light such developments, often unfolding and intensifying at a pace that governments are not designed to deal with, oftentimes leads to governments being perceived as inefficient and unreceptive to change. The governments of the future will be connected, and this is not an option. Governments that are not connected will fall behind. However, efforts in recent years have been limited to connectedness being necessary within and between government entities. This meant initiatives focusing on issues such as effective collaboration across agencies. The emphasis has been mostly on the provision of government services at the front-end, supported by integration and consolidation of back-end processes and IT systems to achieve cost savings and improve service delivery.

Moving forward, governments will be exposed to numerous social, economic, political, legal and technological changes that will bring both opportunities and risks for countries. Governments will be subjected to megaforces that will impact every country in one way or another. These are: globalization, urbanization and structural fluidity; coalitions and political ambivalence; wealth distribution and disparate prosperity; user-driven governance and multi-faceted relationships; digitization, social networks and collaboration imperative; democratic accountability, participation, transparency and legitimacy; demographic transition and population redistribution; rebalancing of power between governments, society and citizens; trust deficit and credibility erosion; and economic uncertainty and multiple futures. These megaforces do not function in isolation from each other in predictable ways, creating a plethora of influences. They act as a complex and unpredictable system, feeding, amplifying or ameliorating the effects of others. They are both the cause and consequence of complexity, which get manifested in different ways when dealing with different national priorities.

The trigger for connected government comes from (or must come from) a strong shared vision. However, to create the shared vision, it is critical to observe discrete events, construct patterns, craft systemic structures and build new mental models. In more practical terms, this means extending the scope of connected government to include linkages that blur international boundaries, public-private boundaries and expand it to a point wherein governments become the platform for co-creation, co-innovation and collaboration; a platform where relationships between governments, society and citizens is one of personalized interactions not service transactions; user-led demand not government-controlled supply and organic emergence not regimented process. To make this happen, the role of leadership, systems thinking and complexity management cannot be overstated. They form the three defining capabilities required to realize connected government. (Systemic) enterprise architecture is the approach and process providing the platform to embrace and build these core capabilities. This chapter

elaborated the EA based approach to connected government with a specific real example from the healthcare sector. The aim of the example was to demonstrate to senior government leaders and decision makers that leadership, systems perspective and ability to tackle complexity (or lack thereof) is a source of risk, cost, management and political challenges.

In summary, these core capabilities constitute the nexus of success, without which it is impossible to deal with the megaforces shaping the future of governments. The ten principles of effectuating systemic enterprise architecture (the crux of this chapter and central theme of this book) are as below. The subsequent chapters demonstrate realization of these principles in varying forms and intensities.

1. The scope and footprint of EA is the enterprise in its entirety.
2. Every functioning enterprise has architecture (formal or non-formal), if it didn't, it wouldn't be able to function.
3. Enterprises are complex adaptive systems, wherein the assumptions of reductionism, linearity, correlation and predictability do not hold true.
4. Enterprises are inherently characterized by diversity, inter-dependence, ambiguity and flux.
5. The emphasis of EA is less on things, and more on interrelationships between things.
6. Enterprises operate in a networked (heterarchical) mode, as opposed to hierarchical mode used for administrative purposes.
7. Complex adaptive leadership, where the power of influence exceeds the power of control, is the most effective architecture leadership style.
8. Alignment makes enterprises more rigid and less agile, because a complex system is approximated as a complicated system; and undesirable limitations and constraints are introduced into the system.

9. Enterprises are characterized by holism, synthesis and systemic paradigms; and any assumption that the effectiveness of the whole will be achieved automatically, as long as the parts are optimal, does not hold true.

10. Enterprises must be architected for emergence and flux, as opposed to being architected for stability and constancy.

ACKNOWLEDGMENT

This innovation project was partly funded by Microsoft Corporation. The author would like to thank Rodrigo Becerra Mizuno of Microsoft Corporation for his support. The author gratefully acknowledges Singapore Healthcare Services (SingHealth) and Integrated Health Information Systems (IHiS) for their involvement and contribution to this work. Their inputs and enthusiastic participation were invaluable.

REFERENCES

Abegunde, D., & Stanciole, A. (2006). *An estimation of the economic impact of chronic noncommunicable diseases in selected countries.* Geneva, Switzerland: World Health Organization.

Armson, R. (2011). *Growing wings on the way – Systems thinking for messy situations.* Devon, UK: Triarchy Press.

Asia and Pacific Centre for Information and Communication Technology (APCICT). (2011). *E-government capability maturity model.* Incheon City, South Korea: United Nations and Asia Development Bank.

Asia-Pacific Development Information Program (APDIP). (2007a). *E-government interoperability: A review of government interoperability frameworks in selected countries.* Bangkok, Thailand: United Nations Development Program Regional Center.

Asia-Pacific Development Information Program (APDIP). (2007b). *E-government interoperability guide.* Bangkok, Thailand: United Nations Development Program Regional Center.

Atkinson, R. D., & McKay, A. S. (2007). *Digital prosperity – Understanding the economic benefits of information technology revolution.* Washington, DC: The Information Technology & Innovation Foundation. doi:10.2139/ssrn.1004516.

Australian Government Information Management Office (AGIMO). (2010). *Engage: Getting on with government 2.0: Report of the government 2.0 taskforce.* Canberra, Australia: Department of Finance and Deregulation, Government of Australia.

Birkinshaw, J., & Heywood, S. (2010, May). Putting organizational complexity in its place. *The McKinsey Quarterly.*

Burton, B., & Allega, P. (2010). Hype cycle for enterprise architecture 2010. *Gartner Industry Research ID Number: G00201646.*

Burton, B., & Allega, P. (2011). Hype cycle for enterprise architecture. *Gartner Research ID Number: G00214756.*

Butland, B., Jebb, S., Kopelman, P., McPherson, K., Thomas, S., Mardell, J., & Parry, V. (2007). *Tackling obesities – Future choices.* London: Department of Business, Innovation and Skills, Government Office for Science.

Chapman, J. (2004). *System failure – Why governments must learn to think differently* (2nd ed.). London: DEMOS.

Cisco Internet Business Solutions Group (IBSG). (2004). *Connected government: Essays from innovators*. London: Premium Publishing.

Cisco Internet Business Solutions Group (IBSG). (2009). *Realizing the potential of the connected republic: Web 2.0 opportunities in the public sector* (Cisco Systems Incorporated White Paper). Cisco.

Corporation, I. B. M. (2009). *The new voice of the CIO – Insights from the global chief information officer study*. Somers, NY: IBM Institute for Business Value, IBM Corporation.

Corporation, I. B. M. (2010a). *Capitalizing on complexity – Insights from the global chief executive officer study*. Somers, NY: IBM Institute for Business Value, IBM Corporation.

Corporation, I. B. M. (2010b). *The world's 4 trillion dollar challenge – Using a system-of-system approach to build a smarter planet*. Somers, NY: IBM Institute for Business Value, IBM Corporation.

DeVol, R., Bedroussian, A., Charuworn, A., Chatterjee, A., Kim, I., Kim, S., & Klowden, K. (2007). *An unhealthy America – The economic burden of chronic disease*. Santa Monica, CA: Milken Institute.

Dooley, K. (2002). Organizational complexity. In Warner, M. (Ed.), *International Encyclopedia of Business and Management* (pp. 5013–5022). London: Thompson Learning.

Doucet, G., Gotze, J., Saha, P., & Bernard, S. A. (2009). *Coherency management: Architecting the enterprise for alignment, agility and assurance*. Bloomington, IN: AuthorHouse.

Dutta, S., & Mia, I. (2010). *Global information technology report 2009-2010 – ICT for sustainability*. Geneva, Switzerland: INSEAD and World Economic Forum.

Dutta, S., & Mia, I. (2011). *Global information technology report 2010-2011: ICT for sustainability*. Geneva, Switzerland: INSEAD and World Economic Forum.

EIU. (2011). *The complexity challenge – How businesses are bearing up*. London: Economist Intelligence Unit.

European Union. (2012). *Redesigning health for Europe for 2020*. Luxembourg: European Union.

Fishenden, J., Johnson, M., Nelson, K., Polin, G., Rijpma, G., & Stolz, P. (2006). The new world of government work: Transforming the business of government with the power of information technology. *Microsoft Public Services and e-Government Strategy Discussion Paper*.

Gall, N. (2010). From hierarchy to panarchy – Hybrid thinking's resilient network of renewal. *Gartner Research ID Number: G00209754*.

Garcia-Lorenzo, L., Mitleton-Kelly, E., & Galliers, R.D. (2003). Organizational complexity – Organizing through the generation and sharing of knowledge. *International Journal of Knowledge, Culture and Change Management*.

Gharajedaghi, J. (2011). *Systems thinking – Managing chaos and complexity*. Burliington, MA: Morgan Kaufmann.

Halstead, D., Somerville, N., Straker, B., & Ward, C. (2009). The way to gov 2.0: An enterprise approach to web 2.0 in government. *Microsoft US Public Sector White Paper*.

Hamel, G. (2007). *The future of management*. Boston: Harvard Business School Press.

Herlands, D., & Brown, K. (2005). *Strategies for chronic disease management*. Washington, DC: The Advisory Board Company.

Heywood, S., Spungin, J., & Turnbull, D. (2007). Cracking the complexity code. *The McKinsey Quarterly*, (2): 85–95.

Himmelstein, D. U., Thorne, D., Warren, E., & Woolhandler, S. (2009). Medical bankruptcy in the United States, 2007 – Results of a national study. *The American Journal of Medicine, 122*(8), 741–746. doi:10.1016/j.amjmed.2009.04.012 PMID:19501347.

Hjort-Madsen, K. (2009). *Architecting government – Understanding enterprise architecture adoption in the public sector.* (Doctoral Dissertation). IT University of Copenhagen, Copenhagen, Denmark.

Homer, J. B., & Hirsch, G. B. (2006). System dynamics modeling for public health – Background and opportunities. *American Journal of Public Health, 96*(3). doi:10.2105/AJPH.2005.062059 PMID:16449591.

Hoogerworst, J. A. P. (2009). *Enterprise governance and enterprise engineering.* Diemen, The Netherlands: Springer. doi:10.1007/978-3-540-92671-9.

Huijboom, N., & Van Den Broek, T. (2011, March/April). Open data – An international comparison of strategies. *European Journal of ePractice,* (12), 4 – 16.

Jackson, M. (2011). *Practical foresight guide.* Retrieved from www.shapingtomorrow.com

Janssen, M., & Hjort-Madsen, K. (2007). Analyzing enterprise architecture in national governments: The cases of Denmark and Netherlands. In *Proceedings of the 40th Annual Hawaii International Conference on Systems Sciences (HICSS'07).* IEEE.

Joffe, M., & Mindell, J. (2006). Complex causal process diagrams for analyzing the health impacts of policy interventions. *American Journal of Public Health, 96*(3). doi:10.2105/AJPH.2005.063693 PMID:16449586.

Johnson, M. W. (2010). *Seizing the white space – Business model innovation for growth and renewal.* Boston: Harvard Business Press.

Kagerman, H., Osterle, H., & Jordan, J. M. (2011). *IT driven business models – Global case studies in transformation.* Hoboken, NJ: John Wiley & Sons.

Kaplan, R. S., & Porter, M. E. (2011, September). How to solve the cost crisis in healthcare. *Harvard Business Review.* PMID:21939127.

KPMG. (2011). *Confronting complexity – Research findings and insights.* KPMG International. Publication Number 110307.

KPMG. (2012a). *Expect the unexpected – Building business value in a changing world.* KPMG International.

KPMG. (2012b). *Transforming healthcare – From volume to value.* KPMG International.

La Trobe University. (2008). *System reform and development for chronic disease management.* Victoria, Australia: Australian Institute for Primary Care.

Leechul, B. (2010). *Building an enterprise architecture for statistics Korea.* Paper presented at Management of Statistical Information Systems (MSIS 2010). Daejeon, Republic of Korea.

Leischow, S. J., Best, A., Trochim, W. M., Clark, P. I., Gallagher, R. S., Marcus, S. E., & Matthews, E. (2008). Systems thinking to improve the public's health. *American Journal of Preventive Medicine, 35*(2S). doi:10.1016/j.amepre.2008.05.014 PMID:18619400.

Liimatainen, K., Hoffman, M., & Heikkilä, J. (2007). *Overview of enterprise architecture work in 15 countries.* Helsinki, Finland: Ministry of Finance, Government of Finland.

Lindgardt, Z., Reeves, M., Stalk, G., & Deimler, M. S. (2009). *Business model innovation – When the game gets tough, change the game*. Boston: Boston Consulting Group.

McGarvey, B., & Hannon, B. (2004). *Dynamic modeling for business management – An introduction*. New York: Springer-Verlag. doi:10.1007/b97269.

Meadows, D. (1999). *Leverage points: Places to intervene in a system*. Hartland, VT: The Sustainability Institute.

Microsoft Corporation. (2009b). *Connected health framework* (2nd ed.). Microsoft Corporation.

Microsoft Corporation. (2010). *Connected government framework – Strategies to transform government in the 2.0 world* (White Paper). Microsoft Corporation.

Microsoft Corporation. (2012). *Connected government framework reference architecture version 1.0*. Microsoft Corporation.

Morecroft, J. (2007). *Strategic modelling and business dynamics – A feedback systems approach*. West Sussex, UK: John Wiley and Sons.

Muehlfeit, J. (2006). *The connected government framework for local and regional government* (White Paper). Microsoft Corporation.

National Information Society Agency (NIA). (2008). *2008 informatization white paper*. Ministry of Public Administration and Security, Government of Republic of Korea.

Nordfors, L., Ericson, B., Lindell, H., & Lapidus, J. (2009). eGovernment of tomorrow – Future scenarios for 2020. *Gullers Group. Vinnova Report VR, 2009*, 28.

Office of Management and Budget. (2007). *Federal enterprise architecture consolidated reference model version 2.3*. Washington, DC: The White House.

Office of Management and Budget. (2012). *Digital government: Building a 21ˢᵗ century platform to better serve the American people*. Washington, DC: The White House.

Office of the Chief Information Officer. (2013). *Stay connected – South Australian government ICT strategy*. Adelaide, Australia: Government of South Australia.

Pardo, T. A., & Burke, G. B. (2008). *Improving government interoperability: A capability framework for government managers*. Albany, NY: Center for Technology in Government, University at Albany.

Perdicoulis, A. (2010). *Systems thinking and decision making in urban and environmental planning*. Northampton, MA: Edward Elgar.

Porter, M. E., & Teisberg, E. O. (2006). *Redefining health care – Creating value-based competition on results*. Boston: Harvard Business School Press.

Reed, G.E. (2006, May-June). Leadership and systems thinking. *Defense AT & L*.

Reisner, R. A. F. (2011). *A leader's guide to transformation – Developing a playbook for successful change initiatives*. IBM Center for the Business of Government Report.

Richardson, K.A. (2008). Managing complex organizations – Complexity thinking and the science and art of management. *E:CO Issuen, 10*(2), 13 – 26.

Ritchley, T. (1991). Analysis and synthesis – On scientific method based on a study by Bernhard Riemann. *Systems Research, 8*(4), 21–41. doi:10.1002/sres.3850080402.

Ross, J. W., Weill, P., & Robertson, D. C. (2006). *Enterprise architecture as strategy: Creating a foundation for business execution*. Boston: Harvard Business School Press.

Rouse, W. B. (2000). Managing complexity – Disease control as a complex adaptive system. *Information Systems Management, 2*(2), 143–165.

Rouse, W. B. (2007). Complex engineered, organizational and natural systems – Issues underlying the complexity of systems and fundamental research needed to address these issues. *Systems Engineering, 10*(3), 260–271. doi:10.1002/sys.20076.

Rouse, W. B. (2008). Healthcare as a complex adaptive systems – Implications for design and management. *The BRIDGE: Linking Engineering and Society, 38*(1), 17–25.

Saha, P. (2007). *Handbook of enterprise systems architecture in practice.* Hershey, PA: IGI Global. doi:10.4018/978-1-59904-189-6.

Saha, P. (2008). *Advances in government enterprise architecture.* Hershey, PA: IGI Global. doi:10.4018/978-1-60566-068-4.

Saha, P. (2012). *Enterprise architecture and connected e-government – Practices and innovations.* Hershey, PA: IGI Global. doi:10.4018/978-1-4666-1824-4.

Sargut, G., & McGrath, R. G. (2011, September). Learning to live with complexity – How to make sense of the unpredictable and the undefinable in today's hyperconnected business world. *Harvard Business Review*, 68–76. PMID:21939129.

Savigny, D., & Adam, T. (2009). *Systems thinking for health systems strengthening.* Geneva, Switzerland: World Health Organization.

Schwaninger, M. (2006). *Intelligent organizations – Powerful models for systemic management.* Berlin: Springer.

Senge, P. (1990). *The fifth discipline.* New York: Doubleday Currency.

Snowden, D. J., & Boone, M. E. (2007, November). A leader's framework for decision making. *Harvard Business Review.* PMID:18159787.

Sterman, J. D. (2000). *Business dynamics – Systems thinking and modeling for a complex world.* Boston: Irwin McGraw-Hill.

Stroh, P. D. (2000). Leveraging change: The power of systems thinking in action. *Reflections: The SoL Journal, 2*(2). doi:10.1162/15241730051092019.

Trochim, W. M., Cabrera, D. A., Milstein, B., Gallagher, R. S., & Leischow, S. J. (2006). Practical challenges of systems thinking and modeling in public health. *American Journal of Public Health, 96*(3). doi:10.2105/AJPH.2005.066001 PMID:16449581.

United Nations Department of Economic and Social Affairs (UNDESA). (2008). *United Nations e-government survey 2008: From e-government to connected governance.* New York: United Nations.

United Nations Department of Economic and Social Affairs (UNDESA). (2010). *United Nations e-government survey 2010: Leveraging e-government at a time of financial and economic crises.* New York: United Nations.

United Nations Department of Economic and Social Affairs (UNDESA). (2012). *United Nations e-government survey 2012: E-government for the people.* New York: United Nations.

Watkins, M. E. (2012, June). How managers become leaders – The seven seismic shifts of perspective and responsibility. *Harvard Business Review*, 65–72. PMID:22741419.

Williams, B., & Hummelbrunner, R. (2009). *Systems concepts in action – A practitioner's toolkit.* Palo Alto, CA: Stanford University Press.

Wilson, B. (1990). *Systems – Concepts, methodologies and applications.* Chichester, UK: Wiley.

World Economic Forum. (WEF). (2011a). *The future of government – Lessons learned from around the world.* Geneva, Switzerland: World Economic Forum.

World Economic Forum. (WEF). (2011b). *The global information technology report 2010/2011 – Transformations 2.0.* Geneva, Switzerland: World Economic Forum.

World Economic Forum. (WEF). (2012a). *Global risks 2012.* Geneva, Switzerland: World Economic Forum.

World Economic Forum. (WEF). (2012b). *Young global leaders – Guide to influencing complex systems.* Geneva, Switzerland: World Economic Forum.

World Economic Forum. (WEF). (2013). *Sustainable health systems – Visions, strategies, critical uncertainties and scenarios.* Geneva, Switzerland: World Economic Forum.

World Health Organization. (2005). *Preventing chronic diseases – A vital investment.* Geneva, Switzerland: Department of Chronic Diseases and Health Promotion, World Health Organization.

Zenghelis, D. (2010). *The economics of network powered growth* (White Paper). CISCO Internet Business Solutions Group (IBSG).

Zokaei, K., Seddon, J., & O'Donovan, B. (2011). *Systems thinking – From heresy to practice.* Hampshire, UK: Palgrave Macmillan.

ADDITIONAL READING

Bittinger, S. (2011). Hype cycle for government transformation – 2011. *Gartner Research ID Number: G00214747.*

Burns, P., Neutens, M., Newman, D., & Power, T. (2009). *Building value through enterprise architecture: A global study.* Booz & Company Perspective.

Department of Health. (2012). *The power of information – Putting all of us in control of the health and care information we need.* London: Department of Health.

Dettmer, H. W. (2003). *Strategic navigation – A systems approach to business strategy.* Milwaukee, WI: ASQ Quality Press.

Dettmer, H. W. (2007). *The logical thinking process – A systems approach to complex problem solving.* New York: ASQ Quality Press.

Gall, N., Newman, D, Allega, P., Lapkin, A., & Handler, R.A. (2010). Introducing hybrid thinking for transformation, innovation and strategy. *Gartner Research ID Number: G00172065.*

Gates, L. P. (2010). *Strategic planning with critical success factors and future scenarios – An integrated strategic planning framework.* Technical Report CMU/SEI-2010-TR-037. Pittsburgh, PA: Software Engineering Institute, Carnegie Mellon University.

Giesen, E., Berman, S. J., Bell, R., & Blitz, A. (2007). *Paths to success – Three ways to innovate your business model.* Somers, NY: IBM Institute for Business Value, IBM Corporation.

Lee, G., & Kwak, Y. H. (2011). *An open government implementation model – Moving to increased public engagement.* Washington, DC: IBM Center for The Business of Government.

Lindgren, M., & Bandhold, H. (2009). *Scenario planning – The link between future and strategy.* London: Palgrave Macmillan.

Mickoliet, A., Kounatze, C. R., Serra-Vallejo, C., Vickery, G., & Wunsch-Vincent, S. (2009). *The role of the crisis on ICT and their role in the recovery. Organization for Economic Development and Cooperation (OECD) Report.* Paris: OECD. doi:10.1787/221641027714.

Microsoft Corporation. (2009a). *Government service center – A Microsoft vision for high performance citizen service* (White Paper). Microsoft Corporation.

Wolstenholme, E. (2004). Using generic system archetypes to support thinking and modeling. *System Dynamics Review*, *20*(4), 341–356. doi:10.1002/sdr.302.

World Bank. (2008). *Global economic prospects – Technology diffusion in the developing world.* Washington, DC: The World Bank.

World Economic Forum. (WEF). (2009). *ICT for economic growth – A dynamic ecosystem driving the global recovery.* Geneva, Switzerland: World Economic Forum.

Zammuto, R. F., Griffith, T. L., Majchrzak, D. J., Dougherty, D. J., & Faraj, S. (2007). Information technology and the changing fabric of organization. *Organization Science*, *18*(5), 749–762. doi:10.1287/orsc.1070.0307.

Section 2
Creating Ecologies of Innovations:
Developments and Convergence

Chapter 2

Enterprises as Complex Systems:
Extended Axiomatic Design Theory and its Application in Enterprise Architecture Practice

Hadi Kandjani
Griffith University, Australia

Peter Bernus
Griffith University, Australia

Lian Wen
Griffith University, Australia

ABSTRACT

The concept of self-evolving/self-designing systems is defined using the notion of life cycle relationships. The authors propose that to design complex enterprises as systems of systems on each level of hierarchy one should maintain a self-designing property, that is, the designers should be part of the system. It is explained that by so distributing the design authority, under certain circumstances the "apparent complexity" of the system visible to any one designer can be reduced. To ensure the success of organised self-design, the approach uses their extension of Suh's axiomatic design theory with the "axiom of recursion." The authors quantitatively demonstrate through two examples the benefits of applying these design axioms in enterprise engineering to reduce the complexity of a system of interest, as well as the complexity of a system which designs the system of interest.

DOI: 10.4018/978-1-4666-4518-9.ch002

1. INTRODUCTION

1.1. Uncontrollability of Human-Engineered Systems

One way to look at the history of homo-sapiens is to consider it as the history of inventing, building, using, continuously improving and reinventing tools to support human endeavour. This history starts with the creation of simple tools, such as weapons for hunting and warfare, through to today's complex engineering objects and production, transport, financial and governmental etc. systems.

With the invention and application of computers, humankind has created the means to design and build systems of unprecedented complexity, solving problems and providing services that were impossible before. However, early in the use of computers it was realised that the creation of ever more complex software systems has limits (Brooks 1982). This is a serious problem, because humankind came to rely on systems of which the complexity makes them harder and harder to invent, specify, design, build, operate and control, and finally, to disestablish.

The field of complexity is gaining more importance in science and engineering and goes beyond traditional disciplines, as all of natural science, engineering, as well as social science must tackle the complexity problem (Suh 2005). Suh (2005) points out that due to the lack of "unifying theories" and terminologies, different disciplines and their constituent fields have defined and viewed complexity differently to respond to their "immediate needs" with a lack of a fundamental approach to complexity. However, Suh (*ibid*) points out that "the field of complexity may emerge as a unified discipline using a common set of principles and theories but with a different knowledge base and constraints, and to achieve this goal, we have to define 'complexity' in an unambiguous manner": an ultimate goal of the complexity field is to replace the "empirical approach" in designing, operating and managing complex systems with a more "scientific approach."

Various disciplines have experienced the problem of having to design and construct more and more complex systems and built tools to handle ever more complex models. Our observation is that while improved design methodologies, modelling languages and analysis tools can decrease the designer's problem, they only extend the complexity barrier that a designer (or group of designers) can deal with – they do not remove the barrier. This is because the desired functionality of the system may be intrinsically complex, i.e. the complexity can only be avoided by giving up on some desired system characteristics. Therefore any designer who needs to model the complete system in its entirety will eventually face a problem.

Our hypothesis is that perhaps the system, or system of systems, and the designer should not be separated: systems should design themselves, out of component systems that have the same self-designing property. This means that while the system of systems may have an intrinsically complex nature – by some significant complexity measure – this complexity would only have to be seen by an omniscient external observer, but not necessarily by any involved design authority.

1.2. Enterprises and Complexity

Enterprises could be looked at as intrinsically complex adaptive systems: they can not purely be considered as 'designed systems', because deliberate design/control episodes and processes, such as 'enterprise engineering' using models in the design of the changed enterprise, are intermixed with emergent change episodes and processes – that may perhaps be explained by models.

In stages of deliberate change during their life history, enterprise may be considered a kind of engineered system, where change is supported by some form of enterprise engineering methodology. However, unless these methodologies adopt appropriate complexity reduction methods, such enterprise engineering efforts may create results that display one or several undesirable systemic properties due to uncontrolled design complexity. Therefore, the main aim of this chapter is to propose a theoretical framework and principles that can be adopted for tackling complexity in enterprise engineering

We intend to apply theories and principles adopted form the complexity field and demonstrate their use in enterprise engineering as 'architecting principles'. These architecting principles can be used as guidelines and help enterprise architects to propose solutions that have desirable systemic properties.

First we shall propose to adopt an existing theory of design of complex systems, Axiomatic Design (AD) – a theory that originated from mechanical engineering (Suh, 2001). Second, we propose an extension to this theory and its principles to cater for the design of enterprises as a special class of complex systems, namely adaptive and self-evolving systems.

In section 1.1 we briefly introduced the problem of uncontrollability of human-engineered systems. Section 2 describes the complexity problem in enterprise architecture practice. Section 2.1 briefly introduces different categories of measures of complexity. In section 2.2, the consequences of the complexity problem are described. In section 2.3 we look at the disciplines that studied how to tackle the complexity problem, and in section 2.4 we introduce a pragmatic measure of complexity.

Section 3.1 discusses complexity from the enterprise engineering point of view and reviews Axiomatic Design Theory and its two axioms. In section 3.2 we introduce the extension to Axiomatic Design and how this theory could be applied in enterprise engineering.

In section 4 we introduce a hypothesis by introducing self-evolution/self-design as a way to tackle the complexity problem and then define a self-evolving system using the concepts of the ISO 15704 standard.

Section 5 reviews Kolmogorov Complexity as a proxy for the complexity of a design, and demonstrates how to estimate this measure, thereby allowing alternative design solutions to be compared.

In section 6, using simple examples, we demonstrate how to apply Extended Axiomatic Design Theory to enterprise engineering. For this purpose in section 6.1 we demonstrate the Application of AD's Axioms I & II in designing a virtual enterprise X (Bernus *et al*, 2002) and in section 6.2 we show the Application of our Axiom III of Design of self evolving systems in designing the project that creates a virtual enterprise X.

2. THE COMPLEXITY PROBLEM IN ENTERPRISE ARCHITECTURE

2.1. Measures of Complexity

Gershenson (2007) points out, that the complexity of the representation of a system depends on the observer (stakeholder). The explanation of this fact is as follows.

When modelling any system, different elements (such as levels of detail, properties, dimensions, states, and probabilities of events and etc.) are considered relevant by different stakeholders of that system (such as user, designer, manager, …).

An omniscient observer 'O' would have to be aware of all such elements, as may be represented by O's model of the system (M_O). However, individual stakeholders (S_i) only need to see appropriate *views* of this model. Each such view is a model M_{Si} of the system seen by the respective stakeholder S_i. Therefore, while it may be possible to define an intrinsic complexity measure of a system (based on M_O), this may not have to be seen by any real stakeholder at all.

Contemporary researchers in architecture, biology, computer science, dynamic systems, engineering, finance, game theory, etc., have defined different measures of complexity for each field: Lloyd (2001) observes that researchers are asking the same or similar questions and that their answers have much in common Following Lloyd, there are three questions posed when attempting to quantify the complexity of an entity, which Lloyd calls a 'thing':

1. How hard is it to describe the entity?
2. How hard is it to create the entity?
3. What is its degree of organization of the entity?

Lloyd (2001) lists the following measures for each:

For (a), the difficulty involved in completely describing the entity (typically quantified in bits): Information; Entropy; Algorithmic complexity or algorithmic information content; Minimum description length; Fisher information; Rényi entropy; Code length, Chernoff information; Dimension; Fractal dimension; Lempel-Ziv complexity. NB. for our treatment here the references to each are not necessary.

For (b), the difficulty involved in constructing or duplicating the entity: Time/space Computational complexity; Information-based complexity; Logical depth; Thermodynamic depth, etc.

For (c), the degree of what Lloyd calls 'organization of the entity'. NB, Lloyd does not elaborate on the dimensions used to quantify these. This measure is subdivided into:

1. The difficulty involved in describing the organizational structure: Effective complexity; Metric entropy; Fractal dimension; Excess entropy; Stochastic complexity; Sophistication; Effective measure complexity.

2. The amount of information shared between the parts of a system as the result of its organizational structure: Mutual information; Channel capacity; Correlation; etc.

2.2. Consequences of the Complexity Problem

What groups (a) and (c) have in common is that they measure the difficulty an observer encounters when describing the entity as a system, for the purpose of analysing, designing or controlling it. This observation is not entirely new: e.g., Gershenson (2007) introduced a relative measure of complexity (see Def 1 below).

Def 1: "The complexity of a system C_{sys} " ... [is a measure, which] ... "scales with the number of its elements #E, the number of interactions #I between them, the complexities of the elements C_{ej}, and the complexities of the interactions C_{ik}." (Gershenson 2002).

This definition is relative, because the description of the system is made from an observer's point of view, so as to be able to make predictions about some properties of the system about which the observer cares. (Gershenson 2004) illustrates this rather abstract measure, using the example of Random Boolean Networks (Kauffman 1993), in which the chance of chaotic behaviour increases with the number of nodes (#E) and the number of interactions determined by the number of connections (#I) between nodes. Namely, with the increase in the number of interactions between nodes slightly different starting states tend to produce increasingly different outcomes, making the prediction of the network's next state very difficult or impossible.

Although this discussion helps us show how system complexity contributes to the difficulty of predicting system behaviour, (Melvin 2003) argues that we need large and complex systems to be able to satisfy all functional requirements of a system. However, it is precisely the complexity of a system that makes it difficult to predict that the system will always do what is required! Indeed, Axiomatic Design Theory (Suh 2001) defines a 'complex' system as one that can not be predicted for certain that it will always satisfy its functional requirements.

We emphasise that Gershenson's and Suh's complexity definitions are relative notions, because depending on the concerns of the observer the same entity may be viewed as having different number of elements / interactions, and the complexity of elements and their interactions may in turn be viewed differently by each observer. We therefore conclude that 'being complex' is not an inherent property of an entity, but it is a property seen by an observer considering the entity as a system.

As an example, in the area of Enterprise Architecture one of the important questions is to maintain a coherent and coordinated investment activity. Complexity is a threat to this endeavour, because it can increase uncertainty and may impose risk (Saha, 2006). Given the relative notion of complexity, while from certain aspects the system may be complex, thus unpredictable, there is scope for finding architectural solutions, *i.e.* solution architectures with appropriate systemic properties, so that while system state may remain to some extent unpredictable, properties of the system that matter for investment efficiency stay predictable.

Smarr (1985) explains that the concept of complexity is multidimensional and multi-disciplinary and there is no single way to define and measure it. A mathematician may define it by the number of degrees of freedom in computational operations, while a physicist may define it by the number and frequency of interactions in a system.

Abraham (2002) analysed the twentieth century history of complexity theory and described the theory's three roots, their interactions and bifurcations as a complex dynamic system itself;

he considers the roots to be cybernetics, general systems theory / theoretical biology, and system dynamics.

Castellani (2009) also identifies three roots of complexity science, but somewhat differently: systems theory, cybernetics and artificial intelligence, and defines derivations of complexity science from these roots, giving a historical perspective of the area.

Complex Adaptive Systems Theory (Holland 1992; Gell-Mann 1994) looks at the problem of a complex system as a system that is created from the interactions of systems – possibly by itself – and which interaction produces emergent properties, without there being a designer at all. We must add though that the problem still exists for the observer who encounters such a system without claiming to have 'designed' it: after all we still may need to know how is it possible to control the system or predict its future behaviour – at least to some desired extent.

2.3. Disciplines that Studied How to Tackle the Complexity Problem

Software Engineering (SE) has been trying to devise methods to reduce apparent complexity. Efforts to reduce the complexity of software include the use of design principles and patterns, encapsulation in Object Oriented software development (Snyder 1986), Object Oriented Analysis and Design (OOAD) (Meyer 1988), Component Oriented Development (Nierstrasz, Gibbs *et al.* 1992), Service Oriented Architecture (Krafzig, Banke *et al.* 2004; Erl 2005) and Multi Agent Systems (Wooldridge and Jennings, 1995), whereupon Software Process Improvement concentrates on the system that develops software manageable (Osterweil, 1987).

Traditional Systems Engineering (SysEng) has been successful at satisfying complex 'design, develop, and deploy' requirements (Dromey 2006;

Wen and Dromey, 2006 and 2009). However, Bar-Yam (2003a, 2003b) argues that there is a transition from procedure-driven to capability-based engineering processes and systems engineering must rely on the self-organising ability of engineering – something traditional system engineering was never proposed to handle.

Systems engineering grew out of the need to tackle the complexity of designing large scale systems and developed various approaches and methods (*e.g.* 'multistage analysis', 'evolutionary engineering' [Bar-Yam, 2002, 2003b]). Systems engineering attempts to overcome the limitations of 'decomposition based' engineering and focuses on planned methods to analyse and design a system of systems rather than a way to remove the complexity of the designed system(s) (Bar-Yam & Kuras, 2003).However, Bar-Yam (2003b) thinks that if the task is intrinsically complex for usual systems engineering processes, then it is better to use an evolutionary process to create an environment within which continuous innovation can be carried out.

Note, that Suh's Axiomatic Design (AD) theory developed an understanding of complex systems, with its own definition of 'complex', explaining reasons of emerging complexity in design (Suh, 1999). AD is also a formal design theory, defining principles that designers of systems need to follow to produce systems with minimal complexity (in Suh's sense).

Enterprise architecture(or 'enterprise engineering') addresses the same problem: enterprises are unquestionably complex systems, but while they can be partly characterised as 'designed systems' they are also 'complex adaptive' in nature because the system being changed/designed is usually an evolving 'living system' – a property also studied in General Systems theory (Bertalanffy, 1968). Enterprise architecture frameworks *e.g.,* GERAM (IFIP-IFAC Task Force, 1999; ISO15704:2000), aim at enlisting a collection of tools, methods and models to be used in enterprise change efforts and effectively become a "toolkit

of concepts for designing and maintaining enterprises for their entire life history" (ISO, 1999a; Bernus *et al.*, 2003).Therefore we expect that EA frameworks may be used to systematize various contributions of the field that address the creation and sustenance through life of the enterprise as a complex system.

Although other architecture frameworks might be applicable to the context of the current paper, we chose GERAM because of its distinct features: a) complete life-cycle coverage of enterprise architecture, b) equally important treatment of the human and technical views of a system, c) ability to cover hybrid systems, like socio-technical systems, and d) ability to demonstrate relationships between life cycle and life history of entities of an enterprise as a complex system – an important distinction not provided by any other systems engineering or enterprise architecture framework.

The GERA modelling framework of GERAM reduces the apparent complexity of enterprise models by introducing the view(point) concept as the generalisation of the view(point) concepts of several other architecture frameworks. Different views constructed on the basis of these viewpoints may highlight certain aspects and level of detail of an enterprise entity and hide the rest of aspects and detail.

It is important to note the completeness of GERA's scope. GERA) uses an 'epistemological trick' inherited from several frameworks (Bernus, Nemes and Williams, 1996) to achieve completeness: the scope is complete by definition because subdivisions in the GERA metamodel are made in a way that preserves completeness – namely GERA considers

- Everything that is done by humans and everything done by non-humans.
- Everything that the system does to satisfy its purpose (i.e., to provide service to, or produce goods for someone else) and everything that the system does for itself (i.e., management and control).

- Everything done by hard systems (i.e., 'hardware') and by non-hardware (i.e., 'software', *or* 'information that controls the state / configuration of the hard system').

- Everything from the system's functional viewpoint (i.e., function and information), as well as the system's structural viewpoint (i.e., constituent resources), and the relationship, or mapping, from resources to functions / information (i.e. the system's organisation).

- Every process that is done *to* the system, pertaining system change, and *by* the system to create or change it, operate it and decommission it, or part of it. These 'life cycle processes' or 'phases' may be performed by the system, or by the environment – which latter may contain other sys-

tems. The processes that create or change the system are further categorised by the same completeness-preserving method: we account for every process that considers the system at a level more abstract than requirements-level: identification and concept, and at the requirements-level, as well as everything that considers the mapping of requirements to structure: architectural design, and finally every process needed to institute the change: detailed design & implementation, building / release to operation. NB, the terminology 'to consider the system' is deliberately vague, because it is intended to mean either 'to describe the system due to design intent' or 'to describe the system due to intent to discover' (see Figure 1).

Figure 1. The GERA modeling framework's viewpoints (adapted from IFIP-IFAC Task Force, 1999)

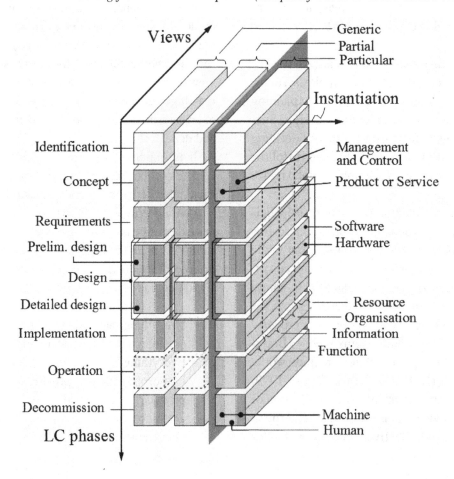

2.4. A Pragmatic Measure of Complexity

As we try to solve the difficulty of having to use complex design descriptions, we turn to Axiomatic Design Theory's complexity measures. AD proposes techniques for reducing complexity in multiple engineering domains, including software development (Suh and Do, 2000).

Suh (2005) divides "the treatment of complexity" into two distinct domains: treating the complexity in the "physical domain" and treating the complexity in the "functional domain." In the first domain most engineers, physicists and mathematicians consider complexity as an "inherent characteristic of physical things, including algorithms, products, processes, and manufacturing systems." Suh (2005) believes that this idea that 'physical things with various parts are inherently more complex' "may or may not be true from the functional point of view." He believes that "the complexity defined in the functional domain is a measure of uncertainty in achieving a set of tasks defined by Functional Requirements (FRs) in the functional domain." The "functional" approach is to treat complexity as a relative concept that evaluates how well we can satisfy "what we want to achieve" with "what is achievable" (Suh 2005). Accordingly Suh believes that: "the complexity based on the physical thinking would have field-specific "dimensions," whereas the complexity based on the functional thinking would be dimensionless regardless of the specific subject under consideration."

Note that some complexity definitions are easy to understand but hard to measure: *e.g.,* Chaitin (1966) and Kolmogorov (1969) proposed a definition of complexity of a software calculated as the length of its most compact description. However, these measures can not be explicitly computed (Suh, 1999; Vitányi, 2007).

What we propose as the measure of complexity is a proxy of the above measure, even though approximation techniques exist to estimate Kolmogorov complexity; see for example Section 5.2of this chapter. For a system to always satisfy its functional requirements it must have 'enough knowledge' of the state of its surroundings (e.g. for software systems this includes the operating system, storage, processor, communication network…), the states of the control information received from other systems, and the possible states of the system's inputs: in each case two states are deemed different if the system must respond to them differently. To function correctly, the system has to know the relevant states of its surroundings. By having to encode these relevant states the minimum length of system description grows with the number of these states: so we can use the number of these relevant states as an approximate complexity measure, and call it 'Information Content' (IC) because it is information the system must have about its environment. Note that 'knowing the state of the environment' may include knowing state history if this is relevant for determining what is the system's appropriate response, and 'state' should interpreted in an abstract sense). Example: consider the environment that contains a counter, which always increments by one, until it reaches 100 after which it resets to zero. Let the functional requirement of the system be to ring a bell when the counter in the environment shows 100. There are two relevant states of the environment: counter=100 and counter<100, though the counter has 100 different states.

The chance of success of a design solution (Suh, 1999) is low if the designer needs to use an overwhelming amount of information to create a design that satisfies the FRs. This is equivalent to having to consider too many states of the environment in which a system must operate. Therefore our Information Content (IC) as a complexity measure is a proxy of what Suh calls information content (whereupon IC_{Suh} = the negative logarithm of the probability that the system always satisfies its FRs).

In addition to this IC being measurable quantity, this concept can be used to devise enterprise engineering methods that exploit the fact that this IC can be made relative. This opportunity is further discussed in Section 4.

3. ENTERPRISE ENGINEERING AND COMPLEXITY

3.1. Enterprise Engineering Principles for Complexity Reduction

We interpret Lloyd's complexity measure classification as:

1. Complexity of the system's function (i.e., the difficulty to describe the function, behaviour, and states of the system).
2. Complexity of the process creating the system (i.e., the difficulty to describe and execute the process creating the system).
3. Complexity of architecture (i.e., the difficulty to describe the relationship between physical and functional structure, *e.g.* due to number of relationships / dynamics of relationships).

Complexity measures a) and c) talk about a 'target system', in our case an 'enterprise', whereupon measure b) talks about the system that creates / changes the enterprise.

To see the relationship between Suh's two complexity domains and Llloyd's three domains we have two observations. Category a) treats the complexity of the target system in the functional domain while category c) treats the complexity of the target system in the "physical domain." Category b) is about a different system, to which therefore complexity categories a) and c) would apply if the system were considered the target.

As enterprise engineering can be considered as a special case of systems engineering, we can try to apply principles of Axiomatic Design (AD), given that AD claims to codify (in a discipline-independent way) what a 'best design' is, therefore it can be expected that AD will contribute important design principles to enterprise engineering.

Suh's two axioms of design are as follows (Suh, 1990):

Axiom I: Independence Axiom

The independence of FRs must always be maintained.

Explanation: a FR_i is independent of other FRs if there exists a solution, i.e. list of 'Design Parameters' (DP), such that if changing one FR_i only one DP needs to be changed.

As mentioned before, the "functional" approach is to treat complexity as a relative concept that evaluates how well we can satisfy "what we want to achieve" with "what is achievable" (Suh 2005). Therefore this approach needs a mapping from the "functional domain" to the "physical domain" to determine the complexity. According to Suh (1990), design is the result of a series of mappings across four design domains. Once we identify and define the perceived customer needs (CA), or the attributes the customers looking for in a product, these must be translated into (FRs), and there may be several ways to do this. After the (FRs) are chosen, we map them into the physical domain to conceive design with specific (DPs) that can satisfy the (FRs). The fourth mapping is to find processes PVs that implement DPs (see Figure 2).

The mapping process is typically a one-to-many process, that is, for a given FR, there can be many possible (DPs) (see Figure 3).

According to Suh, design is a process to find DPs such that [FR] = [[A]] × [DP], where [FR] is the vector of FRs, [DP] is the vector of DPs and [[A]] is a matrix mapping DPs to FRs.

Figure 2. Mappings across four design domains (apdated from Suh, 2003)

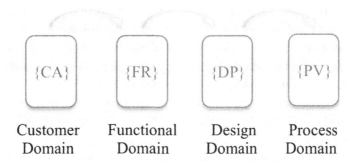

Customer Domain   Functional Domain   Design Domain   Process Domain

Figure 3. Mapping of the design domains in axiomatic design theory to GERA life cycle activities (adapted from Moghaddam, et al., 2008; Kandjani & Bernus, 2011)

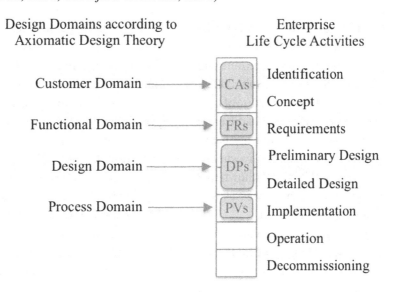

- If [[A]] is a diagonal matrix the design is called uncoupled, meaning that full independence of FRs is achieved.
- If [[A]] is triangular then the design is decoupled, and as a result the implementation process of DPs is 'serialisable'
- If [[A]] can not be rearranged to be triangular then the design is coupled, and consequently the implementation is not 'serialisable'.

Therefore, if an uncoupled design solution is not possible then the number of dependencies must be minimised, through trying to achieve decoupled solutions. If decoupled solutions do not exist then the number of couplings must be minimised.

We see Axiom I as the intent to minimise the complexity of the system's architecture – complexity type 'c' above; examples of this are found in many engineering disciplines.

Axiom II: Information Axiom

Out of the designs that satisfy Axiom I that design is best that has the minimal information content.

Note that Suh defined information content as the negative logarithm of the 'probability of success', we propose to use alternate measures (proxies) for this property, due to pragmatic advantages: namely IC as defined in Section2.4, and IC as the Kolmogorov complexity of the FR → DP mapping matrix (as shown in Section 5.2).

According to these two axioms of design an enterprise as a system must be specified and designed for its FRs to be satisfied by design parameters that are as independent as possible, and where the combined information content is minimal.

AD proposes 'Zigzagging' as a design methodology for producing a design that satisfies the two axioms. Zigzagging is used to simultaneously decompose FRs and DPs in the functional and the physical domains to create FR and DP hierarchies and to make sure that the two design axioms are applied when mapping DPs to FRs (Suh, 2003).

This is because depending on the nature of high level DPs, FRs could be decomposed in different ways, because to decompose a function, one has to devise a process, activities of which are invocations of lower level functions, and it is well known that usually there are many different processes that can perform the same transformation.

Mathematically, if a system S has a function F which could be implemented by a process P, consisting of a set of activities $A=\{A_i\}$, then each A_i must be an invocation of *some* function in the set of functions $L=\{L_j\}$ implemented by the set of DP_P. In this case $L=\{L_j\}$ is a functional decomposition of F. However, an alternative process R may exist, with a different set of activities $B=\{B_i\}$ each being an invocation of some function in $K=\{K_j\}$ of design parameters DP_R. Thus normally there is no single functional decomposition of a function (see Figure 4).

In fact, we should not decompose high level FRs unless we first find some DPs that can satisfy these highest-level FRs, otherwise the feasibility of the design is not ensured.

Therefore, when we define the FRs, we have to "zig" to the physical domain, and after DPs are found and chosen, we have to "zag" back to the functional domain for further decomposition.

NB, enterprises that specify FRs at all levels with no zigzagging between the functional and the physical domains will miss opportunities for innovation (Suh, 2003) (see Figure 5).

These two axioms can be used as architecting principles when considering the structuring or re-structuring of an enterprise, including its Business Model: practically, the way the enterprise is structured from business units, supporting logistics, facilities, and other infrastructure, such as Information Technology. However, as will be discussed in Section 3.2, some of the complexity is not automatically addressed by applying these two axioms as design principles.

A practical consequence of Axiom I is apparent when considering its use as an architecting principle in Service Orientation. A Service Oriented

Figure 4. $L=\{L_j\}$ and $K=\{K_j\}$ are alternative decompositions of F

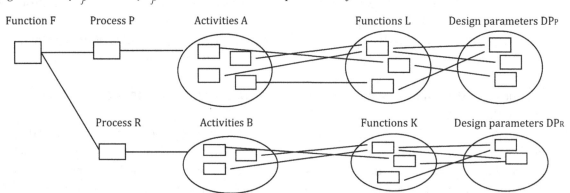

Figure 5. Zigzagging, the result of mapping and decomposition (adapted from Suh, 2003)

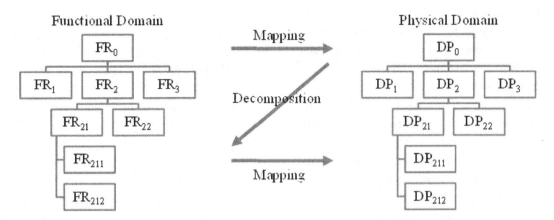

Architecture is believed to foster agility and flexibility of the enterprise. For example, a Service Oriented business is characterised by the business units having clear functional interfaces, such that a service to the customer could be composed by a customer facing unit out of the services of lower level internal or external services. Similarly, the separation of business processes from the underlying functions of software applications using a Service Oriented IT architecture, is believed to allow the configuration of a multitude of new or changed business processes out of underlying application functions. The question is therefore, what methodology can be used to design business- and IT architectures to foster the highest level of agility and flexibility?

The action space of the enterprise is determined by the set of possible combinations of the underlying / available functions, from which services to the customer can be combined. This 'combination' is achieved by a process, which can be ultimately decomposed into activities that in turn are invocations of service functions.

If the first axiom is observed, then the enterprise has the largest action space (i.e. the richest possible combination of [invocations of] functions into processes), because there is no limitation to combining independent functions. In other words,

Axiom I is an essential principle to observe when designing service oriented architectures – either business or IT.

Furthermore, Axiom II insists on the architect selecting the simplest solution out of the ones that satisfy Axiom I. 'Simplest' in this context can be illustrated as 'fewer elements and relationships among elements', thus reducing the number of possible design- and implementation errors and oversights and consequently improving the chances that the implemented system will under all circumstances be operating as expected. As demonstrated in Section 5, there exists a simple mathematical algorithm that can be built into a design system, which calculates an approximation of the information content of alternative designs, so as to enable to designer the select the one which is best from this point of view.

3.2. Extension to Axiomatic Design

Observe, that complexity of type 'b' is not automatically addressed by AD in enterprise engineering. An entity's life history according to GERAM is the representation in time of life cycle activities carried out on the particular entity during its life. *E.g.,* several concurrent design and implementation processes may be executed in one enterprise engineering process, and these work in parallel with the enterprise's operation. Notice that the life history of the target system is a representation in time of the processes of the 'change system' that changes the target system. Given that usually multiple dependencies exist among change activities it is important to address the complexity in the change system as well, in addition to complexity of the target system (see Figure 6).

According to the previously mentioned study of Random Boolean Networks (Kauffman 1993) the more dependency links exist between subsequent states, the higher the probability of chaos in the life of a system. E.g., if the architect produces a draft architectural design, and the designer of a subsystem can work without having to depend on design specifications of other subsystems, progression is predictable. However, if a complete design specification of all subsystems is needed for designers to progress, change in one subsystem's specification propagates, which may cause unpredictability.

The example indicates that there are inseparable dependencies between states of different life-cycle activities throughout the life-history of a system. We suppose that if there are too many dependencies and these dependencies are not controlled, then possibly the evolution of the system during its life history becomes chaotic. Li and Williams (1994) attempted to use AD in enterprise engineering, and demonstrated its use to the development of a master planning methodology (Williams, 1994). In a way their work is an early attempt to address complexity type 'b', *i.e.* to minimise the complexity of the system that creates the system.

While Li and Williams demonstrated the application of AD to the development of a methodology of master planning, typically, in addition to the instantiation of such a methodology in form of a master planning project, there usually exist multiple other change processes, performed on a target system – all at the same time. *E.g.* a long term master planning effort may be parallel with

Figure 6. Parallel processes in the entity's life-history (adapted from IFIP-IFAC Task Force, 1999; ISO15704:2000)

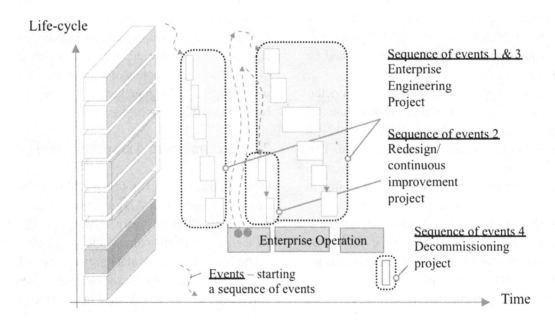

multiple shorter term change processes. These processes all change the entity (often called 'system of interest') on various time horizons.

What we propose below is to define methodology-agnostic principles of change to be satisfied when co-ordinating multiple change projects / processes.

The set of change projects operating on a system could use different methodologies or processes, but their target is the same entity, so there will be dependencies among these projects. The change projects themselves form a 'change system', which could be considered as a complex system in itself. As a consequence, the complexity of the process that creates the system (complexity type 'b') arises from the complexity of type 'a' and 'c' of this change system. We therefore propose that the two AD axioms must also be applied to the change system itself (see Figure 7).

The requirement for a target system (the enterprise) not to deteriorate during its life can be expressed as the recursion axiom, meaning that change projects as a system of systems not only have to use axiomatic design but they must be 'axiomatically designed' (see Figure 8).

Axiom III. Recursion Axiom

The system that designs a system must satisfy Axioms I and II of design.

Explanation: A system (e.g. enterprise) that satisfies Axioms I and II does not necessarily satisfy Axiom III and while at a given moment in time in its life history a system may be considered moderately complex, the same system may be very hard to create or change. E.g., denote three consecutive stages of a system S as S_1, S_2 and S_3.

Figure 7. The relationship between design domains of change system and target system

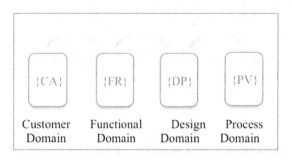

Figure 8. Mapping of design domains to GERA's life cycles and the relationship between the change system's and the target system's life cycle activities

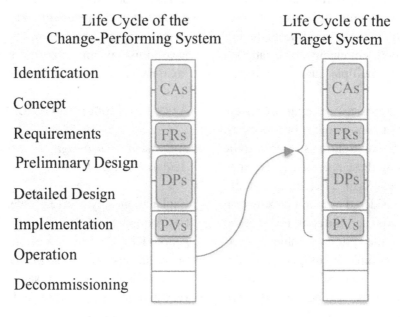

In S$_1$ system S is operating and has a design that either intentionally, or by pure chance, satisfies Axioms I & II. S$_2$ is the stage of change, where the original system has been extended by a change project P. The task of P is to create S$_3$. When S$_1$ creates P it can mandate that P must use Axioms I & II to design S$_3$. However, whether P and thereby S$_2$ satisfy Axioms I and II remains undetermined.

Thus, P can be more complex than necessary and even if its mandate is to design S$_3$, the likelihood of success of this endeavour may be less than desired, *i.e.* P does not satisfy Axioms I & II– even if it applies them to design S$_3$. Axiom III states is that S$_1$ not only has to mandate that P use Axioms I & II, but S$_1$ has to design P using Axioms I & II to improve the probability of successful evolution.

An important note about the independence of Axiom III. One could argue that P is a separate system from S, and as such Axioms I and II apply as the high level functional requirements of designing S, therefore Axiom III is unnecessary. However, notice that Axiom III is really about the

quality of design of S, and *not* about the quality of design of P. What Axiom III is intended to state is that out of the designs of S which satisfy Axioms I and II that one is best which is able to axiomatically design its own change. Thus Axiom III is pertinent to the design of systems that are involved in managing their own change, and its use is to ensure that S does not deteriorate with time. In everyday language: Axioms I and II are about the system being the best design from the point of view of doing what it is supposed to do. Axiom III is about the system being able to change as is intends to change. Thus, we introduced the third Axiom for the design of enterprises as special class of systems, namely self-evolving systems.

As demonstrated, systems at one stage of life may satisfy Axioms I & II but may lose this design quality as they evolve / change, and through reducing the likelihood of success of the change process this quality may even be lost permanently. To prevent such state of affairs we had to introduce Axiom III. Pragmatically: a large and complex system is created by complex systems to the design of which axiomatic design needs to be applied NB, the change system of systems is called the set of 'supporting systems' in systems engineering (see ISO 15288:2000).

4. SELF-EVOLUTION AND COMPLEXITY

A way to minimise the amount of information that a designer needs to have about the states of a system S and its subsystems S_i is to minimise the amount of information the designer has to have about the set of states T_i of each subsystem. There are two ways to minimise the observed information content:

1. The designer of a system elaborates the dependencies of subsystems for each system state in $\Pi_{i=1,...,n}Ti$ and defines the desired system behaviour for each such state (where 'n' is the number of subsystems). Note that in large systems multiple parallel change processes of subsystems may create very large values of Ti. The designer may instead, *stipulate* a set of relevant states t_i of each subsystem, where $|t_i| << |T_i|$, such that dependencies are artificially restricted to avoid chaotic life history. *E.g.,* the designer of a system may stipulate t_i and request a 'controlled release of change' from the subsystem's designer. This technique reduces the chance of undesired system behaviour but does not alleviate the designer's problem, because the designer still has to consider all of T_i.
2. It is known from practice that for the same pragmatic purpose a designer situated outside of the system needs a more detailed model of the system than a designer that is part of the system itself. This is because a designer who is part of the system will have developed tacit knowledge and will have already have the knowledge of how to collapse T_i into t_i – without actually having

to enumerate T_i at all: the designer who is part of the system knows what the relevant distinctions are regarding the system's ability to satisfy its requirements. Thus the apparent information content of the system from this 'embedded designer's point of view is less than the apparent information content.

The Self-Design Hypothesis

The above discussion is the basis for our hypothesis according to which the system (or system of systems) and the designer (or group of designers or design authorities) should not be separated and systems and subsystems should design themselves, out of component systems with the same self-designing property.

Def 2: Self-evolving System

A self-evolving system is a system which can perform its own life-cycle activities by using its own resources or acquiring them from others.

To minimise apparent complexity of a self-evolving system as it appears to any one designer, axiomatic design principles may be used. All of Axioms I, II and III must be satisfied, as the system designs its own change system. Self-evolution can be illustrated by life cycle relationships (see Figure 9).

By satisfying all three axioms the system must attempt to make its life cycle activities as independent, controlled and uncoupled as possible so that the designer can predict the next relevant states of the life history and avoid a chaotic change, i.e. change of *those* states of which the size and direction must be predictable. Note that this still allows behaviour that an external observer may characterise as chaotic.

According to (1) and (2), self-design results in minimised Information Content (IC) and thus creates a 'best design', from the point of view of the likelihood of success. Applying this logic to the change system we derive the conjecture:

Figure 9. Self-evolution and life cycle relationships

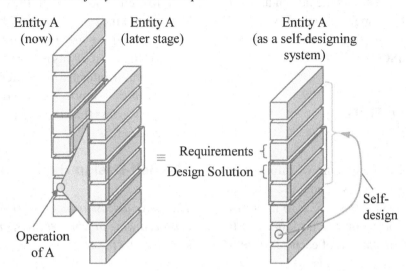

Self-Evolution Conjecture

Among those change systems which satisfy and apply the first two design axioms, that "change system" is the best which is designed by the stakeholders of the system of interest itself.

While we have no formal proof, the rationale for this statement is: *that* change system (change project/ change program) is most likely to succeed whose model used to create and control it is the simplest. The argument behind this conjecture is that management, who are the designers of the system's future, needs to be able to make decisions and plan in light of information about the change environment, and it is the stakeholders themselves with tacit knowledge, who have the least need for explicit information in order to make predictions about and control the change process.

In other words, models used by these 'embedded designers' can be simpler than models necessary for an external observer because the embedded designers know the important distinctions between relevant states. Conversely, embedded designers can recognise two states as identical from the point of view of relevance to the change process, whereupon the same two states

of the change environment would be considered different by 'outsiders' (external observers) who do not have tacit knowledge of this environment.

As a consequence, the requisite variety of the change system (Ashby, 1957; p. 202) can be minimised through the change process being designed by embedded designer agents.

5. KOLMOGOROV COMPLEXITY AS A PROXY FOR THE INFORMATION CONTENT

5.1. Definitions

The concept of Kolmogorov complexity was developed by the Russian mathematician Andrey Kolmogorov (1965). While Kolmogorov is credited with the concept, several other mathematicians appear to have arrived at the same conclusion simultaneously but independently of each other (Nannen 2010) in the 1960s. Kolmogorov complexity is one of the key elements in information theory; it provides a mathematical definition of the information quantity in individual objects, which can be abstracted as binary strings or integers. For about half a century, Kolmogorov complexity has been applied in various disciplines (Li, Vitányi 2008).

The Kolmogorov complexity $K_U(x)$ of a string x with respect to a universal computer U is defined as the length l of the shortest program p running on U that prints x and halts. It is denoted as:

$$K_U(x) = \min_{p:U(p)=x} l(p)$$

If the computer already has some knowledge about x, for example the length of x as $l(x)$, it may require a shorter program that prints x and halt. In this case, we define the conditional Kolmogorov complexity as:

$$K_U(x \mid l(x)) = \min_{p:U(p,l(x))=x} l(p)$$

Theorem 1

If U is a universal computer, $\forall V$ which is another universal computer, $\exists c$ is a constant, so for $\forall x \in \{0,1\}^*$ (i.e. for each binary number x)

$$K_U(x) \leq K_V(x) + c$$

The proof can be found in (Cover, Thomas 2006) and will not be repeated here.

Theorem 1 indicates the universality of the Kolmogorov complexity; it shows that the difference of Kolmogorov complexity with respect to different computers is smaller than a constant. If the string x is long, the difference of Kolmogorov complexity caused by different computers becomes trivial. Therefore, we can discuss Kolmogorov complexity $K(x)$ without referring to a particular computer.

We use $\log n$ to mean $\log_2 n$. We also define

$$\log^* n = \log n + \log \log n + \log \log \log n + \dots$$

until the last positive term.

Theorem 2

For an integer n, the Kolmogorov complexity $K(n)$ satisfies:

$$K(n) \leq \log^* n + c$$

The proof of Theorem 2 can be found in Cover's book (2006). We will explain it in an informal manner here. Generally, we can use a program like "print the integer n" to print n. The program needs the number n, which can be encoded in $\log n$ bits. However, the length of n is unknown, so it requires $\log \log n$ bits to code the length of n and then requires $\log \log \log n$ bits to code the length of the length of n etc.

Theorem 3

For an integer n, if the length of n is known, the conditional Kolmogorov complexity $K(n|l(n))$ satisfies:

$$K(n \mid l(n)) \leq \log n + c$$

The proof of Theorem 3 is similar to the previous theorem.

5.2. Estimating the Kolmogorov Complexity of a Transition Matrix

For a given transition matrix M, which maps Design Parameters to Functional Requirements we propose a simple scheme to calculate an upper boundary of its Kolmogorov complexity.

Let M be a $n \times n$ matrix, where the value of each element in the matrix can only be 1 or 0. The number of ones in M is m. In order to describe the matrix, we need to record the following information: the number n, the number of ones m, and the position of those '1's. Accordingly, we can calculate the Kolmogorov complexity of M as:

$$K(M) \leq K(n) + K(m) + K\binom{n^2}{m} \leq \log^* n$$
$$+ \log^* m + \log \frac{n^2!}{m!(n^2-m)!} + c \qquad (1)$$

If M is a diagonal matrix, because all the non-zero elements are ones, it is an identity matrix. It is obvious that in order to record an identity matrix, the only information we require is its size n. Therefore, the Kolmogorov complexity of an identity matrix can be estimated as:

$$K(I_n) = K(n) \leq \log^* n + c \qquad (2)$$

6. SIMPLE EXAMPLES

We introduce two examples to demonstrate the application of the three design axioms. The first case study demonstrates an example of a coupled design, a bad design which is more complex than necessary, for a virtual enterprise (called 'company X') and applies the first two design axioms which results in an uncoupled design.

The second case demonstrates an example of a decoupled design for a project which creates company X and the application of the 3rd axiom of design, which is the axiom of recursion, to reduce the complexity of the project which designs, creates and implements company X.

We use an upper bound estimation of the Kolmogorov complexity of the design matrix as a proxy of Suh's Information Content to demonstrate the difference between the bad and the good designs by calculating the complexity of the design matrix in both case studies before and after applying design axioms. We therefore demonstrate in both concrete examples how the application of extended axiomatic design theory can reduce the complexity of designing a system of interest, as well as the complexity of a system which designs the system of interest.

Systems, at one stage of life, may well satisfy Axioms I & II but may lose this design quality through uncontrolled change, because uncontrolled change reduces the likelihood of success of the change process and the above quality may even be lost permanently. Therefore the second case study demonstrates the application of the third axiom as a solution to this problem.

6.1. Example One: Application of the Axioms I and II in Designing a Virtual Enterprise X

'Company X', which is actually a virtual enterprise, produces one product including three parts Pt_1, Pt_2 and Pt_3. There are five functional requirements listed below:

- **FR_1:** Each part needs to have a blueprint.
- **FR_2:** Pt_1 needs to be cut and drilled.
- **FR_3:** Pt_2 needs to be cut and painted.
- **FR_4:** Pt_3 needs to be cut, drilled and painted
- **FR_5:** All parts need to be assembled together.

Let the original design parameters to implement these functions as follows:

- **DP1:** Company A provides service of drawing blueprint.
- **DP2:** Company I provides service of cutting.
- **DP3:** Company J provides service of drilling.
- **DP4:** Company K provides service of painting.
- **DP5:** Company L provides service of assembling.

Based on the FRs and the DPs above, we can write the FR to DP mapping formula for company X as:

$$\begin{bmatrix} FR_1 \\ FR_2 \\ FR_3 \\ FR_4 \\ FR_5 \end{bmatrix} = \begin{bmatrix} 1 & 0 & 0 & 0 & 0 \\ 0 & 1 & 1 & 0 & 0 \\ 0 & 1 & 0 & 1 & 0 \\ 0 & 1 & 1 & 1 & 0 \\ 0 & 0 & 0 & 0 & 1 \end{bmatrix} \begin{bmatrix} DP_1 \\ DP_2 \\ DP_3 \\ DP_4 \\ DP_5 \end{bmatrix}$$

It is clear that the design transition matrix is coupled.

According to the first axiom of design, we must maintain the independence of the functional requirements all the times. Therefore to apply axiomatic design principles, we introduce a broker company B which provides the generic service of 'manufacturing parts'. Then we refine the structure of company X to X' with the functional requirements and design parameters as follows:

- **FR1:** Each part needs to have a blueprint.
- **FR2:** Each part needs to be manufactured.
- **FR3:** All parts need to be assembled together.
- **DP1:** Company A provides service of drawing blueprint.
- **DP2:** Company B provides service of manufacturing.
- **DP3:** Company C provides service of assembling.

Then the FR-DP transition matrix for X' is shown below is a diagonal matrix:

$$\begin{bmatrix} FR_1 \\ FR_2 \\ FR_3 \end{bmatrix} = \begin{bmatrix} 1 & 0 & 0 \\ 0 & 1 & 0 \\ 0 & 0 & 1 \end{bmatrix} \begin{bmatrix} DP_1 \\ DP_2 \\ DP_3 \end{bmatrix}$$

The FRs and DPs for the (broker) company B are:

- **FR1:** Some parts need to be cut.
- **FR2:** Some parts need to be drilled.
- **FR3:** Some parts need to be painted.

- **DP1:** Company I provides service of cutting.
- **DP2:** Company J provides service of drilling.
- **DP3:** Company K provides service of painting.

The design transition matrix is a diagonal 3×3 matrix as well.

Let us now calculate the Kolmogorov complexity of each transition matrix of the manufacturing case study. In the original design, the transition matrix M is:

$$M = \begin{bmatrix} 1 & 0 & 0 & 0 & 0 \\ 0 & 1 & 1 & 0 & 0 \\ 0 & 1 & 0 & 1 & 0 \\ 0 & 1 & 1 & 1 & 0 \\ 0 & 0 & 0 & 0 & 1 \end{bmatrix}$$

For this transition matrix, we have $n=5$, $m=9$, so based on inequality (1), we have:

$$K(M) \leq \log^* n + \log^* m + \log^* d$$
$$+ \log \frac{n^2!}{m!(n^2-m)!} + m \times \log d \approx 29.9 \, (\text{bits})$$

For the new design, based on Axiomatic Design principles, we have two diagonal transition matrices and both matrices happen to be 3×3 identity matrices:

$$I_3 = \begin{bmatrix} 1 & 0 & 0 \\ 0 & 1 & 0 \\ 0 & 0 & 1 \end{bmatrix}$$

Based on inequality (2), we have:

$$2K(I_3) \leq 2(\log^* n + n \log d) \approx 4.5 \, (\text{bits})$$

It is clear that the design based on Axiomatic Design principles is much simpler.

6.2. Example Two: Application of Axiom III of Design in Designing the Project that creates a Virtual Enterprise X

Let N be the network which is the aggregation of n enterprise partners $P = \{p_1, p_2, ..., p_n\}$. The network N is managed by a Network Office M. M utilizes N to form a number of projects Pr_X, Pr_Y, Pr_Z... to create Virtual Enterprises (VEs), such as X, Y and Z etc. Each VE consists of a set of enterprise partners collaborating to create the value chain of the respective VEs. We use P_X, P_Y and P_Z to denote the sets of associated enterprise partners for VEs X, Y and Z respectively. Each enterprise partner may participate in zero or more virtual enterprises. Therefore, we have:

$$P_X \subseteq P, \ P_Y \subseteq P, \ P_Z \subseteq P$$

$$\varphi \subseteq P_X \cap P_Y, \varphi \subseteq P_X \cap P_Z, \varphi \subseteq P_Y \cap P_Z.$$

We suppose that the network N that designs, creates and changes VEs (including X) already exists E.g. N may have been created by the network office M.

Now consider the VE creation project Pr_X.

Pr_X has the functional requirements listed below:

- **FR$_1$:** Provide the Identification and Concept of X and specify all its requirements, including functional and non-functional ones.
- **FR$_2$:** Provide the Preliminary or Architectural Design of X: estimate cost, resources needed, selected members etc.
- **FR$_3$:** Provide the detailed design descriptions, and all the tasks that must be carried out to build or re-build and release X into operation.

Let the design parameters to implement this project be the following:

- **DP$_1$:** P_{X1} is the set of participants who together identify and develop the concept, such as principles, business model, etc of X, This would typically require the knowledge of at least some feasible architectural solutions.
- **DP$_2$:** P_{X2} is the set of participants who together develop the Architectural Design ('master plan') of X identifying the list of the selected members, cost and time necessary to build X, etc. This would typically be done by reusing existing designs ['reference models' or 'partial models'] where the feasibility of design and building under the constraints of the non-functional requirements is known.
- **DP$_3$:** P_{X3} detailed design of the common parts of the company with a list of the qualified members creates and the new VE into operation.

Based on the FRs and the DPs above and the life cycle dependencies between project tasks of Requirements Analysis, Architectural Design, detailed Design and Build, the transition between DPs to FRs is as below:

$$\begin{bmatrix} FR_1 \\ FR_2 \\ FR_3 \end{bmatrix} = \begin{bmatrix} 1 & 1 & 1 \\ 0 & 1 & 1 \\ 0 & 0 & 1 \end{bmatrix} \begin{bmatrix} DP_1 \\ DP_2 \\ DP_3 \end{bmatrix}$$

For the transition matrix:

$$M_X = \begin{bmatrix} 1 & 1 & 1 \\ 0 & 1 & 1 \\ 0 & 0 & 1 \end{bmatrix}$$

We have $n=3$, $d=1$, $m=6$. Based on inequality (1), we estimate the information content:

$$K(M_X) \leq \log^* n + \log^* m + \log^* d$$

$$+ \log \frac{n^2!}{m!(n^2 - m)!} + m \times \log d \approx 18.6 \, (\text{bits})$$

According to Axiom III of design: "The system that designs another system not only must apply but also must satisfy the axioms of design."

The project (Pr_X) that creates X could be a system that designs/changes another system (X). Thus Pr_X is itself, based on its life-cycle dependencies shown in the triangular matrix above, a complex system that not only should design another system that has reduced complexity (namely X) by applying axiomatic design theory, but it has to also have reduced complexity and be designed to satisfy axioms I and II.

To achieve the above, we shall reduce the *direct* communication among life cycle activities of Pr_X. Neglecting this communication creates additional complexity in the execution of the life cycle activities (FR_1, FR_2 and FR_3) of Pr_X.

Notice, that practically, the problem is caused by mixing the information dependencies among the life cycle activities with the control of their repeated, iterative invocation.

These dependencies may result in unpredictable chaotic states of Pr_X and decrease the probability of success of the resulting design (the Company X). This effect is well known in managing complex projects and arises if the information flow among life cycle activities is not managed and controlled.

6.3. Separation of Management Functions from Operations

What is required to solve the problem in Section 5.2 is to reduce the complexity of the design of Pr_X itself to guarantee the achievement, or preservation, of the design qualities of X. A solution is to allocate a sub-project manager to each life cycle activity (FR_1, FR_2, and FR_3) and to have them take part in the project management board meetings and to communicate *'just'* at the management level.

Using this method the project manager of Pr_X should make the project's life cycle activities as independent as possible by delegating each life cycle activity to independent sub-projects that communicate just through management of each project and hide the unnecessary operational details of each life cycle activity of creating Pr_X from the rest of the project's operations.

We therefore decompose Pr_X into two parts: Pr_M is the management of the project and Pr_O is the operation of the subproject. Let FR_M be the functional requirement (to 'Manage' Pr), and FR_O the functional requirement(s) describing what Pr has to actually achieve, namely the function of the project's 'Operations'. In this case Pr_M (the project's management) takes care of the control of the communication among operational boundaries. Thus on the high level we have:

$$\begin{bmatrix} FR_M \\ FR_O \end{bmatrix} = \begin{bmatrix} 1 & 0 \\ 0 & 1 \end{bmatrix} \begin{bmatrix} DP_M \\ DP_O \end{bmatrix}$$

The operational function of the project can be further decomposed into three functions (i.e., life cycle activities, or 'phases'):

1. The identification phase.
2. The architectural design phase.
3. The detailed design and building phase of X.

During the three phases, there are three corresponding functional requirements:

- **FR_{O1}:** Provide the Identification and Concept of the virtual company X and specify all its requirements – based on input / control received from Pr_M.
- **FR_{O2}:** Provide the Preliminary or Architectural Design of X– estimates of cost, resources needed, selected members of the company X etc, based on input / control received from Pr_M.

- **FR$_{O3}$:** Provide the detailed design descriptions, and all the tasks that must be carried out to build or re-build and implement the company *X*– based on input / control received from Pr$_M$.

Based on the three functional requirements, we construct three design parameters:

- **DP$_{O1}$:** *Pr$_{O1}$* identifies different VE types, develops their master plan based on existing preliminary design of partial models of the new company *X*, and provides the detailed design of the common parts of the company with a list of the qualified suppliers.
- **DP$_{O2}$:** *Pr$_{O2}$* provides the Architectural Design of *X* with a list of the selected suppliers for Architectural Design of the company;
- **DP$_{O3}$:** *Pr$_{O3}$* creates and operates the new VE, and monitors the results of *X*.

The relationship between the functional requirements and the design parameters can be expressed as:

$$\begin{bmatrix} FR_{O1} \\ FR_{O2} \\ FR_{O3} \end{bmatrix} = \begin{bmatrix} 1 & 0 & 0 \\ 0 & 1 & 0 \\ 0 & 0 & 1 \end{bmatrix} \begin{bmatrix} DP_{O1} \\ DP_{O2} \\ DP_{O3} \end{bmatrix}$$

Under the new design approach, we have two transition matrices which are actually two identity matrices I_2 and I_3.

Based on inequality (2), we have:

$$K(I_2) + K(I_3) \leq \log^* 2 + \log^* 3 \approx 3.3 \, (\text{bits})$$

Compared with the original design, which has the complexity of the design matrix of about 18.6 bits, the design based on the AD principles is significantly simpler.

Note that the reader may suspect a 'trick' in this design, because the internal management process of Pr$_M$ needs to channel the communication among invocations of life cycle activities. This is true of course, however, the separation of content from control has a significant effect: Pr$_M$ only needs to know about the state of the information maintained by the subprojects, not the content. For example, managers of large projects normally use controlled information / version release processes so as to avoid project instability and ensure convergence. Note also that the method is not to be taken as a counter-argument against collaborative design, after all Pr$_{O1,}$ Pr$_{O2}$ and Pr$_{O3}$ possibly share contributors, but their contributions are in different roles.

In this article it was the authors who applied Axioms I and II to ensure that Pr_X is least complex. In reality Pr_X may be a project, created by either the Network *X* itself as a change project, thus effectively *X* being a self designing system obeying Axiom III by mandating Pr$_M$ to satisfy Axioms I and II when creating the operational part of Pr_X.

The authors believe that further work will be needed to study the complexity of project life histories, as opposed to structure that was studied here, i.e., how to apply the above design axioms and associated design methods to reduce the complexity of dependencies among life cycle activity instances. This is because due to iterations and feedback most life cycle activities will be performed several times during the project.

7. CONCLUSION

This chapter reviewed a number of complexity measures that can help characterise how hard it is to design and change a system. By applying Axiomatic Design theory two types of complexity can be avoided or reduced, but we have demonstrated that the third type of complexity—the difficulty to create the system, as defined by Lloyd—is actually the repetition of the other two types of complexity, only targeting the change system not the system of interest.

As a consequence, for enterprises as self evolving systems, we extended the collection of Suh's design axioms with Axiom III – the Axiom of Recursion and demonstrated the application of these three design axioms using two simple examples. The first example shows a coupled design for a virtual enterprise—a bad design which is more complex than needed—and demonstrates how we can apply the first two design axioms to arrive at an uncoupled, less complex design.

The example shows a decoupled design for a project which creates a virtual enterprise X and shows the application of Axiom III to reduce the complexity of the project, i.e., the system, which designs, creates, implements, or changes X.

We applied a known approximation of the upper bound of Kolmogorov complexity to calculate a proxy of AD's Information Content, and compared the bad and the good designs by calculating the approximate complexity / information content of the design matrix. We therefore demonstrated in both concrete examples how the application of extended axiomatic design theory can reduce the complexity of designing a system as well as the complexity of the system which designs the system of interest.

We formulated a conjecture, according to which the reduction of the apparent complexity of systems, such as enterprises, can be achieved if systems design themselves, and the designer is part of the system. This was derived based on logical considerations of how systems and their designers differentiate 'relevant states' of the environment, but further work is needed for a formal proof.

We also introduced the notion of self-evolving systems, a category of evolving systems: those deliberately designing themselves.

REFERENCES

Abraham, R. (2002). *The genesis of complexity*. Retrieved from www.ralph-abraham.org

Ashby, W. R. (1957). *An introduction to cybernetics*. London: Chapman & Hall.

Bar-Yam, Y. (2002). *Large scale engineering and evolutionary change: Useful concepts for implementation of FORCEnet*. Cambridge, UK: NECSI.

Bar-Yam, Y. (2003a). Unifying principles in complex systems. In Roco, M. C., & Bainbridge, W. S. (Eds.), *Converging Technology for Improving Human Performance* (pp. 380–409). Boston: Kluwer.

Bar-Yam, Y. (2003b). When systems engineering fails – Toward complex systems engineering. In *Proceedings of the International Conference on Systems, Man, & Cybernetics*, (Vol. 2, pp. 2021-2028). Piscataway, NJ: IEEE.

Bar-Yam, Y., & Kuras, M. L. (2003). *Complex systems and evolutionary engineering*. Cambridge, UK: NECSI.

Bernus, P., Baltrusch, R., Tølle, M., & Vesterager, J. (2002). Better Models for agile virtual enterprises – The enterprise and its constituents as hybrid agents. In Karvoinen, I. et al. (Eds.), *Global Engineering and Manufacturing in Enterprise Networks* (pp. 91–103). Helsinki, Finland: VTT.

Bernus, P., Nemes, L., & Smith, G. (Eds.). (2003). *Handbook on enterprise architecture*. Berlin: Springer. doi:10.1007/978-3-540-24744-9.

Bernus, P., Nemes, L., & Williams, T. J. (Eds.). (1996). *Architectures for enterprise integration*. London: Chapman and Hall. doi:10.1007/978-0-387-34941-1.

Brooks, F. Jr. (1982). *The mythical man month*. Reading, MA: Addison-Wesley.

Castellani, B. (2009). *Complexity map*. Retrieved from http://www.art-sciencefactory.com/complexity-map_feb09.html

Chaitin, G. J. (1966). On the length of programs for computing finite binary sequences. *Journal of the ACM, 13*, 547–569. doi:10.1145/321356.321363.

Cover, T. M., & Thomas, J. A. (2006). *Elements of information theory* (2nd ed.). Hoboken, NJ: Wiley.

Dromey, R. G. (2006). Formalizing the transition from requirements to design. In Liu, Z., & He, J. (Eds.), *Mathematical Frameworks for Component Software, Models for Analysis and Synthesis* (pp. 173–206). London: World Scientific. doi:10.1142/9789812772831_0006.

Erl, T. (2005). *Service-oriented architecture: concepts, technology, and design*. Hoboken, NJ: Prentice Hall.

Gell-Mann, M. (1994). Complex adaptive systems. In Cowan, G. A., Pines, D., & Meltzer, D. (Eds.), *Complexity: Metaphors, models, and reality* (pp. 17–45). Reading, MA: Addison-Wesley.

Gershenson, C. (2002). Complex philosophy. In *Proceedings of the 1st Biennial Seminar on Philosophical, Methodological & Epistemological Implications of Complexity Theory*. La Habana, Cuba: Academic Press.

Gershenson, C. (2004). Introduction to random Boolean networks. In M. Bedau, P. Husbands, T. Hutton, S. Kumar, & H. Suzuki (Eds.), *Proceedings of the 9th International Conference on the Simulation and Synthesis of Living Systems,* (pp. 160-173). Retrieved from http://arxiv.org/abs/nlin/0408006

Gershenson, C. (2007). *Design and control of self-organizing systems*. Mexico City: CopIt ArXives.

Holland, J. H. (1992). Complex adaptive systems. *Daedalus, 121*(1), 17–30.

IFIP-IFAC Task Force. (1999). GERAM - The generalised enterprise reference architecture and methodology. In Bernus, P., Nemes, L., & Schmidt, G. (Eds.), *Handbook on Enterprise Architecture* (pp. 22–64). Berlin: Springer.

ISO15288. (2000). *Systems and software engineering – System life cycle processes*. Geneva: ISO.

ISO15704. (2000). *Industrial automation systems – Requirements for enterprise reference architectures and methodologies*. Geneva: ISO TC184.SC5.WG1.

Jennings, N. R., & Wooldridge, M. (1995). Applying agent technology. *Journal of Applied AI, 9*(4), 351–361.

Kandjani, H., & Bernus, P. (2011). Engineering self-designing enterprises as complex systems using extended axiomatic design theory. *IFAC Papers OnLine, 18*(1), 11943–11948.

Kauffman, S. A. (1993). *The origins of order: Self-organization and selection in evolution*. New York: Oxford University Press.

Kolmogorov, A. N. (1969). On the logical foundations of information theory and probability theory. *Problems of Information Transmission, 5*(3), 1–4.

Krafzig, D., Banke, K., & Slama, D. (2004). *Enterprise SOA: Service-oriented architecture best practices*. Upper Saddle River, NJ: Prentice Hall.

Li, H., & Williams, T. J. (1994). *A formalization and extension of the Purdue enterprise reference architecture and the Purdue methodology. TR 158 Purdue Lab. of Applied Industrial Control*. West Lafayette, IN: Purdue University.

Li, M., & Vitányi, P. (2008). *An introduction to Kolmogorov complexity and its applications* (3rd ed.). Berlin: Springer. doi:10.1007/978-0-387-49820-1.

Lloyd, S. (2001). Measures of complexity: A non-exhaustive list. *IEEE Control Systems Magazine, 21*(4), 7–8. doi:10.1109/MCS.2001.939938.

Melvin, J. (2003). *Axiomatic system design: Chemical mechanical polishing machine case study*. (PhD Thesis in Mechanical Engineering). MIT, Cambridge, MA.

Meyer, B. (1988). *Object-oriented software construction*. Englewood Cliffs, NJ: Prentice Hall.

Moghaddam, M. R. S., Sharifi, A., & Merati, E. (2008). Using axiomatic design in the process of enterprise architecting. In *Proceedings of the 3rd International Conference on Convergence and Hybrid Information Technology*, (pp. 279-284). ICCT.

Nannen, V. A. (2010). *Short introduction to model selection, Kolmogorov complexity and minimum description length (MDL)*. Retrieved from http://arxiv.org/abs/1005.2364

Nierstrasz, O., Gibbs, S., & Tsichritzis, D. (1992). Component-oriented software development. *Communications of the ACM, 35*(9), 160–164. doi:10.1145/130994.131005.

Osterweil, L. (1987). Software processes are software too. In *Proceedings of the 9th International Conference on Software Engineering*, (pp. 2-13). Los Alamitos, CA: IEEE.

Saha, P. (2006). A real options perspective to enterprise architecture as an investment activity. *Journal of Enterprise Architecture, 2*(3), 50.

Smarr, L. (1985). An approach to complexity: Numerical computations. *Science, 228*, 403–403. doi:10.1126/science.228.4698.403 PMID:17746870.

Snyder, A. (1986). Encapsulation and inheritance in object-oriented programming languages. *ACM SIGPLAN Notices, 21*(11), 38–45. doi:10.1145/960112.28702.

Suh, N. P. (1990). *The principles of design*. New York: Oxford University Press.

Suh, N. P. (1999). A theory of complexity, periodicity and the design axioms. *Research in Engineering Design, 11*, 116–133. doi:10.1007/PL00003883.

Suh, N. P. (2001). *Axiomatic design: Advances and applications*. New York: Oxford University Press.

Suh, N. P. (2003). *Complexity: Theory and applications*. New York: Oxford University Press.

Suh, N. P. (2005). Complexity in engineering. *CIRP Annals-Manufacturing Technology, 54*(2), 46–63. doi:10.1016/S0007-8506(07)60019-5.

Suh, N. P., & Do, S. (2000). Axiomatic design of software systems. *CIRP Annals-Manuf Technology, 49*(1), 95–100. doi:10.1016/S0007-8506(07)62904-7.

Vitányi, P. (2007). Analysis of sorting algorithms by Kolmogorov complexity (a survey). *Entropy, Search, Complexity. Bolyai Society Mathematical Studies, 16*, 209–232. doi:10.1007/978-3-540-32777-6_9.

von Bertalanffy, L. (1968). *General system theory: Foundations, development, applications*. New York: George Braziller.

Wen, L., & Dromey, R. G. (2006). Architecture normalization for component-based systems. *Electronic Notes in Theoretical Computer Science, 160*, 335–348. doi:10.1016/j.entcs.2006.05.032.

Wen, L., & Dromey, R. G. (2009). A hierarchical architecture for modeling complex software intensive systems using behavior trees. In *Proceedings of the 9th Asia-Pacific Complex Systems Conference*, (pp. 292-299). IEEE.

Williams, T. J. (1994). *Purdue guide for master planning & implementation programs*. West-Lafayette, IN: Purdue University.

KEY TERMS AND DEFINITIONS

Axiom I: Independence Axiom: "The independence of FRs must always be maintained." It means that a FR_i is independent of other FRs if there exists a solution, i.e. list of 'design parameters' [DP], such that if changing one FR_i only one DP needs to be changed.

Axiom II: Information Axiom: "Out of the designs that satisfy Axiom I that design is best that has the minimal information content."

Axiom III: Recursion Axiom: The system that designs a system must satisfy Axioms I & II of design.

Axiomatic Design Theory: Is a theory primarily originated from Mechanical Engineering and applied in several other design-related disciplines. AD theory helps to understand and design complex systems, claiming to codify (in a discipline-independent way) what a 'best design' is. AD had its own definition of 'complex', explaining reasons of emerging complexity in design. AD is also a formal design theory, defining principles that designers of systems need to follow to produce systems with minimal complexity (in Suh's sense).

Complex System: According to Axiomatic Design Theory a 'complex' system is one that can not be predicted for certain that it will always satisfy its functional requirements.

Coupled Design: If [[A]] can not be rearranged to be triangular then the design is coupled, and consequently the implementation is not 'serialisable.'

Decoupled Design: If [[A]] is triangular then the design is decoupled, and as a result the implementation process of DPs is 'serialisable'.

Design Matrix: A design or transition matrix [[A]], is a matrix that maps Design Parameters [DP] to Functional Requirements [FR]. According to Suh, design is a process to find DPs such that [FR] = [[A]] × [DP], where [FR] is the vector of FRs, [DP] is the vector of DPs and [[A]] is a matrix mapping DPs to FRs.

Information Content: Suh defined information content as the negative logarithm of the 'probability of success' which is the probability of satisfying all the functional requirements.

Kolmogorov Complexity: The Kolmogorov complexity $K_U(x)$ of a string x with respect to a universal computer U is defined as the length l of the shortest program p running on U that prints x and halts.

Number of Relevant States: An approximate complexity measure, and as the 'Information Content' (IC) of a system, it is the information that the system must have about its environment. Note that 'knowing the state of the environment' may include knowing state history if this is relevant for determining what is the system's appropriate response, and 'state' should be interpreted in an abstract sense.

Self-Evolving System: A self-evolving system is a system which can perform its own life-cycle activities by using its own resources or acquiring them from others.

The Self-Design Hypothesis: The system (or system of systems) and the designer (or group of designers or design authorities) should not be separated: systems and subsystems should design themselves out of component systems with the same self-designing property.

Uncoupled Design: If [[A]] is a diagonal matrix the design is called uncoupled, meaning that full independence of FRs is achieved.

Chapter 3
Complex Adaptive Systems Thinking Approach to Enterprise Architecture

Marc Rabaey
Open-Raxit, Belgium

ABSTRACT

Complex systems interact with an environment where a high degree of uncertainty exists. To reduce uncertainty, enterprises (should) create intelligence. This chapter shows that intelligence has two purposes: first, to increase and to assess (thus to correct) existing knowledge, and second, to support decision making by reducing uncertainty. The chapter discusses complex adaptive systems. Enterprises are not only complex systems; they are also most of the time dynamic because they have to adapt their goals, means, and structure to survive in the fast evolving (and thus unstable) environment. Crucial for enterprises is to know the context/ecology in which they act and operate. The Cynefin framework makes the organization and/or its parts aware of the possible contexts of the organization and/or its parts: simple, complicated, complex, chaotic, or disordered. It is crucial for the success of implementing and using EA that EA is adapted to function in an environment of perpetual change. To realize this, the chapter proposes and elaborates a new concept of EA, namely Complex Adaptive Systems Thinking – Enterprise Architecture (CAST-EA).

INTRODUCTION

The aim of this chapter is to introduce Complex Adaptive System (CAS) and Systems Thinking (ST) into Enterprise Architecture (EA). The combination of CAS and ST is called Complex Adaptive Systems Thinking (CAST) (Lowe & Ng, 2006).

DOI: 10.4018/978-1-4666-4518-9.ch003

Systems Thinking has many forms, but we are basing our concept on the ST defined by Gharajedaghi (2011). In the context of Enterprise Architecture, ST is, in essence, a holistic approach to an enterprise and its environment. Sterman (2010) defines ST as "the ability to see the world as a complex system, in which we understand that 'you can't just do one thing' and that 'everything is connected to everything else'" (p. 4). In this light, we will propose a new concept of EA, which will not only incorporate the Information Technology (IT) view but also a global (holistic) view of the enterprise.

Sterman (2010) wants us to see the world as a complex system, so we will first give a brief overview of complex systems. Senge (2006) states that complex systems have to do with dynamic complexity and not detail complexity. The latter arises where there are many variables, which are difficult (almost impossible) to hold in mind simultaneously to appreciate them as a whole. The former arises where effects over time of interrelatedness are subtle and the results of actions are not obvious, or where short-term and long-term effects are significantly different, or where effects locally are different from effects on a wider scale (Flood, 1999).

Complex systems are interacting with an environment where much uncertainty exists. To reduce the uncertainty, the enterprise will create intelligence. In our discussion, however, we will show that intelligence has two purposes: to increase and to assess (thus to correct) the existing knowledge and to support decision making by reducing the uncertainty. Rabaey and Mercken (2012) are proposing the system of 'Intelligence Base' to organize the intelligence process and the exploitation of knowledge.

After the section on uncertainty and intelligence, we will discuss Complex Adaptive Systems. Enterprises are not only complex systems, but they are also most of the time CAS because they have to adapt their goals, means and structure to survive in the fast evolving (and thus unstable) environment. In this section, we will show the consequence of wanting to implement EA for a CAS.

Crucial for enterprises is to know in which context they are acting and reacting. The Cynefin framework makes the organization and/or its parts aware of the possible contexts of the organization and/or its parts: simple, complicated, complex, chaotic or disordered. Dettmer (2011) uses the Cynefin framework to determine which management methods and tools can be used in

which context. Important to note is that systems can move from one context to another without the enterprise knowing about it (necessity to have an intelligence system).

As a consequence, it is crucial for the success of implementing and using EA, that EA is adapted to function in a context that may permanently change. Therefore, we are proposing a new concept of EA, namely Complex Adaptive Systems Thinking – Enterprise Architecture (CAST-EA).

SYSTEMS

Open Systems

An enterprise or any other organization cannot be a closed system, if it wants to interact with its environment, therefore, it is an open system. Although we will discuss Complex Adaptive Systems (CAS) in more depth later, we will first define what a system is. Russell Ackoff is a Systems Thinking pioneer and organizational theorist. He (Joyce, 2011; Matthews, 2012) states that a system is a whole, that consists of parts, each of which can affect the behavior of the whole or its properties. The parts do not necessarily do it all the time, but they can. Furthermore, each part of the system, when it affects the system, is dependent for its effect on some other parts. In other words, the parts are interdependent; therefore, no part of the system or a collection of parts has an independent effect on it.

As such, a system is a whole that cannot be divided into independent parts. Moreover, the essential or defining properties of a system are properties of the whole which none of its parts have and thus when a system is taken apart it loses its essential properties. As an example, if one takes all of the different cars on the market today, and asks a group of engineers who have the best engine, which has the best transmission, which has the best alternator, etc., and they take these best parts and try to put them together, it is unlikely one would get a working automobile; the parts would not fit, let alone it would be the best car in the world. It is the working together that is the main attribute of systemic thinking.

Moreover, the performance of a system is never the sum of the performance of its parts taken separately. It is the product of its interactions. The performance of a system is based upon how the parts interact and fit, never just on how they act separately. There are many instances where improving the performance of the part will make the performance of the whole worse. This is very well known by the architects.

An architect starts by drawing first the house (the whole) then he/she adds the rooms; the parts. He/she only improves the room in such a way that it also improves the "whole" house. Sometimes a part needs to be made worse to make the whole better. If the architect can make the room worse, but make the house better, then an architect will do it. After all, the objective is to build the best house, not the best rooms.

Ackoff continues: if you have a system of improvement that is directed at improving the parts taken separately, you can be absolutely sure that the performance of the whole will not be improved. The doctrine of the Western world is "divide and conquer"; if every separate part of the organization is managed well, then the whole system will improve. To Ackoff this is absolutely false.

This is completely counter intuitive. The classic western world is committed to managing the actions of the parts, not their interactions. Most improvement programs orientate themselves towards improving the parts separately, not the whole. For continuous improvement, the whole should be the focus.

Deming defines a man-made system as "a network of interdependent components that work together to try to accomplish the aim of the system. A system must have an aim. Without an aim, there is no system. The aim of the system must be clear to everyone in the system. The aim must include plans for the future. The aim is a value judgment" (W. Edwards Deming, n.d.).

However, an organization is not a (static) house; it is a (dynamic) entity that continuously has to reshape itself because of the interactions with its constantly changing environment. As we will discuss later, some organizations are not the only ones that interact (as a whole) with the environment, but also their constituent parts (network of interdependent agents). So another issue is to define the relevant boundaries of a system (Flood, 1999). Nowadays, in this omni-interconnected world with synergies, outsourcing and joint ventures (amongst others), it is hard to determine exactly the boundaries of an organization (system, whole). Donella H. Meadows: "Where to draw a boundary around a system depends on the questions we want to ask" (Matthews, 2012a).

Systems are Co-Creating Their Environment

An organization is an open system because it interacts with its environment for its survival. It will first observe the internal (organization) and external (environment) situation before making decisions to act. These actions will be observed by other actors (agents) in the environment, and they will react upon it (ignore, collaborate, compete, agree, disagree, etc.). Of course, the organization itself will behave in a similar way upon the actions or reactions of the other actors.

All of these actions and reactions will have effects that cannot be fully assessed beforehand. It is possible that the effects are just the opposite of the goals defined by the organizational strategy. A strategy is the balance between goals and means (Bernard, 1976). If a government engages more resources than necessary, then it is not efficient. If the resources are insufficient to attain the objectives, then it will not be effective. This of course also applies to the organizational initiatives, like putting up information systems, which are most of the time very budget intensive projects.

Uncertainty

As already mentioned the actors do not know beforehand if their actions have the desired outcomes, because they do not know how the other players will act, therefore, deciding is making choices under uncertainty. Moreover, the world grows smaller. Therefore, more and more players are coming into the direct environment of the organization, so the number of players is increasing. In addition, the speed of transactions due to Information Technology (IT) is increasing. Uncertainties can be due to wrong information, lack of information, lack of time to analyze information or a wrong collection of information. As a consequence we need a way to reduce the uncertainty and thus to mitigate the risks before making decisions.

Decision making has three dimensions (Gharajedaghi, 2011, pp. 33-37): rational, emotional and cultural. A rational choice is the domain of the self-interest of the decision-maker. It reflects the perceived interest of the decision maker at that certain moment of time and is related to extrinsic values (instrumental).

The emotional dimension of decision-making is the domain of beauty and excitement and deals with intrinsic values (stylistic). In contrast to rational choice, which is risk aversive, emotional choice is not. As a matter of fact, uncertainty is an important attribute of excitement and challenge. An uncertainty can be positive (opportunity), or it can be negative (threat).

The cultural dimension is about ethical norms of the collectivities to which the decision maker belongs. The ethical values are the constraining elements of the decision process. Culture delivers the default values when the decision maker fails to choose one explicitly.

Literature on behavioral economics (Ariely, 2009; Montier, 2010), intuitive management (Burke et al., 1999), psychology (Libet, 2011; Pucket et al., 2011) and naturalistic decision-making (Brooks, 2007; Berryman, 2007; Shattuck & Miller, 2006) confirms that decision-making is not always rational. A lot has to do with how people and their brains are coping with uncertainty and the perception of uncertainty.

In an economic context (see also Rabaey, 2011), rationality has more to do with the ratio of benefits to costs instead of the philosophical meaning of reasoning. Related to the investments and/or resource allocation issue is uncertainty management. Uncertainty is more than risk management, which is the identification, assessment, and prioritization of risks (based on uncertainties) followed by coordinated and economical application of resources to minimize, monitor, and control the probability and/or impact of unfortunate events or to maximize the realization of opportunities. Uncertainty is a state in which the outcomes are unknown and perhaps unknowable. The more distant in time (future), the greater the uncertainty is (Funston, 2010, p. xxiii). The decision horizon is further at the strategic level than at the operational or tactical levels of the organization. For most of the organizations in this ever faster changing environment, the time line at the strategic level is from the present until the long term (at least a year), while the operational level is from now until short term (couple of weeks or months at most).

So, the enterprise as with any other, organization must always be collecting intelligence (Bernard, 1976). The continuous process of observing, creating and disseminating of intelligence is the only rule for this principle. Intelligence is the product resulting from the collection, evaluation, analysis, integration, and interpretation of all available information that concerns one or more aspects of the other actors and their actions in the environment, and that is immediately or potentially significant to the planning and operations of an organization (Rabaey, 2012b).

Analysis and Analysis

The dominant mode of thinking in the western culture is analytical (reductionist) thinking. So it is a common practice to analyze the actions and reactions and the uncertainties in the environment. However, the product of analysis shows you how things are working, never why they are working the way they do. Analysis decomposes the system and shows how it works. It provides knowledge on parts of the system but not understanding of the system itself. Thus, analysis does not answer the question of why a system works in the way that it does.

Analysis has mainly three steps (Joyce, 2012):

- Decomposing the system.
- Studying the behavior of the parts.
- Reassembling the parts and trying to explain the behavior of the (whole) system based on the behavior of the parts.

Flood (1999) observes that the experiment of reductionism in organizational and social settings has not been a full success. On the contrary, it has struggled primarily because it misunderstands the nature of human beings (yet it remains a dominant wisdom). Social settings to Flood are different and exhibit spiritual and systems-thinking qualities. Spiritualism appreciates the wholeness of human being. Systems-thinking builds holistic pictures of social settings.

So the main question of why something is working, is not really answered by analytical thinking. Here we would like to add a Systems Thinking perspective to this matter. Analysis is the intellectual interpretation of the data. According to Gharajedaghi (2011) the intellectual interpretation in ST consists of two other elements than analysis: synthesis and systems design.

As discussed above, analytical thinking has been the essence of classical science, which assumes that the whole is nothing more than the sum of the parts. This implies that understanding of the structure is both necessary and sufficient for the understanding of the whole and therefore, knowing the structure means knowing the system. In ST, structure is only one of the dimensions.

Synthetic thinking is linked to the functional approach. When a system is defined by its outcome, synthesis puts the subject in the context of the environment, which can also be a (larger) system. This corresponds in ST with functions.

Last but not least, Gharajedaghi (2011) added dynamic thinking to the arsenal of intelligence methods. Dynamic thinking is focusing on the processes, so it looks to the how-questions for the necessary answer to define the whole.

Sterman (2010) and Gharajedaghi (2011) state that seeing the whole requires understanding structure, function and process at the same time, and moreover, they are interdependent.

Structure defines components (capabilities) and their relationships. Functions are defining the outcomes or results to be produced. Processes explicitly define the sequence of activities and the know-how to produce the outcomes. The context defines the unique environment in which the system is situated (Gharajedaghi, 2011) which requires permanent observing and intelligence (Rabaey et al., 2012).

Regarding the capability approach (Rabaey et al., 2007) and ST (Gharajedaghi, 2011) a structure can perform more than one function, or different structures can have the same function. The classical view on structure (one function) fails, because of its notion of causality, where the cause is both necessary and sufficient for its effect, proves inadequate to explain the other two non-classical cases.

The assessment of function – structure – process – environment is an iterative inquiry (cycle), which has the framework of interdependent thinking models (analytical, synthetic and design), and they are happening at the same time. Gharajedaghi (2011) refers to the work of Stephen Wolfram when he explains that iteration is the key to understanding complexity. An iterative process of applying simple rules is at the core of nature's mysterious ability to produce complex phenomena so effortlessly.

Single and Double Loop

Since an organization should continuously reshape itself to respond to the permanently changing environment, it should continuously monitor that environment (Bernard, 1976; Rabaey, 2011; Rabaey et al., forthcoming).

However, not only the environment has to be monitored to detect opportunities and risks, but also the organization itself has to be monitored. Since organizations are seen as open and adaptive sociocultural systems, knowledge about its internal operation and construction is equally as important as the mental models of the environment.

Senge (2006) defines mental models as conceptual structures in the mind that drive a cognitive process of understanding. In the context of his learning organizations, the discipline of mental models aims to train people to appreciate that mental models do indeed occupy their minds and shape their actions (Flood, 1999).

The most important item with mental models is that people and organizations are aware that they have mental models, and that they influence the decision-making and the functioning in the organization. Sometimes brilliant ideas are rejected because they are in conflict with the (in this case) implicit mental models.

Of course when people and/or organizations know explicitly their mental models, then they can test them. Therefore, they can adjust quicker these models, which will improve the way they

will observe the environment, interpret the observations and orient the decisions, and thus they could act more appropriate (see OODA below) than in the case, they would not have adapted their mental models.

Korhonen (2012): "The organization is seen as a 'white box'. Intentional design of work and the organization helps enable organizational change. Enterprise governance, in this view, addresses not only the conformance aspect but also the performance aspect of governance and highlights strategic considerations such as value creation and resource utilization. Requisite roles, accountabilities and policies are defined to help maneuver the enterprise in continually shifting contexts. The meaning of 'steering' is returned to governance. Enterprise architecture is seen as the link between strategy and execution. EA addresses all facets of the enterprise in order to coherently execute the strategy. The environment is seen both as a generator of forces to which the enterprise is subject to and something that can be managed. An Enterprise architect is a facilitator, whose challenge is to enhance understanding and collaboration throughout the business."

Since an organization has to continuously monitor itself and its environment, an iterative process to interpret the observed facts is necessary: the intelligence process. As we can observe in previous points, intelligence is not only needed to support decision-making, but it also increases and updates the knowledge of an organization on itself and on its environment. Action Research can be a framework to feed the knowledge base of an organization.

Action Research has the single and the double loop learning. If the results are in line with the action strategies, the intention and the governing variables (or governing values), nothing has to be changed. If the results do not match the intention (of the action strategies), then the first loop learning is activated, meaning that another strategy will be developed, but with respect for the current governing variables. If however there is also a mismatch with the belief system, then the governing variables have to be adapted; this may lead to a redefinition of the scope of the business (market).

Sterman (2010) added mental models to the double loop. Although he defined a double loop-back between (information) Feedback and the mental models, Rabaey (2012b) esteems that this double loopback can be the cause of an (increasing) gap between the models and the awareness (culture, strategy) of the organization, so that loopback is not drawn (Figure 1).

INTELLIGENCE

Information and Knowledge

Before presenting "Intelligence Base," a system to collect and transform information into intelligence to be disseminated towards the clients

and to update the knowledge in an organization, we will first discuss the relationship between information and knowledge.

The term 'information' means any communication or representation of knowledge such as facts, data, or opinions in any medium or form, including textual, numerical, graphic, cartographic, narrative, or audiovisual forms (Whitehouse, 1996). So information is not knowledge but a representation of knowledge. Sanchez et al. defines "knowledge as the set of beliefs held by an individual about causal relationships among phenomena." Causal relationships in this definition are cause and effect relationships between imaginable events or actions and likely consequences of those events or actions. Organizational knowledge is then defined as the shared set of beliefs about causal relationships held by individuals within a group." As we will discuss in the Cynefin framework, some organizations are in complex or chaotic domains and/or are themselves complex or chaotic. In those situ-

Figure 1. Single and double loop

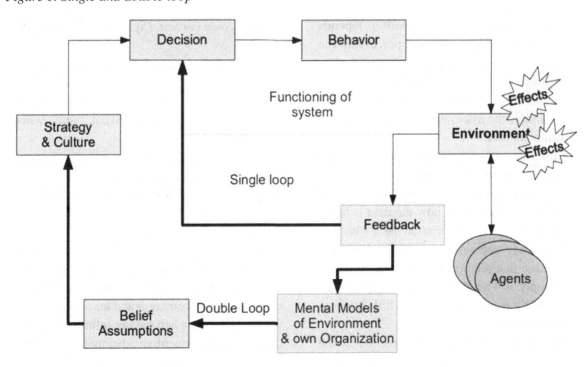

ations cause-and-effect (another high-value item in classic science and management) are irrelevant. And indeed, we can state that both definitions are products of analytical thinking. In the domain of systems thinking, emergent perspectives are noted in the domain of knowledge management.

Based on the idea that the whole is greater than the sum of its parts, on the Website of systems-thinking (n.d.) they start by saying what information and related concepts are not:

- A collection of data is not information.
- A collection of information is not knowledge.
- A collection of knowledge is not wisdom.
- A collection of wisdom is not truth.

Data, which is just a meaningless point in space and time, without reference to either space or time is a fact out of context. Therefore, it is without a meaningful relation to anything else. It only becomes useful when placed in a context. So, a collection of data is not on its own information. The pieces of data may represent information, yet whether or not it is information depends on the understanding of the one perceiving the data in his or her context. Therefore, information is subjective: context of the person and the perception of associations between a collection of data and/or the association between data and other information.

While information entails an understanding of the relations between data, it generally does not provide a foundation for why the data is what it is, nor an indication as to how the data is likely to change over time. Information has a tendency to be relatively static in time and linear in nature. Information is a relationship between data and, quite simply, is what it is, with great dependence on context for its meaning and with little implication for the future.

Beyond relation, there is a pattern, where the pattern is more than simply a relation of relations. Pattern embodies both a consistency and

completeness of relations which, to an extent, creates its own context. Pattern also serves as an Archetype with both an implied repeatability and predictability. (systems-thinking, n.d.)

A pattern has the potential to represent knowledge, when a person can realize and understand the patterns and their implications. The patterns representing knowledge have a tendency to be more self-contextualizing which means that a pattern creates its own context rather than being context dependent to the same extent that information is:

A pattern which represents knowledge also provides, when the pattern is understood, a high level of reliability or predictability as to how the pattern will evolve over time, for patterns are seldom static. Patterns which represent knowledge have a completeness to them that information simply does not contain.

Wisdom arises when one understands the foundational principles responsible for the patterns representing knowledge being what they are. And wisdom, even more so than knowledge, tends to create its own context. (Systems-Thinking, n.d.)

They summarize as follows:

- Information relates to description, definition, or perspective (what, who, when, where).
- Knowledge comprises strategy, practice, method, or approach (how).
- Wisdom embodies principle, insight, moral, or archetype (why).

Gharajedaghi (2011, p. 33) defines in the same way these concepts. He states that the way of doing business also has evolved regarding the usefulness of information and knowledge. There was once a time when having information about clients was a competitive advantage. Nowadays, knowing how clients are thinking 'what they want to do' gives a company a competitive advantage.

It Is All About Known and Unknown

To quote Deming (Wikipedia W. Edwards Deming, n.d.): "The most important things are unknown or unknowable." - "The most important things cannot be measured." The future is full of unexpected events and issues that are most important, long term, cannot be measured in advance.

It is, however, up to the enterprise to define its strategy to act in the future. Flood (1999) discusses the interactive planning of Ackoff. Interactive planning asks what can be done now to create the (desired) future, not what will be the future independently of what an enterprise is doing now. The main aim of interactive planning is to assist members of an organization to "design" a desirable future and to invent ways of realizing it (see also Gharajedaghi, 2011). This reflects Ackoff's firm belief in the maxim "plan or be planned."

Therefore, an organization will collect and transform information into intelligence to enrich its knowledge and/or to support the decision-makers by reducing their uncertainties (to an acceptable level), so that a better awareness and interactive planning are achieved. To better understand intelligence base and the Cynefin framework, we need to relate information and knowledge to what is known and unknown, in other words, their respective states (see Table 1).

Known-Known

Known-known is a situation where the knowledge and the information are available to decide what to do or not do (behavior). This is typical for systems, which are simple and/or in a simple domain. Cause-and-effect is obvious and feedbacks are bringing the systems easily back to the desired state.

Unknown-Unknown

Unknown-unknown is when an organization is not aware of a situation, therefore, it cannot ask to have more information to increase the knowledge or to make (better) decisions in that particular domain. It can be that it is not directly related to the interest of the organization. However, the actual knowledge, culture or belief patterns may cause the sensors of the organization to reject the information, meaning it does not match in its context.

USAF Colonel John Boyd depicts this very clearly in his concept of OODA-loop (Observe-Orient-Decide-Act). OODA (Figure 2) is an important concept on decision-making at the strategic, operational and tactical level. The organization observes the environment, then it considers the new information and orients its thinking into a

Table 1. States of knowledge and information

		State of Our Information	
		Known	**Unknown**
State of our Knowledge	Known	Known-known The information is available and we have it. (Asked and answered)	Known-unknown We know the information we need but we don't have the answers" (Asked and but not answered)
	Unknown	Unknown-known The information we need is out there somewhere, but we don't know what we are looking for. (Not asked but the answer is out there)	Unknown-unknown We don't know what we don't know. (Not asked and not answered)

direction based on cultural traditions, existing knowledge, genetic heritage and the process of analysis-synthesis. In the next step, it will decide, which will result in an action. The organization will observe the effects, and the cycle starts all over again. Rabaey and Mercken (2012) have adapted the OODA-cycle to the context of an organization. Although used in a holistic framework, they did not include the design thinking because it was not fully adapted to systems thinking. So in the picture below (Figure 2) design thinking has been added as described by Gharajedaghi (2011). The term act has been replaced by behavior because a decision can be not to act at all.

There is an implicit guidance and control from the orientation on the observation phase, meaning that the association (relations) of all elements in the orientation phase, is creating a filter for the observation of the environment.

Osinga (2007) stresses that OODA-loop is more than a decision-making process, it is a model of organizational learning and adapting in which the element "Orient" plays an important role in the organizational adaptability. Therefore, OODA is a candidate to implement the single and double loop of action research (Figure 1).

Moreover, Dettmer (2011) in his outstanding paper "Systems Thinking and the Cynefin Framework: A Strategic Approach to Managing Complex Systems'" writes: "Like the Logical Thinking Process, the OODA loop is a qualitative tool. Though it accepts quantitative data in the observation step, it ultimately depends on intuitive knowledge to capitalize on any such data. And like the thinking process, the OODA loop is effective in multiple domains. In fact, it is even more broadly applicable than the LTP" (p. 26).

Figure 2. OODA-loop (adapted from Rabaey & Mercken, 2012)

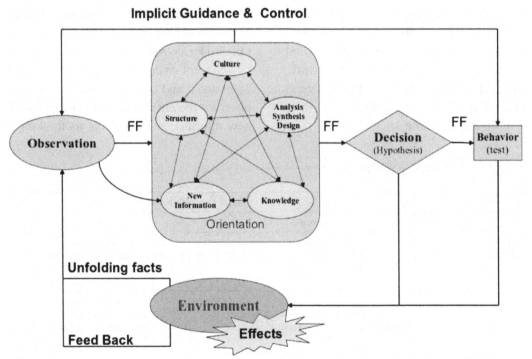

As mentioned above (Double loop), mental models are very important. If an organization is not aware of these models, there is a risk of less good or worse decisions. Senge (2006, p. 164) quotes Chris Argyris, who has worked with mental models and organizational learning for forty years: "Although people do not [always] behave congruently with their espoused theories [what they say], they do behave congruently with their theories-in-use [their mental models]." Indeed mental models are active, and they shape how we act, how we decide, how we think (by definition) but also how we observe. So through the whole OODA-cycle the mental models are active. Reason the more to frequently evaluate these mental models.

Known-Unknown

For one problem there may be more than one answer possible. Although it is more complicated than the known-known, the relationship between cause and effect still pertains, though such relationships may not be obvious. Whether or not they are obvious depends on the depth of people's knowledge about the environment and the system. Variability and uncertainty increase in a complicated environment, increasing the potential range of problems as well as the number of possible right answers. ... we know the questions to ask, but we don't know the answers. Thus, cause-and-effect analysis is only as good as the knowledge of system or environment that one has been available. ... information is usually available somewhere. It's usually just a matter of research to find it" (Dettmer, 2011, p.11).

Unknown-Known

The built knowledge is not sufficient because the environment is changing too fast. However, the information is out there but the organization does not know what exactly it is looking for. As we will see later, this is the domain of complex systems, which typically have multiple agents in the organization.

Dettmer (2011) is quoting Kurtz and Snowden:

... there are cause and effect relationships between the agents, but both the number of agents and the number of relationships defy categorization or analytic techniques. Emergent patterns can be perceived but not predicted; we call this phenomenon retrospective coherence. In this space, structured methods that seize upon such retrospectively coherent patterns and codify them into procedures will confront only new and different patterns for which they are ill prepared. Once a pattern has stabilized, its path appears logical, but it is only one of many that could have stabilized, each of which also would have appeared logical in retrospect. Patterns may indeed repeat for a time in this space, but we cannot be sure that they will continue to repeat, because the underlying sources of the patterns are not open to inspection (and observation of the system may itself disrupt the patterns). Thus, relying on expert opinions based on historically stable patterns of meaning will insufficiently prepare us to recognize and act upon unexpected patterns. (p. 14)

INTELLIGENCE BASE

Components

Intelligence Base is a system to manage, in essence, the unknown and the knowledge (Rabaey & Mercken, 2012). It is composed of:

- Planning and Directing- this cell receives and manages the intelligence needs.
- Collecting cell is responsible for the managing of the network of sensors.
- Network of sensors will collect data on demand or ad hoc.

Figure 3. Intelligence base (internal and external sensoring)

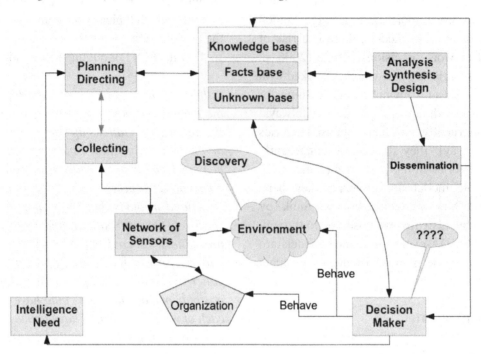

- Knowledge Base is a software system capable of supporting the explicit representation of knowledge in some specific competence domain and of exploiting it through appropriate reasoning mechanisms in order to provide high-level problem-solving performance. The knowledge base, a part of the Intelligence base, stores available knowledge concerning the domain at hand, represented in an appropriate explicit form and ready to be used by the reasoning mechanism (Guida & Tasso, 1994)
- Facts Base is the collection of all raw information. This made a later interpretation of facts possible with new inference rules and/or knowledge.
- Unknown Base supports the management of all requests that are still active.
- Analysis, Synthesis and Design: the intellectual interpretation of the collected data in a context relevant to the user and/or organization.

The "Planning and Directing" cell will look in the knowledge base to see if the intelligence need can be satisfied. If so it will transmit the need to the "Analysis, Synthesis and Design" which will disseminate to the client. If not, the "Planning and Directing" cell will send a request for search to the manager of the sensors "Collecting cell."

Regarding the network of sensors, two events can trigger an interaction between the decision-making process and the intelligence process. Firstly, the decision maker expresses an intelligence need. The second trigger is the transmission of newly detected facts by the sensors.

The case of "Information Pull" is when the decision maker does not find the necessary intelligence (in the Intelligence Base or outside of it), he expresses his need to the "Planning & Direction." As mentioned above, the latter will then define the needed intelligence actions. The needed information may not be in the Intelligence Base in which case the network has to be instructed (push). The resulting information (if any) is, then interpreted

("Analysis, Synthesis and Design"). Additional information may be required if there is not enough information to be integrated into intelligence. Once the intelligence is acquired, then it will be disseminated to the intelligence client. The information and intelligence are stored respectively in the Facts Base and the Interpreted Information Base, and the Unknown Base is updated.

In the case of "Information Push," the sensors are injecting information in the network (push). The transmitted information is then analyzed. If the information can be integrated, then the resulting intelligence is pushed to the concerned people and/or organizations. The information and intelligence (if any) are stored respectively in the Facts Base and the Knowledge Base.

Organization

Regarding the organization of the intelligence process, different types can be used: hierarchical or networked. However, in an interconnected whole a networked structure is preferable. Ackoff has a hybrid solution: the circular organization (Flood, 1999), which of course can also be used for decision making. A circular organization is a democratic hierarchy which has as purpose a more active contribution of people in co-defining their involvement in the organization.

The main structural characteristic is the board. It is a body of people from a local department of an organization. Each person in a position of authority is automatically a member of the board. If a higher hierarchy exists, then he is also a member of the board of the higher hierarchy, idem dito if a lower hierarchy exists. Another example is the system of operation order in the Belgian Defense. An operation order contains in general the mission of the higher level, in detail the own level and in general, the missions of the subordinated units.

In the section on "Evolution of Organizational Views related to Enterprise Architecture," the multi-minded view will be discussed. In essence, it is a whole of interdependent agents where no

real (command and control) hierarchy exists. As a consequence, another type of organization has to be defined.

For a more in-depth discussion, we refer to the work of Rabaey and Mercken (2012) for the general concept and Rabaey and Mercken (forthcoming) for a complex adaptive systems-thinking approach, which brings us to Complex Adaptive Systems (CAS).

COMPLEX ADAPTIVE SYSTEM (CAS)

Characteristics of CAS and Consequences for EA

Holden (2005, p. 654) uses the following definition of CAS: "A complex adaptive system is a collection of individual agents with freedom to act in ways that are not always totally predictable, and whose actions are interconnected so that one agent's actions changes the context for other agents."

As already mentioned, complexity theory deals with systems those are large collections of interacting agents. Despite their diversity, complex systems share certain fundamental behaviors (Gore, 1996; Lowe & Ng, 2006).

"Emergence"

Interactions among agents in complex systems may lead to emerging global (or system-wide) properties that are very different from the behavior of individual agents. These properties which cannot be predicted from prior knowledge of the agents, in turn affect the environment that each agent perceives influencing its behavior is a synergistic feedback loop. Thus, the "whole" of a complex system is far greater than the sum of its parts, and the whole has properties not held by any of its agents.

Therefore the EA analysis of complex systems requires a holistic approach. The study of an organization may thus not be based only on the decomposition into business units (business agents), or the so-called core business. The support of the business processes of these business agents is delivered by resources agents (like Human Resources [HR], Material Resources [MR], Information Technology [IT]). They have also their culture, functions, structure and processes and therefore, must also be considered in the "whole." This is fully aligned to Systems Thinking, as we will see.

"Adaptive Self-Organization"

Complex systems tend to adapt to their environments and to self-organize. Rather than tending toward disorder or entropy, complex adaptive systems spontaneously crystallize into more highly ordered states but with few leverage points.

EA used in (long-term) endeavors or for the global, enterprise must therefore be flexible to adjust to these spontaneous self-organizations. Goals, procedures, processes, stakeholders may change continuously and thus EA must be continuously reviewed (via the processes of Intelligence Base).

"Information Processing"

Complex systems exhibit the ability to process information sensed from the environment and react to it based on internalized models. Information processing is closely related to a system's ability to learn and adapt near the edge of chaos (see above). It creates interacting feedback loops, which cause highly non-linear behavior (Bowser, Cantle, and Allan, 2011). If the CAS is an organization, then the management will be confronted with counter-intuitive and non-intended consequences.

Although EA is modeling information and processes, EA has also to integrate the underlying (hidden) feedback loops, therefore, ST should be integrated with EA.

"Evolution to the Edge of Chaos"

All dynamic systems exist in one of three regimes (see also Cynefin Framework below):

- A stable regime in which disturbances tend to die out.
- A chaotic regime (the province of chaos theory).
- The phase transition between stability and chaos.

Whereas increasing disturbances in the environment cause some systems to move from stability to chaos, complex systems "learn" from their environments and add new functions to cope with previously unknown situations (cause and symptoms are separated in time and space). Thus, they increase their complexity and adapt along the edge of chaos. According to complexity theorists, the same type of growth in complexity occurs in nature, man-made systems as well as societies, business and economies.

Adapting in this case, implies learning. The intelligence base is providing the learning enterprise with a knowledge base. Therefore, the aspects related to knowledge needs to be integrated with EA (see below).

This brings us to CAS and its characteristics.

Large Number of Elements with Rich Interactions

A complex adaptive system is a special case of complex systems. The distinguishing feature of CAS is that a CAS interacts with its environment and adapts in response to a change. As already mentioned, a CAS is resilient; therefore, it can tolerate certain levels of stress or degradation. As a result, sustainability of a CAS can be achieved if the adaptive capacity of it is not destroyed (Gaziulusoy, 2011). The description of the characteristics of complex systems is also relevant when discussing the different domains of the Cynefin framework, especially the complex domain.

Complex systems consist of a large number of elements. When this number is relatively small, the behavior of the elements can often be represented by a formal description in conventional terms. Cilliers (2004) states that when the number becomes sufficiently large, conventional means not only become impractical. They also cease to assist in any understanding of the system. This is a fundamental problem when quantitative tools are used to simulate the organization.

Holden (2005) lists other characteristics as defined by Cilliers. The large number of elements must interact in a dynamic way with much exchange of information. These interactions are rich, non-linear, and have a limited range because there is no over-arching framework that controls the flow of information.

To Cilliers (2004, p. 25), the non-linear nature of the interactions in complex systems has two important consequences. Firstly, it becomes quickly impossible to keep track of causal relationships between components when there are a lot of simultaneous non-linear interactions amongst those components. Secondly, we can deduce that complex systems are incompressible based on the fact of their non-linear nature. Therefore, modeling complex systems is a problem because some parts have to be left out, and we do not know beforehand what the consequence will be. So something that may not appear to be important now may turn out to be very important later, or vice versa, due to the fact that we cannot track a clear causal chain. Thus, no matter how a model of a complex system is constructed, it will be flawed, and worse, we do not know in which way it is flawed. The message for EA-related models is not to stop modeling, but to be aware of its limitations when modeling complex systems.

Dynamic Borders

As already mentioned, complex systems are open systems with feedback loops, both enhancing,

stimulating (positive) or detracting, inhibiting (negative). Both kinds are necessary. Cilliers (2004) remarks that to describe an open system, it is difficult to define the borders. "Instead of being a characteristic of the system itself, the scope of the system is usually determined by the purpose of the description of the system, and is thus influenced by the position of the observer. This process is called framing. Closed systems are merely complicated systems" (p. 24).

So when describing the organization in EA, it must not only be clearly understood what will be described, but also why: what is the purpose of the observer in choosing that particular (sub-) system? However, the organization has to adapt to the environment, so it is possible that the initial motivation and settings are after a while not relevant anymore. Moreover, the complexity in the system is due not only to the feedback loops but also to a result of patterns of interaction between the elements, thus an internal dynamic exists.

Lack of an Equilibrium

Another consequence is that due to the internal and external dynamics (changes), a complex system operates under conditions far from equilibrium, which means that there is continual change and response to the constant flow of energy in the system. Cilliers (2004) remarks that equilibrium is another word for the death of a system.

Complex systems are embedded in the context of their own histories, and no single element or agent can know, comprehend, or predict actions and effects that are operating within the system as a whole.

Mauboussin (2011, p. 89) in his Harvard Business Review article "Embracing Complexity" uses the ant colony as an example of a CAS in nature: 'Complex adaptive systems are one of nature's big solutions, so biology is full of great examples. Ant colonies are solving very complicated, very challenging problems with no leadership, no strategic plan, no Congress."

CAS and Systems Thinking (ST) are complementary for open, social (human) organizations. Both are based on the principle that the whole is greater than the sum of its parts. We state that accordingly the self-organization of a CAS and the fact that ST is a methodology that only can be used by people, CAS and ST can only be applied for human organizations. The combination is called the Complex Adaptive Systems Thinking (CAST).

The effects of CAST for EA are manifold:

- EA must be dynamic because of the continuously changing environment and therefore, continuously changing the organization. Managing EA should be included in the processes of Intelligence Base.
- Knowledge-management must be reflected in EA (see below).
- EA must keep track of the reasons why it has been used, why the models had to be changed during the project.... So the (changing) contexts are at least equally important as the models themselves, therefore, EA should be a part of the systemic models, rather than being outside ST tools and models.
- Links between feedback loops and EA are essential to understand the EA.
- Last but not least, EA must have a holistic approach.

EA is describing enterprises which are (human made) social systems. Gharajedaghi (2011) sees five dimensions of social systems. Since EA should also support the decision making, we will have a closer look at these dimensions.

Dimensions of Social System

The perspectives or aspects of the decision making to systems thinking are: rational, emotional and cultural. This decision making is happening in the context an organization with following five dimensions of a social system: wealth, power, knowledge, beauty and values (Gharajedaghi, 2011). The generation and dissemination of these dimensions forms a comprehensive set of interdependent variables that collectively describe an organization in its totality. All five dimensions must be evaluated at the same time; otherwise, not all interactions can be studied, especially because of the fact that it is quite feasible for any four to become producers of the fifth one.

Recognition of multidimensionality and the imperative of and-relationships among the five dimensions of an organization is one of the most significant characteristics of holistic thinking (Gharajedaghi, 2011). Multidimensionality is the ability to see complementary relations in opposing tendencies and to create feasible wholes with unfeasible parts (Herzog, n.d.)

In a Complex Adaptive System (CAS) it is crucial that not only the five dimensions are created, but that they also are circulating and distributed to the whole organization (system of systems).

CAS and Organizations

Hovhannisian (2001), Bowser, Cantle, and Allan (2011) and Rabaey (2012b) state that organizations are CAS. Those organizations are segmented rather than monolithic, and chararterized by information flows and interactions between the agents. The way this happens is very relevant to understanding the working of the whole and its components because it influences the culture (and subcultures), the hierarchy and the structure and it has an impact on the speed of communication and interpretation of the (internal and external) information.

The system is not the sum of the behavior of its parts. To Russel Ackoff it is on the contrary the product of their interactions. If you have a system of improvement that is directed at improving the parts taken separately you can be absolutely sure that the performance of the whole will not be improved (Matthews, 2012; Flood, 1999).

Hovhannisian (2001) points out that if only the components are analyzed (Taylorian decomposition) and not the whole, analysts are not getting the full picture. (see below, the example of the blind men and the elephant). They are missing the links, the interconnections between agents, and how the whole interacts with its environment. Bowser et al. (2011) emphasize that the study of CAS is interdisciplinary (and so must be the applicable tools) and that emergence requires a holistic approach before studying the parts. Flood (1999) sees a common characteristic of the different approaches by Russel L. Ackoff, C. West Churchman, Stafford Beer, Ludwig von Bertalanffy and himself, namely the interdisciplinary. Sally Bean (2011) names it multidisciplinary.

However Gaharajedaghi (2004) states:

On the other hand, contrary to a widely held belief, the popular notion of a multi-disciplinary approach is not a systems approach. In fact, the ability to synthesize separate findings into a coherent whole seems far more critical than the ability to generate information from different perspectives. Without a well-defined synthesizing method, however, the process of discovery using a multi-discipline approach would be an experience as frustrating as that of the blind men trying to identify an elephant. Positioned at a different part of the elephant, each of the blind men reported his findings from his respective position, as It's a snake; It's a pillar; It's a fan; it's a spear!

Ackoff (1999) goes even further:

Effective research is not disciplinary, interdisciplinary, or multidisciplinary; it is transdisciplinary. Systems thinking is holistic; it attempts to derive understanding of parts from the behavior and properties of wholes, rather than derive the behavior and properties of wholes from those of their parts. Disciplines are taken by science to represent different parts of the reality we experience. In effect, science assumes that reality is structured and organized in the same way universities are.

We do not have to know all the parts of a car to drive it. In this context we can refer to the Chaos theory (Glenn, 1996) upon which the complexity theory has been built. A Chaos system (as a whole) can be controlled by parameters ("control knobs") although the system is not fully described. So, in the case of an organization where a traditional command and control hierarchy exists, if that organization has more than one parameter to control the system (functioning) then it should coordinate the parametrization in the system, otherwise one or more parameters may destabilize its functioning. This phenomenon is also known in CAS (Lowe et al., 2006): "A direct consequence of a Complex Adaptive System's structural heterogeneity and characteristic nonlinear interactions is that some of the nodes and links have a stronger influence on the system by virtue of more or stronger interactions, or by virtue of occupying a point in one or more feedback loops within the system. This gives rise to the concepts of Leverage Points, Centres of Gravity, and the well-known heuristic, the 80/20 rule" (See also Janssen et al., 2006).

Related to the "Edge of Chaos"; systems exist on a spectrum ranging from equilibrium to chaos. The most productive state to be in is at the edge of chaos where there is maximum variety and creativity, leading to new possibilities (see later Cynefin framework). Controls, such as simple rules (Eisenhardt and Sull, 2001) and regulations or institutional and budgetary restrictions, ensure that an agent's behaviors is limited, in this way changing the aggregate behavior and helping the CAS to behave in a predictable way (Janssen et al., 2006).

The different levels of strategy certainly does not imply very complicated and complex rules or processes of developing, maintaining and disseminating these strategies, on the contrary. Eisenhardt et al. are advocating the use of simple rules (in CAS): "Most managers quickly grasp the concept of focusing on key strategic processes that will position their companies where the flow of opportunities is most promising. But because they equate processes with detailed routines, they often miss the notion of simple rules. Yet simple rules are essential. They poise the company on what's termed in complexity theory as 'the edge of chaos', providing just enough structure to allow it to capture the best opportunities. It may sound counterintuitive, but the complicated improvisational movements that companies [like Amazon, Google, Cisco] make as they pursue fleeting opportunities arise from simple rules." (2001, p. 110). Of course, the fact of having to work on different levels (single loop and double loop, see section on Action Research) simple rules may turn an organization into a very complex system.

ENTERPRISE ARCHITECTURE

Overview

Enterprise Architecture is a discipline that aspires to improve enterprise coherence, yet is itself often rather incoherent, mainly due to the fact that it is still relatively immature. There is confusion over its meaning, purpose and scope, and also the role of the EA function. It is often unclear from reading current literature on EA whether an author is referring to a knowledge base, a process/practice or a team of people (Bean, 2011, p.1). So lots of different interpretations of the term Enterprise Architecture (EA) exist (Rabaey et al., 2007). Some hold long lists of technological choices that an organization should make concerning infra-

structure and application design. Others put these technological decisions into sets of guidelines to information architecture and business architecture.

We are proposing a holistic framework based on Complex Adaptive Systems and Systems-thinking. Therefore, EA should be put in a broader context than merely infrastructure architecture and application architecture, because applications are built to support business processes and operate on information gathered through these business processes. Hence, architecture only concerned with infrastructure and application design is insufficient to support a business. The architecture of a building is based on the function that this building will have (store, house, manufacturing, etc.). In the same way an Enterprise Architecture should consider the business and its dynamics so that it can take precautions for changing business requirements or the reuse of certain artifacts in other business domains (Rabaey, 2012).

In this sense, the Enterprise Architecture Research Forum (EARF, n.d.) defines EA as "the continuous practice of describing the essential elements of a socio-technical organization, their relationships to each other and to the environment, in order to understand complexity and manage change."

Stages

Ross (2003) defines four stages: Application Silo Stage, Technology Standardization Stage, Data Rationalization Stage and A Modular Architecture.

Rabaey (2012) describes them as follows. Application Silo Stage can be described as an archipelago. An enterprise needs an information system to manage its functions and responsibilities, but a common characteristic in the beginning of Information Technology (IT) was that these information systems were isolated. They look more like an archipelago with a deep sea in-between than (inter)connected parts of the enterprise.

And although Enterprise Architecture (EA) has already been on the scene for many years, the smooth interfacing of all the different parts and their information systems remains a problematic area in need of further attention. In this stage EA is just the collection of the architectures of isolated applications, most of them implemented in different technologies. The Technology Standardization Stage is the first step towards an EA in which technology gets standardized, and unfortunately often centralization is put in place. The deployment of resources shifts from application development into the development of a shared infrastructure. This phase is further often characterized by the introduction of business intelligence and a first attempt to manage business processes.

The Data Rationalization Stage consists of process and data standardization. The deployment of resources shifts from application development into data management and infrastructure development. The involvement of senior business managers becomes institutionalized by a common forum of IT and business managers. In this phase we see a shift of data ownership from IT towards the business.

The Modular Architecture, characterized by enterprise wide global standards with loosely coupled applications, information and technology components to preserve the global standards while enabling local differences through modules extending the core processes.

Business Process Embedded Information System (BPEIS)

Concept

Rabaey et al. (2006, 2007) have added a fifth stage: business process embedded information systems. As the name implies, the business process has its own information system and moreover it is embedded in the business process. At that moment Grid Computing and Enterprise Application Integration (EAI) were known, but not yet Cloud Computing (as a reality).

Cloud computing (pay per use IT-services) is a relatively new technology which puts whole or partial parts of the Information Technology (IT) infrastructure and services in a virtualized environment inside and/or outside the traditional IT center perimeter. It touches every level of the IT architecture and thus has a big influence on the way the internal and external users via their business processes are interacting with this architecture. Security is a big issue in this context and a lot of business and IT people are reluctant to move to the Cloud. Besides the security, business and architectural issues may increase the risks and create more uncertainties for these kinds of projects (Rabaey, 2012a).

Due to the ever faster changing environment of an organization and increasing interactions with it, a global and central "steering" becomes quite impossible, if the organization aims to have a flexible and rapid response. So the organization delegates to the business units and their processes. Therefore the IT must be federated to obtain the necessary autonomy for the IT-applications. That is why Rabaey et al. (2006, 2007) are propos-

Table 2. Levels of enterprise architecture

Level Architecture	Description
Business Architecture	Is about the description of the business processes as viewed from a business perspective. It should focus on the strategic environment and the business processes, which should attain the objectives.
Knowledge Architecture	Brings the asset of knowledge in chart.
Information Architecture	Describes the information the business is dependent on. This description must pay attention to where information enters the business processes, how this information enters the process, electronically or by other means, who is the owner of the information, and by whom it is to be used.
Application Architecture	Is about how to implement the applications or IT systems in all of its aspects (programming, development environment, quality book of software, etc.).
Infrastructure Architecture	Deals with guidelines concerning hardware platforms, network infrastructure, operating systems.

ing to embed information systems into business processes. Cloud computing in combination with Service Oriented Architecture (SOA) makes BPEIS technically possible. In the context of cloud computing BPEIS can be considered as Business Process as a Service (BPaaS).

All aspects of the information system can be federated without losing the consistency of the information system in the enterprise.

From the point of view of Systems-thinking, business processes are far more than a flow of activities performed by members of the enterprise. As a matter of fact, all agents who are involved in the business process must be included in its domain. Boundaries are drawn creating an action area (Bounded Action Area [BAA]). This BAA will be most of the time partially (thus not the whole) and temporarily (thus limited in time) (Flood, 1999). This is even not exceptionally for EA because most definitions of EA take enterprise to be an organization or business unit. So in practice, EA techniques are often applied to the implementation of an endeavor as a large programme, project (Bean, 2011) or processes. The temporarily and partially aspects of a BAA demands a dynamic approach of EA, which implies a continuously updating of models.

Knowledge and Information Layer

Before going to the fifth stage, an enterprise has to perform a knowledge and information model. Often Enterprise Architecture consists of the following layers (architecture): Business, Information, Application and Infrastructure (Bean, 2011; Rabaey, 2012a). A definition for Enterprise Architecture taking into account the above layers is given by Ross (2003): "An Enterprise Architecture is the organizing logic for applications, data and infrastructure technologies, as captured in a set of policies and technical choices, intended to enable the firm's business strategy" (see Table 2).

The knowledge architecture is an extra level that Rabaey (2012a) is proposing to be inserted into EA. If Cloud Computing will come up to the expectations of the market then IT will become a utility (commodity) and competitive/collaborative advantage will become almost fully dependent from the capability of producing intelligence for decision-making and knowledge management (in systems, processes and human resources). So the differentiation will be made on the level of knowledge assets and therefore knowledge has to be addressed in a specific architecture. That is why this extra level is proposed.

Knowledge becomes a belief system and merging or separating processes (or structures) should be assessed to determine if the cultures of the different parties fit the new organization. Thus at the same time, the structure of the enterprise has to be defined, and the business processes have to be modeled in the Business Process Management tool, which is obviously managed at the level business level of EA.

Once the business model, knowledge model and the conceptual information model are defined, then they need to be merged into a global model (information, knowledge mapping and business processes), where the BAA or business process should manage their own (embedded) information system. But as already mentioned, it has to start with a conceptual information model to solve the problems of information management. Following, the knowledge model should test the cultural compatibilities of the applications with the business.

Since the environment of the organization is permanently changing and thus the organization also, the information system of the organization has to be adapted to the new situation, especially the knowledge infrastructure. So, if a business process could be fully automated and it holds itself the information, then a consistent part of the producible and needed information will be embedded in the business process, in accordance with the culture (customization based on culture and knowledge).

This is confirmed by Bean (2011). As mentioned above, she considers the major goal of EA to be coherency management. EA is evolving from Foundation Architecture (Aligning IT with Business Goals) through 'Extended Architecture' (Codesigning Business and IT change simultaneously in projects) to 'Embedded Architecture', where generically 'architectural' methods and ways of working are embedded in the normal processes of the organization and a level of coherence that is appropriate to the organization's culture and operating model is achieved and maintained organically.

The concept of embedding is not new, Object-Oriented Programming (OOP) keeps methods and data private in objects. Those objects are interfacing with their environment through public functions and data.

Way of Use

Strands of Activity

Bean (2011) defines three strands to EA activity, each of which may have business, information and technology elements. A prescriptive strand that is determining, agreeing and promulgating fundamental design principles, policies and standards in support of organizational strategies, risk reduction and key performance characteristics. These can then be applied to relevant decision-making in business/IT development projects.

The second strand is descriptive. It is creating an aligned set of formal models that define key elements of the business, its information systems and its technologies and managing these in such a way that the relationships between these different elements can be clearly understood. These facilitate understanding of what is involved in business or IT change and can provide a common

starting point for new business or IT development projects.

Thirdly, a programmatic strand is designing a target state architecture and identifying and coordinating the significant projects, commitments, and milestones to move towards it, including the development of core 'building blocks' that can be shared across different projects.

EA teams typically carry out blends of these three strands of activity with varying emphasis on business, knowledge, information, applications and technology architecture (the five layers). However because of the dynamic environment (internally and externally) BPEIS and thus EA need to be continuously updated. Moreover, a BAA can overlap with one or more other BAA's. Therefore it is advisable to implement different BPEIS capable of interfacing with each other and/or other more classic conceived information systems.

EA Frameworks

In the classic use of EA, overall coherence is achieved by the use of guiding principles and an enterprise architecture framework. Bean (2011) states that a formal approach to EA requires that such a framework is underpinned by an underlying metamodel showing how all the different elements of the framework are related to each other. The existing frameworks and methodologies for EA practice are generally very oriented towards the internals of EA content and processes with a specialized set of concepts and vocabulary. As such, this makes it very difficult for business people to grasp how an EA approach will benefit them or their organization. The Zachman framework tries to close the gap between business people and EA teams. It has a clear logic to it which is easily grasped in theory but hardly any organizations have successfully managed to achieve the expected benefits of creating and exploiting Zachman-compliant models in practice.

In her discussion, Bean (2011) continues that the sequence of processes in the TOGAF ADM makes logical sense to an IT person, and can be mapped to IT planning and development life-cycles, but is more difficult to link into the normal processes of an enterprise. Overall this means that the practitioners in a typical EA team often struggle to demonstrate the value of their efforts. She has observed that EA teams frequently fail to achieve the right degree of business involvement, may be out of touch with what's happening on the ground in project deliveries, and viewed as barriers to progress, rather than enablers of change.

EVOLUTION OF ORGANIZATIONAL VIEWS RELATED TO ENTERPRISE ARCHITECTURE

Double Paradigm Shift

The concept of CAS is important for the Command and Control (C2) of an organization (military or civilian). Lowe et al. (2006) state that good military commanders have intuitively understood the nature of complexity and non-linearity on the battlefield. In turn, the complexity theory may reveal the underlying basis of these intuitive truths.

The non-linearity implies that a given input may produce anything from a disproportionately large effect to no effect at all and this may change over time, meaning there is no Newtonian "cause-and-effect" phenomenon (see above). Moreover, the feedback loops may produce effects that propagate and return to impact the original causation in some way (Lowe et al., 2006, p. 5). Another characteristic of CAS is that such a system is very sensitive to initial conditions (Hovhannisian, 2001), as it is for chaos theory (Glenn, 1996).

Classic "formal" management philosophy does not cope with these issues related to CAS. Lowe et al. (2006, p. 9) write: "Continuous change means people, structures and processes need to be able

to adapt appropriately. Study of CAS indicates that an agile organization can be built on the basis of individuals with a simple but effective set of rules and the ability to communicate and adapt."

This concept has an influence on the management of an organization. As will be discussed later, Gharajedaghi (2011) states that two paradigm shifts have happened. One regarding the view on the organization: first the mechanistic view then the biological view and finally the sociocultural view and one paradigm shift from analytical (reductionist) thinking to systems thinking. The latter has a fundamental impact on the way we look at "reality" and how we are reacting, better interacting with the environment. This difference sheds also another light on the way EA is approached and used. For this reason, we will go in more detail by discussing the reflections of Flood (1999, pp. 84-86).

Reductionist vs. Systems Thinking

Reductionism is mainstream thinking that separates science (one form of study of things) from our lives and the world in which we live. It sees practitioners and researchers as independent external observers (a concept that is rejected by quantum physics). "This leads people to think about phenomena as entities that can be fully appreciated as detached real things, behaving according to fixed causal relationships.

Science has in our minds fragmented the world and our lives. It has alienated so-called parts, like people, from the patterns and rhythms of life in which we participate. The richness and mystique of living is deflated to a mental model with an unrealistic and mind-blowing simplicity of the type, 'A caused B'." So socially, when we have a problem then we will look for a black sheep to be the cause of our problem.

"People, especially those ... with formal power, may attempt to detach themselves from patterns of interrelationships and emerging difficulties to which they have a systemic" (Systems-thinking) "attachment and moral responsibility." So reductionist thinking directs people to seek solutions in terms of causal factors.

Flood observes the difficulties of the people conditioned by the mental model of reductionism and causal thinking to flip over to a consciousness of systemic awareness. As a matter of fact, reductionism and holism are two ways of thinking, which are poles apart.

Reductionist thinking is looking for (deterministic or probabilistic) causal laws. This can be possible in non-social sciences, but people are changing and they change the environment, which influences the people, etc. Systemic thinking argues that behavior is most usefully understood as the results of loops where variables are interrelated.

Regarding the feedback principle of Complex Adaptive Systems (CAS), the result of behavior is always scanned and its success or failure modifies future behavior; outputs, outcomes, and impacts are always scanned, and the desirability or undesirability of those items modifies future behavior. (See also Intelligence Base).

The causality principle of CAS has two types of feedback (Independence Partners, 2011): the negative feedback produces stable equilibrium, while the positive leads to instability. In a context of fixed variables, the feedback system is deterministic. However sociocultural systems are composed of agents that can agree to change the context, therefore this dynamic behavior is capable of producing unexpected variety or novelty through spontaneous self-organization. "This is where a complex of variables interrelates with multiple feedback, which spontaneously creates new order. Spontaneous means that what emerges is not predictable. So the emergence is unpredictable because it results from details of dynamics that are inherently unknowable to the human mind.

So not only the environment, but also the organization self is changing in a dynamic and unpredictable way and this is the context in which EA is used. Thus, the EA-framework with its processes must be able to absorb the unpredict-

able internal and external changes, therefore EA must be an enabler and not a de facto inhibitor of change.

EA practitioners must keep the pareto principle in mind: "In any large, complex system, roughly 80% of the effects, outputs, outcomes, and impacts will be the direct result of roughly 20% of the inputs or interactions" (Independence Partners, 2011). Moreover, certain patterns of functioning (structure) recur again and again. Senge (2006) calls them system archetypes or generic structures and are a cyclic chaining of negative and/or positive loops. Senge notes that not many different systems archetypes exist, which indicates that not all management problems are that unique.

The next point discusses the evolution of the views on the organization. The most demanding organizational form is the multi-minded view, for which the dynamic (complex) characteristic is certainly relevant.

View of the Organization

The Mindless View

The mindless system is a mechanistic view of the organization. It is a particular form of known-known, because the mindless system is more or less isolated. Only big "earthquakes" cause the mindless system to change.

Everything is based on efficiency, control and predictability of its operation. The parts of a mindless mechanical system, just like the whole, have no choice to behave how they want, and are therefore energy-bound.

Korhonen (2012) links this approach to EA:

The machinery needs to work predictably and consistently. Variance is reduced and human error is removed from the production process through established work practices, quality standards and policies that regulate discretion. Internal controls are established to ensure that work is conducted 'by the book'.

The behavior of such an organization is treated as a 'black box'. In this view, it is irrelevant what resources the business has and what is its internal design. The organization aims at optimizing its operations by one-dimensional economic indicators. Corporate governance is geared to address the 'agency problem'; it focuses on compliance, internal control and risk management to mitigate conflicts of interest between the shareholders and the management.

As per this view, EA is seen as 'the glue between business and IT'. Focusing on enterprise IT assets, it aims at business-IT alignment, operational efficiency and IT cost reduction. It is based on the tenet that IT planning is a rational, deterministic and economic process. Likewise, the role of the enterprise architect is seen as the master planner/ designer of the architecture.

The Uni-Minded View

In changing and unpredictable environments that call for innovative changes, one could conceive of organizations as living and uni-minded organisms (systems). Gharajedaghi (2011) writes that in this case a system is considered just like a human being, with a purpose of its own, that is survival in its environment. To survive, these systems have not only to interact with the environment (other acting systems) in terms of information, energy, or material permeation through the system boundary, but according to conventional wisdom, biological beings have also to grow (biological view). It is totally under the control of a single brain, the executive function, which receives information (feedback) from a network of sensors and issues directions that activate relevant parts of the system. Most of the time this happens in the single loop.

The organization can be seen as a 'white box' in which intentional design of work and the organization helps enable organizational change. In this view, leadership (the brains of the system) is based on enlightened self-interest that aims at a win-win

outcome. Therefore enterprise governance does not only address the conformance aspect but also the performance aspect of governance and highlights strategic considerations such as value creation and resource utilization. "As per this view, enterprise architecture is seen as the link between strategy and execution. EA addresses all facets of the enterprise in order to coherently execute the strategy. The environment is seen both as a generator of forces the enterprise is subject to and something that can be managed. Enterprise architect is a facilitator, whose challenge is to enhance understanding and collaboration throughout the business" (Korhonen (2012).

The Multi-Minded View

The third and last view is the sociocultural one or the 'Multi-minded' system. The most significant characteristic is purpose. An organization is purposeful if it can produce the same outcome in different ways in the same environment and different outcomes in the same or different environment. It is considered a voluntary association of purposeful members in which the bonding is achieved by a second-degree agreement, which is an agreement based on a common perception. This is formed by the culture, the shared image, which incorporates their experiences, beliefs, attitudes, and ideals; it is the ultimate product and reflection of their history and the manifestation of their identity: man creates his culture and his culture creates him.

One of the characteristics of a learning organization is the shared vision (Senge, 2006), which Gharajedaghi calls shared image. Shared vision provides a focus and energy for learning. "Senge means generative learning rather than adaptive learning, that is, expanding an organization's capacity to create its own future, rather than be created by events of the moment." (Flood, 1999, p. 24). The author of this chapter states that the main difference between CAS and CAST is that a

CAS is capable of adaptive learning, while CAST can learn in an adaptive and generative way.

In the multi-minded view, the agents are very autonomous and have a lot to say about the organization of the whole, consensus is essential to the alignment of a multi-minded system (Herzog, n.d.). As a consequence for the Command and Control (C2), Weijnen, Herder, and Bouwmans (2007) confirm in their paper titled "Designing Complex Systems, A Contradiction in Terms" that a classic C2 is not anymore accepted since no agent is superior to any other, therefore a very good communication system is necessary. Furthermore the authors state that besides the C2, the content-based management by 'expertise of management' is also unlikely to succeed; rather decisions will be based on a negotiated knowledge, which can deteriorate to "negotiated nonsense." (See also Janssen et al., 2006). Intelligence base in the context of CAST is an answer to that problem (Rabaey et al., 2012).

It must be stressed that although it is an evolution in management theory, the enterprise must make a "choice" which system (view) it will use. For instance, during certain military operations it is excluded that soldiers start discussing with their officers what to do next and why.

GOVERNANCE AS A PROCESS

The vast complexity of the context (environment) of an organization far exceeds the comprehension of any single individual or the capabilities of a single organization. EA must transcend a single-organization view and address the organization's long-term resilience and viability in its evolving ecology. Since organizations are co-creators of their environment, the concept of an organization with well defined boundaries is being replaced by the concept of open and co-evolving system-of-agents with fuzzy boundaries (BAA).

Multiple agents are interdependent and because of the emergent properties of the organization com-

ing from the relationships of its agents multiple equilibria (potential alternative states). Moreover the interaction with its environment obliges an organization to be agile. The degree of agility is depending on the ability of the system to absorb perturbations in its stability domain. Therefore it is possible that the transformation as a consequence of being at the edge of chaos, will be far from its actual equilibrium and will endogenously self-organize towards ever-higher orders of complexity and coherence (see section on Cynefin).

In this context, governance is seen as networked, collaborative and loosely-coupled. 'Governance as process' is about coordinating inter-organizational forms such as inter-organizational networks, alliances and public-private partnerships around a shared purpose. EA is seen as the means for organizational innovation and sustainability. In this view, the enterprise and its environment are enmeshed and coevolving; the boundaries are blurred and more permeable. The enterprise architect faces the challenge of fostering pertinent sense-making in the organization and facilitating transformation as needed. (Korhonen, 2012)

Thus an organization can not anymore be seen as a collection of independent parts that have been brought together to act as a machine (mechanical view). Due to the C2 (brain) in a biological organization, the parts are linked in a hub system. In a large company the structure can be a hub of hubs with the agent at the end. However these agents do not have any own purpose and has little or none space for own initiatives. The sociocultural view on organizations gives the agents the possibility to follow their own purpose and the commitment to the whole is a commitment to attain the common purpose(s) of the whole.

Not all of these organizations are complex and even not all contexts are complex, but it is clear that an organization should know what its state is and in which context it is operating. The Cynefin framework with an effective and efficient intelligence base will give those answers. 'Cynefin,' pronounced ku-NEV-in, is Welsh word that signifies "the multiple factors in our environment and our experience that influence us in ways we can never fully understand" (Dettmer, 2011).

CYNEFIN

The Cynefin framework makes the organization and/or its parts aware of which possible contexts the organization and/or its parts can be: simple, complicated, complex, chaotic or disordered. The simple and complicated domains are closer to ordered than unordered. Complex and chaotic domains are more unordered.

It must be stressed that the intention of Snowden and Boone (2007) was not to categorize systems. This would otherwise mean that it is better to be in that particular quadrant (domain) instead of other quadrants. The system is what it is and it is a certain domain, so there is no value or judgmental assessment of the organization. The Cynefin Framework, which originates from Snowden's work in knowledge management but is based on complexity science and is also applicable to strategy formulation, provides a means of exploring different organizational contexts and selecting approaches accordingly. Thus Cynefin is a sense-making framework which allows people and organizations to better understand the contexts within which they are operating (Bean, 2011).

Cynefin helps the organization to assess the necessary knowledge, the cause-and-effect relationships and the role (degree) of uncertainty. This has consequences for the volatility of knowledge; the higher the volatility, the more important the intelligence (process) is. Since dynamics are very important in CAST, we can speak of dynamic knowledge.

But not all systems are CAS and components of CAS are not always complex. In their article in Harvard Business Review Snowden and Boone (2007) state that wise executives should tailor their

approach for decision making to fit the complexity of the circumstances they face. Therefore, although the Cynefin matrix helps visualize and understand how systems operate within a variety of domains, it can also be an indicator of the type of organization it is: mechanical, biological or sociocultural. This will answer the question of whether the organization is fit to survive in a particular domain. Logically a mechanic-based organization will not easily survive in a complex domain, unless it is part of a higher system that is capable of dealing with complexity.

Bean (2011) states that current EA practice (and indeed most management theory) is predicated on an assumption that organizations would be more effective if they exhibited a greater degree of order, but this may or may not be true in a rapidly changing world that is becoming more networked and diverse, as we have discussed in the double paradigm shift (reductionism/systems thinking and organizational view). She refers to Snowden who points out that the nature of CAS renders many current approaches to strategy and planning, where complicated and detailed plans are constructed, to be highly questionable. Snowden also points out that overly constraining a complex adaptive system, treating it as if it were an ordered one, can lead to chaos.

Simple Context

The variability of the environment is narrow. Uncertainty and turbulence are minimal. Here fits the classical C2 where clear cause-and-effect can be detected. The members of the organization know what to expect, and everyone shares a common understanding. It is the domain of the known-known, each event or action carries with it a limited number of potential outcomes that are predictable.

However, there is a danger to oversimplify the situation. In this context, leaders often become complacent and too often react too late which can be catastrophic. The leader should sense the problems, categorize them and then respond with the best practices.

Simple contexts are heavily process-oriented situations typically managed through the application of standard practice. Both managers and employees have access to the information they need. Adhering to best practice makes sense, and for this process re-engineering is a typical tool. Some examples of systems that would fall into this domain would be automobile repair shops, retail merchandise stores, fast food restaurants, municipal government departments, church congregations, and help desks that follow prescribed patterns of questions and answers in responding to common problems (Dettmer, 2011).

EA in a simple context will be more related to the "black box" situation. EA is seen as the glue between business and IT.

Complicated Context

Here also the context is ordered and cause-and-effects exist, only not everybody can see these relationships and therefore experts are needed to detect them, which makes human capital more important for the organization. But in this domain of known unknowns, the experts can be overconfident in their own solutions. The so-called "maverick" solutions of non-experts are mostly rejected.

Dettmer (2011, pp. 11-12) states that an organization can function in a simple context, but that itself can be complicated due to its structure. Specialized subunits (subsystems) have their own tools and methods, and the collaboration between these subsystems can be difficult. Certainly in a complicated domain, the myriad of interacting, interdependent parts can raise considerable issues. This leads to the creation of silos (specialized sub-systems) which are highly specialized and require specialized functional knowledge to operate.

This type of organization esteems that the whole (organization) is the sum of processes. Therefore their EA will focus on the business

processes which have to execute the strategy to attain the aimed goals or objectives. Thus, the organization wants to improve its processes. The organization is a white box and the EA is seen as the link between the strategy and the execution.

Dettmer (2011, p. 12) comes to the same conclusion and he warns against blindly improving the processes without looking at the organization as a whole greater than the sum of the processes. He quotes Deming:

Optimization is a process of orchestrating the efforts of all components toward achievement of the stated aim. Optimization is management's job. Everybody wins with optimization. Anything less than optimization of the whole system will bring eventual loss to every component of the system. Any group should have as its aim optimization over time of the larger system the group operates in. The obligation of any component is to contribute its best to the system, not to maximize its own production, profit, or sales, nor any other competitive measure. Some components may operate at a loss to themselves in order to optimize the whole system, including the components that take a loss.

He continues: "So, while the importance of whole-system thinking and system optimization was clearly important to Deming, that message was largely missed by analytically oriented managers, and the consultants (both internal and external) who sought to serve them. The result has historically been a plethora of process improvement tools and methods, but precious few system-level improvement tools.

As a result, the typical decision-making pattern in the complicated domain, and in complicated systems, boils down to sense-analyze-respond.

Figure 4 shows scenario planning as tool for complicated context. Flood (1999) in his discussion on the different authors in the domain of systems-thinking refers to Ackoff and complex-

Figure 4. Cynefin framework

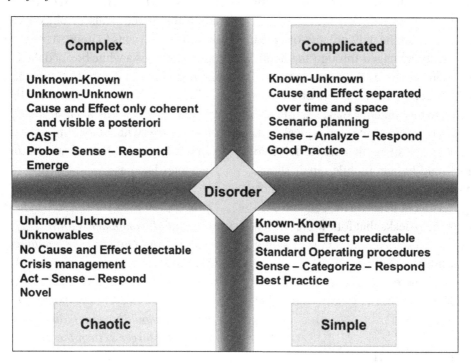

ity theory about scenario-planning as a tool for systems-thinking in a learning organization. Something Flood develops also in his methodology (combined with boundary judgments and subsequently deepening systemic appreciation. Therefore scenario-planning can also be used in the complex context (based on Senge, 2006).

The first two contexts are ordered and base their philosophies on "cause-and-effect." Mauboussin (2011, p. 90) states that this prevents leaders and managers from dealing effectively with complexity. "The biggest issue, in my mind, is that humans are incredibly good at linking cause and effect—sometimes too good. Ten thousand years ago most cause and effect was pretty clear. And our brains evolved to deal with that. But it means that when you see something occur in a complex adaptive system, your mind is going to create a narrative to explain what happened—even though cause and effect are not comprehensible in that kind of system. Hindsight's a beautiful thing. Also, we have a tendency to think that

certain causes will lead to particular effects. …. And we just don't know. I think that's the biggest single bias."

Rabaey et al. (2012) discusses Naturalistic Decision Making (NDM) and the theories of Benjamin Libet on the subconscious mind. Decisions are emerging from the subconscious mind and after a short period are surfacing in the conscious mind. What applies to the complex context is that cause-and-effect and/or patterns cannot be seen a priori. After the fact, it is probable that this cause-and-effect and/or emergent patterns will be revealed (retrospective coherence), only too late to be taken into consideration, so the decision (behavior) is an emergent phenomenon, just like the decision making of a human being (certainly in a stress situation). See also the section on decision-making based on the theory of Gharajedaghi (2011).

Snowden and Boone (2007) stress the risk of entrained thinking, which is a conditioned response that traps decision makers in the practices, policies, techniques and rationales that have successfully put them where they are. Dettmer (2011, pp. 13-14) calls entrained thinking "complacency." It is a danger in the case of a simple context (leaders) and in the case of complicated context (experts). Without a good functioning intelligence system leaders and experts, which of course they also have to respect, such organizations are running behind the facts and the chances are high that they move to a chaotic context.

Complex Context

The two following contexts are unordered and don't have this bias. "Complex context" has unknown unknowns and it is into this domain that much of contemporary business has shifted. There are no right answers and leaders should probe, sense and respond, meaning that the organization should look at emergent, patterns. Snowden et al. (2007, p. 74) warn "If [the managers] try to overcontrol the organization, they will preempt the opportunity for informative patterns to emerge. Leaders who try to impose order in a complex context will fail, but those who set the stage, step back a bit, allow patterns to emerge, and determine which ones are desirable will succeed." Therefore, complex contexts demand a more experimental management approach that admits some failure in the pursuit of understanding (Dettmer, 2011, p. 16).

Effective membership in a multi-minded system requires a role, a sense of belonging, and a commitment to participate in creating the group's future, so much that rolelessness is the major obstruction to integrating a social system. When an individual feels that his or her contributions to the group's achievements are insignificant, or when he or she feels powerless to play an effective role in the system's performance, a feeling of indifference sets in and the individual gradually becomes alienated from the very system in which he or she is supposed to be an active member of (Herzog, n.d.).

Regarding the success of cause and effect in a complex domain, this will depend highly on the depth of resident knowledge about the system and its environment and how much—and how quickly—system agents can learn about them, the known unknowns, and the unknown knowns (Dettmer, 2011, p. 16).

For these reasons, motivation and thus human capital becomes very important, and classical IT-systems alone are not sufficient anymore to support these agents. Systems such as intelligence base will gain importance in (real and virtual) organizations (Rabaey et al., 2012) and the concept of an enterprise architecture needs an extra layer: the knowledge-layer (Rabaey, 2012a). What has to be said about the managers, can also be said about the experts. Dettmer (2011) shows us a critical revelation about knowledge and tools: "in the complex domain, the knowledge of experts may be of limited value, and the effectiveness of cause-and-effect analysis is likely to be marginalized, or of short duration. This is not to say that expert knowledge is useless, only that its value in predicting future events is likely to be limited" (p. 14). The main reason is that CAS is a learning organization in which its agents have also to learn continuously. Furthermore the interactions between agents are multiple and interdisciplinary making it difficult for expert or group of experts to grasp. Therefore the knowledge has to be shared over the network of agents (part of the intelligence base) and EA, when implementing the knowledge layer, becomes of great value to manage the knowledge.

Chaotic Context

It is the realm of unknowables. Chaotic contexts are highly uncertain and changes are so fast that it is nearly impossible to have the time to interpret the facts and to react. A bit counterintuitive, in this case the leader has to act first to create order, so that he/she can sense where stability is or not to make it possible to transform the situation from chaos to complexity; thus act, sense and respond. Dettmer (2011) remarks that waiting for patterns to emerge may be a waste of time, or a recipe for disaster (p. 16). So in this case a leader has not much time to think and must act quickly. George S. Patton can be quoted: "A good plan violently executed now is better than a perfect plan next week."

Companies should look for and explore these contexts because they give the best opportunities. Eisenhardt and Sull write about this phenomenon in their HBR-article "Strategy as Simple Rules" (2001, p. 108): 'The secret of companies like Yahoo! is strategy as simple rules. Managers of such companies know that the greatest opportunities for competitive advantage lie in market confusion, so they jump into chaotic markets, probe for opportunities, build on successful forays, and shift flexibly among opportunities as circumstances dictate. But they recognize the need for a few key strategic processes and a few simple rules to guide them through the chaos." This certainly does not imply that no strategy at all is needed. "Each company follows a disciplined strategy - otherwise, it would be paralyzed by chaos. And, as with all effective strategies, the strategy is unique to the company. But a simple-rules strategy and its underlying logic of pursuing opportunities are harder to see than traditional approaches" (Eisenhardt et al., 2001, p. 109).

Disorder

The fifth context is "disorder." Bean (2011) remarks that Cynefin is a sense-making framework, not a categorization framework. It is intended to be socially constructed as an emergent property of people's interaction and discussion about factors and elements in a particular context. For this reason, there is a fifth domain in the center of the diagram, that of disorder, where people cannot agree on how something fits.

We recommend to break down the situation into constituent parts and assign each to one of the other realms. In this way leaders can make decisions and intervene in contextually appropriate ways.

The fact is that in this continuously (faster) evolving environment, apart from the knowledge network, the organizational structure also needs to be flexible. Therefore in the following part of this chapter we will go in more depth on the capability approach. A capability is composed of modules. Each module can be seen as a capability itself composed of other modules. By digging deeper we reach a certain point where the modules cannot be decomposed any further into other modules. This is the atomic module. It only has resources such as material and human resources to manage. (Rabaey et al, 2007). Of course this reductionist approach is only one step in the iterative process of (holistic) inquiry. Each component can be a Complex Adaptive System (CAS) and will have emergent properties which cannot be explained solely by analyzing the components and/or resources.

The following two sections will be based mainly on the excellent work of William Dettmer (2011): "Systems Thinking and the Cynefin Framework: A Strategic Approach to Managing Complex Systems" except for the EA topics.

Summary Cynefin Framework

The Cynefin framework (Figure 4) is designed to help decision makers—organizational leaders and system managers—understand where their system stands in the external environment. It provides knowledge about the general characteristics of the five domains in which leaders could find their systems. It helps decision makers understand what kinds of methods and tools will be likely to work in their particular organizations, and which ones will not.

The Cynefin concept provides key insight that most leaders have likely been ignorant about:

- The boundaries between simple, complicated, complex and chaotic are indistinct. Consequently, changes in external conditions or internal system modifications may push a given system from one domain to another without being aware of it, if its leaders are not paying attention.

- A particular system may inhabit more than one domain simultaneously. For example, a vertically integrated manufacturing company my find its production subsystem in the complicated domain, but its sales and marketing may be in the complex domain.
- The spatial relationship among the domains emphasizes how easily (or insidiously) an organization might slip from one domain into another, possibly without noticing it. The boundary between complicated and complex is less extreme than the boundary between the simple and the chaotic. Consequently, the failure of management to recognize a shift from complicated to complex, while problematic, is not likely to be as catastrophic as the failure to recognize a shift from simple to chaotic. But all domains are directly exposed to the zone of disorder, which should prompt leaders to heightened awareness of their system s relationship with its external environment.
- Simple and complicated domains assume an ordered universe, where cause-and-effect relationships are perceptible, and right answers can be determined based on facts.
- Complex and chaotic domains are unordered, meaning that there is no apparent relationship between cause and effect. This does not mean that there is no cause and effect, just that it's not apparent or obvious. While the ordered part of the continuum (simple and complicated) can be managed based on facts, the unordered part requires intuition and recognition of patterns. Consequently, the tools and methods that work well in the simple and complicated domains tend to be less effective (or completely ineffective) in the complex and chaotic domains.

What are now the consequences for EA? The Cynefin framework illustrates the principle of bounded diversity; different tools and methods apply in different contexts. So if Enterprise Architecture is to be successful as a discipline, its practitioners must recognize this phenomenon and adapt their practice accordingly (Bean, 2011).

However if the EA practitioners are aware of this then the projects can still fail, because they are confronted with a bigger problem: knowing the whole (enterprise) is not possible. Senge (2006) and complexity theory (Flood, 1999) begin both by acknowledging the interrelated nature of things as well as emergence, where the whole is experienced as being greater than the sum of its parts. A special form is the spontaneous self-organization. It is for a human being impossible to know all the existing interconnections of a complex system. EA therefore cannot fully represent the enterprise. This is based on the incompressibility concept (darkness principle) (Independenc Partners, 2011) which states that no complex system can be known completely. The best representation of a complex system is the system itself; because any representation other than the system itself will necessarily misrepresents certain aspects of the original system. Each individual element in the system is ignorant of the behavior of the system as a whole and can only respond to the information that is available to it locally, that is why BPEIS is proposed. If each element would know what is happening to the system as a whole, all of the complexity of the larger system should be present in that specific element. Related to its environment, it is nearly impossible to know how the system's environment will affect that system.

Flood (1999) states that people have to work local in space and time. Space are the things that one is immediately involved in and time means the not very far into the future. If we look at EA frameworks like TOGAF (n.d.) the purpose of enterprise architecture is to optimize across the enterprise the often fragmented legacy of processes (both manual and automated) into an integrated environment that is responsive to change and supportive of the delivery of the business strategy.

This purpose corresponds to the biological view of an enterprise for which enterprise architecture is seen as the link between strategy and execution. It addresses all facets of the enterprise in order to coherently execute the strategy (see above).

As a matter of fact, TOGAF (n.d.) defines the enterprise as any collection of organizations that has a common set of goals. The term enterprise in the context of EA can be used to denote both an entire enterprise - encompassing all of its information and technology services, processes, and infrastructure - and a specific domain within the enterprise. In both cases, the architecture crosses multiple systems, and multiple functional groups within the enterprise. One can question the effectiveness of such (non-systemic) frameworks. Moreover they extend the enterprise nowadays frequently to partners, suppliers, and customers. If the goal is to integrate an extended enterprise, then the enterprise comprises the partners, suppliers, and customers, as well as internal business units. However for successful projects, bounded action areas has to be defined so that the focused part of the enterprise and its external collaborating agents can easily be served, and as noted before BAA is temporarily and partially (Flood, 1999).

Obviously in addition the unordered domains and the complex systems are not taken into consideration. This implies that changes (and optimizations) are driven by cause-and-effect chains, which have no or few utility in the unordered domains. Moreover the fact that a system can inhabit more than one system simultaneously and that an organization can shift from one domain to another unnoticed, makes this approach to EA a disadvantage rather than an advantage in this fast changing world.

The Enterprise Architecture Research Forum (EARF, n.d.) defines Enterprise Architecture as "the continuous practice of describing the essential elements of a socio-technical organization, their relationships to each other and to the environment, in order to understand complexity and manage change." This definition matches the approach of complex systems, however the author has not found a framework that supports the definition.

IMPLICATION OF THE CYNEFIN FRAMEWORK

Why the Same Management Tool Sometimes Fails and Sometimes Succeeds

William Dettmer's (2011) biggest contribution to the use of the Cynefin Framework is that organizations cannot only determine in which situations they are, but also which management tools can be used in those situations (see above).

The majority of the management methods and tools available have been designed to succeed in simple and complicated domains. The preponderance of these are tactical and quantitative while strategic, qualitative management aids are considerably fewer in number. Some methods and tools have realized significant successes in a variety of situations, while failing to meet expectations in others. The failure to identify and understand the underlying assumptions about these methods made it inevitable. Without extraordinary efforts, their effectiveness begins to deteriorate the deeper into the complex domain the organization is forced to operate. A typical example is the decreasing utility of cause-effect analysis the farther into the complex domain one goes. By the time one reaches the chaotic domain, cause-effect is nearly useless, because the situation changes faster than cause and effect can be determined (complex and chaotic domains). Moreover the closer to the chaotic domain a system or its environment come, the greater the dependence on intuitive decision making, command-control leadership skills, and faster OODA loop cycles (pp. 27-28) (See also Rabaey, 2011).

Without a sense-making framework such as Cynefin, decisions about which methods or tools to use in a particular situation become a trial-and-error, hit-and-miss proposition. How many times has a management team embraced a philosophy or methodology promoted by a particular expert or consulting company, sometimes as a panacea, only to be disappointed with the results? There are obviously other factors instrumental to success, such as organizational psychology and change management. But with an effective foundational understanding of where a particular system resides "in the firmament," the choice of appropriate methods can dramatically enhance the probability of success of the system's improvement efforts, making the jobs of organizational psychologists and change agents much easier (pp. 28-29).

Since EA is also used as a planning tool (TOGAF, n.d.) and therefore can be linked to investment programs (Rabaey, 2012) we will examine the investment techniques in the next section.

Investment Techniques and EA

Investments are sacrifices in terms of money, time and/or manpower to attain goals in the future. It is a consequence of the first principle of the Art of War: the balance between goals and means (Bernard, 1976). The way it will be executed is called the strategy. Interesting for our discussion is that an organization is moving from a situation "as-is" towards a situation "to-be" interacting with its environment to attain goals in the future. Therefore, it will need to acquire and allocate resources for its processes and probably has to reform its structure. However the future is not stable and is unknown (or known) to a certain degree because of the elements described above. Different kinds of investment techniques exist and just like in the Cynefin framework, the range goes from simple to very complex techniques.

It is not the subject of the investment that determines the technique, but rather the context that must determine the investment technique. In the same way the introduction of a new technology can be simple or complicated for company A, while for company B it can be complex and even chaotic (due to a competitive disadvantage that can cause the downfall of the company).

The discussion of all possible investment techniques is out of the scope of this chapter. Only a few will be handled to show the necessary balance between the contexts (organization [internal examination] and domains [external observation]) and investment techniques.

It has to be noted that regarding investments, a company can use a particular investment technique to hide the real choice of the company (make-up) and/or because the managers are not aware of their mental models.

Capital budgeting methods based on the Discounted Cash Flow (DCF) have been the primary instruments for investment decision making. The most commonly used DCF-based method is the Net Present Value (NPV). NPV discounts all cash flows (incoming and outgoing) related to the project or process to the Present Value (PV). If the sum of discounted cash flows is positive then the project is a candidate to invest in. This technique is suited to a simple context (everything is known). "Under static circumstances, DCF-based methods provide reliable results. However, the real world situations are seldom static. Especially in cases of large investments with long economic lives the static DCF-based methods fail to present a highly reliable picture of the profitability" (Wang and Lee, 2010, p. 696).

In this context, EA will also be simple; therefore, EA can support the investment decision-makers.

If business is in a more complex context then it is hard to predict the future, so what about the future cash flows? "[In] a rapidly changing environment, we don't really know how things are going to unfold, so it's difficult to make forecasts or budgets going many years into the future" (Mauboussin, 2011, p. 92). Even tougher mathematical models cannot predict the future: "Complexity theory predicts that we cannot rely on predictions" (Matthews, 2012a).

Shen (2009) and Huang, Kao and Li (2007) write that indeed the evaluation of investments are not trivial, because the costs and benefits may involve uncertainty and vagueness, which make return on investments difficult. Further, projects are assessed from various dimensions and criteria, which need advanced decision tools to aid. Thirdly, solutions may be bundled with some special constraints about the system architecture, budgets, decision preferences, and so on. The authors are proposing a fuzzy multi-objective decision approach for evaluating IT-projects. Fuzzy sets are used because the expertise of specialized people from different domains has to be combined together along with their level of expertise, which situates this techniques more in the complicated context.

In the complicated context management needs more flexibility so that it can postpone, delay, start, and abandon projects. Cobb and Charnes (2007) state that managerial flexibility has value. "The assumption that all investments are irreversible is a fundamental weakness of most DCF methods. … The ability of their managers to make smart decisions in the face of volatile market and technological conditions is essential for firms in any competitive industry" (p. 173). Real Option Analysis (ROA) or Real Option Valuation (ROV) gives management this flexibility and it tackles the problem of uncertainty and risk related to each investment (Trigeorgis, 2002; Fichman, 2004; Brach, 2003; Mun, 2006). Options are the right but not the obligation to execute an action (sell or buy). Translated to real option, it means that management can decide to postpone, stop, start, restart or put on hold a project. The reasons may be because of the lack of relevant information, or to wait for results of some pilot projects.

To be useful for ROV, EA-projects must be linked to risk management and simulation programs and especially the impact analysis of projects on the overall architectures (different layers).

In her study, von Helfenstein (2009) advocates the use of ROV when complexity and risks are involved. Since most of the business has shifted towards complex contexts, it is surprising that ROV is not used more in investment appraisals. General Helmuth von Moltke said once: "No plan survives contact with the enemy." As a matter of fact ROV has a common drawback with the classic investment techniques, being that it does not take into account the interaction of the organization with its environment (market, government, etc.) (Grenadier, 2000; Smit et al., 2009; Fereira et al., 2009). The solution is to combine ROV with game theory, which results in the theory of option games. However option games demand a lot of intelligence and computing power and can only be justified in some cases (see below). The organization can play different games (game theory) at the same time in different domains and/or different levels. Moreover, the underlying organizational elements (agents) can themselves play different games regarding the mother organization (the whole) and regarding each other, even for a same project: Finance can collaborate with third parties, while human resources are in competition with these parties. If there is no superstructure (like project management or business unit), then contradictory signals are sent to the market. So, there is no such thing as a unique strategic game to play. Thus if game options are used, in every node more than two (solution) paths may exist, which may quickly lead into a Chaos system (Glenn, 1996; Rabaey, 2011).

Collan et al. (2009) remark another disadvantage of (probabilistic) ROV by stating that real options are commonly valued with the same methods that have been used to value financial options, that is, with Black-Scholes option pricing formula, with the binomial option valuation method, or with Monte-Carlo-based methods. Most of the methods are complex and demand a good understanding of the underlying mathematics, which make their use difficult in practice. Moreover the pure (probabilistic) real option rule characterizes the present value of expected cash flows by a single number, which is not realistic in many cases (Lee and Lee, 2011). In addition these models are based on the assumption that they can quite accurately mimic the underlying markets as a process, an assumption that may hold for some quite efficiently traded financial securities, but not for investments of a 'singular' organization where every investment is intimately linked to the organization and not to a market.

However, if ROV is not used, classic investment techniques are, and their integration with flexibility and risk is more complex than with ROV (example see Misra et al., 2011).

To overcome the above mentioned problems different authors (Collan, 2008; Collan et al., 2009; Lee et al., 2011; Wang et al., 2010; Tolga et al., 2008) are proposing fuzzy sets (See also Wikipedia Fuzzy Pay-Off Method for Real Option Valuation, n.d.; Bednyagin et al., n.d.).

So if enough statistical data is available then ROV can be used (most of the time in complicated contexts). If not, then fuzzy ROV is preferred (complicated and complex contexts). Although in a complex context the relevancy of experts is not that big, Fuzzy ROV is better suited for making decisions in groups (Tao, Jinlong, Benhai and Shan, 2007) which is certainly useful.

In this case of fuzzy ROV, the knowledge layer of EA, as discussed earlier, is very important. Experts have to feed the knowledge base linked to the concerning processes and information systems. However ROV is not suited for complex and chaos domain projects. Here EA must be fully integrated with CAST as suggested above. Since projects and/or organizations are moving quickly towards the unordered domains, EA and investment techniques suited for these domains are preferably used from the beginning because changing methods during projects can be very time and energy consuming. As opposed to the

ordered domains, EA cannot be used directly to support investments in the unordered domains. Only through the integration with CAST, EA can indirectly support these investments.

HOLISTIC FRAMEWORKS

Interdisciplinary Forum

Benaroch et al. (2007) have observed that mainly two camps of thinking (philosophies) on ROV exist. The first camp favors rigor and the technical aspects of valuing investments using option pricing models. It often overlooks the complexities of applying real options to IT projects. The second camp is more strategy focused and therefore in favor of real options thinking based on managerial heuristics. This camp recognizes the complexities of applying real options in practice. Both camps are confronted with the need to monitor on a permanent base the business environment to assess what should be done with the real options (Weeds, 2006), which certainly is needed in the complex and chaotic contexts (Cynefin framework).

Benaroch et al. (2006) observed that managers are following a logic of real options thinking in managing the risk of their IT investments, but based on intuition. The danger of this intuitive real option thinking may lead to suboptimal or counterproductive results. To the authors, intuition ought to be supplemented by the ability of a formal ROV model to "quantify the value that options add to IT investments in relation to their creation cost and to the mitigation they enable. This ability is a prerequisite to approaching IT risk management from an economic optimization perspective."

It is clear that the followers of the strategy camp are using the "missing information" to compensate to decide. In general, "[d]ecision analysis methods have been used for capital budgeting, and several researchers have proposed an integration of decision analysis tools and ROV. The combination of these concepts may allow models that produce a solution for the value of a project and an optimal investment decision rule more intuitively and efficiently." Whatever combination is used with ROV "the optimal strategies suggested are usually the same" (Cobb et al., 2007, p. 178).

Unfortunately, this does not work in complex and chaotic domains, as for most (quantitative) methods and tools. Rabaey et al. (2004, 2007a, 2007b, 2012) are proposing an interdisciplinary forum to evaluate the business processes and resources allocation at the operational strategic level. The resource managers agree with the business people service levels so that they can guarantee the good functioning of the business processes. Every resource manager will then optimize the usage of his/her resources (investing, disinvesting, reallocation).

EA is used because EA projects deal with the enterprise in all its aspects. Wegmann (2003) writes that as a consequence, EA teams have to be multi-disciplinary. An EA team includes specialists (typically upper management, functional managers and senior staff members) together with architects. The role of the architect is to federate the efforts of the specialists to ensure successful projects.

Although a holistic approach, the interdisciplinary forum is only suited for simple and complicated organizations and domains, since tools like business process management, balanced scorecards are proposed. However Rabaey (2012) in his work "A Public Economics Approach to Enabling Enterprise Architecture with the Government Cloud in Belgium" in "Enterprise Architecture for Connected E-Government: Practices and Innovations" edited by Pallab Saha proposes a more flexible structure and working of the interdisciplinary forum that uses Enterprise Architecture. The philosophy for this flexibility and permanent awareness of the environment (observation) corresponds with the philosophy of the intelligence base and with the OODA (Observe-Orient-Decide-Act) (Rabaey, 2011) of

which Dettmer (2011) writes that it is suitable for all four domains. The latter also concludes that brainstorming can be used in the four domains. This supports the idea of intuitive management.

Agile Enterprise Model

A method proposed by Bilder et al. (2001) is based on Systems Thinking and Process Thinking, the purpose is to model an agile enterprise. "None of the [below] paradigms focuses specifically on the issue of enterprise/business agility – property of an enterprise to function in the highly dynamic world. The agility concerns both being able to adjust the enterprise to changes in the surrounding environment, and discovering new opportunities constantly appearing in the dynamic world for launching completely new products/services. Becoming agile requires a structure that allows discovering changes and opportunities as soon as possible and react on them appropriately" (p. 2).

Bidler et al. (2001) continue; EA is associated with alignment of different parts of the enterprise (physical and non-physical). To complete an EA project requires time and considerable resources which leads to this paradigm normally being used by large enterprises in sectors considered to be stable such as energy, large industrial enterprises, financial sector, large governmental organizations.

ST is associated with a holistic view on the dynamic behavior of the enterprise and its interaction with its environment. It is directed to avoiding situations in which the dynamic behaviors existing in different parts of the enterprise are disconnected.

Business Process Management (BPM) shows the managers how their enterprise is functioning and indicates where processes can be optimized.

The combination of EA, BPM and ST gives an enterprise model that consists of three layers:

- Enterprise assets: people, physical, organizational and information artifacts.

- Sensors: it is not like the sensing part of the Intelligence Base, because they also are triggering the process.
- Business Process Instances (BPI): standardized or ad hoc processes triggered by the sensors:
  - Operational processes: business as usual.
  - Process improvement processes: optimizing the processes.
  - Strategic process: (see below)

The third category of business processes are in fact strategic steering processes. A sensor has a macro view on the whole organizations. If the overall performance is below expectation, a strategic BPI is triggered with the goal of considerably changing the assets layer. "This can include radical changes in process definitions, removing obsolete processes, introducing new ones, rearranging departments, substituting key-managers, introducing new technology, etc. These are the processes where ST is (though maybe too seldom) applied as guidelines for finding the best places to make changes (leverage points). A process here may be completely ad hoc, or use some loose structure, e.g., a series of brainstorming sessions" (Bidler et al., 2001, p. 6). As mentioned before, Dettmer (2011) writes that brainstorming is suitable for all four domains of Cynefin (simple, complicated, complex and chaotic), which supports the idea of intuitive management.

An enterprise behaves as an "adaptive system" through the interplay between the three layers. By constantly interacting with its environment via the operational processes, the enterprise observes the environment and inspects its own functioning and may optimize itself to the current environment through the improvement processes, and can reconfigure itself when the environment changes based on the strategic steering processes.

The idea of EA is implicitly present in this model (alignment of parts of the enterprise, structure), that is why BPM plays an important role in their framework. However the three different types of business processes are so fundamentally different that a simple three layered representation of an enterprise is not without a larger framework, as we will present later.

'Interdisciplinary forum' and 'agile enterprise model' do not fully take the aspect of complex (adaptive) system in consideration, however since they are using respectively OODA and brainstorming, they may produce good results.

CAST-EA

Systems Thinking: Complicated or Complex

The original idea of Cynefin Framework is described in an article of an IBM Journal by Kurtz and Snowden (2003). What is interesting is that the authors put ST in the complicated domain, which they call the domain of the knowables where the thinking is analytical-reductionist. So apparently they use a concept that differs from the concepts of Ackoff or Gharajedaghi. It is clear that the authors had more systems engineering in their mind than (the evolved) ST.

The complex domain is the domain of CAS and patttern management. Kurtz and Snowden (2003) state that it is the "domain of complexity theory, which studies how patterns emerge through the interaction of many agents. There are cause-and-effect relationships between the agents, but both the number of agents and the number of relationships defy categorization or analytic techniques. Emergent patterns can be perceived but not predicted; we call this phenomenon retrospective coherence. In this space, structured methods that seize upon such retrospectively."

However especially for CAS which are interacting with the environment to survive, it is necessary to have a global picture of the system in its environment. Additionally, certain properties cannot be deduced through a study of individual components and interactions (Lowe et al., 2006), thus a holistic view, which is provided by ST (at least the one we have discussed) is needed.

Therefore to make the distinction between the ST versions useful in the complicated domain but not in the complex domain and the ST versions useful in the complex domain, we call the latter the Complex Adaptive Systems Thinking (CAST).

Kurtz and Snowden (2003) emphasize the Cynefin dynamic: "When people use the Cynefin framework, the way they think about moving between domains is as important as the way they think about the domain they are 'in', not least because a move across boundaries requires a shift to a different model of understanding and interpretation as well as a different leadership style. Understanding the differences between the different movements in the framework increases the response sophistication of a decision-making group to rapid change" (p. 14).

It is therefore essential that an enterprise is using a philosophy and framework that can be used in as many possible domains. A system may move from the complicated domain to the complex, thus the management methods and tools may change, however the overall framework should cover both complex and complicated domains (similar logic for the simple domain). Probably this gives another perspective "Why Nobody is Doing Enterprise Architecture" stated by Bloomberg (2011). You have to know which game you are playing.

Combing CAS and ST

Figure 5 "CAST-loop" is based on the to Systems Thinking adapted Sinlge/Double Loop model of Action Research (Figure 1), OODA (Figure 2) and the Intelligence Base (Figure 3).

Action Research has also a triple loop learning. In the single loop an organization makes changes

Figure 5. CAST-loop

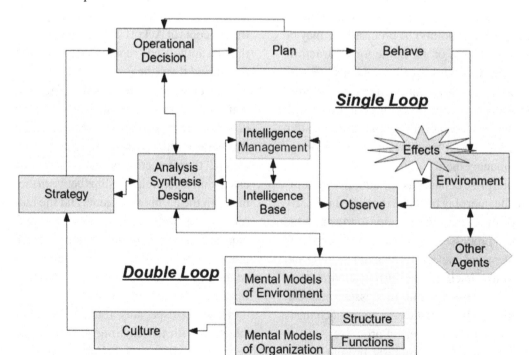

to improve immediate outcomes. In the double loop changes are made either to prevent a problem or to embed a solution. The third loop is focused on ethics (Cram, 2011).

In her paper "Mechanisms to support organizational learning: the integration of action learning tools into multidisciplinary design team practice," Evers (2004) writes that triple loop learning involves three types of management of the learning process: design management (How?), debate management (What?) and might-right management (Why?). These questions correspond to what Gharajedaghi (2011, p. 33) writes on purposefulness of a system: "To influence the actors in our transactional environment we have to understand why they do what they do." Of course, an organization also must understand why it does what it does. Teams need to become aware of and use all three centers of learning, continually looping among these three questions and functions intelligently and responsibly. Evers (2004) makes reference to Argyris who calls this continuous process 'multiloop' learning.

Romme et al. (1999) also reference Argyris: "Double loop learning appears to facilitate the adaptive potential of an organization, but most organizations seem to have great difficulties in actually learning in a double loop manner." They continue "[T]riple loop learning is about increasing the fullness and deepness of learning about the diversity of issues and dilemmas faced, by linking together all local units of learning in one overall learning infrastructure as well as developing the competences and skills to use this infrastructure … Triple loop learning manifests itself in the form of 'collective mindfulness'": members discover how they and their predecessors have facilitated or inhibited learning, and produce new structures and strategies for learning" (p. 440).

The role of the infrastructure which they mention and which is needed for the triple loop is fulfilled by the Intelligence Base, which facilitates learning and increases the knowledge.

As already mentioned above, Sterman (2010) added mental models to the double loop. Although he defined a double loopback between (information) Feedback and the mental models, Rabaey (2012b) esteems that this double loopback can be the cause of an (increasing) gap between the models and the awareness (culture, strategy) of the organization, so that loopback is not drawn (Figure 1). This is however not the case in Figure 5, because the connection is not made between feedback and the mental models, but feed forward and feedback exist between the "Analysis-Synthesis-Design" function and the mental models. So, if necessary the culture and/or the (grand) strategy will be adapted. The (grand) strategy can be directly adapted without having to change the culture and/or fundamentally change the mental models. Therefore a new allocation of resources is possible without changing fundamentally the structure (mental models of the organization).

For the above mentioned reasons a triple-loop is not necessary. Moreover the domains mentioned in the Cynefin framework, will be monitored and will be used in both mental models (environment/ external observation) and organization (internal introspection)) so that the enterprise can use the right set of management tools. Of course, by using the OODA of John Boyd, the organization will always use the right management method and related tools.

Enterprise Architecture

Knowledge Layer

As mentioned in the section overview of EA, lots of different interpretations of the term Enterprise Architecture (EA) exist (Rabaey, 2012). In this context Korhonen (2012) writes that the traditional notion of enterprise architecture assumes information systems as underlying operative resources rather than as core value assets and true business enablers. Actually business-IT alignment exacerbates the business-IT divide. Therefore IT is seen as a separate, value-adding function, relegated to a subordinate role of a mere service and cost center, whose focus is on operational quality and reliability – on producing predictable outcomes on a consistent basis.

However, the knowledge economy forces enterprises to compete at the level of knowledge and not anymore at the level of information (see above). So the differentiation will be made on the level of knowledge assets and therefore knowledge has to be addressed in a specific architecture. We concluded that EA should be put in a broader context than merely infrastructure architecture and application architecture, because applications are built to support business processes and operate on information gathered through these business processes from the environment, therefore EA must cover the business and its dynamics so that it can take precautions for changing business requirements or the reuse of certain artifacts in other business domains.

Rabaey (2012) proposes five levels of Enterprise Architecture: business, knowledge, information, application and infrastructure. Knowledge architecture is an additional level (Ross, 2003). Modeling knowledge brings us to epistemological and ontological models. Bean (2011, p.6) states that "[t]here is an important distinction between ontological models of a reasonably well-understood domain that purport to represent parts of the 'real world'" (mostly developed by subject matters experts), "and epistemological models that are used to explore perceptions of the real world. Epistemological models are not necessarily models of reality but are designed to support discussion, debate and argument about people's perceptions of reality, where the real nature of the problems to be tackled is unclear." Senge (2006) advocates dialogue and discussion to tackle problems. The use of epistemological models will certainly bring implicit mental models to the surface during the processes of dialogue and discussion.

In the context of the Cynefin framework, epistemological models will certainly be used in the complex and chaos domains, while in the complicated and simple domains we will find ontological and epistemological models.

Capability Approach

The above discussed Agile Enterprise Model of Bilder et al. (2001) depicts the enterprise in three layers. Does this match with the idea of EA? Not really but it shows that all assets should be taken into consideration because they are used in all business processes. This brings us to the concept of capabilities.

The general strategy of an enterprise emerges and the organization (structure) is adapted in function of the environment and the own desired effects in the environment. The sum of the effects should be the vision of the organization. The Board obtains these effects on the society (outcomes) by using capabilities (functions), which will then perform actions (output) to obtain these effects. A capability is a logical set of modules (processes) which produce one or more outputs (functions) with a certain service level (Rabaey, forthcoming).

Functions can be performed by external partners (outsourcing). In the extreme case that all functions are outsourced then the enterprise is a complete virtual organization of capabilities. It is a special form of what Gharajedaghi is calling a multi-minded organization, where (quasi-) autonomous but interdependent agents are working together. McHugh et al. (1995) call this the holonic enterprise.

Companies work together in a virtual space called the holonic enterprise. It is a networked organization where (ideally) every company does outsource its non-core business to the other nodes (called holons).

So different companies will join their core forces and outsource their non-core forces to each other (virtual organization), but if they have common strategic interests, even in an emergent way, then the formed capabilities will be used in a holonic enterprise to attain the strategic objectives.

Canter defines the virtual organization as an "enterprise [who] is comprised of the temporary electronic linking, pooling and coordinating of independent enterprises' organizational units, intellectual properties, and production capabilities. It is especially effective in the emerging globally competitive e-marketplace which increasingly is characterized by specialization, fragmentation, and speed and pervasiveness of change - elements which even the largest and most resource-endowed of enterprises find themselves no longer able, on a stand-alone basis, to adequately address. ... The complex inter-dynamics of this environment will place increasing demands for increasingly rapid and accurate OODA loop *[OODA: Observe-Orient-Decide-Act, see Osinga (2007)]* processing... both for each partnering organization in the virtual enterprise, and for the virtual entity as a whole" (Canter, 2000).

In the context of CAST, independent enterprises' organizational units should be replaced by (quasi)autonomous, interdependent organizational units.

So the capability approach shows the emergent synergistic properties of systems: the whole is indeed greater than the sum of its (collaborating) parts. Although the relationship with customers and other stakeholders is important, the internal relationships between the components of an organization (capability) are equally important.

In Figure 6 the different layers have been redefined so that not only IT systems but all systems are taken into account, so it is a whole EA. The knowledge and information layers have been brought together into one "Knowledge and Information Management" KIM due to the fact that

Figure 6. CAST EA

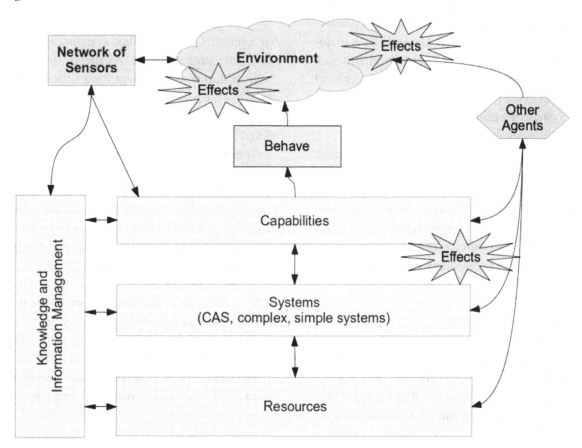

the Intelligence Base holds knowledge, information, data and this in all different forms. Agents of the enterprise are interconnected and have to share the elements of the Intelligence Base. The sensors are detecting the environment. Of course, KIM can be mapped into different layers.

The capabilities form another layer. It represents the functions that are performed outside of the defined enterprise. Defined in this case means from the point of view of the observer (see above). For example the defined enterprise can be a system in a bigger whole, therefore to the bigger whole the enterprise is a system, and for the enterprise the environment can be the bigger whole alone or a combination of the whole with other agents (and conditions).

As such, the underlying layer of systems is partially explained. Systems can be nested, thus a system can be composed of other systems, which then also can be composed of other systems. It is essential that the interactions are also caught. We refer to the definition of EA of EARF (n.d.): "Enterprise Architecture is the continuous practice of describing the essential elements of a socio-technical organization, their relationships to each other and to the environment, in order to understand complexity and manage change."

Systems are using resources and that is the last layer "Resources."

We included also the "Other Agents" because of the possibilities of mutual outsourcing and/or collaboration. If it is on the level of capabilities then the collaboration should be seen as a new enterprise (whole). If it is in the layer of systems then it is more outsourcing, cosourcing or insourcing. Regarding the resources, the other agents are suppliers.

Information Systems

With the evolution of intelligent agents and/or networks software is not anymore only a set of pre-programmed algorithms. As a matter of fact, intelligent agents became CAS and they are ef-

fectively used in processes and/or systems and may even be a capability or a system used with other agents.

CAST EA corresponds also to the traditional layers of EA for IT: business, information, applications, infrastructure. Here also it will depend on who is "observing" the IT. If the observer is the enterprise which owns the IT, then probably the IT will be in the layers of systems and resources. If the IT department is the observer then it will cover the layers from resources to capabilities (and KIM).

So because of the CAST's approach flexibility and interacting and/or integrating models are possible. We would like to stress that the Cynefin framework may not be forgotten so that the IT department (as with any other department) or the whole are aware in which domain they are.

We are referring Bean (2011) and Johnston (2005) for more details.

Bus Structure

All agents (CAS, complex systems, external agents) are interconnected. As already discussed above, a hub is not efficient for a sociocultural entity. We are making an analogy with Enterprise Service Bus and to visualize the nested and inter-related agents we use also a bus structure.

An enterprise forms capabilities with CAS MR and XY. These CAS are composed themselves of other agents. CAS XY has its own Intelligence Base (connected to the other one) and uses CAS -RS, a new CAS 120 and a complex system CBD (composed of Sys C, Sys B, and Sys D). Instead of a dotted line, the Sys C ens Sys B are also used in CAS-MR. CAS-MR has an external agent ABC.

Sys CBD can be a SOA IT-application that supports the logistics of the whole organization. Sys B is the inventory, while Sys C is the invoice and Sys D is the distribution management. This IT application uses IT-infrastructure (network, servers, device) which can also be represented.

RECURSION

General

The description of the capability approach follows the logic of Beer and his Viable Systems Model (VSM). VSM is an organizational representation of the elements and interactions considered essential for any system to be viable or autonomous. A viable system being one that is organized and operates in a manner such as to survive in its changing environment. Adaptability is one of the prime features of systems that survive (Systemswiki, n.d.).

The VSM employs an interdisciplinary law, that all distinct organizations contain themselves. Beer calls this recursion. Another characteristic is that as much as possible autonomy is given to its parts (agents), whilst maintaining the integrity of the whole, thus the multi-minded view of organization (see above).

Recursion means that the whole can be found in the parts. That VSM (whole) itself is part of a larger VSM (Flood, 1999). This corresponds to the recursive-system theorem (each viable system contains, and is contained in, another viable system) and viability principle. The latter is "the ability of a system to fully develop and sustain itself, this is a function of the proper balance between autonomy of subsystems and their integration within the whole system, or of the balance between stability and adaption; systems experiencing chaos (i.e. experiencing random and uncontrolled changes internally and to outputs, outcomes, and impacts) will cease to be integrated by the environment" (Independence Partners, 2011).

Recursion offers a novel way in which shared vision (or for that matter identity) is, at higher levels interpreted within the identity of the whole and is subsequently implemented. The aim of recursive design is to avoid the negative effects of coercive structure (implemented by a traditional, reductionist management authority). Recursion promotes autonomy (viability principle) so the agents or parts have as much independence as is possible given the constraints that exist when coordinating and controlling to maintain a whole (Flood, 1999). This implies the purposeful role of agents, which is in accordance with the multi-minded organizational view of Gharajedaghi (see above). For that reason, the author is proposing the bus-structure for the (communication) needs of coordination and control.

OODA

The Boyd-cycle has four phases, however to work ('act') in every phase OODA is again used. For instance, the observer will also go through an own OODA-cycle to decide (when, where, what, who, why, how) to observe and if the observer find elements (be it in push or pull) then a decision has to be made to inform or not, the network of the made observation.

In a networked (be it virtual or not) organization, different units and subunits must (formally or informally) communicate to act in the context of the whole. Each (sub)unit will have to go through OODA-cycles. Although they may act autonomously, it is preferable that the nested OODA-cycles are based on the same mental models or that the mental models of the different (sub)units and the whole have been made explicit to avoid misunderstandings in the decision process and in the execution. The bottom line is that the main requirement for a successful recurrent OODA is that the mental models are known.

Meta Service Bus and EA Models

The principle of recursion can also be implemented at the IT-level. Since communication in a multi-minded organization is very important, we will focus on the service bus. As we have seen before at the enterprise level the concept of Enterprise Service Bus (ESB) is well known. The concept of service bus can be used for the embedded information system of the business processes (BPEIS).

Programs (modules) of the BPEIS are interacting through Business Process Service Bus (BPSB) with other modules of the own BPEIS or with other applications (can be other BPEIS) inside or outside the enterprise (most likely via the ESB).

To be consistent with the concept of recursion, the programs should also have a (program) service bus with similar management functions of the ESB, which should of course be compatible. The advantage of such service bus is that a program can adapt its version to the request of the client through the business logic management module (multiple versions of a module can reside on the same program service bus). This technique can also be used with service buses at higher levels.

A BPEIS does not necessary have to stay in the physical boundaries of the enterprise. This will be more the exception than the rule. The control can even be outside the main users' enterprise. So an ESB limited to the physical boundaries of an enterprise may cause organizational and/or management problems. Virtual ESB implemented in the cloud, the cloud service bus, is the way ahead (see also Rabaey 2012a, 2012b, 2012c; Rabaey et al., forthcoming).

Figure 8 depicts the concept of recurrent service bus. It has to be noted that more than four levels are indeed possible. In addition, it does not matter for systems thinking if a business process is partially automated or not automated at all.

Separate bodies like authentication agents are controlling the traffic (communication) between the different BPEIS (be it in the CSB, [V]ESB or any other service bus, and other types of information system management). Standardization is a must, the Web services and Service Oriented Architecture (SOA) combined with Cloud Computing are realizing this standardization. In the same context, semantic Web (Rabaey et al. 2007a) and intelligent agents (Rabaey, Vandyck and Tromp, 2003) need to have a standardized platform to communicate and collaborate.

Figure 8 Concept of recurrent Service Bus shows that the information system of the orga-

nization consists of two BPEIS (1.1 and 1.2). They communicate through the (V)ESB which is virtualized in the Cloud Service Bus (CSB). BPEIS 2 and 3 are directly connected to the CSB. BPEIS 4 is composed of the three other BPEIS: BPEIS 1.2, 2, and 3. Analogous to the capability approach, BPEIS 4 without any programs has a management module.

So service buses can be recurrent (recursive-system theorem, modularity and hierarchy principle. The consequence for a systems-thinking EA is that models of the BPEIS in particular and BP in general should also be recurrent.

CONCLUSION

The world grows smaller and the environment changes quickly and continuously. An enterprise has to survive in this context. We have shown that enterprises (or any other man-made sociocultural entity) are a Complex Adaptive System (CAS). This CAS is a whole and the whole is greater than the sum of its parts. Emergent properties of the whole cannot be explained by analyzing the parts of the whole and the whole cannot be detached from its environment.

Therefore EA must take CAST – combination of CAS and Systems Thinking – into consideration. An essential element is the Cynefin Framework, which makes the organization and/or its parts aware in which possible contexts the organization and/or its parts can be: simple, complicated, complex, chaotic or disordered. We have shown that this framework not only determines in which context is, but that Cynefin dynamics can damage the enterprise if it is not aware of the shift from one context to another.

We have proposed CAST-EA (Figure 6) to solve this issue and to support an agile enterprise. The different layers have been redefined so that not only IT systems but all systems are taken into account, so a whole EA. The knowledge and information layers have been brought together into

Figure 7. CAST EA bus structure connection for agents

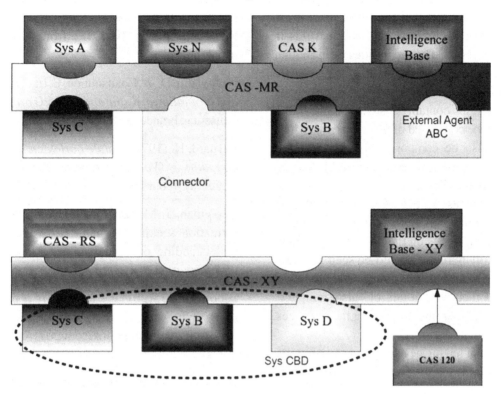

Figure 8. Concept of recurrent service bus

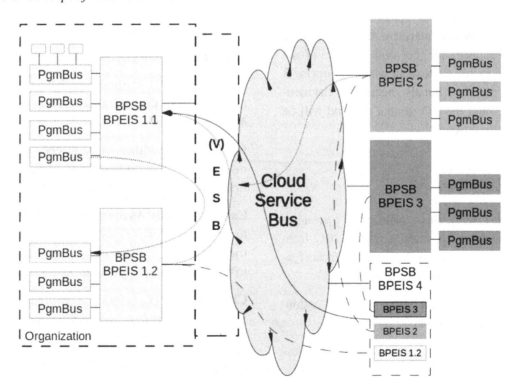

one "Knowledge and Information Management" KIM due to the fact that the Intelligence Base holds knowledge, information, data and this in all different forms. The capabilities form another layer. It represents the functions that are performed outside of the defined enterprise. The underlying layer of systems contains nested systems, thus a system can be composed of other systems, which can then also be composed of other systems. Systems are using resources and that is the last layer "Resources."

"Other Agents" have also been defined because of the possibilities of mutual outsourcing and/or collaboration. If it is on the level of capabilities then the collaboration should be seen as a new enterprise (whole). If it is connected to the layer of systems then we can talk of outsourcing, co-sourcing or insourcing. Regarding the resources, the other agents are suppliers.

The fact of having nested systems (system-of-systems) and the sociocultural form, a bus structure has been proposed to represent the interconnection of the systems (Figure 7).

CAST-EA is a concept and has to be instantiated for every enterprise separately. Copy-paste of a configuration of enterprise A onto enterprise B can be catastrophic, not only because of the different possible contexts in which enterprise B and/or its parts are, but also because of the mental models and the culture that can and will be significantly different.

REFERENCES

Ackoff, R. (1999). *Russell Ackoff: A lifetime of systems thinking*. Retrieved August 7, 2012 from http://www.pegasuscom.com/levpoints/ackoff_a-lifetime-of-systems-thinking.html

Ariely, D. (2009). *Predictably irrational*. London: Harper Collins Publishers.

Bean, S. (2011). *Rethinking enterprise architecture using systems and complexity approaches*. Retrieved August 10, 2012 from http://www.irmuk.co.uk

Bednyagin, D., & Gnansounou, E. (n.d.). *Real options valuation of fusion energy R&D programme*. Lausanne, France. *Ecole Polytechnique Fédérale*..

Bernard, H. (1976). *Totale oorlog en revolutionaire oorlog* (*Vol. I*). Brussels: Royal Military Academy. [course].

Berryman, J. M. (2007). Judgments during information seeking: A naturalistic approach to understanding of enough information. *Journal of Information Science*, 1–11.

Bloomberg, J. (2011). *Why nobody is doing enterprise architecture*. Retrieved August 11, 2012 from http://www.zapthink.com/2011/04/05/why-nobody-is-doing-enterprise-architecture/

Bowser, M., Cantle, N., & Allan, N. (2011). *Unraveling the complexity of risk*. Paper presented at Open Forum of The Actuarial Profession. London, UK.

Brach, M. (2003). *Real options in practice*. Hoboken, NJ: John Wiley & Sons.

Brooks, B. (2007). The pulley model: A descriptive model of risky decision-making. *Safety Science Monitor*, *11*(1), 1–14.

Burke, L. A., & Miller, M. K. (1999). Taking the mystery out of intuitive decision making. *The Academy of Management Executive*, *13*(4), 91–99.

Canter, J. (2000). *An agility based OODA model for the e-commerce / e-business enterprise*. Retrieved June 28, 2012 from http://www.iohai.com/iohai-resources/agility-based-ooda-model.html

Chichilnisky, G. (1998). *A radical shift in managing risks: Practical applications of complexity theory*. Retrieved from http://ssrn.com/abstract=1375437 or http://dx.doi.org/10.2139/ssrn.1375437

Cilliers, P. (2004). A framework for understanding complex systems. In Proceedings of the Workshop on Organisational Networks as Distributed Systems of Knowledge. London: World Scientific Publishing.

Cobb, B., & Charnes, J. (2007). Real options valuation. In *Proceedings of the 2007 Winter Simulation Conference,* (pp. 173-182). IEEE.

Collan, M. (2008). *A new method for real option valuation using fuzzy numbers.* Retrieved April 12, 2011 from http://ideas.repec.org/p/amr/wpaper/466.html

Collan, M., Fullér, R., & Mezei, J. (2009). A fuzzy pay-off method for real option valuation. *Journal of Applied Mathematics and Decision Sciences,* (1): 1–14. doi:10.1155/2009/238196.

Cram, F. (2011). Whānau Or & action research. Paper prepared for Te Puni Kōkiri. Wellington, New Zealand.

Dettmer, H. W. (2011). *Systems thinking and the Cynefin framework: A strategic approach to managing complex systems.* Retrieved August 1, 2012 from http://engine-for-change.com/Weblog/2012/04/link-fuel-3/

EARF. (n.d.). Retrieved July 15, 2012, from http://earf.meraka.org.za/earfhome/our-projects-1/completed-projects/2

Edwards Deming, W. (n.d.). *Wikipedia.* Retrieved August 1, 2012, from http://en.wikipedia.org/wiki/W._Edwards_Deming

Eisenhardt, K., & Sull, D. (2001, January). Strategy as simple rules. *Harvard Business Review,* 106–116. PMID:11189455.

Evers, M. (2004). *Mechanisms to support organizational learning: The integration of action learning tools into multidisciplinary design team practice.* Breukelen: University Nyenrode.

Fereira, N., Kar, J., & Trigeorgis, L. (2009, March). Option games: The key to competing in capital-intensive industries. *Harvard Business Review.*

Fichman, R. (2004). Real options and IT platform adoption: Implications for theory and practice. *Information Systems Research, 15*(2), 132–154. doi:10.1287/isre.1040.0021.

Flood, L. R. (1999). *Rethinking the fifth discipline – Learning within the unknowable.* London: Routledge.

Funston, F., & Wagner, S. (2010). *Surviving and thriving in uncertainty: Creating the risk intelligent enterprise.* Hoboken, NJ: John Wiley & Sons.

Fuzzy Pay-Off Method for Real Option Valuation. (n.d.). *Wikipedia.* Retrieved April 10, 2011, from http://en.wikipedia.org/wiki/Fuzzy_Pay-Off_Method_for_Real_Option_Valuation

Gaziulusoy, İ. (2011). *Complexity and co-evolution.* Retrieved August 10, 2012 from http://systeminnovationforsustainability.com/tag/complex-system/

Gharajedaghi, J. (2004). *Systems methodology: A holistic language of interaction and design - Seeing through chaos and understanding complexities.* Retrieved August 9, 2012 from http://www.interactdesign.com/JGsystems.htm

Gharajedaghi, J. (2011). *Systems thinking: Managing chaos and complexity – A platform for designing business architecture.* Amsterdam: Morgan Kaufmann.

Glenn, E. J. (1996). *Chaos theory: The essentials for military applications.* Newport, RI: Naval War College.

Gore, J. (1996). *Chaos, complexity, and the military.* National Defense University.

Grenadier, S. (2000). Option exercise games: The intersection of real options and game theory. *Journal of Applied Corporate Finance, 13*(2), 99–107. doi:10.1111/j.1745-6622.2000.tb00057.x.

Guida, G., & Tasso, C. (1994). *Design and development of knowledge-based systems: From life cycle to development methodology.* Chichester, UK: John Wiley & Sons.

Herzog, S. (n.d.). *Gharajedaghi.* Retrieved June 28, 2012 from http://www.aleph.at/books/gharajedaghi.html

Holden, L. M. (2005). Complex adaptive systems: Concept analysis. *Journal of Advanced Nursing, 52*(6), 651–657. doi:10.1111/j.1365-2648.2005.03638.x PMID:16313378.

Hovhannisian, K. (2001). *Exploring on the technology landscapes: Real options thinking in the context of the complexity theory.* Paper presented at the DRUID Winter Conference. Aalborg, Denmark.

Huang, C., Kao, H., & Li, H. (2007). Decision on enterprise computing solutions for an international tourism. *International Journal of Information Technology & Decision Making, 6*(4), 687–700. doi:10.1142/S0219622007002666.

Independence Partners. (2013). *Complex adaptive systems theory elements.* Retrieved January 3, 2013 from http://www.dspmatch.com/

Janssen, M., & Kuk, G. (2006). *A complex adaptive system perspective of enterprise architecture in electronic government.* Paper presented at the 39th Hawaii International Conference on System Sciences. Hawaii, HI.

Johnston, A. (2005). *Masters of order and unorder.* Retrieved August 10, 2012 from http://www.agilearchitect.org/agile/articles/order%20and%20unorder.asp

Joyce, D. (2011). *We don't need no frickin architects.* Retrieved August 6, 2012 from http://leanandkanban.wordpress.com/2011/05/18/we-dont-need-no-frickin-architects/

Korhonen, J. J. (2012). *Out-of-box requires lesser mind.* Retrieved August 9, 2012 from http://www.ebizq.net/blogs/agile_enterprise/2012/05/out-of-box-requires-lesser-mind.php

Kurtz, C. F., & Snowden, D. J. (2003, Fall). The new dynamics of strategy sense-making in a complex-complicated world. *IBM Systems Journal*, 1–23.

Lee, Y., & Lee, S. (2011). The valuation of RFID investment using fuzzy real option. *Expert Systems with Applications, 38*, 12195–12201. doi:10.1016/j.eswa.2011.03.076.

Libet, B. (2011). Do we have free will? In Sinnott-Armstrong, W., & Nadel, L. (Eds.), *Conscious Will and Responsibility* (pp. 1–10). Oxford, UK: Oxford Press.

Lowe, D., & Ng, S. (2006). *The implications of complex adaptive systems thinking for future command and control.* Paper presented at 11th International Command and Control Research and Technology Symposium. Cambridge, UK.

Matthews, A. (2012a). *Enterprise architecture & systems thinking.* Retrieved August 7, 2012 from http://www.enterprise-advocate.com/2012/07/enterprise-architecture-systems-thinking/

Matthews, A. (2012b). *Enterprise architecture & complexity theory.* Retrieved August 7, 2012 from http://www.enterprise-advocate.com/2012/07/enterprise-architecture-complexity-theory/

Mauboussin, M. (2011, September). Embracing complexity. *Harvard Business Review*, 89–92.

McHugh, P., Merli, G., & Wheeler, W. A. III. (1995). *Beyond business process reengineering: Towards the holonic enterprise.* Chichester, UK: John Wiley & Sons.

Misra, S., & Mondal, A. (2011). Identification of a company's suitability for the adoption of cloud computing and modelling its corresponding return on investment. *Mathematical and Computer Modelling, 53*, 504–521. doi:10.1016/j.mcm.2010.03.037.

Montier, J. (2010). *The little book of behavioral investing*. Hoboken, NJ: John Wiley & Sons.

Mun, J. (2006). *Real options analysis versus traditional DCF valuation in layman's terms*. Retrieved April 09, 2011, from http://www.realoptionsvaluation.com/download.html#CASESTUDIES

Osinga, F. B. (2007). *Science, strategy and war: The strategic theory of John Boyd (strategy and history)*. Abington, UK: Routledge.

Pucket, S., & Purdy, S. C. (2011). Are voluntary movements initiated preconsciously? The relationships between readiness potentials, urges, and decisions. In Sinnott-Armstrong, W., & Nadel, L. (Eds.), *Conscious Will and Responsibility* (pp. 1–10). Oxford, UK: Oxford Press.

Rabaey, M. (2011). *Game theoretic real option approach of the procurement of department of defense: Competition or collaboration*. Paper presented at the 8th Annual Acquisition Research Symposium. Monterey, CA.

Rabaey, M. (2012a). A public economics approach to enabling enterprise architecture with the government cloud in Belgium. In Saha, P. (Ed.), *Enterprise Architecture for Connected E-Government: Practices and Innovations*. Hershey, PA: IGI Global. doi:10.4018/978-1-4666-1824-4.ch020.

Rabaey, M. (2012b). Holistic investment framework for cloud computing: A management-philosophical approach based on complex adaptive systems. In Bento, A., & Aggarwal, A. (Eds.), *Cloud Computing Service and Deployment Models: Layers and Management*. Hershey, PA: IGI Global. doi:10.4018/978-1-4666-2187-9.ch005.

Rabaey, M. (2012c). A complex adaptive system thinking approach of government e-procurement in a cloud computing environment. In Ordoñez de Pablos, P. (Ed.), *E-Procurement Management for Successful Electronic Government Systems*. Hershey, PA: IGI Global. doi:10.4018/978-1-4666-2119-0.ch013.

Rabaey, M., Hoffman, G., & Vandenborre, K. (2004). *Aligning business- and resource-strategy: An interdisciplinary forum*. Paper presented at the 13th International Conference on Management Technology (IAMOT 2004). Washington, DC.

Rabaey, M., & Mercken, R. (2012). Framework of knowledge and intelligence base: From intelligence to service. In Ordoñez de Pablos, P., & Lytras, M. D. (Eds.), *Knowledge Management and Drivers of Innovation in Services Industries*. Hershey, PA: IGI Global. doi:10.4018/978-1-4666-0948-8.ch017.

Rabaey, M., & Mercken, R. (forthcoming). Complex adaptive systems thinking approach for intelligence base in support of intellectual capital management. In Ordoñez de Pablos, P. (Ed.), *Intellectual Capital Strategy Management for Knowledge-Based Organizations*. Hershey, PA: IGI Global. doi:10.4018/978-1-4666-3655-2.ch007.

Rabaey, M., Tromp, H., & Vandenborre, K. (2007). Holistic approach to align ICT capabilities with business integration. In Cunha, M., Cortes, B., & Putnik, G. (Eds.), *Adaptive Technologies and Business Integration: Social, Managerial, and Organizational Dimensions* (pp. 160–173). Hershey, PA: Idea Group Publishing.

Rabaey, M., Vandenborre, K., Vandijck, E., Timmerman, M., & Tromp, H. (2007a). Semantic web services and BPEL: Semantic service oriented architecture - Economical and philosophical issues. In Salam, A., & Stevens, J. (Eds.), *Semantic Web Technologies and eBusiness: Toward the Integrated Virtual Organization and Business Process Automation* (pp. 127–153). Hershey, PA: Idea Group Publishing. doi:10.4018/978-1-59904-192-6.ch005.

Rabaey, M., Vandijck, E., & Tromp, H. (2003). Business intelligent agents for enterprise application integration. In *Proceedings of the 16th International Conference on Software & Systems Engineering and their Applications.* CMSL/CNAM.

Romme, A., Georges, L., & van Witteloostuijn, A. (1999). Circular organizing and triple loop learning. *Journal of Organizational Change Management, 12*(5), 439–453. doi:10.1108/09534819910289110.

Ross, J. (2003). *Creating a strategic IT architecture competency: Learning in stages.* Cambridge, MA: MIT Sloan School of Management. doi:10.2139/ssrn.416180.

Sanchez, R., & Heene, A. (2000). A competence perspective on strategic learning and knowledge management. In Rob, C., & Sam, I. (Eds.), *Strategic Learning in a Knowledge Economy.* Boston: Butterworth Heinemann. doi:10.1016/B978-0-7506-7223-8.50004-6.

Senge, P. M. (2006). *The fifth discipline.* London: Random House.

Shattuck, L., & Miller, N. (2006). Naturalistic decision making in complex systems: A dynamic model of situated cognition combining technological and human agents. *Organizational Behavior, 27*(7), 989–1009.

Shen, C. (2009). A Bayesian networks approach to modeling financial risks of e-logistics investments. *International Journal of Information Technology & Decision Making, 8*(4), 711–726. doi:10.1142/S0219622009003594.

Smit, H., & Trigeorgis, L. (2009). Valuing infrastructure investment: An option game approach. *California Management Review, 51*(2), 79–100. doi:10.2307/41166481.

Snowden, D., & Boone, M. (2007, November). A leader's framework for decision making: Wise executives tailor their approach to fit the complexity of the circumstances they face. *Harvard Business Review,* 68–76. PMID:18159787.

Sterman, J. D. (2010). *Business dynamics – Systems thinking and modeling for a complex world.* Tata McGraw-Hill.

Systems-thinking. (n.d.). *Knowledge management—Emerging perspectives.* Retrieved August 7, 2012 from http://www.systems-thinking.org/kmgmt/kmgmt.htm/

Systems-wiki. (n.d.). *Viable systems model.* Retrieved January 4, 2013 from http://www.systemswiki.org

Tao, C., Jinlong, Z., Benhai, Y., & Shan, L. (2007). *A fuzzy group decision approach to real option valuation.* Wuhan, China: Huazhong University of Science and Technology. doi:10.1007/978-3-540-72530-5_12.

TOGAF. (n.d.). *TOGAF 9.1.* Retrieved August 10, 2012 from http://pubs.opengroup.org/architecture/togaf9-doc/arch/

Tolga, A., & Kahraman, C. (2008). Fuzzy multiattribute evaluation of R&D projects using a real options valuation model. *International Journal of Intelligent Systems, 23,* 1153–1176. doi:10.1002/int.20312.

Trigeorgis, L. (2002). *Real options and investment under uncertainty: What do we know?* Brussels, Belgium: Nationale Bank van België. doi:10.2139/ssrn.1692691.

von Helfenstein, S. (2009). *Real options 'in' economic systems and the demise of modern portfolio theory.* Paper presented at the 13th Annual International Real Options Conference. Braga, Portugal.

Wang, S., & Lee, C. (2010). A fuzzy real option valuation approach to capital budgeting under uncertainty environment. *International Journal of Information Technology & Decision Making, 9*(5), 695–713. doi:10.1142/S0219622010004056.

Wegmann, A. (2003). Alain Wegmann: On the systemic enterprise architecture methodology (seam). *ICEIS Conference Proceedings, 3,* 483-490.

Whitehouse. (1996). *Management of federal information resources.* Retrieved August 9, 2012 from http://www.whitehouse.gov/omb/circulars_a130

KEY TERMS AND DEFINITIONS

Cloud Computing: Is the delivery of computing as a service rather than a product, whereby shared resources, software, and information are provided to computers and other devices as a utility (like the electricity grid) over a network (typically the Internet).

Complex Adaptive System (CAS): Is a collection of individual agents with freedom to act in ways that are not always totally predictable, and whose actions are interconnected so that one agent's actions changes the context for other agents.

Cynefin: Is a sense-making framework which allows people and organizations to better understand the contexts within which they are operating: simple, complicated, complex, chaotic and disorder.

Financial Options: Are the right but not the obligation to execute an action (sell or buy).

Intelligence: Is the product resulting from the collection, evaluation, analysis, integration, and interpretation of all available information that concerns one or more aspects of the other actors and their actions in the environment, and that is immediately or potentially significant to the planning and operations of an organization.

Intelligence Base: Is a system to collect and transform information into intelligence to be disseminated towards the clients and to update the knowledge in an organization.

Knowledge Base: Is a software system capable of supporting the explicit representation of knowledge in some specific competence domain and of exploiting it through appropriate reasoning mechanisms in order to provide high-level problem-solving performance.

Mental Models: Are conceptual structures in the mind that drive a cognitive process of understanding. The discipline of mental models aims to train people to appreciate that mental models do indeed occupy their minds and shape their actions.

OODA (Observe, Orient, Decide, Act): Is an organic decision-making process and is at the same time a model of organizational learning and adapting in which the element "Orient" plays an important role in the organizational adaptability.

Systems Thinking (ST): Is a way of looking at the world that focuses on the whole and not on the parts. It helps dealing with complex issues, making them simpler and transparent, with the purposes of enabling a better understanding of what is happening, of making visible possible places for taking actions that improve the situation, and of serving as a framework for designing the best vehicles for implementation.

Chapter 4
A Theory for Enterprise Coherence Governance

Roel Wagter
Radboud University Nijmegen, The Netherlands

Henderik A. Proper
Radboud University Nijmegen, The Netherlands

Dirk Witte
Logica, The Netherlands

ABSTRACT

In this chapter, the authors pose a theory for the governance of enterprise coherence. The proposed theory consists of three key ingredients: an Enterprise Coherence-governance Assessment (ECA), an Enterprise Coherence Framework (ECF), and an Enterprise Coherence Governance (ECG) approach. The ECA provides an explicit indication of the degree at which an organisation governs its coherence, while also providing a base to achieve a shared understanding of the level of coherence, and actions needed to improve it. The ECF is a practice-based framework that enables enterprises to make the coherence between key aspects, such as business, finance, culture, IT, etc. explicit. The ECG approach offers the instruments to guard/improve the level of coherence in enterprises during transformations. An important trigger to develop this new theory was the observation that many transformation projects fail. These failures even included projects that used an explicit enterprise architecture to steer the transformation. The theory was developed as part of the GEA (General Enterprise Architecting) research programme, involving twenty client organizations. Based on a survey of the possible causes for the project failures, the requirements for the research programme are identified. In developing the theory on enterprise coherence, the following hypothesis is used as a starting point: the overall performance of an enterprise is positively influenced by a strong coherence among the key aspects of the enterprise, including business processes, organizational culture, product portfolio, human resources, information systems, IT support, etc. The research programme uses a combination of design science-based iterations and case study-based research to develop and iterate the theory for enterprise coherence governance. In this chapter, the authors also discuss one of the conducted (real world) case studies, showing the application of the enterprise coherence theory.

DOI: 10.4018/978-1-4666-4518-9.ch004

1. INTRODUCTION

Developments in the last two decades, such as the globalisation of trade, the fusion of business and IT, the introduction of new technologies, the emergence of novel business models, etc., pose many challenges to modern day enterprises (Op't Land, Proper, Waage, Cloo & Steghuis, 2008). More recently, the economic crises, the growing pains of the Eurozone, also drive companies to find new competitive advantages. As a result, enterprises need to cope with a rapidly changing environment. This means that enterprises need the ability to transform themselves (at least) as quickly as their environment does. Such enterprise transformations may range from changes in value propositions and business processes, via changes to the information systems used to support the business processes, to changes of the underlying IT infrastructures. They may be the result of a 'premeditated' top-down (strategy driven) desire to change, but they can also be the outcome of numerous 'spontaneous' bottom-up changes as a result of locally needed changes. Finally, the required/desired transformations will typically touch upon several additional aspects of the enterprise, such as human resourcing, finance, organisational structures, reporting structures, etc.

To make large enterprise transformations feasible and manageable, they are typically managed as a portfolio of transformation programmes, where these programmes are split further into projects. Even more, the portfolio of programmes and projects that make up an enterprise transformation need to be mutually coordinated, as well as being aligned with the enterprise's strategy. Therefore, a coordination mechanism is needed that connects the strategic considerations at the strategy level to the execution of the different programmes and projects involved in the transformation as a whole. This coordination generally also requires a further elaboration of the enterprise's strategy, since these tend to be too unspecific to indeed steer the programmes and projects within

the transformation (Op't Land, Proper, Waage, Cloo & Steghuis, 2008). In addition, the needed coordination mechanism must allow the coherence between the different aspects of an enterprise to be guarded across the programmes and projects transforming the enterprise (Op't Land, Proper, Waage, Cloo & Steghuis, 2008; Wagter, Berg van den, Luijpers & Steenbergen van, 2005).

Already in 1957, Drucker argued for an integral and complete approach as a pre-requisite to success. Traditionally, project management and programme management are put forward as being responsible for these coordination tasks (The Stationary Office, 2009; The Project Management Institute, 2001). However, these approaches focus primarily on the management of typical project parameters such as budgets, resource use, deadlines, etc. When indeed only considering the typical project parameters, one runs the risk of conducting only local and or partial improvements at the level of specific projects. For example, when making design decisions that have an impact which transcend a specific project, projects are likely to aim for solutions that provide the best cost/benefits trade-off within the scope of that specific project, while not looking at the overall picture. Regretfully, however, in practice such local optimisations do not just remain a potential risk. The risk actually materializes, and consequently damages the overall quality of the result of the transformation (Op't Land, Proper, Waage, Cloo & Steghuis, 2008). This type of risk generally occurs when interests regarding general infrastructural elements of an enterprise collide with local short-term needs. This especially endangers the needed coherence and alignment between different aspects within an enterprise (such as human resources, services, customers, processes, marketing, finance, physical infrastructures, IT, etc.). As a result, more often than not, enterprises fail to actually realise the desired transformation even though it might be the case that all projects are finished on time and within budget. In addition, Bower (2000, p. 83-95) acknowledges the presence of multiple levels of management, such as directing the company, directing management and directing staff and labor. He stresses the need to treat these different management levels in coherence to avoid a partial but rigorous theory in solving business issues.

This raises a key question: How can a company escape from partial improvements on a local scale, and subsequent loss of business value? In finding an answer to this question, we have to expand our (project) managerial dimensions with the governance of enterprise coherence. To be able to do this, we have to make the enterprise coherence explicit and apt to intervene on all levels of decision making, keeping track of the causal effects on these levels as well as between them. Architecture is a school of thought pre-eminently suitable for this purpose.

Slot (2010) has shown that a correlation exists between the performance of IT projects and the use of architecture to steer/coordinate these projects; i.e. projects being implemented under architecture. IT projects implemented under architecture result in 19% less budget over-runs. In principle, one might expect that such a positive effect would be discernable when working under architecture would be applied to enterprise transformations as a whole as well. Regretfully, however, in various transformation assignments in practice, we have been confronted with the situation that transformation projects fail due to budget overruns, or a failure to meet objectives and expectations (Wagter, Proper & Witte, 2011, pp. 28-52). Our informal experiences and observations are also supported by the (Dutch) General Court of Auditors (De Algemene Rekenkamer, 2008), who has produced a report on the cause of failures in ICT projects. In Op't Land et al. (2008), the authors also provide a summary of possible causes for failures of strategic initiatives, as well as the need to develop a solution for them: "The road from strategy formulation to strategy execution, including the use of programmatic steering, is certainly not an easy one to travel. Research

shows that less than 60% of the strategic objectives in organisations are reached (Smit, 2007). When considering the possible failures in strategy execution ... an instrument is needed to support this process." In (Hoogervorst, 2004, pp. 213-233; Hoogervorst, 2009), Hoogervorst also argues in favour of using enterprise architecture as a means to govern coherence in enterprises.

Our own experiences[1], and the above discussed general insights, seem to indicate that achieving and maintaining enterprise coherence between different aspects of an organisation, by applying an architectural line of thinking, is a crucial factor with regard to change processes and the achievement of strategic objectives. Therefore the governance of enterprise coherence deserves a closer study of causes and potential solutions in the field of enterprise transformation.

The general concept of coherence is described in the MacMillan English dictionary (2010) as: "in which all the different parts fit together in a sensible or pleasing way," while the Van Dale (2010) dictionary describes coherence as: "the extent in which several aspects are connected." In line with these definitions, we define enterprise coherence as follows (Wagter, Proper & Witte, 2012a):

Enterprise coherence is the extent to which all relevant aspects of an enterprise are connected, necessary to let the enterprise meet its desired results.

What is to be regarded as relevant aspects, as referred to in the above definition, is organization dependent. Even more, the clarity (and resolve) with which an organization has identified/prioritized these aspects is one of the parameters determining their ability/maturity to govern enterprise coherence. In (Wagter, Proper & Witte, 2011, pp. 28-52) we have discussed the concept of the (organization specific) coherence dashboard, which enables organizations to precisely express the relevant aspects that need to be connected.

Since achieving, and/or maintaining enterprise coherence seems to be an important capability in the realm of enterprise performance (there is a potential positive correlation with the performance) there is a reason to govern enterprise coherence (Wagter, Proper & Witte, 2011, pp. 28-52). This insight triggered the multi-client General Enterprise Architecting (GEA) research programme (Wagter, Nijkamp & Proper, 2007)[2]. The aim of this programme was to make enterprise coherence explicit and to find ways to govern it. The results of the first iterations of this research programme have been reported in (Wagter, 2009)[3]. Important triggers for the GEA research programme were:

- Many enterprise transformation efforts fail.
- Failure to adopt a holistic approach to address key business issues, frequently leading to a unilateral approach from an IT oriented angle.
- Existing architecture methods do not meet their promises because:
  ○ They are set up from an IT perspective only.
  ○ They hardly address the strategic level of the organization.
  ○ They are set up in terms of the Business/IT gap.
  ○ Their underlying IT architectures applied on the enterprise-wide level are unjustly called Enterprise Architectures.

A fundamental first step in the GEA programme was the development of an Enterprise Coherence-governance Assessment (ECA) to attain a clearer understanding of the challenges to enterprise coherence and its associated governance of coherence (Wagter, Proper & Witte, 2011 p. 28-52), as well as the impact of enterprise coherence governance on organizational performance. This assessment has shown that more then 85% of the organisations involved in the first ECA studies lack enterprise coherence governance. This demonstrated the need for further research into enterprise coherence governance and in particular as next step to develop a theory for this issue.

The remainder of this chapter is structured as follows. Section 2 provides a discussion on the research context of this chapter, in terms of the driving research questions and research objectives, the research methodology we used as well as the organisation and planning of the actual research programme. Section 3 provides an extended insight in the requirements for Enterprise Coherence Governnance and the foundation for the further development of a theory for it. Section 4, and 5 describes the development and content of the enterprise coherence governance theory and the relationship with the requirements of section 3. Before concluding, section 6 discuses a case study, which shows the application of this new theory in practice and the results that have been achieved so-far.

2. RESEARCH CONTEXT

The development of the ECA (Enterprise Coherence-governance Assessment) was the first step in the more comprehensive, and still ongoing, GEA research programme. In this section we provide more background to this research programme, as well as the research method used in developing the ECA.

2.1. Focus of the Research Programme

The GEA research programme (Wagter, Nijkamp & Proper, 2007) is based on the aforementioned triggers. The requirements of the programme, and its driving hypothesis, originate from four key research questions:

1. What are the core factors that influence/define enterprise coherence?
2. What is (in practice) the impact of enterprise coherence on the performance of an enterprise?
3. How can enterprise coherence be expressed explicitly?
4. How can enterprise coherence be governed?

More specifically, the research objectives of the GEA programme are:

1. Definition of the core indicators and factors that influence/define enterprise coherence.
2. Identification of the impact of enterprise coherence on the organisational performance.
3. An instrument to assess an enterprise's level of coherence.
4. Instruments to guard/improve the level of coherence in enterprises during transformations.

The Enterprise Coherence-governance Assessment (ECA) was developed to gain initial insight into the first two questions. On the one hand, the answer to these questions provide insight into the need to carry out further research into the governance of enterprise coherence, while on the other hand providing a first refined definition of enterprise coherence and its practical impact on organisational performance.

At its start, the partners in the GEA programme formulated the criterion that if more than 50% of the organisations involved in the first ECA studies lack enterprise coherence governance, it was safe to assume that the lack of enterprise coherence governance is indeed a relevant issue that needs further elaboration. The first ECA study involved seven large Dutch organisations (members of the GEA programme). At the start of the GEA programme, the intention was to execute the ECA assessment (for each of the participating organisations) in three stages:

1. A first assessment at the start of the programme, providing a baseline measure.
2. A second assessment once a shared understanding of enterprise coherence was reached. By comparing the results to the baseline, the effect of having a shared awareness of the forces that influence coherence should be measurable.
3. A final assessment once proper/full governance of enterprise coherence was put in place in a participating organization. By comparing these final assessment results to the earlier ones, the additional effect of coherence governance could be made explicit.

Nevertheless, soon after the start of the programme, it became apparant that doing these three assessments was not feasible. In the time needed for such longitudinal assessments, the composition of the involved organisations, as well as the people involved, would change so much that the results would no longer be comparable. We have therefore modified this idea to only implement the first assessment in the form of the ECA assessment instrument, while using a case based research methodology (Yin, 2009) to further evolve the instrument. See Figures 1, 2, and 3.

The ECA assessment that was carried out at the start of the GEA programme indeed showed that more then 85% of the involved organisations lack enterprise coherence governance (Wagter, Proper & Witte, 2011 p. 28-52). These results convinced the participants of the GEA programme that there was enough evidence that argued for the development of effective instruments to govern enterprise coherence. The resulting set of instruments, based on additional multiple case studies (Wagter, Proper & Witte, 2012b), is called GEA, General Enterprise Architecting, (Wagter, 2009).

In developing the theory, we followed the route as pictured in Figure 3. Based on the triggers and results of the aforementioned ECA we identified

Figure 1. Preliminary research approach for the development of the ECA, based on Yin (2009)

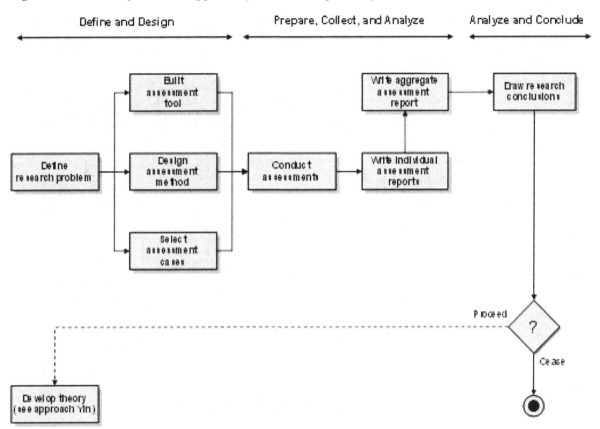

the research questions, and associated objectives, of the GEA research programme. More specifically, in order to meet these research questions, the research programme:

1. Gathered the requirements on enterprise coherence governance,
2. Developed a theorical model, based on these requirements, to make enterprise coherence explicit and governable.

2.2. Organisation of the GEA Research Programme

The GEA programme was organized in terms of four groups:

- A core team consisting of 6 to 8 people.
- A, co-financing, customer reference group of 20 major organizations.
- An expert review team of 30 lead architects.
- A steering committee composed of 7 leading representatives from science and business.

The actual involvement (and composition) of these groups depended on the specific phase of the GEA programme. The core team and the customer reference group performed the actual development activities. The members of the expert review team were charged with the task to attempt to falsify everything the core team and the customer reference group developed. The development strategy was also assessed regurlarly by the steering committee.

Figure 2. Multiple case study research approach, adopted from Yin (2009)

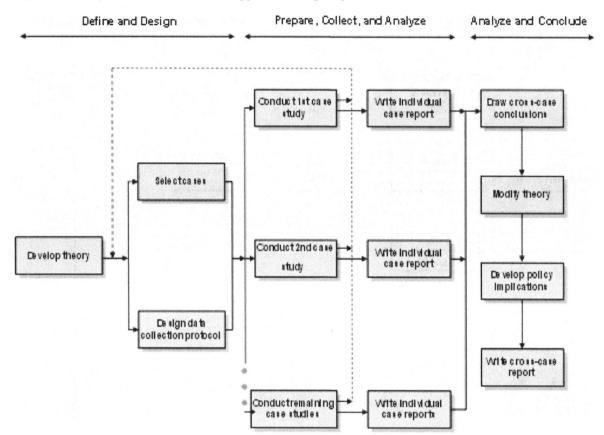

2.2.1. The Development Phases

In 2006, the GEA programme started with the development of the EA-vision, as well as the scientific foundation of GEA. In the ensuing years 2007 and 2008, the EA vision was transformed into an EA governance tool. In 2009, the resulting GEA method was published. Since the start of 2007, the GEA method has been applied in several organizations. Evaluations of these applications resulted in feedback on the GEA method fuelling further improvemets of the method. The GEA method is now also declared to be an open standard. See Figure 4.

2.2.2. Design of the Data Collection Protocol

As mentioned above, the GEA programme used the case-study based research approach from Yin (2009) to improve the GEA method based on input from the different situations in which it was applied. In line with this methodology, we distinguish five levels of questions:

1. Questions to specific interviewees.
2. Questions at the level of an individual case (these are the questions in the case study protocol to be answered by the investigator

Figure 3. Detailed approach of the theory of enterprise coherence governance (ECG)

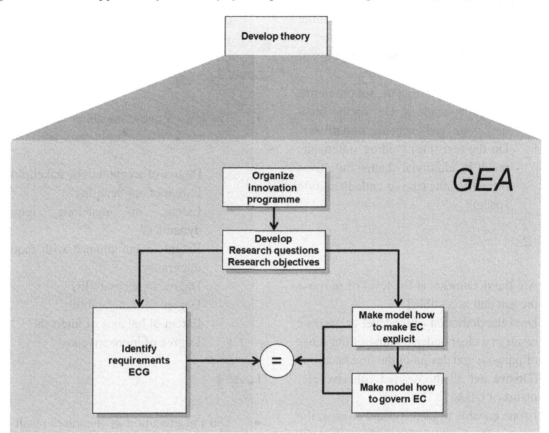

Figure 4. Development phases of the research programme GEA

Development phases					
EA vision	EA governance tool		marketing	application / evolution	
2006	2007	2008	2009	2007	2012

during a single case, even when the single case is part of a larger, multiple-case study).

3. Questions focused on finding patterns across multiple cases.
4. Questions at the level of the entire research effort (for example, calling on information beyond the case study evidence and including literature or published data that may have been reviewed).
5. Normative questions about policy recommendations and conclusions, going beyond the narrow scope of the study.

Below we give, for each level, a few examples of questions as set up by GEA's core team

Level 1

- At the time of the validation process of the ECF:
  - Are the guiding statements valid and up to date?
  - Do the representatives of the perspectives agree with the identified

perspectives, the identified core concepts within it and the related guiding statements?

- At the time of the ECG analysis process of a major business issue:
  - Do the causes, triggers, subproblems, risks, implications, etc. of the business issue lead to change initiatives?
  - Do the (existing) guiding statements result in additional change initiatives or restrictions (the so called solution space)?

Level 2

- Are the documents at the level of purpose present and accessible?
- Does the definition of the level or purpose result in a clear understanding of the sense of purpose and design of the organization? (Do we get all the desired cohesive elements of GEA?)
- Is one capable to identify, and engage, the right representatives for each of the perspectives? This engagement should cover both the identification and validation of the cohesive GEA elements (ECF), and the GEA analysis processes to solve the business issue.
- Are the representatives of the perspectives able to validate the ECF?
- Are the representatives of the perspectives, using the validated ECF, able to execute the analysis processes to solve major business issues?
- Does the development of the ECF lead to increase coherence?
- Does the use of GEA lead to an integral solution that contributes to the coherence of the organization?
- Is the organisation able to, independently, specify a business issue that can serve as input to a GEA based analys?
- Do the owners of the business issue succeed in specifying the business issue in

such a way the representatives of the prospects can perform the complete GEA analysis and develop an integral solution?

Level 3

- The level 3 questions about the pattern of findings across multiple cases are:

  - Degree of acceptance by stakeholders?
  - Extent of applicability?
  - Extent of matching required dynamics?
  - Extent of compliance with required integrality?
  - Degree of accessibility?
  - Degree of transferability?
  - Extent of balance of interests?
  - Degree of innovativeness?

Level 4

- Did the execution of the cases result into detectable performance improvements?
- Does the literature support the answers to the above findings?

Level 5

- What recommendations can be made towards the further development and expansion of the area of enterprise coherence?

For the case as discussed in this chapter, only the questions of level 1 and 2 are relevant.

3. REQUIREMENTS ON ENTERPRISE COHERENCE GOVERNANCE

As argued in (Op't Land, Proper, Waage, Cloo & Steghuis, 2008; Wagter, 2009), architecture offers a means for management to obtain insight in the organizational structure, as well as to make decisions about the direction of enterprise transformations. As such, it should act as a means to steer enterprise transformations, while in particular enabling senior management to govern the enterprise's coherence. We regard enterprise architecture as the appropriate means to make enterprise coherence explicit, as well as controllable/manageable, or at least influenceable.

3.1. General Requirements on GEA

Effective governance of enterprise coherence requires an active involvement of senior management. This, however, implies two important requirements:

1. **Strategy Driven:** It is necessary to take the concerns, and associated strategic dialogues, of senior management as a starting point. In other words, the way in which architecture is integrated into the strategic dialogue should take the concerns, language, and style of communication of senior management as a starting point. When not doing so, it will be difficult to really involve senior management. Even more, the strategic dialogues provide the starting point for steering enterprise transformations and to guard coherence.

2. **Respecting Social Forces:** The social forces, be they of political, informal, or cultural nature, within an enterprise should be a leading element in governing enterprise coherence. As discussed in the introduction, an important reason for using architecture to steer and coordinate enterprise transformations is the fact that those design decisions which, in principle, transcend the interests of a specific project can be guarded/enforced that way. Doing so, however, also requires a strong commitment from senior management to these design decisions. Local business stakeholders, such as business unit managers, who have a direct interest in the outcome of a project, may want to lead projects in a different direction (more favorable to

their own local/short-term interests) than would be desirable from an enterprise-wide perspective. Such divergent forces are also likely to lead to erosion of the desired enterprise coherence. This explains the need to reduce the space for own interpretation on lower management levels by substantiating the decisions, made on strategic level, with unambiguous arguments harmonizing all concerns at stake.

We argue that existing approaches and frameworks, such as, Zachman (Sowa & Zachman, 1992), DYA (Wagter, Berg van den, Luijpers & Steenbergen van, 2005), Abcouwer (Abcouwer, Maes & Truijens, 1997), Henderson & Venkatraman (1993), TOGAF (The Open Group, 2009), IAF (Van't Wout, Waage, Hartman, Stahlecker & Hofman, 2010), ArchiMate (Lankhorst et al., 2005); (Iacob, Jonkers, Lankhorst & Proper, 2009), take an 'engineering oriented' style of communicating with senior management and stakeholders in general. The architecture frameworks underlying each of these approaches are very much driven by 'engineering principles', and as such correspond to a Blue-print style of thinking about change (De Caluwé & Vermaak, 2003).

The above requirements, however, suggest the use of another style of thinking in terms of stakeholder interests, formal and informal power structures within enterprises, as well as the associated processes of creating win-win situations and forming coalitions. In terms of De Caluwé (De Caluwé & Vermaak, 2003), this is more the Yellow-print style of thinking about change. In the GEA programme, this line of thinking was taken as a starting point, by taking the perspective that the actual social forces and associated strategic dialogues within an enterprise should be taken as a starting point, rather than the frameworks of existing architecture approaches suggesting the full makeability of an organization.

In future research, we intent to position governing coherence in relation to the Green, Red and White 'colors' of De Caluwé as well. This does not imply that the existing Blue-print style frameworks and approaches are not useful. On the contrary, the engineering perspective is much needed. At the same time, it needs to be embedded in a Yellow-print oriented process. Architecture models produced from an engineering perspective potentially provide thorough underpinning of the views, sketches and models used in the strategic dialogues with senior management. However, rather than structuring the models and views in terms of 'information architecture', 'application architecture' and 'infrastructure', they would have to be structured based on those domains that are meaningful within the strategic and political dialogue in an enterprise. For example, in terms of 'human resourcing', 'clients', 'regulators', 'culture', 'intellectual property', 'suppliers', etc. Needless to say that this is also highly organisation specific.

This leads to the situation as suggested in Figure 5, where we find on the left hand side the Blue-print style of thinking and associated frameworks, and on the right hand side the Yellow-print oriented approach. Note the (tentative) position of the Zachman framework. More so than frameworks such as IAF, ArchiMate or TOGAF's content framework, the Zachman framework clearly suggests to tune the models and views to the interests/concerns of the stakeholders,

and even suggests a classification of stakeholders. In our view, however, it still does so from a Blue-print thinking perspective and certainly does not take the stakeholder interests, formal and informal power structures in an organisation into account.

The initial application of the Enterprise Coherence-governance Assessment among the GEA members provided a more specific list of requirements regarding enterprise coherence. Combined with the generic requirements as discussed above, this resulted in the list of requirements as shown in Table 1; also referred to as EA success factors (Wagter, Proper & Witte, 2012a).

As a next step, sources from relevant adjacent domains were studied, with the aim to identify additional requirements to strengthen the development of GEA. The adjacent domains were selected based on the daily experience of the GEA members, resulting in three key domains: management control, cybernetics and change management.

3.2. Management Control

One of the leading theories in the field of management control is the work of Simons' "*Levers of Control*" (Simons, 1995). Simons identifies the following levers of control:

Figure 5. Bridging blue-print thinking to yellow-print thinking

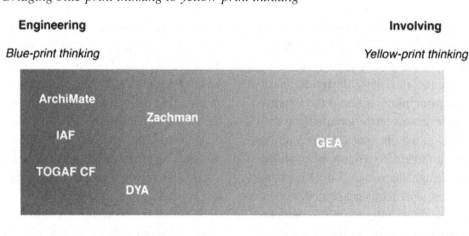

Table 1. EA requirements for the GEA programme

GEA Research Programme	
EA Success Factor	**EA Requirement**
Strategy driven	1. It is necessary to take the concerns, and associated strategic dialogues, of senior management as a starting point.
Social forces	2. Forces, be they of political, informal, or cultural nature, within an enterprise should be a leading element in governing enterprise coherence.
E.A. Vision	3. One must have an EA vision in order to be able to establish EA as a business value driver and make explicit how coherence contributes to both the image and opinion formation phases of the decision-making process and must closely resemble and simulate the way of thinking. One pre-requisite is that the top of the organisation holds this EA vision.
Commitment	4. The added value of EA as a governance tool should be recognized and promoted by all parties concerned. Also the added value of EA compared with other control tools that are in use.
Organisation	5. To establish the EA function, an integral approach to EA vision development, EA processes, EA products, EA people and EA resources needed for EA, is necessary.
Customization	6. EA is a flexible concept, which means that the number and character of organisational angles to govern the enterprise and their associated relationships depend on the situation.
Customer orientation	7. The EA processes and products should support the control processes of the enterprise in a tailor made way, by supplying the necessary results supporting these control processes.
Scope	8. EA moves at a strategic level and gives direction in decision-making on tactical and operational levels by means of lines of policy and must be done in an independent way to include all angles at stake in decision-making processes.
Product distinction	9. From the point of accessibility and understanding it is necessary to distinguish between EA management products and EA specialist products. This means that it is possible to communicate with the right target groups and with the right EA products.
Resource allocation	10. Management must provide the EA function with people with the necessary competencies, time, budget and other resources for EA to realize the added value of EA. In addition to provide EA function with people and other resources, should sufficient authority be given to the EA function so the EA function can implement governance.
Participation	11. Enterprise architects must participate in the organisation's governance processes and must have direct access to managers on a peer-to-peer basis.
Direction	12. The EA governance products must provide direction to change programmes and the existing organisation.
Completeness	13. A complete, and coherent, set of organisational perspectives must be brought together for/by the decision makers.
Permanence	14. EA must be designated as a permanent process whereby coherence is continuously adjusted to the dynamics of the internal and external environment.
Event driven	15. EA must be applied as a governance instrument at the moment major business issues arise in order to establish integral solutions and approaches on time.

1. Diagnostic control systems used to monitor and adjust operating performance.
2. Belief systems that communicate core values such as mission statements, credos and vision statements.
3. Boundary systems that define the limits of freedom, such as codes of conduct and statements of ethics.
4. Interactive control systems that provide strategic feedback and vehicles to update and redirect strategy such as competitive analysis and market reports.

These levers of control led us to the following insights. To give direction on a strategic level we have to distinguish between a 'sustainable' purpose and a 'changeable' shape of an organisation. The purpose is formulated on the level of purpose and the shape is described on the design level. Belief systems typically contribute to the level of purpose. Inspired by these levers of control we derived the following requirements for the development of GEA.

3.3. Cybernetics

The second theoretical foundation concerns the cybernetic perspective, where an organisation is seen as a controllable open system (De Leeuw, 1982). The control paradigm, as introduced in e.g. (De Leeuw, 1982), identifies a set of conditions for effective control. Compliance with these conditions also implies a promise, namely to achieve an effective control situation. These conditions are (De Leeuw, 1982):

1. The controlling system must have a goal to guide it in governing the controlled system.
2. The controlling system must have a model of the controlled system.
3. The controlling system must have information about the controlled system, namely the state of the specified system parameters and subsequent acting environment variables.
4. The controlling system must have sufficient control variety.
5. The controlling system must have sufficient information processing capacity to transform information (3), using a model (2), taking into account the objectives (1) into effective control measures (4).

Inspired by these conditions for effective control we derived the requirements for the development of GEA as listed in Table 3.

3.4. Change Management

A third theoretical foundation for GEA is based on the notion that organisations are a social technical combination of humans and supporting technology. Here we refer to the work of Julia Balogun and Veronica Hope Hailey: "Exploring Strategic Change" (Balogun & Hope Hailey, 2004). The basic idea is that every choice made in a change process should be based on the context and the purpose of the change process. A study conducted in 2004 by Deloitte & Touche "What is the best change approach" (Reitsma, Jansen, Werf van der & Steenhoven van den, 2004) has enhanced this basic idea with the statement that there is a link between the choice of approach and purpose of the change. Since this study concerns successful change processes (in various sectors), the conclusion has been drawn that it is sensible regarding change processes to consider on which organizational aspects the change is essentially focussed and in line with this to choose an appropriate approach.

Inspired by these insights we derived additional requirements for the development of GEA as listed in Table 4.

At the end of this exploration, we were able to establish the basic philosophy of GEA. In this philosophy, the following hypothesis was used as a starting point:

The overall performance of an enterprise is positively influenced by a strong coherence among the key aspects of the enterprise, including business processes, organizational culture, product portfolio, human resources, information systems, IT support, etc.

When indeed taking this hypothesis as a starting point, it is natural to accept that coherence is an important issue. More importantly, an issue that senior management of an enterprise would wants to influence and govern. To govern coherence one needs the levers to adjust the coherence and to be able to do this one has to make coherence explicit. Taking our definition of coherence into account and the fact that organisations are living organisms delivers the insight that coherence has a fluid character, which implies the governance should be carried out permanently. These insights triggered us to pose the question "by means of which concepts, and when, is the coherence of the enterprise improved or decreased?." Coherence will especially be influenced at the moment an organisation formulates answers on major business issues. So coherence governance must be part of, and contribute to, these processes of formulating answers. Using coherence governance in these processes leads to integral solutions and approaches and via this a permanently improvement of the organisational coherence.

These aggregated requirements formed the starting point to develop a new approach to govern enterprise coherence. The first step is to develop a theory for enterprise coherence governance that answers our research questions and meets these requirements.

4. THE ENTERPRISE COHERENCE FRAMEWORK

The Enterprise Coherence Framework (ECF) (Wagter, Proper & Witte, 2012a) defines a series of cohesive elements and cohesive relationships, which together define the playing field for an enterprise's coherence. For a more comprehensive description of the ECF we refer to our earlier work as reported in (Wagter, Proper & Witte, 2012a). By making the definition of these elements explicit in a specific enterprise, a coherence dashboard results in terms of which one can gain insight in the 'state of coherence' while also being able to assess the impact of potential/ongoing transformations. This then enables a deliberate governance of enterprise coherence during/driving transformations.

The ECF is defined in terms of two levels and their connections: the level of purpose and the level of design. At the level of purpose, the cohesive elements that have been identified, correspond to the commonly known concepts from strategy formulation (Senge, 1990; Kaplan, Norton & Barrows, 2008; Thenmozi, 2012; Collins & Porras,

1996; Chandler, 1969; Ahaus, 1998): *Mission, Vision, Core Values, Goals* and *Strategy*. To bring these cohesive elements to life, a few examples are provided in Table 5.

The design level complements the level of purpose, by zooming in to more design oriented concepts. The cohesive elements at the design level are:

- **Perspective:** An angle from which one wishes to govern/steer/influence enterprise transformations. The set of perspectives used in a specific enterprise depend very much on its formal and informal power structures; both internally and externally. Typical examples include culture, customer, products/services, business processes, information provision, finance, value chain, corporate governance, etc.
- **Core Concept:** A concept, within a perspective, that plays a key role in governing the organization from that perspective. Examples of core concepts within the perspective Finance are, for instance, 'Financing' and 'Budgeting'.
- **Guiding Statement:** An internally agreed and published statement, which directs desirable behaviour. They only have to express a desire and/or give direction. Guiding statements may therefore cover policy statements, (normative) principles (Greefhorst & Proper, 2011) and objectives.
- **Core Model:** A high level view of a perspective, based on, and in line with, the guiding statements of the corresponding perspective.
- **Relevant Relationship:** A description of the connection between two guiding statements of different perspectives.

The presence of a well documented enterprise mission, vision, core values, goals and strategy are preconditions to be able to determine the content of the cohesive elements on the design level of the organization and they are the essential resources for this determination. See Figure 6.

In a workshop, the core team of the research program GEA assessed the extend to which the identification (in a specific enterprise) of the five cohesive elements of the design level, would already meet the requirements of the programme. It was established that these cohesive elements contribute to, and substantiate, requirements 1, 2, 8, and 13 of Table 1, requirements 1, 2, 3, and 4 of Table 2, requirements 1, 3, and 4 of Table 3 and requirements 1, 2, and 6 of Table 4.

With the cohesive elements at the design level in place, we now have an integrated framework of cohesive elements that shape an organisation on both the level of purpose and the design level. Later in this chapter we will demonstrate how we utilise this framework as a steering mechanism in order to formulate answers to major business issues and how this way of working strengthens the enterprise coherence. In Figure 7, a visualization is provided on how occurrences of the cohesive elements on the design level of an organisation are derived from the level of purpose. The metaphor shows the transi-

Table 2. EA Requirements from management control theory

Management Control	
Lever of Control	**EA Requirement**
Diagnostic control systems	1. Goals have to be an element of enterprise coherence at the level of the purpose of an organization and objectives an element of enterprise coherence at the design level of an organization.
Belief systems	2. The level of purpose of the organization must be within the scope of EA. This requirement is associated with the previous mentioned requirement 'scope'.
Boundarysystems	3. Boundaries must be made explicit since boundaries define relations between angles of an organization, and as such form a basic asset of enterprise coherence.
Interactive control systems	4. The effect of intended strategic interventions on the enterprise coherence should be made clear interactively and beforehand.

Table 3. EA requirements from a cybernetic perspective

Cybernetics	
Conditions for Effective Control	**EA Requirement**
Specify a goal to the controlled system	1. Objectives have to be an element of enterprise coherence at the design level of an organization. (This requirement is also formulated from the theory of management control in Table 2 requirement no. 1)
Have a model of the controlled system	2. The model of enterprise coherence must represent the dynamics of the design level of an organization.
Have actual information about the controlled system	3. The actual state of enterprise coherence must be represented on a permanent basis including current state as well as future directions.
Have sufficient control variety	4. Enterprise coherence governance must have sufficient levers to influence enterprise coherence on the design level, and support the interdependancy with the level of purpose as well. The latter should include: forward and backward governance, event driven and cyclic governance, single and multi level governance (recursivity and projection).
Have sufficient information processing capacity	5. Restrict the complexity and information overload by differentiating enterprise coherence in several interdependent levels. Allocate sufficient resources to enterprise coherence governance, distinguished by processes, products, peo ple, means, governance, methodology and all based on a clear vision.

Table 4. EA requirements from a change management perspective

Change Management	
Socio-Technical Combinations	**EA Requirement**
Choice made in a change process should be based on the context and the purpose	1. The scope of enterprise coherence governance should include both internal and external angles of the organizational transaction environment. 2. The purpose of a change process should be in line with the goals on the level of purpose and objectives on the design level. 3. The organizational aspects that are dominant in the solution for a business issue, determine the choice of approach. 4. Every change process should be argued by the application of the enterprise coherence governance before execution.
Choice of an appropriate approach determines the success	5. The 'solution direction and choice of approach' should be just one element of the decision. 6. Regarding the decision-making process, enterprise coherence governance should contribute to both the solution direction and choice of approach of a business issue. 7. Enterprise coherence governance should guide the realisation of the 'solution direction and choice of approach' of a business issue. 8. An appropriate approach needs appropriate enterprise coherence products.

Table 5. Examples of cohesive elements on the level of purpose of an organisation

Cohesive Elements	Statements
Mission	• To make people happy (Walt Disney) • To experience the joy of advancing and applying technology for the benefit of the public (Sony) • To bring inspiration and innovation to every athlete in the world (Nike) • To help leading corporations and governments be more successful (McKinsey)
Vision	Walt Disney: • Creativity + Innovation = Profits • One of the world's leading producers and providers of entertainment and information Sony: • We anticipate in the changing relationship between content, technology and the consumer by our four pillars: e-Entertainment, Digital Cinema, High-er Definition and PlayStation Nike: • Sustainable Business and Innovation is an integral part of how we can use the power of our brand, the energy and passion of our people, and the scale of our business to create meaningful change • The opportunity is greater than ever for sustainability principles and practices to deliver business returns and become a driver of growth, to build deeper consumer and community connections and to create positive social and environmental impact in the world
Core values	• Creativity, dreams, imagination, consistency, detail, preservation of the magic (Walt Disney) • Being a pioneer, authentic, doing the impossible, individual ability and creativity (Sony)
Goals	• To build a radically new kind of amusement park, known as Disneyland (in 1950s, Walt Disney) • Become the company most known for changing the worldwide poor-quality image of Japanese products (1950s, Sony)
Strategy	• Continued diversification consistent with Walt Disney's early actions. • The company's increased focus on Sustainable Business and Innovation (SB&I) will be more seamlessly integrated across Nike's business strategies. • Nike utilizes innovation to produce top quality athletic footwear and apparel.

tion from an unstructured set of control information on the level of purpose into a structured coherent set of content, differentiated into the cohesive elements on the design level.

At this stage in the development of GEA, it was possible to make the coherence of a given enterprise explicit. This provided the answer to the research questions 'what are the core factors

Figure 6. Cohesive elements at design level

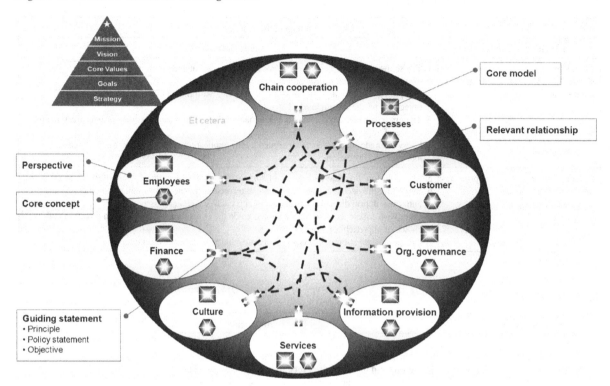

Figure 7. Metaphor for the derivation of cohesive elements on the design level

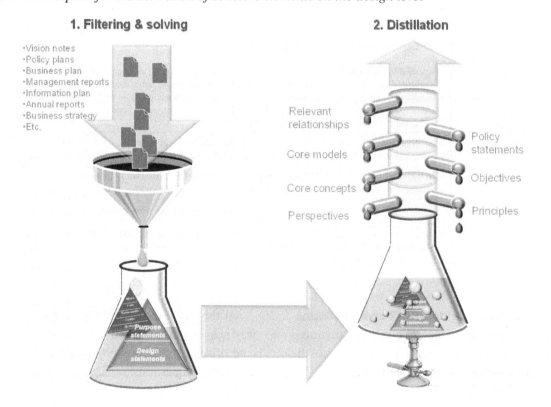

that influence/define enterprise coherence?' and 'how can enterprise coherence be expressed explicitly?'. In doing so, we also met the research objective 'definition of the core indicators and factors influencing/defining enterprise coherence'. In the next section we will answer the research question 'how can enterprise coherence be governed?', while meeting the research objective 'development of instruments to guard/improve the level of coherence in enterprises during transformations'.

5. ENTERPRISE COHERENCE GOVERNANCE

After making enterprise coherence explicit, as discussed above, a survey was conducted to assess the extent to which the original requirements on the GEA programme were indeed met. The results of this survey, held among the core members of the programme, are shown in Table 6.

The survey also shows that solely making the enterprise coherence explicit does not suffice. The necessity to meet all these requirements and the desire to make enterprise coherence governable, led to the initiative to develop the following GEA-components (see Figure 8): EA-vision, EA-processes, EA-products, EA-people, EA-means, EA-governance and EA-methodology. Making a

distinction of these GEA components is based on and in line with the framework for understanding methods for information system development from Seligman, et al. (Seligmann, Wijers & Sol, 1989). We have adopted this framework in the development of the GEA components. This framework was originally developed as a framework to describe, and compare, information system development methods and approaches. It distinguishes the following aspects: a way of thinking, a way of modelling, a way of working, a way of supporting and a way of controlling. In Table 7 we show which method aspect corresponds to the different GEA components.

By developing these components in addition to the cohesive elements, we aimed to achieve the research objective 'development of instruments to guard/improve the level of coherence in enterprises during transformations' and answer the research question 'how can enterprise coherence be governed'. Furthermore, the EA requirements also resulted in the insights needed to develop the GEA-components. More specifically, Table 8 shows which EA requirements stimulated to the development of which GEA-component.

In Table 8, one can see how quite a number of EA requirements, that were already addressed by the cohesive elements, still triggered the development of additional GEA-components. This might seem odd, but can be explained by the fact that

Table 6. Requirements contributed/not contributed by making coherence explicit

Requirement table	Requirement nrs. contributed	Requirement nrs. not contributed
1	1, 2, 3, 5, 6, 7, 8, 9, 12, 13, 14	4, 10, 11, 15
2	1, 2, 3, 4	
3	1, 2, 3, 4,5	
4	1, 2, 3, 6, 7, 8	4, 5
Total	26	6

Figure 8. Coherent set of GEA-components

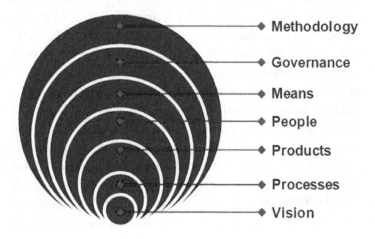

Table 7. Relationship between the "way of" aspects and GEA-components

Way of:	Corresponds with GEA-Components:
Thinking	EA-vision and EA-methodology
Modelling	EA-products
Working	EA-processes and EA-people
Supporting	EA-means
Controlling	EA-governance

the cohesive elements indeed contributed to a large number of EA requirements, but have not fully met them. The GEA components should indeed fully meet these requirements.

There is a strong coherence among the GEA components themselves as well. The promises held by an EA-vision, such as improving the coherence of the organisation, should be achieved through the execution of EA-processes. In their turn, the execution of the EA-processes results in EA-products that will direct change programmes and via this the enterprise coherence. EA-people are needed to carry out the EA-processes and produce the EA-products. The EA-people need, to execute the EA-processes, allocation of means in terms of time, budgets and tools. The EA-people and the execution of EA-processes need to be

Table 8. Overview which EA-requirements led to develop which GEA-components

Tables	GEA Components						
	EA-vision	EA-processes	EA-products	EA-people	EA-means	EA-governance	EA methodology
1	1, 2, 3, 5, 6, 8, 14	1, 2, 3, 5, 7, 8, 11, 14, 15	5, 6, 7, 9, 12, 13, 15	1, 2, 4, 5, 10, 11, 13	5, 10	5	
2	1, 2, 4	3, 4	1, 3, 4				
3	1, 4, 5	3, 4, 5	1, 2, 3, 4, 5	5	5	5	5
4	1	2, 3, 4, 6, 7	1, 3, 5, 6, 7, 8				

governed by EA-governance. And finally to store a maintainable formal description of the formulation of the EA-Vision, EA-processes, EA-products, EA-people and EA-governance there is need for an EA-methodology. In appendix 1 it is shown how each of the GEA components meets specific GEA requirements. In the remainder of this section, we give a brief explanation of the GEA-components.

5.1. EA Vision (Way of Thinking)

An important part of the EA vision is the identification of GEA's essence in terms of three key questions:

1. What is it?

GEA is a set of statements, processes, products, people and resources, that guides the development of an organization with a focus on coherence.

2. What is the intended effect?

The implementation of GEA permanently increase the governnace capacity of an organization and thus its strength, speed and flexibility required in certain situations.

3. How does it meet what it desires?

GEA achieves this guiding by participating the control processes actively and afford insight into the coherence of organizational components and aspects as the relevant environment on a permanent basis.

The EA-vision of GEA consists of the following elements:

1. The triggers and the definition of enterprise coherence as described in section 1.
2. The requirements as shown in section 3.

3. The basic philosophy of GEA as described at the end of section 3.
4. The description of the cohesive elements of enterprise coherence described in section 4.
5. The coherent set of 7 GEA components as show in Figure 8.

Below we give a brief explanation of another number of important aspects of the EA-vision based on the EA-requirements. The other EA-vision aspects are:

- **Scope of GEA:** The cohesive elements on both the level of purpose and the design level of the organization gives direction to the deeper levels behind the perspectives of GEA. See EA-requirement 8 Table 1.
- **Relationship between GEA-Processes/ GEA-Products and the Organisational Control Processes:** The execution processes of GEA that contribute to the organizational control processes and the GEA-products that are involved. See EA-requirement 7 and 12 of Table 1 and EA-requirement 4 of Table 3.
- **Organizational Embedding of GEA:** The way the GEA function is organized. This can be a virtual GEA function or a real allocation of an organizational unit. A special attention is needed for the role of the GEA function in the light of the degree of independency. See EA-requirement 5 and 8 of Table 1.
- **Recursivity of the GEA Governance Instrument:** The possibilities of applying the GEA model in the strategic, tactical and operational levels of the organization and establishing the relationships between these levels. See EA-requirement 4 of Table 3.
- **Projection of the GEA Governance Instrument:** The possibilities of applying the GEA model on a concern level and re-

spective divisions, alliances, supply chains and networks of organizations and their relationships. See EA-requirement 4 of Table 3.

5.2. EA Processes (Way of Working)

Based on the seminal work by Deming (http://nl.wikipedia.org/wiki/Kwaliteitscirkel_van_Deming), we distinguish the following types of processes: planning, execution, review and adjustment; see Figure 9 and Figure 12. The planning, review and adjustment processes (the lowest row in Figure 9) concern the governance of GEA itself and must be tailored to the existing control processes of the organization.

In the context of the execution of GEA, we actually distinguish two types of processes: steering processes (steering the GEA activities) and

performance processes (the actual GEA 'work'). The steering processes are geared towards supporting the control processes of the organization, while the performance processes are aimed at developing and maintaining the GEA deliverables/products. The processes (see Figure 9) 'Make Enterprise Coherence Explicit' and 'Maintain Enterprise Architecture' are performance processes. The processes 'Develop Integral Solutions', 'Develop Program Start Architectures' and 'Check Change Programs by applying PgSA' are steering processes. To understand the working of the steering processes we now give a brief explanation of the process 'Develop Integral Solutions'.

Once an organization has identified the aforementioned GEA cohesive elements, the organisation is able to continue with the process 'Develop Integral Solutions' to solve actual business issues.

Figure 9. Main processes and products of GEA

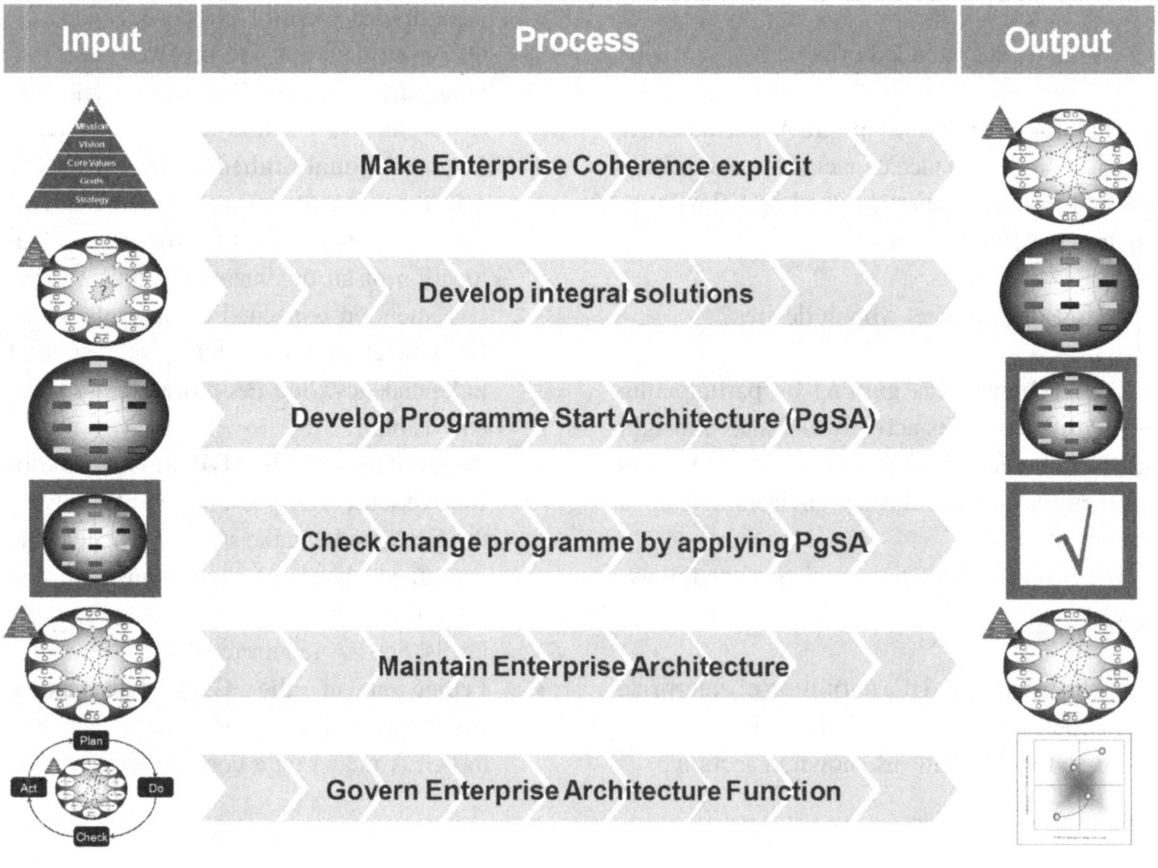

In this process, based on the theory of Sol (Sol, 1988), a business issue will be fully analyzed, aiming to develop the solution and approach to the problem. The analysis of the business issue will be presented in a meeting with the representatives of the different perspectives. This enables each of the participants is able to appreciate the issue and reflect on the consequences and necessary change initiatives to solve the problem. Then, in close collaboration with the representatives of the perspectives, it is determined which of the perspectives should be considered dominant and which ones should be considered sub-ordinate, with respect to the business issue at hand. The reason for this distinction is needed to raise the awareness of which elements of the organization offer the highest possible contribution towards a solution.

After this step, four sub-analyses are to be carried out. In the first sub-analysis, the impact of the issue on the dominant perspectives is determined. The second sub-analysis is used to determine the impact of the issue on the sub-ordinate perspectives. In the third sub-analysis, the possibilities and impossibilities from the viewpoint of the dominant perspectives in relation to the issue are determined. Finally, the fourth sub-analysis is used to determine the possibilities and impossibilities from the viewpoint of the sub-ordinate perspectives in relation to the business issue at hand.

The synthesis between these four analyses leads to the integral solution of the business issue at hand, including an approach to implement the solution. This result serves as a basis for further decisions by the board members of the organization, while serving as a directional framework for the development of a Program Start Architecture (PgSA) (Wagter, 2009), which support the actual change. The integral solution, and associated implementation approach, may also include several scenarios to allow for a final choice to be made by the board members. In the next section, we will discuss a practical (real world) case in which this process was applied.

5.2.1. EA Products (Way of Modelling)

The EA products consist of two main groups: EA control products and EA operational products. The EA control products control the EA function itself and are used to plan, manage and evaluate the EA work. Examples of this type of products are a GEA development plan and a periodic GEA evaluation report.

On their turn the EA operational products consists of two types: the EA performance products and the EA steering products, produced by the performance and steering processes respectively. Examples of EA performance products are: the content of perspectives, core concepts, guiding statements, relevant relationships and core models. These EA performance products form the basis for shaping the EA steering products such as Impact Analysis Reports with recommendations for solutions and approach choices and Program Start Architectures to govern change programmes. This latter category is concerned with products that support the enterprise coherence governance of the organization; i.e. the rationale of GEA. In Figure 9 a summary is given of the main processes and products of GEA and in Figure 10 their relationship including a classification by task areas. This classification will be used in the next section concerning EA People.

5.3. EA People (Way of Working)

The GEA processes, and the corresponding products, require people with specific competencies in terms of knowledge, attitude and skills. These people are known as enterprise architects. This component makes clear how the competencies, responsibilities, powers and duties are to be arranged when working with GEA. In Figure 11 one can see how, based on the theory of Luken (Luken, 2004), we distinguish between a vertical-axis with the task areas of the EA-function and a horizontal-axis with the necessary competencies of the enterprise architects. The task areas are

Figure 10. Task areas, processes, and products of the enterprise architecture function

PROCESSES	PRODUCTS
TASK AREAS	
Initialising & mobilising	
Organising sessions	Enough sessions and a high attendance for realizing enterprise coherence framework
Inventory of cohesive elements	All cohesive elements with appropriate depth
Set up enterprise coherence framework	Coherent enterprise coherence framework, consistent, supported
Advisory	
Integral coherence analyses	Relevant relationships between perspectives, core concepts, etc.
Integral solutions major business issues	Integral solutions including choices of approach
Strategy fit analyses	Strategy impacts
Frameworking	
Programme start architectures	Programme Start Architectures and affiliation with derived Project Start Architectures
Aspect and domain architectures	Relevant sub, domain and aspect architectures
Programme- and project evaluation	Assessment Reports regarding Program Start Architectures
Grant permission	Start Licenses Programme phases
Maintaining	
Enterprise coherence framework actualisation	Releases enterprise coherence framework
Governance	
EA-plan	Enterprise Coherence Development plan, EC annual plan and EC detailed plans
EA-check	Enterprise Coherence Progress reports , Enterprise Coherence Audit reports
EA-act	Decision Enterprise Coherence Change report

distinguished by Initialising & mobilising tasks, Advisory tasks, Frameworking tasks, Maintaining tasks and Governance tasks. The task areas are derived from the above-discussed process activities. In the cells one can see the importance of the competencies for the task areas. In Figure 11, when the relevance of competence for a task exceeds 15 percent, the value is shaded. This allows one to quickly see the major required competencies for a task. The matrix in Figure 11 also includes the management function of the enterprise architecture function.

The GEA competence profile can amongst others be used for:

- Selecting the right people for giving content to the enterprise architecture function.
- Supporting potential candidates in their development process into a role within this function.
- Identifying and giving content to the roles within the enterprise architecture function.

The GEA-competence profile is the result of an extensive study conducted in 2007 at seven major organizations of the research program

GEA. More details of this study can be found in (Wagter, Proper & Witte, 2007; Wagter, Proper & Witte, 2012c).

5.4. EA Means (Way of Supporting)

Templates and other support means, such as reference architectures, indeed play an important role in standardizing and enhancing the EA productivity. Therefore it is necessary to develop advanced tooling to support the EA-function. An important element in this is a clear meta-model of GEA. Therefore, the GEA programme also developed such a meta-model, covering the GEA-processes, the GEA-products as well for the GEA concept as a whole. These meta-models are a part of the EA methodology.

In addition, various architecture frameworks, architecture languages and architecture tools are available to enterprise architects. For instance, the John Zachman framework (Sowa & Zachman, 1992) was one of the first and probably the best-known enterprise architecture frameworks. After this one many followed. In addition, in recent years, tools have been developed that claim to support enterprise architecture. Examples include

Figure 11. GEA competence profile

GEA
ENTERPRISE ARCHITECTURE COMPETENCE PROFILE
Competences / Task areas

COMPETENCES

TASK AREAS	Knowledge & Insight	Subject knowledge	Branche knowledge	Relevant work experience	Academic think & work level	Attitude	Result driven	Organisational sensitivity	Flexibility	Ambition	Professional integrity	Stress resistancy	Service oriented	Visionary	Skills	Planning & Organisation	Networking	Collaboration	Management	Decisiveness	Communicative	Work independence	Persuasiveness	Effective judgement	Creativity	Analytical ability		Number of competence > 10%	Biggest
Basis score Enterprise Architect	12,2	2,2	5,9	1,2	2,9	30,7	3,4	14,6	1,0	0,2	4,9	0,0	1,1	5,5	45,3	0,2	5,5	3,1	0,4	4,7	8,5	0,0	8,3	4,2	3,3	7,1	88		
Percentile score	13,8	2,5	6,7	1,4	3,3	34,8	3,9	16,6	1,1	0,2	5,6	0,0	1,2	6,2	51,4	0,2	6,2	3,5	0,5	5,3	9,6	0,0	9,4	4,8	3,7	8,0	100		
Initialising & mobilising																													
Organising sessions		0	0	18	3		10	17	23	10	2	29	18	2		32	32	7	15	3	17	0	10	2	5	0	255	10	32
Inventory of cohesive elements		5	15	2	7		2	5	5	3	7	4	0	5		0	13	12	2	5	15	7	0	8	7	10	137	4	15
Set up enterprise coherence framework		12	7	8	10		7	7	11	14	15	4	0	22		0	7	10	2	13	13	10	3	5	25	8	211	8	25
Advisory																													
Integral coherence analyses		10	22	5	28		0	19	4	5	10	4	7	13		0	7	15	0	0	8	5	15	12	10	20	218	8	28
Integral solutions major business issues		7	18	8	15		8	14	7	5	7	11	15	18		2	5	10	2	5	12	7	12	15	13	18	233	11	18
Strategy fit analyses		7	22	10	17		5	17	7	15	10	9	9	20		0	5	3	2	2	12	7	13	23	12	17	242	10	23
Frameworking																													
Programme start architectures		20	3	5	8		22	5	7	7	11	5	9	5		2	7	13	2	15	8	8	13	5	8	12	202	7	22
Aspect and domain architectures		18	7	10	7		7	2	4	3	3	5	7	7		2	3	12	5	2	2	18	10	7	10	8	158	3	18
Programme- and project evaluation		2	0	5	0		7	0	4	8	7	7	7	2		2	7	3	2	7	5	13	7	10	0	5	108	1	13
Grant permission		2	2	0	0		3	3	4	3	8	5	7	0		2	3	0	5	22	2	0	5	2	0	0	78	1	22
Maintaining																													
Enterprise coherence framework actualisation		13	0	5	0		5	2	5	2	2	2	18	0		8	0	7	7	2	0	13	2	2	5	0	99	3	18
Governance																													
EA-plan		0	5	10	0		12	5	11	19	2	5	0	7		31	3	3	25	7	2	7	3	0	3	2	161	5	31
EA-check		3	0	5	3		7	0	4	0	7	4	0	0		7	3	2	12	7	3	3	0	8	0	0	77	1	12
EA-act		2	0	8	2		7	5	5	5	11	7	2	0		14	5	3	20	12	2	3	7	2	2	0	123	4	20
		100	100	100	100		100	100	100	100	100	100	100	100		100	100	100	100	100	100	100	100	100	100	100			
Number of competence > 10%		4	4	1	3		2	4	3	4	3	2	3	4		3	2	4	4	4	5	3	4	3	3	4			
Biggest		20	21,7	18,3	28,3		21,7	18,6	23,2	18,6	14,8	28,6	18,2	21,7		32,2	31,7	15	25,4	21,7	16,7	18	15	23,3	25	20			

Figure 12. Overview EA governance

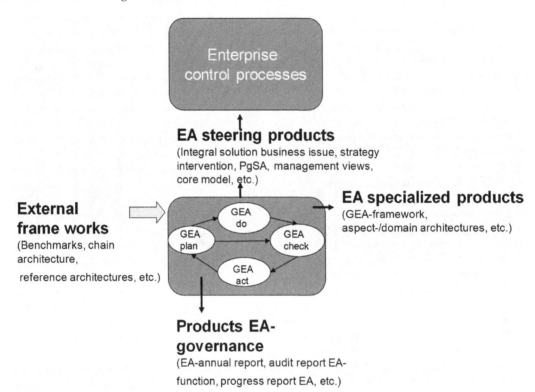

enterprise architecture languages like ArchiMate (Lankhorst et al., 2005) with associated tools such as Architect (http://www.bizzdesign.nl/tools/architect) and ARIS (http://www.ids-scheer.nl/nl/ARIS/ARIS_ARIS_Platform/28569.html), and the enterprise architecture language and associated tool MEGA (http://www.mega.com/en/c/product). However, these languages and tools take a traditionanal 'Business-to-IT' stack perspective, rather than a true enterprise coherence perspective.

5.5. EA Governance (Way of Controlling)

We combine the EA processes planning, review and adjustment (plan, check, act) under the name of EA governance. By carefully performing these processes, organisations can achieve more control over their architecture function. It is important for organizations to achieve this control to obtain the added value of GEA. Key in this remains the question: Does the EA supply the intended added value?

The purpose of EA governance is to have a permanent and critical look if the effects of enterprise architecture can be achieved that will meet the agreed goals. In other words, ensuring that the contribution of EA to the control function of an organization is continuously made explicit in terms of its costs and benefits; see also Figure 12. Depending on the specific situation of an organization, it can be necessary to set up the EA function as a formal organizational unit, while in other cases it may be possible to organize the EA function as a virtual one.

5.6. EA Methodology (Way of Thinking)

The EA methodology includes (1) the formal descriptions of the GEA components EA-vision, EA-processes, EA-products, EA-people, EA-means and EA-governance, (2) all the developed figures of these components as represented in this chapter and, (3) the meta-model of the entire GEA concept including meta-models of both the GEA processes and products. For further details of this meta-models see (Wagter, 2009).

6. CASE STUDY

6.1. Introduction

This section is concerned with a real world case study in Business/IT alignment (or rather enterprise coherence) at the strategic level. The case is situated in the Dutch public sector, involving a Dutch government agency[4] (Dga). This agency has to deal with a business issue on the subject of operational excellence and lack of management control, while carrying out a number of European subsidy arrangements. These subsidy arrangements cover thousands of companies whom, to be eligible for these subsidies, submit an annual application.

For a smooth execution of all this work, about thirty internal and external parties, whose contributions are interdependent and time critical, have to collaborate. Besides these collaborative challenges, the complexity of the process is also increased by outsourcing factors, as well as factors pertaining to the communication channels used to lodge and process the actual applications. In the past, two of the core, massively batch-oriented, processes have already been outsourced. Besides traditional paper-form based subsidy applications, applications are now also lodged by way of the Internet.

The processing of these subsidies has a high degree of political exposure, in the sense that a flaw, or even a drop in the performance, will immediately become public knowledge by way of the national press. This would cause serious damage to the reputation of the organization. Furthermore more non-compliance of the processing of subsidies with, national and EU, laws and regulations will lead to heavy financial fines.

After outsourcing the batch-oriented processes, the outsourcing party remained in default with respect to the quality of the services to be provided. Partly due to the fact that these services were on the critical path, the primary processes got out of control as well. As a result, approximately 60 percent of the client dossiers had to be returned to the applicants without proper processing, while about 20 percent of the subsidy applications resulted in submitted objections by the clients (due to faulty processing of the subsidies). The latter also caused the statutory deadlines to be exceeded, which ultimately resulted in the risk of twenty million Euros in fine. As a result, the very existence of this government agency was put at risk, while the situation quickly raised critical question in the Dutch parlement. As a result, the business issue with which the GEA analysis of the situation at hand was: how can the execution of the subsidy submission, evaluation, and allocation process be made more manageable and efficient? In this regard it was also argued that the failing outsourcing situation was not the only symptom of the real problem, and that more causes were at play.

The case will also illustrate that Business/IT alignment is not only a matter of aligning 'the business' and 'the IT' aspects of an enterprise. The case suggests that a more refined approach is called for. More specifically, we will see how 'the business' is not just a single aspect that needs to be aligned to 'the IT', but rather that it involves many more aspects that need mutual alignment as well. This is actually why we also prefer to use the term enterprise coherence rather than Business/IT alignment. It more clearly expresses the fact that it is more about achieving coherence between multiple aspects, than merely aligning the business and IT aspect. The use of GEA, and the ECF (Enterprise Coherence Framework) as a part of GEA in particular, provided insight into these other elements, as well as their relations and mutual influences (i.e. their *coherence*). This insight allowed the government agency to formulate a strategy to improve matters.

In the case at Dga, just like in other cases, the GEA (General Enterprise Architecting) method was used. As the GEA method was/is developed using a design science driven approach (Hevner, March, Park & Ram, 2004) in combination with case study research (Yin, 2009). The different cases conducted with GEA, also provided feedback on the method. Therefore, we will also explicitly discuss the feedback on the design of the method that follows from this application of the GEA method.

6.2. The Coherence Dashboard for Dga

Since this was the first time for dga to apply/use the GEA method, it was necessary to first develop an organization specific coherence dashboard. To this end, the Dga cases started with an intensive desk research activity, conducted by a small team of architects. This team studied relevant policy documents from Dga, resulting in the first version of the coherence dashboard for the agency, in terms

of a list of the cohesive elements and their definitions, covering both the purpose level and design level. Starting point for creating this list were the strategic documents of the organization such as the mission statement, vision notes, policy plans, business strategy, business plan, etc. In a validation workshop this draft coherence dashboard was then validated with the major stakeholders and approved after some modifications. This validation workshop involved the executives of Dga, complemented with a number of (internal) opinion leaders and key stakeholders.

In Table 10 the perspectives that were selected by Dga are shown, while as an example the core concepts of five of the perspectives are listed in Table 11.

This set of perspectives already illustrates the need to align more aspects of an enterprise rather than just business and IT. The chosen set of perspectives shows that when it comes to alignment, the stakeholders do not think in terms of Business/IT alignment, but rather in a much more refined Web of aspects that need alignment. During the desk research phase more than 200 guiding statements were derived from the aforementioned policy documents. Needless to say that presenting all guiding statements goes beyond the purpose of this chapter. Therefore, as an example Table 12 only shows those guiding statements that turned out to be relevant to the processes perspective.

Table 10. Definitions of perspectives for the Dga-organisation

Perspective	Definition:
ICT	All processes, activities, people and resources for obtaining, processing and delivery of relevant information for Dga.
Chain cooperation	The collaboration of the parties involved in the subsidy arrangement chain.
Processes	A coherent set of activities needed to deliver results of Dga.
Organic structure	The governance and organizational structure of the DGA organisation so that desired goals are attained.
Employees	All persons who execute tasks or activities within the Dga-organization.
Suppliers	Companies or organisations that supplies or sells products and/or serivces at Dga.
Culture	Explicit and implicit norms, values and behaviors within the Dga organization.
Services	All services that Dga within legal frameworks, or through agreed appointments with statutory authorities, establishes and delivers to applicants.
Customer	The applicant of a service of Dga.
Law & regulations	All legal frameworks that form the basis for the task performance of Dga.

Table 11. Core concepts for Dga

Organic structure	Customer	Chain cooperation	Processes	ICT
Governance	Applicants	Collaboration	Formal checks	Standardization
Political leadership	Third parties	Chain test	Material checks	Architecture
Responsibilities & tasks	Channel selection	Chain parties	Seasonal peaks	Integrality
Organizational division	Internet	Chain mandate	Efficiency	Security
Employer ship	Supply coordination	Service level agreements	Effectiveness	Facilities
Policy cores	Objections	Chain management	Predictability	Information
Program management	Switchers		Transparency	Maintenance
Scaling up			Planning	Systems
Combined arrangements			Procedures	Ownership
Works Council			Regulations	Storage

Table 12. Guiding statements relevant to the processes perspective

Processes
Execute three subsidy arrangements through one application'
Execution of the subsidy arrangements should be compliant to legislation
All sub-processes should contribute to sustainability
All processes must be described and provided with work instructions
Of all the processes timely progress reports have to be delivered to the control department
Processes should be implemented more cost efficient
Our aim for Dga is an agile, transparent and fast operation
Factory work as data entry and scanning of maps are outsourced
All process activities must be performed within the statutory time limits
Parallel to the 3rd main process 'judge', the initialization activities of the new subsidy year should start
The processes of the various partners must connect seamlessly
Also determined by the number of subsidy applications received, we aim to compile an optimal size of batches to be processed
Batches of subsidy applications may only move to the next procedure after approval through formal and material checks
Objections should as much as possible be prevented by means of an active application of the possibility of administrative modification
As a result of far-reaching expected changes in European legislation, only the most needed process improvements should be performed.

6.3. The Process Followed in the Case Study

With the dashboard in place, the next step was to organize a workshop, where the business issue at hand was put central and analysed in terms of four questions. During the workshop, each of the ten perspectives of Table 10 had an explicit representative with clear (delegated) ownership of the cohesive elements (in the real organisation, i.e. not just the documentation) of that perspective.

According to the GEA method, at the start of this workshop the owner(s) of the business issue gave a thorough introduction of the issue in terms of causes, degree of urgency, degree of interest, implications, risks, etc. This introduction gave the representatives of the perspectives a deeper insight into the associated issues of this business issue, enabling them to make a translation of the issue to their own perspective. Consequently, the representatives of the perspectives were capable of determining jointly, which perspectives were most affected by/related to the business issue at hand. This resulted in the identification of the dominant and sub-ordinate (for the issue at hand) perspectives.

The core business issue: "How can the execution of the subsidy submission, evaluation, and allocation process be made more manageable and efficient?" was then addressed in terms of four questions, leading to four sub-analyses of the business issue:

1. Determine the impact of the business issue on the dominant perspectives.
2. Determine the impact of the business issue on the sub-ordinate perspectives.
3. Determine the solution space for the business issue from the dominant perspectives.
4. Determine the solution space for the business issue from the sub dominant perspectives.

The first two sub-analyses started from the business issue. This resulted in the identification of the potential impact as well as the necessary change initiatives (originating from the different perspectives) to solve the business issue. The last two sub-analyses were conducted using the guiding statements from the different perspectives as a starting point. This resulted in an identification of the possible/necessary change initiatives, as well as possible limitations (e.g. as a result of

architecture principles) with respect to the solution of the business issue. This was then used as a base to synthesize possible solution scenario's that would fit within the context (as captured in the cohese elements) of the organization. Conversely, the insights gleaned from this exercise also made it clear which cohesive elements should be adjusted to continue giving direction to the further evolution of the organization. The synthesis of the results from these sub-analyses then formed the integral solution and preferred approach to meet the business issue at hand.

The results of the four sub-analysis are given in Table 13, Table 14, Table 15 and Table 16 respectively. As a start, consider Table 13 and Table 14. The second column 'Problem' shows the sub-problems that were expressed by the problem owners. The third column 'Perspective' shows the perspectives, which the representatives perceived as most relevant to a sub-problem. The impact on this perspective is expressed in terms of new or modified guiding statements in the adjacent column 'Guiding statement' (column 4). The impacts resulting from this sub-problem on other possible perspectives (column 5 and 7) are expressed adjacently in terms of guiding state-

Table 13. Sub-analysis 1: impact on the dominant perspectives

Sub-analysis 1: impact on the dominant perspectives								
Nr.	Problem	Perspective	Guiding statement (GS)	Perspective	Guiding statement	Perspective	Guiding statement	Elements of the integral solution
1	Many complaints from customers about not knowing the state of progress	Customer	New GS: status of progress file logistics must always be visible to customer	Processes	New GS: transparency per file in massive processing			Automate logistics on file level
2	Many discussions and problems with suppliers on their payments	Supplier	New GS: No deals with operational staff	Processes	New GS: Manage suppliers by supply management.	Org. structure	New GS: Separation of functions and performance accountability.	Organize professional supply management
3	Major problems due to file loss	Processes	New GS: file loss at all times avoid	Suppliers	New GS: File loss sanction	Services	New GS: Only supply and purchase through SLA	Develop SLA's and sanctions
4	Inadequate cooperation of chain parties led to a lot of money, quality and time loss.	Chain cooperation	New GS: We carry out chain management	Org. structure	New GS: We have the mandate chain management	Processes	New GS: Carry out a chain test prior to the execution.	Organize chain management including chain mandate and development of a chain-test.
5	Execution costs too high	Processes	New GS: Recovery and failure costs are from now in line with the market	Processes	New GS: Checks as early as possible in the process			Redesign the primary processes

Table 14. Sub-analysis 2: impact on the sub-ordinate perspectives

Sub-analysis 2: impact on the subdominant perspectives								
Nr.	Problem	Perspective	Guiding statement (GS)	Perspective	Guiding statement	Perspective	Guiding statement	Elements of the integral solution
1	Awareness of low change ability towards the necessary interventions.	Org. structure	New GS: The change ability must continually adjust our ambitions.	Chain cooperation	New GS: Entire Chain management under program control.			Remove the steering from the line organization and bring it in under program control. Organize program management.
2	Execution is insufficient compliant with international laws.	Laws & regulations	Existing GS: execution should be compliant to legislation	Processes	New GS: Checks should be carried out at the place of execution by authorized officials.	Suppliers	New GS: All outsourced activities shall be performed in the Netherlands.	Renew the outsourcing parties and outsourcing contracts and refocus them on legal regulations.
3	ICT support is insufficient.	ICT	New GS: ICT must support the entire chain.	Chain cooperation	New GS: Support and control the chain at the level of file sharing.	Services	New GS: We communicate only by mail, telephone and internet.	Picture the file exchange and govern this exchange. Organize multi-channel support.

Table 15. Sub-analysis 3: exploring solution space from the dominant perspectives

Sub-analysis 3: exploring solution space from the dominant perspectives								
Nr.	Solution idea	Perspective	Guiding statement (GS)	Perspective	Guiding statement	Perspective	Guiding statement	Elements of the integral solution
1	Applications only via Internet in order to reduce number of objections.	Customer	Existing GS: The customer has free choice of channels.	Services	New GS: Applications preferably via the Internet.			Encourage internet channel, maintaining freedom of choice of channels. Redevelop Internet application.
2	Unbundle the combined subsidy arrangement into 3 separate arrangements to reduce complexity	Customer	Existing GS: Approach the customer as little as possible for gathering data	Processes	Existing GS: 3 subsidy arrangements via one application.	Services	Existing GS: Combine gathering data from multiple arrangements	Proposed unbundling is not accepted, and the status quo maintained.
3	Fill in on forehand previously known information from applicants to reduce many complaints	Customer	New GS: Once gathering, multiple use.	Services	New GS: The applicant receives pre-completed forms and a personalized web site.	Processes	New GS: Forms including logos, etc. are completely printed.	Insert pre-filled forms and complete printing solution at the solution "Redesigning primary processes". Insert personified web site solution at the solution "redevelop internet application".

Table 16. Sub-analysis 4: exploring solution space from the sub-ordinate perspectives

Sub-analysis 4: exploring solution space from the subdominant perspectives								
Nr.	Solution idea	Perspective	Guiding statement(GS)	Perspective	Guiding statement	Perspective	Guiding statement	Elements of the integral solution
1	Work with multiple work shifts to meet the legal deadlines for the subsidy arrangements.	Culture	Existing GS: We will respectful to the interests of our employees.	Processes	New GS: Overtime or multiple shifts only in exceptional circumstances and after approval of the works council.			Working in multiple shifts was no longer seen as a solution.
2	No longer outsourcing of massive routinely sub processes, but carry out these processes themselves to hold more control.	Culture	Existing GS: We will respectful to the interests of our employees.	Processes	New GS: Highly skilled employees carry out highly skilled work.			Maintain the outsourcing, and govern the outsourcing professional.

ments (column 6 and 8). The last column shows the formulated solutions of the sub-problems in which the representatives reached consensus as part of the integral solution.

We continue with an explanation of Table 15 and Table 16. In the column 'Solution idea', ideas are expressed which emerged when determining the solution space. In the third column, 'Perspective,' the perspectives are shown the representatives in the session perceived as most relevant to the solution idea. In the adjacent columns the guiding statements are shown that form the framework for the idea in terms of possibilities and impossibilities. Also newly developed guiding statements are listed here. In the last column the solutions toward the ideas are expressed in which the representatives reached consensus.

To better appreciate the results of the sub-analysis, we will now discuss a concrete example. Consider Figure 13, as an illustration for problem

number 4 from sub-analysis 1: 'The non-cooperative attitude of many parties in the chain resulted in a loss of money, quality and time'. Experience has shown that working together seamlessly with twenty-eight partners, is no simple task. Many of the problems were related to this aspect. Examples include misunderstandings between the parties, not delivering on time, not being able to read each other's file formats, etc. The discussion provided the perspective 'Chain cooperation' with a new guiding statement 'we carry out chain management'. The effect on the perspective 'Processes' was the addition of the guiding statement 'carry out a chain test prior to the execution', and on the perspective 'Organization structure' the addition of the guiding statement, 'we have the mandate on chain management'. The reached solution for this problem was: 'organize chain management including a clear mandate, and develop a chain integration test'. When the mandate for the chain

Figure 13. Sub-analysis nr 1, problem nr 4

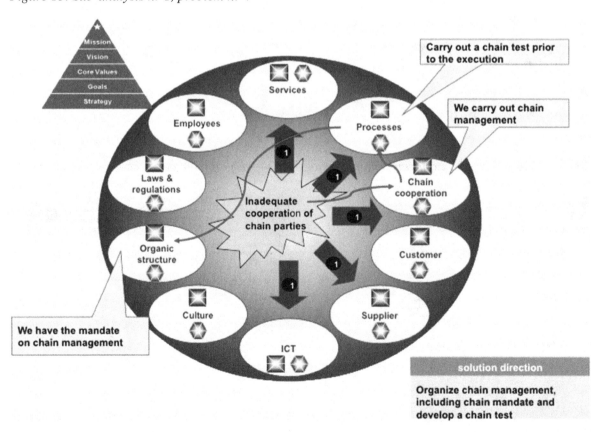

authority had been arranged, all the activities in the chain could be governed in a coherent way. An important consequence of the introduction of a clearer chain authority was the development and execution of a comprehensive test programme to test the integrity of the chain. Many problems regarding the required collaboration of the involved parties, especially in the area of data exchange, could be avoided as a result of having this test.

As a second example, consider sub-analysis 2, problem number 2: 'The execution was not sufficiently compliant with international laws', as illustrated in Figure 14. Every year, a number of checks are conducted by European officials on the degree of compliance with European laws and regulations. There was a need for better anticipation to these checks. This provided a further

confirmation of the existing guiding statement at the perspective 'Laws and regulations': 'the execution should be compliant to the international law'. In addition, a new guiding statement was created at the perspective Processes 'the checks have to be carried out on the place of execution by authorized officials'. Finally, a new guiding statement to the perspective 'Suppliers' was added, 'all outsourced activities shall be performed in the Netherlands'. The reached solution for this problem was: 'Renew outsourcing parties and outsourcing contracts and refocus them on the legal regulations'. This solution meant that the involved suppliers could not re-outsource the activities to a lower wage country and that the outsourced processes could be monitored in an easier way.

Figure 14. Sub-analysis nr 2, problem nr 2

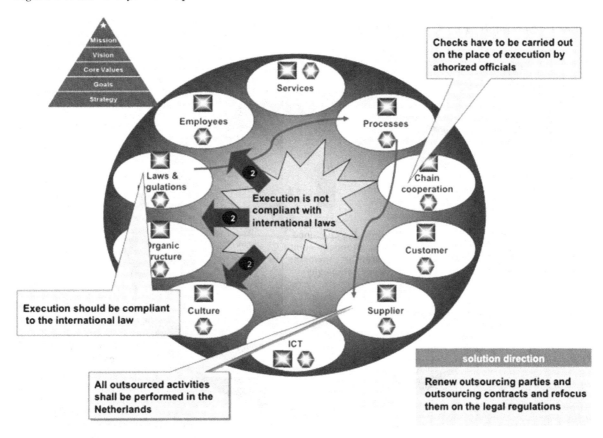

As a third example, consider sub-analysis 3, solution idea number 2: 'Unbundle the combined subsidy arrangement into three separate arrangements to reduce complexity', as illustrated in Figure 15. To try to reduce the overall complexity, some representatives suggested ceasing the current situation in which three (very different) subsidy arrangements were bundled in one application. This would imply that the applicants should be approached three times with subsidy forms. The existing principle from the perspective 'Customer': 'approach the customer as little as possible for gathering data' persisted. From the perspective 'Processes' the guiding statement: 'execute three subsidy arrangements through one application' remained also, as well as the principle from the perspective 'Services': 'combine gathering data from multiple arrangements'. Maintaining the guiding statements here means

a limitation of the solution space. The idea to cease the combination of three subsidy arrangements in one application was not accepted and the final decision for this solution idea was: 'proposal unbundling is not accepted, and the status quo will be maintained'.

As a final example, consider sub-analysis 4, solution idea number 2: 'No longer outsourcing of massive routinely sub processes, but carry out these processes in-house to remain more in control', as illustrated in Figure 16. This discussion concerned the consideration to, given the bad experiences, stop outsourcing critical sub-processes. This situation was rejected based on the principle 'We show respect for the interests of our employee' from the perspective 'Culture'. Apparently there was a mismatch between the fact that the initially outsourced activities had a very massive and routine character, while the employees

Figure 15. Sub-analysis nr 3, problem nr 2

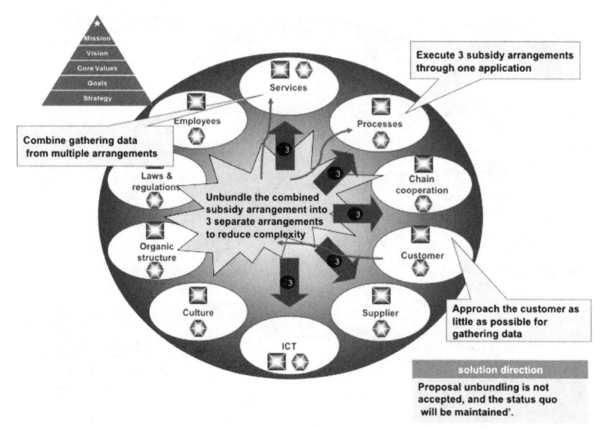

Figure 16. Sub-analysis nr 4, problem nr 2

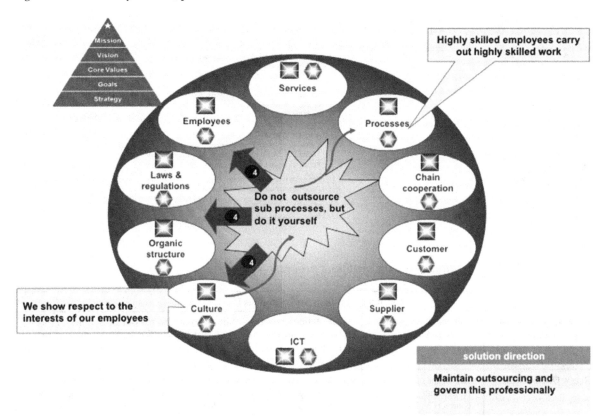

were generally highly educated. This understanding resulted in a new principle in the perspective 'Processes': 'highly skilled employees carry out highly skilled work'. The final outcome for this solution idea was: "continue to outsource, but govern this professionally."

6.4. Results of the GEA Case Study

As a first step in the synthesis process that followed, the participants clustered the sub-solutions of the four sub-analyses (see the right side of Table 17 that corresponds to the elements of the integral solution shown in Tables 13 to 16) into clusters of the integral solution and choice of approach of the business issue at hand (see the left side of Table 17). During this synthesis process, the participants could add sub-solutions. These additions where based, on the one hand, on the new

established guiding statements, and on the other hand, on the overall insight of the integral solution chosen approach. In Table 18 we give some examples of added sub-solutions to the clusters Renew outsourcing and Govern the chain.

At the end of the synthesis process the participants evaluated the GEA approach based on a number of criteria set up by the core team of the GEA programme. See Table 19.

The elaboration of the solution and the associated implementation approach, resulted in a Program Start Architecture (PgSA) for controlling the subsequent change program. A PgSA is a GEA product that is produced to control a change program from an architectural point of view. It is produced after a positive decision on the integral solution and approach is obtained. In the PgSA the integral solution and choice of approach is included, as well as the cohesive elements of the

Table17. Clustering sub-solutions

Clustering sub-solutions	
Clusters of the integral solution	**Sub-solutions from subanalyses**
Organize supply management	• Organize professional supply management • Develop SLA's and sanctions
Govern the chain	• Remove the steering from the line organization and bring it in under program control. • Organize program management. • Organize chain management including chain mandate and development of a chain-test.
Redesign processes	• Redesign the primary processes • Insert pre-filled forms and complete printing solution at the solution "Redesigning primary processes". • Organize multi-channel support. • Automate logistics on file level
Renew outsourcing:	• Renew the outsourcing parties and outsourcing contracts and refocus them on legal regulations. • Maintain the outsourcing, and govern the outsourcing professional.
Govern file exchange	• Picture the file exchange and govern this exchange.
Renew internet application	• Redevelop Internet application. • Encourage internet channel, maintaining freedom of choice of channels. • Insert personified web site solution at the solution "redevelop internet application".
Remain combined data gathering	• Proposed unbundling is not accepted, and the status quo maintained • Working in multiple shifts was no longer seen as a solution

Table 18. Added sub-solutions from the synthesis process

Added Sub-Solutions from Synthesis Process			
Cluster of Integral Solution	**Sub-Solutions, Source Sub-Analyzes**	**Sub-Solutions Added During Synthesis Process Based on Overall Insight**	**Sub-Solutions Added During Synthesis Process Based On New Guiding Statements (GS)**
Renew Outsourcing.	• Renew the outsourcing parties. and outsourcing contracts and refocus them on legal regulations. • Maintain the outsourcing, and govern the outsourcing professional.	• Set the existing outsourcing parties liable for damages suffered. • Retraining of employees.	• Measurements of throughput include in the contract. (see new GS Table 1: status of progress file logistics must always be visible to customer; transparency per file in massive processing). • Sanction of € 5,000 per lost record in the contract file. (see GS Table 1: file loss at all times avoid; file loss sanction). • Suppliers carry out outsource activities under one roof.(see GS Table 1: file loss at all times avoid).
Govern the chain	• Remove the steering from the line organization and bring it in under program control. • Organize program management. • Organize chain management including chain mandate and development of a chain-test.	• Organize a quality assurance project.	

ECF relevant for the change program. Finally the PgSA is supplemented by the organizations accepted norms and standards for relevant aspects of the change program such as eg norms and standards in the areas of security, process design, et cetera. Such a PgSA was the first part of the contract with the designated Program Manager.

The execution of the change program according to the PgSA led to the following results and associated benefits:

• The execution of the subsidy arrangement is now conducted within the set time limits, and agreed budget.

Table 19. Evaluation of the GEA approach

Evaluation GEA Approach			
Criteria	High	Average	Low
Acceptance by stakeholders		*	
Extent of applicability	*		
Matching required dynamics	*		
Extent of compliance with required integrality	*		
Degree of accessibility		*	
Degree of transferability			*
Extent of balance of interests	*		
Degree of innovativeness	*		

- The return of application forms due to application errors was reduced from 62 percent to 35 percent, and now falls within the error tolerance.
- The number of objections was reduced from 22.000 to 7.000 with corresponding reduction in associated costs.
- The Internet based participation of applicants rose from 0.5 percent to 6 percent.
- The European supervisory authority and the Dutch parliament were satisfied about the results and answers on their submitted questions.
- With regard to the new outsourcing parties:
  ○ Their performance was in line with the agreed quality, time and budget.
  ○ Not one client dossier has been lost.
  ○ Given the good performance all contracts were subsequently prolonged.

6.5. Discussion and Conclusions towards the GEA Method

The Dga case study has brought us the following insights on the application of GEA:

- The initial investment by making the enterprise coherence explicit in terms of the ECF is repaid in terms of a better understanding of the enterprise's environment, the stimulation of innovation within (and beyond) the boundaries of the enterprise and a vast improvement of the collaboration of all parties involved.
- Application of GEA leads to achievable and high quality solutions. The execution of the subsidy arrangements was within time and within agreed budget, while substantial savings in operating costs were achieved. More specifically, in the Dga case, a reduction from 22.000 to 7.000 applications, with an average of 10 hours spent per application by lawyers, resulted in a saving of millions Euros.
- Application of GEA implies the involvement of the key social forces in an organization and redirects these into a valuable business asset. More specifically, the key players of the organization, the representatives of the perspectives in this case, did not only know and trust each other more during the design of the GEA framework, but gained also a better insight into and understanding of each other's domains. They were also willing, at the end of sub analysis 1, to transfer the responsibility and the associated power to a chain program manager. At last the decision on the proposed

solution, could soon take place because the decision makers knew that it was developed integrally and supported by all parties involved.

- The process of bringing and keeping the key players together in the workshop sessions does a strong appeal on the required competencies of the facilitators (enterprise architects).

- The quality with which the business issue in all its facets is introduced determines the quality of integrated solution. The business issue at hand has been thoroughly analyzed by the problem owners prior to the impact analysis sessions in terms of causes, degree of urgency and importance, and has been presented clearly at the beginning of the impact analysis sessions. Based on this presentation the perspective-owners were able to make a translation to their own part of the enterprise environment.

- A major business issue can perturb the enterprise coherence in all its facets at the moment an organization decides to react on it. This means that all the preserved, newly added, eliminated and modified cohesive elements must be established in a new actual state of the enterprise coherence at the moment the decision to adopt an integral solution is made! By doing this, the organization is ready to develop an integral solution for a next business issue.

- In the future of the further development of GEA, we should pay more attention to the following lessons learned:
  ○ Application of GEA has a strong increase in transparency as a result. Not all managers are equally happy about it as this offers the possibility for criticizing others on their functioning.
  ○ Success as a result of application of GEA get used quickly, the acquisition of working methods according to GEA requires more effort. The or-

ganization felt relatively soon back to old inefficient behaviour after our departure (See also the low-score on transferability in Table 19).

In summary, we conclude that the case study shows that an incoherent, chaotic situation after application of the enterprise coherence governance instrument GEA, was transformed into a coherent, regulated organization. The presented case study demonstrated that with the application of GEA substantial performance improvements can be achieved. In this real world case study a totally derailed organization has been brought back in control within a single year, while also making substantial savings. In our further research we will, in line with the research methodology used, continue to conduct case studies and based on the findings elaborate and perfect the theory.

7. CONCLUSION

The theory, as proposed in this chapter, was developed by the GEA research programme. The theory answers research questions 1, 3, and 4 as listed in section 2:

- What are the core factors that influence/define enterprise coherence?
- How can enterprise coherence be expressed explicitly?
- How can enterprise coherence be governed?

The triggers of the GEA research programme were discussed in section 1, while these triggers where translated to a set of requirements on the GEA programme as discussed in section 3. Based on the requirements, we developed the theory of enterprise coherence governance (section 4, 5, and 6). With the elaborated case study in section 7, we have shown how this theory has been put into practice. This case also demonstrated that the application of GEA can be used to achieve substantial performance improvements. In this case within one year a totally derailed organization was been brought back into control while also making substantial savings.

This paper is a first step in providing an answer to the aforementioned research questions and achieving our research objectives. In our further research we will, according to our research methodology as described in section 2, execute several cases (see fore instance Wagter, Proper & Witte, 2012b), and based on the findings elaborate and evolve the theory.

ACKNOWLEDGMENT

This work has been partially sponsored by the *Fonds National de la Recherche Luxembourg* (www.fnr.lu), via the PEARL programme.

REFERENCES

Abcouwer, A., Maes, R., & Truijens, J. (1997). *Contouren van een generiek model voor informatiemanagement*. Amsterdam: Universiteit van Amsterdam.

Ahaus, C. T. B. (1998). Balanced scorecard & model nederlandse kwaliteit. Projectgroep bedrijfskunde TNO BV. ISBN 90 267 2477 2

Balogun, J., & Hope Hailey, V. (2004). *Exploring strategic change*. Upper Saddle River, NJ: Prentice Hall.

Bizz Design. (n.d.). Retrieved from http://www.bizzdesign.nl/tools/architect

Bower, J. L. (2000). The purpose of change: A commentary on Jensen and Senge. In Beer, M., & Nohria, N. (Eds.), *Breaking the Code of Change* (pp. 83–95). Boston: Harvard Business school Press.

Chandler, A. D. (1969). *Strategy and structure: Chapters in the history of the American industrial enterprise*. Cambridge, MA: The MIT Press.

Collins, J., & Porras, J. (1996). Building your company's vision. *Harvard Business Review*.

De Caluwé, L., & Vermaak, H. (2003). *Learning to change: A guide for organization change agents*. London: Sage Publications.

De Leeuw, A.C.J. (1982). *Organisaties: Management, analyse, ontwerp en veranderin*. Assen, Germany: van Gorcum.

Deel, B. (2008). *De algemene rekenkamer: Lessen uit ICT-projecten bij de overhead*.

Department of Commerce. (2003). *IT architecture capability maturity model*. Washington, DC: Department of Commerce, Government of the USA.

Drucker, P. F. (1957). *Management in de praktijk*. G.J.A. Ruys Uitgeversmaatschappij N.V..

GEA Groeiplatform. (n.d.). Retrieved from www.groeiplatformgea.nl

Greefhorst, D., & Proper, H. A. (2011). *Architecture principles – The cornerstones of enterprise architecture*. Berlin: Springer. doi:10.1007/978-3-642-20279-7.

Harrison, H. (2009). Togaf™ 9 certified study guide. The Open Group, Van Haren Publishing. ISBN 9 789087 535704

Henderson, J. C., & Venkatraman, N. (1993). Strategic alignment: Leveraging information technology for transforming organizations. *IBM Systems Journal*, *32*(1), 4–16. doi:10.1147/sj.382.0472.

Herzberg, F. (1966). *Work and the nature of man*. Ohio.

Hevner, A. R., March, S. T., Park, J., & Ram, S. (2004). Design science in information systems research. *Management Information Systems Quarterly*, *28*, 75–106.

Hoogervorst, J. A. P. (2004). Enterprise architecture: Enabling integration, agility and change. *International Journal of Cooperative Information Systems*, *13*(3), 213–233. doi:10.1142/S021884300400095X.

Hoogervorst, J. A. P. (2009). *Enterprise governance and enterprise engineering*. Berlin: Springer. doi:10.1007/978-3-540-92671-9.

Iacob, M.-E., Jonkers, H., Lankhorst, M. M., & Proper, H. A. (2009). *ArchiMate 1.0 specification*. The Open Group.

IDS. (n.d.). Retrieved from http://www.ids-scheer.nl/nl/ARIS/ARIS_ARIS_Platform/28569.html

Kaplan, R. S., Norton, D. P., & Barrows, E. A. (2008). *Developing the strategy: Vision, value gaps, and analysis*. Boston: Harvard Business School Publishing Corporation.

Kickert, W. J. M., & Van Gigch, J. P. (1979). A metasystem approach to organizational decision making. *Management Science*, *25*(12). doi:10.1287/mnsc.25.12.1217.

Kwaliteitscirkel van Deming. (n.d.). *Wikipedia*. Retrieved from http://nl.wikipedia.org/wiki/Kwaliteitscirkel_van_Deming

Lankhorst, M. M. et al. (2005). *Enterprise architecture at work: Modelling, communication and analysis*. Berlin: Springer.

Lugtigheid, R. B. (2007). *Architectuur bij PGGM, een praktijkvoorbeeld*. *Technical report*. Ordina.

Luken, J.P. (2004). Zijn competenties meetbaar? Dilemma en uitweg bij het werkbaar maken van het competentiebegrip. *Tijdschrift voor Hoger Onderwijs, 22*.

Macmillan. (2010). *English dictionary for advanced learners* (2nd ed). Hueber.

Mega. (n.d.). Retrieved from http://www.mega.com/en/c/product

NASCIO. (2003). Enterprise architecture maturity model version 1.3. Technical Report. Washington, DC: National Association of State Chief Information Officers (NASCIO).

Op't Land, M., Proper, H. A., Waage, M., Cloo, J., & Steghuis, C. (2008). *Enterprise architecture – Creating value by informed governance*. Berlin: Springer.

Pettigrew, A., Thomas, H., & Whittington, R. (2001). *Handbook of strategy & management*. Thousand Oaks, CA: Sage Publications.

Raadt van der, B., Slot, R., & Van Vliet, H. (2007). *Experience report: Assessing a global financial services company on its enterprise architecture effectiveness using NAOMI*.

Reitsma, E., Jansen, P., Van der Werf, E., & Van den Steenhoven, H. (2004). *Wat is de beste veranderaanpak*. Management Executive.

Rochart, J. F. (1979). Chief executive define their own data needs. *Harvard Business Review*.

Saaty, T. L. (1980). *The analytic hierarchy process*. New York: McGraw-Hill.

Schekkerman, J. (2006). *How to survive in the jungle of enterprise architecture frameworks: Creating or choosing an enterprise architecture framework*. Victoria, Australia: Trafford Publishing.

Schnelle, E. (1978). *Neue wege der kommunikation*. Spielregeln, Arbeitstechniken und Anwendungsfälle der Metaplan-Methode. Number Heft 10. Hanstein, K¨onigstein/Taunus.

Seligmann, P.S., Wijers, G.M., & Sol H.G. (1989). *Analyzing the structure of I.S. methodologies, an alternative approach*.

Senge, P. M. (1990). *The fifth discipline*. New York: Currency.

Simons, R. (1995). *Levers of control: How managers use innovative control systems to drive strategic renewal.* Boston: Harvard College.

Slot, R. G. (2010). *A method for valuing architecture-based business transformation and measuring the value of solutions architecture.* (PhD thesis). Universiteit van Amsterdam, Amsterdam, The Netherlands.

Smit, R. (2007, February 23). Manieren om strategie te verknallen. *Financieel Dagblad.*

Sol, H. G. (1988). Information systems development: A problem solving approach. In *Proceedings of 1988 INTEC Symposium Systems Analysis and Design: A Research Strategy.* Atlanta, GA: INTEC.

Sowa, J. F., & Zachman, J. A. (1992). Extending and formalizing the framework for information systems architecture. *IBM Systems Journal, 31*(3), 590–616. doi:10.1147/sj.313.0590.

Thenmozhi, M. (2012). *Module 9 - Strategic management.* Lecture Notes, Department of Management Studies, IIT Madras.

Van Dale Groot woordenboek van de Nederlandse taal. (2010). *Van dale* (14th ed.). Martinus Nijhoff, Den Haag, The Netherlands.

Van't Wout, J., Waage, M., Hartman, H., Stahlecker, M., & Hofman, A. (2010). *The integrated architecture framework explained.* Berlin: Springer. doi:10.1007/978-3-642-11518-9.

Venkatraman, N., & Henderson, J. C. (1993). Strategic alignment. *IBM Systems Journal, 32*(1), 4–16.

Wagter, R. (2009). Sturen op samenhang op basis van GEA – Permanent en event driven. Van Haren Publishing, Zaltbommel.

Wagter, R., Nijkamp, G., & Proper, H. A. (2007). *Overview 1th phase - General enterprise architecturing.* White Paper GEA-1, Ordina, Utrecht, The Netherlands.

Wagter, R., Proper, H. A., & Witte, D. (2007). *White paper GEA-7.* De GEA Architectuurfunctie: Strategisch specialisme, Ordina, Nieuwegein, The Netherlands.

Wagter, R., Proper, H. A., & Witte, D. (2011). Enterprise coherence-governance assessment. In *Proceedings of the 2nd Working Conference on Practice-driven Research on Enterprise Transformation.* Berlin: Springer.

Wagter, R., Proper, H. A., & Witte, D. (2012a). *A practice-based framework for enterprise coherence.* Berlin: Springer-Verlag.

Wagter, R., Proper, H. A., & Witte, D. (2012b). Enterprise coherence in the Dutch ministry of social affairs and employment. In *Proceedings of the 7th International Workshop on Business/IT-Alignment and Interoperability (BUSITAL2012).* Berlin: Springer.

Wagter, R., Proper, H. A., & Witte, D. (2012c). Enterprise architecture: A strategic specialism. In *Proceedings of 2012 IEEE 14th International Conference on Commerce and Enterprise Computing (CEC 2012).* Hangzhou, China: IEEE.

Wagter, R., Van den Berg, M., Luijpers, J., & Van Steenbergen, M. (2005). *Dynamic enterprise architecture: How to make it work.* New York: Wiley.

Yin, R. K. (2009). *Case study research – Design and methods* (4th ed.). Thousand Oaks, CA: Sage Publications.

KEY TERMS AND DEFINITIONS

Enterprise Coherence Framework (ECF): ECF is an instrument that allows to make the enterprise coherence explicit.

Enterprise Coherence Governance: Enterprise coherence governance is the process of managing, controlling and monitoring the enterprise coherence.

Enterprise Coherence Governance-Approach (ECG): ECG is an instrument that allows to govern the enterprise coherence.

Enterprise Coherence: Enterprise coherence is the extent to which all relevant aspects of an enterprise are connected, in such a way that these connections facilitate an enterprise obtaining/meeting its desired results.

Enterprise Coherence-Governance Assessment (ECA): ECA is an instrument that allows the level of enterprise coherence governance in organizations can be measured.

Enterprise: Enterprise in this thesis is an organization in the public or industrial area with more than 200 employees and a high degree of multiple forms of labor division.

Extended Enterprise Coherence-Governance Assessment (eECA): eECA is an instrument that allows the level of enterprise coherence governance in organizations can be extended measured.

Program Start Architecture (PgSA): A PgSA is a GEA product that is produced to control a change program from an architectural point of view.

ENDNOTES

[1] The authors either currently work for a consultancy firm or have worked for one in the past.

[2] During different stages of the GEA research programme, the members of the programme included: ABN AMRO; ANWB; Achmea; Belastingdienst – Centrum voor ICT; ICTU; ING; Kappa Holding; Ministerie van Binnenlandse Zaken en Koninkrijksrelaties; Ministerie van Defensie; Ministerie van Justitie – Dienst Justitiële Inrichtingen; Ministerie van LNV – Dienst Regelingen; Ministerie van Landbouw, Natuur en Voedselkwaliteit; Nederlandse Spoorwegen; Ordina; PGGM; Politie Nederland; Prorail; Provincie Flevoland; Rabobank; Radboud University Nijmegen; Rijkswaterstaat; UWV; Wehkamp.

[3] For strategic reason, the initial target of the results was the Dutch language community, as most participating organisations where also based in the Dutch language area, while also having a national/local focus. In the near future, these initial results will be made available in English as well.

[4] We cannot disclose the specific government agency. Hence, the anonomized name "Dga."

APPENDIX

As mentioned in section 2 'Research context', the EA requirements form the basis to make the enterprise coherence explicit and to govern the enterprise coherence. In this chapter we have shown that we make the enterprise coherence explicit by cohesive elements and we realize the enterprise coherence governance by applying the GEA components using the cohesive elements. In Table 9 we show the relationships between the cohesive elements and the EA requirements as well as the relationships between the GEA components and the EA requirements.

The confrontation of the Cohesive elements and the GEA-components with the EA requirements, shows that all requirements has been contributed. Conversely, the coherence between the Cohesive elements and the GEA components is made explicit by the requirements that shape both categories. See Table 9.

Table 9. Relationship EA requirements/cohesive elements/GEA components

Table reference	Requirements	On the level of purpose	Perspective	Core concepts	Guiding statement	Core model	Relevant relationship	EA vision	EA processes	EA products	EA people	EA means	EA governance	EA methodology
			Cohesive elements — On the design level					EA function Components						
1.1	It is necessary to take the concerns, and associated strategic dialogues, of senior management as a starting point.	√	√					√	√		√			
1.2	Forces be they of political, informal, or cultural nature, within an enterprise should be a leading element in governing enterprise coherence.	√	√					√	√		√			
1.3	One must have an EA vision in order to be able to establish EA as a business value driver and make explicit how coherence contributes to both the image and opinion formation phases of the decision making process and must closely resemble and simulate the way of thinking. One pre-requisite is that the top of the organisation holds this EA vision.						√	√	√					
1.4	The added value of EA as a governance tool should be recognized and promoted by all parties concerned. Also the added value of EA compared with other control tools that are in use.										√			
1.5	To establish the EA function an integral approach to EA vision development, EA processes, EA products, EA people and EA resources needed for EA is necessary.						√ √	√	√	√	√	√	√	√
1.6	EA is a flexible model, which means that the number and character of organisational angles to govern the enterprise and their associated relationships depend on the situation.		√	√			√	√		√				
1.7	The EA processes and products should support the control processes of the enterprise in a tailor made way, by supplying the necessary results supporting these control processes.					√	√	√	√					
1.8	EA moves at a strategic level and gives direction in decision making on tactical and operational levels by means of lines of policy and must be done in an independent way to include all angles at stake in decision making processes.	√	√	√	√	√	√	√	√					
1.9	From the point of accessibility and understanding it is necessary to distinguish between EA management products and EA specialist products. This means that it is possible to communicate with the right target groups and with the right EA products.						√		√					
1.10	Management must provide the EA function with people with the necessary competencies, time, budget and other resources for EA to realize the added value of EA.									√	√			
1.11	Enterprise architects must participate in the organisation's governance processes and must have direct access to managers on a peer to peer basis.							√		√				
1.12	The EA governance products must provide direction to change programmes and the existing organisation.				√	√		√						
1.13	A complete and coherent set of organisational angles must be brought together by the decision makers.	√	√	√			√	√	√					
1.14	EA must be arranged as a continuous process whereby coherence is permanently adjusted to the dynamics of the internal and external environment.		√	√			√	√	√					
1.15	EA must be applied as a governance instrument at the moment major business issues arise in order to establish integral solutions and approaches on time.							√	√					
2.1	Goals have to be an element of enterprise coherence at the level of purpose of an organization and objectives an element of enterprise coherence at the design level of an organization.	√			√			√	√					
2.2	The level of purpose of the organization must be within the scope of EA. This requirement is associated with the previous mentioned requirement "scope".	√			√			√						
2.3	Boundaries must be made explicit since boundaries define relations between angles of an organization, and as such form a basic asset of enterprise coherence.	√	√	√	√	√	√	√	√					
2.4	The effect of intended strategic interventions on the enterprise coherence should be made clear interactively and beforehand.	√				√	√	√	√	√				
3.1	Objectives have to be an element of enterprise coherence at the design level of an organization. (This requirement is also formulated from the theory of management control in table 2 requirement no. 1)							√	√					
3.2	The model of enterprise coherence must represent the dynamics of the design level of an organization.		√	√	√	√	√		√					
3.3	The actual state of enterprise coherence must be represented on a permanent basis including current state as well as future directions.	√	√	√	√	√	√	√	√					
3.4	Enterprise coherence governance must have sufficient levers to influence enterprise coherence on the design level and support the interdependancy with the level of purpose as well, including: forward and backward governance, event driven and cyclic governance, single and multi level governance (recursivity and projection).	√	√	√	√	√	√	√	√	√				
3.5	Restrict the complexity and information overload by differentiating enterprise coherence in several interdependent levels. Allocate sufficient resources to enterprise coherence governance, distinguished by processes, products, people, means, governance, methodology and all based on an vision.			√				√	√	√	√	√	√	√
4.1	The scope of enterprise coherence governance should include both internal and external angles of the organizational transaction environment.	√	√	√	√	√	√	√		√				
4.2	The purpose of a change process should be in line with the goals on the level of purpose and objectives on the design level.	√			√			√						
4.3	The organizational aspects that are dominant in the solution for a business problem, determine the choice of approach.		√	√				√	√					
4.4	Every change process should be argued by the application of the enterprise coherence governance before execution.							√						
4.5	The "direction of solution and choice of approach" should be just one element of decision.							√						
4.6	Regarding the decision making process, enterprise coherence governance should contribute both the solution direction and choice of approach of a business issue.	√						√	√					
4.7	Enterprise coherence governance should guide the realisation of the "solution direction and choice of approach" of a business issue.				√	√	√	√	√					
4.8	An appropriate approach needs appropriate enterprise coherence products.					√	√		√					

Chapter 5
Architecture Leadership and Systems Thinking

Raghuraman Krishnamurthy
Cognizant Technology Solutions, India

ABSTRACT

Gone are the days when organizations were concerned with increasing efficiency by mastering repetitive tasks. The competitive, boundary-less world of today has dramatically altered the primary challenges of an organization: fluidity, coherence, and connectedness are the hallmarks of successful organizations. Concomitant with this epochal transformation is the emergence of information systems as the backbone for conducting any business. Today, one cannot find any enterprise or government that is not permeated by information systems at all levels. That the role of information systems is so central to any organization is evident from the prescient words of management legend, Peter Drucker, that the future CEO may be the CIO. With extended enterprises so very common, how do we not lose sight at the bigger picture while making decisions? Systems thinking advocates cultivation of viewing the "whole" and seeing the parts (of the whole) in the context of dependence with other parts (of the whole) and their interactions. Architecture should help create necessary artifacts to understand and manage the complexities. Developing insights on how things work together and the influence of one part over the other is at the heart of architectural conversations. There is thus a natural connect between leadership, architecture, and systems thinking. This chapter explores the nature of evolving enterprises and the increasing relevance of systems thinking in architectural activities. The author discusses the importance of systems thinking to enterprise architecture and illustrate, with TOGAF as an example, how to apply the principles of systems thinking. A conceptual case study is presented to illustrate the application of systems thinking in architectural governance.

INTRODUCTION

Technology has been continuously transforming the way we live, work and recreate. The ripples of the waves of technology advancements result in profound effects transforming organizations, governments, military and production of goods and services. In the agricultural era, human and animal power was harnessed for living rendering labor the predominant power. In the industrial age that followed, machine power drove industries in ways unimagined by the earlier generations. Capital was the most important element that drove

DOI: 10.4018/978-1-4666-4518-9.ch005

industrial era. The arrival of Internet heralded the advent of information age. In the information age, knowledge derived from information is the most critical asset. Competitive advantage is no longer derived from land, capital and labor but increasingly from knowledge. Thus, there arose a critical need for managing information in organizations and in personal lives.

The explosion of information is greatly aided by parallel advances in globalization, virtualization and technology (Uhl-Bien et al, 2007). In the industrial economy, organizations faced challenges in maximizing production of physical assets. This was addressed by factory mode of operation – the most often quoted example of Ford which heralded the first of industrial factory floors. This necessitated a command and control structure and organizations evolved a bureaucratic way of operation. Knowledge was in precious few hands and the mass of workers were practically treated machine like – being told what to do. Information age has totally different types of needs but unfortunately our strong roots of industrial age thinking is debilitating and constraining us.

Industrial age was characterized by factory organization of work, specialization of labor, reliance on machine power and strict organizational boundaries. Information age emphasizes on free flow of information, decentralized organizational structures and co-evolutionary ecologies of firms, institutions, and markets. While the age has progressed, have our thoughts and approaches undergone concomitant transformation to deal with the emerging ways? The central theme of this chapter is to explore this question, seek answers and suggest approaches that will better enable to harmoniously blend with the underlying forces.

Thinkers (Stewart, 1998) trace the evolution of information age to 1991 when the corporate capital spending on traditional industrial age goods like turbines, engines and mining equipment was surpassed by spending on information machines like computers and telecom. Since then, the spending

on information machines has seen rapid acceleration and every passing year has further widened the gap between spends on industrial age goods and information machines.

Technological inventions particularly the transistors replacing vacuum tubes, have made computers omnipresent. Today, computers permeate business life (Latham, 2002) and form the backbone of any enterprise. Machines in factory floors are controlled by computers and robots – the steel collared workers – offering higher levels of capability and precision. Transportation machines like sophisticated trains and planes are dependent on electronic control systems. The story gets predictably repeated across industry segments reinforcing the shift of nucleus towards information systems. Truth be told, it is hard to imagine businesses without computers. Social experiment on living with just Internet as the access medium (and shutting out of all other human contacts) to outside world illustrates the pervasiveness, utility and relevance of information systems.

Computer education is no longer an esoteric science; it is taught in elementary schools. Households consider computers as infotainment devices and the market for personal, home computers show robust growth. It is not just technology innovations and affordability that ushered in information age; the coincidence of other events played no less a part in the advent of information age.

Thomas Friedman (2005) argues that the fall of the Berlin Wall allowed people to see the world differently—as "flat" or more global. For Friedman, the fall of Berlin Wall was a far more symbolic event than just a political event – it ushered in a new thinking, one that is based on viewing as seamless whole. In the cold war era, people thought of the world in either-or terms: either capitalist west or communist east. The political and economic split did not simply limit people's ability to communicate or do business; the real deleterious effect was that it limited people's ability to think globally.

With the weakening of physical and ideological walls separating people, free flow of information became a reality. This was greatly aided by technological advancements. For organizations, global access to market, talent and supplies became a reality. This enabled organizations to acquire a truly global hue. Information systems formed the skeletal structure for managing global interactions. Organizations started using information systems beyond the peripheral functions of HR, payroll processing or records maintenance.

With further technological advances and innovative use, information systems acquired a preeminent position powering our everyday life. All core processes that form an enterprise's mission are realized using information systems. Given such widespread use of information systems and the potential future possibilities, the money spent on development of new systems continues to rise. However, it is pertinent to ask, how successful have these endeavors been? Have they resulted in the promised benefits within the budgetary estimates? If there have been considerable failures, is there any trend indicative of deeper malice?

Architecture plays a crucial role in providing an understanding of how the information systems work. In an insightful analysis (Land et al, 2008) of how architecture has evolved and became a discipline by itself, the example of Pyramids was taken for illustration. Pyramids evolved from simple burial sites to historical evidences of power and architectural accomplishments. Great riches were stored in pyramids as safe keeping. With such increasing complexity, it was beyond the role of the engineer or the designer; an architect was required. This led to architecture as a means to obtain and maintain insights into complex relationships.

To retain relevance and to be used powerfully, architecture must evolve in tune with changing times. We will first briefly look at the essential characteristics of information age and discuss about how effectively architectural thoughts fit in and what evolution is necessary.

CONNECTEDNESS AND COMPLEXITY: THE REALITY OF INFORMATION AGE

Newtonian physics has greatly influenced our approach to understand the world: stable, predictable, having discernible cause and effects (Olson & Eoyang, 2001). To every endeavor to build understanding the principles of Newtonian physics were consciously or unconsciously applied. Organization was viewed like a machine having parts and studying parts, it was theorized, will help one understand the whole. Petzinger (1999) notes that "even as it was toppled from unassailableness in science, Newtonian mechanics remains firmly lodged as mental mode of management from the first stirrings of industrial revolution to the advent of modern day MBA studies." Newtonian thinking is effective when the internal and external conditions are stable and predictable. Today's conditions are neither stable nor predictable.

The current times are characterized by incredible possibilities of connections across systems and people. Social networks thrive by creatively connecting people to one another. This connectedness and the attendant proverbial shortening of the world have given rise to unimaginable and unintended consequences of decisions and events in one part of the world over the other. We will illustrate this view point with some examples:

- In 2010, a volcano in Iceland erupted and that resulted in traffic disruptions across the world. This resulted in loss of tourism, disruptions in food supplies, loss in airlines. For instance, press reports indicate that British Airways reported that it was costing them 15-20 million pounds a day because of the disruptions.
- Warming of oceans and impact the changing weather due to drilling of coal and oil fields. Fossil fuels emit carbon dioxide and that contributes to global warming.

- A cartoon appearing in a Danish newspaper that supposedly hurt sentiments of a religious group ended up in an attack on an Italian embassy in Libya months later.
- In Hawaii, the introduction of feral pigs has severely altered the island's ecosystem. The pigs eat rare plants that native birds depend on for nectar. Through their digging, the pigs create large puddles which breed disease-carrying mosquitoes that further decimate the bird population.
- Water quality in Canadian lakes gets negatively impacted due to acid rains which were caused by the pollutants in the US. About half the wet sulphate deposition in eastern Canada is estimated to come from the United States.

We find many such interconnected events – it is hard to separate social, political, economical events. Everything influences 'out of proportion' and triggers a Web of reactions. What may appear superficially unrelated is actually the result of complex interplay of subtle connections. The interconnectedness of our existence is not an alien concept unknown to mankind. In the sacred scripture of the Bhagavad Gita, verse 3.14 (Prabhupada, 1997) speaking about the interrelationship between performance of sacrifices and rainfall, it is said:

annad bhavanti bhutani
parjanyad anna-sambhavah
yajnad bhavati parjanyo
yajnah karma-samudbhavah

The interconnectedness has challenged the notion of six degrees of separation – today, it is perhaps just one or two degrees of separation as local events have global effects. In their well written paper on 'Coping with Complexity', Seijts et al (2010) observe:

The intertwining of organizations' value chains, corporate governance, and financial flows results in exposure to shocks at the periphery that can move to the centre of an organization in rapid succession. As an example, consider the case of Netflix, the online DVD rental giant. With booming sales and profitability over the past five years, it is about to face a major shock to its business model. The United States Postal Service (USPS), struggling with losses, has decided to increase postage rates as well as eliminate Saturday delivery. With Saturday being the biggest delivery day and postage a major cost driver for the Netflix, this move could easily wipe away the firm's profitability and threaten its existence. Netflix will now have to adjust its strategy to compensate for damaging changes in a critical component in its value chain.

It is not just dense connections that characterize today's environment: diversity, interdependence, flux and ambiguity all play an equally powerful and significant role in influencing the current landscape. The sheer diversity of available choices today is staggering. The operating environment changes so rapidly that organizations are usually caught unaware.

The days of vertically integrated organizations are a passé. Extended enterprise (Edward & Spekman, 2003) is the entire set of collaborating companies both upstream and downstream, from raw materials to end user consumption, that work together to bring value to market place. Consider the pharmaceutical industry. New alliances are being forged between pharmaceuticals and care providers and insurance companies that enable pay-as-you-realize-benefit strategy. The fact that now success is a collective performance of the enterprise and not individual firm's actions signals a significant change.

In such complex systems, emergent behavior manifest as a result of interplay of environmental forces with the systems. To appropriately handle and take advantage of these emergent behaviors,

Box 1. Kodak files for bankruptcy protection: Gone in a flash

```
http://www.economist.com/blogs/schumpeter/2012/01/kodak-files-bankruptcy-pro-
tection-1
```

The empire Eastman started to build at the end of the 19ᵗʰ century, and which dominated the 20ᵗʰ, did not last long into the 21ˢᵗ century. On January 18, 2012 Eastman Kodak filed for Chapter 11 bankruptcy protection in New York. The firm was laid low by the rapid shift to digital photography and away from film, where Kodak once earned 70% margins and enjoyed a 90% market share in America.

It is a historic comedown for a firm that once defined American industrial power and inventiveness. Yet its problems were not unlike those that other big American technology near-monopolists had to deal with in the 20th century. National Cash Register (NCR) was once one of the world's top computer makers, but has been reduced to making ATM machines and high-end registers. Xerox, the pioneer of copying machines, is struggling in the competitive market for imaging products and services. Even AT&T, the telecoms giant, was not able replicate the dominance it once enjoyed in handling long-distance calls.

The morale of Kodak's fate is that technology trends are often clearly visible, but changing a successful company is exceedingly hard. NCR was not able to adapt to the world of personal computers. Xerox could not find the right formula to compete in a world with many rivals. AT&T failed to adjust to the Internet.

innovative responses are required. Some principles to keep in mind are:

- Organizations should be viewed as a whole and not as sum-of-parts.
- Boundaries with external world are in a constant state of flux.
- Changes are often seeded from outside.
- Organizations are complex.
- Non linear causes and effect linkages.

As everything connects to everything, we decrease our overall success when we try to design and manage functions within the enterprise independently of each other. This requires that we look at the whole enterprise as a system, rather than as a collection of functions connected solely by information systems. As a discipline, archi-

tecture provides abstraction to facilitate easier understanding of any problem area.

EVOLUTION OF ENTERPRISE ARCHITECTURE AND CHALLENGES

The real value of Enterprise Architecture is not in making better architectures...it's in making better enterprise. (Alexander, 2007 [Gary Doucet, Chief Architect, Government of Canada Treasury Board of Canada Secretariat GC])

Computers, Internet and information systems trace their origins to defense and research organizations. The seed thoughts about the usage possibilities were remotely related to business and mass populace. In the 1980s, radical thoughts of using computers for business purposes took root. The Olympics games in Moscow in 1980 and business implementations by American Express, British Gas, ICI and Philips are some of the harbingers that experimented with using computers for business needs and found huge benefits in working with information systems (Aldrich, 2008).

In the early years, information systems managers for major corporations typically played a secondary role – a service oriented role. They brought technical computing and communications skills, plus management abilities, to the organization. In recent years, the strategic role of information systems has evolved substantially. In information age, unlike the earlier ages, information systems are primary to realization of business strategy. In fact, Peter Drucker has suggested that information and supporting technology is becoming so central to strategy that the CEO of the future will be the CIO (Drucker, 1999).

With increasing usage possibilities and the attendant complexity the need for scientific understanding of how IT systems behave in an enterprise rose significantly. Architecture is well known in the field of construction as a means to understand, guide and control the evolution of buildings. The term software architecture slowly started making an appearance in software as IT industry was confronted with complex structures. In the 1980s and 1990s, people became aware that the development of IT should be done in conjunction with the development of context in which it was used. This is at the heart of the discipline of enterprise architecture. During the last decade, the role of enterprise architecture has expanded from a mere technical blueprint of IT systems and infrastructure to include other aspects related to business-technology alignment. The below partial listing of the evolutionary forces in any enterprise projects a good view of shifts:

- Move from local/country systems to enterprise wide systems.

- Complexity resulting from interconnectedness; for example, integrated health networks have far greater dimension of complexity than simple physician-practice affiliations.
- Need to standardize and move away from 'unique', customized ways of doing things.
- Technology advancements in hosting and advances in end user mobile devices. Any new technology that makes an impact to general public will influence the enterprise.
- Industry getting redefined due to increasingly empowered and aware consumers.
- Constant flux and the need for transformational initiatives.

Architecture is the art and science of building complex structures; it is an indispensable instrument in controlling the complexity of the enterprise and its processes and systems. Enterprise can be defined as any collection of organizations that has common set of goals and/or single bottom line. Enterprise architecture is a coherent set of principles, methods and models that are used to design an enterprise's organizational structure, business processes, information systems and infrastructure (Sessions, 2006). A critical point to note is that the scope is enterprise level – not operational unit level.

In their comprehensive paper on the state of enterprise architecture Winter et al (2010) mention (partial listing) the following as typical goals of EA efforts:

- Standardization.
- Business IT alignment – create layers from enterprise vision to business architecture to information flows to applications/data to infrastructure. It is hoped that this will provide the linkage between business and IT by tracing paths of connections.
- Creating/adopting framework, processes, tools; Governance.

- Building the current state.
- Vision of target state.

This intensely documentation oriented approach to EA tend to be parochial because it does not sufficiently account for the larger the context of the enterprise, the operating environment and numerous other dynamic forces which give rise to emergent behaviors. It is pertinent to remember Dante's famous quote 'art for art's sake' that warned artists not to forsake social responsibility in the name of devotion to the profession. History has a habit of repeating itself: many organizations have a cynical view of enterprise architecture as an ivory tower profession (Saha, 2007).

The initial drivers for EA came from IT in trying to align itself with business and thus EA was approached as an engineering profession with an analytic bent of mind. This gave rise to a colored perception of EA as being an IT centric profession. However, EA should have the focus at enterprise level much beyond the contours of IT. Writing convincingly about the current EA programs, Doucet et al (2009) talk about how EA programs are skewed towards development of frameworks, reference models, maturity models, etc. This has resulted in challenges in gaining wider acceptance of EA programs. Several authors have analyzed and written about the current state of EA. Some of the common findings are:

- Lack of universally accepted view on what is EA.
- Efforts tend to be IT centric; focus on engineering; business focus is at best secondary or sometimes not clearly evident.
- EA artifacts do not have practical utility.
- Governance is not closely linked with EA office.
- Unable to attract business participation in EA efforts.

In the later part of the last century to which the discipline of EA traces its origin, the engineering oriented approach had merits as the external environment was fairly stable and the businesses operated in a vertical fashion and were mostly in control of the external factors. The focus on internal workings of the enterprise was therefore required and justified.

In the annals of evolution of enterprise architecture, 1996 is an important year when the US Congress passed Clinger-Coher act. The act mandated the creation of standards for analyzing, tracking and evaluating risks and results of all major capital investments made by an executive agency for information systems. Ditto in private sector: businesses operate in an environment of faster technology developments, cross boundary information flows and increasing interconnectedness of organizations. A strong frame of reference like enterprise architecture will be of immense aid to manage the onslaught of forces, understand the consequence of decisions and stay in control. Yet, from the lofty theorization, there appears to be a significant gap in how effective enterprise architecture as a discipline has been. Major architectural initiatives in public or private sector face daunting challenges (Charette, 2005) and have gained notoriety for either budgetary overruns or for not meeting the objectives or worse still (yet most common), for both. Examples, from the US government agencies and private sector (Sessions, 2006 & Charette, 2005):

- Internal Revenue Service (IRS) lacks a sound financial management system that can produce timely, accurate, and useful information needed for day-to-day decisions continues to present a serious challenge to IRS management. IRS's present financial management systems ... inhibit IRS's ability to address the financial management and operational issues that affect its ability to fulfill its responsibilities as the nation's tax collector.

- Department of Defense substantial financial and business management weaknesses adversely affect not only its ability to produce auditable financial information, but also to provide accurate, complete, and timely information for management and Congress to use in making informed decisions.
- Department of Homeland Security (DHS) is missing, either in part or in total, all of the key elements expected to be found in a well-defined architecture, such as descriptions of business processes, information flows among these processes, and security rules associated with these information flows, to name just a few. As a result, DHS does not yet have the necessary architectural blueprint to effectively guide and constrain its ongoing business transformation efforts and the hundreds of millions of dollars that it is investing in supporting information technology assets.
- The Federal Bureau of Investigation has sustained heavy criticism for squandering more than $500 million in a failed effort to create a virtual case-filing system.
- In 2007, the integration of ticketing systems between US Airways and American West ran into trouble.
- In 2009, London Stock Exchange crash halted trading.
- The British food retailer giant J Sainsbury PLC had to write off its US $526 million investment in an automated supply-chain management system.

A discernible trend in all the failures is the increasing scale and complexity of systems. Issues that need to be addressed for large, complex enterprise architectures have to do with the interactions between applications, not the implementations of the applications themselves. Some of the recent areas where enterprise architecture is examined for potential application include regulatory compliance, risk management, shared models, etc. These are briefly discussed below:

- In the past decade, the dual pressure of corporate governance and regulatory compliance has significantly risen. Though regulatory compliance is generally associated with data and access, it is slowly enmeshing the whole of the enterprise – in the interconnected world it is very difficult to isolate the impact. In the conceivable future, innovative approaches using EA as the fulcrum for compliance are likely to emerge.
- As enterprises are transforming from delivering services to delivering experiences, it is critical that the contribution of EA be measured in business outcomes. Delivering experiences require broader thinking and the ability to maintain razor sharp focus on the desired outcomes. EA should guide the enterprises towards the enterprises transformation from services to experience; from process driven to value driven.
- Operational excellence is no longer possible in enterprises by optimizing on internal processes. EA guided by systems thinking is necessary as enterprise boundaries need to be transcended - enterprises are no longer insulated or be able to deliver most of the customer experiences by themselves. As a way to foster greater collaboration and inculcate a shared sense of ownership, enterprises are pioneering risk reward models in the ecosystem. Enterprise architecture can help the collaborators identify the strengths and weaknesses and take appropriate decisions.
- As collaboration and extended enterprises are increasingly becoming prominent, con-

siderable focus has shifted to how security concerns can be addressed. Models are being attempted in weaving security within the enterprise at design time itself (contrast to afterthought, run time). Maturity model of EA is receiving significant attention in the recent years. For instance, the US Office of Management and Budget (OMB) have prioritized 'Share First' policy to promote reuse. In the private sector, firms going through mergers and acquisitions or internal consolidations look at Shared Services as a way to cut costs, promote standardization. Architecture governance informed by systems thinking is essential to help enterprises move towards higher realms of maturity and benefits realization.

Charette (2005) poses the uncomfortable introspective question when he writes: "Like electricity, water, transportation, and other critical parts of our infrastructure, IT is fast becoming intrinsic to our daily existence. In a few decades, a large-scale IT failure will become more than just an expensive inconvenience: it will put our way of life at risk. In the absence of the kind of industry wide changes that will mitigate software failures, how much of our future are we willing to gamble on these enormously costly and complex systems?"

Architecture tends to have a componentized view of the system. For example, a business process centric view will show the business processes, an infrastructure centric view will show the infrastructure, an application centric view will show the applications. Foundational thinking in this approach is that multiple views, aimed at analyzing from various perspectives, will together help understand the entire enterprise. However, such an approach is flawed as the interrelationships which give rise to emergent behaviors are lost when one studies just the components.

As we saw earlier in the chapter, today's businesses are characterized by interconnectedness, complexity, open boundaries and are highly influenced by the operating environment. Cost reduction, waste elimination, efficiency and productivity gains are not enough to be successful. Businesses now need to exhibit high level of thinking, being able to form perspectives, discern the trends in the operating environment, create new value propositions and do bold experimentations. A couple of great examples of success stories are Nike Plus and Rolls Royce offering of jet engines as product with service. To survive and thrive in current era, the need is for a different type of approach, a fundamentally different thinking.

APPLYING SYSTEMS THINKING IN ENTERPRISE ARCHITECTURE AND GOVERNANCE

From an early age, we're taught to break apart problems in order to make complex tasks and subjects easier to deal with. But this creates a bigger problem … we lose the ability to see consequences of our action, and we lose a sense of connection with the whole. - Senge P (1990)

Systems thinking place emphasis on understanding of the whole. Breaking apart to analyze and understand might not always build the full understanding. A computer cannot be understood as key board, mouse, CPU, etc. While it can provide some level of understanding, the most comprehensive knowledge is not possible using analysis approach. Dismembered parts have, often times, no meaning without connection to the whole. A CPU alone has no utility unless it is connected with input and output devices. Analysis may end up trivializing or more often, not able to explain the synergistic contributions of the parts while in dynamic action. Therefore, what is important is not only the parts, but the interrelationships between the parts.

To illustrate the difference in approaches between analytic and systems thinking, consider a bridge across a river. How will an analytic thinker and a systems thinker define the bridge? To an analytic thinker, the bridge will be seen as number of columns, composed of what materials, the strength of the material, the force of water and wind current it has to withstand, etc. To a systems thinker, the bridge will be seen as connecting two parts of the city/town/ village, the needs for people to move from one part to the other, any strategic importance of the bridge, etc. While both the perspectives are important, analysis should not lose sight of synergistic understanding of the whole and the relative place in the larger scheme of things. Systems thinking equip one with that broader grounding. Broad principles of systems thinking are shown in Table 1.

A full treatment of systems thinking is beyond the scope of this chapter. We have attempted to cover as much as necessary to equip the reader with a fair knowledge of application of important principles in systems thinking.

As we discussed earlier, the information age is characterized by complexity brought about various combinatorial factors. Our systems are highly interconnected, exposed to impact on global scale and changes occur in lightening speed. These give rise to heightened complexity that was never experienced before. Like people, the modern systems of the world are getting more and more interconnected than ever before.

Modern systems have the following characteristics (Savigny & Taghreed, 2009): self-organizing, constantly changing, tightly linked, governed by feedback, non linear, counter intuitive. Trying to understand parts and integrating that knowledge (of all parts) cannot yield a clear understanding of the system; it can help understand the parts, it can reveal the structure but not the complete function. Even if we make each part perform as effectively as possible, there is no guarantee that

Table 1. Principles of systems thinking

S.No.	Principle	Explanation
1	Influence of Operating Environment	Systems are open and are highly influenced by the environment in which they operate.
2	See the Whole	Having contextual understanding of the whole is essential
3	Non Linear Influence	It is hard to predict the extent or impact of how change in one part influences the whole
4	Multiple Interrelationships	The parts of the whole share complex interrelationships with one another
5	Emergent Properties & Feedback Loops	Properties manifesting from whole; individual parts do not exhibit it. Feedback loops can help understand the emergent behavior.

the system will perform effectively; it might bring unintended detrimental effect to the whole.

The U.S. health care system is an example of a system that is optimized in parts yet perhaps the most expensive patient care system with unsatisfactory patient care. The health care system has highly optimized and highly profitable subsystems of insurance, doctors, hospitals, pharmaceuticals, laboratories, and others, yet provide the most expensive but by some measures the lowest quality patient care in the industrialized world (Common Wealth Fund, 2010).

Keeping the whole picture is extremely critical for any optimization efforts. Although made in the context of building architecture, Finnish builder Alvar Aalto's quote (italics added) has abiding significance for software/enterprise architecture as well: 'Nothing is dangerous in architecture as *dealing with separated problems*. If we split life in separated problems, we split the possibility of making a good building art'.

Enterprises have found advantage with systems thinking approach to architecture.

The Institute of Systemic Leadership (2012) suggests the following as some of principles

Box 2. Systems thinking in architecture @ Ford motor company: Project Edison

http://www.appliedsystemsthinking.com/supporting_documents/Leveraging_Ford.pdf

In the fall of 2003, Ford Motor Company's Information Technology Group began to look at the organization's fragmented IT infrastructure. This undertaking was named the "Edison Project" in hopes that it would "shed some light" on the complexities of the group's business of warehousing, building, and transferring data throughout the company. Everyone agreed that IT fragmentation was a costly and time consuming issue that needed to be dealt with, but not on the definition of the problem trying to be solved. Some saw it as a problem of data integration across a shared network of servers. Others saw it as a problem of mixing legacy systems with modern day applications. And everyone had questions. How would they know if they were solving the "right" problem? In solving it, would they create a whole host of new issues? Were they willing to bet their reputation with the business on their instincts about the right solution?

The champion, or sponsor, of the project suggested taking a systemic approach so that the group could see the interrelations of the system and gain a better understanding of the issue. Participants in the project first created an accurate picture of Ford's IT infrastructure. This included what the system looked like to customers, the complexity of the servers, and the complexity of the types of applications. Using systems thinking tools – which included causal loop diagrams and stock-and-flow computer models – helped them articulate and build a shared understanding of the (then-current state) of the organization's IT infrastructure without assigning blame or trying to "fix" a problem.

Armed with this information and a greater understanding of the system at large, group members were able to explain the change in a way that customers could understand, encouraging adoption of the new methodology, and allowing better partnerships between IT and the business.

(partial list) that can help in systems thinking. These will be extremely useful in EA activities.

- Concentrate on the whole, and the interconnections between the parts.
- Explain things in terms of the system's overall purpose.
- Focus on the system's purpose ahead of its processes and procedures.
- Don't let short-term pressures get in the way of understanding the system.
- Build and make use of feedback loops.
- Understand complex dynamics through patterns and feedback loops rather than cause-effect links.
- Facilitate and value emergence.
- Be aware of natural oscillations.
- Embrace the edge of chaos.

The paradox is that should systems thinking precede architectural initiatives or should architectural initiatives enrich systems thinking? How do we ensure that such broad, systemic thinking has been applied in the enterprise architecture initiatives?

Applying Systems Thinking in Enterprise Architecture Development

There are several frameworks available to help and guide enterprise architecture activities. Prominent among them are Zachman, TOGAF, FEAF. TOGAF is a popular open framework for developing, approaching and maintaining enterprise architecture. TOGAF suggests a methodology (including guidelines and techniques) for developing enterprise architecture, outlines typical architectural deliverables, provides reference model, suggests way of organizing architectural artifacts and discusses how architectural capabilities can be managed in an enterprise. At core of TOGAF, is its Architectural Development Method (ADM), which is an eight phase iterative process for developing and maintaining enterprise architecture. Each phase is defined by objectives, approach, inputs, steps and outputs. Excellent reference materials are available for TOGAF.

We suggest Table 2's seven points to bring in systems thinking while using TOGAF as the framework for guiding enterprise architecture.

Table 2. TOGAF architecture development method and integration of systems thinking

TOGAF Framework	Activity	What Can Be Done?	Rationale
ADM: Preliminary Phase	Defining Enterprise	Create a map of interrelationships in the extended enterprise.	Enhanced 'Scope of Organizations Impacted' document.
ADM: Phase A – Architecture Vision Stakeholder Analysis	Stakeholder Analysis	Stakeholders should be broad enough to include representation from ecosystem players.	Stakeholder Matrix to show ecosystem players
ADM, Phase C: Information Systems Architecture	Develop data and application architecture	Whether explicitly required or not, prepare an output for 'Data Exchange' and list out how data can move in and out of systems.	No systems can live in isolation. Integration should be an inbuilt capability.
ADM, Phase H: Architecture Change Management	Process of managing changes to architecture	In the business drivers for architecture change, suggest that we include 'Ecosystem Changes' to specifically bring in systems thinking focus.	Model and think about possibilities of change originating from the environment.
Architecture Principles	Develop principles for development of enterprise architecture	Like Business Principles, Data Principles, Application Principles, Technology Principles have a section for 'Collaboration Principles'. Principles like Open Standards, Granular Data Access can be included as examples.	Architecture Principles must be inherently tuned towards collaboration as a reality rather than built for it as an afterthought.
Architectural Artifact: View Point	To describe architecture in various views	Include a viewpoint for 'Ecosystem/Extended Enterprise'	Important to understand the large context.
Architecture Skills Framework	Skills and Experience norms for staff undertaking enterprise architecture work	Include a skill area for 'Systems Thinking'.	Current focus is heavily focusing inside the enterprise to do architecture work. Architects should have broader, contextual understanding.

Irrespective of the methodology used to approach enterprise architecture, at effective intervention points the enterprise architects must ensure that the principles of systems thinking are applied. Generally, the office of enterprise architecture is mandated with governance. Governance offers a very good influencing position and leadership opportunities for enterprise architects.

Architecture Leadership by Governance

The word governance is derived from Greek verb kubernao, meaning to steer. Steering is a leadership activity; hence governance, quite naturally, is a leadership activity. Architecture leadership finds a strong expression in governance activities. Our proposal is that systems thinking must be the lens through architecture is effectively governed. Architecture prepares enterprises for the constantly changing environment by giving a frame of reference. Governance is an important mechanism towards managing transformation.

Architectural governance is a set of mechanisms through which architecture is enacted in the enterprise (Aziz et al., 2005). There are three main components to architecture governance as depicted in Figure 1.

All the three are closely enmeshed. Processes are required to ensure adherence to principles and processes need appropriate organizational structure to implement. For governance models to be most successful, the organizational structure should be home grown. This will ensure that it is built in line with the culture of the organization and has executive management blessings.

The Open Group suggests a similar approach as key strategic elements for successful functioning of governance. In the parlance of The Open Group (Architecture Governance, 2012) the main elements for governance are: cross organizational Architecture Board, a comprehensive set of architectural principles and an architecture compliance strategy. While elaborating on the merits of archi-

Figure 1. Components of architecture governance

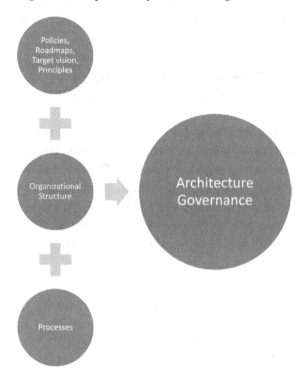

tecture governance, The Open Group (Architecture Governance, 2012) lists the following:

- Links IT processes, resources, and information to organizational strategies and objectives.
- Integrates and institutionalizes IT best practices.
- Aligns with industry frameworks such as COBIT (planning and organizing, acquiring and implementing, delivering and supporting, and monitoring IT performance).
- Enables the organization to take full advantage of its information, infrastructure, and hardware and software assets.
- Protects the underlying digital assets of the organization.
- Supports regulatory and best practice requirements such as auditability, security, responsibility, and accountability.
- Promotes visible risk management.

In the information age characterized by interconnectedness and complexity, the governance policies and principles must be inspired by systems thinking. Awareness of the overall extended enterprise is critical for policy makers. For example, in an extended enterprise, the data consumers will have varying needs. Conformance to multidimensional role based security controls and the ability to audit data feeds will form a critical principle while taking any decision.

Solution context is extremely important while formulating architecture governance. Governance is ultimately for business and it is not just IT governance. Hence the context of operating environment is critical.

Success of efforts in enterprise architecture usually hinges on governance. Gartner (Gartner, 2012) identifies 'not establishing effective EA governance early' as one of the top 10 reasons for EA failures. We posit that unless the principles

and policies that guide governance are themselves informed and enriched by systems thinking, failure rates are unlikely to abate. Solution context should be driven by systems thinking.

Enriching EA with Systems Thinking

We see three major areas where systems thinking can help enrich EA: coherence, horizontal perspective and decision making.

Consider the case of purchase of an automobile – car. The purchaser will eventually be requiring periodic services and may be using the manufacturer's authorized service centers. For the car manufacturer, selling and services are usually two different business units; the manufacturer separately optimizes on business units. This compromises coherence and jeopardizes customer delight by inadvertently offering varying levels of customer experience. In the intensely competi-

Box 3. Clinical governance model at the UK National Health Service: Evidence of systems thinking

```
http://home.health.tvu.ac.uk/richardwells/pdfs%20and%20documents/Healthcare%20
goverance%20and%20the%20modernisation%20of%20the%20NHS.pdf
```

```
The NHS was established in 1948 to provide comprehensive healthcare for all citi-
zens based on need, not the ability to pay. Its principal aim was to ensure the
highest level of physical and mental
```

```
health within available resources by promoting health and preventing ill-health,
diagnosing and treating injury and disease and caring for those with long-term
illness and/or disability. Half a century later, the NHS has become one of the
great British institutions, employing around a million people in England alone
and costing over £50 billion a year to run (rising to £69 billion by 2005).
```

```
A framework through which NHS organizations are accountable for continuously
improving the quality of their services and safeguarding high standards of care
by creating an environment in which excellence in clinical care will flourish.
```

```
As each of the components of clinical governance develop, they have a knock-on
effect on other sections of the organization. Systems thinking is critical to
coordinating developments and taking advantage of growing strengths in different
sectors of the organization.
```

tive world characterized by multiple choices for customers, coherence is a preeminent priority for enterprises. Systems thinking can help EA by facilitating coherence as it offers a panoramic perspective.

Connectedness is not sufficiently modeled or given attention to in EA efforts. Linkages are very important to understand the cause and effects. EA focuses on vertical linkages – from business capability to business process to applications to information/data to infrastructure. The crucial missing element is the horizontal linkages – how different entities are influencing one another. Feedback loops of systems thinking offer the horizontal perspective and it can dramatically improve the utility of EA artifacts in understanding the whole picture.

The office of EA is often required to take decisions and systems thinking will fundamentally change the approach and greatly enhance the quality of decisions. Best decisions are made when we know as much as possible about the situation and the solution options. But that alone is not enough. What is also critically required is systemic thinking that is not satisfied with superficial or point solutions. As will be illustrated in the following section, decisions that are made when trying to optimize one component of the system tend to have unintended detrimental consequences or tend to be suboptimal.

CASE STUDY: PERSONALIZED MEDICINES – SYSTEMS THINKING AND ARCHITECTURE LEADERSHIP

This case study is a conceptual approach on how architecture that is governed by systems thinking can be effectively used to manage complexity and the interconnectedness. For the purposes of the case study, we will maintain the view that the pharmaceutical enterprise is at the center of scheme of things – the discussions are around how could the pharmaceutical enterprise benefit from systems thinking and architecture leadership?

Pharmaceutical industry has traditionally made business by inventing new medicines. The industry enjoys patent protection for many years giving them, at times, extraordinarily attractive returns. Famous blockbuster drugs like Lipitor, Humira, Plavix generate upwards of US $5 billion a year. Unlike consumer goods industry, the influencers in pharmaceutical industry are not the end consumers; it is the prescribers who decide on what medicine is effective to the patients. Expectedly, the industry has spent a lot of energy in trying to understand the prescription behavior and how to influence the prescribers. The entire sales force was tuned towards this goal and incentivized by targets such as new prescriptions, identification of key opinion leaders, visits to prescriber, holding of scientific events for prescribers, etc. In the recent past, payers have emerged as a major influencer as well. The focus on patients and their outcomes was not a direct goal of the pharmaceuticals in the sense that it was beyond their immediate circle of influence.

With increasing interconnectedness and extended enterprises, a welcome change is being witnessed. Pharmaceuticals are talking about how to bring patient focus by aligning with firms that deliver healthcare and firms that pay for healthcare. Consider the following interesting developments:

- Leo Pharma, is known in the industry for its extensive patient reach programs that aim to engage with patients. Psoriasis, a skin condition that Leo Pharma's medicines target, needs a good level of patient compliance in managing the condition. Leo Pharma has provided not only educational services but nurse consultation services as well.
- Merck Pharmaceuticals tied up with insurance company Cigna to announce an outcome based pricing model for their oral diabetic drugs Januvia and Janumet.

- Sanofi SA has announced a partnership with Medco Health Solutions, a pharmacy benefit manager, to provide Sanofi SA with a broader perspective on the needs of governments and health insurers. Typically, regulatory approval for marketing new drugs is based on placebo trials and does not mandate comparative efficacy studies. However, health insurers and governments would like to have scientific details on how effective and comparable the new drug with existing ones in the market.

- Novartis established a partnership with patientslikeme.com, an online community, to work with people who have received organ transplant. Novartis expects that it can get closer to patients as the online setting might allow patients to be more open and share their experiences in a personal way.

- Merck Pharmaceuticals has established a collaboration with Weight Watchers to help physicians (their patients) fight obesity through lifestyle management approach. This is in recognition that mere advice to patients to lose weight is not good enough – patients need intensive assistance and resources.

- Roche has launched a personalized medicine Zelboraf for a particular type of skin cancer. This requires the prescriber to run diagnostic checks on patients for their genetic makeup before prescribing. The regulatory authorities also approved the diagnostic test developed by Roche to identify patients eligible for treatment with Zelboraf.

Each of the above examples, illustrate the innovative reach outside of the traditional realm of pharmaceuticals. These trends will accelerate in the coming years as the convergence will be towards patient care and benefit. Trends like the ones indicated above, require one to think totally differently and architect systems that have inherent characteristics for collaboration. We will examine the emergence of personalized medicine as a reference problem for our discussions.

Personalized medicine is based on scientific understanding that medicines may not always act the same for all patients. Several factors influence the way medicine works: genetic variations, existing ailments/conditions, lifestyle habits, etc. Traditional approach of 'one-size-fits-for-all' is not the safest or the most effective way of prescribing medicines. For instance, Iressa and Tarceva are drugs for treatment of non-small cell lung cancer, but they are effective only in tumors that express the epidermal growth factor receptor gene (West, 2011).

With scientific understanding of human genomes reaching sophisticated levels and technology moving towards commercialization, there is a spurt of interest in personalized medicines. Recognizing the tectonic shifts, FDA recently issued guidelines for drugs based on biomarkers (FDA, 2011). The successful availability of personalized medicines requires that patient's genetic markup is considered during the evaluation of fitment of medicines. This requires close collaboration between labs (Campbell, 2011) that provide genetic markups and the pharmaceutical and the prescribing community. The important players in the personalized medicines and their dynamic influences are depicted in Figure 2 (a simplistic representation).

We will discuss the following:

- How systems thinking principles can help us build a holistic understanding.

- Once the holistic picture is formulated how to use that understanding to device a set of architecture principles.

- How the implementation of architecture principles founded on the basis of systems thinking can be ensured by effective architectural leadership - governance.

Figure 2. Illustrative healthcare eco-systems (key stakeholders and their interactions)

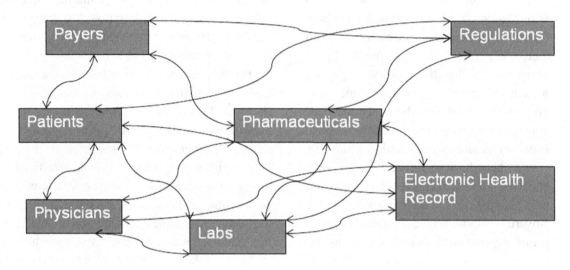

We will discuss about how systems thinking principles help build a broader understanding.

Principle 1: Influence of Operating Environment

Personalized medicine is an emerging trend and there will be a lot of dynamic forces in action. Consider the players: the pharmaceutical trying to device a more effective medicine that can guarantee better outcome, the payer who will ultimately pay for the medicines, the prescriber who needs convincing and who will be working closely with the patient, the labs which will be doing the tests, the systems that maintain patient records, the regulator who is ultimately responsible for patient safety and fairness in business.

Any system that the pharmaceutical wants to create to manage personalized medicine must take into cognizance the extraordinary influence of environment and extended enterprise forces that will create changes in the functionality.

Principle 2: See the Whole

Systems thinking enjoin to use systemic understanding as opposed to purely analytic understanding. In the increasing connected world, where isolation of systems or people is nonexistent, it is very important to cultivate a bigger picture understanding. The diagram shown above illustrates the wider context of personalized medicines and the influence of one another.

Principle 3: Non Linear Influence

All the players do not have equal influence. It will be hard to predict the impact of any change happening in the operating system. Consider a fictitious scenario where the payer decides to change the way effectiveness of medicines is judged. This will impact the pharmaceutical, the labs, the patient, the prescriber. Each impact is bound to cascade further impacts in the ecosystem. The cumulative effect will be nonlinear.

Principle 4: Multiple Interrelationships

The players in the extended enterprise have multiple interrelationships that increase the complexity of the system:

- Regulators influence pharmaceuticals on what can be done or cannot be done.
- Labs that conduct diagnostic test will be governed by regulatory mandates.
- Pharmaceuticals are dependent on labs to provide diagnostic services for personalized medicines.
- Prescribers are dependent on pharmaceutical for medicines.
- Labs are dependent on prescribers for references.

There can be several such relationships and new relationships also emerge with changes in the operating environment.

Principle 5: Feedback Loops and Emergent Behaviors

Due to multiple interrelationships, it is hard to predict the influence of one over the other. Feedback loops are essential mechanism to understand what types of relationships govern between the systems. Table 3 attempts to a give this flavor.

As a result of complexity, emergent behaviors are to be expected. An example could be that the payer decides that the costs of genetic markup tests will not be reimbursed and that could result in lesser references to labs by physicians which in turn might hurt the revenue sharing agreements between pharmaceutical and the labs.

Architectural Principles

Systems thinking perspective provides a broader view of extended enterprise and the influence of one player over the other. Ultimately, the software architecture must facilitate integration of systems.

Paramount architectural principle in any collaboration oriented architecture is data privacy and security. The participating players should be assured that there is no compromise in data security. Architectural considerations must be giving to multiple levels of protection of data as-

Table 3. Healthcare stakeholders and plausible feedback loops

Players	Feedback Loops
Payers and Pharmaceuticals	Health Economics
Pharmaceuticals and Regulators	Establish safety of medicines
Pharmaceuticals and Labs	Establishing understanding of patients genetic makeup
Labs and Prescribers	Biomarket tests, Dosage determination, Safety
Patients and Prescribers	Efficacy and Safety
Patients and Payers	Payment for health care

sets, levels of data access. Parts of functionality may be required by extended enterprise for collective operation and hence consideration must be given if the architecture is modular and service enabled. It is hard to predict the number of tests required and the prescriber references. Scalability is an important principle that must be kept in mind while architecting systems for personalized medicines. Another important principle is the need for real time data exchange. As soon as the lab results are ready, it must be made accessible to the prescriber. As there are multiple players and the possibility for more players joining the extended enterprise cannot be ruled out, it is critical that open standards are followed for all interfaces. For instance, a pharmacy that sells personalized medicines might join the extended enterprise. Having open standards will facilitate easier integration. Extensibility is another important capability that will be required and architectural principles must enable that. An instance could be that of a new payer joining the extended enterprise.

While formulating architectural principles, it is essential that clear reasoning for principles is documented. The impact of lack of compliance to standards must be documented so that the underlying thought process can be understood. Such an understanding will greatly aid in decisions in governance.

Architecture Leadership by Governance

As discussed earlier, governance is assuming a very critical role especially in extended enterprises as the complexity is high. The forces on extended can originate from outside the influence of pharmaceutical. It must be ensured that the architectural principles that were outlined earlier are complied with.

Let us consider the case of a new lab, Best Diagnostics, joining the extended enterprise. Let us say that the pharmaceutical has already developed system interfaces for existing labs that are based on open standards. Best Diagnostics, is the most powerful player in the industry and uses its size as the influencing power and mandates that the pharmaceutical should interface with its system in the way it wants. Business did not abhor the idea considering the clout of Best Diagnostics. The matter was presented to architecture governance board for deliberations and direction.

The governance board is guided by the principles of extended enterprises: open standards is one of the mandated principles. Although in the microscopic view, the interface requested by Best Diagnostics seemed to make business sense, it will create unintended consequences. Consider the situation when the payer requests lab results. Having multiple types of standards will create roadblocks for systemic integration in the overall extended enterprise.

In the absence of architectural principles that are based on systems thinking, probably, the pharmaceutical would not have thought of the overall impact of the decisions. Systems thinking provide enterprises with a much clearer view of the dynamic world and the extent of interconnectedness. This should be used to formulate architectural principles with a clear reasoning so that governance can effectively be accomplished.

RESEARCH TOPIC: FRAGILITY OF COMPLEX SYSTEMS

An interesting research area in complex systems is in analyzing how and when these systems fail. Such an insight will be extremely valuable to identify hidden vulnerabilities. On the whole, the complex system is extremely sophisticated and so are the subsystems that are part of the complex system. Nonetheless, failure due occur in complex systems. The failures occur due to nonlinear interactions in subsystems resulting in emergent behavior which was not anticipated.

In an elegantly researched article Crutchfield (2009) writes that complex systems are inherently fragile. Crutchfield believes that bigger is not better and it is naïve to assume that systems are always composed of independent modules. It may have been designed that way but due to dynamic interactions, the modularity of the systems gets lost and that forms the basis for manifestation of emergent behavior. Understanding of the emergent behavior and the loss of modularity of systems pose interesting challenges for software architecture. Architectures are needed to provide a common foundation for understanding, maintaining and analyzing complex systems.

For the subsystems that are part of complex systems, one can consider that the critical functional features and interfaces that link with other subsystems are the critical capabilities. By identifying and synthesizing such critical capabilities in each subsystem, an architectural understanding of complex system can be realized.

CONCLUSION

In this chapter, we saw how systems thinking provide the much needed holistic perspective to the enterprise architecture initiatives. Information age is characterized by extended enterprises united by common objectives. Interconnectedness of enterprises gives rise to complexity; complexity

Box 4. New approach needed to prevent major 'systemic failures'

http://www.purdue.edu/newsroom/research/2011/110131VenkatasubramanianF.html

A Purdue University (2011) researcher, Venkatasubramanian, is proposing development of a new cross-disciplinary approach for analyzing and preventing systemic failures in complex systems that play a role in calamities ranging from huge power blackouts to the BP Deepwater Horizon disaster and the subprime mortgage crisis.

While these are different disasters that happened in different domains, in different facilities, triggered by different events, involve different ingredients, and so on, there are, however, certain common underlying patterns behind such systemic failures. There is an alarming sameness about such major accidents, which underscores important fundamental lessons that need to be learned in order to prevent such events from recurring. To understand these patterns and learn from them, one needs to go beyond analyzing them as independent one-off accidents and examine them in the broader perspective of the potential fragility of all complex engineered systems. One needs to study all these disasters from a common systems engineering perspective, so that one can thoroughly understand the commonalities as well as the differences, in order to better design and control such systems in the future.

"Typically, systemic failures occur due to fragility in complex systems," Venkatasubramanian said. "Modern technological advances are creating a rapidly increasing number of complex engineered systems, processes and products, which pose considerable challenges in ensuring their proper design, analysis, control, safety and management for successful operation over their life cycles"

"In particular, the nonlinear interactions among a large number of interdependent components and the environment can lead to what we call 'emergent' behavior," Venkatasubramanian said. "In other words, the behavior of the whole is different than the sum of its parts and can be difficult to anticipate and control."

gives rise to dynamic and hard to predict behaviors. Traditional notions of enterprise architecture were based on enterprises operating in a relatively stable condition. Novel ways to deal with complexity and building a holistic picture is essential for ensuring an architecture led evolution.

The chapter discussed about how the complex systems behavior is hard to predict. A sophisticated complex system which is made up of several sophisticated individual systems can have

hidden vulnerabilities. Synergistic contributions that manifest in dynamic conditions cannot be understood by reductionist approach of analysis. Architectural decisions that derive contextual understanding from systems thinking are likely to make architecture a living, dynamic tool for governing and managing an enterprise. We looked at how possibly TOGAF can be enriched by systems thinking. The relevance and acceptance of architecture as a profession with immense practicality can be substantially enhanced by applying the principles of systems thinking.

As enterprises become more and more extended, the need for architecture as a way to manage the complexity will become acute. During the next few years we anticipate significant progress in understanding of emergent behavior, impact of that on architecture, ways of modeling the same and governance that places emphasis on systems thinking.

Attesting to the relevance of systems thinking and need to cultivate such skills in young minds, academic institutions are showing great interest in systems thinking and its application. Interesting research work on novel applications of systems thinking is happening in MIT. The hallowed institute is offering a graduate program on Systems Design and Management. That leadership powered by architecture is poised for very interesting times is evident from the wide array of ongoing, inter-disciplinary research involving organizational structures, business management, complexity science, leadership theories, information science and public administration.

REFERENCES

Aldrich, M. (2008). *Innovative information systems 1980-1990*. Retrieved from http://www.aldricharchive.com/innovative_information.html

Alexander, J. (2007). *The value of enterprise architecture*. Retrieved from http://www.statcan.gc.ca/conferences/it-ti2007/pdf/alexander04a-eng.pdf

Aziz, Obitz, Modi, & Sarkar. (2005). *Enterprise architecture: A governance framework -- Part I: Embedding architecture into the organization*. Technical report. Infosys Technologies Ltd.

Cambell, C. D. (2011). *Systems thinking in personalized medicines*. Paper presented in 2011 MIT SDM Conference on Systems Thinking for Contemporary Challenges. Retrieved on July 30, 2012 from http://sdm.mit.edu/systemsthinking-conference/2011/docs/Campbell_2011-Systems-Thinking-Conference.pdf

Charette, N. R. (2005). Why software fails. IEEE Spectrum. Retrieved from http://spectrum.ieee.org/computing/software/why-software-fails/0

Common Wealth Fund. (2010). *US ranks last among 7 countries on health system performance*. Retrieved from http://www.eurekalert.org/pub_releases/2010-06/cf-url062210.php

Crutchfield, J. P. (2009). The hidden fragility of complex systems—Consequences of change, changing consequences. In Ascione, G., Massip, C., & Perello, J. (Eds.), *Cultures of change: Social atoms and electronic lives* (pp. 98–111). Barcelona, Spain: ACTAR D Publishers.

Davis, E. W., & Spekman, E. R. (2003). *The extended enterprise: Gaining competitive advantage through collaborative supply chains*. FT Press.

de Savigny, D., & Taghreed, A. (Eds.). (2009). Systems thinking for health systems strengthening. Geneva: Alliance for Health Policy and Systems Research, WHO.

Doucet, G., Gtze, J., Bernard, S., & Saha, P. (2009). *Architecting the enterprise for alignment, agility and assurance*. International Enterprise Architecture Institute.

Drucker, P. (1999). *Management challenges for the 21st century*. New York: Harper Business Press.

FDA. (2011). Building the infrastructure to drive and support personalized medicine. Retrieved on July 30, 2012 from http://www.fda.gov/AboutFDA/ReportsManualsForms/Reports/ucm274440.htm

Friedman, T. L. (2005). *The world is flat: A brief history of the twenty-first century*. New York: Farrar, Straus and Giroux.

Gartner. (2012). *Garter identifies ten enterprise architecture pitfalls*. Retrieved from http://www.gartner.com/it/page.jsp?id=1159617

Land, M., Proper, E., Waage, M., Cloo, J., & Steghuis, C. (2008). *Enterprise architecture: Creating value by informed governance*. Berlin: Springer Publishing Company, Incorporated.

Latham, R. (2002). Information technology and social transformation. *International Studies Review*, *4*, 101–115. doi:10.1111/1521-9488.t01-1-00254.

Olson, E. E., & Eoyang, H. G. (2001). *Facilitating organization change: Lessons from complexity science*. Hoboken, NJ: John Wiley & Sons.

Open Group. (2012). *Architecture governance*. Retrieved from http://pubs.opengroup.org/architecture/togaf8-doc/arch/chap26.html#tagfcjh_32

Petzinger, T. Jr. (1999). *The new pioneers: The men and women who are transforming the workplace and marketplace*. New York: Simon & Schuster.

Prabhupada, S. (1997). *Bhagavad gita as it is*. Bhaktivedanta Book Trust.

Purdue University. (2011). *New approach needed to prevent major 'systemic failures'*. Retrieved on July 30, 2012 from http://www.purdue.edu/newsroom/research/2011/110131Venkatasubramanianf.html

Seitjs, G., Crossman, M., & Billou, N. (2010). Coping with complexity. *Ivey Business Journal*. Retrieved from http://www.iveybusinessjournal.com/topics/leadership/coping-with-complexity

Senge, P. M. (1990). *The Fifth Discipline: The Art and Practice of the Learning Organization*. New York: Currency Doubleday.

Sessions, R. (2006). *A better path to enterprise architecture*. Retrieved from http://msdn.microsoft.com/en-us/library/aa479371.aspx#sessionsfinal100_topic3

Stewart, A. T. (1998). *Intellectual capital: The new wealth of organizations*. Crown Publishing Group. doi:10.1002/pfi.4140370713.

The Institute of Systematic Leadership. (2012). *The historical link between systems thinking and leadership*. Retrieved from http://www.systemicleadershipinstitute.org/systemic-leadership/theories/the-historic-link-between-systems-thinking-and-leadership/

Uhl-Bien, M., Marion, & McKelvey. (2007). Complexity leadership theory: Shifting leadership from the industrial age to the knowledge era. *The Leadership Quarterly*, *18*, 298–318. doi:10.1016/j.leaqua.2007.04.002.

West, M. D. (2011). *Enabling personalized medicine through health information technology: Advancing the integration of information*. Retrieved on July 30, 2012 from http://www.brookings.edu/research/papers/2011/01/28-personalized-medicine-west

Winter, K., Buckl, S., Matthes, F., & Schweda, C. M. (2010). Investigating the state-of-the-art in enterprise architecture management methods in literature and practice. In *Proceedings of MCIS*. Retrieved from http://aisel.aisnet.org/mcis2010/90

ADDITIONAL READING

Daft, R. L., Murphy, & Willmott. (2010). *Organization theory and design*. Cengage Learning EMEA.

Doucet, G., Gotze, J., Saha, P., & Bernard, S. (2008). Coherency management: Using enterprise architecture for alignment, agility, and assurance. Journal of Enterprise Architecture. Retrieved from http://siteresources.worldbank.org/extedevelopment/Resources/JEA_May_2008_Coherency_Management.pdf?resourceurlname=JEA_May_2008_Coherency_Management.pdf

Edson, R. (2008). *Systems thinking: Applied: Primer*. Arlington, VA: Applied Systems Thinking Institute.

Filder. (2007). Architecture amidst anarchy. Global Health Governance, 1(1). Retrieved from http://diplomacy.shu.edu/academics/global_health

Fritjof, C. (2002). *The hidden connections: A science for sustainable living*. New York: Doubleday.

Gharajedaghi, J. (2011). *Systems thinking: Managing chaos and complexity: A platform for designing business architecture* (3rd ed.). London: Elsevier Inc..

Hoverstadt, P. (2008). *The fractal organization: Creating sustainable organizations with the viable system model*. Hoboken, NJ: John Wiley & Sons.

Khan, M. (2012). Archetypes of organisation: Laying systemic enterprise architecture foundations at an upstream oil and gas company. *Journal of Enterprise Architecture*. Retrieved from http://aeajournal.info/article/archetypes-of-organisation-laying-systemic-enterprise-architecture-foundations-at-an-upstream-oil-and-gas-company/

Laszlo, E. (1996). *The systems view of the world: A holistic vision for our time* (2nd ed.). New York: Hampton Press.

Luftman, J. N. (2002). *Competing in the information age: Align in the sand* (2nd ed.). Oxford, UK: Oxford University Press.

Lyytinen, K., & Robey, D. (1999). Learning failure in information systems development. *Information Systems Journal, 9*, 85–101. doi:10.1046/j.1365-2575.1999.00051.x.

MacCormack, A., Baldwin, C., & Rusnak, J. (2012). *The architecture of complex systems: Do core-periphery structures dominate?* Harvard Business School. Retrieved on July 30, 2012 from http://www.hbs.edu/research/pdf/10-059.pdf

Mueller, L., & Phillipson, A. (2007). *The emerging role of IT governance*. Retrieved from http://www.ibm.com/developerworks/rational/library/dec07/mueller_phillipson/index.html

National Research Council. (1985). *Information technologies and social transformation*. Washington, DC: The National Academies Press.

Niemann, K. D. (2006). *From enterprise architecture to IT governance*. Berlin: Springer.

Nightingale, D. J., & Rhodes, D. H. (2004). *Enterprise systems architecting: Emerging art and science within engineering systems*. Paper presented at the MIT Engineering Systems Symposium. Cambridge, MA: MIT.

Reed, E. G. (2006). *Leadership and systems thinking*. Retrieved from http://www.au.af.mil/au/awc/awcgate/dau/ree_mj06.pdf

Ross, W. J., Weill, P., & Robertson, D. (2006). *Enterprise architecture as strategy: Creating a foundation for business execution*. Boston: Harvard Business Review Press.

Rouse, B. W. (2007). *Healthcare system as a complex adaptive system: Implications for design and management*. Retreived from http://medicine.utah.edu/internalmedicine/patient_empowerment/papers/Rouse%20NAEBridge2008%20HealthcareComplexity.pdf

Saha, P. (Ed.). (2007). *Handbook of enterprise systems architecture in practice*. Hershey, PA: IGI Global. doi:10.4018/978-1-59904-189-6.

Saha, P. (Ed.). (2009). *Advances in government enterprise architecture*. Hershey, PA: IGI Global.

Saha, P. (2010). *Enterprise architecture as platform for connected government*. Retrieved from http://unpan1.un.org/intradoc/groups/public/documents/unpan/unpan039390.pdf

Schneider, V. (2007). *Johannes M Bauer governance: Prospects of complexity theory in revisiting system theory*. Paper presented at the Annual Meeting of the Midwest Political Science Association. Chicago, IL.

Sessions, R. (2008). Simple architectures for complex enterprises (pro-best practices) (best practices (microsoft)). Microsoft Press.

Stephen, H., Gail, A.-S., & McKinlay, J. (2005). *Enterprise-wide change: Superior results through systems thinking*. Hoboken, NJ: John Wiley & Sons.

Taylor, C. (2009). *Systemic leadership*. Retrieved from http://www.theknowledge.biz/resources/Systemic-Leadership.pdf

Venkatasubramanian, V. (2011). Systemic failures: Challenges and opportunities in risk management in complex systems. *AIChE Journal. American Institute of Chemical Engineers*, *57*, 2–9. doi:10.1002/aic.12495.

KEY TERMS AND DEFINITIONS

Architecture Governance: A way of managing that uses/relies artifacts from architecture efforts.

Complexity: Something with many parts in intricate arrangement. Hard to predict the behavior.

Enterprise Architecture (EA): An architectural approach that links all aspects of an enterprise primarily business and IT.

Extended Enterprise: A set of enterprises coming together for a purpose.

Interconnectedness: Enterprises linked together by business and have a dependence on each other.

Operating Environment: The social and business environment where the system works.

Systems Thinking: Thinking that is based on holistic approach.

Chapter 6
Enterprise-in-Environment Adaptation:
Enterprise Architecture and Complexity Management

James S. Lapalme
École de Technologie Supérieure, Canada

Donald W. de Guerre
Concordia University, Canada

ABSTRACT

Enterprise Architecture (EA) is a consulting practice and discipline intended to improve the management and functioning of complex organizations. The various approaches to EA can be classified by how they define what is to be architected and what, as a result, is the relevant environment. Traditionally, management has been understood as "Planning, Organizing, Command, Coordinating, and Controlling" (POCCC), that is, the role is bounded within the organization. The corresponding EA approach suggests architecting IT systems to support management, with the implicit environment being members of the organization as well as partner organizations. As the objective of EA practice expands to include organizational members, technical systems, and a wider set of stakeholders, so too does the complexity it must address. This results in an enlarged domain of issues and concerns. Finally, if the objective of EA is a sustainable enterprise, then physical, societal, and ecological environments radically increase the complexity of actualizing this goal. Corresponding to this increase in scope is a parallel shift in the scope of management concerns. With the goal of pushing EA towards concerns regarding enterprise sustainability, an open socio-technical system design perspective of EA, which we have named Enterprise-in-Environment Adaptation (EiEA), is discussed. EiEA offers a comprehensive approach to respond to the demands for complexity management that arise when working towards enterprise sustainability; yet, it requires that organisations also embrace deep culture changes, such as participative design, worker empowerment, as well as shared accountability and responsibility, to name a few.

DOI: 10.4018/978-1-4666-4518-9.ch006

INTRODUCTION

The world has become an increasingly challenging place to live in, especially in the last decade. Modern information and communication have played key roles in shrinking the previously perceived "large world" into a "global village" (McLuhan, 1962). Virtually speaking, your next-door neighbour could be halfway across the planet and be contacted through the click of a button. Keeping cultures and ways of living relatively separate in a "large world" was challenging in the past, especially nations in close geographical proximity. However, in a relatively "small global village," it is impossible to avoid a mingling between the residents of the various "global neighbourhoods." Consequently, as cultures mix, ways of living and thinking are changing across the globe; but there are many more challenges in the world besides cultural transformation. At one time, governments were considered almost as solid as bedrock; they were the foundation on which societies and civilisations were built. One could hardly imagine the fall of a government or a country as an outcome of a civil or intercountry war. Today, these once rock-like governments are recognized as large piles of pebbles that can be toppled by the winds of social change, population uprisings, and market turbulence. Just in the last couple of years, significant countries, such as Greece, Italy, Egypt, and Tunisia, have been profoundly shaken. People are now face-to-face with the fact that governments will not necessarily last throughout their lifetime and that they have the power to instigate change.

As the world has become a challenging place to live in, it has also become a very challenging place in which to manage an organisation! Similar to people, organisations now face "global markets" that are subject to ongoing cultural transformation and impacted by governmental instabilities. In addition to being affected by the turbulence that comes from outside of their boundaries, organisations are also faced with the complexities of the world's challenges within their boundar-

ies. As organisations span across the globe, their personnel have become richly multicultural and are constantly evolving. Modern personnel must be able to function with the challenges of cultural diversity as well as the resulting plurality of perspectives. Today's organisations must "survive" in the modern world where, in the blink of an eye, allies become foes and foes become allies. As an example from the business sector, the customer of the past, who was faithful and content with procuring the goods and services that companies decided to make available, has now become a sophisticated consumer who wants what they want and when they want it. Moreover, the contemporary consumer will, when possible, approach competitors in the "global village neighbourhood" in a heartbeat if he/she is not satisfied.

Put simply, the world has become a complex place within which complex organisations operate. How are organisations to cope with such pervasive complexity? Enterprise Architecture (EA) is a practice and discipline intended to improve the management and functioning of complex organisations. In the literature and in practice, there are many different, and at times contradicting, perspectives on the nature of EA, especially with regards to its scope and the nature of its activities. We interpret the term "scope" to mean the breadth of elements that are considered inputs, constraints, and items to be architected, in other words, that which is encompassed by, and is relevant to, the enterprise. We interpret the term "nature" to refer to the characteristics of the activities encompassed by the act of architecture. This chapter will focus on a particular perspective of EA for the management of complexity. The perspective is grounded in open socio-technical system theory, which is a specific system thinking theory about organisations. Our intent is to present how open social-technical systems theory can serve as a foundation for the management of organisational complexity and dynamism and how it would inform the operationalization of enterprise architecture.

In this chapter, we will present a systemic perspective on EA based on the modern form of socio-technical systems design: open socio-technical systems design. According to open socio-technical systems design, our stance, entitled Enterprise-in-Environment[1] Adaptation (EiEA), is concerned with enterprise sustainability and the management of the associated complexity. Through this narrative, it is our intent to expose the assumptions, implications, and limits of our perspective.

In order to present our ideas, we will first discuss how we interpret the meaning of complexity management in the context of EA. To aid us in this discussion, we will share a framework about complexity and its management. The framework will then be used as a cornerstone for a discussion about various schools of thought on EA found in the literature and their associate perspectives on complexity management. This will be followed by an explanation of open socio-technical systems design. We will then explain the key ramifications for EA if it were to be grounded in the EiEA design approach. A comparison between typical EA methodologies and EiEA will be presented. The comparison will be followed by a discussion on complexity management in the context of EiEA. We will conclude with a discussion of the benefits and the challenges of EiEA as well as the implications for governance and organisational leadership.

It must be noted that our intent is not to give an exhaustive explanation of open socio-technical systems theory and design; such an endeavour would require an entire book. We would rather refer the reader to the many books and articles that are available on this topic. In addition, our intent is not to offer a step-by-step guide for the execution of EA according to open socio-technical systems theory, for again this would require a vastly more substantial text in order to be of practical use. Rather, we offer important guidelines that should serve as the grounding for EA practice and execution if one wishes to address the complexities of enterprise sustainability.

COMPLEXITY AND MANAGEMENT

In order to discuss the concept of complexity management, it is important that we first define our interpretation of the terms "complexity" and "management." We will interpret the term "complexity" in a very general sense as meaning beyond absolute and complete understanding; hence, something that is complex cannot be perfectly understood. In the context of our discussion on EA, we are particular interested in the notion of complex systems. A special edition of the magazine *Science* offers a number of informal and complementary definitions of the term "complex systems":

- A complex system is a highly structured system that shows structure with variations (Goldenfeld and Kadanoff, 1999);
- A complex system is one whose evolution is very sensitive to initial conditions or to small perturbations, one in which the number of independent interacting components is large, or one in which there are multiple pathways by which the system can evolve (Whitesides and Ismagilov, 1999);
- A complex system is one that by design or function or both is difficult to understand and verify (Weng, Bhalla, and Iyengar, 1999);
- A complex system is one in which there are multiple interactions between many different components (Rind, 1999);
- Complex systems are systems in process that constantly evolve and unfold over time (Arthur, 1999);

As the reader can see, our general interpretation is very similar to that of Weng et al. (1999). For the intent of our discussion, it is sufficient to understand a complex system as a system that:

- Cannot be perfectly understood through analysis;
- Has properties that emerge from the interactions of the system's sub-parts;
- Is in a process of constant evolution over time.

There are many complex systems that can be considered in the context of organizations and enterprises, as summarized by Table 1.

Table 2 gives a summary of the complexities that emerge from the interrelations between the various complex systems. Together, Table 1 and Table 2 offer a framework for discussions about complexity in the context of EA.

Complexity Management

The term management has been traditionally understood as "Planning, Organizing, Command, Coordinating, and Controlling" (POCCC), that is, the role of management is bounded within the organization (Fayol, 1917). However, in the context of complexity, the concept of management must be adapted. A POCCC approach is viable in the absence of complexity and when it is possible to perfectly understand a system as well as predict its evolution. When faced with complexity, POCCC is not possible because both perfect understanding

Table 1. Basic complexity sources in the context of organisations and enterprises

Basic sources	Informal Descriptions
Environmental (market) Complexities	The environmental complexities encompass all of the elements and their interactions that are considered by the enterprise to lie of its boundaries, for example: customers, governments, competitors, technologies, cultures, etc.
Social System	The social system encompasses all of the elements and their interactions with regards to the human aspect considered by the enterprise to be within its boundaries, for example, personnel, organizational culture, psychological needs, etc.
Technological System	The technological system encompasses all of the elements and their interactions with regards to the technologies used within the boundaries of the enterprise, for example, IT assets, knowledge, automation tools, work design, etc.
Operational System	The operational system encompasses all of the elements and their interactions with regards to how day-to-day work is designed and executed. This system can be considered to be a sub-system of the technological system.
Strategic System	The strategic system encompasses all of the elements and their interactions with regards to how the enterprise strategy is defined. This system can also be considered to be a sub-system of the technological system.

Table 2. Interrelation complexities

Interrelation Complexities	Informal Descriptions
Socio-technical complexity	The complexity that emerges from the interactions between the social and technical systems of an enterprise.
Strategy execution complexity	The complexity that emerges from the interactions between the strategic and socio-technical systems.
Enterprise-in-environment complexity	The complexity that emerges from the interactions between the enterprise and the environmental systems.

and evolution prediction are not possible. In such contexts, organisations must shift towards "mindfulness"; they must become considerate rather then controlling. An example of such mindfulness is the concept of High Reliability Organisations (HRO) (Weick & Sutcliffe, 2007).

Weick and Sutcliffe (2007) define five key characteristics that HROs possess:

- Preoccupation with failure;
- Reluctance to simplify interpretations;
- Sensitivity to operations;
- Commitment to resilience;
- Deference to expertise.

HROs function through fostering mindfulness.

In summary, there are various sources of complexities that can be considered in the context of EA. Moreover, with regards to complexity management, we can conceptualise a continuum between a traditional management approach (POCCC) at one end and mindfulness at the other. This continuum is depicted in Figure 1. Moving from the traditional management end of the continuum to mindfulness represents a shift in beliefs from determinism to indeterminism.

ENTERPRISE ARCHITECTURE SCHOOLS OF THOUGHT AND COMPLEXITY MANAGEMENT

As proposed by Lapalme (2012), there are multiple schools of thought with regards to EA that can be identified in the literature. Each school of thought perceives the realities that are the enterprise and the practice of EA through the lens of its own belief system; this lens filters and/or puts emphasis on various types of complexity.

Enterprise IT Architecting (EITA) School: According to this school of thought, EA is about aligning the IT assets of the enterprise (through strategy, design, and management) to achieve effective organizational strategy execution and operations by developing the proper IT capabilities. This school of thought is very techno-economic centric in that it is particularly concerned with achieving IT cost reduction through technology reuse and de-duplication. This school of thought is guided by the practices of software engineering, which promote a reductionist approach through mantras such as "divide-and-conquer." Consequently, its process of architecting, through the use of models and views, often tries to neatly separate the IT assets of the enterprise into components and sub-components, which are then designed and assembled according to software engineering best practices. The lens of this school of thought filters all but a subset of the complexities related to the enterprise's technological system; only the architecture and strategic management of IT assets are considered. This school of thought promotes a traditional POCCC approach to complexity management.

Enterprise Integrating (EI) School: According to this school of thought, EA is about designing all of the facets of the enterprise so that enterprise strategy may be executed by maximizing the overall coherency (in regards to the strategy) between all of its facets, of which IT is one. This school of thought is grounded in systems thinking and, hence, approaches the design of enterprises

Figure 1. Complexity management strategy continuum

220

holistically or systemically. The guiding principle of the school of thought is that a reductionist approach to enterprise design and strategy execution is not adequate; therefore, all of the aspects of the organization, which form a complex fabric of reinforcing and attenuating dynamics, must be globally optimized and designed. Because of its grounding in systems thinking, this school of thought is capable of designing comprehensive solutions that take into account all of the various known aspects of enterprises. The lens of this school of thought filters the complexity related to the environmental system and the enterprise-in-environment complexities, as well as a portion of the strategic system (the strategy formulation). This school of thought also promotes a POCCC approach to complexity management, but because it is not reductionist in nature, it is positioned in the middle of the continuum depicted in Figure 1.

Enterprise Ecological Adaptation (EEA) School: According to this school of thought, EA is about fostering organizational learning by designing all of the facets of the enterprise and its relationship to its environment to enable innovation and enterprise-in-environment adaption. The guiding principle of this school of thought is that a systemic approach alone is not sufficient to enterprise design; it is necessary to achieve environment and enterprise coevolution by purposefully changing the environment and designing both the enterprise and its relationship to its environment systemically. Coevolution is achieved in three ways; firstly, by making the environment friendlier for the desired goal of the enterprise. This is achieved by reinforcing pockets of desired futures within the environment and by reducing unwanted forces. The second way is by adapting the desired goals of the enterprise to ensure compatibility with the environment of the enterprise. Through environmental learning, the enterprise can learn from the environment and determine desired goals based on desirable futures that already exist in the environment. The third way, similar to the EI school of thought, is through intra-organizational coherency. Because

of its grounding in systems-in-environment thinking; this school of thought is capable of fostering enterprise-in-environment coevolution as well as enterprise coherency. Enterprises designed by this school of thought are conducive to innovation and sustainability. The lens of this school of thought does not filter any of the complexity; it is holistic from the perspective of the complexities identified in Table 1 and Table 2. This school of thought promotes a considerate approach with regards to complexity management. Mindfulness is implicit in the principles that guide its approach to enterprise design.

Table 3 offers a summary of our discussion on the EA schools of thought and complexity management.

EiEA is based on the EEA school of thought; consequently, it inherits its complexity management perspective. The next section will discuss some key aspects of socio-technical systems thinking, analysis, and design that will be relevant to our later discussion of EiEA.

OPEN SOCIO-TECHNICAL SYSTEMS DESIGN

EiEA is concerned with enterprise-in-environment coevolution as well as enterprise coherency. These concerns emerge from its grounding in open socio-technical systems.

Table 3. EA schools of thought and complexity management

Schools of Thought	Considered Complexities	Management Approach
EITA	Subset of technical system (design and strategic management of IT assets)	Traditional POCCC
EI	Social System Technological System Operational System Subset of Strategic System Socio-technical complexity Strategy execution complexity	System-oriented POCCC
EEA	All	Mindfulness

According to Emery (1972), an open socio-technical system is a purposeful system composed of an interrelated social (people, culture, norms, interactions, roles, etc.) and technical component (technology, tools, materials, etc.), which is embedded in a broader context (an environment) that the system is both influenced by and influences. Consequently, from the perspective of enterprise ecological adaption, enterprise architecture is concerned with the integration of open socio-technical systems (people and technology) or, more simply, open socio-technical systems design.

At the heart of open socio-technical systems design is socio-technical systems theory, a theory grounded in a number of principles but, just as importantly, in a number of espoused values and human ideals (Emery, 1976). People are seen as purposeful systems that can be ideal seeking (Ackoff and Emery, 1972). Organizations are seen as purposeful, but not as pursuing ideal seeking behaviour based on a set of common human ideals. Consequently, socio-technical systems theory is not aesthetically or value neutral. Having said this, all theories are aesthetically or value laden whether implicitly or explicitly (Popper, 1959). Furthermore, as practitioners, we have our own biases that shape the way we approach a design challenge, especially one related to organisational design. Currently, other worldviews exist that contrast with that of socio-technical systems theory. Probably the most prominent of which is mechanism (Pepper, 1961), which can be described as Tayloristic or technologically driven and which sees organizations as big machines and people as unpredictable parts. That is, this worldview perceives that if people are not stopped by the system design, they will make mistakes and so it would be best to eliminate them completely from the system. However, since organizations cannot completely eliminate people, designs based on mechanism try to anticipate all eventualities and program them into the machines (Cherns, 1976). Contextualism is an alternative worldview to mechanism.

According to Pepper (1961), mechanism is analytical and integrative. Consequently, from its perspective, the world is understood by breaking up problems into sub-problems (reductionism) as well as by bringing order to individual facts by defining integrative laws. The latter laws are often used as stepping-stones for making predictions. Unlike mechanism, contextualism is synthetic and dispersive (Pepper, 1961). It approaches problems systemically (holism), thus rejecting reductism and hence its consideration for the system in its environment. Moreover, contextualism, being dispersive, expects the novel and acknowledges the particulars of each context, hence rejecting universalism. Consequently, contextualism accepts indeterminism and unpredictability. Socio-technical systems theory, being grounded in contextualism, approaches the design of socio-technical systems holistically, accepts novelty, and embraces the particularities of contexts and people. Consequently, it strives to design social systems that allow for more effective human relations at work, hence allowing for better control of the technical system. The organizational expression of mechanism is Tayloristic and, consequently, socio-technical systems analysis and design can be seen as developing a new paradigm of organizing that is more aligned with a contextual worldview.

Social System Analysis and Design

The social system is comprised of the work related transactions and inter-dependencies among people. The four following variables or processes must be well managed for any social system to express the ideals of contextualism (Parsons, 1951):

- Goal setting and attainment (e.g., daily or weekly goals or targets linked to long-term strategic goals);
- Adaptation to the external environment (e.g., changes demanded by new regulations or new customer requirements);

- Integration of the activities of people within the system (e.g., how they resolve their differences);
- Long-term development to ensure the future survival and growth of the system (e.g., through recruitment, training, etc.).

In socio-technical systems theory, each of these variables is assessed with respect to a particular key variance in the technical system and, in general, for each of the four most probable social system interactions, namely:

- Superior/subordinate or vertical relationships;
- Intra-group relations or horizontal relationships within the work group involved in the control and coordination of work to control key variances in the technical system;
- Inter-group relations or horizontal relationships between the work group and the groups they interact with to carry out their work tasks;
- Organizational goals or relationships across the larger organization that contains the social system under study.

The analysis of these social system variables and their key variances with respect to the technical system can be achieved by using the GAIL analysis tool (Taylor & Felten, 1993).

Technical System Analysis and Design

The technical system is comprised of the system inputs, throughputs, and outputs (product or service). While technical system analysis and design varies by the nature of the work (e.g., knowledge work vs. manufacturing), at its most simple, there are three steps involved in conducting a technical system analysis (Trist, 1981). First, the technical system is mapped to identify a complete workflow analysis and identify unit operations. Next, the steps in the process and their variances

within each unit operation are identified and key variances are mapped on a chart showing how the key variances affect other variances. The bridge between the technical system and the social system in socio-technical systems analysis and design is the variance control table, which shows how the social system will keep that key variance in range. This necessarily involves information system design, as it is related to the question of what information the social system needs to control the key variance. There is also the question of whether control of variance can be automated and what impact this may have on the social system. In some cases, in order to maintain the socio-technical system principles (see below) and ensure joint optimization, an intermediate technology may be the best choice. In any case, it is a kind of to-and-fro between the technical system design and its impact on the social system that technical system design choices are made always in the context of the social system and vice versa.

Joint Optimization

Socio-technical systems theory insists that optimal system design is achieved by joint optimization of the social and technical systems. Optimizing the techno-economic system sub-optimizes the social system, which often confirms mechanistic assumptions about people because people are not able to pursue their ideals in such a system. Optimizing the social system at the expense of the technical system results in sub-optimized production and quality. In order to achieve joint optimization of the social and technical systems rather than optimizing one and sub-optimizing the other, as described above, they must be jointly analyzed and designed (Emery. 1959).

Socio-technical systems theory complements Parsons' (1951) model by offering a set of principles that guide the joint optimization of socio-technical systems. These principles (outlined below) should serve as a design guide but not a blueprint (Cherns, 1976).

1. **Compatibility:** The process of design must be compatible with its objectives.

2. **Minimal Critical Specification:** No more should be specified than is absolutely essential.

3. **Socio-Technical Criterion:** If they cannot be eliminated, variances must be controlled as near to their point of origin as possible.

4. **Redundancy of Function:** Use redundancy of function rather than redundancy of parts. The intent must be to rely on a redundancy of skills (function) in each person instead of a redundancy of people (parts) as a way of dealing with flexibility needs and work design.

5. **Boundary Location:** Departmental boundaries should be drawn, usually to group people and activities, on the basis of one or more of three criteria: technology, territory, and time.

6. **Information Flow:** Information systems should be designed to first provide information to the point in the system where action is dependent on this information.

7. **Support Congruence:** The systems of social support should be designed so as to reinforce the behaviours that the organization structure is designed to elicit.

8. **Design and Human Values:** An objective of organizational design should be to provide a high quality of work life.

9. **Incompletion:** Design is an iterative process.

We will further explain principles 1, 2, 8, and 9. Principle 1 basically states that the process used to create a design should embody the objectives that the design tries to accomplish. Consequently, if one wishes to achieve joint optimisation of the social and technical systems, then it is important to address both of these systems in the design process. If it is important that the people who will implement the new socio-technical system understand the design, then they need to be involved in the design process.

Principle 8 states that the final design should allow for a high quality of work life. This is measured by the following six psychological factors required for productive human activity. Each person should have the right amount of autonomy to make decisions so that their work challenges them; the opportunity to set learning goals and receive feedback on their progress towards achieving their goals; and the right amount of variety so that their work does not become routine and boring. The organization should provide an atmosphere or climate where there is mutual trust and respect; meaningful work so that people can see their contribution to the whole, are proud of it, and see it contributing to society; and some sense of a desirable future that is not dependent on promotion (Emery & Thorsrud, 1969).

In order to take principle 8 into account in the design process, it becomes necessary to allow the people that will be affected by the design to participate in creating their working conditions. The principle of incompletion is also relevant here. Design teams leave the design somewhat incomplete so that the people who have to live with the new system need to become involved in completing the design of the system. If we add the latter point to what was stated previously about joint optimisation, it becomes clear that the design process must address both the social and technical systems and, furthermore, the people who will be impacted by the design must be participants in the design process; hence, participative design is necessary. The process should also be democratic in order to transfer responsibility of the design process outcome to the system because the design must be optimized according to the needs of those who it will affect, not those of a third party.

Open socio-technical systems design is also grounded in open systems theory. As mentioned previously, an open system is a system-in-context, that is, a system in its environment. The system and environment are co-implicative (Emery, 2000). An open system is not independent of its environment; as the system changes the environment is influenced to change and vice versa. If we reconsider principle 1 in this light, then the design process must also address the influence of the system's environment as well as the influence of the system on its environment in order to achieve coherence between them. If this is not done, one can imagine a system that is irrelevant to the needs of the environment or a system that hopes to redesign itself without addressing environmental pressures that contradict the desired vision. Co-evolution of the system and its environment is a reality that designers need to take into account.

ENTERPRISE-IN-ENVIRONMENT ADAPTION AS OPEN SOCIO-TECHNICAL SYSTEMS DESIGN

We have previously proposed the following characteristics that an open socio-technical systems design process should possess:

1. Participative and democratic;
2. Addresses jointly both the social and technical systems to achieve joint optimization;
3. Addresses system-in-context coherence and co-evolution.

The question is now "what would an enterprise architecture process possessing these characteristics look like?"

The first characteristic would entail that the EA outcome be owned by the organisation (or sub-organisation) under design. (For the reminder of the text, we will use the expression *system* to replace organisation (or sub-organisation) under design.) Moreover, the members of the *system* would be full participants in the process, co-determining the outcome by making design decisions.

The second characteristic would entail two elements. The first element is that the EA process would address both the social system (people, culture, norms, interactions, roles, etc.) and the technical system (technology, tools, materials, etc.). In modern organisations, IT technologies play a key role in technical systems; hence, the traditional IT domains (data, application, and infrastructure) must be addressed. The traditional business architecture would be separated into three portions: the social system (people, culture, roles, etc.), the technical system (process), and the system-in-environment coherence (objectives, vision, competition, etc.). The second element is that current *system* boundaries might have to be redrawn in order to achieve a coherent and stable system. Consequently, all of the organisational entities that interact with the *system* must participate in the process in order to help determine new boundary relations.

The third characteristic would require that the EA process addresses a number of points: (1) determining the new boundaries of the *system* (including members), (2) learning about the environment (stakeholder needs, competition, expectations, etc.), (3) learning about the historical context of the *system* (how has the past shaped the current state and what to leave behind and what to carry forward), (4) determining the vision and objectives of the *system*, and (5) influencing its environment in order to achieve co-evolution.

A consequence of the EA outcome being owned by the *system* is that an enterprise architect cannot be responsible for the outcome per se. The responsibility of the enterprise architect is to nurture and uphold the design process itself in order to maintain the socio-technical systems principles and open socio-technical systems design process characteristics. A corollary of this latter point is that the enterprise architects must have a solid grounding in both how machines/technology behave as well as how people and social groups behave. Since this double specialty is rare, an engineer-social scientist pairing is required.

Ideas similar to those presented above, but in the context of software systems design, informed open socio-technical systems theories and have been proposed in the literature (Mumford, 1995).

KEY EXECUTION GUIDELINES FOR ENTERPRISE ARCHITECTURE

The following section offers a number of key guidelines that should be followed in order to ground EA in open socio-technical systems theory. These guidelines are not intended to address the full complexity of undertaking EA. A comprehensive EA intervention design would require complete descriptions of elements such as: the various phases of the intervention, the task groups, the activities of the task groups, the member composition of the task groups, the recruitment/selection methods for the task groups, etc. However, the presented guidelines will offer anchor points that should guide the enterprise architect in adjusting current ways of working and designing workshops.

Facilitation and Group Dynamics: Beware of group dynamics and the importance of proper group process design and facilitation. The role of the enterprise architect is above all to develop and facilitate the design process, which must be a sound group process. He/she may act as a subject matter expert in certain instances, but it is important that the decision is made by the members of the systems under design who will "live" with the decision.

An enterprise architect should have an understanding of how people and groups behave. Consequently, a minimum understanding of group dynamics and processes as well as a minimum level of skills in group facilitation is necessary if an enterprise architect plans to design and facilitate the design process. If he/she does not have such skills or knowledge (and even if he/she does), given the organisational significance and importance of the outcome, the aid of a social scientist should seriously be considered. It is important to note that the poor performance of a working group is not indicative of the general performance of

group-centric (vs. individualist) work processes, but rather is indicative of the lack of knowledge and skills underlying group workshop design and facilitation.

Participative and Democratic: The members of the *system* must be the primary participants and decision makers in the process in order to gain their commitment as well as ensure that the final design meets their psychological and social needs. This cannot be achieved effectively if the members of the *system* are not participants in the process and if they are not making key decisions. This is not to say that all of the members of the *system* should be active participants. However, an adequate recruiting approach should be used (Taylor & Felten, 1993). The EA process itself could be achieved according to Emery's two-step participative organizational design process (Search Conference and Participative Design Workshops) (de Guerre, Noon, & Salter, 1997; Emery, 1993).

Holistic: If necessary, the EA process must consider the possibility of redesigning a number of domains that cannot be addressed in a piecemeal fashion. A divide-and-conquer approach would be inconsistent with the systemic nature of the design problem. The domains that should be addressed are the typical IT domains (applications, data, infrastructure, and other automation/mechanisation technologies) in addition to an extensive business architecture (strategy, education, work processes, work team design, organisational boundaries, planning, pay system, human resource policies, labour management, capital investment system, etc.). Addressing any of the IT and business architecture sub-domains separately and trying to adapt the other sub-domains accordingly will probably produce an ineffective and unsustainable outcome. In addition to scanning the environment (opportunities, competition, industry trends, etc.), it is equally important to scan the history of the organisation in order to achieve shared understandings of how the current organisation was shaped by past events and how the past will continue to influence the organisation in the future.

Learning: It is important to remember that the most important outcome of the EA process is not a perfect, elegant design (especially not according to industry dictated best practices), but rather is a system that is capable of continuous learning and adaptation. It is much more important to enable continuous learning because one can rarely predict the future, hence, a perfect design could easily become dysfunctional before it is delivered as a result of changes within and/or outside of the organisation (Mintzberg Lampel, & Ahlstrand, 1998). The EA process should be viewed as a never-ending iterative process. In addition, learning to learn is important for participants. Organizational members that participate in the design process not only understand and are ready to implement the new design, they also have implicitly learned design thinking and, therefore, are prepared to go on learning and changing the new design as necessary. Over time, this iterative process leads to elegant solutions (de Guerre, 2000).

Shared Tools: It is important that the tools used during the EA process are understood by everyone who will use them. Moreover, it is important that the tools used in the design process be relevant for the continuous management and improvement of the *system*. Consequently, the design process must allow the necessary time for the participants to learn, adapt, and create the necessary tools for the design. In addition to the already existing tools available in current EA methodologies, the following, previously presented, analysis tools of socio-technical systems (see open socio-technical systems design section) should be considered: (a) workflow analysis and unit operations identification, (b) key variance matrix and control analysis, and (c) GAIL model analysis.

A COMPARISON WITH CONVENTIONAL ENTERPRISE ARCHITECTURE APPROACHES

In order to further deepen the meaning of EiEA, let us compare it with current approaches to EA. Our intent is not to make side-by-side comparisons, but rather to highlight and contrast some of the predominant characteristics of mainstream approaches to EA to those of EiEA.

Participative vs. Top-Down

In many organisations, the execution of EA is often given to an elite group of senior IT specialists (sometimes management specialists), which are typically positioned in the higher levels of the organisational hierarchy. This select group has the mandate, guided most often by EA methodologies rooted in strategic planning (Ansoff, 1965) and strategy design (Christensen, Andrews, Bower, Hamermesh, & Porter, 1982), to define the desirable future state of the *system*. The members of the *system* are typically involved in only a limited capacity, usually for requirements gathering and final design validation. The EA team usually solicits the involvement of the members of the *system* for input regarding requirements, future organisational objectives, as well as current irritants. In addition, the gathering of potential solutions is often avoided; it is not rare to hear requests from the EA team such as: "please give us requirements and not solutions; we will propose the solution that will take the larger picture into consideration." This separation between those with the needs of those determining the solutions usually creates misunderstandings and resistance. It is not rare to have the *system* reject (or even sabotage) the proposed solution. The challenges with regards to both gaps and acceptance are often exacerbated by the fact that the people solicited for input regarding the requirements are not those doing the work but rather are the supervisors, who: (a) are not always aware of the details of workarounds that workers have long since informally implemented and/or (b) have divergent views from their team regarding how the work should be improved. EA teams typically try to get around these challenges by using an iterative two-step design and validation process. They also develop a very keen sales aptitude in order to get their ideas across. However, currently, most EA teams do not have deep support within their organisations; according to Forrester, only 15% of EA teams are recognised by their organisations (DeGennaro, 2010). This very low rate seems to support the likely resistance of a top-down process outlined above.

EA as EiEA would be necessarily participative in nature. As described earlier, EiEA is based on a design process that is democratic and participative. In this context, enterprise architects are guardians of the process, not the outcome. It is the *system* that owns the outcome.

Mechanist vs. Contextualist

Most EA methodologies have been designed and supported by the fields of engineering and computer science. These fields typically have a mechanistic view of the world. According to Pepper (1961), mechanism is a worldview that is based on the metaphor of a machine. Because of this underlying metaphor, the engineering and computer science communities often hold implicit assumptions and beliefs that an organisation can be viewed as a machine that can be engineered to achieve ultimate perfection. Taken to the extreme, this worldview perceives that it would be ideal to engineer out people (if that were possible) because people are inherently unpredictable and perfect machines should be predictable. These assumptions often lead to an overemphasis on the technical system to the detriment of the social system. Often the objective is to adapt or coerce the social system to fit the optimised technical

system according to "best practice." Consequently, these methodologies and their outcomes reflect these assumptions.

In contrast, EiEA is grounded in explicit ideals and values that are humanistic. It is also very much influenced by the social science research communities that have a more ecological or contextual view of the world and of organisations (Pepper, 1961). EiEA tries to achieve joint optimisation between social and technical systems, while not overemphasising either. The underlying objective is to achieve coexistence between people and technology, while not replacing one with the other. The emphasis is on developing technologies for smart people, rather than smart systems to replace people.

Task vs. Process

Many EA methodologies explain the various steps and/or artefacts that should be produced in great detail. They are very focused on the outcomes and the tasks or steps to achieve these outcomes. However, they often offer very little information with regards to how to conduct the tasks in order to achieve the best outcome given that it is people who are doing the tasks. In other words, current methodology might clearly explain what steps must be done and describe the inputs/outcomes of these steps, but they offer very little information as to how to get people involved in actually executing the steps of the process. It is not rare to see such preoccupations swept into the concept of "governance."

In contrast, EiEA is firmly grounded in the theoretically sound, participative, open socio-technical systems design process. The process guides both design accomplishment and group dynamic management. Moreover, the process is designed to uphold the socio-technical systems principles and process characteristics, which are key to achieving joint optimisation. Consequently, equal consideration is given to task accomplishment and process management.

Piecemeal vs. Holistic

Most EA methodologies that propose a process offer one that is fairly linear. Moreover, it is not rare for them to choose a starting point, such as process redesign or IT ecosystem design, and then, in a linear fashion, adapt the other dimensions of the *system* one at a time, building on the previous decision. This linear approach complemented with an underlying mechanistic worldview goes a long way to explain why most EA approaches are techno-centric and socially coercive in nature. However, what underlies these shortcomings is caused by a much deeper assumption: divide-and-conquer. Based on the problem solving tools of the engineering community most EA methodologies assume that the design of a system can be addressed in a piecemeal, linear fashion. The strategy is to recursively divide the larger problem into independent sub-problems, solve these sub-problems, and reconstitute the combined solution. At best, most mainstream EA methodologies propose iterative processes that try to refine an optimal solution by using multiple gap-and-fix steps. It is very rare to find an EA methodology that explicitly acknowledges that the design process cannot use a linear problem solving approach, but rather requires a more holistic approach.

Most EA methodologies are also piecemeal in regards to the domains that they consider. Many dimensions, such as education/training, pay system, human resource policies, and important historical events, are swept aside because they are perceived to be unimportant to the final design. In order to achieve an optimal, coherent, and stable system, all systemic dimensions must be addressed together as a whole. This holistic nature of EiEA is probably one of its most challenging components because a large number of domains must be considered. However, its avoidance is an avoidance or denial of the systemic nature of the problem at hand as well as the co-implicative nature of the system-in-environment relationship.

Process vs. Artefact

Most current EA methodologies implicitly or explicitly use one of three following stances when defining EA: EA as a process, EA as an artefact, or EA as both a process and an artefact.

The stance taken by EiEA is that EA is a process and artefact, since the key outcomes of the process are a redesigned open socio-technical system that is capable of learning and influencing its environment as well as the creation of the necessary shared tools (artefacts) that are required to support the management and future evolution of the system. Two things are particular about this stance. The first is that the outcome is not a repository of artefacts or a redesigned system, but rather a system that is capable of learning, which is the basis for continuous active adaptation. The corollary of this is that the redesign process is never really finished, but rather is embedded in the day-to-day activities of the system as it strives to better itself. The second particularity of this stance is that, to ensure continuous evolution, the tools used to guide analysis and decision-making must be adopted by the system both during and after the design process. Since the tools serve to help the participants in the process (the *system*) make decisions, this necessarily means that the participants must understand how to use the tools as well as understand their meaning and implications. In order to achieve this, an enterprise architect cannot merely use a pick-and-choose approach to selecting the best practice tools and selling them to the *system* through coercion. An inquiry and learning process must be planned, as must be time for tool creation, adaptation, and adoption. It is important to understand that the objective is not to use the latest fad of analytic or modeling tools, but rather to foster learning and appropriation of system design.

In practical terms, the stance taken by EiEA on modelling artefacts and tools is that that the majority of people designing and implementing the new EA must understand the design as well as be able to use the tools/artefacts to redesign their system as necessary. Consequently, having only a select few EA experts is neither appropriate nor desirable. In contrast, it could be said that current EA methodologies give too much importance to creating comprehensive (and most often very complex) tools and artefacts that hinder conversation, consequently hindering EA. According to EiEA, conversation, teamwork and ongoing organisational learning are the key tools of EA... the rest is secondary.

ENTERPRISE-IN-ENVIRONMENT ADAPTATION AND COMPLEXITY MANAGEMENT

EiEA is mindful with regards to a wide range of sources of complexity. By using the theoretical framework of open socio-technical systems design, it is possible to gain a better understanding of how EiEA addresses such complexities.

Social and Technological Systems and Socio-Technical Complexities: These complexities are addressed by the design process itself, which focuses on joint-optimisation and participative democracy. By having the people of the enterprise participate as designers, the social and technological systems are jointly addressed both implicitly and explicitly. Moreover, joint-optimisation will foster solutions that will allow the social system to mitigate the complexities of the technological system. As technological systems become increasingly complex, it becomes crucial that social systems serve as a mitigation tool for the technological systems so that the unavoidable unexpected can be managed (Perrow, 1999; Weick & Sutcliffe, 2007).

Strategic and Operational Systems and Strategy Execution Complexities: These complexities are mainly addressed by transferring accountability and responsibility for the final design to the people who are redesigning their work. By not separating the tasks of decision-making, decision implementing, and ongoing execution between multiple people or groups, there is little possibility for misalignment. Moreover, this integrative approach allows for ongoing rapid adjustment of strategies, designs, and operationalization in order to address unexpected results and change.

Environmental System and Enterprise-in-Environment Complexities: These complexities are addressed by the enterprise-in-environment co-evolution concerns of the design process. Moreover, with the transfer of accountability and responsibility for the design, more people in the enterprise become mindful of the evolution of the enterprise's environment as well as the need for co-evolution. Consequently, the enterprise gains a more vast number of environmental "sensors" and adaptation agents compared to the low number in traditional enterprises, which is comprised typically of only executive, marketing, and EA teams. Moreover, the continuous adaptation characteristic of the design process fosters ongoing co-evolution, which is critical in turbulent environments.

In summary, the process of open social-technical systems design addresses complexity management by fostering pervasive mindfulness in the enterprise, which is accomplished by making everybody accountable and responsible for managing the unexpected and contributing to adaptation.

Table 4 offers a summary of the complexity management strategies used by EiEA.

BENEFITS AND CHALLENGES OF ENTERPRISE ECOLOGICAL ADAPTATION

The breadth of management concerns increase greatly when attempting to achieve enterprise sustainability; there are more complexities to acknowledge and manage. Through its grounding in open socio-technical systems design, EiEA is capable of managing a wide range of complexities, hence fostering enterprise innovation, adapta-

Table 4. Summary of complexity management strategy for EiEA

Complexities	How it is Addressed
• Social System • Technological System • Socio-technical Complexity	• Joint-optimisation • Participative democracy • Continuous evolution • Mindfulness
• Strategic System • Operational System • Strategy execution Complexity	• Integrative approach • Participative democracy • Continuous evolution
• Environmental Complexities • Enterprise-in-Environment Complexity	• Co-evolution • Pervasive environmental sensors • Pervasive adaptation agents • Continuous evolution • Mindfulness

tion, and sustainability in the midst of constantly changing unknown and unavoidable unexpected factors. In addition, the participative nature of the design process minimizes resistance to change.

However, the benefits of EiEA are not free, they come at the steep "price" of cultural transformation, which many organisations will not be willing to pay even at the risk of the sustainability of their enterprise. With regards to traditional organisations, three paradigm shifts are required: reductionism to holism, closed system to enterprise-in-environment, and top-down to participative democracy.

The shift towards holism requires that organisations set aside all silo ways of seeing, thinking, and acting. It requires that organisations acknowledge that not all problems can be solved in a "divide-and-conquer" fashion. For many organisations, accepting that one cannot separate design from implementation will be close to unimaginable because it goes against the principle underlying bureaucratic forms of organisations: the management of work is separated from the work.

The shift from closed system thinking and enterprise-in-environment is not made any easier because it requires that organisations put aside their belief in perfect control. Enterprise-in-environment co-evolution implies that organisations evolve jointly with their environment and not as

executives see fit or according to the wishes of the personnel. For many, such a sense of loss of utter control in one's destiny will be unacceptable.

Last but not least, the shift from top-down to participative democracy will probably be the most difficult hurdle for organisations. For participative democracy to be possible, personnel must be trusted, respected, nurtured, and appreciated. In order to transfer accountability and responsibility from management to the people doing the work, it goes without saying that management must trust the workers motives, skills, and judgement. Moreover, in order for workers to make the best decisions possible as well as execute their work as best as they can, management must invest significantly and continuously in the workers' training and development. When subject to the complexities of turbulent enterprise environments, ongoing training and development are not luxuries; they are necessities for organisational sustainability and adaptation. Such responsibilities can longer be merely implicitly "outsourced" to the education systems or shifted to workers to be done on personal time. Despite the fact that many organisations say that their people are their most important resource, they function based on belief systems that label workers as lazy, untrustworthy, and incompetent (McGregor, 1960). Again, many organisations will not be capable of putting aside their negative beliefs about workers, such as workers cannot be trusted, hence must be directed and controlled from above.

In summary, EiEA offers a great deal of complexity management capacity at the "price" of shifting enterprises ways from bureaucratic "ideals" to management sharing decisional power.

ORGANIZATIONAL LEADERSHIP AND GOVERNANCE

As discussed previously, EiEA requires an organisational shift towards participative democracy. This shift does not imply that anybody can decide anything at any moment, nor does it imply that organisations should fire all managers! What is does imply is that the "rulebook" on organisational governance and leadership, as well as the role of management, must be revisited.

With EiEA, strategy formulation, decision-making, and enterprise sustainability become the concerns of all organisational members, not just management. However, it is neither necessary nor desirable to have everybody participate in all of the decisions. The guiding principle is that those impacted by a change must participate actively in designing and implementing the change and be held accountable and responsible for the change, as well as for continuous improvement.

With the decentralisation of accountability and responsibility, the role of management must necessarily shift away from traditional POCCC because it is no longer their responsibility to command and control all ongoing activities. Rather, the role of management must center around three key tasks: *fostering mindfulness, fostering learning,* and *offering services* to those making the decisions. The task of fostering mindfulness is about fostering an organisational culture that keeps members accountable for monitoring and adjusting to internal and external enterprise changes. All members of the organisation must be sensitive to the unavoidable unexpected. The task of fostering learning is about creating a working environment and making the necessary resources available so that workers can maintain their knowledge, skills, and competencies at the necessarily levels. The last task is about offering services to workers that allow them the control and coordination of work at their level. It is management's responsibility to make sure that the workers have all that is needed for them to do their jobs. Examples of such services could be information, facilitation, mediation, coordination, etc. Since it is impossible and impractical that everyone be involved in all decisions, some decisions remain part of the workload of managers. However, differently from traditional management practices, the distribution of such decision-making tasks is subject to discussion between management and workers. Moreover, through the process of evolving the enterprise in order to achieve co-evolution and intra-coherency, past distribution may be redesigned. This is in stark contrast with traditional management approach, where the top decides what is delegated to the bottom. Participative democracy requires that members of the enterprise be recognized as equal citizens.

FURTHER RESEARCH

Despite the many decades of ongoing research on open socio-technical systems and system thinking, it is still unclear how to foster sustainable enterprises. One only has to be aware of the daily news to know that mammoth enterprises, such as GM, and governments, such as Greece and Italy, are in precarious situations.

We still must gain further insight into how to transform the cultures and beliefs of modern enterprises so that they may embrace the necessary paradigm shift required to move towards systems thinking and participative democracy. Without this shift, there is little hope that much sustainable transformation will occur in organisation and that EA will become an effective tool for the management of complexity.

Since the principles underlying EiEA require that people work together, we must become effective at fostering dialogues within organisations. It is striking to notice how little (although not a complete lack of) concern is giving in most modern EA methodologies regarding the design and facilitation of effective, rich dialogues. We believe that it is paramount that such concerns be embedded in the next generation EA methodologies, especially if they wish to be effective at complexity management. In this ways, enterprises must become effective at deliberation (Pava, 1983).

On a more practical level, within this narrative, we have given very little insight into the concrete steps required to conduct EiEA. A comprehensive

EA intervention design based on EiEA should contain a complete description of elements such as: the various phases of the intervention, the task groups, the activities of the task groups, the member composition of the task groups, and how to design opportunities that inspire effective dialogue. Such an intervention should draw upon the knowledge available in the literature from fields such as psychology, anthology, sociology, and organisational sciences, etc.

On a more philosophical level, we must explore the question "what should be designed and what should not be designed?" Does enterprise coherency necessarily mean an absence of contradiction or paradox? Ulanowicz (2009) proposes that in a system without a certain level of disorder, entropy is brittle because it is within the rich basin of entropy that mutation and adaptation can emerge. If this is the case, how should EA foster and manage such entropy in the design of an enterprise?

CONCLUSION

The world has become a complex place for everyone. Modern organisations are faced with the challenge of surviving in conditions of high relevant uncertainty (Emery & Trist, 1965). Moreover, since organisations have permeable boundaries with regards to their environment, they cannot escape the increasing turbulence within their own boundaries, which mirrors the reality of their environment (Ashby, 1958).

EA should be a tool that allows modern organisations to cope and thrive within these turbulent times. The past decades have been plagued by two dominant realities. The first is the low life expectancy and high early mortality of organisations (de Geus, 2002). The second is the unresolved challenges surrounding IT project delivery (Eveleens & Verhoef, 2010). In light of these facts, one is forced to wonder if current EA methodologies are adequately adapted to current realities and complexity. Very few conventional

EA methodologies are based on a worldview other than mechanism. Mechanism offers many insights when coping with a world that is predictable, can be broken down into separate parts, is based on cause and effect, and is linear. The constant, unexpected, and sometimes dramatic change that we all experience in our daily lives does not seem to be accounted for by the mechanistic worldview. Hence, how are tools built on the foundations of a mechanistic worldview supposed to be effective in contemporary contexts? How can enterprises cope and manage the complexity which they face?

Within this narrative, we have explained that the practice of complexity management may differ dramatically depending on one's definition of complexity and management. The crux of complexity management is the lens one uses to identify the relevant complexities to be managed as well as determine what constitutes the act of management. We presented three schools of thought on EA that emerge from the literature. Each school of thought has an underlying belief system that determines what complexities are relevant and how they can be managed. We have proposed a taxonomy of sources of complexity in order to facilitate the discussion on the approach to complexity management outlined by each school of thought. Our discussion was a stepping stone for the introduction of EiEA, an open social-technical system design perspective of EA. We have discussed the theories of open systems and socio-technical systems in a discourse about EA. Through the discourse, we have presented how previous theories inform the practice of EA from the perspective of EiEA. EiEA is an alternative path to conventional EA methodologies; it is an alternative grounded in explicit theory that is supported by many decades of fieldwork and research regarding open socio-technical systems theory (Mumford, 2006; Trist, 1981). We believe that the worldview of contextualism underlying open socio-technical systems theory serves to provide a firm basis for new EA methodologies that can better account for the inner and outer turbulence of contemporary and future organisations. It also offers a better vantage point for the management of complexity.

Finally, we discussed the challenges facing enterprises in the adoption of EiEA, which requires a three-pronged paradigm shift towards holism, enterprise-in-environment, and participative democracy. At the heart of the challenges underlying the acceptance of these paradigms is the acceptance by management that control is not possible in the midst of complexity and that the best solution is through shared accountability, personnel empowerment, as well as ongoing dialogue between organisational members. The future success of such an approach will lie in the ability to transform current managerial beliefs concerning power and control and to design opportunities that inspire effective dialogue.

To conclude, we must strive to create enterprises and systems for smart people as opposed to trying to replace them with smart technologies.

REFERENCES

Ackoff, R., & Emery, F. (1972). *On purposeful systems: An interdisciplinary analysis of individual and social behavior as a system of purposeful events*. Chicago: Aldine-Atherton.

Ansoff, H. I. (1965). *Corporate strategy*. New York: McGraw-Hill.

Arthur, W. B. (1999). Complexity and the economy. *Science, 284*(5411), 107–109. doi:10.1126/science.284.5411.107 PMID:10103172.

Ashby, W. R. (1958). Requisite variety and its implications for the control of complex systems. *Cybernetica, 1*(2), 83–99.

Cherns, A. B. (1976). Principles of socio-technical design. *Human Relations, 29*, 783–792. doi:10.1177/001872677602900806.

Christensen, C. R., Andrews, K. R., Bower, J. L., Hamermesh, G., & Porter, M. E. (1982). *Business policy: Text and cases* (5th ed.). Homewood, IL: Irwin.

de Geus, A. (2002). *The living company*. Boston: Harvard Business Press.

de Guerre, D. (2000). The codetermination of cultural change over time. *Systemic Practice and Action Research, 13*(5), 645–663. doi:10.1023/A:1009529626810.

de Guerre, D., Noon, M., & Salter, S. (1997). *Syncrude Canada limited: A Canadian success story*. Paper presented at the Association for Quality and Participation Annual Spring Conference. Clevland, OH.

DeGennaro, T. (2010). *The profile of corporately supported EA groups: Tactics for improving corporate management's support for EA in large firms*. Forrester.

Emery, F., & Trist, E. (1965). The causal texture of organizational environments. *Human Relations, 18*, 21–32. doi:10.1177/001872676501800103.

Emery, F. E. (1959). *Characteristics of socio-technical systems: The emergence of a new paradigm of work*. Canberra, Australia: ANU/CCE.

Emery, F. E. (1972). Characteristics of socio-technical systems. In Davis, L. E., & Taylor, J. C. (Eds.), *Design of Jobs* (pp. 157–186). Harmondsworth, UK: Penguin Books.

Emery, F. E. (1976). *In pursuit of ideals*. Canberra, Australia: ANU/CCE.

Emery, F. E., & Thorsrud, E. (1969). *Form and content in industrial democracy*. London: Tavistock.

Emery, M. (1993). *Participative design for participative democracy*. Canberra, Australia: ANU/CCE.

Emery, M. (2000). The current version of Emery's open systems theory. *Systemic Practice and Action Research, 13*(5), 685–703. doi:10.1023/A:1009577509972.

Eveleens, J. L., & Verhoef, C. (2010). The rise and fall of the chaos report figures. *IEEE Software Journal, 27*, 30–36. doi:10.1109/MS.2009.154.

Fayol, H. (1917). *Administration industrielle et générale, prévoyance, organisation, commandement, coordination, controle.* Paris: H. Dunod et E. Pinat.

Goldenfeld, N., & Kadanoff, L. P. (1999). Simple lessons from complexity. *Science, 284*(5411), 87–89. doi:10.1126/science.284.5411.87 PMID:10102823.

Lapalme, J. (2012). Three schools of thought on enterprise architecture. *IT Professional, 14*(6), 37–43. doi:10.1109/MITP.2011.109.

McGregor, D. (1960). *The human side of enterprise.* New York: McGraw-Hill.

McLuhan, M. (1962). *The Gutenberg galaxy: The making of typographic man.* Toronto, Canada: University of Toronto Press.

Mintzberg, H., Lampel, J., & Ahlstrand, B. (1998). *Strategy safari: A guided tour through the wilds of strategic management.* New York: Free Press.

Mumford, E. (1995). *Effective systems design and requirements analysis: The ETHICS approach.* London: Macmillan.

Mumford, E. (2006). The story of socio-technical design: Reflections on its successes, failures and potential. *Information Systems Journal, 16*, 317–342. doi:10.1111/j.1365-2575.2006.00221.x.

Parsons, T. (1951). *The social system.* London: Routledge and Kegan Paul.

Pava, C. H. P. (1983). *Managing new office technology: An organizational strategy.* New York: The Free Press.

Pepper, S. (1961). *World hypotheses: A study in evidence.* Los Angeles, CA: University of California Press.

Perrow, C. (1999). *Normal accidents: Living with high-risk technologies.* Princeton, NJ: Princeton University Press.

Popper, K. (1959). *The logic of scientific discovery.* London: Hutchington & Co..

Rind, D. (1999). Complexity and climate. *Science, 284*(5411), 105–107. doi:10.1126/science.284.5411.105 PMID:10102804.

Taylor, J. C., & Felten, D. F. (1993). *Performance by design: Socio-technical systems in North America.* Englewood Cliffs, NJ: Prentice Hall.

Trist, E. (1981). *The evolution of socio-technical systems: A conceptual framework and an action research program.* Issues in the Ontario Quality of Working Life Center Occasional Paper No. 2. Toronto, Canada: Ontario Ministry of Labour.

Ulanowicz, R. E. (2009). *A third window: Natural life beyond Newton and Darwin.* West Conshohocken, PA: Templeton Foundation Press.

Weick, K. E., & Sutcliffe, K. M. (2007). *Managing the unexpected: Resilient performance in an age of uncertainty* (2nd ed.). San Francisco, CA: Jossey-Bass.

Weng, G., Bhalla, U. S., & Iyengar, R. (1999). Complexity in biological signaling systems. *Science, 284*(5411), 92–96. doi:10.1126/science.284.5411.92 PMID:10102825.

Whitesides, G., & Ismagilov, R. F. (1999). Complexity in chemistry. *Science, 284*(5411), 89–92. doi:10.1126/science.284.5411.89 PMID:10102824.

KEY TERMS AND DEFINITIONS

High Reliability Organization: An organization that exhibits: a) Preoccupation with failure, b) Reluctance to simplify c) Sensitivity to operations, d) Commitment to Resilience, and e) Deference to Expertise.

Mindfulness: The combination of ongoing scrutiny of existing expectations. Continuous refinement and differentiation of expectations based on newer experiences, willingness and capability to invent new expectations that make sense of unprecedented events, a more nuanced appreciation of context and ways to deal with it, and identification of new dimensions of context that improve foresight and current functioning (Weick and Sutcliffe, 2007).

Open Socio-Technical System: A purposeful system composed of an interrelated social (people, culture, norms, interactions, roles, etc.) and technical component (technology, tools, materials, etc.), which is embedded in a broader context (an environment) that the system is both influenced by and influences.

Purposeful System: A system which can produce the same outcome in different ways given the same context and can produce different outcome given the same or different contexts. In addition, the system is ideal-seeking in that it makes choices with the intent of attaining an ideal.

ENDNOTES

[1]   We have chosen the term Enterprise-in-Environment in order to reflect a concern with the larger environmental field (social, political, ecological, economical, technical, etc.) in which enterprises operate.

Chapter 7

A Systemic View on Enterprise Architecture Management:
State-of-the-Art and Outline of a Building Block-Based Approach to Design Organization-Specific Enterprise Architecture Management Functions

Sabine Buckl
Technische Universität München, Germany

Christian M. Schweda
Technische Universität München, Germany

ABSTRACT

Multiple approaches for Enterprise Architecture (EA) management are discussed in literature, many of them differing regarding the understanding of the EA as well as of the performed management activities. Applying a cybernetic point of view, the differences between these approaches can be mitigated, a more embracing perspective can be established, and fields for future research that lack support in current EA management approaches can be identified. In this work, the authors apply the Viable System Model (VSM) as reference for elaborating an overarching conceptualization of the EA management function. In comparison to the VSM reference, they discover that system five of the VSM—the identity system—is underrepresented in prevalent EA management approaches. Using a building block-based approach that makes reuse of existing best practices for EA management, the authors outline a development method that addresses the challenge of identity of an EA management function by enabling an organization-specific design thereof. The development method can be used to govern the EA management function by providing means and techniques to configure and adapt, that is, to design and to re-design an EA management function tailored to the specific situation of an organization.

DOI: 10.4018/978-1-4666-4518-9.ch007

1. MOTIVATION

Enterprise Architecture (EA) management forms a research subject, which has been approached from various directions and groups of differing origin over more than two decades (cf. Langenberg and Wegman 2004; Mykhashchuk et al. 2011). These prescriptions differ regarding the pursued EA-relevant goals and taken foci. Against this background many researchers in this field doubt that a one-size-fits-it-all EA management process or function exists, but expect these processes to be company-specific (Buckl et al. 2010a). In general, enterprises form complex systems consisting of various elements with a large number of inter-dependencies. In special, each enterprise differs regarding the industry branch, internal culture, situation, or strategy. Aside all these difficulties enterprises have to adapt to changes in the environment, e.g. changing markets or legal regulations, in order to survive. The VSM, developed by Beer (cf. Beer 1979, Beer 1981, Beer 1985) provides a framework to describe such complex systems that have to survive in a changing environment. According to Beer such systems consist of five interacting subsystems—*operation, coordination, control, planning, and identity*. The VSM has been beneficially applied in various contexts, e.g. project management (Britton and Parker 1993) or organizational modeling (cf. Espejo and Harnden 1989 and Brocklesby and Cummings 1996). The VSM can be used according to Brocklesby and Cummings (1996) as a tool to support an enterprise during the implementation of large scale organizational change. Whereas, a definition and description for each of the systems of the VSM is given in e.g. Beer (1979) no such common understanding about the constituents of the EA management function exists.

In this work, we seek to understand the constituting activities of EA management functions as the management subsystems of the Viable System Model (VSM). Building on this understanding, we review existing EA management approaches and identify the coverage of the different management subsystems, which they provide. As a key result of the analysis, we identify that the approaches do only partially cover system five of the VSM. This system, called *identity system*, is responsible for keeping the management system serving the purpose that it is intended for. In order to promote the discussion on this weakness we outline a development method for organization-specific EAM functions. This method is based on an organized collection of best-practice building blocks as found in literature and practice.

2. A VSM PERSPECTIVE ON EAM

EA management itself is concerned with the management of the EA, i.e. the documentation, analysis, and transformation planning pertaining to the architecture of the enterprise. We apply the generic understanding of architecture, as presented in Ernst (2008), to the entire enterprise on an abstract level in order to derive the following definition of EA:

The enterprise architecture is the fundamental organization of an enterprise, embodied in its components ranging from business to IT infrastructure, their relationships to each other, and to the environment. The enterprise architecture exists at any point in time and is planned as well as changed via projects in the boundaries given by principles. The change heads towards a target state, outlined by goals, which are measured via metrics.

Different enterprise-level management functions, e.g. project portfolio management, or demand management, transform the organization of an enterprise, more precisely relevant parts thereof. These transforming management functions can be identified with *system one—operation—*of the VSM. This system contains the primary activities of the system under consideration, which directly interact with the environment. The enterprise-level management functions form the systems that change the EA via projects, which have been initiated in the demand management, aligned in the strategies and goals management, selected in the project portfolio management, scheduled in the synchronization management, and realized with standards from the IT architecture management. A description of the function of EA management therefore must consider the role of related enterprise-level management functions.

The different enterprise-level management functions pursue different goals and perform the transformations independent from each other. EA management – in a more narrow sense – seeks to establish a consistent planning of the enterprise transformations in a holistic and integrated manner. This poses a particular challenge, which is not addressed by an all-embracing management function that supersedes existing management functions targeting different aspects of the organization. In contrast, EA management is designed to integrate with the existing enterprise-level management functions and to act as "glue" between the processes to conjointly manage and develop the EA towards aligned business and IT

(cf. Matthes 2008). Basically, this refers to *system two—coordination—*of the VSM. This system contains the information channels and bodies, which ensure that the primary activities of *system one* work harmoniously in coordination. As one part EA management provides a common basis and the means for communication between the various stakeholders with business and IT background involved in the enterprise-level management functions. Figure 1 illustrates this central principle of EA management, by showing how the EA management function integrates with selected other enterprise-level management function via the exchange and provision of information.

Beyond the communication level of EA management, the EA management function also provides additional guidance to the other enterprise-level management functions by resolving conflicts, which cannot be addressed on a peer-level. This part of EA management represents *system three—control—*of the VSM, and establishes the responsibilities and rights to maintain the resource allocation of system one. Thereby, system three monitors the primary activities as well as the communication and coordination tasks of system two and adapts them according to the

Figure 1. EAM as glue between enterprise-level management processes

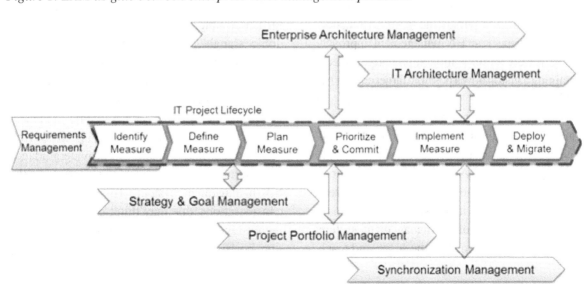

holistic view on the primary activities. If, for example, newly agreed standards from IT architecture management are not available for the project portfolio management, the projects considered therein cannot be checked for standard compliance. System three should therefore set up a structure, e.g. an intranet, where the standards can be viewed and communicated to the respective stakeholders. System three can be referred to as reactive EA management and should be considered in the description of the management function.

Further, EA management is expected to take into account environmental influences, e.g. changing markets, regulations, or industry standards. These influences are processed in that part of EA management that represents *system four—planning*—of the VSM. It establishes the EA intelligence function and is concerned with a holistic and future-oriented perspective to support strategic decision making. Whereas system three is capable of dealing with immediate concerns, system four focuses on future aspects, which emerge from the system's environment and also considers strategic opportunities, threats, and possible future directions. Typical processes in system four in the context of EA management include the analysis of the status quo of the architecture, the development of a target architecture representing the envisioned state in the future, and planning the transformation of the enterprise to pursue the target. Alongside the reactive aspect, an EA management approach must cover the aforementioned proactive aspect, containing a vision how a possible target enterprise should look like.

System five—identity—is responsible for managing the overall policy decisions. It should provide clarity about the overall direction, values, and purpose of the system under consideration. The main goal of system five is to balance present and future efforts, and to steer the system as a whole. In the context of EA management, system five addresses concerns like the scope and reach

(sometimes also referred to as the width and depth) of EA management. Typically, a piloting project is performed in the initial phase of an EA management endeavor, e.g. starting with a limited number of concerns, e.g. compliance issues, availability aspects, or with restricted reach e.g. within one business department. Nevertheless, after the initial phase, when the EA management has matured and become more adopted, EA management governance is established to redefine the initially selected scope and reach of EA management. According to the typical quality control cycle as discussed by Deming (1982) and Shewart (1986), the EA management governance aspect should be part of a description of the EA management function.

Summarizing, the systems one to three can be regarded as managing the "inside and now" of the EA whereas system four and five manage the outside and the future of the EA and the EA management endeavor respectively. In the context of EA management, the former systems relate to the operative EA management tasks – running the enterprise – while the latter ones consider the strategic EA management tasks – changing the enterprise. The application of the VSM to the EA management function as described above is illustrated in Figure 2.

This systemic view on EA management is further complemented with the concept of algedonic signals from the VSM. These signals, originating from systems one to three, provide an alerting mechanism, which is employed, if one of these systems is not able to perform as intended in the current situation. Such a signal is escalated to system five, which then can adapt the overall management function and can provide guidance to maintain the identity, i.e. the purpose of the EA management system. To exemplify these considerations, one may think of an EA getting increasingly heterogeneous albeit a standardization board has been established. At the point,

Figure 2. The EAM-VSM

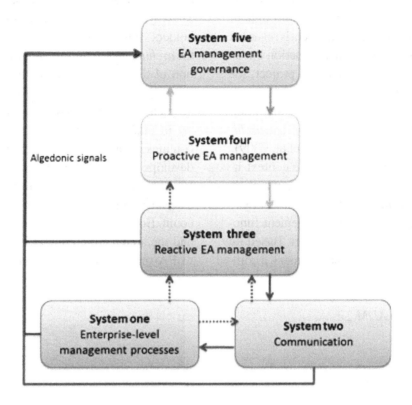

where this board notices that it has no means to counteract the tendency; an alert is escalated to the EA management governance. The governance function then has to redesign the governance structures, e.g. to empower the board to stop non-standard conform projects, in order to enact the envisioned homogenization, or to raise the question, if a standardized EA is necessary in the future.

3. A VIABLE SYSTEM PERSPECTIVE ON DIFFERENT APPROACHES IN LITERATURE

In the following we analyze selected EA management approaches and frameworks from practice and literature regarding the coverage of the different systems of our EAM-VSM.

3.1. The Open Group Architecture Framework

One of the most prominent frameworks for EA management is The Open Group Architecture Framework (TOGAF) (The Open Group (2009). This framework has been developed since 1995 and matured to version 9.0 in October 2009. TOGAF 9 consists of six main parts, of which the following three are relevant for our subsequent analysis:

- The *architecture development method (ADM)* describes an iterative process for EA development.
- The *ADM guidelines* and *ADM techniques* cover aspects of adapting and configuring the ADM to different process styles.
- The *content framework* provides a conceptual meta-model for describing architectural artifacts.

TOGAF's perspective on EA management is strongly project-centric, meaning that throughout the recommendations, EA management is regarded not as a continuous management function but as a transformation project. The ADM project, see Figure 3, can be split into different iterations – *architecture context iteration*, *architecture definition iteration*, *transition planning iteration*, and *architecture governance iteration* (Josey et al. 2009).

A core aspect of the architecture context iteration is *stakeholder management*, which is concerned with the identification of stakeholders from related enterprise-level management functions and with winning their support. Based on the output from stakeholder management, a communication plan for EA related topics is developed. Thereby, different viewpoints reflecting the stakeholders' information demands are designed. In the *architecture definition iteration* a documentation of the current architecture is created. This can be regarded as a basis for reactive EA management, although no additional mechanisms are set in place. The *transition planning iteration* contains an architectural planning process that develops a target EA and derives roadmaps for EA evolution. Thereto, requirements driven by external changes are proactively taken into account. Both the architecture governance iteration and the architecture context iteration contribute to EA management governance: the former by

Figure 3. TOGAF's ADM

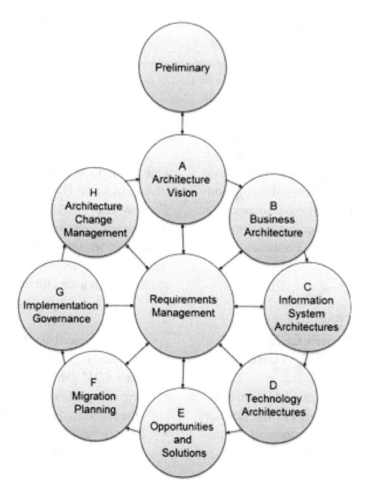

establishing responsibilities and boards, whereas the latter is concerned with scoping EA management. Nevertheless, TOGAF does not provide concrete guidelines or best practices on how to enact architecture plans and ensure that architecture principles are adhered to. The *content framework* thereto provides limited mechanisms of extensibility, allowing the using organization to omit or include certain concepts in the EA metamodel. Scoping and re-scoping is triggered by *requirements management*, which drives the ADM project via feeding new, updating, and discontinuing requirements.

3.2. Systemic Enterprise Architecture Methodology

The Systemic Enterprise Architecture Methodology (SEAM) roots in the work of Wegmann (2003), where he elaborates on the multi-disciplinary

nature of EA projects and the resulting need to support these projects with methods and models. Central to SEAM is the notion of the *EA project*, which is initiated by an organization to react or to anticipate change. A stepwise method is applied by SEAM to federate the knowledge of specialists from different enterprise-level management functions, see Figure 4.

The first step of the basic design process of SEAM is to create a consistent *as-is* model that reflects project-relevant entities. From this perspective, EA management according to SEAM acts as "glue" between the different functions, although information is only gathered, but not communicated between the functions. Based on a federated perspective on the as-is of the EA a to-be EA is designed and finally handed over to implementation. According to the discussions in Langenberg and Wegmann (2005) the design process covers both the reactive aspect, which

Figure 4. Basic design process of SEAM according to Wegmann et al. (2008)

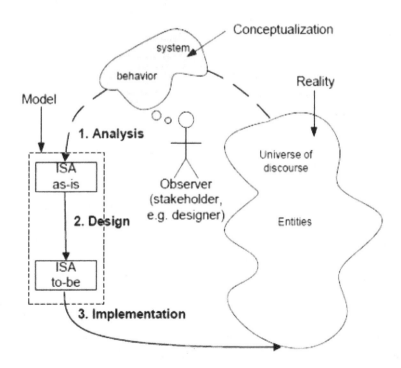

deals with necessary business and technology changes ex post, and the proactive aspect. Central to proactive management is not only to anticipate future changes, but also to prepare the enterprise to potential changes by increasing agility and flexibility. Regarding the "downward" communication, i.e., the communicative actions taken to facilitate implementation, the guidelines provided by SEAM remain abstract and vague. The same applies to the guidelines for setting up an EA management function. The approach discusses that EA such function is a multi-disciplinary endeavor, but abstains from discussing questions of how to establish and govern an EA management function.

3.3. The ArchiMate Approach

The ArchiMate modeling language for EAs has a long development history starting with the early work of Jonkers et al. (2003) who outline the key principles of their language for coherent EA descriptions. With the books of Lankhorst (2005) and (2009) ArchiMate has become more than a language but a method for EA management. Central to this method is the architecture life cycle consisting of the phases *design*, *communication*, *realization*, and *feedback*. During design different stakeholders of EA management derive the to-be architecture that addresses the organization's strategic goals. In particular, the relevant architecture transformations are described based on the gap identified between the as-is and the to-be EA. For the aspect of communication, Lankhorst et al. (2004) take an integration perspective. This means that prevalent communication facilities of related enterprise-level management processes have to be taken to an integrated and consistent level of communication. Lankhorst (2009) describes different architectural conversation techniques which can be used to attain different knowledge goals regarding the EA descriptions. One particular knowledge goal—commitment of knowledge—transcends the boundary from com-

munication to realization, such that the associated conversation techniques contribute to the realization phase of the architecture life cycle. For the feedback phase, different analysis techniques are described to measure, whether the EA relevant goals have been attained or not. These goals are accordingly derived from high level business visions and strategies and are conversely used to shape the understanding of the EA. As the EA management function is executed, feedback from the stakeholders and a changing environment influence the specific purpose (concern) of EA management and can necessitate adaptations of the function. Lankhorst discusses these adaptations for the context of the involved EA modeling languages, but leaves out the process perspective. Further, other governance-related aspects of EA management, like roles and responsibilities, are not covered by the approach.

3.4. Dynamic Enterprise Architecture (DYA)

A group of researchers at Sogeti Netherlands started in 2001 to develop the approach of *DYnamic Architecture for modeling and development (DYA)*. This approach helps architects to determine, which parts of the architecture should be designed when, which stakeholders should be consulted in doing so, and how the architecture designs are used (Wagter et al. 2005). By doing so, stakeholders are supported in facing and balancing two central challenges: 1) *fostering coherence* between the various processes and 2) *increasing agility* of the organization in the market. DYA proposes an iterative, continuous, "just-enough," and just-in-time process that guides architecting and allows deviations, where necessary (cf. Wagter et al. 2005).

The process of DYA consists of three distinct sub-processes that support an organization in its evolution with the full benefits of using EA. These sub-processes affect the dynamic architecture of the enterprise and are complemented by a governance structure as illustrated in Figure 5:

Figure 5. Architecture processes of DYA

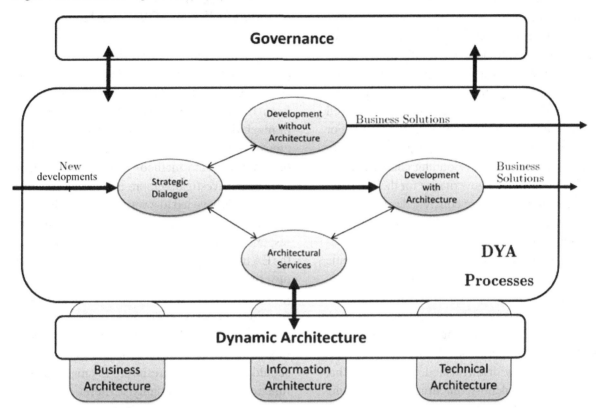

- In the process of *strategic dialog*, the business objectives are determined and are refined by business and IT management to project proposals.
- The process *architectural services* is triggered, if a change on the strategic level is decided. It develops principles, guidelines, and models that enable realization of the business case.
- The processes *development with/without architecture* implements the concrete project proposals with desired time frame, level of quality and acceptable costs. Both processes represent alternatives at which *with architecture* represents the standard:
  - In the process *development with architecture* each project proposal is furnished with a project-start architecture, i.e. a description of concrete

standards, norms, and guidelines to be followed by the project (anticipatory strategy).
  - If specific circumstances apply, the process *development without architecture* is chosen setting certain aspects of architecture out of order. This exceptional way concludes in a consensus on how and when the temporary solution is replaced by a permanent architecture-conform one (defensive or offensive strategy).

A critical success factor of the DYA processes according to the authors is the integration of the architectural process with related enterprise-level management functions of the organization (cf. Berg and Steenbergen 2006). Such integration targets especially the reactive EA management, in which the management function coordinates between the enterprise-level management functions by means of architecture prescriptions. For architecture governance, especially the *architecture maturity matrix* is important. This matrix defines eighteen key areas of architectural maturity, among others *roles and responsibilities* as well as *maintenance of the architectural process*. For each of these areas, different stages of maturity are described via corresponding characteristics. While this frames a governance for the EA management function, more concrete descriptions of the governance process itself are not given.

Summarizing, the approaches from literature as discussed above can be analyzed from a systematic perspective as given by the VSM. Thereby, System *one* and *two* are emphasized by all approaches. System *three* and *four* – the re-active and pro-active aspects of EA management – are also alluded to by the different approaches although they are typically not clearly distinguished. System *five* that represents the identity function complementing the lower level EA management systems is only partially alluded to. As system *five* is needed to ensure that EA management keeps performing the function, which it is intended for, it can be considered important to prevent EA management from degenerating to a worthless exercise in data collection and analysis. Thereby, especially the reaction to alerts from systems *one* to *three* is of importance, which can give indications of failing management instruments. Changing these instruments e.g. setting up new policies and roles that influence the related enterprise-level management functions, forms one of the most important tasks of system *five* and represents the governance aspect of EA management. Additionally, it is this system, which has to be considered during the setup of an EA management function, whose central enterprise-specific purpose and understanding is encoded into system *five*.

4. REQUIREMENTS FOR EA MANAGEMENT GOVERNANCE

The analysis of the state-of-the-art in EA management approaches reveals that neither system five, i.e. the identity system, nor algedonic signals from EA management activities are discussed in much detail in current approaches. This may ascribe to the novelty of the field. Only recently, the processes and methods of EA management have been investigated more in-depth. These investigations have led to a variety of contributions for describing not only the EA, but also the corresponding management system, i.e. for describing the EA management function. Such description in turn provides the conceptual basis on which the governance processes for the EA management function can build. These governance processes correspondingly define the EA management function and well-designed governance processes should ensure that the resulting EA management function is of high quality. Criteria of quality pertaining to the EA management function can be derived from the approaches analyzed above:

- **Q1 Suitable:** The EA management process must be applicable to the key problems that the stakeholders of EA management want to address.
- **Q2 Executable:** The EA management process must rely on well-defined roles and responsibilities of the involved actors and stakeholders.
- **Q3 Combinable:** The EA management process does not exist in isolation but receives and provides input to existing enterprise-level management processes.
- **Q4 Measurable:** The performance of the EA management process, i.e., its effectiveness regarding the solution of the relevant problems, must be controlled.
- **Q5 Sustainable:** The EA management process must remain executable or be

adaptable in case of changing organizational set-ups.

The analyzed approaches further help to identify the typical activities of which an EA management function consists. These activities resemble the ones in a management cycle, like the one discussed by Deming (1982) and Shewart (1986):

- Develop and describe both the current state of the EA and a planned future state of the EA in terms of the concepts and abstractions relevant to the stakeholders.
- Communicate and enact the current state and the planned one, by providing appropriate artifacts to and by exerting influence over the stakeholders of EA management and of related enterprise-level management processes.
- Analyze and evaluate the different EA states regarding their degree of fulfillment of EA management goals, and their adherence to established EA principles and set standards.

Describe, *communicate* and *evaluate* therein target mainly the current state and are hence activities of systems 2 and 3 in the VSM of EA management. *Develop*, *enact* and *analyze* have a strong focus on the future state of the EA and contribute to system 4 in the VSM of EA management. The aforementioned activities develop and describe, communicate and enact, and analyze and evaluate are linked to each other, providing output to subsequent activities and receiving input from preceding ones. Nevertheless, they should not be considered as "states" of overall EA management, as the management of a particular part of the EA may currently analyze this part, while for another part the results of the previous analysis are currently communicated. Each of these activities is further embedded into an ongoing activity to monitor the performance and effectiveness of EA management. This activity of *configure and*

Figure 6. Activities constituting an EA management function

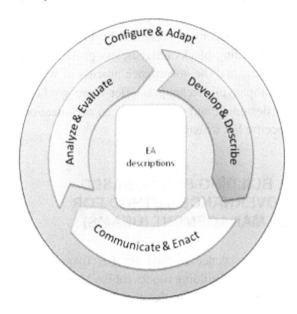

adapt identifies with system 5 of the VSM of EA management and forms the core of EA management governance. Figure 6 displays the framework of EA management activities from a systemic perspective, covering systems 2 to 5 of the VSM.

The EA management governance can design the EA management function conforming to above framework in a way that all criteria Q1-Q5 are met. Given a set of key problems and their rising stakeholders, a list of actors to be involved, and an overview of the current organizational context including existing enterprise-level management processes, the EA management governance defines the processes of EA management. A resulting process can subsequently be described in terms of the activities, roles and responsibilities, and the artifacts exchanged. As a suitable technique for such description, we assume the BPMN-like notation introduced by Buckl et al. (2010b).

In the following, we present a method for EA management governance. This method consists of a governance process together with a library of building blocks that constitute best-practice knowledge about EA management extracted from both practice and literature. With this emphasis on building blocks, the presented method furthers the idea outlined by the pattern-based approach to EA management presented by Ernst (2010). The building blocks nevertheless provide more structure and the governance process as well as accompanying techniques offer more guidance for designing and re-designing an organization-specific EA management.

5. BUILDING BLOCK-BASED GOVERNANCE METHOD FOR EA MANAGEMENT (BEAMS)

Our governance method for EA management (BEAMS – Building Blocks for EA Management Solutions) builds on the notion of the building block, which reflects a best-practice collected from literature or practice. A building block not only describes and names the best-practice solution, but provides an example of the solution in action and outlines the consequences of applying the solution, i.e., lists well-known wanted and not-wanted side-effects of the solution. Thereby, the building block provides much additional information to determine, whether it should be applied in a given context or not. We distinguish two types of building blocks, namely

- **Method Building Blocks (MBBs):** Present practice-proven method prescriptions, i.e. describe who has to perform which tasks in order to address a problem in the situated context and
- **Language Building Blocks (LBBs):** Present practice-proven EA modeling languages, i.e. refer to which EA-related information is necessary to perform a task and how it can be visualized.

This differentiation of the two types of building blocks follows the central dichotomy of any management function in general: the dichotomy of process and subject. The language provides the basis for describing the EA, i.e., the subject of EA management. It introduces the relevant concepts, establishes their semantics, and relates to the visual primitives used to designate and represent these concepts. The process describes the steps and tasks that are performed in managing the subject. The EA management governance has to define both the process and the language and to align them to each other, to form an executable EA management.

The overall governance process, shown in Figure 7, consists of three major activities: 1) characterize situation, 2) configure EA management function, and 3) analyze EA management function. In the first activity (characterize situation) relevant stakeholders and the given organizational context are identified, and an EA management-related problem is selected. Based on the problem, a relevant LBB is determined and reflected against available sources of EA information. This LBB becomes then part of the organization-specific configuration of the EA management function. Based on the selection of stakeholders and organizational contexts, the available library of MBBs is filtered, i.e., MBBs are considered as black-boxes. During the second activity (configure EA management function) MBBs admissible under the given context are selected, customized, and integrated to an executable process. The LBBs, which have been of primary interest in the first step, are subsequently only fine-tuned, i.e., their supplied visualizations and representations are adapted to the needs of the using stakeholders. Activities 1) and 2) are repeated for any remaining EA management-related problem. After the last problem (for the time being) has been addressed, the resulting EA management function can be subjected to an analysis. The analysis shows not only, whether the configured management process is executable, but also reveals the informational relationships between the stakeholders.

Figure 7. Activity diagram of the governance process

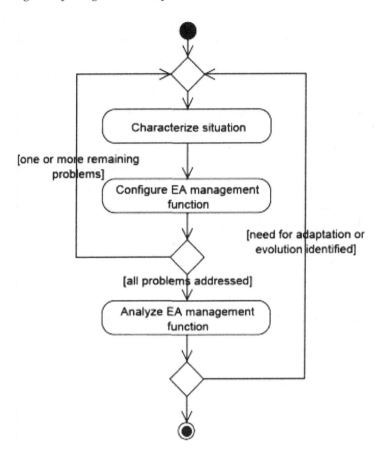

Subsequently, we detail the single steps of the governance method and designate the involved participants. While we assume the enterprise architect to be the typical user of the method other stakeholders of the EA management initiative need to be consulted during the governance method in order to identify the problems that should be addressed. The development method is subsequently presented in a twofold way: an overview on parts of the method is given by an UML activity diagram and the single activities of the diagram are described textually.

5.1. Characterize Situation

The first activity of the governance process centers on a stakeholder-specific EA management-related problem. In a first step the organizational context, in which the particular problem occurs, is identified, e.g. the structure of existing lines-of-command and the availability of EA management-experts in the particular environment is determined. The library of MBBs helps to characterize the situation with a catalog of organizational contexts. This analysis also prepares the second step, in which the stakeholders raising or otherwise relating to the particular problem are identified. These stakeholders are further characterized regarding their interest in the problem. In particular two kinds of stakeholders are relevant, namely the *information consumers* actually wanting the problem to be addressed and the *information providers*, who can offer the information relevant for addressing the problem.

Involving at least both these stakeholder groups, the third step develops an operationalization of the EA management-related problem. Such operationalization centers around a set of language constructs for describing and modeling the states under consideration, and has to fit with the already existing language constructs in the same context. The LBBs support the establishment and definition of these language constructs, as they provide well-defined sets of constructs categorized by the EA management-related problems that they have shown to address. The mechanisms of the BEAMS governance method filter the LBBs against the context of the already established language, such that building blocks making contradictory assumptions about the EA are ruled out. Different admissible LBBs are analyzed in the third step to identify the one best balancing the informational demands of the consumers and the effort caused for the information providers, given the importance of the problem under consideration. Thereto, in particular already existing information sources are considered. Finally, the selected LBBs are integrated into the existing configuration of the EA management function and the activity *characterize situation* regarding a particular problem is completed.

5.2. Configure EA Management Function

During the activity *configure EA management function* appropriate MBBs are selected and customized by the enterprise architect in an iterative way. The set of available MBBs is filtered using the following criteria stored in the organization-specific configuration to determine the MBBs applicable in the current situation:

- The selected EA management goal.
- The defined organizational context.
- The fulfillment of pre-conditions by the information already covered.

Pre-conditions of an MBB are described by meta-attributes. Meta-attributes represent properties of associated concepts of the information model. If for instance no method is currently selected to document business processes, the business process concept has no meta-attribute defined. After selecting an MBB from the develop and describe activity to gather information on business processes, the meta-attribute "businessProcess.documented" is set to true. Different meta-attributes like ".documented," ".communicated," or ".published exist" that describe whether a respective process to document, communicate or publish the respective information exists.

From the set of applicable MBBs the enterprise architect has to select an admissible one. The choice can be supported by taking into account the participants involved in executing the tasks described by the MBB as well as the described consequences of applying it. The selected MBB is subsequently customized to organization-specificities. Customization thereby means that

- The trigger of the MBB is detailed taking into account possible limitations that are already specified by the MBB.
- The participant placeholder delineated by the MBB has to be replaced by an organization-specific role.
- For each involvement of a participant in a task the used viewpoint has to be defined; i.e. detailed by LBBs. While the constraints provided by the type of viewpoint have to be accounted for, the recommendations and dissuasions can optionally be considered.

After the enterprise architects have finished customization of the selected MBB, the organization-specific configuration is updated to incorporate the customized method and the conditions on the information model are updated accordingly. This activity of selecting and customizing appropriate MBBs is iteratively repeated until all EA management activities of the framework introduced in Figure 6 are covered. The output of the activity *configure EA management function* part of the development method is a coherent and self-contained EA management function that addresses the defined set of problems stored in the organization-specific configuration.

The enterprise architects can either start to characterize the next situation and problem to be addressed (configuration cycle) or continue the development method with the analysis of the EA management function.

5.3. Analyze the EA Management Function

The incremental governance process incorporated in BEAMS allows to develop and enhance the EA management function in a step-by-step fashion, and to respond to changing organizational contexts as well as EA management-related problems proactively. After a series of increments, the activity *analyze the EA management function* is helpful to determine, whether the overall function is in good shape or is critical from some perspective. In particular two questions are relevant in this context:

● Is every relevant step of the EA management function still triggered? (Applies in

particular, if the language was greatly extended or adapted.)

● Is the informational structure of the EA management function backed by a supportive organizational structure?

Question one can be considered a liveliness-analysis of the EA management-process in particular considering the triggering events. Such analysis can rely on existing techniques in the field of process liveliness, wherefore we focus on the second kind of analysis targeting the second question. The informational structure relates the information providers, required to supply EA-relevant information, and the information consumers, drawing benefit from this information in addressing problems relevant to them. Understanding the nature of these relationships is elementary to analyze and ensure sustainability and viability of the EA management function. Any consumer draws benefit from a corresponding provider and latter should receive something in return for offering the information. If nothing is returned, the providing stakeholder is likely to give up information provision in favor of more rewarding activities. The relationship between information provider and information consumer can be expressed in terms of language constructs, in particular the concepts forming the abstract

Figure 8. Provider-consumer relationships for EA management-relevant information

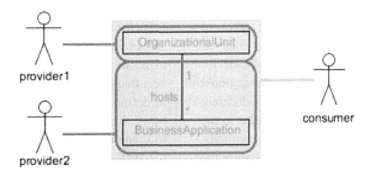

syntax of the language. Figure 8 gives an example of such relationship.

Juxtaposing the information dependencies with the organizational control structures in the enterprise allows analyzing, which dependencies are organizationally supported. In particular, the following relations between organizational control and informational dependencies can exist, which we use to classify the different organizational situations of an organization:

- **Line-of-Control:** The information consumer is a superordinate of the information provider and can exert direct control over the subordinate to demand the necessary information. In this case organizational control and informational dependencies are aligned.
- **Tits-for-Tats:** The information consumer can exchange information needed for one EA management-related problem with information for another problem, where the consumer acts as provider. In such case, informational dependencies form a circle or become circular, when including downward organizational control flows.
- **Social Competition:** The information consumer can raise peer-level competition between the information providers. In such case, the consumer is in a well-respected but not empowered role in the organization, and can create transparency about information provision among the equally-leveled information providers.

Above classification of possible types of organizational situations derived from informational dependencies can be used to decide for the most appropriate supportive organizational implementation. Based on the results different organizational interventions are provided in the final step of *propose organizational interventions*. In this vein, different mechanisms to ensure the supply of information can be established.

6. CONCLUSION AND OUTLOOK

In this chapter, we discussed how the Viable System Model (VSM) of Beer (1979) can be used to establish a systemic perspective on EA management. Identifying system 1 with the existing enterprise-level management processes, like project portfolio management or risk management, we outlined the different levels of integration mediated in systems 2 to 4. The communicative function of EA management (system 2) facilitates peer-level coordination between the different processes via providing transparency about the enterprise in a holistic source of information. Reactive EA management (system 3) steps in, when peer-level coordination does not suffice to maintain the status-quo, whereas proactive EA management (system 4) actively shapes the structure of the future enterprise by creating vision and plans of the overall EA. The state-of-the-art EA management approaches and frameworks put different emphasis on the different levels of systems, as do the companies systematically managing their EA. In particular, we diagnose that lower level systems (communication) are usually more well-established than higher level ones (proactive planning). A critical omission in the state-of-the-art approaches targets system 5 (EA management governance) necessary to define the identity, i.e., the "why?" of EA management. An EA management function without explicit statements about the stakeholders that are satisfied or involved, without reference to the organizational context in which it is meant to operate, and without a description of the problems that should be addressed, is spell-bound to failure and may not sustain in a changing enterprise environment. In response to this omission, we presented a governance process that uses Method Building Blocks (MBBs) to define the activities of the EA management function and Language Building Blocks (LBBs) to shape the conceptualization of the enterprise used in EA management. The Building Blocks for EA Management Solutions (BEAMS) forms an organized library of such building blocks useful for supporting the governance process. While the LBBs are selected in response to identified EA management-related problems, the MBBs are selected to fit the organizational context, in which the EA management function should operate. Complementary analysis techniques can be used to assess viability and organizational implementability of the designed EA management function. BEAMS has successfully been applied in several case studies (c.f. Buckl 2011; Buckl et al. 2011).

Future work can build on the BEAMS approach by extending the library of building blocks with LBBs for novel EA management-related problems or MBBs for unforeseen organizational contexts. Further, the presented governance process demands some critical reflection, in particular regarding the algedonic signals, raising the need to re-iterate the governance. Future work could collect a list of such signals, i.e., identify organizational situations and behaviors hinting towards difficulties with the execution of the current EA management function.

REFERENCES

Baskerville, R., & Pries-Heje, J. (2008). The design theory nexus. *Management Information Systems Quarterly, 32*(4), 731–755.

Beer, S. (1979). *The heart of enterprise.* New York: John Wiley.

Beer, S. (1981). *Brain of the firm* (2nd ed.). New York: John Wiley.

Beer, S. (1985). *Diagnosing the system for organizations.* New York: John Wiley.

Britton, G. A., & Parker, J. (1993). An explication of the viable system model for project management. *Systems Practice, 6*(1), 21–51. doi:10.1007/BF01059678.

Brocklesby, J., & Cummings, S. (1996). Designing a viable organization structure. *Long Range Planning, 29*(1), 49–57. doi:10.1016/0024-6301(95)00065-8.

Buckl, S. (2011). *Developing organization-specific enterprise architecture management functions using a method base.* (PhD Thesis). Technische Universität München, Munich, Germany.

Buckl, S., Dierl, T., Matthes, F., & Schweda, C. M. (2010b). A modeling language for describing EA management methods. In *Proceedings of Modellierung betrieblicher Informationssysteme (MobIS2010).* Dresden, Germany: MobIS.

Buckl, S., Matthes, F., & Schweda, C. M. (2010a). A situated approach to enterprise architecture management. In *Proceedings of the IEEE International Conference on Systems, Man, and Cybernetics,* (pp. 587-592). Istanbul, Turkey: IEEE.

Buckl, S., Matthes, F., & Schweda, C. M. (2011). A method base for EA management. In *Proceedings fo the IFIP Working Conference on Method Engineering (ME 2011).* Paris, France: IFIP.

Deming, E. W. (1982). *Out of the crisis.* Cambridge, MA: MIT Press.

Ernst, A. (2008). Enterprise architecture management patterns. In *Proceedings of the Pattern Languages of Programs Conference 2008.* Nashville, TN: PLoP.

Ernst, A. (2010). *Pattern-based approach to enterprise architecture management.* (PhD thesis). Technische Universität München, München, Germany.

Espejo, R., & Harnden, R. (1989). *The viable system model: Interpretations and applications of stafford beer's VSM.* Chichester, UK: John Wiley.

Jonkers, H., van Burren, R., Arbab, F., de Boer, F., Bonsangue, M. M., Bosma, H., & ter Doest, H. (2003). Towards a language for coherent enterprise architecture descriptions. In *Proceedings of the 7th IEEE International EDOC Conference (EDOC 2003)*. Brisbane, Australia: IEEE Computer Society.

Josey, A. et al. (2009). *TOGAF version 9 – A pocket guide* (2nd ed.). Amsterdam: Van Haren Publishing.

Langenberg, K., & Wegmann, A. (2004). *Enterprise architecture: What aspect is current research targeting? (Technical report)*. Lausanne, Switzerland: Laboratory of Systemic Modeling, Ecole Polytechnique Fédérale de Lausanne.

Lankhorst, M. M. (2005). *Enterprise architecture at work: Modelling, communication and analysis*. Berlin: Springer.

Lankhorst, M. M. (2009). *Enterprise architecture at work: Modelling, communication and analysis* (2nd ed.). Berlin: Springer. doi:10.1007/978-3-642-01310-2.

Lankhorst, M. M., van Buuren, R., van Leeuwen, D., Jonkers, H., & ter Doest, H. (2004). Enterprise architecture modelling-The issue of integration. *Advanced Engineering Informatics, 18*(4), 205–216. doi:10.1016/j.aei.2005.01.005.

Le, L.-S., & Wegmann, A. (2005). Definition of an object-oriented modeling language for enterprise architecture. In *Proceedings of the 38th Annual Hawaii International Conference on System Sciences*. IEEE.

Matthes, F., Buckl, S., Leitel, J., & Schweda, C. M. (2008). *Enterprise architecture management tool survey 2008*. Munich, Germany: Technische Universität München.

Mykhashchuk, M., Buckl, S., Dierl, T., & Schweda, C. M. (2011). *Charting the landscape of enterprise architecture management – An extensive literature analysis*. Paper presented at Wirtschaftsinformatik. Zürich, Switzerland.

Shewart, W. A. (1986). *Statistical method from the viewpoint of quality control*. New York: Dover Publication.

The Open Group. (2009). The open group architecture framework (TOGAF) enterprise Ed. version 9. San Diego, CA: The Open Group.

van den Berg, M., & van Steenbergen, M. (2006). *Building an enterprise architecture practice – Tools, tips, best practices, ready-to-use insights*. Dordrecht, The Netherlands: Springer.

Wagter, R., van den Berg, M., Luijpers, J., & van Steenbergen, M. (2005). *Dynamic enterprise architecture: How to make IT work*. Hoboken, NJ: John Wiley.

Wegmann, A. (2003). On the systemic enterprise architecture methodology (SEAM). In *Proceedings of the International Conference on Enterprise Information Systems 2003 (ICEIS 2003)*, (pp. 483–490). ICEIS.

Wegmann, A., Kotsalainen, A., Matthey, L., Regev, G., & Giannattasio, A. (2008). Augmenting the Zachman enterprise architecture framework with a systemic conceptualization. In *Proceedings of the 12th IEEE International EDOC Conference (EDOC 2008)*, (pp. 3–13). EDOC.

Section 3

The New Science of Practice:
Experiments, Cases, and Examples

Chapter 8

Enterprise Architecture of Sustainable Development:
An Analytical Framework

Roberto Villarreal[1]
United Nations, USA

ABSTRACT

The Outcome Document of the recent international diplomatic conference on sustainable development, Rio+20, portrays it as a multi-stakeholder process aimed at increasing the wellbeing of present and future generations in a dynamic, inclusive, equitable, safe, lasting, and environmentally balanced fashion, emphasizing that it should lead to poverty eradication, social development, the protection of all human rights and the elimination of human-provoked damage to the natural environment and resource-base. This reflects a highly complex process. Whereas the wording of its features and purposes exhibits considerable progress in the international policy dialogue, it appears that, among analysts, policy-makers, and practitioners around the world, there could be still large dispersion in the precise understanding of many underlying notions, the main issues, and their interrelationships. Consequently, there is not yet enough clarity among all stakeholders as to how to proceed on the implementation of coherent and coordinated strategies and policies for sustainable development. This chapter presents an analytical framework to look at these matters from a systemic perspective, with the intention of inspiring non-specialists to consider the advantages of the Enterprise Architecture approach to generate more clarity, facilitate communication, enhance policy coherence, and foster cooperation and partnerships for improving sustainable development. Some practical uses of the systems approach to enhance strategy, organization, and management for sustainable development are suggested.

1. INTRODUCTION

Sustainable development can be described for the purposes of this paper, in non-technical language consistent with the notions of the *Outcome Document* of *Rio+20*[2], as the process through which

human beings improve over time their standards of living, with all people benefiting in equitable terms, including the persons in poverty and others that have chronically been at a disadvantage—like women, rural inhabitants, indigenous populations, etc.—from expanding production activities that make available to them more numerous and bet-

DOI: 10.4018/978-1-4666-4518-9.ch008

ter jobs as well as more abundant and affordable higher quality goods and services to satisfy their needs, and from social development activities that increase their individual and social capacities—health, education, cohesion, solidarity, etc.—and warranty their enjoyment of all human rights, in ways which can be continued into the more distant future and thus benefit both present and future generations, because technical and socio-economic innovation secure that such activities do not create imbalances and permanent damage in the natural environment and resource base, and also because the overall process is conducted effectively and reliably through societal and government institutions that facilitate coherent decision-making and coordinated implementation of actions by all stakeholders, while being collectively prepared to cope with and recover from economic and sociopolitical crises and from natural disasters that may occur and negatively affect the process over time. Thus, sustainable development is a highly complex multi-stakeholder process, with economic, social and environmental aspects, which is influenced not only by diverse factors in each of these dimensions but also by the evolution of technology and public institutions adopted by the people and government.

The understanding of sustainable development in these terms emerged along several decades in the international development forums, reflecting an evolving socio-economic and environmental context in diverse countries and at the world level, combined with an increasingly multi- or inter-disciplinary conceptualization from academic and research communities[3]. Initial views that highlighted in the past the interactions between economic activities and the natural environment and resulted in concepts like green economy, have been progressively enriched with a variety of notions from different scientific disciplines and professional practices to arrive at the more complete and meaningful understanding described above[4]. Yet, whereas the diverse empirical and cognitive backgrounds of analysts, policy-makers,

practitioners and stakeholders involved positively contribute to interpreting and weighting differently the core notions encompassed in this complex process and their action-oriented implications—in its three main dimensions, namely economic, social and environmental—duly acknowledging the different contexts they operate in, that same diversity presents the risk of overlooking the numerous inter-linkages between the many specific issues relevant for sustainable development, hence losing to some degree the integrated vision on the process altogether, which is essential to its current understanding in the international policy dialogue.

A systemic vision of the process of sustainable development is ultimately necessary for the design of coherent public policies, as well as for their effective implementation, to pursue economic growth, poverty eradication, social development, human rights and a continuous improvement in the standards of living of all people in inclusive and equitable terms, while maintaining a stable and lasting balance between human activities and the natural environment, at the local, national, regional and global levels[5]. Moreover, a systemic view is also needed to facilitate communication among the different types of stakeholders at all these levels and to bring together their roles and actions in ordered and synergetic fashions, promoting effective partnerships and cooperation[6]. A systemic vision is indispensable as well to assess progress towards sustainable development overtime, at all levels, with due consideration to all its particular aspects. And last, but not least, a systems visualization of the overall process is fundamental for the sake of public governance, or in other words, for the people and their organizations—in the private sector, civil society and in government—to make adequate collective decisions and effectively enforce these to secure over time the gradual consolidation of sustainable development. In sum, a systemic approach is useful and necessary in these several respects, whose importance has been underscored at *Rio+20*[7].

The objective of this chapter is to motivate sustainable development analysts, policy-makers, practitioners and stakeholders to further adopt integrative approaches and tools for sustainable development. A conceptual framework is offered to this aim, building on the notions put forward at *Rio+20*. The chapter presents in a simplified yet comprehensive way the set of issues most prominently raised in the international policy dialogue, highlighting some of their most evident inter-relationships, with a systems approach. The framework is depicted in the form of diagrams encompassing the elements and relationships deemed most important from a systems-dynamics perspective. This is useful to facilitate policy-analyses and coordinated implementation, including the construction of adequate indicators to monitor progress and strengthen public governance. Ultimately, readers should be encouraged by these ideas to further learn about the possible utility of using the approaches and tools of Enterprise Architecture, among other ones to best conduct sustainable development: whereas the sustainable development stakeholders can gain from the utilization of Enterprise Architecture, as appropriate, the practitioners of Enterprise Architecture can further contribute in action-oriented ways to sustainable development at the local, national, regional and global levels.

Leading scientists, government authorities and social leaders all over the world increasingly call attention to the imperative of taking urgent steps to foster sustainable development—encompassing its economic, social and environmental dimensions-, as the environmental challenges—such as global climate change and the loss of natural ecosystems and biodiversity- are accelerating at the same time that poverty and social exclusion are major lasting and painful phenomena for mankind[8]. Hence, it is important and timely to further foster innovations in technology, social institutions and public policies in order to advance

faster towards overcoming these challenges and achieving sustainable development.

The structure of the chapter is as follows. Section 2 summarizes some important notions about sustainable development and how it is understood nowadays in international development forums. Section 3 points out some aspirations concretely identified by countries around the world with regard to the implementation of the agreed principles and notions of sustainable development. Section 4 describes a simplified framework to portray with a systems approach the main issues and their interrelationships. Section 5 offers some discussion on practical steps to apply this framework in the international dialogue and in public management. Finally, section 6 contains some final remarks.

2. EVOLVING NOTIONS ABOUT SUSTAINABLE DEVELOPMENT

The concept of sustainable development has evolved very noticeably since the seventies[9], when leading international think-tanks raised awareness on the constraints for long-run economic growth presented by the fast depletion of non-renewable natural resources and the over-exploitation of renewable ones, and their eventual exhaustion[10]. The arguments on the challenges for growth mostly from the fast decrease of world oil reserves at that time—just as, much earlier, the notions of Malthus about constraints in the supply of food for the population, and similar concerns about soft water in our time[11]—were followed by enriching debates and analyses which highlighted that such constraints were not rigid, but malleable, because: technical innovation could increase the productivity of extractive industries—and agriculture—and improve technical efficiency in the utilization of natural resources in production activities, all this contributing to ease the constraints from the supply side; and raising relative prices of increasingly scarce natural resources could induce substitution towards less scarce and cheaper inputs for production and final consumption, raising economic efficiency about the use of natural resources to satisfy human needs, thus helping to cope with the restrictions from the demand side[12]. In addition, the evolving thoughts on the constraints for growth from imbalances between human and environmental activities eventually included considerations about pollution in many forms—like solid waste, disposal of chemicals[13] and gas emissions—and its effects on the quality and productivity of natural resources, the costs and safety of productive activities, the health of life species and biodiversity[14]; in this respect, a most prominent issue addressed has been global climate change, underscoring that the scale and space of these phenomena are not always local or national, but in some important sense also encompass large regions with different countries or the entire planet[15]. This set of ideas—oversimplified here for didactic exposition purposes—underlined the interdependencies between the economy and the environment, and, after considerable refinement over the next decades to incorporate numerous related issues—for instance, regarding public policies and regulations that affect, in positive or negative ways, public knowledge and information on environmental matters, research and development for technical innovation, inputs utilization in production, market prices, financial institutions and more generally investment and consumption due to taxes and subsidies—translated into a corpus of notions and policy prescriptions often denoted as green economy[16].

In parallel, social scientists and development practitioners from diverse countries introduced a broader comprehension of diverse interrelated phenomena, beyond the narrower economy-environment scope of the green economy. Among other contributions, a key one was that the assumptions about rational choice by producers and consumers, which could implicitly be embedded in the understanding of the green economy in advanced countries—where the people on average have higher education and training, are more supported by solid scientific institutions and public information media or networks, and usually operate in well-functioning and reasonably complete and efficient markets—were constructively complemented with analyses on the different conditions which exist in developing countries, in ways that make clear that public strategies and policies for sustainable development have to be tailored to the existing social context in each country, rooting in the local realities to be fully effective[17].

This social perspective put forward the necessity to consider social development and poverty alleviation together with notions about the green economy, given their many relevant interrelationships. In the case of social development, interdependencies with the green economy run in several directions; for example, more education and, in general, institutional and human resources capacity building, facilitate the adaptation and adoption of environmental-friendly production and consumption patterns; and vice versa, a safe and balanced natural environment influences public health and increases human lifespan, making investments in human capital more productive.[18] Similar interdependencies exist about poverty, the environment and the economy: people in poverty often deplete natural wealth—forests, grasslands, fisheries, endangered animal and plant species, etc.—and provoke dangerous pollution, because no options are available for them to survive on alternative productive activities; and, vice versa, the depletion of natural resources in poor communities exacerbates poverty and challenges of survival at the local level, directly from the exhaustion of resources, or indirectly from imbalances in biodiversity and increased risks of natural disasters out of the erosion of soils, floods, permanent damage to underground water deposits, etc.[19] Furthermore, these negative interactions between the environment, the local economy and poverty induce out-migration of certain social groups –like young males- to seek employment and make remittances for the survival of their families and communities from elsewhere, thus generating disruptions in local networks for social protection and diminishing local resilience, while increasing demographic pressures on the economy and the environment in other parts of the territory at the regional level.

For reasons like these—again, the interrelationships between economic, social and environmental phenomena are illustrated here in over-simplified fashion for expository efficiency—the contributions from researchers, policy-makers and practitioners of sustainable development have widened very significantly the understanding of the concept beyond the green economy.

Last, but not least, coming from disciplines like sociology, political science, Law studies and public administration, two other perspectives have progressively converged on the concept of sustainable development and continue to do so: resilience and public governance. Resilience refers to the capacity of a society or community to prevent, react upon and recover from major contingencies that threaten development in any of the three pillars of sustainability, such as macroeconomic crises, large social or political conflicts, and natural disasters; elements that influence resilience comprise, among the most important: the protection of human and property rights, the administration of justice, the existence of public welfare safety nets for vulnerable groups, and the prevalence of societal values, social cohesion and solidarity attitudes that further strengthen the outcomes from public interventions in these regards[20]. In turn, public governance is about the effectiveness of the diverse social, political and juridical institutions and practices in place for the orderly conduct of people's regular activities—in the private sector, civil society and the public sector—including among the most relevant: the rule of law and effective enforcement of laws and public regulations, the operation of diverse

mechanisms for participation of diverse stakeholders in collective decision making, a responsive and accountable government, etc.

Indeed, logic and experience have progressively pointed out that to the extent that there is more resilience and better governance, sustainable development is facilitated on all its three pillars. Otherwise, it could be negatively affected by economic, social, political and environmental risks to a very considerable degree—from massive losses of income, wealth, and infrastructure; upsurges in poverty; popular uprisings; military coups; civil or international wars; crime; natural disasters for which the people are not well prepared, etc.—that are faced with weak public and societal foundations. Hence, to successfully cope with economic, social and environmental risks and maintain conditions that are conducive to enhance the wellbeing of all the people over the longer term, resilience and public governance need not only to be constantly present, but to be improved over time[21].

Thus, the evolution of the notions succinctly pointed out above has been conducive over time to generalize the understanding of sustainable development in the international policy dialogue, specifically to comprise three important pillars—its economic, social and environmental foundations[22]—and their interrelationships.[23] Box 1 presents some language from the *Outcome Document* of *Rio+20* in this regard.

3. CALL TO BE ACTION-ORIENTED AND USEFULNESS OF A SYSTEMIC VISION FOR SUSTAINABLE DEVELOPMENT

The accumulation of scientific data and the growing record of major environmental problems registered in countries around the world—pollution of soils, water and air; loss of biodiversity and damage to ecosystems; climate change and

Box 1. Some key notions on sustainable development in the outcome document of Rio+20

In the Outcome Document of Rio+20 countries expressed: "We recognize that poverty eradication, changing unsustainable and promoting sustainable patterns of production and consumption and managing the natural resource base of economic and social development are the overarching objectives of and essential requirements for sustainable development. We also reaffirm the need to achieve sustainable development by promoting sustained, inclusive and equitable economic growth, creating greater opportunities for all, reducing inequalities, raising basic standards of living, fostering equitable social development and inclusion, and promoting the integrated and sustainable management of natural resources and ecosystems that supports, inter alia, economic, social and human development while facilitating ecosystem conservation, regeneration and restoration and resilience in the face of new and emerging challenges" (United Nations General Assembly, 2012, paragraph 4).

In a related manner, countries also indicated: "We also reaffirm the importance of freedom, peace and security, respect for all human rights, including the right to development and the right to an adequate standard of living, including the right to food, the rule of law, gender equality, women's empowerment and the overall commitment to just and democratic societies for development" (United Nations General Assembly, 2012, paragraph 8). And countries also expressed: "We acknowledge that democracy, good governance and the rule of Law, at the national and international levels, as well as an enabling environment, are essential for sustainable development, including sustained and inclusive economic growth, social development, environmental protection and the eradication of poverty and hunger. We reaffirm that to achieve our sustainable development goals we need institutions at all levels that are effective, transparent, accountable and democratic." (United Nations General Assembly, 2012, paragraph 10).

And, with equal importance, countries acknowledged that there is no just one unique way or model for sustainable development, and thus each country has to pursue what is effective in its own context, committed to this as a national and global endeavor but with differentiated responsibilities, given the disparities in economic, social and environmental terms that exist across countries: "We reaffirm that there are different approaches, visions, models and tools available to each country, in accordance with its national circumstances and priorities, to achieve sustainable development in its three dimensions which is our overarching goal. In this regard, we consider green economy in the context of sustainable development and poverty eradication as one of the important tools available for achieving sustainable development and that it could provide options for policy making but should not be a rigid set of rules. We emphasize that it should lead to eradicating poverty as well as sustained economic growth, enhancing social inclusion, improving human welfare and creating opportunities for employment and decent work for all, while maintaining the healthy functioning of the Earth's ecosystems." (United Nations General Assembly, 2012, paragraph 56).

increasing frequency and impacts of natural disasters like hurricanes, floods, droughts, etc.—have progressively raised awareness among the people worldwide on the urgency to introduce changes in the patterns of production and consumption (including in societal values and behavior of families and communities, and processes and products of private firms), in laws and regulations, and in governance institutions, to induce sustainable development.

This has gradually created a context for governments at the local and national levels to take more decisive actions, adapt and adopt public policies, transform public administration and engage the people and their private and social organizations for the sake of promoting sustainable development. Yet, these trends have not been swift in most cases due to the diversity of stakeholders and actors, the asymmetric distribution of potential wins and losses, and the political complexities of reform in many aspects[24]. Hence, political pressures are multiplying on governments, and public commitment is steadily building at the local and national levels in all countries to different extent, depending on their particular context.

As the call for action to promote sustainable development has multiplied around the world, with growing support from non-government and government stakeholders, this has been reflected as well in the international policy dialogue. Box 2 summarizes some views expressed in the *Rio+20 Outcome Document* in this respect, and comments on the pertinence for countries to adopt a systemic approach in conducting the necessary actions from all stakeholders.

4. A FRAMEWORK TO INTEGRATE THE MANY ELEMENTS OF SUSTAINABLE DEVELOPMENT AND THEIR INTERRELATIONSHIPS

This section presents schematically a simple integrative framework of the most important notions underscored in the international policy dialogue about sustainable development. The framework brings together in a conceptual fashion a number of important elements and some basic interrelationships among them, which have been prominently acknowledged in the leading documents agreed by governments of countries around the world over the last decade, with particular emphasis on the *Outcome Document* of *Rio+20*. Building on the notions highlighted in the international policy dialogue, the system encompasses three major subsystems[25], corresponding to: the interplay between production activities and the natural environment; the interplay between economic activities and society, with particular attention on poverty and inequality; and the interplay between society and the natural environment, with special emphasis on resilience and public governance.

To present the relevant ideas, systems analysis is used to describe the main elements and interrelationships under consideration in each subsystem, as well as to map these within the broader integrative system. In other words, the specific dynamics that correspond closely to the cause-effect notions highlighted by the international policy dialogue are presented for each of the three subsystems, and subsequently these partial descriptions are put together to provide a comprehensive perspective on the whole complex process of sustainable development. The framework is simplified to focus only on a relatively few issues of central importance[26] and their inter-linkages, portraying these as a core system which could subsequently serve to further integrate additional elements and interrelationships[27].

A diagrammatic exposition is used, providing a graphic representation of each of the subsystems. The main issues are represented by circles, and the linkages between them are denoted by arrows, pointing from the cause to the effect. In connection with those interrelationships, where pertinent, the potential influences from relevant variables to be modulated by adequate public policies are symbolized by a couple of opposing triangles[28].

Box 2. How countries look forward to advance into sustainable development

The Outcome Document of Rio+20 is comprehensive and addresses a large number of issues that have been progressively incorporated into the international policy dialogue over the last twenty five years. It covers challenges as well as elements of strategy for the consideration of government and non-government actors in all countries. The following are only some few quotes related to the latter, which highlight the pertinence of adopting integrative approaches and tools in the countries, as appropriate, to facilitate coherent policy-making and effective implementation, with the participation of a multiplicity of stakeholders, in informed and coordinated manners. Indeed, the countries expressed, among many other matters:

"We recognize the opportunities for people to influence their lives and future, participate in decision-making and voice their concerns are fundamental for sustainable development. We underscore that sustainable development requires concrete and urgent action. It can only be achieved with a broad alliance of people, governments, civil society and the private sector, all working together to secure the future we want for present and future generations." (United Nations General Assembly, 2012, paragraph 13). Thus, it is fundamental to facilitate a common understanding of sustainable development among very diverse stakeholders.

"We recognize that effective governance at the local, sub-national, national, regional and global levels, representing the voices and interests of all is critical for advancing sustainable development. The strengthening and reform of the institutional framework should not be an end in itself, but a means to achieve sustainable development. (…). We therefore resolve to strengthen the institutional framework for sustainable development, which will, inter alia: (a) promote the balanced integration of all the three dimensions of sustainable development; (b) be based on an action- and results-oriented approach giving due regard to all relevant cross-cutting issues with the aim to contribute to the implementation of sustainable development; (c) underscore the importance of inter-linkages among key issues and challenges and the need for a systemic approach to them at all relevant levels; (d) enhance coherence, reduce fragmentation and overlap, and increase effectiveness, efficiency and transparency, while reinforcing coordination and cooperation; (e) promote full and effective participation of all countries in decision-making processes; (f) engage high-level political leaders, provide policy guidance and identify specific actions to promote effective implementation of sustainable development, including through voluntary sharing of experiences and lessons learned; (g) promote the science-policy interface through inclusive, evidence-based and transparent scientific assessments, as well as access to reliable, relevant and timely data in areas related to the three dimensions of sustainable development (…); (h) enhance the participation and effective engagement of civil society and other relevant stakeholders in the relevant international

continued on following page

Box 2. Continued

forums and, in this regard, promote transparency and broad public participation and partnerships to implement sustainable development; (i) promote the review and stocktaking of progress in the implementation of all sustainable development commitments, including commitments to means of implementation." (United Nations General Assembly, 2012, paragraph 76). Therefore, a systemic vision is needed, in which all different aspects -economic, social and environmental- of sustainable development are included and their inter-relationships are explicit. This need is twofold. First, to facilitate that key elements and interrelationships are comprehended with enough clarity by all the diverse stakeholders, so as to make dialogue among them more productive and strengthen their respective willingness to act motivated by a larger understanding of everyone's responsibilities in a mutual accountability setting. And, second, to ease the participatory design and implementation of numerous public policies aimed at making these more coherent, better coordinated and effective.

"We also underscore that sustainable development goals should be action-oriented, concise and easy to communicate, limited in number, aspirational, global in nature and universally applicable to all countries, while taking into account different national realities, capacities and levels of development and respecting national policies and priorities. We also recognize that the goals should address and be focused on priority areas for the achievement of sustainable development, being guided by the present Outcome Document. Governments should drive implementation with the active involvement of all relevant stakeholders, as appropriate." (United Nations General Assembly, 2012, paragraph 247). "The goals should address and incorporate in a balanced way all three dimensions of sustainable development and their interrelationships." (United Nations General Assembly, 2012, paragraph 256). Hence, a systemic view is important to establish goals in the different aspects of sustainable development in ways that facilitate traceability of actions and accountability relationships by making it easier for all stakeholders to map their different but common responsibilities with respect to said goals.

"We recognize the importance of the evaluation of the range of social, environmental and economic factors, and encourage, where national circumstances and conditions allow, their integration into decision making. We acknowledge that it will be important to take into account the opportunities and challenges, as well as the costs and benefits, of green economy policies in the context of sustainable development and poverty eradication, using the best available scientific data and analysis. We acknowledge that a mix of measures, including regulatory, voluntary and others applied at the national level and consistent with obligations under international agreements, could promote green economy in the context of sustainable development and poverty eradication. We reaffirm that social policies are vital to promoting sustainable development." (United Nations General Assembly,

continued on following page

Box 2. Continued

2012, paragraph 63). Thus, the advantages of a systemic approach pointed out above are again perceived with regard to appraising results along the process, not only for accountability sake, but for promoting learning and an ever improving understanding by all stakeholders on how they manage to promote sustainable development both individually and collectively.

4.1. Interrelationships between Production and Consumption Activities and the Natural Environment

The international policy dialogue has highlighted, as the main overall aspirations for sustainable development in these particular matters:

1. Reaching a pace of economic growth that suffices to satisfy the short-run and durable consumption needs of the population (whether this is increasing, constant or diminishing) and to generate enough jobs to fully employ the working labor force; and
2. Arriving at aggregate consumption levels and a balance of primary energy sources that, first, stop global climate change; second, generate pollution levels that don't harm the health of human and any animal or plant species and thus secure biodiversity; and third, permit to maintain stable stocks of natural resources due to simultaneous offsetting technological innovations.

Indeed, these aspirations are minimalistic fundamental conditions for the natural environment to be sustainable and safe while the economy satisfies the basic requirements of human needs and jobs creation. Yet, for many sustainable development actors and stakeholders it is not clear enough how these aspirations can be achieved as goals, what are the technical and human behavioral issues at play and how these are inter-related, and which are some of the public

policy interventions that may help conduct the private and collective processes of production and consumption towards said goals.

So, a simple conceptual analytical framework or model is helpful to improve the understanding of these matters by the different actors and stakeholders, as a point of departure to facilitate better shared knowledge and coordination of particular efforts to advance towards these goals. To these aims, Figure 1 depicts the issues, interrelationships and policies deemed most important with regard to the interplay of the economy and the natural environment[29].

The narrative of Figure 1, reading the series of cause-effect relationships that altogether connect the consequences from economic activities for the natural environment, is the following[30]. The total volume of economic activity, consumption and production in the economy grows (diminishes)[31] over time as an *immediate*[32] result of two main phenomena. First, due to the increase (decrease) of the population and the labor force, which reflect demographic trends and labor-market participation decisions of individuals and families; whereas these decisions depend on a myriad of conditions faced by the people—including the age-structure of the population, gender roles for males and females about production and reproduction, etc.—some public policies can influence to certain degree the growth rate—and over time the size—of the population and the labor force—such as immigration policies, public information on family planning, taxes that affect work decisions of individuals, and so on. And, second, the aggregate volume of economic activ-

Figure 1. Main issues and inter-linkages between economic activities and the environment

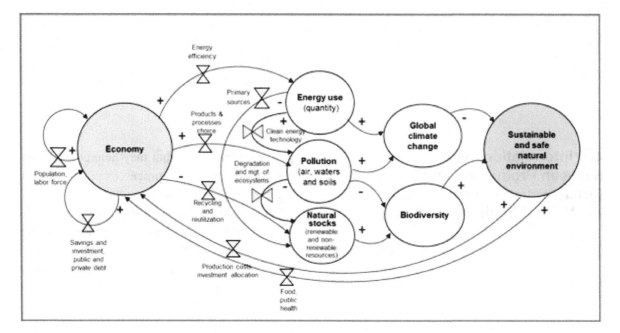

ity, consumption and production increases (decreases) from the accumulation (depletion) of the physical capital stock, which results from the decisions made by the people and their organizations in the family, private and public sectors, regarding savings, investment and net borrowing -from other economies or from future generations-; while these decisions depend on a variety of conditions met by the people—consumer confidence and more generally expectations about the future-, they can also be affected by public policies—for instance, about taxes and subsidies, financial interest rates, financial sector regulations, etc.[33]

In turn, the levels of economic activity, production and consumption cause *direct* and *indirect* effects[34]. On one hand, a direct effect is that higher (lower) volumes of economic activity, consumption and production provoke more (less) energy consumption, because energy is an input for generating practically all goods and services consumed by people. Yet, the average energy use per unit of production is not fixed, but depends on the energetic efficiency of the respective produc-

tion and consumption activities, as energy waste can be diminished by innumerable technological innovations, as well as by energy-saving behavioral change of consumers. In these regards, total energy consumption can be modulated by influencing energy efficiency, through public policies -such as government regulations, information and education for the public on technical issues and good practices, taxes on energy use, taxes or subsidies for technical change including research and development and also new or replacement investment in energy-efficient equipment and infrastructure, etc.[35]

Moreover, *indirectly*[36], energy consumption in turn affects pollution levels and the depletion of natural resources: more (less) energy consumption generates higher (lower) quantities of pollution, as a consequence of the disposal to the environments of byproducts—such as monoxides and dioxides of carbon, sulfur and nitrogen[37]—that come out from the generation and use of energy to a larger or smaller degree. This depends mostly on two factors. First, the chemical characteristics of the primary sources used to produce energy, which can be more or less polluting, or in other words, cleaner or dirtier—coal and oil of different qualities being in the high range of pollutants, and wind, solar radiation, geothermal, and atomic nuclear fusion in the low range, with a variety of fuels like natural gas and biomass in-between. And, second, the technologies used to convert primary sources into final energy, because the alternative technical processes for this provoke different amounts of the various pollutants. Both the decisions people and firms make, as to the primary energy sources used and the corresponding technologies, depend on their availability, safety and cost factors[38], and can be influenced by the same public policies mentioned in the preceding paragraph.

And, concomitantly, another *indirect* effect derived from what has been discussed above is that more (less) energy consumption depletes at a faster (slower) pace the stocks of natural energy resources. As above, this also depends on the choice of primary energy sources—renewable ones like solar, wind, geothermal and biomass, or non-renewable ones such as coal, oil and gas-, which are available in larger or smaller amounts of natural stock and usable reserves[39]; and the technical efficiency with which exhaustible energy resources are transformed into final energy and products, given that a primary source decays more slowly the more efficiently it is technically exploited and transformed. In these respects, the decisions by people and firms as to the primary energy sources used and the corresponding technologies depend on availability, reliability and cost factors, and can be influenced by public policies like those mentioned in the previous paragraphs.

A second *direct* effect from the levels of economic activity, production and consumption is on pollution, not only in the manners already mentioned already around energy use, but in more general forms. Indeed, larger (smaller) amounts of pollution to the air, waters and soils result from the disposal of a large variety of liquid and solid waste, including a large variety of toxic chemicals from agricultural activities (fertilizers, pesticides,

etc.) and mining and manufacturing activities (heavy metals, detergents, etc.), as well as solid waste (packaging materials, used products, etc.).

And, *indirectly*, related with this, larger (smaller) amounts of pollution to the air, above- and underground waters, and land, degrade more (less) markedly the quality and quantity of reserves of renewable natural resources, including ecosystems, wild plant and animal varieties, agriculture, and so on[40]. The extent of these effects can be moderated by varying the choice of goods and services produced and consumed—preferring those with an overall lesser impact on the environment, or in other words, with a lower human footprint on nature. And, concurrently, the volumes and types of pollution from these sources can also be affected by technologically improving the production and distribution processes and modifying behavioral patterns of consumption to favor reuse, recycling and reduction of excessive consumption. Public policies that can modulate the choice of products and processes in production and consumption activities include, for instance: dissemination of technical and environmental information and knowledge to better inform production and consumption decisions by firms and people; public regulations; differential taxation on goods that provoke different degrees of pollution; taxes or subsidies as incentives for reducing consumption, reusing and recycling of goods that generate these types of residuals; grants for the production of natural environmental services[41]; subsidies for research and development leading to better products, and so on.

Furthermore, other *transcendental* effects, from more (less) energy consumption, combined with the higher (lower) amounts of pollution, and with the faster (slower) degradation and exhaustion of the stocks of natural resources, are: more (less) pronounced impacts on global climate change and on biodiversity loss. *Ultimately*, these impacts result in a less (more) sustainable and safe natural environment at the local, national and global levels.

All this, at the end, feedbacks into the economy in two ways. First, because the changes of the natural environment affect food production, public health and systemic costs (external economies), which influence the size, growth and characteristics of the population and the labor force. And, in parallel, a second effect is that the reactive public policies applied to mitigate the consequences from economic activities onto the environment result in economic costs that impact on investment decisions and capital accumulation. Hence, through these demographic and economic channels, the quality of the natural environment affects economic activities.

By putting together the notions mentioned above, Figure 1 constitutes a simple analytical framework and modeling tool for one of the three main pillars of sustainable development, namely the green economy. This, even if only presented here in an overly-simplified manner for expository reasons, can help diverse development actors and stakeholders to have a systemic perspective on the several interrelated processes, the cause-effect linkages between them, and the use of a variety of public policies to advance towards sustainability.

And, with great importance, the systemic perspective largely facilitates the design, effective implementation and monitoring of coherent and coordinated policy packages. The importance of this cannot be exaggerated, particularly recalling that most often specific policies are put in place by separate public authorities and implemented by disperse public agencies, that do not communicate and cooperate optimally and, thus, not rarely apply their function-specific policies in ways that result in overall low efficacy to harness economic, production, consumption, and technological processes for sustainable development.

4.2. Interrelationships between Economic Activities and Society, with Attention on Poverty and Inequality

As it comes to this other dimension of sustainable development, the international policy dialogue has highlighted that the major challenge in this respect implies attaining the following aspirations[42]:

1. Sufficient jobs are created to occupy the entire working population and pay adequate wages so that with existing socio-demographic characteristics (family size, male and female labor participation, dependency ratio, etc.) every family is capable of satisfying more than mere basic needs, or in other words, every family and individual is out of poverty;

2. Said jobs are also decent[43], in the sense that they offer legal and social protection vis a vis risks faced by workers, such as unemployment, illnesses, work accidents, death and other hazards that may cause their families suffer major economic losses, or even fall into poverty; and

3. Those jobs are also accessible for all population groups with equity and in ways that do not cause offensive social or economic inequalities.

These aspirations represent the fundamental conditions that need to be secured in order that, as the economy operates to satisfy the short-run and durable consumption needs of the population, the economic performance is such that permanent decent jobs are created with equity for all, while eliminating poverty and narrowing inequality. The importance of these notions is so high, that throughout the *Rio+20 Outcome Document*, wherever reference is made to balancing the interactions between the economy and the environment, this is immediately followed by a remark that it is to take place simultaneously in the context of eliminating poverty and reducing inequality[44]. Thus, in the global international policy dialogue both building blocks—green economy and equitable/inclusive society—are deemed equally necessary to attain sustainable development.

Yet, it is useful for development actors and stakeholders to have a comprehensive perspective on these matters as a basis for adopting diverse public policies that are coherent and altogether conducive to sustainable development in all three of its dimensions—economic, social and environmental. A conceptual analytical framework is presented next in the form of a simplified model of inclusive and equitable economic growth with poverty reduction.

Using the same expository method introduced in the preceding section, Figure 2 presents graphically the issues and interrelationships deemed most important with respect to the interactions between economic activities and an inclusive and equitable society.

The story line of Figure 2 is as follows[45]. The total volume of economic activity, particularly the amount of production, as mentioned already, increases (decreases) over time as an *immediate* result of the evolving features of the population and the labor force—size, age, and sex structures, skills, etc.—and also due to the accumulation of capital from savings, investment and net borrowing determined by the people, private firms and the public sector. In turn, bigger (smaller) volumes of economic activity, i.e., production, *directly* diminish (increase) poverty—that is, the head-count of individuals who cannot meet basic human needs—if the goods and services to satisfy generalized basic needs are produced more (less) abundantly and distributed more (less) efficiently, thus lowering (augmenting) the price index of basic products, also denoted as the cost of living index. In this regard, public policies that influence the relationship between production levels and poverty include those that maintain favorable production and market conditions for staple foods, medicines, public services—such as water and

sanitation, public transportation, safety, etc.—and other basic needs; for instance, policies that prevent anticompetitive behavior or monopolistic/oligopolistic practices in the production and distribution of private goods and services, policies that ease the expansion of public services as economic activity raises[46], etc.

This effect from the volume of economic activity on poverty is strengthened (weakened) by another most important *direct* effect, consisting in that, as more (less) quality jobs are created, their features are such that they are not only accessible to privileged workers and their families—like those more educated, living in determined regions, or with determined social backgrounds—but all social groups in an inclusive way. The inclusiveness of decent employment depends on the distribution of skills and labor productivity across the population, and societal institutions which shape labor relations. Public policies that can influence this encompass: adequate labor laws and regulations that avoid discrimination—in any form, including by gender, ethnicity, religious beliefs, etc.—and protect legitimate rights of workers and employers, without imposing excessively costly obligations and procedures on employers; active labor policies that support the well-functioning of labor markets through training and retooling workers, as well as adequate employment-opportunities information systems; and policies that promote the development of a competitive and dynamic private sector, including through public regulations, efficient financial institutions, innovation systems, quality public services and infrastructure, agile courts and law- and contract-enforcement institutions, and efficient taxation and fiscal institutions.

Indirectly, the extent to which more (less) quality jobs decrease (increase) poverty, depends on several factors. Among these are the characteristics of families—for example, the ratio of dependents to income earners and the male-female participation in extra-domestic activities; the skills of the working-age population in poverty; the costs of commuting between poor neighborhoods or

Figure 2. Main issues and inter-linkages between economic activities and an inclusive and equitable society

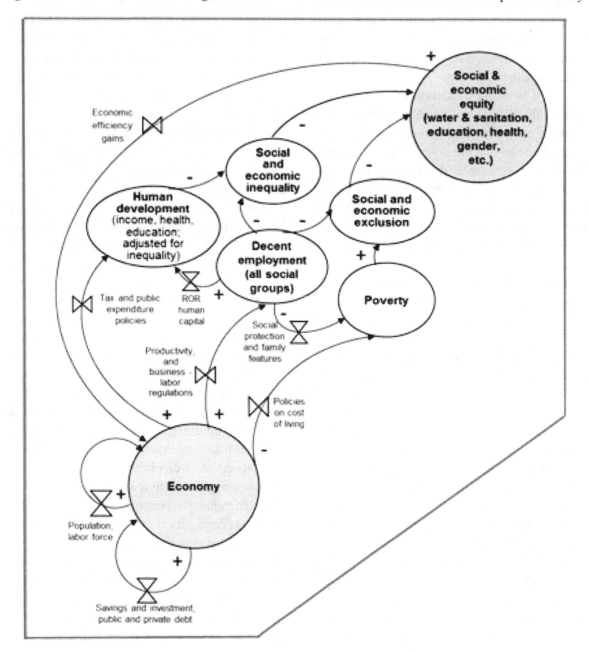

communities and the geographical zones where most jobs are created; and the institutions in place to provide public services and social protection. Hence, not only general employment growth is needed, but especially pro-poor and inclusive growth[47]. Public policies useful in this sense comprise: deregulation to eliminate any administrative or legal requirements that may make excessively costly to create decent low-skills jobs; adequate spatial planning of regional development, to facilitate that decent jobs are well distributed over geography and lagging communities are well connected to dynamic economic centers through sufficient transportation infrastructure, etc. In addition, to increase the ratio of income earners to dependents in poor households, as a means to increase average per capita income and lower the headcount under the poverty rate as well as the depth of poverty, female extra-domestic remunerated work needs to be supported; this can be done, in the short-run, by antidiscrimination laws and institutions, as well as by facilities that provide working females in all localities and social groups with efficient care support institutions for children and elderly family members; and, in the mid- and long-runs, through more effective dissemination of information and means for family planning to all population groups, including evidently the poor.

Alongside, the creation of more (less) decent jobs *indirectly* facilitates (constraints) improvements in human development—in other words, for attaining more income, schooling, training, health, equality of opportunities for women and men, etc.—for the disadvantaged population groups. This comes about because the enlarged (reduced) productive opportunities to attain higher living conditions stimulate (face with negative incentives) all the people, including the poor, to permanently invest more (less) in personal health, education and labor skills. This relationship depends crucially on the economic returns to health, education and training from well remunerated jobs. Thus, public policies relevant in this respect are those that affect net or after-tax wages—particularly marginal income tax rates for workers in different levels of human development—and the cost of health, education, and training services, including the opportunity cost of staying in the school system instead of having a wage job—for instance, subsidies for low-income groups, school grants for low-income students, and so on.

In addition, there are other *transcendental* effects, as more (less) decent jobs for all social groups, less (more) poverty, and more (less) equal opportunities for social development, clearly translate into lower (higher) socioeconomic inequality and diminish (augment) socioeconomic exclusion. Altogether, these generate more (less) social and economic equity, which should be observed not only in access to private goods, but also in more even access to public services—such as water and sanitation, education, healthcare, etc.

This final outcome, moreover, influences *back* the evolution of economic activity, production and consumption levels, because a more (less) equitable and egalitarian society propitiates systemic efficiency gains in the form of "external economies"[48], like lower (higher) transactions costs, less (more) markets segmentation and larger (smaller) market scale economies in production and distribution, and so on. This feedback effect is of utmost importance because it can generate a "virtuous circle," by which equitable and inclusive pro-poor growth brings about external economies that further promote additional growth.

The simplified description of the issues and inter-linkages presented above is useful to analyze and model how the second major pillar of sustainable development can be strengthened, namely, an inclusive and equitable society. In particular, the simplified description portrayed in Figure 2 facilitates that an adequate mix of different public policies are designed, implemented and monitored in coherent and coordinated ways for the economy, social equity and inclusion, and poverty eradication, to evolve as necessary for attaining sustainable development.

4.3. Interrelationships between Society and the Natural Environment, with Emphasis on Resilience and Public Governance

The international development policy dialogue has increasingly addressed over the past two decades the importance of adequate public governance, the rule of law, justice, the protection of all human rights, the existence of participatory and democratic institutions for the people to be involved in public affairs including in decision-making, and preparedness and effective response to diminish and recover from risky negative events. In particular, the following stand out as major aspirations related to public governance and social resilience[49]:

1. That people have adequate societal and public institutions that permit them to enjoy ample freedoms and rights, and to live in peace and safety, benefiting from orderly social and political conditions to foster their individual and collective efforts to improve their living conditions; and

2. That people count on social and public institutions that allow them to protect all forms of wealth—human and physical capital, social solidarity, natural wealth, etc.—or in other words, to reasonably maintain what they have achieved through past development, even when adversity hits in different forms, including sociopolitical or armed conflicts, economic or financial crises, and natural or human-caused disasters.

Accomplishing this over time requires not only actions from government and community leaders and civil society organizations, but also the direct participation of the people, communities and grassroots organizations to support one another, reciprocally protect their rights and altogether defend the fundamental societal and political institutions that serve all to live well. This is a multifaceted matter, in which a plethora of interactions among very large numbers of diverse actors eventually advance public trust, respect for the rule of law and human rights, and democratic and participatory institutions, learning from their collective experience as to how these factors effectively lead to better development and living conditions for all. The cause-effect relationships that underlie in this are often not totally clear, although the social sciences have succeeded somehow in elucidating some of their features[50].

Proceeding with the same terminology and expository method of previous sections, Figure 3 summarizes in a stylized fashion some important inter-linkages between human activities and the natural environment, beyond the ones of an economic or productive character already described. The additional set of behavioral and learning processes addressed next encompasses those stemming from the form in which society gets structured over time—by inequality, exclusion, and a variety of institutions—and which translate in stronger or weaker resilience and public governance. Thus, Figure 3 represents a simplified conceptual framework to analyze these matters, even if with a considerable degree of intellectual speculation given the state of the art in social and political research.

The plot depicted in Figure 3 is as follows[51]. Higher (lower) social and economic equity contributes *directly* to increase (decrease) social cohesion, even more (less) so if the people enjoy effective fundamental freedoms and human rights, recognizing the intrinsic merits that everyone has as a member of society and as a human person; and, in the opposite direction, more (less) social cohesion leads to further augment (diminish) social and economic equity, to the extent that higher (lower) solidarity among people is conducive for everyone to persevere in (detach from) seeking fairness in economic and social opportunities for all members of society. Public policies conducive to strengthen these processes include shaping adequate legal and judicial institutions, and effective public administration practices, to attain high levels of freedoms and rights, including all human rights, in a context of equality before the law. Indeed, a leveled playing-field in rights matters is deemed fundamental for building cohesion and solidarity; yet, as a necessary but not sufficient condition, the outcomes are also the result of how societal values are shaped by past collective experiences, on which public policies have subtle but important effects as referred to below, including policies and leadership to conduct public administration and politics in accordance with society's ethical principles, fairness, inclusiveness, responsiveness to all people's needs—

Figure 3. Main issues and inter-linkages between an inclusive and equitable society and the natural environment

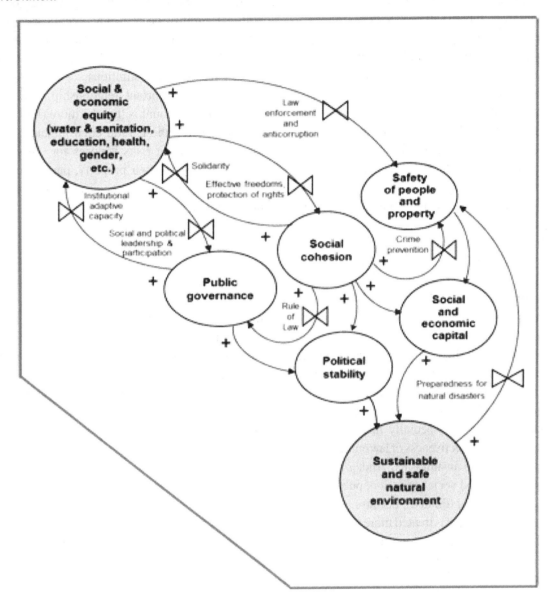

especially of the weakest and most disadvantaged and vulnerable groups—and adherence to the rule of law, evidently comprising effective law enforcement, justice administration and countering of corruption.[52]

Furthermore, as an *indirect* effect from equity and inclusion, stronger (weaker) social cohesion facilitates (makes it less likely) that the safety and property of persons are effectively protected, especially when reciprocity to these aims among the people is compounded with more (less) effective public institutions and policies to prevent and combat crime. Similarly, higher (lower) social cohesion is favorable (contrary) to public governance, because it underscores (undermines) the collective observance of public norms and institutions, to an extent that is influenced by the public policies in place for enforcing the rule of law. And, concomitantly, more (less) social cohesion contributes as well, in more *transcendental* forms, to increase (decrease) social capital for all persons[53] and to strengthen (weaken) political stability, both of which ultimately create better (worse) enabling conditions for the people to maintain a safe and sustainable natural environment. Indeed, the natural environment can result largely damaged in circumstances in which the people are loosely interconnected on social grounds and exhibit low levels of mutual support and when there are serious political or armed conflicts.

The harmonious and cohesive functioning of society, supported by enabling public institutions, is thus an important factor of resilience vis a vis environmental, social and economic challenges[54].

Also, *directly* as an effect from higher (lower) equity, there is better (worse) protection and safety for the people and their property, because when people recognize that they are treated more (less) fairly in economic and social terms they tend to engage to a smaller (larger) degree in illicit or criminal behaviors[55], especially more (less) so depending on the effectiveness of law enforcement and anticorruption institutions. And, *indirectly* through more (less) social cohesion, public governance is enhanced (diluted), because as people perceive that everyone is treated more (less) fairly in economic and social terms, they tend to be altogether more supportive of the rules and institutions by which society harnesses such activities, and even more (less) so when they take part in the collective shaping of such rules and institutions and when they trust the capacity of public leaders to enforce these effectively and fairly. In the opposite direction, more (less) effective public governance generates better (worse) general conditions for socioeconomic equity if public rules and institutions are successfully adapted over time to warranty equity as the conditions of the economy and society evolve. Also, more

(less) effective public governance is conducive as well, *transcendentally*, to maintaining (eroding) political stability, because when public rules and institutions render benefits for all there is less or no need to alter the power relationships that support such rules and institutions.

One final important relationship that must be taken into account is that the more (less) safe and sustainable the natural environment is, the lower (higher) the risks it poses for the safety of the people and their property, particularly to the extent that there is social and institutional preparedness to prevent, mitigate and overcome natural disasters[56].

The succinct description of the issues and inter-relationships considered above helps to analyze and model the building block of sustainable development consisting in societal and public institutions for resilience and public governance to maintain sustainable development. As in the case of the other building blocks, this conceptual analytical framework is useful to design, implement and monitor the corresponding public policies and to promote that these are coherent and well-coordinated to advance more swiftly towards sustainable development.

4.4. Other Interrelationships

The many different inter-linkages described in the previous sections have the characteristic of being circumscribed to each of the three conceptual blocks utilized in this chapter to depict sustainable development, namely: a green economy, an equitable and inclusive society, and societal and government institutions for resilience and public governance. Next, Figure 4 puts together the preceding three, and, thus, offers a fully integrated yet simplified vision of sustainable development, following the main notions that are highlighted nowadays in the international development dialogue.

However, there are additional inter-linkages of considerable importance that run between the three main blocks previously described. These are depicted by dashed arrows in Figure 4, as follows:

- Less (more) poverty is conducive to increase (decrease) the volumes and qualities of the stocks of natural resources, depending on the availability of alternative production opportunities for the poor to sustain their livelihoods[57].

- Diminish (augment) the depletion- and degradation-rate of the stocks of natural resources propitiate (more) political stability, as conflicting claims over their property rights and alternative uses moderate (intensify)[58].

- Greater (lower) political stability creates conditions more (less) favorable for the reduction of poverty, to the extent that the poor and vulnerable groups of population are less (more) exposed to the negative consequences of abuses and violent behav-

Figure 4. Main issues and inter-linkages encompassed within and between the main conceptual blocs of sustainable development: green economy, equitable, and inclusive society, and institutions for resilience and public governance

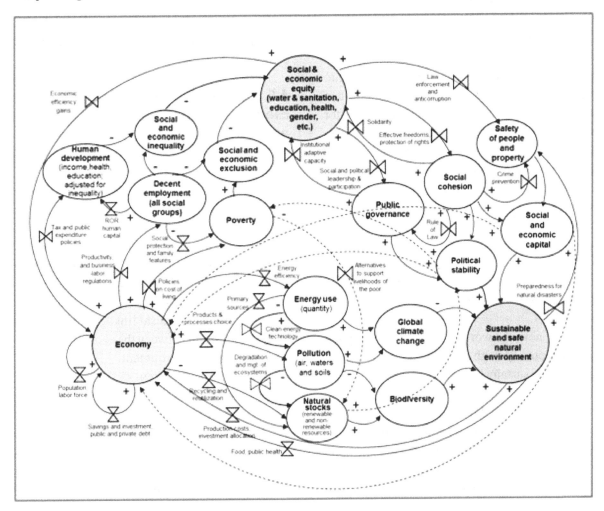

ior, such as death of family income earners, displacements of people as refugees, and destruction or stealing of their property[59].

- More (less) social capital, and higher (lower) political stability, generate more confidence for consumers and investors and, hence, are favorable (unfavorable) for increasing economic activity levels[60].

It is worth mentioning that these linkages between the subsystems described in the last three sections are only a few examples of what in reality may be a much larger number of system-wide cause-effect relationships. It is not surprising that much better identification of pertinent interrelationships has been attained by scholars and practitioners within each of the subsystems, than between these: this is largely a consequence of the compartmentalized way in which research and the generation of scientific knowledge has been structured in the past, going deeply into relatively narrowly defined subjects, more than addressing cross-cutting phenomena that call for wider multi-disciplinary research[61], which is similar to a "silos" organizational model encountered in other collective human activities[62]. Hence, the less (more) multidisciplinary the generation of knowledge to harness sustainable development becomes, and the less (more) its practical application to solve sustainable development matters is, the larger (smaller) uncertainty development actors and policy makers will have as to how to modulate or control the overall system depicted in Figure 4.

As of now, the world seems to be undergoing a transition, although still at early stages, about addressing sustainable development challenges with integral approaches. In this situation, it should humbly be admitted that there are still many issues and inter-relationships, mostly between its subsystems, that are not completely understood, or in other words, strategy and policy design and implementation are made still under significant

limited knowledge and hence uncertainty. This is not in any way to paralyze necessary actions, even if undertaken with incomplete information; on the contrary, the urgency to advance towards sustainable development to avoid major and costly crises on economic, social and environmental grounds, as acknowledged in the international policy dialogue, makes it advisable to move ahead with what we already know and continue learning along the way, even stressing that learning-as-we-go should be an explicit priority process in seeking sustainable development[63].

The same is valid about transforming the overall organization among diverse actors and stakeholders, including prominently government or the public sector: new models of organization, including better use of information and communication technologies, are indispensable to enhance the effectiveness of public management in the context of sustainable development[64].

4.5. Evolution of the Different Elements of the System as Time and Development Go On

The graphic description of sustainable development in Figure 4 underscores how complex it is. Yet, its intricate characteristics are not artificially the result of abstract theories, or of accommodating in a patchwork fashion diverse views that emerge in the international development dialogue: the complexity of sustainable development is intrinsic to it because of the myriad of relevant causal linkages that exist in reality within and between the economy, society and the natural environment.

The integrated system description encompasses a wide view of all the issues and inter-relationships comprised within the multidimensional concept of sustainable development, yet combined with precise perspectives on the particular issues and inter-linkages within and between the subsystems or conceptual building blocks. As such, the system description constitutes an analytical tool that is useful to establish, as a point of departure, an effective shared understanding of the overall picture among development actors and stakeholders who may have diverse disciplinary approaches, expertise and general cognitive backgrounds. That enhanced shared vision can, moreover, facilitate communications, action-oriented negotiations and alliances, and the setting of goals that clearly highlight the mutually agreed aspirations of said actors and stakeholders. And, especially about collective goal-setting, the systemic analytical framework can help selecting those that are not only notionally and politically important, but which have also an operational character in the sense that a sufficiently reliable connection can be recognized with certain degree of certainty between said goals, the actions to be undertaken by the multiplicity of actors and stakeholders, and the public policies that could effectively contribute to reaching those goals. Thus, the framework is a holistic resource for conceptual analyses and for articulating the multi-stakeholder policy dialogue, without being prescriptive or rigid.

Metaphorically, the systemic description of sustainable development offered in this chapter can serve as a large meeting hall with different entry points, where interested individuals can come from diverse sites to engage with many others into mutually beneficial exchanges of knowledge, joint reflections, possible partnerships, and gradual consensus building as to the relative priorities among their aspirations to achieve sustainable development in its economic, social, and environmental dimensions.

Nevertheless, the framework under consideration has to be used wisely and not mechanically. The precise features of the numerous cause-effect relationships involved, and the strength and importance of the many inter-linkages commented in the preceding sections, are not fixed over time. Thus, whereas the conceptual

framework presented may be robust to certain extent over some considerable period of time, the very set of connections between the issues and variables pointed out should not be deemed as a rigid model that is to remain unaltered over time and equally useful at all future dates, or in any particular context or level—global, national, sub-national. Indeed, with the exception of the cause-effect relationships of a pure technical nature, whose regular consistency has been demonstrated by the natural sciences, the ones predicated on human behavioral and institutional grounds typically change over time and are considerably context-specific[65].

Confronting this inescapable fact, and risking major disruptions in all three pillars of sustainable development—economic, social and environmental- if past trends continue indefinitely into the future, human activities, behaviors and institutions need to be adequately modified and monitored for their gradual modulation, to significantly improve on the past record of sustainable development at all levels. Development actors and stakeholders -from the public, private and social sectors, and the people in the broader sense- need to identify, implement and adapt over time, in their own local demarcations, countries and at the global level, effective courses of action and coherent public policies to secure and consolidate in the future a green economy, an inclusive and equitable society, and robust institutions for resilience and public governance. The framework presented in this chapter can be a useful tool in this regard, with the caveat just made that it falls short from being an ideal structural universal model.

The next section further elaborates on the usefulness of a systems approach for diverse groups of actors and stakeholders to embrace more fully a comprehensive action-oriented view on sustainable development and to undertake decisive steps to accelerate progress to consolidate it at the global, national and sub-national levels.

5. APPLYING THE FRAMEWORK TO THE STRATEGIZING, ORGANIZATION, AND MANAGEMENT OF SUSTAINABLE DEVELOPMENT

Sustainable development is so challenging because of its inherent complexity and due to the many different actors involved in its manifold specific processes. Indeed, sustainable development management is about pursuing orderly strategies that encompass government, the private sector and society—the people at large—to simultaneously induce economic growth, reduce poverty and inequity, create opportunities for all population groups—especially the ones that are more disadvantaged and vulnerable—to benefit from the effective enjoyment of all human rights, gender equality, health, education, public services, etc., and to maintain adequate public governance and resilience while protecting fundamental freedoms, ultimately assuring a permanent balance between all kinds of human activities and the natural environment.

As mentioned in section 4.5, it is deemed that the system approach provides an explicit framework in which diverse actors and stakeholders can interrelate, with many entry-points suited to their different concerns, viewpoints and expertise, in a way that propitiates and can lead to multi-stakeholders inter-disciplinary work, specifically through facilitating coherent and convergent discussions, analyses, policy proposals and collective action for implementation, monitoring and continuous policy adaptation, innovation and improvement. Some considerations in these regards are presented next.

5.1. Establishing Goals, Milestones, and Indicators for Advancing towards Sustainable Development

The framework proposed in this chapter is convenient to explicitly map the *priorities* that are often only implicit in the minds of diverse stakeholders and actors. In connection with this, the framework can help stakeholders to agree on a number of relevant sustainable development *goals* that provide clarity to all as to the direction in which each and every one is to advance. And, with great importance, the framework helps to identify narratives, logically anchored on concrete cause-effect *processes* which are controllable to certain extent in some determined aspects and thus are the ground for establishing milestones and *indicators*.

In this respect, the *aspirations* that have been highlighted in the preceding sections with regard to a green economy, an inclusive and equitable society, and societal and public conditions and institutions for adequate public governance and resilience, can be further elucidated through *deliberations* among stakeholders, who with the use of a systemic framework like the one presented here can move forward with a better shared understanding of all the issues and interrelationships.

The framework offers in this respect several advantages. It is helpful, on one hand, to define not only the desirable future outcomes in a fashion that appeals to the diversity of stakeholders with different contexts and priorities, but also to meaningfully communicate how specific goals are interrelated, and how respective processes, efforts and progress towards each of these, being more (less) successful, contribute (complicate) to advance in respect of the other goals. Thus, the framework facilitates inter-disciplinary discussions and negotiations among stakeholders from different contexts, and it also helps them to identify the highest *priorities* for all of them and for groups in rather unique or different contexts. Indeed, while offering generality, the analytical framework presented before can also accommodate particularities.

Furthermore, the systemic framework is useful for those deliberations to translate the identified priorities into more focused *goals*, that, as already mentioned, are not only notionally and politically important, but which have also an operational character in the sense that a sufficiently reliable connection can be recognized with certain degree of certainty between said goals, the *actions* to be undertaken by the multiplicity of *actors* and *stakeholders*, and the *public policies* that could effectively contribute to reaching those goals.

Based on reasonable empirical knowledge about the diverse issues and cause-effect relationships involved in advancing towards said goals, *milestones* can be qualitatively or quantitatively established by all actors and stakeholders, to monitor progress over time, not only about the more transcendental issues and relationships, but also about specific ones that stakeholders may consider appropriate either because of their intrinsic importance (substantive milestones) or because these may reveal how particular processes and actors are proceeding (process milestones). In other words, useful milestones would be relevant not only about progress towards substantive important ends, but also about the advance attained in adapting behavior and institutions along the process of moving towards the goals; these process milestones, for instance, could be about the evolving awareness and values among actors, their participation according to their typical roles, the steps taken for policy-making and implementation, the ongoing institutional reforms, and so on.

In this fashion, both sets of milestones—about ends and about process—would provide all actors and stakeholders with pertinent references to maintain clear shared expectations and to adapt not only the policies and resources devoted to reach the end-goals, but also to fine-tune along the way the actions pursued by the relevant actors. This is tantamount to acknowledging that the desired changes to attain sustainable development are not only to get results, but also about people and their organizations learning to do things differently and cooperating together to be better prepared to address challenges. In these respects, underscoring that mankind faces real uncertainties as to how numerous processes affect sustainable develop-

ment, the systems model offered in this chapter can contribute to pursue a rational search strategy of options to reach sustainable development, emphasizing both rationality about the *outcomes* sought and with equal importance about the *processes* to reach these[66].

Finally, assessments of how progress is made relative to those milestones can be made through the values attained at different dates by adequate *indicators*. Thus, the framework proposed in this chapter can also facilitate to identify where additional *data- and information-collection efforts* must be done, enriching the possibilities of introducing highly pertinent indicators, instead of being circumscribed to where statistical activities are already ongoing.

5.2. Policy Coherence and Coordination

The systemic framework helps as well to link generic public policies to the several goals. In this regard, the framework makes clear to considerable extent, for every group of stakeholders and actors, the regulatory, social, economic or political processes that seem adequate to move towards each goal; in this technical sense, the framework facilitates policy-makers attaining an overall use of different public policies that promise the highest possible outcomes about sustainable development. Yet, the framework at the same time preserves for each group the necessary room to define, in the same technical fashion, the particular policies about such processes that fit best in each particular context (in cultural, social, economic, political and legal terms)[67]. Thus, the value of the framework for policy coherence and coordination, and thereof policy effectiveness.

In particular, the analysis contained in section 4 has pointed out to specific public policy types that can influence to some degree concrete processes and modulate them to converge in sustainable development, in an overall way. These are recapitulated here for easy reference:

- **Fiscal Policies:** including taxes, subsidies, grants, public investments and debt finance. Combined, the framework highlights that sustainable development fiscal policies would have, among their distinctive characteristics: 1) the use of tax instruments for public revenue purposes, geared to finance the expenditures on grants, public investments and the delivery of public services; 2) with equal importance, the use of tax and subsidy instruments for incentives sake as powerful tools to influence the behavior of very large numbers of firms and consumers[68]; 3) the use of grants to compensate different actors for their efforts to fill-in investment gaps in matters of social equity—poverty alleviation, education, health, gender equality, etc.— scientific and technological research, and provision of environmental services; and 4) the use of public investments and public debt finance for the construction of infrastructure and the provision of public services with positive social rates of return in the long run, either directly by public entities at the corresponding levels of government or by public-private-people partnerships, as appropriate, in cases where competitive markets are likely to fail. The analytical framework offered in this chapter, by highlighting a series of important issues and cause-effect linkages, can serve fiscal specialists to generate guidelines, as well as fiscal planning and programming spreadsheets and simulation models, for a coherent and effective use of this variety of fiscal instruments to facilitate decision-making by governments at the national and sub-national levels.

- **Public Information and Awareness-Raising Policies:** These comprise: 1) increasing and disseminating existing public knowledge and propitiating efficient private knowledge generation and sharing in all matters of sustainable development which could help individuals, communities and firms to make pro-sustainability choices on consumption, production, investment and technology decisions, and family planning; and 2) building capacities, through education and training, for consumers, entrepreneurs, investors, workers, public officials at all government levels, and researchers, to generate, obtain and use useful knowledge for making informed decisions and partnerships for sustainable development.

- **Legal and Regulatory Policies:** These imply not just the enactment of laws and regulations, but also their effective application through law-enforcement by administrative and judiciary authorities— including inspectors, tribunals, courts, ombudspersons, etc.—and preventing corruption through shared efforts between government and non-government actors, in a variety of matters related to sustainable and inclusive development[69]. Most importantly, the principles, rules and procedures introduced throughout the different laws and regulations should look not narrowly at the specific issues addressed, but at aspects of coherence and coordination to improve over past tendencies to concentrate normative and regulatory activities in vertically-designed single-purpose public entities that had created incentives for fragmentation of the public administration and the dispersion of policies and norms across public entities operating as "silos," thus being ultimately less effective to address the inter-sectoral aspects of sustainable development.

- **Policies for Scientific and Technological Research and Development:** These would address issues of funding, consortia and public-private partnerships, diffusion of technologies, etc. for sustainable development.

Combining public policies of these different kinds, adequate policy-packages can be put together in a technical sense by policy-makers with the opinions and advice from diverse actors and stakeholders.

Yet, the framework also contributes to enhance policy effectiveness in a political or contextual way. Indeed, to the extent that it comprehensively articulates the different aspects of sustainable development, and leads to accommodating the priorities of all constituencies into interrelated goals, it can bring them closer together and facilitate their converging efforts to advance sustainable development. By propitiating a balance of interests in relation to those goals, the framework helps maintain productive coalitions of diverse groups about sustainable development, generating stronger public support and continuity over time for public policies adopted in this regard, and facilitating multi-stakeholders partnerships for their implementation. Given the importance of this for policy effectiveness, it has been argued in section 5.1 that it should be monitored in itself by means of targets and indicators on process aspects.

5.3. Foundations for Better Strategy and Organization for Sustainable Development

It is important to stress that designing a balanced, meaningful, viable and shared set of sustainable development goals, as an image of what is desired by all stakeholders in the future, is necessary but not sufficient to achieve effective progress. The overall process to move in the desired direction needs as well to be firmly and efficiently established in reference to what the different groups of actors are to contribute with, and how they will get organized to do it not simply together—which would be in itself a very important accomplishment, considering the complexity and multi-stakeholder character of sustainable development—but using everyone's special characteristics and comparative advantages to the best possible extent.

In this respect, the framework seems also helpful to map the *comparative advantages* of diverse groups of actors, regarding the different issues and inter-linkages encompassed in sustainable development. Indeed, rather than inviting the participation of all groups of stakeholders and actors, in a broad sense and without specific reference to the particular issues about which their contributions could be the highest and possibly also unique, the framework presented can help deliberations among stakeholders and actors on who does what better than others and, therefore, it can serve to distribute responsibilities on the grounds of their comparative advantages. The specific merits and special capabilities of diverse actors and stakeholders can be of different kinds and originate in distinct sources, such as: economic and natural resources, technology, sociopolitical leadership, scientific research, public information and communications, data gathering and monitoring, holding specific actors publicly accountable, and so on. By sharing common but differentiated responsibilities, stakeholders and actors are likely to commit more effectively to collective action based on roles that are determined in finer ways, which would appear not only logical and fair, but that would lead to secure both specialization and coordination, and, ultimately, greater efficiency and effectiveness from their joint endeavor to make development sustainable.

The adoption of adequate organization among the multiplicity of actors and stakeholders—at the global, regional, national and local levels—to fully utilize the proven advantages from specialization, with robust governance for coordination and convergence of particular efforts, is crucial for sustainable development, as in any other field of human collaboration. Proceeding along these lines would contribute to both the organization of sustainable development and the development of sustainable organization.

In an isomorphic fashion, just as the diagrams used in this chapter help describe the inherent issues and inter-linkages of sustainable development, they can be used as blueprints to build new or better organizations and institutions by which human beings, at the local, national, regional and global levels, can act together more effectively to ensure sustainable development. Enterprise Architects are uniquely qualified professionals to contribute in these organizational and institutional transformations.

5.4. Conceptual Support to Enhance Public Administration and Development Management

Systemic descriptions of sustainable development like Figure 4 are valuable not only for the strategic and organizational purposes discussed above, but also for tactical day-to-day functions in public administration and development management. Descriptions like Figure 4 can be applied in different ways to these aims. For instance, to guide public entities at the national and sub-national levels, to: identify the variables to measure, the statistics to gather and the indicators to build; to inspire the design of balanced scorecards for monitoring and decision making; to guide the construction of full-fledged indicators systems to be made publicly available to all stakeholders for transparency and mutual accountability sake and for assessing the effective leadership of government; to facilitate the design of measurement, evaluation and simulation models; and so on.

However, it is seldom the case that bureaucracies in any public entity act mechanically to achieve established goals, improve performance and follow rules, as it is sometimes assumed. In real life, bureaucrats need to face incentives strong enough to deliver outputs and outcomes up to the aspirations of the people they are to serve, and whose very resources they use through public budgets. Thus, whereas the technical tools and techniques described in the previous paragraph are important for public administration to enhance sustainable development management, they often

need to be complemented by other managerial methods to attain better results.

In particular, a widespread problem observed in countries around the world is that the public sector has tended to be organized mostly in vertical ways, with departments, ministries and similar entities conceived as single-purpose organizations, and the overall public sector lacking means adequate enough to look for cross-cutting concerns and deliver integrated outcomes through the cooperation of different entities. This is especially problematic for addressing sustainable development, because its multidimensional character requires effective, coherent and coordinated interventions from diverse public entities.

Two mutually complementary approaches are often used in public administration to cope with the problems of administrative silos. One consists in multi-entity commissions, cabinets, councils or similar instances, lead and supervised by high-level government officers, where the different public entities jointly analyze the public policy challenges that must be addressed through integrated actions, and agree on communication, reporting and evaluation procedures, while each entity operates on its own budget and follows its own procedures for resource allocation and accountability. The other, which is impending but gaining attention about sustainable development[70], relies in the use of integrated budgets, by which public resources are allocated to systemic goals and managed with the use of targets and indicators that comprise the actions from different public entities, instead of those resources being allocated to determined departments, ministries, programs, and so on. This second approach also introduces shared accountability methods and procedures for allocating pooled resources to shared goals through the most competent entities that are to work together with other relevant ones[71].

The use of systems descriptions, like those offered in this chapter, can help in both ways, to maintain commissions and multi-entity taskforces adequately looking at the broader challenges beyond the narrow missions of their particular member entities, and to manage pooled resources from integrated budgets, deciding jointly on their allocation to specific actions and programs while pursing effectively the cross-cutting goals.

6. CONCLUSION

The concept of sustainable development has evolved significantly over the past fifty years, from an original focus on avoiding environmental constraints on economic growth and human wellbeing which result from the deployment of natural resources, to a holistic understanding that encompasses three major inter-related notions: green economy, equitable and inclusive society, and institutions for adequate public governance and resilience. Each of these three notions represents an intricate set of relationships among specific phenomena, including, respectively: 1) effects from human economic activity, particularly consumption and production, on energy use, pollution, and degradation of renewable and non-renewable natural resources, that impact climate change, biodiversity and the overall quality of the natural environment, and, if unattended, cause increasing threats for the life of many animal and life species in the planet, including human beings; 2) effects from different types of economic and productive activities, on the creation of jobs of different quality and on trends of poverty and human development, which may improve -or not- aspects of equity and socioeconomic inequality; and 3) effects of socioeconomic inclusion and equity on social cohesion, observance of the rule of law and human rights, and safety and protection for people and their assets, in ways that contribute—or not—to adequate public governance and resilience and altogether influence the forms in which institutional capacities evolve and different types of capital are accumulated. The interactions among all these phenomena determine how the

features of development vary over time and how it becomes more or less sustainable.

Public policy makers and development managers in countries around the world are generally aware of these issues, yet it appears that the international policy dialogue and international cooperation in this context would be well served by a basic conceptual map linking these diverse elements in explicit, clear and meaningful ways, with a systems approach. This chapter has aimed to contribute in this regard by presenting a systemic description of sustainable development as it is generally understood nowadays in the international policy dialogue, in order to attract and facilitate the contributions from practitioners of enterprise architecture.

The systemic description of sustainable development presented in the chapter constitutes a comprehensive conceptual framework that facilitates a shared understanding of the many issues and interactions involved for diverse development actors and stakeholders, as a basis to help them deliberate on relative priorities and establish partnerships to promote sustainability on economic, social and environmental dimensions, notwithstanding their diverse disciplinary backgrounds and their expertise gathered from very different contexts—economic, social, political, environmental, cultural and institutional. Ultimately, the framework is useful for diverse actors and stakeholders to elucidate goals, determine mileposts, design indicators, identify effective public policies and agree on collective actions to be pursued with differentiated responsibilities—considering their different contexts and comparative advantages—implement them coherently, and monitor and modulate them over time as may be necessary, to foster sustainable development.

The description of the system should not be taken as a structural model that fixes over time the numerous cause-effect relationships embedded in it, or that can be used mechanically to analyze any particular context. Only a few such relationships of a pure technical character remain unchanged, while those based on human behavior and institutions evolve over time. Thus, the conceptual framework provided should be thought of as a general description of the issues and inter-relations most relevant for sustainable development, but which requires to be adjusted with flexibility to different contexts and periods in time.

The explicit consideration of every stakeholders group's particular concerns and respective actions about the different issues encompassed, within a comprehensive balanced picture in which everyone else's concerns and actions are similarly considered, is also useful to promote results-oriented and lasting partnerships more effectively than traditional advocacy efforts which invoke general shared notional or political goals but make less visible the inherent partnership or combination of efforts from all stakeholders and the fairness that underlies in linking each one's roles to those of the widest constituency.

Whereas diagrams as the ones offered in this article look as cartoons, compared to the complex realities they attempt to describe and characterize, both diagrams in system analyses, and cartoons in popular political media, effectively convey important messages, highlight sensitive attributes of reality, and connect different people to the underlying themes. Hopefully, the diagrams and discussions presented in this article are useful to development actors and stakeholders to further advance in these regards.

REFERENCES

Adger, W. N. (2000). Social and ecological resilience: Are they related? *Progress in Human Geography*. doi:10.1191/030913200701540465.

Ashford, N., & Hall, R. (2011). *Technology, globalization and sustainable development: Transforming the industrial state*. Cambridge, MA: MIT Press.

Asian Development Bank. (2012). Green urbanization in Asia. In *Key Indicators for Asia and the Pacific 2012*. Retrieved from http://www.adb.org/sites/default/files/pub/2012/ki2012-special-chapter.pdf

Bachus, C. (2005). Governance for sustainable development and civil society participation. In L. Hens & B. Nath (Eds.), *The World Summit on Sustainable Development: The Johannesburg Conference*. Retrieved from http://link.springer.com/book/10.1007/1-4020-3653-1/page/1

Barber, J. (2005). Production, consumption and the world summit on sustainable development. In L. Hens & B. Nath (Eds.), *The World Summit on Sustainable Development: The Johannesburg Conference*. Retrieved from http://link.springer.com/book/10.1007/1-4020-3653-1/page/1

Barber, J. (2007). Mapping the movement to achieve sustainable production and consumption in North America. *Journal of Cleaner Production*. doi:10.1016/j.jclepro.2006.05.010.

Bates-Eamer, N., Carin, B., Lee, M. H., Lim, W., & Kapila, M. (2012). *Post-2015 development agenda: Goals, targets and indicators*. Retrieved from http://www.cigionline.org/sites/default/files/MDG_Post_2015v3.pdf

Begossi, A., & de Avila-Pírez, F. D. (2005). World summit on sustainable development 2002: Latin America and Brazil, biodiversity and indigenous people. In L. Hens & B. Nath (Eds.), *The World Summit on Sustainable Development: The Johannesburg Conference*. Retrieved from http://link.springer.com/book/10.1007/1-4020-3653-1/page/1

Bennett, E. M., Peterson, G. D., & Gordon, L. J. (2009). Understanding relationships among multiple ecosystem services. *Ecology Letters*. Retrieved from http://onlinelibrary.wiley.com/doi/10.1111/j.1461-0248.2009.01387.x/full?goback=%2Egde_788017_member_181915703

Berkes, F., Colding, J., & Folke, C. (Eds.). (2003). *Navigating social–ecological systems: Building resilience for complexity and change*. Cambridge, UK: Cambridge University Press.

Boulanger, P.-M. (2010). Three strategies for sustainable consumption. *Sapiens*. Retrieved from http://sapiens.revues.org/1022

Canadian Environmental Assessment Agency. (2004). *Cabinet directive on the environmental assessment of policy, plan and program proposals*. Ottawa, Canada: Author.

Christopoulos, S., Horvath, B., & Kull, M. (2012). Advancing the governance of cross-sectoral policies for sustainable development: A metagovernance perspective. *Public Administration and Development*. Retrieved from http://onlinelibrary.wiley.com/doi/10.1002/pad.1629/pdf

Commission on Growth and Development. (2008). *The growth report: Strategies for sustained growth and inclusive development*. Retrieved from http://cgd.s3.amazonaws.com/GrowthReportComplete.pdf

Commissioner of the Environment and Sustainable Development Canada. (2009). *Managing sustainable development*. Retrieved from http://www.oag-bvg.gc.ca/Internet/English/sds_fs_e_33574.html

de Oliveira, P., & Antonio (Eds.). (2012). *Green economy and good governance for sustainable development: Opportunities, promises and concerns*. United Nations University.

Department of Environment, Food and Rural Affairs, United Kingdom. (2012a). *Adapting to climate change: Helping key sectors to adapt to climate change*. Retrieved from http://www.defra.gov.uk/publications/files/pb13740gov-summary-adapt-reports.pdf

Department of Environment, Food and Rural Development, United Kingdom. (2012b). *Adapting to climate change: Evidence-based plan 2011/12*. Retrieved from http://www.defra.gov.uk/publications/files/pb13486-ep-adapting-climate-change.pdf

Dornbusch, R., Fischer, S., & Startz, R. (2010). *Macroeconomics*. New York: McGraw-Hill/Irwin.

Dryzek, J. S., Downes, Hunold, & Schlosberg. (2003). *Green states and social movements: Environmentalism in the United States, United Kingdom, Germany and Norway*. Oxford, UK: Oxford University Press. doi:10.1093/0199249024.001.0001.

Eurostat. (2007). Measuring progress towards a more sustainable europe: 2007 monitoring report of the EU sustainable development strategy. Eurostat.

Fajnzylber, P., Lederman, D., & Loayza, N. (2002). Inequality and violent crime. *Journal of Law and Economics*. Retrieved form http://siteresources.worldbank.org/DEC/Resources/Crime&Inequality.pdf

Folke, C. Carpenter, Elmqvist, Gunderson, Holling, Walker, … Svedin. (2002). *Resilience and sustainable development: Building adaptive capacity in a world of transformation*. Retrieved from http://www.sou.gov.se/mvb/pdf/resiliens.pdf

Folke, C. Colding, & Berkes (2002). Building resilience for adaptive capacity in social-ecological systems. In F. Berkes, J. Colding, & C. Folke (Eds.), Navigating Social-Ecological Systems: Building Resilience for Complexity and Change. Cambridge, UK: Cambridge University Press.

Folke, C. Carpenter, Elmqvist, Gunderson, Holling, & Walker. (2002c). *Resilience and sustainable development: Building adaptive capacity in a world of transformations*. Retrieved from http://era-mx.org/biblio/Resilience.pdf

Gaballah, A. D., & Tondeur. (2002). Education, employment and sustainable development in the European Union. *Jounal of Materials*. Retrieved from http://iWeb.tms.org/ED/JOM-0211-24.pdf

Gallopín, G. (2003). *A systems approach to sustainability and sustainable development*. Retrieved from http://www.eclac.org/publicaciones/xml/8/12288/lcl1864i.pdf

Glemarec, J., & de Olivera. (2012). The role of the visible hand of public institutions in creating a sustainable future. *Public Administration and Development*. Retrieved from http://onlinelibrary.wiley.com/doi/10.1002/pad.1631/pdf

Grimm, M. Klasen, & McKay (Eds.). (2007). Determinants of pro-poor growth: Analytical issues and findings from country studies. New York: Palgrave Macmillan.

Herring, H., & Sorrell (Eds.). (2009). *Energy efficiency and sustainable consumption: The rebound effect*. New York: Palgrave McMillan.

INSEE & OECD. (2008). *Survey of existing approaches to measuring socio-economic progress*. Commission on Measurement of Economic Performance and Social Progress. Retrieved from http://www.stiglitz-sen-fitoussi.fr/documents/

International Labor Organization (ILO). (2007). *Decent work for sustainable development*. Retrieved from http://www.ilo.org/public/english/standards/relm/ilc/ilc96/pdf/rep-i-a.pdf

Jackson, T. (2005). *Motivating sustainable consumption: A review of evidence on consumer behavior and behavioural change*. Retrieved from http://www.c2p2online.com/documents/MotivatingSC.pdf

Jreisat, J. E. (2002). *Comparative public administration*. Westview Press.

Kanie, N. Betsil, Zondervan, Biermann, & Young. (2012). A charter moment: Restructuring governance for sustainability. *Public Administration and Development*. Retrieved from http://onlinelibrary.wiley.com/doi/10.1002/pad.1625/pdf

Kemp, R. Parto, & Gibson. (2005). Governance for sustainable development: Moving from theory to practice. *International Journal of Sustainable Development*. Retrieved from http://kemp.unu-merit.nl/pdf/IJSD%208(1)%2002%20Kemp%20et%20al.pdf

Kemp, R., & Martens. (2007). Sustainable development: How to manage something that is subjective and never can be achieved? *Sustainability: Science, Policy and Practice*. Retrieved from http://sspp.proquest.com/archives/vol3iss2/0703-007.kemp.html

Komiyama, H. Takeuchi, Shiroyama, & Mino (Eds.). (2011). Sustainability science: A multidisciplinary approach. United Nations University Press.

Krugman, P., & Wells. (2012). *Microeconomics*. World Publishers.

Láng, I. (2005). Sustainable development: A new challenge for the countries in Central and Eastern Europe. In Hens & Nath (Eds.), *The World Summit on Sustainable Development: The Johannesburg Conference*. Retrieved from http://link.springer.com/book/10.1007/1-4020-3653-1/page/1

Langford, M. (2012). *Measurement choices and the post-2015 development agenda*. Retrieved from http://post2015.files.wordpress.com/2013/01/art-of-the-impossible-langford-final.pdf

Lebel, L., Anderies, Campbell, Folke, Hatfield-Dodds, Hughes, & Wilson. (2006). Governance and the capacity to manage resilience in regional social-ecological systems. *Ecology and Society*.

Levin, S.A., Barrett, Aniyar, Baumol, Bliss, Bolin, ... Sheshinsky. (1998). Resilience in natural and socioeconomic systems. *Environment and Development Economics*. doi:10.1017/S1355770X98240125.

Lorek, S., & Fuchs. (2011). Strong sustainable consumption governance: Precondition for a degrowth path? *Journal of Cleaner Production*. Retrieved from http://www.academia.edu/1573624/Strong_sustainable_consumption_governance_-_precondition_for_a_degrowth_path

Maddison, A. (2001). *The world economy: A millennial perspective*. Paris: OECD Development Centre. doi:10.1787/9789264189980-en.

Manning, R. (2009). *Using indicators to encourage development: Lessons from the millennium development goals*. Danish Institute of International Studies, Report 2009/1. Retrieved from http://www.diis.dk/graphics/Publications/Reports2009/DIIS_Report_2009-

Masika, R., & Joekes. (1997). *Environmentally sustainable development and poverty: A gender analysis*. Report for the Swedish International Development Agency. Retrieved from http://www.bridge.ids.ac.uk/reports/re52.pdf

McGuire, C. (2012). Public policy frameworks in environmental settings: An argument for new policy frameworks to support new policy directions. *Environmental Management and Sustainable Development*. Retrieved from http://www.macrothink.org/journal/index.php/emsd/article/view/1537

Meadows, D. Meadows, Randers, & Behrends. (1972). The limits of growth. Universe Books.

Meier, G., & Stiglitz. (2001). *Frontiers of development economics: The future in perspective*. World Bank and Oxford University Press.

Merritt, A., & Stubbs. (2012). Complementing the local and global: Promoting sustainability action through linked local-level and formal sustainability funding mechanisms. *Public Administration and Development*. Retrieved from http://onlinelibrary.wiley.com/doi/10.1002/pad.1630/pdf

Mestrum, F. (2005). Poverty reduction and sustainable development. In Hens & Nath (Eds.), *The World Summit on Sustainable Development: The Johannesburg Conference*. Retrieved from http://link.springer.com/book/10.1007/1-4020-3653-1/page/1

Morita, S., & Zaelke. (2005). *Rule of law, good governance and sustainable development*. Paper presented at the Seventh International Conference on Environmental Compliance and Enforcement. Retrieved from http://www.inece.org/conference/7/vol1/05_Sachiko_Zaelke.pdf

Morrison, T., & Lane. (2005). What 'whole of government' means for environmental policy management: An analysis of the 'connecting government' initiative. *Australasian Journal of Environmental Management*. Retrieved from http://www.tandfonline.com/doi/abs/10.1080/14486563.2005.9725071

Mudacumura, G. Mebratu, & Hague. (2005). Sustainable development policy and administration (public administration and public policy). New York: Taylor and Francis.

Mwanza, D. (2005). Water for sustainable development in Africa. In Hens & Nath (Eds.), *The World Summit on Sustainable Development: The Johannesburg Conference*. Retrieved from http://link.springer.com/book/10.1007/1-4020-3653-1/page/1

Najam, A., & Cleveland. (2005). Energy and sustainable development at global environmental summits: An evolving agenda. In Hens & Nath (Eds.), *The World Summit on Sustainable Development: The Johannesburg Conference*. Retrieved from http://link.springer.com/book/10.1007/1-4020-3653-1/page/1

Nath, B. (2005). Education for sustainable development: The Johannesburg summit and beyond. In Hens & Nath (Eds.), *The World Summit on Sustainable Development: The Johannesburg Conference*. Retrieved from http://link.springer.com/book/10.1007/1-4020-3653-1/page/1

Neumayer, E. (2011). *Sustainability and inequality in human development*. Human Development Research Paper, United Nations Development Program. Retrieved from http://hdr.undp.org/en/reports/global/hdr2011/papers/HDRP_2011_04.pdf

Nunan, F. Campbell, & Foster. (2012). Environmental mainstreaming: The organizational challenge of policy integration. *Public Administration and Development*. Retrieved from http://onlinelibrary.wiley.com/doi/10.1002/pad.1624/pdf

Olken, B. Dell, & Jones. (2012). Temperature shocks and economic growth: Evidence from the last half century. *American Economic Journal: Macroeconomics*. Retrieved from http://economics.mit.edu/files/7642

Olson, L. (2005). Management of chemicals for sustainable development, menutextcount, class_name, data_text = 1556, asharticle. In Hens & Nath (Eds.), *The World Summit on Sustainable Development: The Johannesburg Conference*. Retrieved from http://link.springer.com/book/10.1007/1-4020-3653-1/page/1

Organization for Economic Cooperation and Development. (2002). *Governance for sustainable development: Five OECD case studies*. Retrieved from http://www.ulb.ac.be/ceese/nouveau%20site%20ceese/ documents/oecd%20 governance%20for%20sustainable%20development%205%20case%20studies.pdf

Organization for Economic Cooperation and Development. (2003). *Policy coherence: Vital for global development*. Paris: OECD.

Organization for Economic Cooperation and Development. (2008). *Gender and sustainable development: Maximizing the economic, social and environmental role of women*. Paris: OECD.

Organization for Economic Cooperation and Development. (2010a). *Perspectives on global development, 2010*. Retrieved from http://www.oecd.org

Organization for Economic Cooperation and Development. (2010b). *Environmental performance review of japan 2010*. Retrieved from http://www.oecd-library.org/docserver/download/fulltext/971012e.pdf

Overseas Development Institute. (2013). *Tracking proposals on future development goals*. Retrieved from http://post2015.org/2013/01/08/tracking-proposals-on-future-development-goals/

Pautz, M., & Rinftet. (2012). *The Lilliputians of environmental regulation: The perspective of state regulators*. London: Routledge.

Peeters, H. (2005). Sustainable development and the role of the financial world. In Hens & Nath (Eds.), *The World Summit on Sustainable Development: The Johannesburg Conference*. Retrieved from http://link.springer.com/book/10.1007/1-4020-3653-1/page/1

Pisano, U. (2012). *Resilience and sustainable development: Theory of resilience, systems thinking and adaptive governance.* Retrieved from http://www.sd-network.eu/quarterly%20reports/report%20files/pdf/2012-September-Resilience_and_Sustainable_Development.pdf

Princen, T. Maniates, & Conca. (2002). Confronting consumption. Cambridge, MA: MIT Press.

Ranis, G. (2004). *The evolution of development thinking: Theory and policy.* Paper delivered at the Annual World Bank Conference on Development Economics. Washington, DC. Retrieved from http://siteresources.worldbank.org/DEC/Resources/84797-1251813753820/ 6415739-1251814066992/ Gustav_Ranis_Evolutiion_of_Thinking_formattd.pdf

Reitz, J. G. Breton, Dion, Dion, Phan, & Banerjee. (2009). Multiculturalism and social cohesion: Potentials and challenges of diversity. Berlin: Springer.

Rival, L. (2012). *Sustainable development through policy integration in Latin America: A comparative approach.* Retrieved from http://www.unrisd.org/80256B3C005BCCF9/httpNetITFramePDF?ReadForm&parentunid=DA1744ED6C1FFD03C12579F3002A5769&parentdoctype=paper&netitpath=80256B3C005BCCF9/(httpAuxPages)/DA1744ED6C1FFD03C12579F3002A5769/$file/7%20Rival-Web.pdf

Roberts-Schweitzer, E. Greaney, & Duer (Eds.). (2006). *Promoting social cohesion through education: Case studies and tools for using textbooks and curricula.* World Bank Institute. Retrieved from http://www.iiep.unesco.org/fileadmin/user_upload/Cap_Dev_Technical_Assistance/pdf/2010/Promoting_Social_Cohesion_through_Education.pdf

Rothboeck, S. (2010). *Skills for green and decent jobs and sustainable development: The ILO perspective.* Retrieved from http://iveta2010.cpsctech.org/downloads/materials /full%20papers/2.%20Skills%20for%20Green%20and%20Decent%20Jobs%20and%20Sustainable%20Development.pdf.

Sachs, J. (2012). From millennium development goals to sustainable development goals. *The Lancet.* Retrieved from http://www.thelancet.com/journals/lancet/article/PIIS0140-6736(12)60685-0/fulltext#article_upsell

Simon, H. (1978). Rationality as a product and a process of thought. *American Economic Review.* Retrieved from http://www.jstor.org/discover/10.2307/1816653? uid=3739832&uid=2129&uid=2&uid=70& uid=4&uid=3739256&sid=21101715134507

Smith, L. B., & Thelen (Eds.). (1993). *A dynamic systems approach to development: Applications.* Cambridge, MA: MIT Press.

Srivastan, R. (2012). *History of development thought: A critical anthology.* Routledge India.

Stern, N. (2006). *The economics of climate change: The stern review.* Cambridge, MA: Cambridge University Press.

Stewart, A., & Wilkison. (2005). Health: A necessity for sustainable development. In Hens & Nath (Eds.), *The World Summit on Sustainable Development: The Johannesburg Conference.* Retrieved from http://link.springer.com/book/10.1007/1-4020-3653-1/page/1

Stiglitz, J. Sen, & Fitoussi. (2009). *Report by the commission on the measurement of economic performance and social progress.* Retrieved from http://www.stiglitz-sen-fitoussi.fr/documents/rapport_anglais.pdf

Stringl. (2005). Science, research, knowledge and capacity building. In Hens & Nath (Eds.), *The World Summit on Sustainable Development: The Johannesburg Conference*. Retrieved from http://link.springer.com/book/10.1007/1-4020-3653-1/page/1

Swedish Environmental Protection Agency. (2008). *Sweden's environmental objectives in brief*. Author.

Swedish International Development Agency (SIDA). (1995). *Promoting sustainable development likelihoods: A report from the taskforce on poverty*. Author.

Tester, Drake, Driscoll, Golay, & Peters. (2005). *Sustainable energy: Choosing among options*. Cambridge, MA: MIT Press.

Tester, J. W. Drake, Driscoll, Golay, & Peters. (2012). *Sustainable energy*. Retrieved from http://mitpress.mit.edu/sites/default/files/titles/content/9780262201537_sch_0001.pdf

Tukker, A. Emmert, Charter, Vezzoli, Sto, Andersen, … Lahlou. (2008). Fostering change to sustainable production and consumption: An evidence-based view. *Journal of Cleaner Production*. Retrieved from http://www2.lse.ac.uk/socialPsychology/research_activities/publications/saadi_lahlou/fosteringchange.pdf

United Nations. (2002). *Global challenge, global opportunity: Trends in sustainable development*. United Nations Johannesburg Summit. Retrieved from http://www.un.org/esa/sustdev/publications/critical_trends_report_2002.pdf

United Nations Conference on Sustainable Development Rio+20. (2012). *The future we want – Outcome document of the conference*. Retrieved from http://daccess-dds-ny.un.org/doc/UNDOC/GEN/N12/381/64/PDF/N1238164.pdf?OpenElement

United Nations Conference on the Environment and Development. (1992a). *Rio declaration*. Retrieved from http://daccess-dds-ny.un.org/doc/UNDOC/GEN/ N92/836/55/PDF/N9283655.pdf?OpenElement

United Nations Conference on the Environment and Development. (1992b). *Conference report*. Retrieved from http://daccess-dds-ny.un.org/doc/UNDOC/GEN/N92/836/55/PDF/N9283655.pdf?OpenElement

United Nations Department of Economic and Social Affairs. UNDESA. (2010a). *Trends in sustainable development: Chemicals, mining, transport, waste management*. Division for Sustainable Development, UNDESA. Retrieved from http://www.uncsd2012.org/content/documents/205Trends_chem_mining_transp_waste.pdf

United Nations Department of Economic and Social Affairs. UNDESA. (2010b). *Trends in sustainable development: Sustainable production and consumption*. Division for Sustainable Development, UNDESA. Retrieved from http://www.uncsd2012.org/content/documents/15Trends_in_sustainable_consumption_and_production.pdf

United Nations Department of Economic and Social Affairs. UNDESA. (2012). *A guidebook to the green economy, issue 1: Green economy, green growth, and low-carbon development, history, definitions and a guide to recent publications*. Division for Sustainable Development, UNDESA. Retrieved from http://www.uncsd2012.org/content/documents/528Green%20Economy%20Guidebook_100912_FINAL.pdf

United Nations Development Program. (2011). *Human development report 2011: Sustainability and equity: A better future for all*. Retrieved from http://hdr.undp.org/en/reports/global/hdr2011/download/

United Nations Development Program. (2012a). *Triple wins for sustainable development: Case studies of sustainable development in practice.* Retrieved from http://www.undp.org/content/dam/undp/library/Cross-Practice%20generic%20theme/Triple-Wins-for-Sustainable-Development-Web.pdf

United Nations Development Program. (2012b). *Governance for peace: Securing the social contract.* Retrieved from http://www.beta.undp.org /content/undp/en/home/librarypage/crisis-prevention -and-recovery

United Nations Development Programme. (2009). *Fighting climate change: Human solidarity in a divided world. Human Development Report 2007/2008.* UNDP.

United Nations Economic Commission for Europe. Organization for Economic Cooperation and Development, & Eurostat. (2008). *Measuring sustainable development: Report of the joint UN-ECE/OECD/Eurostat working group on statistics for sustainable development.* Retrieved from http://www.oecd.org/dataoecd/30/20/41414440.pdf

United Nations Environmental Program, UNEP. (1995). *Poverty and the environment: Reconciling short-term needs with long-term sustainability goals.* UNEP.

United Nations Environmental Program. UNEP. (2011). *Towards a green economy: Pathways to sustainable development and poverty eradication.* Retrieved from http://www.unep.org/greeneconomy/Portals/88/documents/ger/ger_final_dec_2011/Green%20EconomyReport_Final_Dec2011.pdf

United Nations General Assembly. (1987). *Our common future.* Retrieved from http://www.un.org/documents/ga/res/42/ares42-187.htm

United Nations General Assembly. (1992a). *Resolution on the report of the united nations conference on environment and development.* Retrieved from http://www.un.org/documents/resga.htm

United Nations General Assembly. (1992b). *Rio declaration on environment and development.* Retrieved from http://www.un.org/documents/ga/conf151/aconf15126-1annex1.htm

United Nations General Assembly. (1992c). *Agenda (Durban, South Africa), 21.* Retrieved from http://www.un.org/documents/resga.htm.

United Nations General Assembly. (2012a). *Resolution adopted by the general assembly endorsing the outcome document of the united nations conference on sustainable development entitled the future we want.* Retrieved from http://daccess-dds-ny.un.org/doc/UNDOC/GEN/N11/476/10/PDF/N1147610.pdf?OpenElement

United Nations General Assembly. (2012b). *Note of the secretary general on submitting the report resilient people, resilient planet: A future worth choosing.* Retrieved from http://www.un.org/ga/search/view_doc.asp?symbol=A/66/700&referer=/english/&Lang=E

United Nations Secretary General's High Level Panel on Global Sustainability. (2012). *Resilient people, resilient planet: A future worth choosing.* Retrieved from http://www.un.org/gsp/sites/default/files/attachments/GSPReport_unformatted_30Jan.pdf

Urban, F., & Nordensvard. (2013). *Low carbon development.* London: Routledge.

Vale, R., & Vale. (2013). *Living with a fair share ecological footprint.* London: Routledge.

Van Zeijl-Rozema, A. Corvers, Kemp, & Martens. (2008). Governance for sustainable development: A framework. *Sustainable Development.* Retrieved from http://www.onlinelibrary.wiley.com/doi/10.1002/sd.367/abstract

Villarreal, R. (2012a). *Regulatory quality improvements for preventing corruption in public administration: A capacity building perspective.* Retrieved from http://unpan1.un.org/intradoc/groups/public/documents/un-dpadm/unpan049594.pdf

Villarreal, R. (2012b). *Countering corruption from one or two sides? Opportunities and Challenges in cooperation between government and civil society.* Retrieved from http://www.surrey.ac.uk/sbs/events/COUNTERING%20CORRUPTION%20FROM%20ONE%20OR%20TWO%20SIDES%20-%20GOVERNMENT%20AND%20CIVIL%20SOCIETY%20Roberto%20Villarreal.pdf

Walker, B., Carpenter, Anderies, Abel, Cumming, Janssen, Lebel, & Pritchard. (2002). *Resilience management in social-ecological systems: A working hypothesis for a participatory approach.*

Walker, B., & Salt. (2006). *Resilience thinking: Sustaining ecosystems and people in a changing world.* Island Press.

Weber, E. (2003). *Bringing society back in grassroots ecosystem management, accountability and sustainable communities.* Cambridge, MA: Massachusetts Institute of Technology Press.

Wilkinson, R., & Pickett. (2010). *The impact of incomes inequalities on sustainable development in London.* Report for the London Sustainable Development Commission. Retrieved from http://www.londonsdc.org/documents/The%20impact%20of%20income%20inequalities%20on%20sustainable%20development%20in%20London.pdf

Williamson, O. (1994a). The institutions and governance of economic development and reform. In *Proceedings of the World Bank Annual Conference on Development Economics.* Washington, DC: World Bank.

Williamson, O. (1994b). Visible and invisible governance. *The American Economic Review.* PMID:10134748.

World Bank. (2003). *Sustainable development in a dynamic world. World Development Report 2003.* Washington, DC: World Bank.

World Bank. (2010). *Development and climate change. World Development Report 2010.* Washington, DC: World Bank.

World Commission on Environment and Development (Brundtland Commission). (1987). *Our common future.* Report of the Brundtland Commission. Retrieved from http://www.un-documents.net/our-common-future.pdf and http://www.un.org/documents/ga/res/42/ares42-187.htm

World Summit on Sustainable Development. (2002a). *Report of the world summit on sustainable development: Political declaration.* Retrieved from http://www.un.org/esa/sustdev/documents/WSSD_POI_PD/English/POI_PD.htm

World Summit on Sustainable Development. (2002b). *Report of the world summit on sustainable development: Plan of implementation.* Retrieved from http://www.un.org/esa/sustdev/documents/WSSD_POI_PD/English/POIToc.htm

Yusuf, S. Deaton, Derviş, Easterly, Ito, & Stiglitz. (2009). *Development economics through the decades: A critical look at 30 years of the world development report.* World Bank. Retrieved from http://www-wds.worldbank.org/external/default/WDSContentServer/WDSP/IB/2009/01/14/000334955_2009011 4045203/Rendered/PDF/471080PUB0Deve101OFFICIAL0USE0ONLY1.pdf

ENDNOTES

[1] The author's academic background is in development economics, public management

and systems engineering. At the time of contributing this chapter he was Inter-Regional Advisor at the United Nations Department of Economic and Social Affairs. This chapter was prepared in the author's personal capacity and reflects his own professional views and not necessarily those of the United Nations member countries, the organization or the department. Communications about this paper may be sent to Roberto.Villarreal-Gonda@hotmail.com.

2   The *Outcome Document* contained the conclusions arrived at by countries from around the world along the international *Conference on Sustainable Development* and which have been subsequently endorsed by the United Nations General Assembly. The conference was held under the auspices of the United Nations in Rio de Janeiro, Brazil, in June 2012, and followed a series of previous ones hosted over the past two decades in different places, including one at the same venue in 1992, hence the short name for the recent conference: *Rio+20*. For additional information see: United Nations General Assembly (2012) and http://www.uncsd2012.org/.

3   For a comprehensive discussion, see Ashford and Hall (2011).

4   For more information on the concept at different epochs, see: Commission on Growth and Development (2008); Komiyama, et al. (2011); Meier and Stiglitz (2001); Organization for Economic Cooperation and Development (2010a); Puppim de Oliveira (2012); Ranis (2004); Srivastan (2012); Stiglitz, et al. (2011); United Nations (2002); United Nations Conference on the Environment and Development (1992a, 1992b); United Nations Development Program (2009, 2011, 2012); United Nations General Assembly (1987, 1992a, 1992b, 1992c, 2012a, 2012b); United Nations Secretary General's High Level Panel on Global Sustainability (2012); World Bank (2003, 2010); World

Commission on Environment and Development (Brundtland Commission) (1987); World Summit on Sustainable Development (2002a, 2002b); and Yusuf et al. (2009).

5   On the use of systems analysis in matters related with sustainable development, see for example: Gallopín (2003); Pisano (2012); and Smith and Thelen (1993).

6   Consider for example the large number of diverse initiatives and proposals contributed in the recent past to shape the international sustainable development agenda, as summarized in Overseas Development Institute (2013). See also http://www.iddcconsortium. net/joomla/index.php/component/content/ article/38-news-and-events/886-european-consultation-starts-shaping-the-post-2015-framework#proposals.

7   See Box 2 later in this chapter.

8   The *Outcome Document* of *Rio+20* indicated this urgency, for instance, in paragraphs 12, 17, 25, 26, 33, 61, etc.

9   Relevant bibliography is listed in endnote 5.

10   For instance, *The Limits to Growth* was in this sense a very influential study around the world. See: http://www.clubofrome. org/?p=326.

11   For example, see Mwanza (2005).

12   Broader analyses are available in: Barber (2005); Najam and Cleveland (2005); and United Nations Department of Economic and Social Affairs UNDESA (2010b).

13   For additional discussion, see Olson (2005).

14   See for example United Nations Department of Economic and Social Affairs UNDESA (2010a).

15   A comprehensive discussion on the economics of climate change can be found in Stern (2006) and World Bank (2010).

16   See for instance United Nations Department of Economic and Social Affairs UNDESA (2012) and United Nations Environmental

Program UNEP (2011). See also http://www.uncsd2012.org/rio20/index.php?menu=62.

[17] Broader explorations of these matters can be found in: Láng (2005); Nath (2005); Peeters (2005); and Strigl (2005).

[18] A more complete analysis is offered in Stewart and Wilkinson (2005).

[19] For additional discussion, see: Begossi and Díaz de Avila-Pírez (2005) and Mestrum (2005).

[20] For a comprehensive analysis, see Folke, et al. (2002a, 2002b).

[21] See for example: Bachus (2005); Mestrum (2005); Sachs (2012); and United Nations General Assembly (2000a, 2000b, 2000c, 2000d, 2012a, 2012b).

[22] See for instance: United Nations (2002); United Nations Conference on the Environment and Development (1992a, 1992b); United Nations General Assembly (1987, 1992a, 1992b, 1992c, 2012a, 2012b); United Nations Secretary General's High Level Panel on Global Sustainability (2012); World Bank (2010); World Commission on Environment and Development (Brundtland Commission) (1987); and World Summit on Sustainable Development (2002a, 2002b).

[23] See for example United Nations General Assembly (2012), paragraph 3.

[24] For further information, see United Nations Secretary General's High Level Panel on Global Sustainability (2012).

[25] For related information, see section IV.A of the *Rio+20 Outcome Document*, devoted to "Strengthening the three dimensions of sustainable development," and also paragraphs 3, 11, 25 and 30. In addition, see United Nations Secretary General's High Level Panel on Global Sustainability (2012), page 6, and paragraphs 3, 94, and 139-142.

[26] The *Outcome Document* of *Rio+20* addressed a very large set of issues, which had been introduced into the international policy dialogue at the several related global conferences over the past twenty years. The variety of issues related to sustainable development that are included in the *Outcome Document* comprise, among others: food security and nutrition and sustainable agriculture; water and sanitation; energy; sustainable tourism; sustainable transport; sustainable cities and human settlements; health and population; full and productive employment, decent work and social protection; oceans and seas; small islands developing states; least developed and land-locked developing countries; Africa; regional efforts; disaster risk reduction; climate change; forests; biodiversity; desertification, land degradation and drought; mountains; chemicals and waste; sustainable consumption and production; mining; education; gender equality and women's empowerment; trade; technology; capacity building; finance; sustainable development goals; institutions; and implementation.

[27] For instance, Bennett, et al. (2009) analyzed the inter-linkages between diverse ecosystems and environmental services. Their analysis connects to the notion of biodiversity included only coarsely in the core framework of this article, and can well be incorporated as a detailed description of the corresponding elements and causal relationships within this matter, and of their effects on other parts of the overall sustainable development system, such as human health, safety of the people and their property, social cohesion, and so on.

[28] Thus, the issue at the end point of an arrow is modeled as a dependent variable, influenced by both an independent variable (which is also somehow endogenous because in turn it is influenced by other variables in the system) and a control variable that is affected by policy. Besides these symbols, additional terms, used to interpret the symbolic language of the diagrams, are explained

subsequently as they are introduced along the chapter.

[29] For a related discussion, see, in particular, section III of the *Rio+20 Outcome Document*, on "Green economy in the context of sustainable development and poverty eradication," and also paragraphs 4, 30, 60, 61, 109, 111, 112, 113, 122, 124, 127, 128, 130, 132, 163, 193, 197, 201, 205, 206, 213, 218, 219, and 224-226. In addition, see United Nations Secretary General's High Level Panel on Global Sustainability (2012), paragraphs 25-42, 89-128, and 143-163.

[30] For explanations and in-depth analyses of the relationships listed next, see for example: Asian Development Bank (2012); Barber (2005, 2007); Begossi and Díaz (2005); Bennett, et al. (2009); Boulanger (2010); Commission on Growth and Development (2008); Herring and Sorrell (2009); Jackson (2005); Lorek and Fuchs (2011); Mwanza (2005); Najam and Cleveland (2005); Olson (2005); Organization for Economic Cooperation and Development OECD (2010b); Peeters (2005); Puppim de Oliveira (2012); Princen (2002); Stern (2006); Stringl (2005); Tester, et al. (2005); United Nations Department of Economic and Social Affairs, UN-DESA (2010a, 2010b, 2012); United Nations Environmental Program UNEP (2011); and World Bank World Bank (2003, 2010).

[31] Here and in the rest of the paper, causal relationships are described in opposite directions, such as increasing (decreasing), more (less) and so on. The first direction is to be read in every sentence ignoring all terms in parenthesis, whereas the opposite direction is to be read by considering the latter instead of the corresponding ones immediately preceding the parentheses.

[32] The terms "immediate," "direct," "indirect," and "ultimate" are used hereafter to indicate the relative position in the diagram of the issues under consideration, particularly their proximity to the departing point of the analysis. Thus, the socio-demographic and economic processes denoted in this sentence as "immediate" are labeled so because these are the closest in the diagram to the start of the storyline on how the economy is related to the sustainability and safety of the natural environment; similarly, in what follows, other processes are considered as "directly," "indirectly," and "ultimately" affected, the farther they appear along the narrative describing the diagram.

[33] This paragraph is a considerable simplification of how the economy functions. Detailed analyses of the phenomena mentioned here can be found in any textbook in macro- and microeconomics. See for example Dornbusch et al. (2010) and Krugman and Wells (2012).

[34] What follows in the next bullets is a large simplification of how the energy-engine of the economy functions. Detailed analyses of the phenomena mentioned here can be found in any textbook in energy economics and sustainable development. See for example Tester et al. (2012).

[35] The different costs of this are not included in the analysis for simplicity. Including these in a more detailed modeling exercise should go in hand with adding causal effects on the production costs of goods and services, and on poverty.

[36] See endnote 45.

[37] The effects from these different pollutants on the environment are not equal. Whereas carbon oxide and dioxide emissions ("coxes," as slang for their chemical formulae CO and CO_2) impact largely on greenhouse atmospheric conditions and global climate change, sulfur and nitrogen emissions ("soxes" and "noxes," SO and SO_2 and NO and NO_2, respectively) result in acid rain and impact on agriculture and natural ecosystems. Altogether, health and

biodiversity are affected. Numerous analyses can be found, in technical and non-technical language, in journals like The Lancet, Journal of Sustainable Development, International Journal of Innovation and Sustainable Development, etc., or in textbooks like Urban and Nordensvard (2013) and Vale and Vale (2013).

38 Reliability and safety considerations are weighted by people, firms and governments because the supply of these primary sources can be affected by natural and technical risks, and by economic and geopolitical factors. I turn, cost factors may be distorted by inadequate accounting practices or norms that may consider only some productive-process costs (extraction, transformation, transportation, etc.) but no other systemic costs that are provoked through broader ecological processes and have also the character of negative externalities (i.e., costs not entirely borne by the suppliers and users of energy, but by the people and the natural environment) on health and the qualities of nature. If these not-accounted-for costs are not clearly perceived by development actors and stakeholders, their decisions on the use of different natural energy resources are ill-informed and result in excessive demand and use, and in lower economic efficiency in the use of energy.

39 Simply put, a natural stock is the volumetric amount or the primary energy resource that exists naturally, and a usable reserve represents the part of that physical amount that can be effectively used for energy generation given existent cost-efficient technologies for extraction, processing, etc.

40 Other effects not included in the diagram, so as to maintain the system simple for exposition purposes, are those on human health and life expectancy, and thus the higher and costly use of economic resources for health services.

41 Private owners of land and water areas can devote these alternatively to produce goods for consumption, or to keep well-functioning ecosystems where living species can effectively reproduce themselves and absorb and transform pollutants at adequate rates through natural biological processes, thus producing environmental services. As the use of resources to produce consumption goods generates economic income for the owners, whereas maintaining healthy natural ecosystems ordinarily does not generate economic income, their decisions to produce instead environmental services need to be stimulated through grants that compensate the owners of those land and water areas for the opportunity cost of not producing consumption goods.

42 For a related discussion, see the *Rio+20 Outcome Document*, in particular paragraphs 105-107 on poverty eradication, and also paragraphs 2, 3, 4, 23, 24, 30, 31, 63, 120, 126, 139, 147-156 and 229. In addition, see United Nations Secretary General's High Level Panel on Global Sustainability (2012), paragraphs 5, 17, 43-46 and 58-88.

43 The expression "decent jobs" refers to jobs where workers have fair wages, work safety, legal rights established by legislation and contracts, and social security, in contrast to informal jobs or occupations where these conditions are usually not observed. See the International Labor Organization (ILO) Website at http://www.ilo.org/global/topics/decent-work/lang--en/index.htm.

44 The phrase "a green economy in the context of sustainable development and poverty eradication" is reiterated verbatim along the *Rio+20 Outcome Document*. See, for instance, paragraphs 12, 56, 57, 58, 60, 64, 66, 74, etc.

45 For explanations and in-depth analyses on the inter-relationships listed next, see for example: Gabalah, et al. (2002); Grimm, et

al. (2007); International Labor Organization ILO (2007); Masikal and Joekes (1997); Mestrum (2005); Nath (2005); Neumayer (2011); Organization for Economic Cooperation and Development OECD (2008); Rothboeck (2010); Swedish International Development Agency SIDA (1995); United Nations Environmental Program UNEP (1995); and Wilkinson and Pickett (2010).

[46] For example, in fast growing localities, upward economic activity and employment trends often create situations of constrained supply relative to excess demand (colloquially referred to as "bottle-necks") in public services. Hence, the importance of regional and local planning and financing for the necessary expansions of the supply of public services, particularly for the poor, cannot be overlooked.

[47] Indeed, economic growth can sometimes have only small effects in lowering poverty, for example when the jobs it creates are mostly for qualified workers which are rarely found among the poor, or offered in zones that are remote to impoverished communities, or that offer wages that are not commensurate with the socio-demographic characteristics of households. Thus, pro-poor growth is required.

[48] "External economies" come about when costs are lowered due to factors that surround production units.

[49] Resilience and public governance were succinctly explained in section 2 of this paper. For additional considerations on these matters, see the *Rio+20 Outcome Document*, paragraphs 8, 10, 22, 31, 42-46, 50, 63, 67, 71, 76, 98, 99, 101, 135, 148, 237, and 238. In addition, see United Nations Secretary General's High Level Panel on Global Sustainability (2012), paragraphs 5, 17, 47-51, 58-66, 81, 129-138, and 164-244.

[50] See, for instance: Folke, et al. (2002a, 2002b, 2002c); Reitz, et al. (2009); and Roberts-Schweitzer, et al. (2006).

[51] For discussions and analyses on the inter-relationships indicated next, see: Adger (2000); Bachus (2005); Berkes, et al. (2003); Commissioner of the Environment and Sustainable Development Canada (2009); Department of Environment, Food and Rural Affairs, United Kingdom (2012a, 2012b); Dryzek, et al. (2003); Folke, et al. (2002b); Jreisat (2002); Kemp, et al. (2005); Langford (2012); Lebel, et al. (2006); Levin, et al. (1998); McGuire (2012); Morita and Zaelke (2005); Morrison and Lane (2005); Mudacumura, et al. (2005); Organization for Economic Cooperation and Development OECD (2002); Pautz and Rinfret (2012); Pisano 2012); Rival (2012); United Nations Development Program (2009, 2011, 2012b); United Nations Secretary General's High Level Panel on Global Sustainability (2012); Van Zeijl-Rozema, et al. (2008); Walker and Salt (2006); Walker, et al. (2002); Weber (2003); and Williamson (1994a, 1994b). See also the papers submitted to the Seventh International Conference on Environmental Compliance and Enforcement, at http://www.inece.org/conference/7/vol1/index.html.

[52] Corruption is a phenomenon that consists in the intentional breaching of laws and regulations by individuals in the public or other sectors, in order to obtain personal gains or advantages. By violating the principle of equality before he law, these corrupt individuals harm the trust of others on existing legal institutions and work against a rights-based leveled playing field in which all individuals can improve their living conditions with equal opportunities. For in-depth discussion of these issues, see Villarreal (2012a, 2012b).

[53] The notion of social capital, based on the pioneering work of Robert D. Putnam, refers to the eventual support or help in various forms that an individual (the owner of said capital) can receive from others on the basis of the connections and relationships they have developed. The larger the social capital of an individual, the more resourceful he or she is for improving his or her living conditions and the more protected he or she is against the negative consequences of adverse economic, social or natural phenomena. Social capital, in the same way as other types of capital (physical, natural, intellectual, etc.) can be enlarged through investment (in this case, about maintaining and improving social relations), can decrease if not adequately maintained, and provides positive returns or benefits for the individual who has it. Social cohesion, in turn, consists in the prevailing values and attitudes within members of a social group that move them to respond regularly with empathy to the needs and challenges faced by its members; social cohesion can be understood as synonymous o solidarity, in less technical language. Thus, social capital is individual-specific and social cohesion is group-determined. Common sense indicates that in contexts where there is more social cohesion it is easier for any individual to build for himself or herself more social capital; in contrast, when there is low social cohesion, as for instance after a social conflict, accumulating social capital is a more difficult challenge.

[54] The use of the term "resilience" in this chapter refers to all three dimensions of sustainable development, denoting the capacity of the people and its societal and public institutions, including sociopolitical arrangements and juridical or legal frameworks, I order to be prepared, to orderly react, and to successfully overcome, in inclusive and fair manners, the eventual occurrence of risky phenomena such as economic crises, sociopolitical disruptions or natural disasters.

[55] See for example Fajnzylber, et al. (2002).

[56] For a related discussion, see paragraphs 186-189 of the *Rio+20 Outcome Document*.

[57] For a related discussion, see paragraph 30 of the *Rio+20 Outcome Document*.

[58] For example, see United Nations Secretary General's High Level Panel on Global Sustainability (2012), paragraph 29.

[59] Ibidem, paragraphs 45, 46, and 205.

[60] Ibidem, paragraph 50.

[61] This is drastically changing in recent years because of the intrinsic challenges of sustainable development. Indeed, whereas in the academic literature in many disciplines it was rather infrequent to find journal articles authored by more than three researchers, in matters related to sustainable development it is remarkably more frequent nowadays to find articles authored by more than six researchers, and occasionally even up to a dozen. Some examples can be recognized in the bibliography included at the end of this chapter.

[62] Section 5 of this chapter refers to this in the case of public administration, which over the last century got increasingly organized vertically in the form of a large number of function-specialized agencies, with comparatively few horizontal inter-agency communication and coordination relationships. The parallelism between the structural models of scientific research, on one hand, and public management, on the other hand, is then used to argue that for attaining in the future a more comprehensive or integral public management of sustainable development it will be necessary to adapt the overall organization of knowledge management, specifically making it more inclusive of diverse stakeholders, less compartmentalized and thus more integrated, and better mainstreamed into public administration.

63   Section 5 recognizes the pertinence that one explicit goal about sustainable development should be about this collective learning process and its application into practical actions and policies. This goal, as others mentioned therein, can be sought effectively by following guideposts and using relevant indicators to monitor progress.

64   This is further discussed in Section 5. The most promising trends in this respect, in more developed countries, point in the directions of transparency and openness to a diversity of actors and stakeholders outside government, and close communication and coordination inside government; these approaches are known in the literature on public administration as open government and whole-of-government, respectively.

65   The adjective "technical," from the Greek etymological root "texne," precisely refers to the transformation of matter and energy that exist in nature. Particularly, in modern times, technology is understood as the application of knowledge from the natural sciences –like physics, chemistry, biology, etc.- to human production processes. Technological cause-effect relationships, thus, reflect constant phenomena considered as "rules of nature" and which remain valid at all times and in all contexts (if properly specified to include all relevant natural factors that affect each particular technical relationship). In big contrast, relationships based on human behavior and institutions are fluid, evolve over time and differ considerably across contexts, due to a variety of factors that affect human conduct and interactions, such as availability of new data and information, social learning, evolving philosophies or ideologies, changing social values and culture, re-composition of social groups, varying power of actors and stakeholders, and so on. Incorporating this practically infinite number of factors to describe individual and collective human behavior and institutions, either in a static or a dynamic way, is an impossible challenge and has prevented the social sciences—sociology, political science, psychology, economics, law studies, etc.—in the majority of cases, to arrive at absolute structural explanations on these matters, applicable in every context at any time: omitted variables are a pervasive methodological problem that results generally in misspecifications of social models and just make these applicable—quite usefully, nevertheless—to concrete contexts at determined moments in time.

66   For a similar analysis of rationality as a product and process of thought, although referred to individual rather than collective rationality, see Simon (1978).

67   Because of this, the framework could help the international policy dialogue for sustainable development to overcome some limitations which have been perceived about the MDGs agreed by all member countries of the United Nations in 2000, namely, (1) that the MDGs were portrayed in a piecemeal fashion; and that the political necessity to maintain ample policy space for each country for the achievement of the MDGs resulted in many cases in (2) lack of attention by policy-makers and stakeholders to the interrelationships and synergies that must be considered by the policies put in place.

68   The use of taxes and subsidies is of particular importance in this sense to "correct" market prices when positive or negative externalities are not adequately accounted for in private economic calculations and, unless market prices are not adjusted in net terms by taxes or subsidies, consumers and producers would lack adequate signals to make rational decisions leading to a green economy. For example, the market prices of fuels do not reflect the social and environmental costs provoked for human health and natural eco-

systems because of pollution from carbon and sulfur emissions, and as a consequence the aggregate use of such fuels ends being higher than it would be if he later costs were made clear to consumers and producers; by applying taxes on these fuels, their higher net prices in the market will better induce energy users to substitute for cleaner energy sources.

[69] For instance: 1) integrated planning and management to maintain ecosystems and biodiversity, health and environmental protection and safety, and for the efficient use of water and determined non-renewable and renewable resources ; 2) energy use, emissions and pollution; 3) recycling and disposal of consumption products and by-products; 4) all human rights -including the right to development-, labor regulations and social protection, and simplified regulatory and tax regimes for small businesses; 5) property rights, with adequate special provisions about rights and obligations regarding public goods; 6) competition policy, including in markets for goods and services that affect most the cost of living, and in matters related to natural resources rent-seeking activities, encompassing public access to related information or transparency; 7) financial markets and institutions, addressing financial services for the poor and marginalized, and for investments geared to innovations for sustainable development and productive activities to substitute for non-sustainable ones, including in agriculture and manufacturing; 8) regional—including urban—planning for sustainable development, considering public service delivery with special attention to the poor and marginalized; 9) prevention, preparedness and recovery from natural disasters; and so on.

[70] See for instance United Nations Secretary General's High Level Panel on Global Sustainability (2012).

[71] See, for example: Christopoulos, et al. (2012); Glemareck, et al. (2012); Kanie, et al. (2012); McGuire (2012); Merritt and Stubbs (2012); Morrison and Lane (2005); Mudacumura, et al. (2005) and Nunan, et al. (2012).

Chapter 9
Competitive Pattern–Based Strategies under Complexity:
The Case of Turkish Managers

Gürdal Ertek
Sabancı University, Turkey

Selin Tokman
Sabancı University, Turkey

Nihat Kasap
Sabancı University, Turkey

Özcan Bilgin
Sabancı University, Turkey

Mert İnanoğlu
Sabancı University, Turkey

ABSTRACT

This chapter augments current Enterprise Architecture (EA) frameworks to become pattern-based. The main motivation behind pattern-based EA is the support for strategic decisions based on the patterns prioritized in a country or industry. Thus, to validate the need for pattern-based EA, it is essential to show how different patterns gain priority under different contexts, such as industries. To this end, this chapter also reveals the value of alternative managerial strategies across different industries and business functions in a specific market, namely Turkey. Value perceptions for alternative managerial strategies were collected via survey, and the values for strategies were analyzed through the rigorous application of statistical techniques. Then, evidence was searched and obtained from business literature that support or refute the statistically supported hypothesis. The results obtained through statistical analysis are typically confirmed with reports of real world cases in the business literature. Results suggest that Turkish firms differ significantly in the way they value different managerial strategies. There also exist differences based on industries and business functions. The study provides guidelines to managers in Turkey, an emerging country, on which strategies are valued most in their industries. This way, managers can have a better understanding of their competitors and business environment and can develop the appropriate pattern-based EA to cope with complexity and succeed in the market.

DOI: 10.4018/978-1-4666-4518-9.ch009

1. INTRODUCTION

The primary goal of this study is to introduce the concept of pattern-based Enterprise Architectures (EA), and to illustrate how this new concept augments the traditional EA. The intermediate goal to serve this primary goal and illustrate the need for patter-based EA is to reveal the value of alternative managerial strategies across different industries and business functions in a specific country. This value assessment is revealed through both survey based research and thorough investigation of business practices, and motivates the adoption of systemic pattern-based EA.

Complexity, in the context of management science, emerges from diversity, interdependence, ambiguity, and flux (Maznevski et al., 2007). Enterprise Architecture (EA) is a fundamental framework that can be adopted by all types of organizations, including business enterprises, government organizations, and other institutions to tackle with complexity and create and sustain coherent enterprises (Saha, 2007). EA is "the system of applications, infrastructure, and information that support the business functions of an organization, as well as the processes and standards that dictate and guide their evolution" (O'Neill et al., 2007). There exist an multitude of schemas in literature that describe the possible approaches to establishing an EA, such as the Zachman Framework (http://www.zachmanframeworkassociates. com/) and the specific EAs that can be or have been implemented, such as the EA of the Internal Revenue Service (IRS) (Bellman, 2012).

In this chapter, upon suggesting pattern-based EAs, we focus on the competitive pattern-based strategies that influence the design of EAs. O'Neill et al. (2007) introduce a visual representation of how organizational strategies, business process strategies and Information Technology strategies interact with EA (inside the dashed circle in Figure 1). Our work extends this view with competitive pattern-based strategies, which can be visualized to form a layer that wraps the EA and the above

three categories of strategies (the complete picture in Figure 1). The main contribution of our novel extended view is two-folds: Firstly, we can now incorporate multi-functional strategies that fall into not only one of the above three categories but can encompass two or three of them. Secondly, we can now link the EA to the business environment through these pattern-based strategies, which each find applicability only under certain set of business conditions.

The specific set of strategies that we consider in this study is taken from an influential business book, *Profit Patterns*, by Adrian Slywotzky (Slywotzky et al., 1999). Slywotzky et al. (1999) consider pattern recognition as the essence of business strategy and the primary skill in dealing with complexity. Patterns in this book have been systemically formulated based on extensive case studies and hence are supported by evidence from the real world, and this was the main reason for the selection of this source for constructing the strategy layer that wraps the EA (Figure 1). This pattern-oriented approach for dealing with complexity is particularly helpful for organizations in managing complexity: Instead of having to design exhaustive systems that consider every possible case and take into account every possible environmental variable, the EA needs to be designed only around capturing and understanding the patterns that trigger the selected list of strategies. In Figure 1, the environmental variables that need to be considered by the EA are shown for a given competitive strategy, namely the "collapse of the middle." Therefore, in order to embrace and implement Slywotzky's listed strategies, the appropriate organizational setup and the EA are those that cater the information needed to identify the patterns and to launch the mentioned strategies.

In pattern-based EA, the strategy that should be applied in a particular business situation is found through the application of strategy rules. Figure 2 illustrates a particular set of rules related with Customer. The questions about the different aspects of the business environments reveal which

Figure 1. Competitive pattern-based strategies under complexity and the supporting pattern-based EA (enterprise architecture). This framework augments the classic EA, which consists of only the region inside the dashed circle.

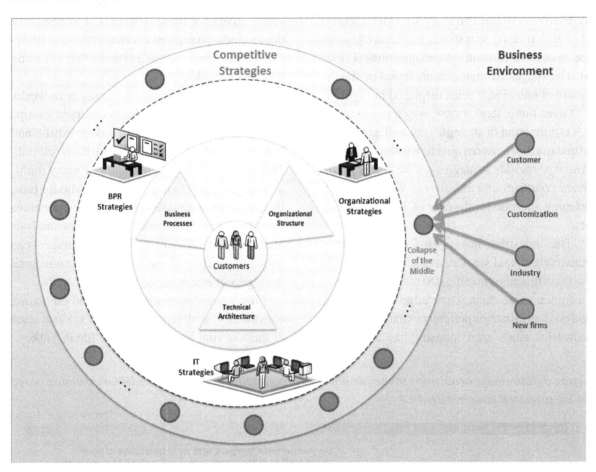

Figure 2. A database of strategy rules, supporting the pattern-based EA

	A	B	C	
1	Module_No	Module_Name	Node_Type	Text
94	2	Customer	Question	Is the effect of market on value chain economics changed or unaffected?
95	2	Customer	Question	Is the effect of product on commodization changed or unaffected?
96	2	Customer	Continue	
97	2	Customer	Start	
98	2	Customer	Question	Is there a 20%-80% rule (ABC rule) in profit , or is it dispersed among customers?
99	2	Customer	Question	Is the segment range of purchase behaviour wide or limited?
100	2	Customer	Question	Is the segment range of priorities wide or limited?
101	2	Customer	Question	Is the segment range of cost to serve wide or limited?
102	2	Customer	Question	Is the variation level of customer priorities high or low?
103	2	Customer	Question	Are customers consolidated into powerful segments or buyer groups?
104	2	Customer	Question	Is there a shift to new actors at players of decision making?
105	2	Customer	Question	Is profitability of traditional customers high or low?
106	2	Customer	Module Continue	
107	2	Customer	Suggestion	* Invest the time and effort to build a customer profitability system. Update it quarte
108	2	Customer	Suggestion	* Anticipate the power balance between your customer and supplier successfully. * (
109	2	Customer	Suggestion	* Identify the most profitable customers. * Offer them perfectly tailor-made options

H ◀ ▶ H NODE ANSWER_NODE ARC **NODE_Rule_Based** ANSWER_NODE_Rule_Based ARC_Rule_Based Rule_Based_3.6 Que ◀

strategies should be suggested by the EA. Figures 3 and 4 illustrate an example enterprise application, a strategic management Decision Support System (DSS) named StrategyAdvisor (Irdesel et al., 2012), that suggests strategies (Figure 4) given the answers to domain-related questions (Figure 3). The suggested strategies are based on the database of knowledge rules displayed in Figure 2.

Given this extended view, which suggests that EA is a function of strategies, as well as a driver, a fundamental research question is the following: *Which particular strategies are prevalent in different countries and industries?* We answer this research question for the case of Turkish managers.

The industries investigated include textile, construction, and service, as well as others. The business functions investigated consist of channel, customer, value chain, knowledge, organization, and product. Strategic preferences may vary across industries since each industry has a different

business environment and set of requirements. In this study, we explore most preferred strategy for different industries in Turkey, and compare the values given for these strategies. The results of this exploration suggest which competitive strategies Turkish managers select under the prevailing business complexity.

Turkey is the 16th largest economy in the world, and is the third most populous country in Europe behind Russia and Germany (Cakanyildirim and Haksoz, 2012). IMF and World Bank classify Turkey as an emerging market, and many multinational companies today run their Middle East, Balkan, Africa, and/or Central Asia operations from their headquarters in Turkey. The analysis of strategy preferences of Turkish managers can be considered part of understanding of managerial strategies in emerging economies.

Firstly, we give some background on textile, construction and service industries, since each of them is vital for the economic life in Turkey.

Figure 3. Knowledge acquisition in the sample enterprise application (StrategyAdvisor), running based on the proposed pattern-based EA

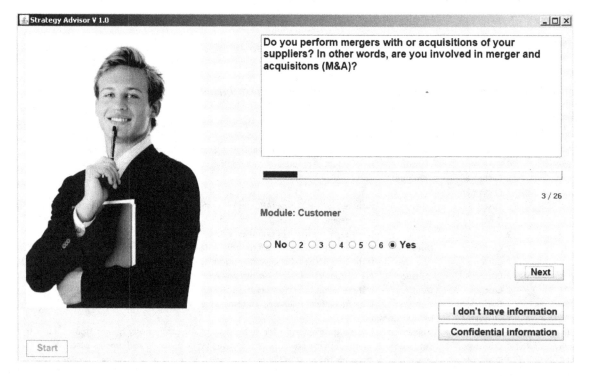

Figure 4. Strategy suggestion in the sample enterprise application (StrategyAdvisor), running based on the proposed pattern-based EA

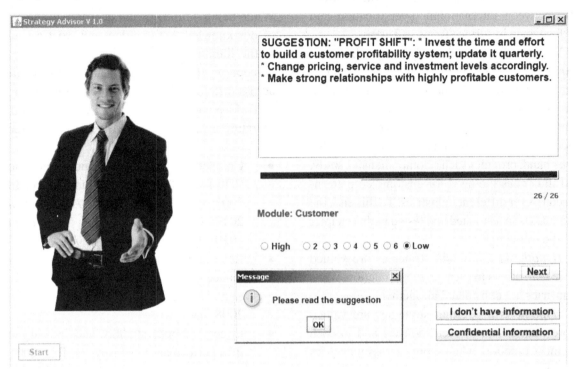

Atilgan (2006) mention that the *textile and apparel* industry, which comprise about 11-12% of the gross national product, 30% of the export and 12% of total employment, has great importance on Turkey's development and growth. However, the industry is experiencing problems due to poor managerial decisions and business practices, as well as macro factors affecting the industry. Adverse developments in such a large industry would inevitably affect the national economy in the same way. Turkey is the 9th biggest textile producer and the 5th biggest apparel producer in the world, and strategies are being developed to improve and maintain this position. With this objective, while endeavoring to improve the quality of both product and production, Turkish government launched the "Turquality" project (Turquality, 2012), to acquaint the world with high-quality Turkish brands. The Turquality project aims at actualizing the benefits of some of the well-known business strategies, such as product to brand and reintegration.

With regards to the *construction* industry, Dikmen and Birgonul (2003) reveal that the most prioritized important objective in the Turkish construction industry is building a positive company image, which is seen as a way of enhancing long-term profitability. Companies doing work for the private sector declare quality of services as their major strength. Company image and innovation in services are denoted as major strength factors by companies that utilize a differentiation strategy. When average values are considered, differentiation appears to be the most frequently used managerial strategy. Moreover, companies having a long-term profitability objective focus on differentiating their services, whereas others that aim at maximizing short-term profits focus on achieving cost advantage.

Service industry has become the dominant element in the global economy, especially in the industrialized nations, over the past three decades (Akbaba, 2006). Service quality is a prerequisite for success and survival in today's competitive environment. Capar and Kotabe (2003) report the first attempt to empirically examine the relationship between international diversification and performance in service firms in Turkey.

While Atilgan (2006), Dikmen and Birgonul (2003), Akbaba (2006), and Kotabe (2003) provide insights on the prioritization of specific strategies in certain industries, a cross-industry study covering all the major industries was not encountered in the literature. This chapter, on the other hand, provides such a comprehensive study, and illustrates the need for customized pattern-based EA for different industries. To this end, the hypotheses investigated and tested in this chapter are the following:

Hypothesis 1: Certain strategies are valued more than others in each business function, when industries are considered altogether.

Hypothesis 2: Certain strategies are valued more than others in each industry and in each business function, when scores across industries are considered.

The research process that we followed is given in Figure 5. In the survey conduct, the participants were provided with a list of strategies to choose from in each business function, and were asked to assign an importance value (on a Likert scale of 1 to 7) for each of these strategies. As mentioned earlier, the listed strategies come directly from Slywotzky *et al.* (1999). Once the survey data was acquired and cleaned, statistical data analysis was applied to identify strategy preferences, especially across industries. Given these differences, business application literature was scanned to find support or refutation regarding the findings from the survey.

The remainder of the paper is organized as follows: section 2 provides a brief literature review; section 3 describes the methodology followed including the data collection process and the statistical methods employed for the data analysis; section 4 presents the analysis results; and finally, section 5 summarizes the research conclusions and outlines further work.

2. LITERATURE

While being a fundamental question, to the best of our knowledge, there does not exist a study in the literature, for any country, on the value perceptions for alternative managerial strategies across different industrial sectors. With regards to Turkish companies, most of the studies in the literature investigate one of the following three:

- Competitive strategies and innovation (Ulusoy, 2003; Ulusoy and Yegenoglu, 2007; Ulusoy *et al.*, 2007; Alpkan *et al.*, 2010; Gunday *et al.*, 2011; Erbil *et al.*, 2010),
- Relation between strategy and firm performance (Bayraktar and Tatoglu, 2010; Koh *et al.*, 2007; Taslak, 2004; Glaister *et al.*, 2008) and
- Effects of both strategy and industry on firm performance (Ulusoy and Ikiz, 2001).

Our literature survey is structured along these groups of studies, and especially focuses on the case of Turkey. We also introduce and discuss the profit patterns of Slywotzky *et al.* (1999), which is the theoretical framework for the analyzed strategies.

2.1. Competitive Strategies and Innovation

The studies in the first group focus on strategy only in the context of innovation. These studies identify innovation and EA that promotes innovation as the pillars of strategic management: Ulusoy (2003) reveal that the manufacturing industry in Turkey bases its competition strategy mainly on low price, rather than product differentiation (even though the latter is promoted by Porter, 1980). Still, companies are reported to be inclined to increase the weight of the product differentiation strategy within their mixed strategy in near future, particularly through more knowledge-intensive products. In successive

Figure 5. The research process followed in the study

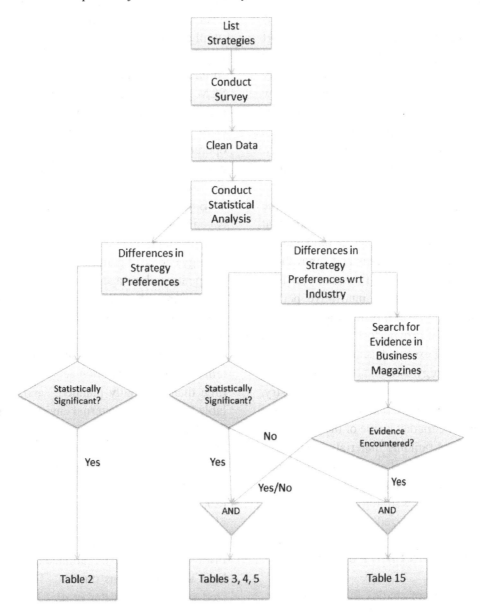

studies, Ulusoy and Yegenoglu (2007) and Ulusoy *et al.* (2007) demonstrate that the manufacturing industry in Turkey has indeed increased the weight of the product differentiation strategy against low cost strategy within their mixed strategy. Ulusoy and Yegenoglu (2007) highlight that emphasis on innovation and particularly new product development is steadily increasing. Ulusoy *et al.* (2007) suggest that besides brand reputation or an extensive sales and service network, product differentiation can be achieved through proprietary technology or through new products. More investment and organizational innovation are needed for R&D projects and new product development. Organizational innovations such as collaboration with other firms are also important for the product differentiation strategy to be successful.

Alpkan *et al.* (2010) expose the factors that contribute to innovative performance: An internal supportive environment providing support (especially management support), tolerance for risk-taking entrepreneurs, and a high quality human capital. When human capital is of low quality, the organizational support was shown to still influence innovative performance positively. However, when human capital is of higher quality, the marginal impact of organizational support on innovative performance diminishes. Gunday *et al.* (2011) report on an innovativeness study in the Turkish manufacturing industry. They show that organizational innovations play a fundamental role for innovative capabilities and innovations performed in manufacturing firms have positive and significant impacts on innovative performance. Hence, they show that innovation strategy is a major driver of firm performance and should be developed and executed as an integral part of the business strategy.

In an analysis of the construction industry, Erbil *et al.* (2010) suggest that introducing new products into the market is one of the main business strategies of building materials suppliers.

While innovation and strategies that expand innovation are critical, innovation is not the only source of competitive strategy. Other types of strategies should be analyzed, as we do in our study.

2.2. Strategy and Firm Performance

The second group of studies focuses on establishing the relation between strategy and firm performance:

There are several studies about strategy and firm performance in the context of Turkish companies in general, or specifically Turkish Small and Medium Size Enterprises (SMEs). Koh *et al.* (2007), determine the relation between Supply Chain Management (SCM) practices and operational performance by focusing on SMEs

in Turkey. The SCM practices with the highest level of usage by the sample firms included "JIT supply," "many suppliers," and "holding safety stock." The finding that both "JIT supply" and "holding safety stock" were the two most cited SCM practices in terms of the level of usage appears to be somewhat surprising. The analysis of the relationship between SCM practices and operational performance indicates that SCM practices might directly influence operational performance of SMEs.

Bayraktar and Tatoglu (2010) study the link between strategy choice and operational performance of Turkish companies. They show that a firm's strategy choice of gaining a differentiation-based competitive advantage improves firm's operational performance. Taslak (2004) shows that the most important formulation problem is "uncertainties arising from national economic conditions," and the two of most important implementation problems are "implementation activities taking more time than originally planned," and "uncontrollable factors in the external environment" for the Turkish textile firms. Many firms had much more difficulty in making realistic strategic decisions and successfully implementing them because of national economic uncertainty. Glaister *et al.* (2008) provide new evidence to explain the nature of the strategic planning-performance relationship, drawing on data from Turkish companies. Prior studies that have examined this relationship have tended to focus on firms from industrialized countries. Glaister *et al.* (2008) is one of the first studies that has explicitly modeled and empirically tested the relationship in an emerging country context. Their findings show that there exists a strong and positive relationship between formal strategic planning and firm performance, which confirms the arguments of the prescriptive strategic management literature.

In a related study, Ağca and Uğurlu (2008) investigate the impact of strategic orientation and strategy choices. The authors consider the orientation typologies suggested by Porter (1980) and Miles *et al.* (1978), and reveal that strategic orientations of Turkish manufacturing companies have significant effect on strategy formation capability and business performance.

The mentioned studies in the second group show that strategy choices in Turkish companies have a significant impact on performance. Our study is thus relevant and applicable, since it reveals the strategy valuations in Turkish companies, both on an industry basis, and as a whole.

Several other studies about strategy and firm performance are related to our study, even though they are not in the context of Turkish firms. These are summarized in Appendix A.

While the studies in the second group show the link between strategy selection and industry, they do not analyze how strategy valuations change across industries. Our study specifically investigates and reveals this critical link.

2.3. Strategy and Industry Effects Together

The third group of papers analyzes strategy and industry effects together: Ulusoy and Ikiz (2001) show that there is no appreciable difference between industrial sectors in implementing best manufacturing practices and in achieving high operational outcomes for Turkish firms. The leaders that adopt the best practices are rewarded by higher business performance. In comparison to foreign competitors, the ability to adopt products is stated to be a key advantage of Turkish companies.

Okumus (2003) presents a comprehensive review of strategy implementation, arguing that strategy implementation is too complex to be explained by prescriptive linear models. The framework he developed can be used for a retrospective analysis of past, future and current cases of strategy implementation.

Gulev (2009) examines to what extent cultural dimensions influence management behavior in different European Union (EU) countries. He identifies the strategic differences stemming from location and culture, as well as other factors. Gulev (2009) argues that variances in culture can have a profound impact on management behavior. He shows that there are some direct linkages between capitalistic and authoritarian cultures on managerial aspects of multi-national corporations.

Other studies that analyze strategy and industry together, that are not in the context of Turkey, are given in Appendix B.

2.4. Profit Patterns

The strategies included in our study are taken from the list of strategies in the *Profit Patterns* book, written by Adrian J. Slywotzky and his colleagues at Mercer Management Consulting (Slywotzky *et al.*, 1999; Mercer Consulting). These patterns/ strategies are listed in Table 1, and are explained in Table 6 in Appendix C. The names either directly refer to the strategies themselves or to the pattern under which the strategies are applied. The rationale behind the selection of this book is detailed in Appendix D.

Slywotzky *et al.* (1999) consider pattern recognition as the heart of business strategy and as the heart of managing complexity: Detecting and understanding the key strategic patterns playing out in an industry enables the mapping of the business landscape, and selection of the most appropriate strategy for the observed pattern. An example profit pattern, namely "collapse of the middle," is explained in Appendix E.

Weill *et al.* (2005) investigates whether business models, such as the profit patterns of Slywotzky, can have a significant impact on company success. The study introduces MIT Business Model Archetypes (BMA), a typology of four basic types of business models, and 16 variations based on these basic types. It is shown that a company's

Table 1. List of profit patterns (profit strategies)

Function	Strategy	Strategy Name	Function	Strategy	Strategy Name
1-Channel	158	Concentration	5-Mega	557	Collapse of the middle
1-Channel	159	Multiplication	5-Mega	558	Convergence
1-Channel	160	Compression	5-Mega	559	Technology shifts the board
1-Channel	161	Reintermediation	5-Mega	560	De Facto standard
2-Customer	245	Profit Shift	5-Mega	561	Back to profit
2-Customer	246	Power Shift	6-Organization	643	Skill Shift
2-Customer	247	Microsegmentation	6-Organization	644	Pyramid to network
2-Customer	248	Redefinition	6-Organization	645	Corner-stoning
3-Value Chain	349	Deintegration	6-Organization	646	Digital business design
3-Value Chain	350	Strengthening the weak link	7-Product	783	Product to brand
3-Value Chain	351	Value chain squeeze	7-Product	784	Product to pyramid
3-Value Chain	352	Reintegration	7-Product	785	Product to solution
3-Value Chain	353	Downstream	7-Product	786	Product to blockbuster
4-Knowledge	441	Operations to knowledge	7-Product	787	Product to profit multiplier
4-Knowledge	442	Product to customer knowledge			
4-Knowledge	443	Knowledge to product			
5-Mega	556	No profit			

business model is a substantially better predictor of its operating income, compared to the company's industry and other control variables.

Slywotzky's profit patterns have been subject of a multitude of academic papers (Slywotzky *et al.*, 1999b; Slywotzky and Morrison, 2001), and have been central to countless strategy applications over the years by Mercer Consulting. Since the strategies were identified through the investigation of global companies (besides local ones), they are globally applicable: Peng *et al.* (2009) apply the value network profit pattern for a Chinese telecom operator and Rodrigues *et al.* (2006) explains how this strategic pattern has been applied by Brazilian banks in the adoption of Automated Teller Machines (ATM) successfully.

3. METHODOLOGY

3.1. Data

Our research was conducted based on real world data collected through a field study survey. The field work has been carried out in Spring 2008, and involved 244 participants from 159 companies in 12 main industries. Each participant was assisted by a Sabanci University student as s/he answered all the 237 questions in a strategic management decision support system (StrategyAdvisor) and the 139 questions in an accompanying survey. A sample size of 244 can be considered reasonable with respect to goals of this study, which investigates the preferences for various strategies by different industries. Benchmark survey-based studies on strategic management, such as the one by Güleş *et al.* (2011) analyze samples of similar or smaller size.

This paper presents the analysis of the following 15 of these 139 questions, across seven business functions:

Q1: "Which industry do you operate in?"

Q2-8: "Which strategy within the business function X do you find most useful?" (X∈{channel, customer, value chain, knowledge, mega, organization, product})

Q9-15: "Which score would you assign to the value (benefit) of this strategy (7 being most useful)?"

3.2. Contingency Tables

Once the data has been systematically cleaned based on the taxonomy of dirty data in Kim *et al.* (2003), the next step was summarizing the frequencies and average scores of strategies. Firstly, contingency tables (Pearson, 1904) were constructed for the strategies in each of the business functions, across all industries. These are given in Table 7 in Appendix F. Then, they were created for each of the industries, for the strategies in each of the business functions. These are given in Tables 8 – 14 in Appendix F. A strategy has been included in a contingency table only if its frequency (the number of times that strategy was selected by the respondent as the most valuable strategy) was greater than or equal to five.

3.3. Statistical Tests

Once the contingency tables were constructed, statistical analysis was carried out to test for differences between scores given for the strategies. Even though the counts for the strategies could have been compared using Friedman test (Friedman, 1937, 1939), this was not pursued. We have instead focused on the score values given by the managers for the strategies.

A fundamental issue was the selection of the appropriate statistical tests for measuring the statistical significance of the hypothesized differences in strategy scores (Conover, 1998; Cassidy, 2005). The first decision to be made was whether parametric (t-test, ANOVA) or non-parametric tests (Mann-Whitney, Kruskal-Wallis) should be applied. When applicable, parametric tests are preferred due to their power, their requirement for smaller sample sizes to draw conclusions with the same degree of confidence. However, parametric tests are applicable only when the data follows parameterized distributions, such as the requirement of normal distribution for the t-test and ANOVA. Non-parametric test such as Mann-Whitney and Kruskal-Wallis, on the other hand, use the rank data to compute the test statistics, and do not require the data to come from a particular distribution (Conover, 1998).

Throughout the study, Shapiro-Wilk test (Shapiro and Wilk, 1965) was applied to test normality. t-test was applied for comparing differences among two samples that both follow normal distribution; ANOVA test was applied for comparing differences among three or more samples that both follow normal distribution (Conover, 1998). When any of the distributions were not following normal distribution, Mann-Whitney (Mann and Whitney, 1947) and Kruskal-Wallis (Kruskal and Wallis, 1952) tests were applied instead of t-test and ANOVA test, respectively.

3.4. Validation of Results

Any empirical study is bound by the data that it is based on, as well as the assumptions it makes. The assumptions regarding the selection of statistical tests have been tested thoroughly, as described in the preceding section. The validity of the results and insights is a major issue, and should be supported with observations, before being suggested as actionable facts. In our study, this validation was carried out through an in-depth analysis of the Turkish business literature, covering issues of the periodical business magazines Capital (http://www.capital.com.tr/), CNBC-e Business (http://www.cnbce.com/business/), Inc. Türkiye, Infomag (http://www.infomag.com.tr/), Turkishtime (http://www.dijimecmua.com/turkishtime/), within the years 2008 and 2009. This approach of searching for empirical proof or disproof in the business periodicals was very time-consuming. Yet, our study is the first study in related literature to conduct this methodological approach.

4. RESULTS

4.1. Overall Preferences

The first question to ask is whether there exist differences in the evaluations for the strategies'

values, ignoring the cross-industry effects. This analysis is important in designing a pattern-based EA that can be deployed in any industry within a given country. The augmented pattern-based EA that we propose in this chapter (Figure 1) supports such a country-specific customization. Hypothesis tests were carried out based on the contingency table (Table 7 in Appendix F) for comparing the scores of strategies that have been selected by at least five respondents for that function-industry combination.

Table 2 shows the results of the statistical tests, at p=0.05 level of confidence. The non-parametric Kruskal-Wallis test (Kruskal and Wallis, 1952) was carried out for testing the statistical significance of the differences in the average value scores. This test was used since the Shapiro-Wilk test (Shapiro and Wilk, 1965) rejected normality for at least one of the score vectors. Under the "Strategy Pair" column, the first strategy in the pair has a higher average value score, with statistical significance.

Table 2. Statistically-supported observations regarding the valuation of different strategies, across all industries

Observation	Function	Strategy Pair	Observed Diff	Critical Diff
1	1	158-159	19.72	14.74
1	1	158-160	37.11	15.85
1	1	158-161	29.72	17.65
1	1	159-160	13.64	12.42
2	2	248-245	35.16	16.31
2	2	248-246	27.48	13.61
2	2	248-247	14.48	10.39
3	3	350-349	26.50	14.15
3	3	350-351	25.39	13.40
3	3	350-352	12.76	12.50
3	3	353-349	23.80	15.12
3	3	353-351	18.11	12.82
4	5	556-557	21.26	21.06
4	5	556-559	27.52	20.33
4	5	560-559	13.97	13.77
5	7	785-783	24.05	15.04
5	7	785-787	11.77	10.18

For example, the first line of Table 2 shows that strategy 158 (Concentration) is preferred compared to strategy 159 (Multiplication).

It is very hard to validate these general findings through an investigation of the business literature, since the information regarding the value of a strategy can always be industry-specific. So, the insights are given without any supporting evidence from industry, while such evidence is later presented in the analysis for each function-industry pair.

Following an overall analysis, the hypothesis supported by statistical tests (and the insights obtained) when all industries are considered is the following:

Hypothesis 1: Certain strategies are valued more than others in each business function, when industries are considered altogether.

The statistically significant observations that support Hypothesis 1 are as follows, and are given in Table 2: (1) Among the strategies in the "Channel" function, Concentration strategy (158) is the *most* valuable one. The only other significant difference relates to Multiplication (159) having higher value than Compression (160). (2) Among the strategies in the "Customer" function, Redefinition strategy (248) is the *most* valuable one. (3) Among the strategies in the "Value Chain" function, both Strengthening the weak link (350) and Downstream (353) strategies are *more* valuable than Deintegration (349) and Value chain squeezing (351). Moreover, Strengthening the weak link (350) is also more valuable than Reintegration (352). (4) Among the "Mega" strategies, both the strategies under the No profit (556) pattern and the De Facto standard (560) strategy are *more* valuable than the strategies under the Technology shifts the board (559) pattern. Moreover, strategies under the No profit (556) pattern are also more valuable than the strategies under the Collapse of the middle (557) pattern. (5) Among the strategies in the "Product" function, Product to solution strategy (785) is *more* valuable than Product to brand (783) and Product to profit multiplier (787) strategies.

4.2. Value Evaluation for Each Industry

We next analyze the value of alternative strategies for each industry. This analysis is important when designing a pattern-based EA that provides customization for a specific industry. The pattern-based EA that we propose in this chapter (Figure 1) supports such a customization, just as it supports country-specific customization (Section 4.1). The analysis begins with contingency tables (Tables 8-14 in Appendix F) for all the business functions and industries.

Tables 3, 4, and 5 present the statistically significant insights obtained. The Test Type column tells whether a parametric (P) or non-parametric (NP) test was used. The Test column tells whether Kruskal-Wallis (KW) test, t-test (T) or Mann-Whitney (MW) test was used. Under the Strategy pair column, the first strategy in the pair has a higher average value score, with statistical support.

Both supporting and refuting evidence regarding the insights in this section have been searched and found from business magazines. The information on the related evidence has been given under a new column in Tables 3, 4, and 5, which gives the reference to the source of the evidence, and names the companies for which this insight is true (supporting the insight) or false (refuting the insight), with the refutations marked with X.

The tables list only the differences that satisfy one of the following two conditions: 1) Differences that are found to be statistically significant at p=0.05, *regardless of* whether related evidence exists in literature. 2) Differences that are found to be statistically significant at p=0.10, given that there *is* related evidence from business magazines.

For example, the first line of Table 3 tells that in the Channel function (Fn=1) of companies in Turkish construction industry, strategy 158 is preferred to strategy 160. One example company, as reported in Inc. Türkiye magazine, is ODE Yalıtım (Inc. Türkiye, 2009a).

Table 3. Statistically-supported observations regarding the valuation of different strategies in different industries

Obs	Fn	Industry	Test Type	Test	Strategy Pair	Obs Diff	Crit Diff	p	Evidence
6	1	Construction	NP	KW	158-160	5.48	4.88	0.1	ODE Yalıtım (Inc. Türkiye 2009a)
7	1	Consumer Products	NP	KW	158-160	9.31	8.51	0.05	(X) BANVIT (Inc. Türkiye 2009c), Tuborg & Efes (CNBC-e Business 2008d), Tekin Acar Cosmetics (CNBC-e Business 2008e), Marmaris Büfe (CNBC-e Business 2008h)
7	1	Consumer Products	NP	KW	158-161	12.87	9.59	0.05	(X) BANVIT (Inc. Türkiye 2009c), Tuborg & Efes (CNBC-e Business 2008d), Tekin Acar Cosmetics (CNBC-e Business 2008d), Marmaris Büfe (CNBC-e Business 2008h)
8	1	Textile	NP	KW	158-160	4.95	4.37	0.1	Koton, Park Bravo, Damat, Kiğılı (CNBC-e Business 2008c)
9	2	Construction	NP	KW	245-246	6.14	5.74	0.05	Hoffmann İnşaat (Infomag 2008a), TOKİ (Infomag 2008b)

Table 4. Statistically-supported observations regarding the valuation of different strategies in different industries

Obs	Fn	Industry	Test Type	Test	Strategy Pair	Obs Diff	Crit Diff	p	Evidence
10	2	Consumer Products	NP	KW	248-245	16.3	7.39	0.0500	Skullcandy (Inc. Türkiye 2008)
10	2	Consumer Products	NP	KW	248-247	4.75	4.67	0.0500	Skullcandy (Inc. Türkiye 2008)
11	2	Textile	NP	KW	248-246	6.97	5.70	0.0500	
12	3	Consumer Products	NP	KW	350-349	13.54	7.70	0.0500	Pepsico (Turkishtime 2009)
12	3	Consumer Products	NP	KW	350-351	7.21	6.49	0.0500	Pepsico (Turkishtime 2009)
13	5	Construction	NP	KW	559-557	7.48	6.54	0.0500	Hoffmann İnşaat (Infomag 2008a)
13	5	Construction	NP	KW	561-557	7.11	5.91	0.0500	Hoffmann İnşaat (Infomag 2008a)
14	5	Service	P	T	561-559			0.0783	Dursun İnanır ve Güzellik Merkezleri (CNBC-e Business 2008a), Alaçatı Beach Resort, Taş Otel, Sardunaki Konak Otel, Lale Lodge (CNBC-e Business 2008b)

Table 5. Statistically supported observations regarding the valuation of different strategies in different industries

Obs	Fn	Industry	Test Type	Test	Strategy Pair	Obs Diff	Crit Diff	p	Evidence
15	6	Consumer Products	NP	KW	646-643	9.20	8.18	0.0500	Procter & Gamble (Capital 2008a)
15	6	Consumer Products	NP	KW	646-644	8.12	7.27	0.0500	Procter & Gamble (Capital 2008a)
16	7	Consumer Products	NP	KW	785-784	11.86	8.21	0.0500	Procter & Gamble (Capital 2008a), Godiva (Capital 2008c)
16	7	Consumer Products	NP	KW	786-784	9.50	7.88	0.0500	Procter & Gamble (Capital 2008a), Godiva (Capital 2008c)
16	7	Consumer Products	NP	KW	787-784	9.16	6.75	0.0500	Procter & Gamble (Capital 2008a), Godiva (Capital 2008c)
17	7	Service	NP	MW	785-784			0.0516	
18	7	Textile	NP	MW	785-784			0.1092	(X) Yelda İpekli (Inc. Türkiye 2009b), (X) Louis Vuitton (Capital 2008b)

The hypothesis supported (and the insights obtained) through this analysis is the following:

Hypothesis 2: Certain strategies are valued more than others in each industry and in each business function, when scores across industries are considered.

The statistically significant observations that support Hypothesis 2 are as follows, and are given in Tables 3, 4, and 5:

(6) For the construction industry, among the strategies in the "Channel" function, Concentration strategy (158) is *more* valuable than Compression (160). (7) For the consumer products industry, among the strategies in the "Channel" function, Concentration strategy (158) is *more* valuable than Compression (160) and Reintermediation (161). (8) For the textile industry, among the strategies in the "Channel" function, Concentration strategy (158) is *more* valuable than Compression (160). (9) For the construction industry, among the strategies in the "Customer" function, Profit shift strategy (245) is *more* valuable than Power shift (246). (10) For the consumer products industry, among the strategies in the "Customer" function, Redefinition (248) is *more* valuable than

Profit shift (245) and Microsegmentation (247) strategies.

(11) For the textile industry, among the strategies in the "Customer" function, Redefinition (248) is *more* valuable than Power shift (246) strategy. (12) For the consumer products industry, among the strategies in the "Value chain" function, Strengthening the weak link (350) is *more* valuable than Deintegration (349) and Value chain (351) strategies. (13) For the construction industry, among the "Mega" strategies, Technology shifts the board (559) and Back to profit (561) are both *more* valuable than Collapse of the middle (557). (14) For the service industry, among the "Mega" strategies, Back to profit (561) is *more* valuable than Technology shifts the board (559). (15) For the consumer products industry, among the strategies in the "Organization" function, Digital business design (646) is *more* valuable than Skill shift (643) and Pyramid to network (644) strategies. (16) For the consumer products industry, among the strategies in the "Product" function, Product to solution (785), Product to blockbuster (786), and Product to profit multiplier (787) are all *more* valuable than Product to pyramid (784). (17) For

the service industry, among the strategies in the "Product" function, Product to solution (785) is *more* valuable than Product to pyramid (784). (18) For the textile industry, among the strategies in the "Product" function, Product to solution (785) is *more* valuable than Product to pyramid (784).

Some of the observations above are also supported with evidence from the academic literature. One example is for the textile industry: The textile and clothing sectors, which comprise about 11-12% of the gross national product, 30% of the export and 12% of total employment, have great importance on Turkey's development and growth (Atilgan, 2006). The problems in this industry were alleviated by the "Turquality" project launched by the Turkish Government (Turquality, 2012), which acquaints the world with high-quality national brands. The Turquality project corresponds to the combination of Concentration (observation 8 under Hypothesis 2) and Redefinition (observation 11 under Hypothesis 2) strategies, which are shown to be more valuable than (certain) other strategies in their respective functions with statistical support.

Some of the function-industry combinations were observed to contain only a single strategy selected at least five times. Statistical analysis was not carried out for comparing the scores of the strategies in these cases. So these observations are not statistically supported, but instead they are given in Table 15 in Appendix G for these cases simply state that the strategy was the most frequently selected one.

5. CONCLUSION AND DISCUSSIONS

The main novelty of the paper is the introduction of the pattern-based Enterprise Architecture (EA), which augments existing EAs. The main finding in this paper is that managers in different industries have differing perceptions of the value of various managerial strategies. This will play an important role in the design and implementation of the proposed pattern-based EAs. Our study confirms this expected result and identifies these differences with statistical rigor and support from real-world case studies. The insights obtained through statistical data analysis are validated through findings from academic and business literature. The references to the business literature name the specific companies that have preferred certain strategies over other alternative ones. While the search for the business literature was carried out, the cases that *refute* the statistical findings (besides those that *support*) were also searched and revealed, but were seldom encountered. Hence, objectivity was maintained at the risk of having some of the statistically significant differences being refuted by real world cases.

The presented study can be extended in several directions through future research:

- The sample was too small for some industries, which makes it impossible to carry out hypothesis testing or causes many score differences to appear statistically insignificant. So, additional data collection, as in all empirical research, would be helpful in future replications of this study.
- The sample should include a more balanced representation of industries, so that hypothesis testing will be possible for more industries. However, since this would require the collection of more data, the study can focus on selected industries.
- Recently emerging profit patterns, reported by Slywotzky in his more recent books can be included. The pattern-based EA introduced in this chapter is flexible and can incorporate any set of patterns.

ACKNOWLEDGMENT

The authors thank İlter İrdesel, Damla Uygur, Ceylin Özcan, Özge Onur, Ceren Atay, and Gizem Kökten for their help in managing the field studies; the 20 Sabanci University undergraduate students who conducted the field studies; and to all the anonymous respondents that participated in the fieldwork. The authors thank Gülce Karslı, Berker Şaşmaz, and Ayşegül Kama for searching business magazines to find real world cases that support or refute the hypotheses; Ahmet Demirelli and İlter İrdesel for designing and developing the StrategyAdvisor software; Dr. Pallab Saha for his valuable suggestions in improving the chapter; and finally Soner Ulun and Kamil Çöllü for their help in editing the documents and preparing the figures.

REFERENCES

Ağca, V., & Uğurlu, Ö.Y. (2008). Türk imalat işletmelerinde stratejik eğilimin strateji oluşturma yeteneği ve performans ilişkisine etkisi. *İktisat İşletme ve Finans, 23*(273), 79-103.

Akbaba, A. (2006). Measuring service quality in the hotel industry: A study in a business hotel in Turkey. *Hospital Management, 25*, 170–192. doi:10.1016/j.ijhm.2005.08.006.

Alpkan, L., Bulut, C., Gunday, G., Ulusoy, G., & Kilic, K. (2010). Organizational support for intrapreneurship and its interaction with human capital to enhance innovative performance. *Management Decision, 48*(5), 732–755.

Atilgan, T. (2006). The effects of the textile and clothing sector on the economy of Turkey. *Fibres & Textiles in Eastern Europe, 14*(4), 16–20.

Bayraktar, E., & Tatoglu, E. (2010). Assessing the link between strategy choice and operational performance of Turkish companies. In *Proceedings of the 14th International Research/Expert Conference in Trends in the Development of Machinery and Associated Technology TMT 2010,* (pp. 805-808). Mediterranean Cruise.

Bellman, B. (2012). *Managing organizational complexity: Enterprise architecture and architecture frameworks with an overview of their products, artifacts and models.* Retrieved from http://ertekprojects.com/url/4

CNBC-e Business. (2008a, May). Kişisel bakım dünyasının kralı. [The king of the personal care world]. *CNBC-e Business,* 110-112.

CNBC-e Business. (2008b, May). Butik olsun benim olsun. [Let it be boutique, but let it me mine. *CNBC-e Business,* 128-130. CNBC-e Business. (2008c, August). Türk hazır giyimini zirveye taşıyanlar. [Those who crown the Turkish apparel industry]. *CNBC-e Business,* 42-52.

CNBC-e Business. (2008d, August). Tuborg'un havasının kaçış öyküsü. [The story of how the air went off Tuborg]. *CNBC-e Business,* 54-56.

CNBC-e Business. (2008e, August). Kozmetikte ikinci yatırım dalgası. [Second wave of investment in cosmetics]. *CNBC-e Business,* 70-72.

CNBC-e Business. (2008f, August). 10 metrekarede büyük yarış. [Big race on the 10 meter-square]. *CNBC-e Business,* 74-76.

CNBC-e Business. (2008g, August). Gripin al bir şeyin kalmaz. [Take a Gripin pill and you will be all right]. *CNBC -e Business,* 108-110.

CNBC-e Business. (2008h, August). Taklitle uğraşmak düşman başına. [Fighting imitation? I wouldn't wish it on my worst enemy]. *CNBC-e Business,* 110-111.

Cakanyildirim, M., & Haksöz, C. (2012). *CSCMP global perspectives – Turkey.* Council of Supply Chain Management Professionals.

Capar, N., & Kotabe, M. (2003). The relationship between international diversification and performance in service firms. *Journal of International Business Studies, 34*, 345–355. doi:10.1057/palgrave.jibs.8400036.

Capital. (2008a, February). Dünya devi P&G B&G ile büyüyor. [World giant P&G grows with B&G]. *Capital*, 114-124.

Capital. (2008b, February). Lüks devi çift haneli nasıl büyüyor?. [How does the luxury giant show two-digit growth?]. *Capital*, 140-144.

Capital. (2008c, May). Hesaplar yeniden yapılıyor. [Recounts being made]. *Capital*, 136-144.

Cassidy, L. D. (2005). Basic concepts of statistical analysis for surgical research. *The Journal of Surgical Research, 128*(2), 199–206. doi:10.1016/j.jss.2005.07.005 PMID:16140341.

Conover, W. J. (1998). *Practical nonparametric statistics*. New York: John Wiley & Sons.

Dikmen, I., & Birgonul, M. T. (2003). Strategic perspective of Turkish construction companies. *Journal of Management Engineering, 19*(1), 33–40. doi:10.1061/(ASCE)0742-597X(2003)19:1(33).

Erbil, Y., Acar, E., & Akinciturk, N. (2010). Evidence on innovation as a competitive strategy in a developing market: Turkish building material suppliers' point of view. In *Proceedings of the Second International Conference on Construction in Developing Countries (ICCIDC-II)*. Retrieved from http://acare2.tripod.com/academic/Erbil_et_al_2010.pdf

Falshaw, J. R., & Glaister, K. W. (2006). Evidence on formal strategic planning and company performance. *Management Decision, 44*(1), 9–30. doi:10.1108/00251740610641436.

Friedman, M. (1937). The use of ranks to avoid the assumption of normality implicit in the analysis of variance. *Journal of the American Statistical Association, 32*(200), 675–701. doi:10.1080/01621459.1937.10503522.

Friedman, M. (1939). A correction: The use of ranks to avoid the assumption of normality implicit in the analysis of variance. *Journal of the American Statistical Association, 34*(205), 109.

Glaister, K. W., Dincer, O., Tatoglu, E., Demirbag, M., & Zaim, S. (2008). A causal analysis of formal strategic planning and firm performance: Evidence from an emerging country. *Management Decision, 46*(3), 365–391. doi:10.1108/00251740810863843.

Güleş, H.K., Türkmen, M., & Özilhan, D. (2011). Tekstil ve otomotiv yan sanayi küçük ve orta ölçekli işletmelerinde üretim ve işletme performansı. *İktisat İşletme ve Finans, 26*(304), 79-112.

Gulev, R. E. (2009). Cultural repercussions. *Industrial Management & Data Systems, 109*(6), 793–808. doi:10.1108/02635570910968045.

Gunday, G., Ulusoy, G., Kilic, K., & Alpkan, L. (2011). Effects of innovation types on firm performance. *International Journal of Production Economics, 133*(2), 662–676. doi:10.1016/j.ijpe.2011.05.014.

Hawawini, G., Subramanıan, V., & Verdin, P. (2003). Is performance driven by industry- Or firm-specific factors? A new look at the evidence. *Strategic Management Journal, 24*, 1–16. doi:10.1002/smj.278.

Infomag. (2008a, October). Devremülke alternatif geliyor!. [Alternative arriving to timeshared residences!. *Infomag*, 32-34.

Infomag. (2008b, October). TOKİ'nin gelmesi gereken noktayı hayal eden başkaları var. [There are others who imagine where TOKİ should reach]. *Infomag*, 115-118.

Irdesel, I., Ertek, G., & Demirelli, A. (2012). *A graph-based methodology for constructing expert systems and its application in the strategic management domain* (Working Paper).

Kim, W., Choi, B. J., Hong, E. K., Kim, S. K., & Lee, D. (2003). A taxonomy of dirty data. *Data Mining and Knowledge Discovery*, 7(1), 81–99. doi:10.1023/A:1021564703268.

Koh, L., Demirbag, M., Bayraktar, E., Tatoglu, E., & Zaim, S. (2007). The impact of supply chain management practices on performance of SMEs. *Industrial Management & Data Systems*, 107(1), 103–124. doi:10.1108/02635570710719089.

Kruskal, W. H., & Wallis, W. A. (1952). Use of ranks in one-criterion variance analysis. *Journal of the American Statistical Association*, 47(260), 583–621. doi:10.1080/01621459.1952.10483441.

Mann, H. B., & Whitney, D. R. (1947). On a test of whether one of two random variables is stochastically larger than the other. *Annals of Mathematical Statistics*, 18(1), 50–60. doi:10.1214/aoms/1177730491.

Maznevski, M., Steger, U., & Amann, W. (2007). *Perspectives for managers* (white paper). Lausanne, Switzerland: IMD.

Mercer Consulting. (n.d.). Retrieved from http://www.mercer.com

Miles, R. E., Snow, C. C., Meyer, A. D., & Coleman, H. J. (1978). Organizational strategy, structure and process. *Academy of Management Review*, 3(3), 546–562. PMID:10238389.

O'Neill, T., Denford, M., Leaney, J., & Dunsire, K. (2007). Managing enterprise architecture change. In Saha, P. (Ed.), *Handbooks of Enterprise Systems Architecture in Practice*. Hershey, PA: IGI Global. doi:10.4018/978-1-59904-189-6.ch011.

Okumus, F. (2003). A framework to implement strategies in organizations. *Management Decision*, 41(9), 871–882. doi:10.1108/00251740310499555.

Pearson, K. (1904). *On the theory of contingency and its relation to association and normal correlation*. Cambridge, UK: Cambridge University Press.

Peng, Y., Iiu, H., Tao, H., & Ming, F. (2009). A study on the value network of telecom service and the organization change of Chinese telecom operator. In *Proceedings of the 6th International Conference on Service Systems and Service Management (ICSSSM '09)*, (pp. 493-497). Xiamen, China: ICSSSM.

Porter, M. E. (1980). *Competitive strategy: Techniques for analysing industries and competitors*. New York: Free Press.

Prajogo, D. I. (2007). The relationship between competitive strategies and product quality. *Industrial Management & Data Systems*, 107(1), 69–83. doi:10.1108/02635570710719061.

Raymond, L., & Croteau, A. (2006). Enabling the strategic development of SMEs through advanced manufacturing systems. *Industrial Management & Data Systems*, 106(7), 1012–1032. doi:10.1108/02635570610688904.

Rodrigues, L. C., Lancellotti, M., & Riscarolli, V. (2006). ATM technology as Brazilian banks strategy. In *Proceedings of the 15th International Conference on Management of Technology (IAMOT 2006)*. Beijing, China: IAMOT.

Saha, P. (2007). A synergistic assessment of the federal enterprise architecture framework against GERAM (ISO15704:2000). In Saha, P. (Ed.), *Handbook of Enterprise Systems Architecture in Practice*. Hershey, PA: IGI Global. doi:10.4018/978-1-59904-189-6.ch001.

Shapiro, S. S., & Wilk, M. B. (1965). An analysis of variance test for normality (complete samples). *Biometrika*, 52(3/4), 591–611. doi:10.2307/2333709.

Slywotzky, A., & Morrison, D. (2001). Becoming a digital business: It's not about technology. *Strategy and Leadership*, 29(2), 4–9. doi:10.1108/10878570110387671.

Slywotzky, A. J., Morrison, D. J., Moser, T., Mundt, K. A., & Quella, J. A. (1999a). *Profit patterns: 30 ways to anticipate and profit from strategic forces reshaping your business.* New York: John Wiley & Sons Ltd..

Slywotzky, A. J., Mundt, K. A., & Quella, J. A. (1999b, June). Pattern thinking. *Management Review*, 32–37.

Spanos, Y. E. (2004). Strategy and industry effects on profitability: Evidence from Greece. *Strategic Management Journal, 25*, 139–165. doi:10.1002/smj.369.

Taslak, S. (2004). Factors restricting success of strategic decisions: Evidence from the Turkish textile industry. *European Business Review, 16*(2), 152–164. doi:10.1108/09555340410524256.

Turkishtime. (2009a, April). Pepsi'nin yüzü hep gülecek mi?. [Will Pepsi always smile?]. *Turkishtime*, 92-95.

Turkishtime. (2009b, April). Yeni yatırımlar için ısınıyor. [He is warming up for new investments]. *Turkishtime*, 110-111.

Türkiye. (2008, December). Ses kafanızın derinliklerinde titreşerek gözlerinizden dışarı akar. [The sound blinks in the depth of your head and flows out of your eyes.]. *Türkiye*, 123.

Türkiye. (2009a, April). Dünya krizle çalkalansa bile ilaç sektörü kendine güveniyor: Hem de haklı sebeplerle. [The pharmaceutical industry trusts itself: Due to valid reasons]. *Türkiye*, 84-92.

Türkiye (2009b, January). Sıfır sermaye ile yola çıkan Orhan Turan, bugün 40 milyon dolarlık yatırım yapabilen ODE Yalıtım'ı yarattı: En büyük sermayesi, büyük düşünebilmesi.... [Orhan Turan started with zero capital, and he created ODE Insulation, which can make an investment of 40 million dollars: His biggest capital is thinking big....]. *Türkiye*, 52-55.

Türkiye. (2009c, February). Bedavalar da yetmiyor, 'İndirim' yeniden tanımlanacak. [Even the free giveaways are not enough, 'Sale' will be redefined]. *Türkiye*, 21-23.

Türkiye. (2009d, April). Yolunuzu bulmak için tüketicinin sesini dinleyin. [Listen to the consumer to find your way]. *Türkiye*, 53-67.

Turquality. (2012). Retrieved from http://www.turquality.com

Ulusoy, G. (2003). An assessment of supply chain and innovation management practices in the manufacturing industries in Turkey. *International Journal of Production Economics, 86*, 251–270. doi:10.1016/S0925-5273(03)00064-1.

Ulusoy, G., Çetindamar, D., Yegenoglu, H., & Bulut, Ç. (2007). An empirical study on the competitiveness and innovation in four sectors of the Turkish manufacturing industry. In *Proceedings of the 14th International Annual EurOMA Conference,* (pp. 438-447). Ankara, Turkey: EurOMA.

Ulusoy, G., & İkiz, İ. (2001). Benchmarking best manufacturing practices: A study into four sectors of Turkish industry. *International Journal of Operations & Production Management, 21*(7), 1021–1043. doi:10.1108/01443570110393478.

Ulusoy, G., & Yegenoglu, H. (2007). Innovation performance and competitive strategies in the Turkish manufacturing industry. In *Proceedings of the 8th International Research Conference on Quality, Innovation and Knowledge Management,* (pp. 907-915). New Delhi, India: IEEE.

Weill, P., Malone, T. W., D'Urso, V. T., Herman, G., & Woerner, S. (2005). *Do some business models perform better than others? A study of the 1000 largest US firms.* Cambridge, MA: MIT Press.

APPENDIX A

Several other studies about strategy and firm performance are related to our study, even though they are not in the context of Turkish firms.

Falshaw et al. (2006) establish the link between formal strategic planning and company performance for companies in UK. They consider not only financial measures, but also measures such as quality and employee satisfaction for appraisal of company. Prajogo (2007) examines the underlying strategic target of quality performance and investigates the impacts of differentiation and cost leadership on quality performance in the context of Australian manufacturing firms. He shows that quality is primarily predicted by differentiation strategy and this relationship is moderated by cost leadership strategy. Raymond and Croteau (2006) examine the use of advanced technology in SMEs. Since Advanced Manufacturing Systems (AMS) could help creating new distribution channels, products, services etc., the development strategies of small manufacturing firms can be associated with AMS. They consider three types of SMEs as local, transition and world-class and they conclude that compared to transition SMEs, local SMEs show equal levels of market and network development, but higher levels of product development, and higher levels of AMS integration. In addition, transitions SMEs have the capacity to benefit more from advanced manufacturing technologies but are not yet capable of reaching the same level of performance as world-class SMEs. Each one seems to follow a distinct logic of strategy that leads them to attain higher performance. The authors suggest that SMEs should integrate IT considerations with company-wide strategic development and put this principle into action through IT management policies and practices.

APPENDIX B

Hawawini et al. (2003) study the relative importance of industry- and firm-level effects on performance. They show that for most firms in an industry, i.e., for those that are not leaders or losers in their industry, the industry effect turns out to be more important for performance than firm-specific factors. Spanos (2004) examines the impact of firm and industry-specific factors on profitability, using census data on Greek manufacturing. The author shows that the more generic strategy dimensions included in the strategy mix, the more profitable the strategy is, provided that one of the key components is low cost. Pure strategies generally appear to produce below-average results. Firms pursuing pure differentiation strategies are found less profitable even when compared with firms having no clear strategy.

APPENDIX C

Table 6. Strategy explanations, taken directly from Slywotzky et al. (1999) and Mercer consulting website

Function	Strategy	Strategy Name	Strategy Explanation
1-Channel	158	Concentration	Model future situations before competitors. Consolidate some of the operations. Consider acquisition of smaller players. Provide better product/service selections to your customers at lower prices.
1-Channel	159	Multiplication	If you are the manufacturer, use new channels earlier than your competitors; become the default choice of your customers. If you are a traditional channel, design new business models and channels that respond to how your current and potential customers want to buy. Pioneer new channels ahead of your competitors to satisfy customer priorities. Grow rapidly in where, when and how customers buy products and services.
1-Channel	160	Compression	Create early direct connections with your suppliers to achieve lower sourcing costs. If you are still "the old channel," create new value added offerings, or disinvest. Simplify and eliminate the redundant processes in your distribution operations.
1-Channel	161	Reintermediation	Use the new channels early. Maximize your value added. Accelerate your investment in the new channels to minimize the free space available for other new entrants. Serve customers that are dissatisfied with the current business practices by introducing new alternatives, by enabling more efficient transactions and new value-added services. Integrate your products by using multiple vendors.
2-Customer	245	Profit Shift	Invest the time and effort to build a customer profitability system; update it quarterly. Change pricing, service and investment levels accordingly. Make strong relationships with highly profitable customers.
2-Customer	246	Power Shift	Anticipate the power balance between your customer and supplier successfully. Choose the right side that you need to control carefully.
2-Customer	247	Microsegmentation	Identify the most profitable customers; offer them perfectly tailor-made options; build a barrier around them, so that your competitors find them too expensive to convert. Use technology, share information, and customize in the market.
2-Customer	248	Redefinition	Look beyond your current customer set. Search the broader system for the most important and the most profitable customers. Build your business design around them. Target untapped customers or segments.
3-Value Chain	349	Deintegration	Dominate an important cell of the new, broken-up value chain and specialize in it. Make specialists serve on formerly secure position of the chain. Outsource non-core operations. Perform cost-cutting activities.
3-Value Chain	350	Strengthening the weak link	Assist the members (suppliers, intermediate customers, distributors) in terms of investment, equity positions, volume shifting, system standardization, information sharing, training and alliance. Perform exclusive contracts in order to fix the weak link.
3-Value Chain	351	Value chain squeeze	Improve your performance faster than your neighbours do. Limit the strength of their position by encouraging new entrants. Perform differentiation and consolidation in current chain steps.
3-Value Chain	352	Reintegration	Control the industry over customer relationships and product presentations. Enhance the attractiveness and uniqueness of customer's offerings. Rebalance the power equation between customer and supplier. Move closer to the customer. Use contracts, relationships or minority ownership.

continued on following page

Table 6. Continued

Function	Strategy	Strategy Name	Strategy Explanation
3-Value Chain	353	Downstream	Help carriers plan and network. Supply technical support to end users. Deal with finance, logistics management, distribution and training beyond the factory gate.
4-Knowledge	441	Operations to knowledge	Translate operations into unique knowledge. Create a form (contract or a database) for selling it and sell it.
4-Knowledge	442	Product to customer knowledge	Minimize cost by mass marketing, inventory reduction or stockout reduction. Perform just-in-time management. Perform targeted sales. Perform category management. Try to perform successful innovation. Listen to your transactions for your customer and get the message. Then apply this message to create new offerings, develop new systems, and improve the customer's economics and your own.
4-Knowledge	443	Knowledge to product	Identify the most valuable knowledge of your organization. Try to make it have a highly replicable structure that is easy to sell, easy to train and easy to improve. Advertise it, sell it, and most importantly improve it.
5-Mega	556	No profit	Invent a new way of doing business.
5-Mega	557	Collapse of the middle	Be the first to go to the extremes. Be a high end specialty and low cost focused firm by tailor solutions and systems integration.
5-Mega	558	Convergence	Identify the new rules of competition. Define your best oppurtunity space. Become its leader. Eliminate all other options for your customer and motivate your new rivals to look elsewhere.
5-Mega	559	Technology shifts the board	Exploit the new strategic landscape. Go to where the power will be.
5-Mega	560	De Facto standard	In terms of the art of optimal coalition building, sell product for profit margin, use these products' differentiated performance technology and try to create a standard in the part of the value chain.
5-Mega	561	Back to profit	Observe the customer base again; see the undiscovered and unmet needs; build a new business design to meet these.
6-Organization	643	Skill Shift	Look at how the customer is changing. Identify tomorrow's skill, and try to build it today.
6-Organization	644	Pyramid to network	Maximize your external exposure; use whatever organizational change it takes.
6-Organization	645	Corner-stoning	Be the optimum at something. Search for the next best space; experiment to find it; go there first; then find the next best space.
6-Organization	646	Digital business design	Shift the nature from an episodic encounter to a electronically continuous flow of customer information by transactions, customer services and customer communications.
7-Product	783	Product to brand	Realize the customers' need and request of valuable brand; increase the mindshare of this brand.
7-Product	784	Product to pyramid	Create multiple product levels according to different functionality, different performance attributes, different styles and different price points. Maximize profitability by using upper levels to bring in profits. Protect profitability by using lowest level to keep competitors out.
7-Product	785	Product to solution	Study your customers' system and understand better than they do. Create solutions for your customers such as reducing customer costs, reducing complexity of operations for customers, reducing time-to-market or enhancing utility to customers.
7-Product	786	Product to blockbuster	Design a new pipeline or system focusing resources on selected products with blockbuster potential and consistently generating blockbuster products.
7-Product	787	Product to profit multiplier	Organize to identify how your product, brand or skill can be sold; find the most profitable ways and build a system that puts them to work.

APPENDIX D

Slywotzky, a well-known business thinker and management consultant, was listed in 2007 among the top fifty business thinkers in the world (http://www.thinkers50.com). His *Profit Patterns* book (Slywotzky *et al.*, 1999). book was selected as the knowledge source, mainly because the book is structured after "profit patterns," observed recurring patterns across industries, together with their corresponding strategies. This book was selected also because it includes newly emerged profit patterns (such as *Microsegmentation*), due to the developments in information technology, as well as classic patterns (such as *Convergence* and *Collapse of the Middle*).

APPENDIX E

Slywotzky et al. (1999) consider pattern recognition as the heart of business strategy: Detecting and understanding the key strategic patterns playing out in an industry enables the mapping of the business landscape, and selection of the most appropriate strategy for the observed pattern. For example, the "collapse of the middle" pattern in the "Channel" business function refers to the collapse of the middle player along a value chain, which offers differentiated product/service performance at premium price. This value proposition is neighbored by the players that offer acceptable quality at lowest price and superior products at an equal or premium price. The realization of this pattern can be detected from several indicators: The customer being polarized with respect to priorities, needs for customization, or level of knowledge; the industry being mature or moving from average to extremes; new firms entering the market with high-end specialy focus or low cost focus. The strategic solution for the middle player about to be collaped is to choose a non-middle position on both product and information. The company should create a new business design with which it can successfully compete for future value in its industry, pushing its boundary towards the value propositions of its neighbors (Slywotzky et al., 1999).

APPENDIX F

Table 7 presents the contingency tables for all the business functions, that contain the frequencies and average value scores for each of the strategies. The strategies with the highest average value score for each business function are shown in bold. Frequency of selection and average scores are given for each strategy, grouped by business function.

Tables 8 through 14 contain the frequencies and average value scores for each of the strategies for each function-industry pair. The strategies with the highest average value score for each business function are shown in bold. Since a breakdown was made based on industry, some function-industry pairs had only one strategy selected at least five times. Therefore, Tables 8 through 14 also give us insights on which strategies are valued most for those function-industry pairs.

Table 7. Contingency table for the strategies in each of the business functions across all industries

Function	Strategy	Strategy Name	Frequency	Avg Score
1	158	Concentration	32	6.13
1	159	Multiplication	61	5.61
1	161	Reintermediation	27	5.30
1	160	Compression	42	5.17
2	248	Redefinition	32	6.31
2	247	Microsegmentation	48	5.58
2	246	Power Shift	41	5.46
2	245	Profit Shift	55	5.44
3	350	Strengthening the weak link	27	6.15
3	353	Downstream	21	6.10
3	352	Reintegration	43	5.77
3	349	Deintegration	30	5.63
3	351	Value chain squeeze	31	5.23
4	443	Knowledge to product	37	5.78
4	442	Product to customer knowledge	93	5.61
4	441	Operations to knowledge	39	5.51
5	556	No profit	12	6.00
5	560	De Facto standard	29	5.93
5	558	Convergence	24	5.67
5	561	Back to profit	49	5.59
5	557	Collapse of the middle	31	5.32
5	559	Technology shifts the board	41	5.07
6	646	Digital business design	52	5.77
6	645	Corner-stoning	42	5.60
6	643	Skill Shift	41	5.37
6	644	Pyramid to network	36	5.25
7	785	Product to solution	37	6.03
7	784	Product to pyramid	46	5.65
7	786	Product to blockbuster	19	5.63
7	787	Product to profit multiplier	33	5.61
7	783	Product to brand	30	5.43

Table 8. Contingency table for the strategies for business function "channel" (1) for each industry

Function	Industry/Sector	Strategy	Strategy Name	Frequency	Avg Score
1	Construction	159	Multiplication	10	6.00
1	Construction	158	Concentration	7	6.00
1	Construction	160	Compression	8	5.25
1	Consumer Products	158	Concentration	6	6.17
1	Consumer Products	159	Multiplication	15	5.53
1	Consumer Products	160	Compression	13	5.00
1	Consumer Products	161	Reintermediation	7	4.43
1	Manufacturing	159	Multiplication	7	5.00
1	Mining	159	Multiplication	5	4.80
1	Service	159	Multiplication	8	5.63
1	Textile	158	Concentration	6	6.50
1	Textile	159	Multiplication	8	6.00
1	Textile	160	Compression	5	5.20

Table 9. Contingency table for the strategies for business function "customer" (2) for each industry

Function	Industry/Sector	Strategy	Strategy Name	Frequency	Avg Score
2	Construction	245	Profit Shift	8	6.00
2	Construction	247	Microsegmentation	7	6.00
2	Construction	246	Power Shift	10	5.10
2	Consumer Products	248	Redefinition	8	6.75
2	Consumer Products	247	Microsegmentation	8	5.38
2	Consumer Products	245	Profit Shift	20	5.20
2	Consumer Products	246	Power Shift	6	5.17
2	Manufacturing	245	Profit Shift	7	5.14
2	Manufacturing	247	Microsegmentation	6	5.00
2	Mining	245	Profit Shift	6	5.17
2	Service	248	Redefinition	5	6.60
2	Service	246	Power Shift	7	6.00
2	Service	247	Microsegmentation	7	5.71
2	Textile	248	Redefinition	7	6.57
2	Textile	247	Microsegmentation	8	6.25
2	Textile	246	Power Shift	5	5.60

Table 10. Contingency table for the strategies for business function "value chain" (3) for each industry

Function	Industry/Sector	Strategy	Strategy Name	Frequency	Avg Score
3	Construction	349	Deintegration	8	5.50
3	Construction	352	Reintegration	8	5.00
3	Consumer Products	350	Strengthening the weak link	5	6.80
3	Consumer Products	352	Reintegration	10	6.10
3	Consumer Products	351	Value chain squeeze	9	5.78
3	Consumer Products	349	Deintegration	8	5.63
3	Manufacturing	351	Value chain squeeze	6	4.67
3	Service	352	Reintegration	8	5.63
3	Textile	353	Downstream	6	6.33
3	Textile	352	Reintegration	7	5.86

Table 11. Contingency table for the strategies for business function "knowledge" (4) for each industry

Function	Industry/Sector	Strategy	Strategy Name	Frequency	Avg Score
4	Chemical	442	Product to customer knowledge	9	5.89
4	Construction	443	Knowledge to product	10	5.90
4	Construction	442	Product to customer knowledge	16	5.69
4	Consumer Products	443	Knowledge to product	14	6.00
4	Consumer Products	442	Product to customer knowledge	10	5.60
4	Consumer Products	441	Operations to knowledge	16	5.38
4	Energy	442	Product to customer knowledge	5	6.00
4	Manufacturing	442	Product to customer knowledge	11	4.45
4	Mining	442	Product to customer knowledge	7	6.00
4	Service	442	Product to customer knowledge	12	5.75
4	Textile	441	Operations to knowledge	7	6.29
4	Textile	442	Product to customer knowledge	14	5.79

Table 12. Contingency table for the strategies for business function "mega" (5) for each industry

Function	Industry/Sector	Strategy	Strategy Name	Frequency	Avg Score
5	Construction	559	Technology shifts the board	7	6.57
5	Construction	561	Back to profit	10	6.50
5	Construction	557	Collapse of the middle	11	5.45
5	Consumer Products	560	De Facto standard	10	5.90
5	Consumer Products	558	Convergence	8	5.63
5	Consumer Products	557	Collapse of the middle	8	5.25
5	Consumer Products	561	Back to profit	9	5.00
5	Mining	559	Technology shifts the board	5	3.40
5	Service	561	Back to profit	7	6.14
5	Service	559	Technology shifts the board	7	5.29
5	Textile	559	Technology shifts the board	5	6.40
5	Textile	560	De Facto standard	5	6.20

Table 13. Contingency table for the strategies for business function "organization" (6) for each industry

Function	Industry/Sector	Strategy	Strategy Name	Frequency	Avg Score
6	Chemical	646	Digital business design	7	5.71
6	Construction	646	Digital business design	7	6.00
6	Construction	645	Corner-stoning	9	5.89
6	Construction	644	Pyramid to network	10	5.30
6	Consumer Products	646	Digital business design	8	6.13
6	Consumer Products	645	Corner-stoning	14	5.43
6	Consumer Products	644	Pyramid to network	9	5.22
6	Consumer Products	643	Skill Shift	10	5.20
6	Manufacturing	646	Digital business design	7	5.29
6	Manufacturing	643	Skill Shift	7	4.57
6	Service	643	Skill Shift	6	6.00
6	Service	646	Digital business design	6	5.50
6	Textile	646	Digital business design	9	5.89
6	Textile	643	Skill Shift	5	5.80

Table 14. Contingency table for the strategies for business function "product" (7) for each industry

Function	Industry/Sector	Strategy	Strategy Name	Frequency	Avg Score
7	Construction	784	Product to pyramid	7	6.00
7	Construction	785	Product to solution	9	5.67
7	Construction	783	Product to brand	5	5.40
7	Consumer Products	785	Product to solution	6	6.17
7	Consumer Products	787	Product to profit multiplier	15	5.87
7	Consumer Products	786	Product to blockbuster	7	5.71
7	Consumer Products	783	Product to brand	8	5.50
7	Consumer Products	784	Product to pyramid	7	4.71
7	Manufacturing	784	Product to pyramid	5	5.20
7	Service	785	Product to solution	6	6.50
7	Service	784	Product to pyramid	6	5.50
7	Textile	785	Product to solution	5	6.80
7	Textile	784	Product to pyramid	11	5.91

APPENDIX G

Some of the function-industry combinations were observed to contain only a single strategy selected at least five times. Statistical analysis was not carried out for comparing the scores of the strategies in these cases. So these observations are not statistically supported, but instead these observations given in Table 15 for these cases simply state that the strategy was the most frequently selected one.

Table 15. Observations without statistical support but with support from business literature regarding the valuation of different strategies

Observations	Fn	Industry	Strategy	Strategy Name	Evidence
19	1	Manufacturing	159	Multiplication	Arçelik (CNBC-e Business 2008g)
20	3	Manufacturing	351	Value chain squeeze	Baytek (Turkishtime 2009)
21	3	Service	352	Reintegration	Alaçatı Beach Resort, Taş Otel, Sardunaki Konak Otel, Lale Lodge (CNBC-e Business 2008b)
22	4	Chemical	442	Product to customer knowledge	Gripin (CNBC-e Business 2008g), Bilim İlaç, Merck Sharp & Dohme, Pfizer (Inc. Türkiye 2009)
23	4	Manufacturing	442	Product to customer knowledge	Baytek (Turkishtime 2009)

(19) Multiplication (159) is the most selected strategy in the "Channel" function for the manufacturing industry, within the selected sample. (20) Value chain squeeze (351) is the most selected strategy in the "Value Chain" function for the manufacturing industry, within the selected sample. (21) Reintegration (352) is the most selected strategy in the "Value Chain" function for service industry, within the selected sample. (22) Product to customer knowledge (442) is the most selected strategy in the "Knowledge" function for chemicals industry, within the selected sample. (23) Product to customer knowledge (442) is the most selected strategy in the "Knowledge" function for the manufacturing industry, within the selected sample.

Chapter 10
Federated Enterprise Architecture:
Meaning, Benefits, and Risks

Edward M. Newman
National Defense University, USA

ABSTRACT

The purpose of the chapter is to provide clarity on what a Federated Enterprise Architecture (FEA) is and what the benefits as well as risks are in contrast to a non-federated enterprise architecture. The chapter draws upon organizational theory, federalist theory, and case studies to explicate what constitutes a federated model and the expected federated EA benefits. There are a number of challenges with the concept of a FEA. Two are focused on in this chapter: the meaning of federated EA and associated benefits and risks. The first is the use of the term "federated," which occurs rather frequently in ICT literature, such as "federated search" or "federated database design," and in the context of IT governance, "federal model" in Drs. Weill and Ross's book IT Governance. The term also appears in the non-ICT context such as "federated insurance." However, the term "federated" is frequently not defined and when defined speaks to a decentralization concept. This distinction is relevant to the understanding and success of a federated EA implementation. In reviewing federalist theory, there is a clear difference between decentralization and federalism. It is argued that the so-called federal or federated "model," as described, is not federated but is a form of decentralization. The second challenge within the EA discipline is the lack of benefits attributed to a FEA. In the few sources that exist for FEA benefits are either not stated or the stated benefits could equally apply to a non-FEA. It is argued that scalability is the singular key benefit that FEA provides over a non-FEA, and the following non-FEA benefits are enhanced: 1) agility and IT innovation, 2) process consolidation and business process standardization and discipline, and 3) interoperability. However, while there are clear benefits to FEA, there are inherent risks.

DOI: 10.4018/978-1-4666-4518-9.ch010

INTRODUCTION

Within the discipline of Enterprise Architecture (EA) there is an emergence of an EA style or archetype – Federated Enterprise Architecture (FEA) or hybrid (Allega, 2009; Burke & Tuft, 2012; DoD CIO, 2007; Drecun, 2003; Fernandez, Zhao, & Wijegunaratne, 2003; Ross & Beath, 2005; Roy, 2006; Wilson, 2012; Zachman, 2006). The advancement of this new form of EA has been argued as a response to today's complex organizational structures such as networked Multinational Corporations (MNC), M-form, and large federal government entities (*i.e.,* Cabinet level Departments) (Allega, 2009; Zachman, 2006) who through competitive pressures and/or scale are attempting to optimize centralization and decentralization structures and management controls to improve organizational performance (Chandler & Mazlish, 2005; Prahalad & Doz, 1981).

There is pragmatic interest in a FEA, based on a recent informal survey taken by Gartner during a Webinar of 74 responses 11% indicated they are pursuing a federated EA approach (Burton, 2010). There is also in interest in FEA by the public sector. The United States' Department of Defense (DoD CIO, 2007) and the Department of Health and Human Services (United States, 2010) are pursuing a FEA and the national governments of Canada (Ministry of Information and Communications Technology, 2006), Jordan (Roy, 2006), and Uganda (Rwangoga & Baryayetunga, 2007) have proposed the use of a FEA as a component of their respective E-Government programs. Curiously enough, at least in these public sector examples, justification for selecting an FEA approach rather than a classical or non-FEA is omitted. Given that the empirical evidence for the benefits of classical EA is wanting (Boucharas, van Steenbergen, Jansen, & Brinkkemper, 2010). What empirical or theoretical evidence is there to support the adoption of an FEA over a non-FEA? Are there additional risks and do they outweigh the benefits? If the scope is extended to include IT Governance as a compliment to enterprise architecture (Sambamurthy & Zmud, 1999; Weill & Ross, 2004; Weill & Ross, 2005; Willson & Pollard, 2009), additional key insight is revealed.

Weill and Ross (2004) in their book *IT Governance* observed, for 74 government and not-for-profit organizations, most used a federal approach (as described similar to federated) for IT Governance input (to include IT principles, IT architecture, IT infrastructure), but not for the corresponding *decision execution*. Furthermore, of the six archetypes identified, they state "The federal model is undoubtedly the most difficult archetype for *decision making* because enterprise leaders have different concerns from business unit leaders" (p. 61). Returning to the private sector, of the top three IT governance performance strategies only two include a federal archetype and only for one of the five decision criteria – Business Application Needs (Weill & Ross, 2004), a narrow application of a federal strategy. In a separate study of 356 multibusiness firms, Tanriverdi (2006), focused on the performance effects of IT synergies and found that of three IT governance modes (centralized, decentralized and hybrid), the hybrid mode was statistically the least effective, supporting prior observations by Brown (1998; 1999). As described, the hybrid IT mode combined central and decentralized decision-making and shares characteristics of a federal model or federated structure. Taken all together, not a resounding affirmation for a FEA approach – what then is the allure?

Where is the empirical or theoretical evidence to support a FEA approach? None in the Government examples above provided evidence and the advocates of an FEA do not provide empirical evidence and theoretical arguments are inconsistent. Perhaps confidence in a federated approach lies in other disciplines. Does the answer reside in the IT discipline, based on some familiarity with federated databases or search design concepts that have demonstrated promise in addressing the challenges of heterogeneous and autonomous environments (Haas, Lin, & Roth, 2002; Hsiao, 1992; Lu & Callan, 2006; Sheth & Larson, 1990)?

However, an understanding of "federated" through the IT lens is misleading as it essentially ignores the confounding organizational social networks behaviors (i.e., people) and, as it turns out, violates key principles of federalism from which federated is derived from. For example, a database system, as a constituent of a federated database system, can unilaterally become unavailable for host of reasons (e.g., upgrades), an aspect of autonomy/decentralization. This behavior, while necessary for IT systems, violates a fundamental principle of federalism. By analogy, sub-nation constituents (i.e., States) cannot unilaterally withdraw from the Union, witness the United States's Civil War. If a constituent can, then we have a confederation, a different governmental polity, and one reason why the founding fathers of the United States Constitution aggressively moved to petition for a federated government (Federalist, 1966).

Alternatively, are the virtues of an FEA derived from organization design literature? It appears few organizations have formally declared themselves federated or are based on a federal model by senior leadership that were not characterized as federal/federated by external reviewers (as examples see O'Donnell, 2009; Stewart & Raman, 2008; Taylor, 1991). Organizational theorist Handy echoes this finding and laments "Few businesses are consciously federal..." (p. 111). And for those examples that were found, as described, while exhibiting characteristics of federalism were missing essential elements. The organizational design literature was overwhelmingly focused on decentralization and horizontal organization mechanisms (Chandler, 1962,1991; Fenton & Pettigrew, 2000; Galbraith, 1995; Mintzberg, 1979; Ostroff, 1999; Pettigrew & Fenton, 2000; Porter, 1985) and while sharing characteristics of federalism does not make it federalism as will be demonstrated. Researchers have explored federated or federative organizational models, primarily from a descriptive perspective (Ghoshal & Bartlett, 1990; Provan, 1983) and management control issues, vis-á-vis the MNC Headquarter/Subsidiary relationship (Andersson, Forsgren,

& Holm, 2007; Yamin & Forsgren, 2006). Few examples were found that explicitly advocated, with supporting rationale, a federated or federerative organizational model as a formal design (Ackoff, 1994; Andersson et al., 2007; Drucker, 1954; Ghoshal & Bartlett, 1990; Handy, 1989; Handy, 1994; Provan, 1983), with Handy (1989, 1994) being the most ardent advocate. In general, it is advanced that a federated/federative organizational design can offer are alternative agility mechanisms, necessary governance controls, and strategies to address today's complex and hyper competitive environments.

Returning briefly to the use (or misuse) of the terms federal and federated in the IT community, which are frequently ambiguous as to the explicit definition of "federation" (see Ariyachandra & Watson, 2006; Baldwin, Mont, Beres, & Shiu, 2010; Denning & Hayes-Roth, 2006; Hasselbring, 1997; On, Vanborre, Stanick, & Williams, 2006; Wilson, 2012; Wilson, Mazzuchi, & Sarkani, 2010) or when defined (see Brown, 1999; Peppard, 1999; Rockart, Earl, & Ross, 1996; Sambamurthy & Zmud, 1999) are not consistent with many of the essential concepts that characterize federalism and federation as defined or characterized in political science literature. Consider two related governmental polities federation and confederation – what are the explicit differences and which one is considered a more viable system? Having an explicit understanding of federalism/federation will be necessary to distinguish a classical EA from a FEA with regard to benefits.

IT and organizational design disciplines, with few exceptions, provided limited empirical evidence for the support of a FEA approach. We are left with, what appears to be, a normative assumption that federalism and federation are universally "good" and in some manner a FEA is imbued with qualities and characteristics associated with the United States as a federation. After all the United States is one of the few long standing continuous governments and is the polity strategy of choice in contemporary times for a variety of reasons (Watts, 1999). Political science, organizational, and economic scholars have described federalism/ federation's effectiveness with regard to flexibility, asymmetric information in decentralized decision-making, social (i.e., knowledge), and economic benefits (Breton, 2000; Elazar, 1973; Federalist, 1966; Handy, 1994; Hayek, 1945; Kincaid, 2001). Therefore, not surprisingly, the most promising evidence for a FEA resides in the political science domain based on the federalism and federated governments. This is not to suggest that federalism and federation are not without faults, quite the contrary (Filippov, Ordeshook, & Shvetsova, 2003; Qian & Weingast, 1997; Rodden, 2004; Wibbels, 2000, 2001) and the pursuit of a federated approach should be mindful of those issues.

To this point, the advancement of a FEA is largely argued as a response to the emergence of complex organizations such as MNC and the presumed advantages of federalism/federation. Complementary view of the EA practitioner also has merit. Although not stated, that classical EA or non-FEA methodologies (as distinct from an EA framework) were not effective, otherwise why introduce a new approach? This strongly suggests the non-FEA methodologies were not either extensible or scalable to address the needs of complex organizations. An alternative approach was needed and, as will be argued under the FEA benefits section, turns out to be a primary driver.

Returning to the utility of an FEA, given the paucity of supporting evidence either theoretical or empirical for a FEA several questions present themselves: Are there indeed benefits (i.e., improved performance) unique or enhanced by a FEA? Can federalism/federation, as a political science construct, be "dropped in" or adopted directly into organizational and EA design without context modification? If the federation is modified, how much can it be modified before it is something other than a federation from a political science perspective? How is a FEA different from a non-FEA? In this chapter we will argue, on primarily on theoretical grounds as well as heuristic grounds, there are essential benefits and characteristics of federated EA that will contribute towards or enable organizational transformation and agility in the information age. However the adoption of a FEA has a number of challenges. This position is derived from political science and organizational design disciplines. Also addressed is the fit or organizational alignment with a FEA approach and leadership's role in embracing a federated EA. This chapter is organized as follows. Through the eyes of political science, we examine pertinent characteristics of federalism/federation for without a firm understanding of political federalism and federation concepts, the discussion on FEA benefits may appear axiomatic. The meaning of federalism/federation is introduced by contrasting three governmental polities to provide a broader context and is followed by a deeper exploration of federalism and federation to include definitions and key elements of the federation structure. With the concepts of federalism/federation succinctly stated, the focus shifts to enterprise architecture and its alignment with organizational structure, in particular MNCs. Not surprisingly MNCs exhibit aspects of a federation and have been characterized as a federal model, but this characterization while understandable is not entirely accurate, as a result a brief overview on MNCs is provided from a federalism/federation perspective. Next from a political science view of federalism and federation, a definition and a notional structure of a FEA is advanced to provide a basis for the discussion of FEA benefits. With the foundation and context established benefits ascribed to EA in general are presented followed by benefits and admonitions unique to a FEA. It will be argued that there is only one principle benefit, scalability, which is unique to a FEA approach. Two additional benefits are also discussed, which are equally characteristic of a non-federated EA approach, but due to federalism/federation concepts, are enhanced or in some other way different. As to the admonitions, a FEA approach, while there is value, has a number of risks which must be considered before being engaged.

FEDERALISM AND FEDERATION AS A POLITICAL SCIENCE CONSTRUCT

Given the ambiguity of the use of the term "federated" and "federation" by the IT community, it would be instructive to clarify the fundamental concepts of federalism and federation. But first an apology to the students of political science, the author has taken liberties with this overview and has necessarily selected aspects of federalism and federation that are germane to the chapter (and presumed tolerance of the reader). Before proceeding with an exploration of federalism and federation definition and characteristics let us first consider why choose federation as an organizational construct for EA development? Why not another governmental system? The next section briefly compares federation and two other governmental polities and serves as a preliminary introduction to the meaning of a federation.

Governmental Polities: Unitary, Confederation, and Federation

While there are many forms of governmental polities, political science scholars generally agree on three broad categories: unitary, confederation, and federation (see Elazar & Merkaz ha-Yerushalmi le-`inyene tsibur u-medinah, 1991; Karmis & Norman, 2005; Watts, 1999). Contrasting these three governmental polities will serve as an initial introduction to the underlying characteristics of a federation. For our purposes, while there are many aspects and important nuances concerning these governmental polities, from a political science perspective, we will consider the following characteristics: 1) administration verse politics, 2) structure and constituents, and 3) decentralization and power distribution.

A unitary polity is a hierarchical model often characterized as a pyramid and can also be viewed as concentric circles or center-periphery model. The efficient administration of the pyramid takes

priority over politics that is to mean the ability to exercise maximum control over the subordinate governments and communities (i.e., subnational entities) (Elazar, 1997). While confederation and federation are focused primarily on politics and secondarily administration (Elazar, 1997). Therefore by design confederation/federation are not necessarily efficient as they are concerned with resolving differences and achieving compromise, which could present challenges when implemented in non-governmental systems seeking to maximize performance or revenue.

The hierarchical organizational structure of a unitary polity contrasts markedly from a "hub & spoke" like-structure of a confederation/federation which, establishes a new central or national governmental entity to focus on the abdicated shared-rule power, while subnational entities retaining all residual powers as self-rule (i.e., sovereign). Furthermore, for a confederation the primary relationship is between the subnational entities and the central government (Watts, 2001). The subnational entities provide funding and determine leadership for the central government. In contrast, a federation's primary relationship is between the central government and the citizen followed by the subnational entities (Karmis & Norman, 2005). The citizen, rather than the subnational entities, is the primary revenue source (i.e., taxes) as well as elects political officials.

With regard to the third characteristic, there are two aspects of centralization/decentralization that concern us: 1) the distribution of power; and 2) the degree of autonomy of subnational entities within the political system. In a unitary system the power and strategic decision-making resides or is owned by the top and may be distributed, that is decentralized, and can be redistributed or withdrawn at the sole discretion of the central government (or nation-state) (Breton, 2000; Elazar, 1997). In a confederation polity subnational entities (e.g., states) confer or delegate power, typically a limited set of competencies, to a central "entity" (i.e., the opposite direction), but do not give up ownership (Watts, 2001) as in a unitary polity . The central "entity" is therefore not sovereign. In contrast to a federation, the subnational entities abdicate a limited set of powers to the newly formed central entity and once powers are distributed within they are owned by the respective governmental entities to include the newly formed central "entity" (Riker, 1964; Watts, 1999). The national-center can enjoy a minimum of one competency or a maximum of all but one (if it were *all* then it would be unitary government), with most federations lying somewhere in between (Riker, 1964, p. 6). For confederation and federation, powers not explicitly stated are considered residual and are retained by the subnational entities.

Preserving subnational identity or sovereignty (i.e., autonomy) is essential. As the power structure suggests in unitary polity, subnational entities have little or no autonomy and certainly cannot unilaterally secede from the central government. On the other hand, subnational entities in a confederation system have few restrictions and enjoy the most autonomy (i.e., weak center). Indeed, to the extent a subnational entity may unilaterally withdraw from agreement or even the confederation, while not suffering significant consequences. Within a federation, subnational entities, once joined as a nation, are less autonomous (i.e., strong center) for two primary reasons. First, they become dependent for services of the competencies or powers abrogated to the national entity. Second, with few exceptions federations, as in unitary governments, do not permit any subnational entity once joined, to unilaterally secede from the federation, or unilaterally infringe on or withdraw support for abdicated powers (King, 1982; Rousseau, 2005).

As an additional comparison a government polity that has been demonstrated to be more durable and sustainable would, given all things equal, be more desirable. The durability and sustainability of a confederation has historically been far less than a federation (Watts, 2005, p. 241). This is due primarily to a lack of leadership by the sub-

national entities. The founding fathers also held this view and argued for a federation through the various Federalist Papers (Federalist, 1966, No. 15-22). As Handy (1994) succinctly states "A confederation is not an organization that is going anywhere, because there is no mechanism or will to decide what the anywhere might be" (p. 112).

In summary, as unity polity does not typically include sovereign organization entities and while able to devolve powers can unilaterally rescind those powers. A confederation is distinguished from federation in the form of the centralization/decentralization and sovereignty – the relationship with the various constituents and the degree of central government empowerment. The confederation has a weak central governmental entity and the federation has a strong central governmental entity. With the general characteristics a federation now clarified a definition is advanced next.

Federalism and Federation: Defined

Broadly speaking, federalism, as an ideology, is an arrangement of subnational entities or communities (e.g., State, ethnic, cultural, or distinct organizational entities) that cooperate within the same political environment to form at least two levels of government, a Nation-state composed of the subnational communities (King, 1982, p. 21). Federation is the structure, an outcome of implementing the ideology. Taking a closer look at the origin of the word federation, Proudhon (2005) reminds us of its Latin roots -

… foedus, genitive foederis, which means pact, contract, treaty, agreement, alliance, and so on, is an agreement by which one or more heads of family, one or more towns, one or more groups of towns or states, assume reciprocal and equal commitments to perform one or more specific tasks, the responsibilities for which rests exclusively with the officers of the federation. (p. 176-177)

Therefore, a formal contract (i.e., constitution) of some nature is essential to the existence of a federation. An organization venturing into a federal arrangement must formalize the agreement in a contract, stipulating roles and responsibilities, resulting in administrative governance processes and organization (e.g., legislative, executive, and judicial). Needless to say, there is an additional "cost of doing business" in a federal arrangement that is greater than in a unitary polity.

We can now turn our attention to the formal definition of federalism. Unfortunately, there are numerous definitions of federalism coinciding with much controversy and ambiguity (Cobb & Bean, 2006; Dye, 1990, pp. 4-5; Filippov et al., 2003, p. 5; Riker, 1975, p. 106; Watts, 1999). No less equivocal, three definitions are presented. The first by Filippov and his colleagues (2003), as their definition supports a framework/process to construct a political federation.

[T]hat a sate is federal if its government structure can be characterized by multiple layers (generally national, regional, and local) such that at each level of the chief policy makers – governors, presidents, prime ministers, legislatures, parliaments, judges – are elected directly by the people they ostensibly serve or (as with judges) appointed by public officials thus directly elected at that level. (p. 9)

The second by Riker (1975), while controversial in his own right (Riker, 1969; Stepan, 2001), was considered to be the leading theorist on federalism.

Federalism is a political organization in which the activities of government are divided between regional governments and a central government in such a way that each kind of government has some activities on which it makes final decisions. (p. 101)

And the third by Watts (1999):

[The] basic notion of involving the combination of shared-rule for some purposes and regional self-rule for others with a single political system so that neither is subordinate to the other.... (p. 7)

Based on these definitions federalism is a political system which involves a multi-structure (i.e., hierarchical or networked), typically two levels, that seeks to balance centralization and decentralization (i.e., interdependence and independence) while preserving the identity and autonomy of each constituent institution through combined components of "shared-rule and regional self-rule." However, Filippov and his colleagues (2003), focus on the aspect of elected officials by citizens, embracing a broader concept of democracy. While Riker (1975, p. 156), on the other hand, is of the resolute position that there is no association between federalism and democracy, instead focuses on delegation of activities and the execution of those activities an aspect of decentralization exhibited by federalism. While Watt (1999) is apparently silent on the role of democracy in federalism, his definition is absent of any reference to "elected" and suggesting democracy is not an essential component.

Implicit in this generalized description, among others, is the notion of being simultaneously big and small (Handy, 1994), and as a result derived benefits from "the coming-together" in forming the federated Nation (Stepan, 1999). Historically, the impetus to form a federation was to forestall incursions by hostile nations/states external and/or internal (i.e., factions) to the political environment (Dikshit, 1975; Federalist, 1966, No. 10; McKay, 1996, pp. 27-35; Riker, 1964; Rousseau, 2005, p. 60). Two secondary drivers include local responsiveness to citizen needs due to distance and geography (Aalesina & Spolaore, 1997; Oates, 1999; Wilkins, 2004), and economic considerations, such as Interstate Commerce (Riker, 1975, p. 110). Since the 1990s the impetus has shifted markedly to focus on macroeconomic considerations (Maxwell School of Citizenship and Public Affairs, 2003; McKay, 1996; Watts, 1999), such as preserving market incentives through inter-governmental competition (Breton, 2000; Qian & Weingast, 1997) or to address the balkanizing-tendencies of regional ethnic or multicultural communities, while still preserving the advantages of being "big" (Karmis & Norman, 2005; Requejo, 2004). With federalism reasonably defined, the institutional elements of a federation are explored next.

Federation: Structural Elements

The definitions of federalism provide insight into the construction of a federation, but do not describe the key structural elements of a federation, which would be the basis for evaluating structural alignment of a FEA or fit with a governmental federation. The common structural elements of a federation model are drawn principally from Watts (1999, p. 7):

- Two or more orders of government (e.g. national and subnational, and federal and state), each acting directly on their citizens. This arrangement can be referred to as an "N+1," where sovereign entities (the "N") agree to join and create a new central entity – the "1" (Filippov et al., 2003, pp. 26-31). The decision to join by a sovereign entity is a non-trivial act. The sovereign entity is a willing participant and contractually bound (i.e., Constitution) and will consciously abdicate selected powers to the federal center and is therefore subordinate to (or dependent on), the federal center for those explicit powers (Auer, 2005). Additionally, once the federation is formed for all practical purposes the prior sovereign entity can

no longer unilaterally secede. While federations have procedures in place to include subnational entities that elect (or forced) to be part of the federation after its initial formation (i.e., adding States). Federations, however, rarely have procedures for secession (King, 1982, pp. 108-120; Watts, 1999, pp. 107-108) and have demonstrated great distain for any subnational entity who attempts to withdraw from the federation (e.g., US Civil War). Generally, all political constituents, national and sub-national, are of equal "power" – no constituents are subordinate, at least at the on-set (there are exceptions see asymmetric federation below). It should be noted, that the creation of the national center by the constituents is not the only approach, the reverse direction can also occur. There are governmental cases where unitary polity, through a process of devolution formed federations such as Belgium and Nigeria, that is "1+N" (Watts, 2005, p. 249). A final point is that citizens are now a critical element of two governments. In federation the citizen plays an essential role in choosing governmental leaders, source of income (i.e., taxes), and consumer of services for both the federal-center and the subnational entities. A challenge for federations is that citizens, who are affiliated with a subnational entity, must now identify with both government entities otherwise balkanizing behaviors emerge favoring subnational entities at the expense of the federal-center.

- The distribution of powers resulting in subnational self-rule (i.e., autonomy) and national shared-rule (Riker, 1975). The distribution of powers to the national-center generally focuses on economies of scale, integration (i.e., interoperability), and general oversight of the nation, the later point is influenced by social contract theory.

Historically, the national powers or competencies include defense, relations and contracts with international entities, and interstate commerce to include such items as a standard currency, weights and measures, and interstate transportation (Mill, 2005, p. 169; Watts, 1999). Riker (1964, Chapter 3) provides a more contemporary list in an attempt to order federations on the continuum from minimum to maximum, identified 17 "areas of action" or powers. Sufficient for our purposes, the additional powers that may concern us include communication, utilities, production and distribution, economic development and knowledge creation (Riker, 1964, p. 83), areas that focus on the general welfare and sustainability of the federation at large. The now subnational entities retain all residual powers (Watts, 1999, p. 39) and in the national-center should not infringe on those powers.

- A "supreme" constitution is created that codifies the power distribution that cannot be unilaterally amended and requires the consent of all sovereign constituents (Auer, 2005; King, 1982; Riker, 1964; Rodden, 2004, p. 490), an expression of social contract theory, is an essential artifact of any federation. The contract rarely is ever complete and is subject to frequent renegotiation (Rodden, 2004, p. 493).

- The formation of an "umpire" or judiciary entity to arbitrate disputes between the governmental entities (Riker, 1975; Rodden, 2004, p. 490; Watts, 1999, p. 39). Auer (2005) observes that, "...every single federal state structure appoints some sort of umpire who is called to resolve federal-type conflicts" (p. 426), as a means to enforce the social contract. In the same manner that a constitutional contract must exist as a feature of a federation, an independent judiciary entity must also exist.

Federation: Relevant Characteristics

Besides Riker's coercive reason for adopting a federation there are other desirable characteristics or benefits that make a federation approach attractive and are relevant to a FEA approach. As will be shown, key federation benefits will ring true in today's business world. Behind the definition of federalism is the need to be responsive to the citizens while at the same time addressing national and international concerns.

Related to the formation of the "national-center" the challenge with being exclusively big, as in a unitary polity, is the general lack of responsiveness to local needs (Dye, 1990) and is attributed to imperfect or asymmetric information. Hayek (1945), in his seminal paper *The Use of Knowledge in Society*, argues if a unitary polity had perfect information, that is, complete knowledge, they would be able to make informed or rational decisions, negating the need to decentralize or federate, that is, to abrogate or delegate the decision to sub-national entities. How would the decision-makers in the unitary polity have knowledge of the relevant information to make a decision and take subsequent action? Information/knowledge would need to be first communicated to a central entity followed by a decision and subsequent action which would involve communicating most if not all the relevant knowledge so that the action would be implemented in a timely manner, correctly, and consistently. A difficult challenge even with today's ICT. The solution requires some form of decentralization. Another facet of asymmetric information is geographical distances and scale. Countries with a large geographic foot print constrained the central government's ability react or provide services due to distance and thus the need to be "small" or decentralized (Aalesina & Spolaore, 1997). That is, in general, even if the national-government had "perfect information" its ability to administratively provide the service would be strained and uneven.

Federations exhibit a high degree of flexibility and adaptability to such an extent that Nations have chosen to adapt these instruments to suit their particular needs, frequently taking great liberties and interpretations with the underlying principles of federalism. Elazar (1991) in an exhaustive review of the world's polities proposed ten federative categories. Within the more narrow interpretation of federalism/federation there are two types. For the first type, there is a general assumption of general homogeneity on many aspects of the subnational entities, such as language, religion, natural resources, and geography (Stepan, 1999; Tocqueville, 2005, p. 161). The United States original thirteen colonies is an example and results in a less complex federal arrangement. However, in contemporary times, Nations are more apt to be heterogeneous, the second type, with regard to language, religion, resources, and minority representation. The subnational entity's federal arrangements in Canada and India are the typical examples. Within Canada, special dispensations have been afforded to Quebec over the other providences (Stepan, 1999; Watts, 1999, p. 67). In the case of India, language and secular differences resulted in unbalanced distribution of powers (Manor, 1998). In these situations, the idiosyncratic accommodations result in more complex federal bargains. As was referenced in the introduction, these two types of federal bargains are referred to as symmetric and asymmetric, with the asymmetric federations the preferred contemporary strategy (Stepan, 1999; Watts, 1999). The additional point to be drawn from this discussion is that the initial structure and subsequent evolution of the federation structure is highly dependent (i.e., path-dependence) on the initial conditions (Breton, 2000). While the general federation model or "genus" is varied and therefore flexible, understanding the initial conditions is essential to selecting a specific type or "species" of federation.

The prior discussion focused to a great extent on the subnational entity's (e.g., States) horizontal representation within the federation. Vertical relationships between the federal-center and sub-national entities are equally dynamic and may evolve over time. For example the evolution of the United States Federation, at inception the federal-center and the States were considered equal, with distinct competencies and referred to as "Dual Federalism." Then through various circumstances this neutral network eventually evolves to a hierarchical network called "Centralized Federalism," where the national entity is more powerful and the subnational entities become administrative agents (Peterson, 2003; Riker, 1964; Watts, 1999).

Continuing with the nature of the vertical/horizontal relationships, an aspect of flexibility and adaptability is scalability. Whether symmetric/asymmetric or dual/centralized there are at least two generalized organizational components - the federal-center and the quasi-autonomous subnational entities. Within each subnational entity there are often additional lower-levels of government (i.e., local government) and while often not formally acknowledged (Gibbins, 2001), adding at least two to three more levels, implicit if not explicit. Upwards, federated Nations can themselves be part of other federations or suprafederations (Watts, 1999). For example, while not strictly a federation, consider the European Union, consisting of several Nations, federated and non-federated (Auer, 2005).

Competition and experimentation, terms more likely associated with Adam Smith and capitalism, are as much a part of federalism/federation (see Dye, 1990). Tiebout (1956) in his seminal paper on local government expenditures, argued that citizens are able "vote with their feet" when selecting a jurisdictional residence based on available public goods and services. Thus jurisdictions, acting as marketplaces, compete amongst themselves for taxpayer dollars and are obliged to offer "better" public goods more efficiently. Breton (2000) argues that the horizontal competition that Tiebout describes is characteristics of any decentralized governmental system and what makes federalism unique is the competition between vertical layers for power or competencies to provide for citizen needs. Regardless of whether the competition is vertical or horizontal, jurisdictions will experiment to create alternative or innovative approaches (Dye, 1990; Foster, 1978; Gray, 1973; Menzel & Feller, 1977; Walker, 1969), to such an extent that subnational entities have been describe as "Laboratories of Democracy" by Louis Brandeis, then Supreme Court Justice (Tarr, 2001). This suggests that a federation approach would at least be benevolent towards innovation from an organizational and EA perspective.

Continuing with the competition theme, powers frequently delegated to the federalist center such as commerce (domestic and international), finance and transportation to: 1) promote inter-regional commerce (Dye, 1990; Riker, 1964) and 2) prevent regional governments from aggrandizing behaviors such as economic rent seeking (Qian & Weingast, 1997), cross-regional and international value-destroying spillovers (Sykes, 1995) and negative externalities (Filippov et al., 2003). An outcome of these powers is the establishment and regulation of standards such as weights, measures, and currency to promote commerce and economic growth (Mill, 2005; Proudhon, 2005). For example, standard coinage establishes, in economic terms, an "Optimum Currency Area" (OCA) which promotes regional economic efficiencies (Mundell, 1961). Notwithstanding the current European Community's (EU) economic problems, the OCA theory was the basis for adopting the Euro as a common currency (Anonymous, 1999). In general, national government technical and product standard setting and regulation are essential for inter-regional and international macroeconomic stability (and market preservation) by reducing barriers and promoting greater efficiencies (e.g., interoperability) (Sykes, 1995). Related to Standards is the establishment and regulation of infrastructure. A contemporary example is India's recent electrical grid power failure where Government has not shown leadership and now

brings doubt as to India's ability to compete in the global economy (Denyer & Lakshmi, 2012). Similarly there are repeated reports in the general news regarding the United States aging infrastructure such as bridges, power grids, and air traffic control. Therefore it is the federalist center's responsibility and desirability for establishing standards and infrastructure for the federation. How well they execute that responsibility is of course the concern.

Two aspects with regard to the prior discussion, a federation in overly simplistic terms is balancing centralization and decentralization structures to address conflicting goals, but is not strictly a centralize/decentralize debate, as unitary governments also struggle with this same challenge (Breton, 2000; Elazar, 1997). The act of determining centralized/decentralized structures is a function of power distributions and is guided by the principle of subsidiarity in federalist models. Subsidiarity is frequently a misunderstood concept, while appearing to be straightforward is rather complex as to its meaning and outcomes (see Bermann, 1994; Handy, 1992). Simply stated subsidiarity directs the distribution of powers at the most local level to be responsive to local needs, which could be interpreted as a delegation action. However, subsidiarity is more than a delegation of authority. Once the authority or power is distributed it cannot be withdrawn unilaterally (Handy, 1999). Further, it preserves "self-determination" or autonomy of the subnational entity among others (Bermann, 1994). Further, the subnational entities while no longer completely sovereign do retain a high-degree of autonomy or quasi-independence (at least at conception) in this decentralized-like arrangement. Therefore decentralization under a federal system is different than decentralization under a unitary system. Regarding the second aspect, flexibility and scalability characteristics of federations align with today's understanding of networks and system-of-systems (i.e., self-organizing systems) that have demonstrated resilience and sustainability in dynamic environments (see Camazine, 2001).

An underlying theme for federalism concerns, to a large extent, is the eternal struggle between centralization and decentralization - the ebb and flow of control and power with respect to balancing global and local needs, but as was demonstrated, is more than a simple debate between centralization and decentralization. This concludes the exploration of the meaning of federalism and federations from a political science perspective. Next, we turn our focus to the applicability and ramifications of applying federalism to organizations and enterprise architecture.

ENTERPRISE ARCHITECTURE ALIGNMENT WITH THE ORGANIZATION'S STRUCTURE

It would be ill advised to have a discussion on enterprise architecture structure and utility, such as our focus on FEA, without addressing its relationship to the firm's structure or organizational alignment. First, researchers have advanced that overall firm performance, private or public, necessitates alignment of the enterprise *structure* (Chandler, 1962; Egelhoff, 1982; Galbraith, 1973, 2000; Porter, 1985). Second, IT strategy and infrastructure should be aligned with the firm's business strategy and operations infrastructure to improve performance (Henderson & Venkatraman, 1993; Venkatraman, Henderson, & Oldach, 1993). While the empirical evidence supporting this last assertion has been varied (see Markus, Kien Sia, & Soh, 2012), research on MNCs has generally supported the IT-Business alignment (Aral & Weill, 2007; Kearns & Sabherwal, 2006; Lai, 2008; Markus et al., 2012; Tanriverdi, 2006). Third, a complementary topic of research has focused on what is the best way to organize and align the structure of the IS organization to improve firm performance. While there is debate as to the "best structure," there is general agreement that the IS

function, must be aligned with the organization's structure (Brown & Magill, 1994; Brown, 1999; Hodgkinson, 1998; Agarwal & Sambamurthy, 2002; Von Simson, 1990). Forth, with regard to enterprise architecture alignment, empirical research appears to be wanting with the following notable exception. Ross and her colleagues (2006), based on a review of over 200 businesses, observed that key components of the enterprise architecture are different for each target organizational business model, suggesting that the enterprise architecture aligns with the structure associated with a specific target end-state. Fifth, Ross and her colleagues further state for complex organizations, expect enterprise architectures at different levels of maturity for each business unit as they have different business objectives, (2006, pp. 88-89), supporting the notion of a multi-business unit firm consisting each having an embedded enterprise architecture that must all interoperate. This observation is advanced by other researchers as a federated enterprise architecture (Burke & Burton, 2011; Burke & Tuft, 2012; Martin, 2012; Zachman, 2006). Based on the forgoing five arguments, it is reasonable to conclude that the EA approach and structure should exhibit a high-degree of fidelity to the organization's desired end-state structure. As was stated previously, for any Nation adopting a federal model, the initial conditions strongly influence or determine the type of federal model to select. Therefore, a FEA (as well as other enterprise architecture types) cannot be used by just any organizational structure and it follows that the benefits attributable to a FEA are restricted to a specific class of organizational structure. That is, a FEA will inherent benefits typically attributed to a non-FEA, but will also have additional unique benefits that emerge based on a complementary organizational structure.

As to the type of organizational structure that a FEA would best support or "fit," should come as no surprise. We return to IS management/function and IT systems/infrastructure organizational structure alignment discussion. In a review of this literature Brown (1999) states

In particular, many multidivisional companies have adopted a federal design for the IS organization in which IT infrastructure responsibilities are centralized in order to respond to enterprise-level pressures for connectivity and economies of scale, but systems development responsibilities are decentralized to business units in order to respond to division-level pressures for autonomy over strategic IS resources. (p. 422)

Her assertion regarding multidivisional companies and federal-like model for either the IS function or IT systems/infrastructure is supported by other researchers (Hodgkinson, 1998; Karimi & Konsynski, 1991; Lai & Wong, 2003; Lai, 2008; Martin, 2012; Peppard, 1999; Tanriverdi, 2006) and includes global firms, multi-business-unit firms which are characterized generally as MNCs. The next section will explore briefly MNC characteristics.

MULTINATIONAL CORPORATIONS: OVERVIEW

In today's world, corporations with a global presence are influenced or constrained by internal and external factors such as knowledge, economic, political, environmental, technology, geographical distance, and culture. These same factors are also many of the major driving forces for *global integration* which is strongly influenced by economies of scale and *local responsiveness,* the specialization or adaptation to local needs and provision of services and goods to local markets (Prahalad & Doz, 1987). The tension created by global/local pressures influence, if not drive, corporate strategies and organizational design with regard to centralization/decentralization decisions. Traditional organizational structures such as bureaucratic, autocratic (i.e., unitary), and multidivisional

(M-form) organizational structures are not able to scale, learn, and adapt in response to threats/ opportunities resulting from information asymmetry (Galbraith, 1973) and have given way to the MNC structures (Chandler & Mazlish, 2005; Prahalad & Doz, 1987). MNCs are composed of decentralized quasi-autonomous sub-business units such as subsidiaries, strategic business units, divisions and affiliates (and are referred to broadly as subsidiaries in this chapter) and the corporate parent (Chandler, 1962; Johnston & Menguc, 2007), analogous to the federation model "N+1." While corporations typically form top down (unusual for a federal model, but permissible), that is the parent company exists first and acquires/creates or divests subsidiaries rather than pre-subsidiaries agreeing to form as one corporation and create the parent entity. The parent-subsidiary should not be viewed simply as a dyadic structure, as MNCs inter- and intra-firm relationships more closely resemble a network (Bartlett & Ghoshal, 1993; Gooderham & Ulset, 2002; Ruigrok, Achtenhagen, Wagner, & Rüegg-Stürm, 2000). The nature of the form, process, and role of MNC is dynamic, responding and adapting to global and local conditions. As a result MNCs are becoming flatter, more agile, and highly information intensive (Fenton & Pettigrew, 2000; Ghoshal & Bartlett, 1990; Ruigrok et al., 2000), and are viewed as "social communities that serve as efficient mechanisms for the creation and transformation of knowledge into economically rewarded products and services." (Kogut & Zander, 1993, p. 627). To such an extent they have been referred to as knowledge-based organizations (Kogut & Zander, 1993, 2003), where competitive advantage of MNC places importance on the ability of subsidiaries to incorporate new knowledge from their respective environments (Ghoshal & Bartlett, 1990). This arrangement results in increased regionalized authority, responsiveness, adaptation, learning, and innovation, strengthening the competitive advantages and performances of subsidiaries

(Galbraith, 1995; Pettigrew & Fenton, 2000; Prahalad & Doz, 1987) and ultimately the competitive strength of the whole corporation.

Returning briefly to the use of the term federated to describe the structure of MNCs, while structurally exhibiting federation characteristics it is not technically federated. Why? Based on the prior description of political federation, at least two essential components are absent: 1) the contract and 2) the independent judicial entity. A contract is a primary characteristic of firms or parties entering into either an equity or non-equity *alliance* and adjudicated through an array of governance mechanisms (Ariño & Reuer, 2004; Reuer & Ariño, 2007; Slowinski & Sagal, 2003), which may include the legal system, the ultimate referee. In contrast, MNCs appear not to enter into formal contact relations between the parent and subsidiaries. A review of literature by leading organizational leaders found no reference to the term contract (see Chandler, 1962; Chandler & Mazlish, 2005; Galbraith, 1973, 2000; Mintzberg, 1979; Prahalad & Doz, 1987), instead governance was frequently viewed in the broad context of control and managed through a set of conflict resolution tools consisting of task forces or committees, procedures, and polices (Galbraith, 2000; Prahalad & Doz, 1987), but are nonetheless, not a formal "supreme" contract. Furthermore, the judiciary entity, represented by committees, does not meet the requirement for an independent arbitrating organization. Therefore, MNCs while having some characteristics of a federation are not technically federated - they are something else. The choice of the term *federative* by Andersson (2007) to describe MNCs is perhaps a more accurate connotation.

In the preceding sections the definition and structure of a federation in political science terms was explored and while federalism and federation are concerned with the national economies of scale and local responsiveness or centralization vs.

decentralization of powers, so are other political models such as unitary and confederation. How the powers are distributed through the principle of subsidiarity and key features such as the "supreme" contract and an independent judiciary distinguish centralization/decentralization under federation from those other political forms. This point was belabored to at least inform, if not correct the misuse of the term federated in the IT community. Characteristics of MNCs were then examined as they are frequently viewed as embracing a federated model and therefore, are likely candidates for the use of FEA. This concludes the background discussion of this chapter and we are now prepared to explore the structure and benefits of a FEA.

FEDERATED ENTERPRISE ARCHITECTURE: STRUCTURE

Now that we have an understanding of political federalism and federation a reasonable question to ask is how is a FEA structurally different from a non-FEA or classical EA? Even though the discipline of EA has been with us for a couple of decades, there is still no singular standard for an EA definition (Kappelman, McGinnis, Pettite, & Sidorova, 2008; Wilson, 2012) or structure. From a strict frameworks perspective two of the more popular frameworks are the Zachman (Zachman, 1987), and the United States Department of Defense Architecture Framework (DoDAF) (United States Department of Defense, 2012). From a methodology perspective, there is the TOGAF (Open Group, 2011) and Enterprise Architecture Planning (EAP) (Spewak & Hill, 1993). In a review of these frameworks and methodologies the generally include the following:

- The scope is the organizations enterprise rather than a subset such as a business area, line of business or segment. The scope generally focuses on organizations with one primary mission or business area. It is important to note that many of these frameworks/methodologies have their roots in the 1980s when business were generally smaller, less complex, and few had an international footprint as compared today's corporations.

- An organization has one EA and one implementation/transition plan (vis-à-vis the roots).
- The architecture is not exclusive to IT and includes at least business, data, applications, technology, technical standards and principles.
- The EA typically includes a governance mechanism.

Various FEA structures have been advanced by EA researchers and practitioners, two will be briefly discussed. Zachman (2006) advances a structure based on optimizing "common" functions and distinguishes functions that are not common in complex organizations such as the previously described MNCs. Although primarily focused on the challenge of identifying common or "sameness" clusters across business units he depicts a federated architecture where each business unit has an EA as does the headquarters (Zachman, 2006). His focus then is to integrate and/or standardize common areas or functions across the business units. This certainly addresses the identification of "powers" in a federation, but does not address the principle subsidiarity that is, the abreaction of common functions to headquarters. Zachman wisely speaks to the importance of governance as the means for consistency within an FEA, but not in terms of federalism/federation – as there is no discussion of a "contract" or a judiciary entity. Further, a discussion on technical standards that promote interoperability, while perhaps implied is the lower level primitives, is absent. However, by

implementing the Zachman framework across all organizational entities as a means to describe and analysis explicitly establishes a "common" standard or language, a key component of a symmetric federation. Zachman's approach for FEA does exhibit characteristics of federalism/federation, however essential components are absent.

Gartner, like Zachman, also advocates the use of a FEA for complex organizations, such as MNC who are seeking advantages of economies of scale while also remaining agile – that is preserving business unit[1] or subsidiary autonomy (Burke & Tuft, 2012). Gartner advances a FEA structure that is hierarchical in nature consisting of three levels of processes: Core, Common, and Distinct. Core and Common processes are managed under the stewardship of corporate leadership and Distinct remain under the leadership of the business unit. Functions under Core and Common are based on interoperability, replication, and shared. While Distinct functions are autonomous. From a federalism/federation perspective this categorization supports both the identification of "powers" and the distribution of those powers (i.e., principle of subsidiarity). Each level consists of one or more architectures and governance is required for all architectures (Burke, 2011). However, the governance discussion does not address federalism/federation concepts such as contract or a judiciary entity and unlike, the Zachman approach, does not address a common language through standard EA framework.

The primary difference between the FEA and non-FEA is that the FEA includes multiple EA's structured loosely on a hierarchy with the corporate parent having functions and capabilities that have a high commonality across the various business units, while the business units retain some degree of autonomy over unique functions. Based on the exploration of federalism/federation from a political science perspective these FEAs need to include the concept of a contract, judiciary entity, standard methods as a common language, and technical standards to promote interoperability. This overview should be sufficient to permit a discussion on the benefits of a FEA.

FEDERATED ENTERPRISE ARCHITECTURE: BENEFITS AND RISKS

Armed with an understanding of political federalism and federation, and a rudimentary understanding of a FEA structure, we are now ready to explore the benefits of a FEA. Our primary focus is on benefits unique to and, in some manner, enhanced by a FEA structure or approach, while also considering competitive adage of the organization as viewed from an EA perspective. A review of benefits ascribed to a non-FEA or classical EA would provide reference point. Boucharas et al. (2010) conducted an exhaustive and systematic review of EA benefits studies and found over 100 EA benefits grouped under four broad categories: Learning & Growth, Internal, Financial, and Customer. A rather daunting number and even summary review would be cumbersome. Therefore, in the interest of brevity we leave it to the reader to review this noteworthy report and instead speak conditionally to benefit differences. Furthermore, given the few FEA studies available and absents of references to FEA in the Boucharas research, it is assumed the benefits identified are applicable only to non-FEA or classical EAs.

The benefits attributable to a FEA, as a function of the federation or federative structures of MNCs and perhaps other M-form structures are necessarily a small set. The primary benefit that is unique to an FEA is scalability, that can accommodate multiple or networked EAs that a non-federated or classical EA frameworks and methodologies does not acknowledge. And through the lens of federalism/federation, we have identified five additional classical EA benefits in three groups: 1) Agility and IT Innovation, 2) Process Consolidation and Business Process Standardization and Discipline,

and 3) IS/IT Interoperability, which are in some manner enhanced in a FEA design.

Scalability – Federation of EAs and Federation of Federations. This is the one unique benefit that can be derived from a FEA approach. A review of the 100 plus benefits attributed to an EA by Boucharas and his colleagues (2010) did not address scalability. The support for this assertion will first focus on the challenges with the classical EA approaches from a methodology perspective and then consider the scalability advantages of a FEA from an organizational perspective.

Complex organizations such as MNCs or other M-forms to include government cabinet-level agencies that are pursuing an EA strategy will find the implementation of a non-FEA approach to be especially challenging due to fundamental issues with classical EA methodologies, and practicalities of scalability and associated pre-existing conditions. The discussion on EA methodology at this juncture is likely to be surprising. However the original EA methodologies had a fundamental problem when applied in MNC environments that has not been previously acknowledged and has bearing on contemporary EA methodologies. Enterprise architecture structure, in classical methodologies and frameworks depict the enterprise architecture as a unified object, that is there is only one monolithic EA for a firm (Bernard, 2004; Cook, 1996; Martin, 1989; Spewak & Hill, 1993; Zachman, 1987). This was due to the relatively small size of the firms of the day, which were mostly single-missioned and non-global. The three primary founding EA methodologies, Information Engineering (Martin, 1990), Enterprise Architecture Planning (Spewak & Hill, 1993) and Texas Instruments Information Engineering Facility (IEF) are all data-driven in mathematical terms. This means all three had in common, literally, a pivotal diagram the CRUD (i.e., Create, Read, Update, and Delete) matrix and an associated affinity/cluster analysis to derive the data architecture, target application architecture, and "idealized" implementation plan (see Martin, 1990, pp. 173-181; Spewak & Hill, 1993, pp. 242-248). If an architect applied these classic EA methodologies to a MNC or M-form organization he/she would violate the underlying implied assumption (i.e, single missioned) and experience difficulties – primarily the CRUD matrix would be invalid. The data-driven approach is only applicable to single value-chain or single-missioned organization. While these methodologies have fallen into disuse by EA practitioners the CRUD matrix is still present in contemporary EA methodologies, but stands alone, its pivotal role long since forgotten (for example see Open Group, 2011; United States, 2012).

In addition to the methodology problem, there are practical/feasibility constraints with the classical approaches. First, completing the CRUD matrix requires a total view of the firm, highly impractical for complex organizations such as MNCs both in time and resources. To illustrate this point, conservative estimates will be used, assume that our hypothetical MNC consists of nine subsidiaries or agencies (many MNCs and U.S. cabinet-level Departments have twenty or more subsidiaries), resulting in a total of ten component organizations (9 subsidiaries + 1 headquarters); the development of an EA takes one year; and the cost is one million dollars (many cost more). The last two assumptions are based on available data from U.S. federal government EA implementations (United States. General Accounting Office, 2003, Appendix II). In the two extremes either ten million dollars is required to complete the EA in one year or at one million per year for ten years. In the first extreme a funding commitment of this magnitude is typically impractical (but possible). In the other extreme by the time the EA was developed content developed in first phases will have likely have changed and general interest will have been lost (Theuerkorn, 2004). Second, given that EA has been advanced as a means to improve firm performance since the 1980s it should be expected that components of complex organiza-

tions have implemented EAs and are at various maturity stages (Martin, 2012; Ross et al., 2006, pp. 88-89). Reversing-out these local EAs in the pursuit of a monolithic EA would be impractical technically and politically. As a result of these challenges a new EA methodology as well as a supporting EA framework is necessary for MNC's and other types of M-Form organizational structures found in contemporary firms with national and international footprints – the FEA.

As political federations are able to integrate subnational entities and facilitate multiple federations, an EA based on federalism/federation, or a FEA, is theoretically designed to scale, accommodating multiple EAs within an enterprise and multiple-levels of FEAs (see prior discussion on FEA structure). The scalability permits subsidiaries to tailor EA to local conditions (the decentralized aspect) while still interoperating within the larger global firm. FEAs by design can accommodate pre-existing EAs as well as EAs acquired through mergers (this not to suggest this is a straightforward process). Furthermore, FEA enhances scalability, in part, through the flexibility and adaptability of symmetric and asymmetric structures described previously under political federations. From an organizational perspective the scaling of multiple EAs must consider at least the subsidiary "size" (e.g., revenue or employees), mission disparity relative to the enterprise as a whole, and/or geographical dispersion. Consider the U.S. Department of Treasury consisting of twelve bureaus (i.e., subsidiaries), in 2009 had a discretionary budget authority of $12.5B, with one bureau, the Internal Revenue Service (IRS), controlling 91% of the total discretionary budget (United States, 2008). Likewise, asymmetries have been observed in subsidiaries of MNC (Ghoshal & Bartlett, 1990; Johnston & Menguc, 2007). In either case a symmetric FEA approach where all subsidiaries have the exact same representation would seem unlikely, however an asymmetric FEA, that in some manner accommodates the major peculiarities of the subsidiaries, would seem likely when considering successful strategies adopted by other asymmetric federated nations (Stepan, 1999; Watts, 1999). In theory a FEA is sufficiently flexible to scale regardless of whether the subsidiaries of an enterprise are symmetric or asymmetric form or multiple layers. While the prior argument advances scalability as a key benefit of a FEA, the argument should not be misconstrued to suggest developing a FEA is by any means straightforward. Complex problems found in MNCs require complex strategies.

Classical EA Benefits Enhanced or Altered by a FEA Approach

Agility – Organization and Enterprise Architecture and IT Innovation – Experimentation and Learning. Agility is an essential, if not the foundational, characteristic of today's hyper competitive global organizations who are responding to regional market-based threats and opportunities. The MNC structure is a means to achieving agility and is largely in response to balancing centralization/ decentralization needs. A FEA approach can enhance organizational agility in at least two ways. First, organizational agility is sustained through innovation and subsequent adaption and diffusion – organizational learning (Han et al., 2012; Wilson & Doz, 2011). Innovation occurs through experimentation. As explored previously, a federated design, promotes experimentation on multiple dimensions. The quasi-autonomy afforded by FEA would support subsidiary experimentation in functions/processes that are unique or "Distinct," competing to develop new novel and innovative strategies, and share those findings with the other subsidiaries, while not adversely impacting the enterprise strategic direction (Adler & Hashai, 2007; Gupta & Govindarajan, 2000). By extension, subsidiaries would also experiment with IT innovation (Kien, Soh, & Weil, 2010; Swanson, 2012). The semi-autonomous subsidiaries would be permitted to experiment with new and novel

uses of IT and be able to diffuse successes more readily through the federated structure. This would be in contrast to the top-down driven diffusion in a non-FEA. Second, a FEA and its approach accelerate organizational agility through process standardization and consolidation and semi-autonomous of process unique to a subsidiary or business unit. This enhancement is address under the next benefit group.

Process consolidation and business process standardization and discipline – strategic effectiveness and effectiveness, and agility have been linked with business process standardization from an enterprise perspective (Davenport, 2005; Hammer & Stanton, 1999; Hammer, 2007; Malnight, 2001). Ross (2006) observed that organizational strategic agility is not achieved until the fourth and final EA maturity phase – Business Modularity. Each phase may take three to five years, with an optimistic total time span of twelve years, perhaps beyond the discipline of many organizations. Attempts to reduce the total duration by leap-frogging a phase have proven ineffective (Curtis, Hefley, & Miller, 2001; Ross et al., 2006; Shpilberg, Berez, Puryear, & Shah, 2007). The Business Modularity phase involves the modularization of business process and the separation of core-enterprise processes and business unit processes identified in the prior third phase. The identification and separation for core-enterprises aligns exactly with federation's separation of powers. As was discussed previously fundamental to a governmental federation is the distribution of powers. Likewise, a FEA also includes a "power" identification and separation activity typically of processes (Burke & Tuft, 2012; Zachman, 2006) and therefore enhances this non-FEA benefit.

To explore this benefit further from an EA practitioner perspective, IT capabilities and processes are strategically aligned in large-scale organizations, achieving economies of scale and business and IT alignment. EA is a comprehensive and systematic mechanism and/or approach to achieve organization alignment and steer's organizational transformation (Gregor, Hart, & Martin, 2007; Hoogervorst, 2011; Ross et al., 2006; United States Government Accountability Office, 2010). A challenge for EA practitioners is few large-complex organizations (e.g., Cabinet-level agencies or MNC) have formally acknowledge the federated model, but nonetheless exhibit federative characteristics (Andersson et al., 2007; Ghoshal & Bartlett, 1990). The assumption is, at least the near-term, implementing major changes in process, competency, or organization structure (i.e., the power redistribution) is not realistic due to the complex relationships and often independent subsidiaries. This dilemma can be turned into an opportunity for the practitioner. In a federated model, EA practitioners identify firm-wide business processes that are frequently occurring. The horizontal functions in Porter's Value Chain (Porter, 1985) are typical candidates such as human resources, finance, and IT infrastructure (i.e., backbone networks). The headquarters EA practitioner achieves in one strategy, a reduction of EA scope risk by focusing only on the functions and infrastructure essential to firm interoperability and opportunities for economies of scale. The other business functions and capabilities are deferred or are addressed by the respective subsidiaries. While non-federated and federated EAs, certainly share these aspects, they are enhanced under a FEA.

Interoperability – Standards. In political federalism/federation, a key activity is to promote interstate commerce. This is accomplished by establishing a limited set of key "standards" such as currency, weights, and measures (Mill, 2005; Watts, 1999). Today's national governments value the economic importance of standards to facilitate *global* integrated goods markets (Sykes, 1995), and the ability to promote IT and communications interoperability (Garcia, 1993; Open ePolicy Group, Harvard Law School, & Berkman Center for Internet and Society, 2005). Technical and product standards figure prominently in businesses seeking a competitive advantage by either establishing a standard or to improve

network coordination (Besen & Farrell, 1994; Carlton & Klamer, 1983; Shapiro & Varian, 1999). Similarly EA practitioners rely on technical standards to promote interoperability, decrease platform diversity, and improve IT management (Boh & Yellin, 2006). Furthermore, with respect to the emergent qualities of business agility, EA practitioners can leverage technical standards to improve Information Systems Development (ISD) to reduce the restraining effects of "stable system drag" (Truex, Baskerville, & Kelin, 1999), as one example. Therefore an EA, federated or not, without a standards component, is woefully incomplete. These benefits and issues with standards should not be a revelation to experienced EA practitioners. What the practitioner may not be aware of, are benefits derived from a FEA model that could enhance the organization's ability to implement and manage standards.

While all components of the enterprise should embrace standards as part of the corporate DNA, in a federated model the headquarters would primarily (but not exclusively) be concerned with the technical standards that promote enterprise-wide interoperability. This constrained or prioritized focus provides two benefits to the EA practitioner (in addition to interoperability). First, "simplified" management, not that standards management is anything but simple (Nielsen, 1996), headquarters would focus limited resources on a reduced set of standards associated with firm-wide interoperability. There are not "hundreds" of standards. What is often not fully appreciated is that the adoption of just one standard can have profound cascading economic and coordination effects. For example, in the 1800s, railroad gauges (the width of the track) were diverse - freight had to be off-loaded and re-loaded between rail-carriers - slowing delivery and introduced additional costs, in effect restraining interstate commerce and domestic growth (Cook, 1996). This is reminiscent of the nascent Internet, characterized by an array of gateways to translate the various communication protocols (recall GOSIP) – today TCP/IP is essentially the only game in town, our attention can now focus on more important topics such as resolving the issues surrounding semantic Web. Consequently, only a limited number of standards are essential to promote and sustain interoperability. And headquarters would not necessarily be concerned with the standards selection activities of the subsidiaries (except when some subsidiary standard exhibits undesirable behaviors). As a result standards management is simplified from a numbers perspective and scope. Likewise, a subsidiary's standards management would be simplified, as a subsidiary would be obligated, vis-à-vis "the common language," to abide by the firm-wide standards. Subsidiaries now know where the "water-line" resides and are able to select technical standards, without being required to consult or obtain approval from the enterprise-center, that are harmonious, at least benign, with the firm-wide standards and do not harbor any negative network externalities (e.g., incompatible communications of first responders). Decentralized standard decision-making simplifies and expedites the management and coordination processes.

The second aspect of this benefit is experimentation with emerging standards. To a great extent, emerging standards are identified and adopted through subsidiary experimentation to solve local opportunities, providing a broader spectrum of standard evaluations, than the enterprise-center would necessarily be able or inclined to – innovation and agility. Local standards exhibiting characteristics that would enhance enterprise performance would then, through the formal adoption process, be promoted to enterprise-wide standards.

FEA Risks

While there are distinct benefits to an FEA and its approach, it is not without risks that the EA practitioner must be mindful of. First and foremost, as was discussed previously federalism/federa-

tion as governmental construct is "messy." It is inherently focused on compromise and through the principle of subsidiary releases control by the corporate parent. In a for-profit situation to the degree this can be tolerated is questionable.

There is sufficient evidence that an EA structure (and implied the supporting EA methodology) should alignment with the organizational structure (Ross et al., 2006). However, as was discussed few complex organizations have formally declared themselves as federated (Handy, 1994, p. 111). This situation presents at least N challenges. While the FEA facilities the identification and selection of processes/functions (such as common, core, and distinct). This separation and redistribution of processes/functions would seem especially difficult if the organization "business process/function" managers and leadership have not bought into this approach.

The second concern is related to governance. Weill (2004) and Tranriverdi (2006) both observed major challenges with a federal model for governance. The author advances that the challenges are a result of an incomplete implementation of a federalism due to an incomplete understanding of federalism and suggest at least two mechanism are absent: 1) the "contract" that stipulates the power distribution of processes/functions and 2) an independent judiciary entity. A FEA structure and approach must include these two critical components of a governance process.

The third concern is related to the "common" language that is generally necessary in a federation. A uniform EA methodology and supporting methods is necessary to identify the business processes and functions (Zachman, 2006). This specifically focused on preexisting EAs by the federation constituency who may have both different EA maturity levels, (Ross et al., 2006, p. 88-89) and different approaches (i.e., TOGAF vs. Zachman) or methods. Backing these preexisting EAs out will be challenging.

CONCLUSION

Through the concepts of federalism such as subsidiarity and the distinction of shared-rule and regional self-rule, the FEA, while including the benefits attributed to a non-federated EA, is primarily on theoretical grounds, distinguished by the primary benefit *scalability* to inherently support multiple EAs both horizontally and vertically, and the two enhanced non-federated EA benefits *agility* and *interoperability*.

A FEA is not a solution for most organizations and its adoption should not be taken in a cavalier manner. First, a FEA is not the substitute for poor leadership in resolving chronic inter-organizational conflicts or apparent "uniqueness" of mission or infrastructure. Second, the identification and execution of competencies or organizational responsibilities (i.e., decision-rights) is difficult to implement as there are both vertical and horizontal considerations that must be formalized (i.e., the constitution). Third, arbitration of infringements of competencies necessitates a strong governance mechanism and should be mediated through a neutral third party adding additional transaction costs. Fourth, the necessary alignment with the organizational structure represents a critical challenge for EA practitioners and the success of the FEA endeavor. The success rate is likely to be low. However, given that most EA initiatives fail and that the classical EA approaches are not appropriate for MNCs, there appears to be little recourse.

With regards to the necessity of the last two points in forming a FEA and returning to the opening remarks regarding the *ineffectiveness* of a federation approach, attributed to ambiguity regarding decision rights, by Weill and Ross (2004) and Tanriverdi (2006). The supporting discussions suggest that the "power redistribution" was not formally documented in a contract, resulting in considerably more ambiguity then there would have been otherwise and that the use of the term federated or federation is incomplete at best and worse a substitute for decentralization without leadership. As Handy (1989, p. 125) cautions, "Unfortunately, federalism misunderstood can be worse than no federalism. Federalism misunderstood becomes inefficient decentralization...." That is, there is much more to a federation then just accommodating autonomy and decentralization!

REFERENCES

Aalesina, A., & Spolaore, E. (1997). On the number and size of nations. *The Quarterly Journal of Economics*, *112*(4), 1027–1056. doi:10.1162/003355300555411.

Ackoff, R. L. (1994). *The democratic corporation: A radical prescription for recreating corporate America and rediscovering success*. New York: Oxford University Press.

Adler, N., & Hashai, N. (2007). Knowledge flows and the modeling of the multinational enterprise. *Journal of International Business Studies*, *38*(4), 639–657. doi:10.1057/palgrave.jibs.8400284.

Agarwal, R., & Sambamurthy, V. (2002). Principles and models for organizing the IT function. *MIS Quarterly Executive*, *1*(1), 1–16.

Allega, P. (2009). *Defining the span of control for enterprise architecture. No. G00172267*. Gartner.

Andersson, U., Forsgren, M., & Holm, U. (2007). Balancing subsidiary influence in the federative MNC: A business network view. *Journal of International Business Studies*, *38*(5), 802–818. doi:10.1057/palgrave.jibs.8400292.

Anonymous. (1999). Finance and economics: Economics focus: Man of the hour. *The Economist, 353*, 82.

Aral, S., & Weill, P. (2007). IT assets, organizational capabilities, and firm performance: How resource allocations and organizational differences explain performance variation. *Organization Science, 18*(5), 763–780. doi:10.1287/orsc.1070.0306.

Ariño, A., & Reuer, J. J. (2004). Designing and renegotiating strategic alliance contracts. *The Academy of Management Executive, 18*(3), 37–48. doi:10.5465/AME.2004.14776166.

Ariyachandra, T., & Watson, H. J. (2006). Which data warehouse architecture is most successful? *Business Intelligence Journal, 11*(1), 4–6.

Auer, A. (2005). The constitutional scheme of federalism. *Journal of European Public Policy, 12*(3), 419–431. doi:10.1080/13501760500091166.

Baldwin, A., Mont, M. C., Beres, Y., & Shiu, S. (2010). Assurance for federated identity management. *Journal of Computer Security, 18*(4), 519–550.

Bartlett, C. A., & Ghoshal, S. (1993). Beyond the m-form: Toward a managerial theory of the firm. *Strategic Management Journal, 14*, 23–46. doi:10.1002/smj.4250141005.

Bermann, G. A. (1994). Taking subsidiarity seriously: Federalism in the European community and the United States. *Columbia Law Review, 94*(2), 331–457. doi:10.2307/1123200.

Bernard, S. A. (2004). *An introduction to enterprise architecture* (1st ed.). Bloomington, IN: Authorhouse.

Besen, S. M., & Farrell, J. (1994). Choosing how to compete: Strategies and tactics in standardization. *The Journal of Economic Perspectives, 8*(2), 117–131. doi:10.1257/jep.8.2.117.

Boh, W. F., & Yellin, D. (2006). Using enterprise architecture standards in managing information technology. *Journal of Management Information Systems, 23*(3), 163. doi:10.2753/MIS0742-1222230307.

Boucharas, V., Van Steenbergen, M. E., Jansen, R. L., & Brinkkemper, S. (2010). *The contribution of enterprise architecture to the achievement of organizational goals: Establishing the enterprise architecture benefits framework*. No. Technical Report UU-CS-2010-014. Utrecht, The Netherlands: Department of Information and Computing Sciences, Utrecht University.

Breton, A. (2000). Federalism and decentralization: Ownership rights and the superiority of federalism. *Publius, 30*(2), 1–16. doi:10.1093/oxfordjournals.pubjof.a030076.

Brown, C. V. (1999). Horizontal mechanisms under differing IS organization contexts. *Management Information Systems Quarterly, 23*(3), 421–454. doi:10.2307/249470.

Brown, C. V., & Magill, S. L. (1994). Alignment of the IS functions with the enterprise: Toward a model of antecedents. *Management Information Systems Quarterly, 18*(4), 371–403. doi:10.2307/249521.

Brown, C. V., & Magill, S. L. (1998). Reconceptualizing the context-design issue for the information systems function. *Organization Science, 9*(2), 176–194. doi:10.1287/orsc.9.2.176.

Burke, B. (2011). *Is a federated architecture the right approach? No. G00219399*. Gartner.

Burke, B., & Burton, B. (2011). *What is the right approach to developing an enterprise architecture? No. G00219400*. Gartner.

Burke, B., & Tuft, B. (2012). *Federated architecture diagnostic: Understanding the four levels of enterprise architecture consolidation. No. G00234790*. Gartner.

Burton, B. (2010). *Survey results: Which EA approach are organizations using? No. G00174847.* Gartner.

Camazine, S. (2001). *Self-organization in biological systems.* Princeton, NJ: Princeton University Press.

Carlton, D. W., & Klamer, J. M. (1983). The need for coordination among firms, with special reference to network industries. *The University of Chicago Law Review. University of Chicago. Law School, 50*(2), 446–466. doi:10.2307/1599497.

Chandler, A. D. (1962). *Strategy and structure.* Cambridge, MA: MIT Press.

Chandler, A. D. (1991). The functions of the HQ unit in the multibusiness firm. *Strategic Management Journal, 12,* 31–50. doi:10.1002/smj.4250121004.

Chandler, A. D., & Mazlish, B. (2005). *Leviathans: Multinational corporations and the new global history.* Cambridge, UK: Cambridge. doi:10.1017/CBO9780511512025.

Cobb, C., & Bean, K. B. (2006). Unitary: A concept for analysis. *Journal of Theory Construction & Testing, 10*(2), 54–57.

Cook, M. A. (1996). *Building enterprise information architectures: Reengineering information systems.* Upper Saddle River, NJ: Prentice Hall.

Curtis, B., Hefley, W. E., & Miller, S. (2001). *People capability maturity model.* Pittsburgh, PA: Carnegie Mellon University, Software Engineering Institute.

Davenport, T. H. (2005). The coming commoditization of processes. *Harvard Business Review, 83*(6), 100–108. PMID:15942994.

Denning, P. J., & Hayes-Roth, R. (2006). Decision making in very large networks. *Communications of the ACM, 49*(11), 19–23. doi:10.1145/1167838.1167852.

Denyer, S., & Lakshmi, R. (2012, August 1). In India, although power is restored, doubts remain. *Washington Post.*

Dikshit, R. D. (1975). *The political geography of federalism: An inquiry into origins and stability.* New York: Wiley.

Dod, C. I. O. (2007). *Global information grid (GIG), architecture federation strategy, version 1.2.* Department Of Defense.

Drecun, V. (2003). *Federated enterprise offers a breakthrough for supply chain collaboration.* D.H. Brown Associates, Inc..

Drucker, P. F. (1954). Building the structure. In *The Practice of Management.* New York: Harper & Row.

Dye, T. R. (1990). *American federalism: Competition among governments.* Lexington, MA: Lexington Books.

Egelhoff, W. G. (1982). Strategy and structure in multinational corporations: An information-processing approach. *Administrative Science Quarterly, 27*(3), 435–458. doi:10.2307/2392321.

Elazar, D. J. (1973). Curse by bigness or toward a post-technocratic federalism. *Publius, 3*(1), 239–298.

Elazar, D. J., & Merkaz Ha-Yerushalmi Le-`Inyene Tsibur U-Medinah. (1991). *Federal systems of the world: A handbook of federal, confederal, and autonomy arrangements.* Harlow, UK: Longman Current Affairs.

Elazar, D. J. (1997). Contrasting unitary and federal systems. *International Political Science Review, 18*(3), 237–251. doi:10.1177/019251297018003002.

Federalist. (1966). *The federalist papers, a collection of essays written in support of the constitution of the United States.* Garden City, NY: Anchor Books.

Fenton, E. M., & Pettigrew, A. M. (2000). Theoretical perspectives on new forms of organizing. In Pettigrew, A. M., & Fenton, E. M. (Eds.), *The Innovating Organization* (pp. 1–46). Thousand Oaks, CA: Sage. doi:10.4135/9781446219379.n1.

Fernandez, G., Zhao, L., & Wijegunaratne, I. (2003). Patterns of federated architecture. *Journal of Object Technology*, 2(3), 135–149. doi:10.5381/jot.2003.2.3.a4.

Filippov, M., Ordeshook, P. C., & Shvetsova, O. (2003). *Designing federalism: A theory of self-sustainable federal institutions*. New York: Cambridge University Press.

Foster, J. L. (1978). Regionalism and innovation in the American states. *The Journal of Politics*, 40(1), 179–187. doi:10.2307/2129981.

Galbraith, J. R. (1973). *Designing complex organizations*. Reading, MA: Addison-Wesley Pub. Co..

Galbraith, J. R. (1995). *Designing organizations: An executive briefing on strategy, structure, and process*. San Francisco: Jossey-Bass Publishers.

Galbraith, J. R. (2000). *Designing the global corporation*. San Francisco, CA: Jossey-Bass.

Garcia, L. (1993). A new role for government in standard setting? *StandardView*, 1(2), 2–10. doi:10.1145/174690.174691.

Ghoshal, S., & Bartlett, C. A. (1990). The multinational corporation as an interorganizational network. *Academy of Management Review*, 15(4), 625–626.

Gibbins, R. (2001). Local governance and federal political systems. *International Social Science Journal*, 53(167), 163–170. doi:10.1111/1468-2451.00305.

Gooderham, P. N., & Ulset, S. (2002). 'Beyond the m-form': Towards a critical test of the new form. *International Journal of the Economics of Business*, 9(1), 117–138. doi:10.1080/13571510110103010.

Gray, V. (1973). Innovation in the states: A diffusion study. *The American Political Science Review*, 67(4), 1174–1185. doi:10.2307/1956539.

Gregor, S., Hart, D., & Martin, N. (2007). Enterprise architectures: Enablers of business strategy and IS/IT alignment in government. *Information Technology & People*, 20(2), 96–120. doi:10.1108/09593840710758031.

Gupta, A. K., & Govindarajan, V. (2000). Knowledge flows within multinational corporations. *Strategic Management Journal*, 21(4), 473–496. doi:10.1002/(SICI)1097-0266(200004)21:4<473::AID-SMJ84>3.0.CO;2-I.

Haas, L. M., Lin, E. T., & Roth, M. A. (2002). Data integration Through database federation. *IBM Systems Journal*, 41(4), 578–596. doi:10.1147/sj.414.0578.

Hammer, M. (2007). The process audit. *Harvard Business Review*, 85(4), 111–123. PMID:17432158.

Hammer, M., & Stanton, S. (1999). How process enterprises really work. *Harvard Business Review*, 77(6), 108–118. PMID:10662000.

Han, K., Oh, W., Im, K. S., Oh, H., Pinsonneault, A., & Chang, R. M. (2012). Value cocreation and wealth spillover in open innovation alliances. *Management Information Systems Quarterly*, 36(1), 291–316.

Handy, C. (1992). Balancing corporate power: A new federalist paper. *Harvard Business Review*, 70(6), 59–72. PMID:10122692.

Handy, C. B. (1989). *The age of unreason*. Boston, MA: Harvard Business School Press.

Handy, C. B. (1994). *The age of paradox*. Boston, MA: Harvard Business School Press.

Handy, C. B. (1999). Subsidiarity is the word for it. *Across the Board*, 36(6), 7–8.

Hasselbring, W. (1997). Federated integration of replicated information within hospitals: System design and architecture. *International Journal on Digital Libraries*, *1*(3), 192–208. doi:10.1007/s007990050016.

Hayek, F. A. (1945). The use of knowledge in society. *The American Economic Review*, *35*(4), 519–530.

Henderson, J. C., & Venkatraman, N. (1993). Strategic alignment: Leveraging information technology for transforming organizations. *IBM Systems Journal*, *32*(1), 4–16. doi:10.1147/sj.382.0472.

Hodgkinson, S. L. (1998). The role of the corporate IT function in the federal IT organization. In Earl, M. J. (Ed.), *Information Management: The Organizational Dimension* (pp. 247–269). New York: Oxford University Press.

Hoogervorst, J. (2011). A framework for enterprise engineering. *International Journal of Internet & Enterprise Management*, *7*(1), 5–40. doi:10.1504/IJIEM.2011.038381.

Hsiao, D. K. (1992). Federated databases and systems: Part 1 - A tutorial on their data sharing. *The VLDB Journal*, *1*(1), 127–179. doi:10.1007/BF01228709.

Johnston, S., & Menguc, B. (2007). Subsidiary size and the level of subsidiary autonomy in multinational corporations: A quadratic model investigation of Australian subsidiaries. *Journal of International Business Studies*, *38*(5), 787–801. doi:10.1057/palgrave.jibs.8400294.

Kappelman, L., Mcginnis, T., Pettite, A., & Sidorova, A. (2008). Enterprise architecture: Charting the territory for academic research. In *Proceedings of the Fourteenth Americas Conference on Information Systems*. Toronto, Canada: IEEE.

Karimi, J., & Konsynski, B. R. (1991). Globalization and information management strategies. *Journal of Management Information Systems*, *7*(4), 7–26.

Karmis, D., & Norman, W. J. (2005). *Theories of federalism: A reader*. New York, NY: Palgrave Macmillan.

Kearns, G. S., & Sabherwal, R. (2006). Strategic alignment between business and information technology: A knowledge-based view of behaviors, outcome, and consequences. *Journal of Management Information Systems*, *23*(3), 129–162. doi:10.2753/MIS0742-1222230306.

Kincaid, J. (2001). Economic policy-making: Advantages and disadvantages of the federal model. *International Social Science Journal*, *53*(167).

King, P. T. (1982). *Federalism and federation*. Baltimore, MD: Johns Hopkins University Press.

Kogut, B., & Zander, U. (1993). Knowledge of the firm and the evolutionary theory of the multinational corporation. *Journal of International Business Studies*, *24*(4), 625–645. doi:10.1057/palgrave.jibs.8490248.

Kogut, B., & Zander, U. (2003). A memoir and reflection: Knowledge and an evolutionary theory of the multinational firm 10 years later. *Journal of International Business Studies*, *34*(6), 505–515. doi:10.1057/palgrave.jibs.8400066.

Lai, V. S. (2008). The information system strategies of MNC affiliates: A technology-organization-environment analysis. *Journal of Global Information Management*, *16*(3), 74–96. doi:10.4018/jgim.2008070104.

Lai, V. S., & Wong, B. K. (2003). The moderating effect of local environment on a foreign affiliate's global is strategy-effectiveness relationship. *IEEE Transactions on Engineering Management*, *50*(3), 352–361. doi:10.1109/TEM.2003.817290.

Lu, J., & Callan, J. (2006). Full-text federated search of text-based digital libraries in peer-to-peer networks. *Information Retrieval, 9*(4), 477–498. doi:10.1007/s10791-006-6388-2.

Malnight, T. W. (2001). Emerging structural patterns within multinational corporations: Toward process-based structures. *Academy of Management Journal, 44*(6), 1187–1210. doi:10.2307/3069396.

Manor, J. (1998). Making federalism work: India defies the odds. *Journal of Democracy, 9*(3), 21–36. doi:10.1353/jod.1998.0048.

Markus, M. L., Kien Sia, S., & Soh, C. (2012). Mnes And information management: Structuring and governing IT resources in the global enterprise. *Journal of Global Information Management, 20*(1), 1–17. doi:10.4018/jgim.2012010101.

Martin, A. (2012). Enterprise IT architecture in large federated organizations: The art of the possible. *Information Systems Management, 29*(2), 137–147. doi:10.1080/10580530.2012.662103.

Martin, J. (1989). *Information engineering: Introduction (book I)*. Englewood Cliffs, NJ: Prentice-Hall.

Martin, J. (1990). *Information engineering: Planning & analysis (book iI)*. Englewood Cliffs, NJ: Prentice-Hall.

Maxwell School of Citizenship and Public Affairs. (2003). *Evolving federalisms: The intergovernmental balance of power in America and Europe*. Syracuse, NY: Maxwell School of Syracuse University.

Mckay, D. H. (1996). *Rush to union: Understanding the European federal bargain*. New York: Clarendon Press, Oxford University Press. doi:10.1093/acprof:oso/9780198280583.001.0001.

Menzel, D. C., & Feller, I. (1977). Leadership and interaction patterns in the diffusion of innovations among the American states. *The Western Political Quarterly, 30*(4), 528–536. doi:10.2307/447654.

Mill, J. S. (2005). Of federal representative governments. In Karmis, D., & Norman, W. J. (Eds.), *Theories of Federalism: A Reader* (pp. 165–172). New York, NY: Palgrave Macmillan.

Ministry of Information and Communications Technology. (2006). *E-government strategy*. Jordan E-Government Program. Retrieved October 14, 2012 from http://www.thieswittig.eu/docs/mpc_strategies/jordan/jordan_e-governmenstrategy.pdf

Mintzberg, H. (1979). *The structuring of organizations: A synthesis of the research*. Englewood Cliffs, NJ: Prentice-Hall.

Mundell, R. A. (1961). A theory of optimum currency areas. *The American Economic Review, 51*(4), 657–665.

Nielsen, F. (1996). Human behavior: Another dimension of standards setting. *StandardView, 4*(1), 36–41. doi:10.1145/230871.230878.

O'Donnell, A. (2009). The big picture. *Insurance & Technology, 34*(8), 34–35.

Oates, W. E. (1999). An easy on fiscal federalism. *Journal of Economic Literature, 37*(3), 1120–1149. doi:10.1257/jel.37.3.1120.

On, P., Vanborre, F., Stanick, K., & Williams, J. (2006). Experts' perspective. *Business Intelligence Journal, 11*, 25–29.

Open Epolicy Group Harvard Law School, & Berkman Center For Internet And Society. (2005). *Roadmap for open ICT ecosystems*. Cambridge, MA: Berkman Center For Internet & Society at Harvard Law School.

Open Group. (2011). *TOGAF version 9.1*. Open Group. Retrieved December 12, 2012 from http://www.opengroup.org/architecture/togaf91/downloads.htm

Ostroff, F. (1999). *The horizontal organization: What the organization of the future looks like and how it delivers value to customers*. New York: Oxford University Press.

Peppard, J. (1999). Information management in the global enterprise: An organizing framework. *European Journal of Information Systems, 8*(2), 77–94. doi:10.1057/palgrave.ejis.3000321.

Peterson, P. E. (2003). The changing politics of federalism. In Maxwell School Of Citizenship And Public Affairs (Ed.), *Evolving Federalisms: The Intergovernmental Balance of Power in America and Europe* (pp. 25-42). Syracuse, NY: Maxwell School of Syracuse University.

Pettigrew, A. M., & Fenton, E. M. (2000). *The innovating organization. London*. Thousand Oaks, CA: Sage.

Porter, M. E. (1985). *Competitive advantage: Creating and sustaining superior performance*. New York: Free Press, Collier Macmillan.

Prahalad, C. K., & Doz, Y. L. (1981). An approach to strategic control in MNCS. *Sloan Management Review, 22*(4), 5–13.

Prahalad, C. K., & Doz, Y. L. (1987). *The multinational mission: Balancing local demands and global vision*. New York: Free Press, Collier Macmillan.

Proudhon, P. (2005). The principle of federation. In Karmis, D., & Norman, W. J. (Eds.), *Theories of Federalism: A Reader* (pp. 173–188). New York, NY: Palgrave Macmillan.

Provan, K. G. (1983). The federation as an interorganizational linkage network. *Academy of Management Review, 8*(1), 79–90.

Qian, Y., & Weingast, B. R. (1997). Federalism as a commitment to preserving market incentives. *The Journal of Economic Perspectives, 11*(4), 83–92. doi:10.1257/jep.11.4.83.

Requejo, F. (2004). Value pluralism and multinational federalism. *The Australian Journal of Politics and History, 50*(1), 23–40. doi:10.1111/j.1467-8497.2004.00318.x.

Reuer, J. J., & Ariño, A. (2007). Strategic alliance contracts: Dimensions and determinants of contractual complexity. *Strategic Management Journal, 28*(3), 313–330. doi:10.1002/smj.581.

Riker, W. H. (1964). *Federalism: Origin, operation, significance*. Boston: Little Brown.

Riker, W. H. (1969). Six books in search of a subject or does federalism exist and does it matter? *Comparative Politics, 2*, 135–146. doi:10.2307/421485.

Riker, W. H. (1975). Federalism. In Greenstein, F. I., & Polsby, N. W. (Eds.), *Handbook of Political Science, Governmental Institutions and Processes* (pp. 93–172). Reading, MA: Addison-Wesley.

Rockart, J. F., Earl, M. J., & Ross, J. W. (1996). Eight imperatives for the new IT organization. *Sloan Management Review, 38*(1), 43–55.

Rodden, J. (2004). Comparative federalism and decentralization: On meaning and measurement. *Comparative Politics, 36*(4), 481–500. doi:10.2307/4150172.

Ross, J. W., & Beath, C. (2005). *The federated broker model at the DOW chemical company: Blending world class internal and external capabilities. No. CISR WP No. 355 And Sloan WP No. 4559-05*. Cambridge, MA: Center For Information Systems Research, Sloan School of Management.

Ross, J. W., Weill, P., & Robertson, D. C. (2006). *Enterprise architecture as strategy: Creating a foundation for business execution*. Boston: Harvard Business School Press.

Rousseau, J. (2005). A lasting peace through the federation of Europe: Exposition and critique of St. Pierre's project. In Karmis, D., & Norman, W. J. (Eds.), *Theories of Federalism: A Reader* (pp. 59–85). New York, NY: Palgrave Macmillan.

Roy, J. (2006). E-government and local governance in Canada: An examination of front line challenges and federal tensions. *Public Administration and Management*, *11*(4), 306–350.

Ruigrok, W., Achtenhagen, L., Wagner, M., & Rüegg-Stürm, J. (2000). ABB: Beyond the global matrix towards the network multidivisional organization. In Pettigrew, A. M., & Fenton, E. M. (Eds.), *The Innovating Organization* (pp. 117–143). Thousand Oaks, CA: Sage. doi:10.4135/9781446219379.n4.

Rwangoga, N. T., & Baryayetunga, A. P. (2007). E-government for Uganda: Challenges and opportunities. *International Journal of Computing and ICT Research*, *1*(1), 36–46.

Sambamurthy, V., & Zmud, R. W. (1999). Arrangement for information technology governance: A theory of multiple contingencies. *Management Information Systems Quarterly*, *23*(2), 261–290. doi:10.2307/249754.

Shapiro, C., & Varian, H. R. (1999). The art of standards wars. *California Management Review*, *41*(2), 8–32. doi:10.2307/41165984.

Sheth, A. P., & Larson, J. A. (1990). Federated database systems for managing distributed, heterogeneous, and autonomous databases. *ACM Computing Surveys*, *22*(3), 183–236. doi:10.1145/96602.96604.

Shpilberg, D., Berez, S., Puryear, R., & Shah, S. (2007). Avoiding the alignment trap in IT. *MIT Sloan Management Review*, *49*(1), 51–58.

Siew Kien, S. I. A., Soh, C., & Weil, P. (2010). Global IT management: structuring for scale, responsiveness, and innovation. *Communications of the ACM*, *53*(3), 59–64. doi:10.1145/1666420.1666449.

Slowinski, G., & Sagal, M. W. (2003). *The strongest link: Forging a profitable and enduring corporate alliance*. New York: American Management Association.

Spewak, S. H., & Hill, S. C. (1993). *Enterprise architecture planning: Developing a blueprint for data, applications, and technology*. New York: John Wiley-QED Pub..

Stepan, A. (1999). Federalism and democracy: Beyond the U.S. model. *Journal of Democracy*, *10*(4), 19–34. doi:10.1353/jod.1999.0072.

Stepan, A. C. (2001). Towards a new comparative politics of federalism, (multi)nationalism, and democracy: Beyond Rikerian federalism. In *Arguing Comparative Politics* (pp. 1–369). Oxford, UK: Oxford University Press.

Stewart, T. A., & Raman, A. P. (2008). Finding a higher gear. *Harvard Business Review*, *86*(7), 68–76. PMID:18543809.

Swanson, E. B. (2012). The managers guide to IT innovation waves. *MIT Sloan Management Review*, *53*(2), 75–83.

Sykes, A. O. (1995). *Product standards for internationally integrated goods markets*. Washington, DC: Brookings Institution.

Tanriverdi, H. (2006). Performance effects of information technology synergies in multibusiness firms. *Management Information Systems Quarterly*, *30*(1), 57–77.

Tarr, G. A. (2001). Laboratories of democracy? Brandeis, federalism, and scientific management. *Publius*, *31*(1), 1–37. doi:10.1093/oxfordjournals.pubjof.a004880.

Taylor, W. (1991). The logic of global business: An interview with ABB's Percy Barnevik. *Harvard Business Review*, *69*(2), 90–105.

Theuerkorn, F. (2004). *Lightweight enterprise architectures*. Boca Raton, FL: Auerbach Publications. doi:10.1201/9780203505311.

Tiebout, C. M. (1956). A pure theory of local expenditures. *The Journal of Political Economy*, *64*(5), 416–424. doi:10.1086/257839.

Tocqueville, A. D. (2005). Federal theory in democracy in America. In Karmis, D., & Norman, W. J. (Eds.), *Theories Of Federalism: A Reader* (pp. 147–163). New York, NY: Palgrave Macmillan.

Truex, D. P., Baskerville, R., & Kelin, H. (1999). Growing systems in emergent organizations. *Communications of the ACM*, *42*(8), 117–123. doi:10.1145/310930.310984.

United States. (2008). *Budget of the U.S. government: fiscal year 2009*. Office of Management and Budget. Retrieved October 15, 2012, from http://www.whitehouse.gov/omb/budget/fy2009/pdf/budget.pdf

United States. (2010). *HHS enterprise architecture — framework version 16.0*. U.S. Department of Health and Human Services. Retrieved October 8, 2012, from http://www.hhs.gov/ocio/ea/documents/hhseaframeworkpdf.pdf

United States. (2012,). *The common approach to federal enterprise architecture*. Executive Office of the President. Retrieved January 10, 2013, from https://cio.gov/wp-content/uploads/downloads/2012/09/common_approach_to_federal_ea.pdf

United States Department of Defense. (2012). *DoD architecture framework version 2.02*. Retrieved January 8, 2013, from http://dodcio.defense.gov/dodaf20.aspx

United States General Accounting Office. (2003). *Enterprise architecture: Leadership remains key to establishing and leveraging architectures for organizational transformation*. No. GAO-04-40. Washington, DC: U.S. General Accounting Office.

United States Government Accountability Office. (2010). *Organizational transformation: A framework for assessing and improving enterprise architecture management (version 2.0)*. No. GAO-10-846G. Washington, DC: Government Accountability Office.

Venkatraman, N., Henderson, J. C., & Oldach, S. (1993). Continuous strategic alignment: Exploiting information technology capabilities for competitive success. *European Management Journal*, *11*(2), 139–149. doi:10.1016/0263-2373(93)90037-I.

Von Simson, E. M. (1990). The 'centrally decentralized' IS organization. *Harvard Business Review*, *68*(4), 158–162. PMID:10107960.

Walker, J. I. (1969). The diffusion of innovations among the American states. *The American Political Science Review*, *63*, 880–889. doi:10.2307/1954434.

Watts, R. (2001). Models of federal power sharing. *International Social Science Journal*, *53*(1), 23–32.

Watts, R. L. (1999). *Comparing federal systems* (2nd ed.). Montreal, Canada: McGill-Queen's University Press.

Watts, R. L. (2005). Comparing forms of federal partnerships. In Karmis, D., & Norman, W. J. (Eds.), *Theories of Federalism: A Reader* (pp. 233–253). New York, NY: Palgrave Macmillan.

Weill, P., & Ross, J. W. (2004). *IT governance: How top performers manage IT decision rights for superior results*. Boston: Harvard Business School Press.

Weill, P., & Ross, J. W. (2005). A matrixed approach to designing IT governance. *MIT Sloan Management Review*, *46*(2), 26–34.

Wibbels, E. (2000). Federalism and the politics of macroeconomic policy and performance. *American Journal of Political Science*, *44*(4), 687. doi:10.2307/2669275.

Wibbels, E. (2001). Federal politics and market reform in the developing world. *Studies in Comparative International Development*, *36*(2), 27–53. doi:10.1007/BF02686208.

Wilkins, R. B. (2004). Federalism: Distance and devolution. *The Australian Journal of Politics and History*, *50*(1), 95–101. doi:10.1111/j.1467-8497.2004.00323.x.

Willson, P., & Pollard, C. (2009). Exploring IT governance in theory and practice in a large multi-national organisation in Australia. *Information Systems Management*, *26*(2), 98–109. doi:10.1080/10580530902794760.

Wilson, J., Mazzuchi, T., & Sarkani, S. (2010). Federating enterprises architectures using reference models. In *Proceedings International Conference on Information Warfare and Security* (pp. 481-488). IEEE.

Wilson, J. A. (2012). *Evaluating the effectiveness of reference models in federating enterprise architectures*. (Dissertation). The George Washington University, Washington, DC.

Wilson, K., & Doz, Y. L. (2011). Agile innovation: A footprint balancing distance and immersion. *California Management Review*, *53*(2), 6–26. doi:10.1525/cmr.2011.53.2.6.

Yamin, M., & Forsgren, M. (2006). Hymer's analysis of the multinational organization: Power retention and the demise of the federative MNE. *International Business Review*, *15*(2), 166–179. doi:10.1016/j.ibusrev.2005.07.006.

Zachman, J. A. (1987). A framework for information systems architecture. *IBM Systems Journal*, *26*(3), 454–470. doi:10.1147/sj.263.0276.

Zachman, J. A. (2006). *Federated enterprise architecture*. Retrieved August 3, 2011 http://www.intervista-institute.com/zachman-fa.php

ENDNOTES

[1.] Both Zachman and Gartner refer to components of complex organizations, such as MNC, as business units rather than subsidiaries as used in this chapter. In keeping with the meaning of these two examples business unit is retained.

Chapter 11
Transitioning to Government Shared Services Centres:
A Systems View

Torben Tambo
Aarhus University, Denmark

Lars Bækgaard
Aarhus University, Denmark

ABSTRACT

Services are fundamental to the provisioning of business activities. Enterprise Architecture (EA) is maintaining the relationship between strategy, business, and technology. A clear definition and agreed understanding of services is critical to realising information technology artefacts. Services, however, tend to be more complex than the mere act of interaction or working processes, and should be seen out of the cultural, organisational, and managerial factors surrounding them. This chapter uses a service model consisting of execution, context, and intention with an underlying claim that all three elements must be present to make services meaningful. EA must be seen in the light of this. This chapter addresses the issues related to combined transformation of organisations, service systems, and consequently, EA. The transformation changes loosely coupled, distributed organisations into Shared Service Centres (SSCs). A case study of a far-reaching SSC transformation from Denmark is presented where eGovernment services are moved from local government level into a national SSC structure referred to as Udbetaling Danmark (lit. PayDK). Major findings include: (1) When eGovernment reaches a certain level of maturity, it dissolves its original reason and no longer follows a progressive maturity model. Instead, it leads to a more radical reorganisation emphasising operational efficiency. (2) Development and management of complexities and uncertainties in governmental administrative services are closely associated with the development of eGovernment through ongoing refinement of EA and service frameworks. (3) The policy-driven reshaping of governmental services, originally themselves being SSCs, can lead to itera

DOI: 10.4018/978-1-4666-4518-9.ch011

tive SSC formations, each seeking to establish a professional logic of its own. (4) The systemic perception connected to EA and service science provides valuable insight into service transformation before, during, and after the transformation. This chapter aims at a deeper understanding and discussion of services in developing eGovernment policies and architectures, but findings are readily applicable in general business environments.

INTRODUCTION

Administrative and information processing work is increasingly viewed as services when enterprises search for operational effectiveness and development (Bardhan et al., 2010; Alter, 2010; Goldkuhl, 2006). Enterprise architecture (Bernard, 2005; Lankhorst et al., 2009; Ross et al, 2008) has to convert these services into systems and structures. Services are being developed and maintained within specific disciplines of service science and service design (Bækgaard, 2009; Maglio et al., 2006; Cherbakov & Galambos, 2005). Well-defined services can better be routinised and undergo decision-making process of organisational restructuring, outsourcing or redundancy (O'Sullivan et al., 2002). Enterprises working on adapting offerings to markets also need to structure and adapt direct or underlying services to be aligned with market expectations. Many enterprises consider organising well-defined services as shared services (Bergeron, 2003; Deloitte, 2011; Forst, 1997; Seal & Herbert, 2009) and establish or contract Shared Service Centres (SSCs) (Schulz & Brenner, 2010; Janssen & Joha, 2006; PWC, 2008; Rothwell et al., 2011). Until now, governmental services have needed a degree of vicinity to citizens to retain justification and relevance and to avoid perceived unjust barriers; widespread implementation of eGovernment changes the interaction form and suggests reorganising services (Birkmeier et al., 2012; Janssen & Wagenaar, 2004). In such changes, Enterprise Architecture (EA) plays a critical role in continuous aligning strategic and operational objectives (GAO, 2010; Hjort-Madsen, 2009). However, where EA generally supports management and technology transition well, it is interesting to review the completeness of the services transition implications for both the ceding and receiving organisational contexts.

Since Zachmann (1987), EA has dealt with capturing, documenting, planning and changing services (Hausman, 2011). By approaching services directly and basing EA analytics on design of services, complexity is assumed to be better managed. Formation of SSCs in the industry tentatively dissolves Zachmann's notions of "where," "who," and "when" into a global cloud of service providers; even "why" is often seen as separated from the original organisational context and into routinised delivery structures. A challenge to this is services as an abstraction of intention and the lack of guarantee of usefulness of services.

The processes in question relate to the moving of the executing organisation from an existing organisation and the re-assembly of services as shared services in SSCs. This creates issues of precision in the distinction and isolation of the service, the character and role of the ceding organisation as well as the qualitative and quantitative performance of the receiving organisation. Services are generally not only regarded as processes, but require environments rendering the service meaningful. In a broader perspective, a service is performed within a line of relationships, expectations and agreements. Overall service design and service architecture policies should be formulated in shared service centre formations as both the new established services provided, but also the organisational and relation interface to the ceding organisation, and obviously to the immediate consumer of the service.

In the following, a deeper background of the service, EA and organisation structure will be presented. Then, a theoretical account of particularly services but also architectures in services and services transition in light of governmental organisational dynamics is given. A case will be presented on a large-scale service reorganising process from the governmental sector in Denmark. A model view on the relation between services and actors will be suggested based on the case. The classical eGovernment services architecture maturity models are discussed together with a systemic and transformational approach to organisation of services architectures. Finally a number of suggested future research activities are being proposed.

BACKGROUND

The notion of service as discussed in this chapter relates to the providing of 'something', typically an act of usefulness to somebody. Quality is closely related to service, but typically, it is not a matter of good or bad but within a window of quality regarded acceptable by at least one part in a provider-consumer framework. Service is often defined as everything not of physical nature and may thus relate to issues of time, space, interaction and context; however, many services are closely associated with supporting making, managing and maintaining physical artefacts. Information, knowledge and experience play a distinctive role in services where parties of interaction are typically asymmetrical and strive for a more symmetrical balance through the service provided.

Power, necessity, attractiveness and voluntarity are also defining elements of services (Evans, 2007). The police provide a service of power enjoyed by some and disliked by others.

A hospital provides services necessary in certain circumstances. A hairdresser delivers a service if this hairdresser is more attractive than competitors around. A religious or cultural service can be succumbed voluntarily upon desire. Social elements of interrelation and reciprocity attribute to services.

Roles and motives must not be overlooked in understanding services. The individual provider and consumer of services are normally guided in hierarchical structures. The professor provides education service to the students, because the dean wants the service to be provided in this way; and the dean acts accordingly because it is what the management wants. The management in turn, is guided by societal necessity and financial incentives. Much scientific interest in service goes to the immediate provider-consumer relation often at an individualistic level. This might overshadow services largely provided without consumers, particularly services internal to an organisation. Common strategic management rhetoric is to discard services 'not providing customer value', but services are constructed of fabrics of necessity, tradition, habit and training and, as such, disregarded services are not easily identifiable due to their embedded nature. To verbally make certain services unwanted, illicit or disregarded might worsen the odds in capturing of these services in regular analysis.

Management, governance or motivation is characteristic to most services provided (Evans, 2007). In business-to-business relationships, management on both sides is easily recognised. In business-to-consumer relationships, the guiding hierarchy of the consumer is made by the essential rules of the society: law, cultures, social motivations, market. In governmental services, law and necessity will often constitute the skeleton of the hierarchy. Democracy is largely founded on agreements made on a strategic level in what the citizens can expect. New public management did make it popular to introduce a clear provider-consumer relationship where these were not readily obvious. A model view could be expressed as Figure 1.

Figure 1. Exchange of service

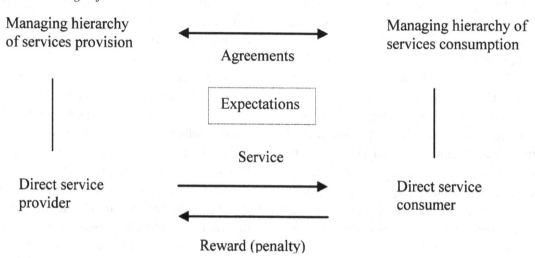

The subsequent discussion is based on a model where the provisioning of the service is viewed as execution (E), the expectations together with the agreements and the management directives of the hierarchies are seen as intentions (I), and the background in the form of human behaviour, education, corporate culture, governing laws are formed as context (C). A service (Se) can then be abstracted to this form:

$$Se = f(E, I, C)$$

This model is an adaption of a further model perspective, NICE, (Bækgaard, 2005) where use cases are abstracted into cases of activities. NICE is a case-oriented containment referring to services out of name (N), intention (I), content (C), and environment (E).

EA should be underpinning each of these factors. In relation to e.g. the EA3 Cube model of Bernard (2005), this abstraction addresses the relationship between 'Goals & Initiatives' and 'Products & Services' with a wider scope towards driving factors (I), and surrounding influencing factors (C). The service execution is coinciding with 'Products & Services', but might include services not encompassed by the EA model, e.g.

'subjective assessment' or 'asking a colleague of her opinion'. This discussion follows part of the pragmatic EA proposition of Smith (2011), but here we suggest elaborating further on the character of services related to EA.

Services and provisioning of services are becoming increasingly volatile and geographically unbound. Network technologies are readily enabling access to the most desired non-physical service, and physical services struggle to maintain a digital presence.

The perception of governmental enterprise architecture as a service construct, the formal, informal and technical organisation of these services, and the management of service architectures under change are the key issues in the case study presented below.

MAIN FOCUS OF THE CHAPTER

Broadly defined, services in any granularity and in any degree of technical or business perception are materialised in EA. EA is to ensure coherence between business and technology, but also to maintain and sustain the strategic change perspective. In discussing eGovernment development and challenges of organisational transformation or adaption, the theories of service, service orientation and EA, yield relevance.

What is Service?

The notion of a service is a business concept encompassing a value proposition (to someone). Service-orientation represents an organising principle in which everything immaterial that is offered by a business is thought of as a service (Vargo & Lusch, 2008b). The inherent perspective of service-orientation is that a process is viewed as a set of services offered to consumers or entities that interact with the services. Each service may itself be the consumer of other services. Thus, a process is viewed as a network of interacting services and consumers. Businesses engage in such networks of services. The notion of services has been studied in areas like financial services (Dandapani 2004; Kumar and van Hillegersberg 2004; Mallat, Rossi et al. 2004; Pan and Vina 2004; Rabhi, Yu et al. 2007) and Web services (van Hillegersberg, Boeke et al. 2004; Roman, Keller et al. 2005; Currie and Parikh 2006; Umapathy and Purao 2007).

Ideally, services are defined as deliveries with a purpose adding or reproducing value individuals and organisations. Alter (2010) presents a number of definitions mostly derived from purpose, value, intent and expectation. Alter (2010) phrases a more simplistic definition: Services are acts performed for someone else, including providing resources that someone else will use. Studies of efficiency (McIvor et al. 2011), however, typically claim that at least some services provided within and between organisations are obsolete, formalistic only, not adding value and can be removed without harming a broader outcome of an organisation. Contrarily defined, services may be part of a larger service delivery where the defined service enters a broader context of meaningfulness (Alt et al., 2010; Barros & Dumas, 2005).

Inefficiency might be desired e.g. in providing certain services decentralised to give a local

autonomy and experience of a higher service level. A portfolio of services is thus made up of any degree of value-adding or politically desired elementary services in the sense that some services are not driven by fundamental economic necessity but remain due to more historical and non-economic decision-making. Services may thus be reorganised in any constellation that can be accepted in a political, moral and economical context. Such reorganisation may lead to extraction of services from one organisational context and into another organisational context. In the case of systematic regrouping of services from many organisational units and into one, the term Shared Service Centre (SSC) is often used (Turle, 2010; Grant et al., 2007; Ulbrich, 2010; Ulbrich, 2006).

According to Hill, a service is a "… change in the condition of a person, or a good belonging to some economic entity, brought about as the result of the activity of some other economic entity, with the approval of the first person or economic entity" (Hill 1977). This implies that the essence of a service is work activities that are performed in order to change the state of something. It is more important to be able to create a product than to possess the material resources that constitute a car.

Sheth and Verna view a service as a provider-consumer interaction that creates and captures value (Sheth, Verna et al. 2006). An organisation can offer services using assets comprised of humans and software that interact with service consumers. This implies that a service is executed by a combination of human beings and IT systems in interaction with the service's consumer. Service scenarios can be used to model service as socio-technical systems and the roles played by human beings and technology in such systems.

Maglio and Spohrer view service as the application of competences for the benefit of another (Maglio and Spohrer 2008). Service science is the study of service systems, which are dynamic value co-creation configurations of resources, i.e. people, technology, organisations and shared information. This implies that the consumer does much more than merely receiving the result of a service in a passive manner. The consumer's actions contribute to the value-creation in a significant and active way. Service scenarios explicitly emphasise the interactive actions of service consumers and thus, they can be used to represent the ways in which consumers participate in the co-creation of service effects.

The service-dominant logic supports this view with the assumption that the ability to act is a more fundamental resource than the resources that are transformed into physical products (Vargo and Lusch 2004; Arnould 2008; Madhavaram and Hunt 2008). The ability to produce an effect, i.e. to change the state of something, is more important than the resources that constitute that which is changed. This implies that services are inherently perishable and intangible (Sampson and Froehle 2006). Service science suggests research that focuses on the essential characteristics of services (Chesbrough and Spohrer 2006; Paulson 2006; Spohrer and Riecken 2006; Lusch & Vargo, 2008a).

Grefen (Grefen, Ludwig et al. 2006) elaborates further on the proportions of the consumer/user opposed to the provider using an abstract or concrete intermediary directory ensuring generic interaction and internal processes in the confronting between a service-providing system and a service-using system. Sampson and Froehle have proposed a unified service theory that emphasises the following elements (Sampson and Froehle 2006):

1. Customer involvements, inputs and selection and consumption of outputs.
2. The customer.
3. The production process.

They emphasise the importance of co-creation in terms of the customers' contribution. Sampson and Froehle do not pay attention to concepts like meaning, quality or business issues, such as marketing and business models.

Kaner and Karni (Kaner and Karni 2007) characterise service systems in terms of the following aspects, some coinciding with EA (Bernard, 2005), such as goals, meaning, input and output. But also wider aspects are introduced, such as human enablers, social infrastructure as well as information and knowledge. Karner and Karni focus intensively on the human and non-human resources that are involved in the execution of service-related issues of quality, marketing and business models secondary.

The following service characteristics can be derived from the preceding discussion of service concepts:

1. Service is delivered by means of provider-consumer interaction.
2. Humans and technology may act as operants.
3. Value is co-created when provider and consumer interact.
4. Services are executed in networks of interacting services.
5. The provider and the consumer interact with a shared service target.
6. Service execution is constrained and supported by the interaction structures of the involved services.
7. Service execution is constrained and supported by the operants' skills, potential behaviour and available information.
8. Service implementations are hidden from the consumer by means of service information hiding.

In an analytical approach to services, delicate respect must be taken upon 'services' as an extremely generic term with a vast range of meanings. The proposed model takes into account services without clear and immediate request, but still intentions from the agent executing the services. Likewise, services are asserted meaningless without a context even if atomic of generic services tend to decontextualise ("What's the clock?"), the context remains within the provider – consumer axis. The intentionality of services includes the desire for reward or avoidance of penalty in order to identify high level drivers.

Subsequently, we argue from the model view of services consisting of intention, context and execution to promote a broader, but targeted research lens into services providing organisational environments.

Service and Enterprise Architecture

EA is to establish appropriate links between business and technology including business as a portfolio of services governed by a strategy (Bernard, 2005; Lankhorst et al., 2009; Holt & Perry, 2010). Doucet et al. (2009) emphasise on continuous adaptation between business and technology as coherency management. Business strategy is the bearing point, but EA often must deal with discrepancies between strategy and operations with full alignment as long term goal. With technology also being infrastructure and integration, EA supports complex, long-term change processes (Ross et al., 2008). The management plan for transition is therefore not definite, but object of ongoing updating. With the thoughts of (Bernard, 2005), this is illustrated in Figure 2. Jensen (2010) points at the cost of plan revisions, and the following requirements for an appropriate balance between cost-of-update and cost-of-lack-of information. Booch (2010) comments on EA and change, and quotes from a definition from The Open Group of EA as: "The continuous practice of describing the essential elements of a sociotechnical organization, their relationships to each other and to the environment, in order to understand complexity and manage change." Management plans are thus associated with a frequency of update, a level of detail into the technical design, scope, organisational responsibilities and top management involvement.

Individual changes in existing technology are requiring close EA monitoring to deal with dependencies and to converge properly to future state plans. Van den Bergh and van Steenbergen (2010) discuss an architectural vision comprising reason, purpose, definition, organisation and services. Ross et al. (2008) suggest management of shared services as a critical factor of EA.

Figure 2. Core processes interaction and management plan of enterprise architecture

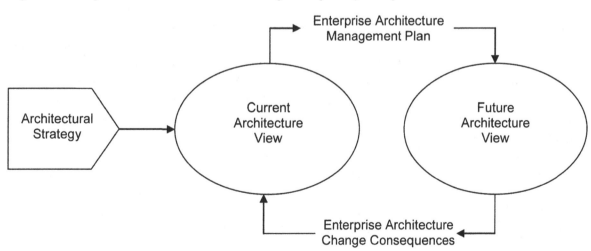

EA is not always only related to positive progression towards better technological support of the enterprise (Afshani et al., 2012; Jahani et al., 2010). EA must also deal with consequences of organisational restructuring such as cost cutting, mergers, divestures, redundancies, conflicts and mishaps in the wake of rapid decision-making (Anupindi & Coady, 2011; Smith, 2011). EA must manage new technology that might be less mature than old technology and shifts from old narrowly adapted technology to new standardised technology. New externally imposed requirements might contradict with the EA vision, but must be implemented professionally.

Bouwmann et al. (2011) present the necessity of having explicit abstractions of strategy, business architecture, enterprise [IT] architecture and implementation to create the required alignment between (technical) services and (business) services in the public sector. . TOGAF suggests designing the EA with a service orientation and it has been commonplace to establish a service-oriented architecture (SOA) (Dico, 2012; Glissman & Sanz, 2009). However, this will normally address narrowly technical requirements.

Shared Service Centres for eGovernment

With eGovernment, governmental services are generally exposed through Internet-based applications (Birkmeier et al, 2012; Hjort-Madsen, 2009; Janssen & Wagenaar, 2004). Internal governmental services are thus combined in fabrics between desired business services and underlying technical services. Governmental services are generally not driven by market mechanisms, but business perception of services and cost of services should not differ from commercial environments. Governments are thus 'competing' on developing electronic services to cut costs and harness com-

plexity, and most governments in industrialised countries have reached various level of electronic service enabling. Also governments in developing economies are utilising eGovernment to some extent. The eGovernment services must normally be strongly integrated and properly organised with existing back-office and transactional systems to provide relevance and value.

Schulz & Brenner (2010) elaborate on the understanding of the notion of SSC, and find common characteristics within consolidation of processes, cost cutting as major driver, a schism between internal and external customers, being separate organisational units, operates like a business. They furthermore emphasize SSC as an empirical phenomenon with ad hoc definitions; importantly is a distinction between SSC in governmental and private enterprise requiring different governance and inability to swap between these.

From an accountancy view, Mohan (2006) suggest pragmatic approaches to SSC in the governmental sector as a key factor in development of effectiveness and major cost reductions, but also underlining that the human factor of SSC staffing is critical in deriving success. Su et al. (2009) propose an economic value perspective to SSC decisions especially viewing SSC over time to model consequence analysis and valuation of earnings/savings. Mercer (2011) is describing important factors in developing success within SSCs in USA for local governments among other using public-private partnerships (PPP) (Joha & Janssen, 2010); initiating processes and operational agreement is also a topic in this contribution. Murray et al. (2008) shed light a particular case of SSC namely procurement offices for small local governments in UK. Niehaves & Krause (2010) are presenting a case study from Germany in how local governments collaboration naturally can reshape into SSC; they conclude SSC seems to develop from a central structure where the locally driven alternative in network collaboration. Boglind et al. (2011) present cases of human resource management done within SSC in Sweden. Borman (2010) and Dollery et al. (2009) are showing cases of successful SSC in Australia. David (2005) suggests a well organised cost control around SSC both on transition and operation.

In Figure 3 are the key roles and relations illustrated in the non-SSC (e-) governmental service delivery model. eGovernment and "physical" government services would both front the citizens, in some contributions called clients, but obviously it could be houseowners, patients, schoolkids, inmates, etc. The overall architectural perception is to include an underlying infrastructure for e.g. citizen registration, motor vehicle owners register, etc. Importantly in the case study below are common citizen portals and single-sign on systems.

Over the years, a number of authors have proposed various maturity models for eGovernment (Schendel et al., 2011; Windley, 2002). Karokola and Yngström (2009) present models from a.o. United Nations, Asia-Pacific, Deloitte and World Bank. All models whether 3, 4, 5, or 7 stages display a progression from simplistic email governmental services and up to integrated, citizen-centric, highly automated governmental information services.

During the last 20 years, SSCs have gained much attention materialising the concentration and standardisation—formerly characterising physical manufacturing—in the service industry (Janssen et al., 2009; Janssen & Joha, 2006; PWC, 2008; Infosys, 2011). Some SSCs have been identified with shifting from low to medium complexity services from high-wage countries to low-wage countries (Chandrasekaran & Ensing, 2004). Nevertheless, SSCs can be situated in any organisational and geographical setting. SSCs can also aim at high-level professional services along with lower complexity routinised work, e.g. in HR services were both salary processing and legal services could be organised in the same SSC. Wagenaar (2006) states, "The implementation of shared service centers is claimed to be a valuable organizational redesign that will lead to less redundancy in operations, less staff and more concentrated knowledge accumulation." Furthermore is the risk of failure highlighted due to complex and confusing multi-parametric enterprise design of the SSC.

In establishing SSC, Smith et al. (2008) propose a number of problems needing attention. Loss of control and identity is stressing the ceding organisation. Cost containment is often only handled as direct costs, but indirect costs can be much higher. HR management in both the ceding and the continuing organisations need close attention no matter if staff or only processes are transferred. Funding structures and models are complex – are we talking unit costs, objective costs, initial cost

Figure 3. The service and electronic service structure of eGovernment

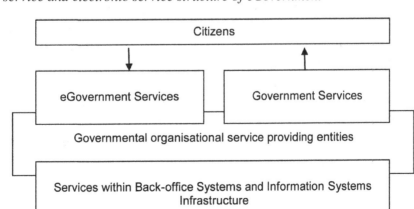

sharing, cost of different service levels, bespoke adaption, etc. Finally, exit strategies are embossed as important to the strategic management of the SSC relation.

The literature indicates a breadth of potential governmental SSC design styles. Cross-cutting SSC can be established on specific areas, e.g. HR and procurement. Generic SSC is also a design style making broad centres able to take off "any" service that reasonably can be transferred from ceding contexts. Reflecting upon generally known Business Process Outsourcing (BPO) market actors in predominantly India, transfer should relate more to the strategic decision on cost and service than certain requirements within the SSC actor.

There are now a number of references in the literature to failed projects of governmental SSC establishments. Expectations from policy makers and citizens have not been met. Cost saving agendas have been obscured by service level expectations. The level of preparedness has not been in place from the ceding organisation to the SSC, or the technological foundation has not required quality in time.

The SSC will itself be a service providing organisation, and Wilson (2004) discuss the SSC's necessity to develop itself not to be the continuation of the transferred services, but to gain a professional identity of its own. Wilson (2004) suggest a number of contrast, e.g. a switch from cost control into service excellence and high performance, also a switch from absence of service management and into application of service level agreements. Farndale et al. (2012) are talking about SSC in the HR domain as drivers of new emergent roles in management of the inter-organisational collaboration with e.g. demand management, service/value chain management, service level management, and procurement of services. Also new delivery models derived from the externalisation of the SSC and the development with the SSC of new

professional logics is discussed (Ulrich & Grochkowski, 2012). This all together suggest SSC as a generally empirical and emergent phenomenon still lacking from solid definitions and practices.

A Systemic Perspective

EA processes ideally interrelates business and technology into supporting operational structures as indicated in Figure 2. Maintaining the duality and insisting on the open-ended character of these processes, a systemic perspective ensures optimal non-a priori alignment. Out-of-the-box enterprise systems do necessarily compromise with alignment and henceforth reduces this to unidirectional alignment with the system as a more single-ended driver. In contrast to this will more chaotic organisational contexts result in shortcomings in any suggested architecture.

In his contribution on systemic EA, Wegmann (2003) introduces a *systemic EA philosophy* constructed of an epistemology within the EA, an ontology and an ethics. This leads to an iterative approach of EA built upon multi-level modelling, multi-level design, and multi-level deployment. Pulkkinen (2006) directs the systemic understanding into a two-dimensional EA-grid consisting of the confluence of architectures on business, information, systems and technology with the multi-level perception proposed as the enterprise level, the domain level, and the systems level. Going further in (governmental) organisational analysis in, Jensen (2010) argues for the importance of systemic thinking and action learning in government management, also arguing for EA as intrinsically systemic to its context. Jensen (2010) additionally states that: "*A more nuanced approach to enterprise modelling, which accepts that organisational life is a hybrid of both hard and soft business problems, demanding a varied, systemic meta-modelling approach to coherently modelling and understanding a government agency based on both learning, enquiry, engineering, and logic."* Kudryavtsev and Grigoriev (2011) discuss a systemic orientation in developing EA with an onset in functional decomposition thereby suggesting organising guiding systems in value creation. Jensen (2010) and Kudryavtsev & Grigoriev (2011) differ in observing governmental respectively commercial organisations; importantly here is the lack of external value-drivers in governmental contexts.

The EA practice must orientate itself within systemic, contextual conditions and external factors. The EA thinking should thus support a dynamic view from strategic drivers and "down" to operational artefacts. The service model of *Se = f (E, I, C)* is likewise proposing to identify the systemic character of the object organisation, with Jensen (2010) governmental organisation are forming a special case with its probable tendency to develop differentiated implementation of *Se* given only slight differences in intention and context. Here the distributed nature and local autonomy are attributing factors.

Issues and Controversies

The service abstraction of intention, context and execution, should be beneficial to case research when observing services or organisation under transition. The transition obviously means that execution is moved from the ceding to the receiving organisation. The intention is less clear. If a service is changed without full consent of all parties, will the service then retain its original validity or will it just materialise again as a new service with a separate validity? Also, the relationship between organisations and services is interesting when looking at validity of case of shifts.

The understanding of service is complex. Providers and consumers will look differently at services (as "good" and "bad") depending on intuitive or opportunistic views. Analysts are mostly

struggling with the paradoxical nature of services that the architectural artefacts must converge towards an atomic nature with a trade-off that this might decontextualise the service. Context can thus be preserved with the risk that the service is too complex, or a new organisational context can be created along with an implementation of a service system.

Popular and professional confusion of the different notions of service can promote unclear and ambiguous architectural design. *Service orientation* is frequently confused between a business-inspired understanding of providing services in provider-consumer relations, and a more technical understanding of a certain design style of information systems architecture using designated Internet protocols and well-defined interfaces. In the following, we will aim at the more business-oriented understanding but having the *technical service orientation* as the key technology proportion of the business (Booch, 2010). Business services can be translated into technical services and technical services can be assembled to support or create business.

Any inter-personal service is suggesting its own complexity in how at least the service provider interprets his/her role. A mapping of services described below indicated that strictly law-based, objective services had highly different implementations in different local governments. In service management, it is fundamental that any service no matter level of detail can be performed good or bad. Selection, training and management are often assumed to be able to improve quality. The individual interpretation may result in executing the clearest defined goals and initiatives highly different in practice.

A classic controversy in service transformation through organisational or architectural change is should the service remain where it is, or it is more feasible to move it? Generally, EA should be indifferent to where a service is being provided as long as someone can answer "why," "how," and "where." This does, however, not change the idea that service design and organisational design are two of a kind, and EA sometimes might lack the ability to develop the necessary organisational assumptions.

CASE STUDY

Governmental information systems are typically some of the most transaction intensive in many countries and the impact of any system to the society can be immense. Politicians and senior government officials will be viewed by the public for their ability to manage and develop information systems and might lose their seats in case of failed projects. IT, however, remains attractive in transforming and streamlining the governmental sector at all levels. With an ever increasing number of governmental and governmentally accessible information services, it is interesting to work on combining these in new ways to gain cost effectiveness or improve service offerings.

In the following, a case study is presented on an ongoing project in Denmark. Selected services provided by all local governments are being transferred into one single, national organisational entity using both predefined architectural framing but also strong ad hoc approaches in the transformation process.

In 2010, the Danish government started a process of centralising payment of social benefits, welfare and pensions. Previously 98 municipalities were managing the payment of €25bn of smaller and larger benefits for two million citizens using 2,000 employees (full-time equivalents, FTE). By removing these services from the existing units and consolidating them into one unit, the expected savings after four years is assumed to be €50m mostly by reducing the workforce by 500 employees. The new unit is called PayDK (org. *Udbetaling Danmark*).

The services transferred are classified as 'objective' services where administrative staff without personal interviewing or other verbal interaction should be able to grant a welfare benefit to a citizen based on an application. Decisions are made on quantifiable data of the citizen. The data should normally be retrievable from various governmental data sources like the citizens register, the housing register or the tax register. Thus, the services provided ideally encompass receiving of applications from citizens mostly entered in eGovernment self-service systems, validation of applications, some exception handling, granting of the benefit, payment authorisation and account payables reconciliation.

The benefits granted are all based on the national laws of social security. The political rationale behind the laws is to sustain social balance, e.g. between home owners and tenants, persons with government-funded pension versus private pension and families with children. Many benefits have a long history closely associated with the foundation of the European style of the welfare state in the 1960ies. Objectiveness and perceived simplicity are important from the national political level to avoid allegations of anti-social sentiments and bias pro or con important voter groups.

The services are executed by administrative staff with a vocational background and probably months to years of on-the-job training. Persons with more than five years on the job are regarded as highly experienced. For some years, local governments have addressed the administrative processing as an area of cost cutting. Administrative processing is normally counted together with administrative expert services where the latter is growing due to generally higher complexity and judicial requirements. Administrative staff in local governments has increasingly been organised in cross-disciplinary administrative centres, either as front offices where citizens inquiries are being processed, or as back offices where either more complex issues are being resolved or repetitious tasks are prepared. A service is therefore carried out by one or more persons to whom the service is a smaller or larger part of this person's overall workload.

PayDK is to receive 1,500 persons from the local governments. These 1,500 persons are to be placed in five regional centres with a certain distance from the original workplace. The business case is developed out of an assumption that the headcount can be reduced by 500 persons during the first three to four years of operation. Another 500 persons associated with the services are to remain in the local governments to deal with mainly digitally illiterate citizens, mostly elderly, handicapped and otherwise socially impaired persons. One of the five centres will have complex services and general management of PayDK. All five centres are to receive staff from all areas of the services, but over time, there are indications that each centre will have specialised assignments, e.g. child benefits.

At a certain deadline, the local governments could only identify 920 persons to be transferred to PayDK. The concept of transfer was based on persons predominantly associated with a service. The interdisciplinarity of the existing organisations has, however, made it difficult to come up with the required number of singular-service persons. Existing staff has been reluctant in seeking transfer to PayDK, as their place of work may be located further away from home, and the planned staff reduction would make the general position unsecure. In some cases, older employees have requested early retirement. PayDK will have to start using 300-500 employees with a time-limited contract. A success criterion of retaining knowledge seems problematic.

Seven core services with objective character are identified to be transferred from the local governments to PayDK:

- Child and youth benefits
- Housing support
- General governmentally-funded pension
- Payment and adjustment of pension of early retirement

- Added pension benefits
- Maternity support
- Alimonies

No legal body has been founded to manage the creation of PayDK Instead, the governmentally controlled organisation for generalised pension savings (abbreviated ATP) has been granted the assignment of the hosting and project management of PayDK. The project organisation has publicised a number of documents of the planning and intentions on PayDK on the Website http://www.atp.dk/wps/wcm/connect/udbetalingdanmark/ud.dk. A number of quality requirements are made for the project including citizens' satisfaction, operations and project cost control, realised savings, employee satisfaction and retaining of qualifications.

The matter of enterprise architecture is addressed very specifically. With limited time, little local insight, a relatively weak business case and a host of failed governmental IT projects, the PayDK project is defined conservatively as a HR project and not an IT project. Existing platforms are to be transferred from the local governments and into PayDK with minimal modifications. Contributing to this is a dominance of systems in the area from one system provider (abbreviated KMD). KMD is granted sole IT responsibility of the PayDK project. KMD is providing PayDK a help desk where issues on systems from other vendors are also to be addressed. KMD is thus providing consultancy, software solutions, operational services as well as infrastructure and help desk. Basically, favouring one private actor without public tendering is not legal. To avoid legal issues, there have been made a plan sending each of the work packages (systems, services) in tendering from 2014 and onwards. KMD used to be owned by the local governments but was divested in 2008 to a private equity fund.

The enterprise architecture is thus being characterised by risk minimising, one strong vendor, a non-competitive environment, an operational continuation approach and an existing architecture with many identical platforms.

Generally, eGovernment and Internet self-service are regarded cornerstones of the PayDK project with several of the services already, to some extent, Internet-based, and a mandated use of a general citizen single sign-on service.

A number of issues are pointed out by the administrative staff. Local governments have been running different versions of main systems, and some have been 'development partners' receiving and using newer versions much earlier. This means a rapid upgrade of IT in the local governments 'lagging behind'. Old software versions might have been part of a coherent infrastructure locally, but lack integration to core systems during and after rapid upgrades.

Fraud and unrightfully claimed benefits are always a risk. In the presentation of PayDK, it is clearly stated that correct and lawful payment is the responsibility of PayDK. Fraud counter-measures have been difficult to materialise alone from the physical distance introduced and the more "silo"-oriented administrative processing. Currently, administrative staff will e.g. drive to a house to verify the legal and actual status, if central registers give reason for concern. Likewise with the other services, where fraud or unrightful claims are possible. The existing administrative centres have given the option of sharing knowledge across disciplines and data mining approaches are among the measures to deal with fraud. The staff is, however, pointing at issues of faulty reference databases on e.g. housing data. The senior project manager of PayDK pointed to the necessity of collaboration with local governments to do proper controlling and avoid fraud.

Several stakeholders have been very straight-forward on the risks, potential disadvantages and meager business case of PayDK, but the point-of-no-return has long been claimed by the hosting organisation, ATP, and the government. At an early point in time ATP requested the 5 centres to be build and signed 25 years irrevocable lease agreements.

Issues discussed in public have a.o. included: Alienation through loss of contact between citizen and local government, loss of local qualifications and uniform business processes (standard instead of best practices). A number of disadvantages are discussed in the legislation and implementation guidelines – also counter-measures to avoid the worst issues. A another critical issue relates to the fact that the 2,000 affected employees are actually not employees but man-years covering an unrecognised number of actual employees, potentially up to 10,000 employees each engaged more or less in providing of the services in question. Qualifications thus have a much broader base than those individuals assigned as key operatives on each of the 7 services.

Services Considerations

The services complex transferred from the local governments to PayDK can be described as

$$S_t = f (S_1, S_2, S_3, S_4, S_5, S_6, S_7)$$

Each services is characterised by a foundation in a law (Fl), regulations enacting the law (Fr), regular practices (Frp), processes related to the services (Fp), processes necessitated by adjacent services (Fa), fraud detection (Fd) and exception handling (Fe), thus making the service as:

$$Sn = f (Fl, Fr, Frp, Fp, Fa, Fd, Fe)$$

Large parts of these frameworks have been described in an online business process management system called the Work Flow Bank (abbreviated AGB), largely using Business Process Model and Notation (BPMN) (Weske, 2012) flow diagram and syntax (see Figure 4).

According to the involved persons in the development of the formal service models, consensus for many critical services was never reached. The modelling facilitators insisted on models as

Figure 4. Example from the work flow bank on housing support

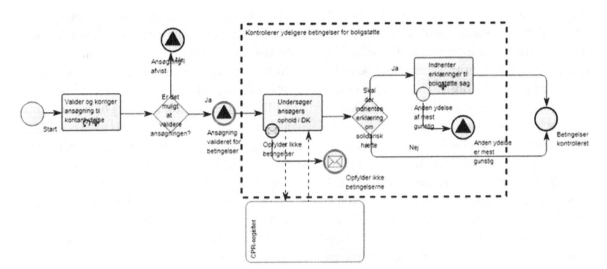

current state with potentials for improvement. The business case of PayDK was therefore based on relatively inefficient models and discarded best practices. The granularity of the models remain at a rather high level not including concrete data, reporting and most specifics of interfaces. More importantly, the intentions of the service 'consumer' are generally omitted, and the operating context is mostly left open. Skills, cross-functional insight, communication channels, exception handling, etc. are not emphasised.

The desire to make things work, the professional attitude of service agents and the political necessity of welfare payments are all important contributing factors in securing ongoing operations. The intentional and contextual side of the service provision adds well to the fundamental theoretical stance of services as more formalistic provisioning.

Enterprise Architecture Considerations

Besides the pragmatic, organisation-oriented EA approach, a number of architectural methodologies have been established for development of digital solutions within local governments and between national governmental bodies and local government levels. A cross-local government frame architecture has been established (Kombit, 2012) guiding decision-making processes, standards and patterns, cross-cutting systems, methods and communication.

The cross-local government architecture is aligned to the central governmental enterprise architecture and shares a common reference model. Remarkable is, that by transferring architectural components from local to central level, the resulting architecture is expected to remain unchanged. The idea of having a static EA is following the strategy of the PayDK implementation with strict focus on risk minimising. It can, however, be claimed that architecture and organisation is so closely related that any change in organisation must result in a changed architecture. Interviewed enterprise architects of some local governments were also astonished to find that the project perspective changed a few months before go-live from 'system preservation' to an actively realised requirement for a modified EA. This is furthermore interesting in our general service framework pointing to a change of context as a change of service.

The process is therefore characterised by mature EA viewpoints. The project lead is only seeing organisational and HR changes, as the technical service agents contracted to the project have all tools required to navigate the required processes. This raises an interesting discussion on whether EA can reach a level of maturity where is becomes self-evident and process-intrinsic. The maturity of EA also applies to numerous systems probably affected and most likely needing adaption even though the view of 'this is not a software development project' might prove correct. Contradicting with the maturity perception, administrative staff indicates that substantial amounts of manual processes still exist. Typically, transfer of data from one system to the next, e.g. in child support, the agents need to manually retrieve verdicts from the family court on these cases; in housing support, data is transferred as files between approval systems, welfare systems and accounts payable systems.

EA segmentation is interesting. Given e.g. Bernard's (2005) EA3 cube, the local governments have organised themselves as one cube with the welfare services as segments. PayDK organises itself as another cube, "slicing" out the segments of the local governments. Segmentation could thus indicate a potential of transferability with due reservations. Segmentation is to support clarity and sustain a relevant context. Segmentation suggests a relevance, adherence and consistency of the organisation. On the other hand, segmentation can render the individual, overall organisational structure obsolete at any time. EA should be considered for if it should improve or limit 'plug-in /plug-out' segmentation. In this case, most back-office and citizens self-service systems are kept static during the transition to maintain risk minimising.

The establishing of SSC is generating an EA of its own addressing new organisational boundaries, goals, products as well as technical architectures and infrastructure. The carving out of services from the ceding organisation is often overlooked as impose new architectural requirements within this organisation as the future state is different from the past. In this case, a number of financial services must be adjusted as the services transferred are no longer in the architecture. Assumptions related to completeness must be adjusted in case of planned future incompleteness. Termination of service contract, software subscriptions, infrastructure obsolescence, "de-training" of staff, incomparable KPI's and time-series, lowering of buying power and critical mass, etc. are factors to be considered in transition of services from one organisation to another. Enterprise architecture could beneficially consider end-of-life issues on services. The services extraction leaves the ceding organisation with an EA *phantom pain* requiring meticulous analysis to address dependencies, data sufficiency, cross-segment use, changes in authorisations and role of services as intermediaries between other services to pursue relevant remediation.

Solutions and Recommendations

Service transformations generally take place in a field of organisational tension and technological change. Motives (Janssen & Joha, 2006) for transformations are likewise multifaceted mixing cost cutting with professionalisation, harmonisation and political horse-trading. Rothwell et al. (2011) discuss SSC as a general emergent organisational type highly related to learning and establishing its exact role and required set of competencies. The emergent character underlies the following discussions with an emphasis on how a service understanding and more active enterprise architecture thinking could improve the process. From the literature, the outcome of SSC establishment and transformation is highly unpredictable. The resultant services-providing organisations might be much more streamlined services organisation than the departing organisation. But sometimes they are realised as dysfunctional or commercially infeasible and new transformation processes are started. Subsequently, considerations on solutions and recommendations for analysis, architecture and management of service transformations are presented.

EGovernment Transformation

EGovernment transformation must in all cases have its point of departure in a workable consensus of the services expected to be object for the transformation. The judicial foundation seems to be one out of many aspects, but other aspects such as organisational structure, tradition, culture, interpretation, demography and training also need close consideration. The important contribution from maturity models relates to an incremental nature of transformation: Any transformation is based on the existence of past components that are used as stepping stones or building blocks whether it is services targeted directly at the citizens, or it is back office services, case office services, transaction systems or integration infrastructure.

A general critique of maturity models in eGovernment is, however, the aspect of undisputed continuous progression towards "better" services. Such models overlook, e.g. (1) organisational changes disrupting established services, (2) technological obsolescence of systems in operations, (3) failed projects and (4) abrupt changes in laws and basic societal mechanisms, e.g. austerity. A maturity model based on EA management plans (Bernard, 2005; Afshani et al., 2012) would cover the open, iterative character of maturity development better. The motion towards a management plan contrary to maturity models would better suit management of uncertainties and complexities during transition.

The service approach and the linkage of services and EA seem to suffer from the breadth of meanings of the notion of service. A multi-parametric approach would suggest human versus digital services, consumer-provided services versus internal/supportive/atomic services, back-office versus front-office services, integrative services (human or digital), reporting and performance services, etc. A systemic approach to management of complexity should highlight the difference in perception and positioning of services as well as the interchangeable and dualistic character of

services. Within this understanding, obsolete or redundant services could be recognised better.

EGovernment transformation aims at re-architecting services. Management and politicians' view of services is likely to differ from professional view of services. In the PayDK case politicians promised a continued analogue channel to digital illiterate citizens; the professional view is that multichannel services are complex, costly and undesired. Several more examples exist where professionals cannot see practice implemented with the loose and informal strategic service views. Such conflicts are classical and could at best be elevated in the analytical processes, ideally supported as a mapping of stakeholder intentions and opposing stances at every level of interest.

The aforementioned Work Flow Bank is interesting in the eGovernment process. The Work Flow Bank defines and visualises the services object to eGovernment. The responsibility for this repository was formerly with the local governments IT service provider, KMD, but after it was sold, a new entity Kombit (Kombit, 2012) was formed to exercise ownership of the services. The services could have various local implementations, but the generic service has the overall governance based on the mentioned workable consensus. The high degree of transparency and controlled management of the services are thus making the creation of national SSC more obvious.

The studies of PayDK indicate that the high-level strategy of the organisation is clear and relatively indisputable. However, the primary business case is not strong. The low-level operational processes are, among others, relatively well-defined through the Work Flow Bank and work instructions. The managerial levels between the high-level and process-level are more unresolved. The PayDK management talks about evolvement of collaboration (with departing organisations), ongoing role refinement, risk-minimising and continuation of operation. The fraud detection formerly exercised differently at the local level is now stated as more systematically implemented through the use of data mining with wide access to a broad line of databases. This exemplifies fraud detection as a service moving from a front office capability and into the transaction systems.

The governing EA frameworks (Kombit 2012a; Kombit 2012b) play a relatively limited role in the PayDK process. Furthermore, the EA process has been included at a late stage in the process; at one point enterprise architects were included just three months before go-live. The EA processes have been asymmetrical given so that one vendor, KMD, has a dominant role, the departing organisations were engaged sporadically, and the key project organisation did not consider itself related to EA. The externally defined strategy might be related to this as the PayDK organisation has limited influence on its overall business objectives, and these objectives are weakly linked to services and work practices.

Thus, EA could beneficially address:

- Degree of externalised strategy formation.
- Relationship or lack of relationship between services and strategic objectives.
- The technological and organisational leeway to independently or collaboratively connect services and EA.
- Symmetry in engagement of parties and actors in the process.
- Awareness of frequency of updating the management plan.
- The ruggedness of the interconnection between strategic, tactical and operational layers of the business in question.

The emergent organisational character of eGovernment SSC and the general "hourglass" organisation of SSC as suggested by Rothwell et al. (2011) should therefore be included in the EA processes to harvest the benefits of EA along with the ad hoc thinking used in the PayDK case.

Management of Uncertainties and Complexities

Bardhan et al. (2010) state that "*IT-based service delivery systems span multiple business functions, enterprises, and geographies, resulting in new levels of complexity. They are difficult to evaluate, implement, and manage successfully. Managers, meanwhile, are faced with developing effective service-sourcing strategies.*" As such, complexity challenges are omnipresent. The case suggests several approaches to reduce complexity:

- Transfer existing staff and qualifications as intact as possible.
- Assume EA and IT core systems as static well knowing they are not, thereby contributing to a strategic and semi-tactical means of minor change, but supporting necessary lower-tactical and operational means of transformation.
- An a priori definition of services as steady with a contingent approach to ongoing adaptation.
- A dynamic alignment of service interfaces and distribution of responsibilities with the ceding organisations in form of the 98 local governments.

McIvor et al. (2011)'s proposal on organising SSC in three layers of (1) contact layer, (2) transaction support and (3) case management has largely been verified in the case and must be regarded as mainstream in services organisations. In the case, it has furthermore been acknowledged that staff should only be exposed to the contact layer for a limited time on a working day to ensure qualifications and avoid burn-out phenomena. The case questions if case management needs to reside at local SSC level or if it could be further centralised in a SSC within the SSC organisation. The recursive nature of SSC is also interesting in the management of complexity. PayDK tentatively connects services in different patterns: The five regional SSCs can e.g. be focused on a specific service, they can assume the responsibility for a service in certain hours or days of the week, take a percentage or a number of ingoing phone calls, cases or email, or they can retain a geographic responsibility. This emphasises the necessity to harmonise and generalise services and the strong reduction of uncertainties and complexities needed.

Together with governmental and local governmental organisations PayDK makes process descriptions of the new services. These process descriptions are meticulous. In an example of Housing Support (KL, 2012), the work instructions are 69 pages with many manual processes related to lack of integration between systems. These work instructions are very interestingly related to the Work Flow Bank previously described. The work around the Work Flow Bank generally resulted in several workflows for the same governmental process with differences typically stemming from differences in organisation in local governments, different administrative hierarchies, different IT systems, etc. With one organisation, the complexity of different workflows for the same process needs, at least temporarily, to be managed into one workflow . Tacit knowledge and trained, intrinsic knowledge likewise need to be made explicit, maybe losing some details, but creating transparency and uniformity in workflow and business process. Eventually, there can be a correspondence between the Execution element of the service model and the Intention. SSC establishment can therefore conclusively be said to require and create uniform services with a full fledge drive towards systemic management of complexity. Local innovation and self-organisation are lost, but the overall cost-base will be significantly reduced due to this fact alone.

Reviewing Transformation Policies

Rightfully used EA and services perspectives can well support an improved understanding of potential risks and advantages in governmental service transformation. With Janssen & Joha (2006), the perceived and realised motives for changes are complex and strongly interrelated. In the Danish context, only cost mattered as the political base-justification. In a political game between local and central governments, efficiency can come into play. In the PayDK case local politicians lost the PayDK services by saving potentially €50 m, but got opportunity to spend €200 m more in other areas.

The literature describes several cases of transformation of governmental services into SSC based on voluntary and local initiatives (Boglind et al., 2011; Borman, 2010; David, 2005; Dollery et al., 2009; Krecklow & Kinney, 2007; Niehaves & Krause, 2010; Selden & Wooters, 2011; Smith et al., 2008; Ulbrich, 2010). The local initiative is somewhat idealised to better understand and contain processes as implemented. The voluntary character is emphasised as inviting and inclusive to the parties. The case presents the opposite: The 98 local governments are not even asked to improve, participate or engage, but simply to transfer staff on a pro rata basis. EGovernment therefore needs to be understood not only as a technology-based transformation mechanism, but also as a potential mean for a comprehensive reorganisation of governmental services where both technological and social systems can come into play.

Strong discussions on digital divide, digital literacy and multi-channel governmental services are lying behind the PayDK formation. With Denmark being among world leaders in digital literacy, still 15% of the adult population are not using the Internet. The decision on PayDK was augmented with a decision of retaining 500 FTE around in the local governments to support digitally "impaired" citizens with sticks and carrots.

As mentioned above, in reviewing the international discussion on SSC in the literature,, PayDK seems different. The literature normally talks about "bottom up" approaches where local governments choose a SSC partner. In PayDK, the national government basically gave no alternative to the local governments. The local governments were originally critical to the change, but accepted after getting different fiscal compensations. The local governments had until then fiercely protected their local autonomy, their political integrity and their right to design and organise administrative processes to local requirements. There are no indications that the PayDK decision can be reverted, so local governments have permanently given up their control of the broad interaction with citizens. There is little in the literature on this scale of SSC, and the long-term effects will be highly interesting to study.

A final transformation consideration has been "equal to the law." The claim from local governments that local conditions should influence local service design has annoyed national politicians. The press and NGOs have claimed that national politicians accepted inequality by giving local government too much autonomy. The Work Flow Bank project demonstrated adversity to harmonisation in processes among local governments. The evolvement of the governmental reference models based on EA has, however, obscured the local government's arguments. When the application, information and technology architectures of the implemented eGovernment infrastructure are identical, local governments' claim of local design is rendered empty. The SSC rationale of effectiveness must therefore be supplemented with a rationale related to harmonisation, standardisation, well-defined assumptions of equal treatment and assumed objectivism.

Systemic Perspectives of the Transformation Journey

The described work on prior local SSCs and the national Work Flow Bank made a foundation for the service transformation into PayDK and can thus be seen as the functional decomposition and framework of compliance as suggested by Kudryavtsev & Grigoriev (2011). The identification of 'objective services' as a lead object for SSC came out of past work to align services across local governments. Systemic perspectives strongly relate to emphasising the SSC transformation more as a HR project than an EA or IT project by moving a social system and creating a new social organisation with the original set of qualifications. With Pulkkinen (2006), the *enterprise level* changes from 98 enterprises to one enterprise; the *domain level* is consequently much more singular, and the *systems level* relies on one main systems architecture and not several. However, the systemic character must be assumed first to gain momentum when the organisation takes shape, i.e. when the actual transfer of staff and services starts from the departing organisation and into the SSC.

Already implemented eGovernment systems are used as a foundation for far-reaching changes like in the case. For years, the local governments had "competed" in making the best eGovernment service offerings. In the end, this suggests the option of radical change. Conclusively, eGovernment dissolves the requirement for governmental services associated with geography, as the context is already the Internet. The systemic nature of eGovernment should, thus, be seen as a potential "game changer" in the physical counterparts in the form of front office, back office and case management. From Pulkkinen (2006), the Information, Application and Technology Architectures of the local governments were already largely identical, so a national governmental pressure the change and streamline the Business Architecture seemed logical.

The SSC is normally characterised as being an independent organisation having a distance from its customers, owners or contributing partners. This mean that the SSC will do what is necessary to develop a professionalism of its own with its own organisational dynamics forming specialist teams, transaction support teams, etc. The systemic nature of the SSC thereby follows the emergence of the organisation. In PayDK, the hosting organisation ATP indicates a roadmap of new services put into the umbrella of PayDK. Any eGovernment service reaching a certain threshold of the overall transactional activity is susceptible to be transferred into an SSC-like organisation as a physical front service is no longer required, and with Pulkkinen (2006), the Information, Application and Technology Architectures have their own systemic logic of transferability.

With PayDK as a SSC hosting objectivised services from departing organisations and basically with the society as customer, the overall service system is influenced by both internal and external factors. The systemic character of PayDK is suggested to be found in the individual constituents of the core services as well as in the organisational confluence of these. Looking at the generic form of the services presented above:

$$Sn = f (Fl, Fr, Frp, Fp, Fa, Fd, Fe)$$

The legal, operationalised, practice-driven, process-related, adjacent services, fraud detection and exception handling services all have an evolving logic which influences and attributes to the dynamics of the SSC. For example, a change in laws of cross examination of governmental databases can suddenly give the fraud detection new possibilities; likewise, changed organisation of work and specialisation can create new forms of practices different from was known from the departing organisation.

The service construct of intention, context and execution is interesting in the SSC process.

The intention is much more open to interpretation and modelling than in running organisations on the other hand, intention split from context and execution is artificial. Context setting in green field organisation must be expected to reside within the enterprise architecture activities, but with the questionable approach of partially neglecting EA in the current case.

The systemic nature of SSC is interesting when it comes to securing a positive outcome and continuous improvement. Since the literature describes several examples of problematic cases of SSC, the PayDK case is interesting while it has long crossed its point of no return; it has an externalised business case, it is basically a green field organisation, and it will issue tenders for all transaction systems over the next five years. General observations seen in the discussion of this case are:

- Grant et al (2007) suggest that *"without systemic feedback and feed-forward channels of communication from constituents, hierarchies in either the public or private sector do not have reliable and sustainable processes to identify, let alone, increase effectiveness and responsiveness."* Balanced Scorecard is here proposed as the framework of communication. Other references are just highlighting general use of relevant Critical Success Factors (CSFs) and Key Performance Indicators (KPIs) when relating services architectures and services performance.

- Adaptation to external environments is expected to be easier in the creation of SSCs than when pursuing systemic change in ongoing organisations following the arguments of dynamic capabilities of Teece et al. (1997). The organisational remodelling might alone be considered as a driving argument for the SSC.

- The systemic perception of the SSC formation is the reverse form of other similar "organisational internal" developments where systemic nature is a forthcoming object to design and architecture, but also continuously shaped by internal and external factors.

- In governmental services, the reference model is beneficially found in domain-specific laws, the general administrative act, administrative orders as well as recognised, administrative practices. The immense adaptation of the governing laws following establishment of PayDK serves an inspiration that legal systems and enterprise architecture can provide mutual support.

Conclusively, systemic services transformation must focus on both the services architecture and on the governing principles of the organisational transformation. Inclusion of external factors, drivers and barriers, i.e. the emergent extended context, seem to augment the "narrow" enterprise architecture planning positively.

FUTURE RESEARCH DIRECTIONS

The involved staff of the PayDK case participated in several years to capture the services in the BPMN notation in the governmental Work Flow Bank, but did never reach a definite point regarding consensus or level of detail. Now PayDK is being established on vaguely defined business processes with vaguely defined administrative interfaces to the ceding local governments. At the same time, much experience and knowledge is being discarded due to the lack of identifiable staff motivated to join. It is assumed to work anyhow. In some cases, organisational realignment needs to work despite difficult odds because there is no point of return, this paradoxical balance is also discussed by Wagenaar (2006). Learning from these cases is extremely interesting, since pragmatism and willingness of constant small rapid changes must

be at its highest here. The senior project manager stated that "it all comes down to collaboration and teamwork."

There have been several claims in the public debate on PayDK that the business case was made before the local governments themselves implemented local shared service centres, and the PayDK as a large organisation will be significantly more expensive than the service provided today. Furthermore, the ability to find faults and fraud based on local communication will disappear assuming a growth in fraud. The idea of extracting shared services from one SSC and moving these services to other SSCs must be relevant to many organisations. But is the business case sufficiently strong? And how does it affect EA? Future research could beneficially review EA under change and distributed versus centralised design considerations.

The model approach of intention, context and execution of services offer a fundamental toolkit for the systemic understanding of transformation. Thus it can support the development of an EA by going behind the formal organisational construct. As a matter of future research, *intentions* display a paradoxical nature that would be interesting to review further: The intentional tension between the strategic and operational layers is an issue potentially both on the provider and consumer side. In a research perspective, this might contribute to the reason why services are seen differently at management level and the level of the immediate service provider.

Further research into the meaning of context could include parallel contexts, influence of distributed contexts, cross-culturalism in contexts and management versus operations view on context. Organisational shift of context and necessary transformation in design of new contexts would support the formation of business entities, such as SSC, better.

On *execution*, further research should address services not directly associated with the primary provider-supplier relation, but underlying, internal, supportive or habitual services. Popular rhetoric is often deeming these services obsolete, of a non-value creation type, and not contributing to customer experience. But the usefulness must be seen broader. E.g. human data validation, as a service, might be useful, if technology support of this is insufficient or error prone. Non-technology services may also be beneficial for the integration of otherwise technological services. In the critique of SSC, the loss of informal knowledge, informal lines of communication and casual non-compliance detection has often been raised. Architectural design processes would benefit from better insight in this domain.

Very interesting is also, as briefly indicated above, the efficiency of moving of services from one SSC to another. Included in this are the possibilities to decontextualise a service, to transfer a context, to find a minimal set of common contexts or to simply aim for a new, "blank" context out of necessity. The degree of decontextualisation may also be researched along with failed or successful cases of SSC formation.

CONCLUSION

The growth in complexity and the drive for cost cutting is similar in governmental and commercial organisations. A services view is interesting as the universal nature of the service notion ideally can encompass technical as well as business services. The composite and combinatorial character of services makes it straightforward to suggest changes and continuous realignment.

The case of PayDK exemplifies an edge of services perception, services delivery, shared services and (Governmental) SSC where existence of eGovernment and legislative adjustments form foundation for creating one organisation for servicing around 50% of a population and around 10% of the GDP. PayDK is a somewhat radical approach to an expected new generation

of eGovernment typically placed differently as projected in maturity models: PayDK changes citizen's interaction with a broad range of services to a single channel digital service. Local insight and networked, distributed SSCs are given up and focus is on economies of scale and harvesting the fruits of a high level eGovernment maturity. The perceived and desired quality of services change focus into a transaction cost perspective far more than local insight, local government autonomy, and face-to-face interaction. The next level of eGoverment can both include a stronger and more professional service production, but also a services impoverishment and alienation in the relation between citizens and government.

The approximation between citizens and systems driven by eGovernment changes the game of governmental services from physical citizen interaction and into a more abstract character of information and applications architectures. SSC will develop a new logic of service thinking with an inevitable specialisation and professionalization. SSC will never be static; the SSC is likely to develop SSCs within the SSC, move selected services to other partners, move certain responsibilities back to the ceding organisations or any other business partner. The fundamental systemic character of SSC is its dynamics strongly associated with the service model making services abstract and transferable although only meaningful with its intention and context. Selected activities in services transformation are superficially seen as execution-oriented but under the surface developed of intention and adaption with context is prevalent.

Broader considerations of the service proportion of enterprise architecture are expected to provide a deeper and more systemic foundation for the architectural processes. The distinction between intention, context and execution suggest abstracting from formal, potentially digital services and into purpose, reason and meaningfulness. In other words, the management accepts and emphasise the ability to use informal communication, tacit knowledge, experience and non-technical approaches opposed to comprehensive IT solutions to any issue. Thereby, technical services and business services can translate and exchange, augment or replace each other in any order. Obsolescence, end-of-life and purpose-less services have been discussed and are proposed to be included in the architectural considerations.

REFERENCES

Afshani, J., Harounabadi, A., & Dezfouli, M. A. (2012). A new model for designing uncertain enterprise architecture. *Management Science Letters*, *2*, 689–696. doi:10.5267/j.msl.2012.01.005.

Alt, R., Abramowicz, W., & Demirkan, H. (2010). Service-orientation in electronic markets. *Electronic Markets*, *20*, 177–180. doi:10.1007/s12525-010-0047-6.

Alter, S. (2008). Service system fundamentals: Work system, value chain, and life cycle. *IBM Systems Journal*, *47*(1), 71–85. doi:10.1147/sj.471.0071.

Anupindi, N. V., & Coady, G. A. (2011). *Enterprise architecture turnaround*. Trafford Publishing.

Arnould, E. J. (2008). Service-dominant logic and resource theory. *Journal of the Academy of Marketing Science*, *36*, 21–24. doi:10.1007/s11747-007-0072-y.

Bækgaard, L. (2005). *From use cases to activity cases*. Paper presented at ALOIS'2005 - Action in Language, Organisation and Information Systems. Limerick, Ireland.

Bækgaard, L. (2009). Service scenarios - A socio-technical approach to business service modeling. In *Proceedings of ECIS'2009 - European Conference of Information Systems 2009*. Verona, Italy: ECIS.

Bardhan, I. R. et al. (2010). Information system in services. *Journal of Management Information Systems*, *26*(4), 5–12. doi:10.2753/MIS0742-1222260401.

Barros, A., & Dumas, M. (2005). *Service interaction patterns: Towards a reference framework for service-based business process interconnection*. Queensland University of Technology.

Bergeron, B. (2003). *Essentials of shared services*. Hoboken, NJ: John Wiley & Sons.

Bernard, S. (2005). *Enterprise architecture*. Bloomington, IN: AuthorsHouse.

Birkmeier, D., et al. (2012). The role of services in governmental enterprise architecture: The case of the German federal government. In Saha (Ed.), Enterprise Architecture for Connected E-Government – Practices and Innovations. Hershey, PA: IGI Global.

Boglind, A., Hällstén, F., & Thilander, P. (2011). HR transformation and shared services: Adoption and adaptation in Swedish organizations. *Personnel Review*, *40*(5), 570–588. doi:10.1108/00483481111154441.

Booch, G. (2010, March/April). Enterprise architecture and technical architecture. *IEEE Software*, 95–96.

Borman, M. (2010). Characteristics of a successful shared services centre in the Australian public sector. *Transforming Government: People. Process and Policy*, *4*(3), 220–231.

Boukhedouma, S., et al. (2012). Adaptability of service based workflow models: The chained execution architecture. *BIS*, 96-107

Bouwman, H., van Houtum, H., Janssen, M., & Versteeg, G. (2011). Business architecture in the public sector: Experiences from practice. *Communications of the Association for Information Systems*, *29*(1), 411–426.

Chandrasekaran, N., & Ensing, G. (2004). ODC: A global IT services delivery model. *Communications of the ACM, 47*(5), 47–49. doi:10.1145/986213.986237.

Chang, C. M. (2010). *Service systems management and engineering – Creating strategic differentiation and operational excellence.* Hoboken, NJ: Wiley. doi:10.1002/9780470900208.

Cherbakov, L., & Galambos, G. et al. (2005). Impact of service orientation at the business level. *IBM Systems Journal, 44*(4), 653–668. doi:10.1147/sj.444.0653.

Chesbrough, H., & Spohrer, J. (2006). A research manifesto for services science. *Communications of the ACM, 49*(7), 35–40. doi:10.1145/1139922.1139945.

Currie, W., & Parikh, M. (2004). Exploring the supply-side of web services: The need for market positioning. In *Proceedings of ICIS*, (pp. 339-350). ICIS.

Dandapani, K. (2004). Success and failure in web-based financial services. *Communications of the ACM, 47*(5), 31–33. doi:10.1145/986213.986233.

David, I.T. (2005). Financial management shared services: A guide for federal users. *Journal of Government Financial Management*, 55-60.

Deloitte. (2011). *2011 global shared services survey.* Retrieved from http://www.deloitte.com/assets/Dcom-UnitedStates/Local%20Assets/Documents/IMOs/Shared%20Services/us_sdt_2011GlobalSharedServicesSurveyExecutiveSummary.pdf

Dico, A. S. (2012). Towards whole-of-government EA with TOGAF and SOA. In Saha (Ed.), Enterprise Architecture for Connected E-Government – Practices and Innovations. Hershey, PA: IGI Global.

Dollery, B., Hallam, G., & Wallis, J. (2009). Shared services in Australian local government: A case study of the Queensland local government association model. *Economic Papers, 27*(4), 343–354. doi:10.1111/j.1759-3441.2008.tb01048.x.

Doucet, G., Gøtze, J., Saha, P., & Bernard, S. (2009). *Coherency management – Architecting the enterprise for alignment, agility and assurance.* Bloomington, IN: AuthorsHouse.

Evans, C. (2007). Modelling service. *Business Strategy Review*, 53-59.

Farndale, E., Paauwe, J., & Hoeksema, L. (2009). In-sourcing HR: Shared service centres in the Netherlands. *International Journal of Human Resource Management, 20*(3), 544–561. doi:10.1080/09585190802707300.

Forst, L. I. (1997, January). Febraury). Fulfilling the promises of shared services. *Strategy and Leadership.* doi:10.1108/eb054578.

Galliers, R., & Currie, W. (Eds.). (2011). The Oxford handbook of management information systems. Oxford, UK: Oxford.

GAO. (2010). *Organizational transformation - A framework for assessing and improving enterprise architecture management (version 2.0).* Washington, DC: United States Government Accountability Office.

Glissman, S., & Sanz, J. (2009). *A comparative review of business architecture: IBM research report.* San Jose, CA: IBM.

Goldkuhl, G. (2006). Action and media in interorganizational interaction. *Communications of the ACM, 49*(5), 53–57. doi:10.1145/1125944.1125975.

Graham, A. (2012). *The enterprise data model – A framework for enterprise data architecture* (2nd ed.). Koios Associates.

Grant, G., McKnight, S., Uruthirapathy, A., & Brown, A. (2007). Designing governance for shared services organizations in the public service. *Government Information Quarterly, 24*, 522–538. doi:10.1016/j.giq.2006.09.005.

Graves, T. (2012). *The enterprise as story*. Essex, UK: Tetradian Books.

Grefen, P., Ludwig, H., Dan, A., & Angelov, S. (2006). An analysis of web services support for dynamic business process outsourcing. *Information and Software Technology, 48*(11), 1115–1134. doi:10.1016/j.infsof.2006.03.010.

Hausmann, K. (2011). *Sustainable enterprise architecture*. Boca Raton, FL: CRC Press. doi:10.1201/b10793.

Hill, T. P. (1977). On goods and services. *The Review of Income and Wealth, 23*(4), 315–338. doi:10.1111/j.1475-4991.1977.tb00021.x.

Hjort-Madsen, K. (2009). *Architecting government understanding enterprise architecture adoption in the public sector. (PhD-Thesis)*. Copenhagen, Denmark: The IT University.

Holt, J., & Perry, S. (2010). *Modelling enterprise architectures*. The Institution of Engineering and Technology.

Howcroft, D., & Richardson, H. (2012). The back office goes global: Exploring connections and contradictions in shared service centres. *Work, Employment and Society, 26*(1), 111–127. doi:10.1177/0950017011426309.

Infosys. (2011). *Infosys partners with Philips in the journey to transform their shared service centers (SSC)*. Bangalore, India: Infosys.

Jahani, B., Javadein, S., & Jafari, H. (2010). Measurement of enterprise architecture readiness within organizations. *Business Strategy Series, 11*(3), 177–191. doi:10.1108/17515631011043840.

Janssen, M., & Joha, A. (2006). Motives for establishing shared service centers in public administrations. *International Journal of Information Management, 26*, 102–115. doi:10.1016/j.ijinfomgt.2005.11.006.

Janssen, M., Joha, A., & Zuurmond, A. (2009). Simulation and animation for adopting shared services: Evaluating and comparing alternative arrangements. *Government Information Quarterly, 26*, 15–24. doi:10.1016/j.giq.2008.08.004.

Janssen, M., & Wagenaar, R. (2004). An analysis of a shared services centre in e-government. In *Proceedings of the 37th Annual Hawaii International Conference on System Sciences (HICSS'04)*. IEEE.

Jensen, A. Ø. (2010). *Government enterprise architecture adoption: A systemic-discursive critique and reconceptualisation*. (MSc Thesis). IT University, Copenhagen, Denmark.

Joha, A., & Janssen, M. (2010). Public-private partnerships, outsourcing or shared service centres? Motives and intents for selecting sourcing configurations. *Transforming Government: People. Process and Policy, 4*(3), 232–248.

Kaner, M., & Karni, R. (2007). Engineering design of a service system: An empirical study. *Information Knowledge Systems Management, 6*, 235–263.

Karokola, G., & Yngström, L. (2009). Discussing e-government maturity models for the developing world - Security view. *ISSA*, 81-98.

KL. (2012). Work instructions, form-based application, housing support, first-time application. *Association of Danish Local Governments*. Retrieved August 20, 2012 from http://www.kl.dk/ImageVault/Images/id_53025/scope_0/ImageVaultHandler.aspx

Kombit. (2012a). *Fælleskommunal rammearkitektur – Konkurrence, digitalisering og sikker drift*. Retrieved June 1, 2012, from http://www.kombit.dk/rammearkitektur

Kombit. (2012b). *Fælleskommunal rammear-kitektur – Godkendelse af centrale elementer.* Retrieved June 1, 2012, from http://www.kombit.dk/rammearkitektur

Kreklow, S. R., & Kinney, A. S. (2007). The effective organization of administration functions through shared services. *Government Finance Review, 23*(3), 61–62.

Kudryavtsev, D., & Grigoriev, L. (2011). Systemic approach towards enterprise functional decomposition. In *Proceedings of the 2011 IEEE Conference on Commerce and Enterprise Computing*, (pp. 310-317). IEEE.

Kumar, K., & Hillegersberg, J. V. (2004). New architectures for financial services. *Communications of the ACM, 47*(5), 27–30.

Lankhorst, M. et al. (Eds.). (2009). *Enterprise architecture at work.* Berlin: Springer Verlag. doi:10.1007/978-3-642-01310-2.

Longepe, C. (2007). *The enterprise architecture IT project – The urbanisation paradigm.* London: Kogan Page.

Lusch, R. F., & Vargo, S. L. et al. (2008). Toward a conceptual foundation for service science: Contributions from service-dominant logic. *IBM Systems Journal, 47*(1). doi:10.1147/sj.471.0005.

Madhavaram, S., & Hunt, S. D. (2008). The service-dominant logic and a hierarchy of operant resources: Developing masterful operant resources and implications for marketing strategy. *Journal of the Academy of Marketing Science, 36*, 67–82. doi:10.1007/s11747-007-0063-z.

Maglio, P. P., & Spohrer, J. (2008). Fundamentals of service science. *Journal of the Academy of Marketing Science, 36*, 18–20. doi:10.1007/s11747-007-0058-9.

Maglio, P. P., & Srinivasan, S. et al. (2006). Service systems, service scientists, SSME, and innovation. *Communications of the ACM, 49*(7), 81–85. doi:10.1145/1139922.1139955.

Mallat, N., & Rossi, M. et al. (2004). Mobile banking services. *Communications of the ACM, 47*(5), 42–46. doi:10.1145/986213.986236.

McIvor, R., McCracken, M., & McHugh, M. (2011). Creating outsourced shared services arrangements: Lessons from the public sector. *European Management Journal.* doi:10.1016/j.emj.2011.06.001.

Mercer, M. (2011). Shared services & cost saving collaboration deserve respect. *Public Management,* 8–12.

Mohan, S. (2006). Making the case for shared services in the public sector. *Accountancy Ireland, 38*(4), 14–15.

Murray, J. G., Rentell, P. G., & Geere, D. (2008). Procurement as a shared service in English local government. *International Journal of Public Sector Management, 21*(5), 540–555. doi:10.1108/09513550810885822.

Niehaves, B., & Krause, A. (2010). Shared service strategies in local government - A multiple case study exploration. *Transforming Government: People. Process and Policy, 4*(3), 266–279.

O'Sullivan, J. et al. (2002). What's in a service? Towards accurate description of non-functional service properties. *Distributed and Parallel Databases, 12,* 117–133. doi:10.1023/A:1016547000822.

Pan, A., & Vina, A. (2004). An alternative architecture for financial data integration. *Communications of the ACM, 47*(5), 37–40. doi:10.1145/986213.986235.

Paulson, L. D. (2006). Services science: A new field for today's economy. *IEEE Computer, 39*(8), 18–21. doi:10.1109/MC.2006.277.

Pulkkinen, M. (2006). Systemic management of architectural decisions in enterprise architecture planning: Four dimensions and three abstraction levels. In *Proceedings of the 39th Hawaii International Conference on System Sciences – 2006*. IEEE.

PWC. (2008). *Point of view shared service center 2nd generation: Taking the next step to reach a more efficient level of evolution.* PriceWaterhouseCoopers.

Quartel, D. A. C., & Steen, M. W. A. et al. (2007). COSMO: A conceptual framework for service modelling and refinement. *Information Systems Frontiers, 9*, 225–244. doi:10.1007/s10796-007-9034-7.

Rabhi, F.A., Yu, H., Dabous, F.T., & Wu, S. (2007). A service-oriented architecture for financial business processes. *Information Systems and e-Business Management, 5*(2), 185-200.

Roman, D. et al. (2005). Web service modeling ontology. *Applied Ontology, 1*(1), 77–106.

Ross, J. W., Weill, P., & Robertson, D. C. (2008). *Enterprise architecture as strategy*. Boston: Harvard Business School Press.

Rothwell, A. T., Herbert, I. P., & Seal, W. (2011). Shared service centers and professional employability. *Journal of Vocational Behavior, 79*, 241–252. doi:10.1016/j.jvb.2011.01.001.

Rust, R. T., & Miu, C. (2006). What academic research tells us about service. *Communications of the ACM, 49*(7), 49–54. doi:10.1145/1139922.1139948.

Sampson, S. E., & Froehle, C. M. (2006). Foundations and implications of a proposed unified services theory. *Production and Operations Management, 15*(2), 329–343. doi:10.1111/j.1937-5956.2006.tb00248.x.

Schendel, R. et al. (2011). *ICT project guidebook: E-government capability maturity model*. Manila: Asian Development Bank.

Schulz, V., & Brenner, W. (2010). Characteristics of shared service centers. *Transforming Government: People. Process and Policy, 4*(3), 210–219.

Seal, W., & Herbert, I. (2009, Spring). The role of shared services. *Management Services*, 43-47.

Selden, S. C., & Wooters, R. (2011). Structures in public human resource management: Shared services in state governments. *Review of Public Personnel Administration, 31*(4), 349–368. doi:10.1177/0734371X11408698.

Sheth, A., & Verna, K. et al. (2006). Semantics to energize the full services spectrum. *Communications of the ACM, 49*(7), 55–61. doi:10.1145/1139922.1139949.

Smith, C., Henschel, E., & Lefeber, R. (2008). Consolidation and shared service. *Government Finance Review, 24*(5), 14–20.

Smith, K. L. (2011). *An introduction to PEAF – Pragmatic enterprise architecture framework*. Great Notley: Pragmatic EA.

Spohrer, J., & Riecken, D. (2006). Service science. *Communications of the ACM, 49*(7), 31–34.

Su, N., Akkiraju, R., Nayak, N., & Goodwin, R. (2009). Shared services transformation: Conceptualization and valuation from the perspective of real options. *Decision Sciences, 40*(3), 381–402. doi:10.1111/j.1540-5915.2009.00243.x.

Teece, D., Pisano, G., & Shuen, A. (1997). Dynamic capabilities and strategic management. *Strategic Management Journal, 18*(7), 509–533. doi:10.1002/(SICI)1097-0266(199708)18:7<509::AID-SMJ882>3.0.CO;2-Z.

Turle, M. (2010). Shared services: An outline of key contractual issues. *Computer Law & Security Report*, 2(6), 178–184. doi:10.1016/j.clsr.2010.01.009.

Ulbrich, F. (2006). Improving shared service implementation: Adopting lessons from the BPR movement. *Business Process Management Journal*, 12(2), 191–205. doi:10.1108/14637150610657530.

Ulbrich, F. (2010). Adopting shared services in a public-sector organization. *Transforming Government: People. Process and Policy*, 4(3), 249–265.

Ulrich, D. (1995). Shared services: From vogue to value. *Human Resource Planning*, 18(3), 12–23.

Ulrich, D., & Grochowski, J. (2012). From shared services to professional services. *Strategic HR Review*, 11(3), 136–142. doi:10.1108/14754391211216850.

Umapathy, K., & Purao, S. (2007). A theoretical investigation of emerging standards for web services. *Information Systems Frontiers*, 9(1), 119–134. doi:10.1007/s10796-006-9021-4.

Van den Berg, M., & van Steenbergen, M. (2010). *Building an enterprise architecture practice*. Berlin: Springer.

Van Hillegersberg, J., Boeke, R., & Van den Heuvel, W. J. (2004). Potential of webservices to enable smart business networks. *Journal of Information Technology*, 19(4), 281–287. doi:10.1057/palgrave.jit.2000027.

Vargo, S. L., & Lusch, R. F. (2004). Evolving to a new dominant logic for marketing. *Journal of Marketing*, 68, 1–17. doi:10.1509/jmkg.68.1.1.24036.

Vargo, S. L., & Lusch, R. F. (2008a). Service-dominant logic: Continuing the evolution. *Journal of the Academy of Marketing Science*, 36, 1–10. doi:10.1007/s11747-007-0069-6.

Vargo, S. L., & Lusch, R. F. (2008b). Why service? *Journal of the Academy of Marketing Science*, 36, 25–38. doi:10.1007/s11747-007-0068-7.

Wagenaar, R. (2006). Governance of shared service centers in public administration: Dilemma's and trade-offs. In *Proceedings of ICEC'06*. ICEC.

Wegmann, A. (2003). *The systemic enterprise architecture methodology, business and IT alignment for competitveness*.

Weske, M. (2012). *Business process management – Concepts, languages, architectures*. Berlin: Springer. doi:10.1007/978-3-642-28616-2.

Wilson, D. A. (2004). Shared services: A strategy for reinventing government. *Government Finance Review*, 20(4), 37–44.

Windley, P. (2002). *eGovernment maturity*. Retrieved June 1, 2012, from http://www.windley.com/

Zachmann, J. A. (1987). A framework for information systems architecture. *IBM Systems Journal*, 26(3), 276–292. doi:10.1147/sj.263.0276.

ADDITIONAL READING

Baskerville, R. (2009). What design science is not. *European Journal of Information Systems*, 17(5), 441–443. doi:10.1057/ejis.2008.45.

Carlsson, S. A. et al. (2011). Socio-technical IS design science research: developing design theory for IS integration management. *Information Systems and E-Business Management*, 9(1), 109–131. doi:10.1007/s10257-010-0140-6.

Daigneau, R. (2011). *Service design patterns: Fundamental design solutions for SOAP/WSDL and RESTful web services*. Upper Saddle River, NJ: Addison-Wesley.

Daskin, M. (2011). *Service science*. Hoboken, NJ: Wiley.

Duggan, D. (2012). *Enterprise software architecture and design: Entities, services, and resources.* Hoboken, NJ: Wiley. doi:10.1002/9781118180518.

Felten, J. (2011). *Service design: Essay.* Norderstedt: GRIN Verlag.

Foorthuis, R. et al. (2012). Compliance assessments of projects adhering to enterprise architecture. *Journal of Database Management, 23*(2), 44–71. doi:10.4018/jdm.2012040103.

Lockwood, T. (2009). *Thinking: Integrating innovation, customer experience, and brand value.* New York: Allworth Press.

Macintyre, M., Parry, G., & Angelis, J. (2011). *Service design and delivery.* London: Springer. doi:10.1007/978-1-4419-8321-3.

Møller, C. (2008). Complex service design: A virtual enterprise architecture for logistics service. *Information Systems Frontiers, 10*(5), 503–518. doi:10.1007/s10796-008-9106-3.

Payne, A. F., & Storbacka, K. et al. (2008). Managing the co-creation of value. *Journal of the Academy of Marketing Science, 36,* 83–96. doi:10.1007/s11747-007-0070-0.

Salomonson, N., & Lind, M. (2006). *IT in service encounters - Studying conversations to determine IT-enabled actions.* Paper presented at the Conference on Action in Language, Action in Language, Organisations and Information Systems (ALOIS'06). Borås, Sweden.

Tan, X., Alter, S., et al. (2008). *Integrating lightweight systems analysis into the unified process by using service responsibility tables.* Paper presented at the Americas Conference on Information Systems - AMCIS'08. Toronto, Canada.

Vidgen, R., & Wang, X. (2006). From business process management to business process ecosystem. *Journal of Information Technology, 21,* 262–271. doi:10.1057/palgrave.jit.2000076.

Wulf, J., & Zarnekow, R. (2010). Technologies for the electronic distribution of information services - A value proposition analysis. *Electronic Markets, 20,* 3–19. doi:10.1007/s12525-010-0027-x.

KEY TERMS AND DEFINITIONS

Business Process Outsourcing: BPO is the idea of buying non-core business activities from vendors specialised in the specific fields of services typically related to administrative business processes. Examples include phone services, telemarketing as well as accounting and human resource management. The term has intensively been linked to the Indian offshoring industry, but there is no physical limitation to BPO, and numerous small and large players characterise the market.

Quality of Service (QoS): QoS originates from telecommunication as a guaranteed communication bandwidth sold by a network owner to a network consumer. QoS describes a range of physical and electrical features which the consumer should expect. The term is now colloquially used in a much broader sense where the level of details in any service needs to be unambiguously defined.

Service Architecture: The relationship between service execution, current/future state operational organising, technology and business strategy. Service architecture will normally be supported by information technology, but can also exist without. Likewise, service architecture can also purely address a technological construct.

Service Context: The organisational ambience including tangible and intangible factors supposed present in providing and requesting services. Social, cultural and behavioural issues can, very broadly, be seen as influence factors. Also existence of regular patterns of business practices, knowledge, formal and informal skills as well as balance of power of relations would be part of the context making a service meaningful.

Service Design: Service design is the process of creating, detailing and modifying service execution. It is primarily driven by service intention and must properly manage service contexts. Service design can address any type of service with any degree of inclusion or exclusion of technology. Furthermore, it requires close attention to cost, and part of the design can be the reward/penalty system.

Service Execution: The act of the service at any organisational level and in any granularity and complexity. A consumer role is not necessarily involved, and the service execution can thus be disputed for either providing value or being inert. Persons, organisations and systems can all provide service execution.

Service Intention: Motivations, desires and governance of the provider-consumer scheme both at organisational and individual levels. Intention embodies expectations, assumptions, circumventions and opportunisms. Reward or penalties would be associated with intention and expected outcome.

Service Level Agreement (SLA): Originally a contract stating mutual obligations of buying and selling of information technology services, but in recent years, SLA's are being used in most types of services provisioning, including services not related to information technology. The SLA is typically regulating the relationship between cost and the quality of services seen as e.g. workforce allocated, provider latency, escalation, skills and information. Most often, the SLA is associated with a performance measurement regime, also occasionally supported by a reward and penalty system.

Shared Service Centre: An organisational unit hosting shared services. It can be within the same overall organisation consuming the services or it can be externalised into specialised operators. Shared service centres are often associated with cost reduction, internal specialisation and geographical concentration.

Shared Service: A generalisation of an individual service to a level where several consumers of the service can request service execution under sufficiently overlapping contexts and intentions. Shared services are mostly relating to routinised administrative business processes.

Chapter 12
Navigating Complexity with Enterprise Architecture Management

Haiping Luo
Department of Commerce, USA

ABSTRACT

Enterprises are like living creatures in the ecosystem – there are vast varieties of species; each individual in any species is unique, complex, dynamic, and constantly interacting with its ever-changing environment. Also, like living creatures, enterprises have many commonalities. These commonalities exist in all enterprises, regardless of their business, size, environment, culture, lifecycle stage, or any other factor. Enterprise Architecture (EA) management helps enterprises discover their commonalities, adopt best practices to manage the commonalities, and apply holistic and systemic approaches to tackling unique complexity encountered by enterprises. This chapter extracts thinking from many thought leaders in the EA discipline and consolidates a dynamic and multi-dimensional alignment approach to managing an enterprise's architecture as a living system. This integrated approach utilizes the "Fractal" concept in Chaos Theory and identifies six common alignment dimensions in enterprises. This approach includes dynamic alignment mechanisms to help enterprises navigate the increasingly complex and ever-changing world. This approach bridges individual alignments with enterprise optimization. A fictional example of a disaster relief operation is used to illustrate how the EA approach could help a relief enterprise navigate through the complexity and dynamics of the disaster relief operation to achieve life-saving results.

DOI: 10.4018/978-1-4666-4518-9.ch012

1. INTRODUCTION

A Chinese proverb says, *Even a tiny bird has all the guts*. Any individual enterprise, regardless of its type and size, is a complex system. An *Enterprise* is defined in this chapter as *a set of people who are related by a common goal or goals formally or informally, permanently or temporarily, explicitly or implicitly*. An enterprise can be a company, a project, a program, a government, a mass movement, a military operation, a religious mission, a community, a group of nations, the human species, and much more. Enterprises are like living creatures in the ecosystem – there are vast varieties of species; each individual in any species is unique, complex, dynamic, and constantly interacting with its ever-changing environment. Managing any such enterprise is a highly complex pursuit.

This chapter integrates different schools of Enterprise Architecture (EA) thinking to address enterprise complexity through utilizing commonalities and applying dynamic alignment. The sections will discuss the dimensions of enterprise complexity, the unique benefits of the EA approach, the different schools of EA thinking, and an integration of the EA methods to manage enterprises holistically and agilely. The use of the EA approach will be illustrated through a fictional disaster relief operation.

The objectives of this chapter are:

- Integrating different schools of EA thinking to manage the many dimensions of enterprise complexity.
- Demonstrating how to apply the EA approach to tackle complexity and dynamics in real world problems.
- Identifying directions for future development and applications of the EA management approach.

2. BACKGROUND

To tackle the complexity of managing enterprises, an arsenal of management theories and approaches have been developed over thousands of years, with their flourish coming mainly in the 20th century. These management theories and approaches can be grouped into the following categories according to the perspectives they take:

2.1. Functional Perspective

This thought group views enterprise management as a set of responsibilities or activities that can be generalized into basic management responsibilities such as forecasting, planning, organizing, commanding, coordinating and controlling; or common functional branches such as human resource management, operations or production management, strategic management, financial management, information technology management.

The thinking and approach of this group emphasizes defining scope, roles and responsibilities of management activities and functions, identifying guiding principles that apply to management in general and to specific functions, and defining best-practice approach to perform and coordinate these management activities and functions.

Influential authors and works in this group include Henri Fayol's works on general theory and principles of management (Fayol, 1918); Alexander Church's works on the science and practice of management (Church, 1914); and Harvard Business School's Business Administration textbooks since 1921.

2.2. Psychological and Sociological Perspective

This thought group investigates the human and social aspects of enterprise management. It applies psychological and sociological approaches to address management issues such as personnel recruitment and selection, performance appraisal, remuneration and compensation, motivation in the workplace, organizational culture, group behavior, job satisfaction and commitment, and organizational change/development.

This group emphasizes developing and leveraging human characteristics, human needs, human behavior, and social relationships in an organization to address management challenges. The thinking and approach of this thought group contributes to an organization's success by improving the performance and well-being of its people.

Influential authors and works in this group include Ordway Tead's works on industrial relations (Tead, 1916); Walter Dill Scott's works on human efficiency in business (Scott, 1911); Kurt Lewin's works on group dynamics (Lewin, 1948) and action research; Elton Mayo's works on social relations in industrial civilizations (Mayo, 1945); Mary Parker Follett's works on dynamic, matrix-style organizations (Follett, 1927); Max Weber's works on economic sociology during the 1900's to 1920's (Weber, reassembled in 1999); Rensis Likert's works on management patterns (Likert, 1961); and Chris Argyris' works on action science (Argyris, 1982).

2.3. Engineering and Analytical Perspective

This thought group applies engineering and analytical approaches to maximize the productivity of any task and activity. Originated by Frederick Taylor and later evolved into various process engineering, quality control, operation research, and other productivity improvement approaches, this thought group dissects work activities into small components, collects productivity data for each components, and seeks the best possible way to improve the performance of each individual component as well as the overall process.

This group emphasizes that the prosperity of the enterprise as well as of its members depends on the productivity of the enterprise and that the optimization of this productivity can only come from data-driven scientific analysis and process discipline.

Influential authors and works in this group include Frederick Taylor's works on scientific management (Taylor, 1911); Henry Gantt's work charts (Gantt, 1903); Ronald Fisher's works on modern statistics and experimental design (Fisher, 1925); Patrick Blackett's works on operation research initiated in WWII (Kirby & Rosenhead, 2011); Kaoru Ishikawa's works on quality control (Ishikawa, 1988); Goldratt's works on theory of constraints (Cox & Goldratt, 1986); and Michael Hammer's works on process reengineering (Hammer, 1990).

2.4. Systemic Perspective

This thought group applies systems and complexity theories and approaches to address the complexity of the enterprises. An enterprise is viewed as a system which maintains its existence through the mutual interaction of its parts. Systems have characteristics which cannot be found as characteristic of any of the individual parts. Enterprise managers must recognize systems' characteristics and manage relationships and interactions. This thought group uses structure models, process patterns, information volume and quality, communication loops, control mechanisms, and other systemic tools and approaches to examine and assist enterprise management.

This group emphasizes that enterprises can evolve and improve through maintaining an open structure; increasing the degree of organization; establishing all-way communication loops; and strengthening the adaptive and progressive capability to process information, manage change, keep learning from experience, and pursue excellence. The optimum state of an enterprise is not a static point. Rather, the optimum state is a self-disciplined, active process that interacts with environmental and internal conditions and changes dynamically and agilely, and keeps pursuing higher forms of the enterprise's existence.

Influential authors and works in this group include Ludwig von Bertalanffy's General Systems Theory (Bertalanffy, 1969); Wiener's works on Cybernetics (Wiener, 1948); Boulding's works on eco-dynamics (Boulding, 1953); and Santa Fe Institute's works on complex adaptive systems (Holland, 1992) (Gell-Mann, 1994).

Enterprise architecture's approach takes the systemic perspective to enterprise management, despite the fact that EA is more of an encompassing integration framework that connects and incorporates all management perspectives to help enterprises tackle complexity through holistic methods. The next section will discuss the EA approach in detail focusing on tackling enterprise complexity.

3. THE ENTERPRISE ARCHITECTURE APPROACH

3.1. Sources of Enterprise Complexity

The term "Complexity" is defined as the number of factors and their connections that need to be considered by a decision maker. The complexity faced by enterprises comes from many sources:

- The business they are in could involve many components, processes, and highly intertwined interactions and interdependencies internally and externally;
- There are many internal functions and activities to manage;
- There are infinite types of environments or situations an enterprise could encounter;

- There are endless external and internal non-managerial factors to consider at any time and by any level of the enterprise;
- Everything is constantly changing, both within and outside the enterprise;
- Everything is interconnected; and
- Every source of complexity above not only contains factors and challenges that are known or knowable to the enterprise, but also encompasses factors that are completely unknown and unforeseeable by any enterprise.

EA management is an information-based, holistic, and dynamic approach to tackling enterprise complexity from all these sources.

- "Information-based" means that the EA management depends on systematically collected, maintained, and analyzed information to make informed decisions. More precisely, EA management depends on "metadata," rather than "data," to make management decisions.
- "Holistic" means EA has a systemic way to take all things into consideration when making decisions, rather than handling management challenges in silos.
- "Dynamic" means EA establishes interactive and adaptive capabilities to monitor the environment and the situations constantly, and to re-optimize the enterprise continuously according to the situations.

In his Cynefin framework (Snowden, 2000), Snowden distinguished organizational complexity into five domains, ranging from Simple, Complicated, Complex, Chaotic, to Disorder. Such distinction is based on how a cause relates with its effects, what sequence of response is possible, and what type of management practice is suitable. While the EA discipline can help manage all five domains, the complexity targeted by EA management goes one step further. Using the thought pattern in the Cynefin Framework, a term "Interconnected Complexity" can be defined as situations in which causes and effects are inter-related and cross-impacted, requiring analysis and retrospective investigation to guide decisions using the approach of *Probe – Connect – Sense – Coordinate Responses*. Only a holistic practice, such as EA management, can help manage inter-connected complexity.

The EA approach can be presented from two perspectives: 1) extracting and utilizing enterprise commonalities; 2) establishing mechanisms to embody dynamic progress and optimization into the enterprises.

3.2. Commonalities

As indicated above, there are infinite known or unknown factors contributing to enterprise com-plexity. The EA approach applies systems thinking and believes that there exist models, principles, and laws that apply to generalized systems or their subclasses, irrespective of their particular kind, the nature of their component elements, and the relationships or "forces" between them (Bertalanffy, 1969). Through investigating the sources of enterprise complexity, the EA approach has extracted six common dimensions that apply to all enterprises. These common dimensions provide the base to develop a holistic and feasible approach to common management challenges, as well as to the unique complexity of any particular circumstance.

Below are some definitions for the terms that will be used in the rest of the chapter:

An "Enterprise Architecture Dimension" is defined as *a problem field of an enterprise entity that contains all possible, known or unknown, problems or needs which can be addressed by a specific alignment effort*. This definition may not mean anything right now, but we will revisit this definition later in this section (near the end of 3.4.1) to shed more light on its meaning.

An "Enterprise Entity" is *any enterprise or its element*. An enterprise comprises elements that are connected by various relationships and mutual interactions. Any enterprise itself is always an ele-ment of a larger enterprise. The terms "enterprise," "enterprise element," and "enterprise entity" will be used inter-changeably in this chapter.

"Architecture Alignment" is a dynamic process that establishes and maintains appropriate in-teroperability and fitting among related enterprise entities and components.

3.2.1. The Attribute Dimension

When we study a thing, we must always ask "what it is." The Attribute Dimension of an enterprise contains all information about "what it is." John Zachman, recognized by the enterprise architects' circle as the "father of enterprise architecture," initiated the entity attributes dimension in the *Zachman Enterprise Framework* (Zachman J. A., 1987).

As Zachman calls it "the fundamentals of communication [are] found in the primitive inter-rogatives: *What, How, When, Who, Where, and Why*" (Zachman J., 2008), the first dimension of his framework describes an enterprise entity through the following sets of interrogative attributes:

- **What:** What this entity is. For example, the United Nations (UN) is an international organization aiming at facilitating coop-eration in international law, international security, economic development, social progress, human rights, and achievement of world peace.
- **How:** How this entity functions/works. For example, from its offices around the world, the UN and its specialized agencies decide on substantive and administrative issues in regular meetings held throughout the year.
- **When:** The time aspects of this entity. For example, the UN was founded in 1945 af-

ter World War II; or, the presidency of the UN Security Council is rotated alphabetically each month.

- **Who:** Who are involved with this entity in what way. For example, the UN Security Council is made up of 15 member states, while 5 of the 15 are permanent members; the five permanent members hold veto power over substantive but not procedural resolutions.
- **Where:** The location aspects of the entity. For example, four of the five UN principal organs are located at the main UN Headquarters located on international territory in New York City. The International Court of Justice is located in the Hague, while other major agencies are based in the UN offices at Geneva, Vienna, and Nairobi.
- **Why:** The *raison d'etre* of this entity, or why it exists. For example, because of the widespread recognition that humankind could not afford a third world war, the United Nations was established to replace the flawed League of Nations in 1945 to maintain international peace and promote cooperation in solving international economic, social and humanitarian problems.

Defining and documenting these W's and H are not simply word exercises. These interrogative attributes describe the key characteristics of the entity and enable the connection and alignments of enterprise architecture building blocks.

3.2.2. The Reification Dimension

The second dimension of the enterprise entity answers the question of "how much we want/need to know." People at different levels of work function or in different circumstances may care about different kinds of information about a same thing. An enterprise as a system has "hierarchical orders," which is a basic characteristic of any system (Commons & Richards, 1984). The viewpoints, functions, characteristics, and type of complexity vary when moving from the high level of a system to its lower levels. In the Zachman Framework, the enterprise's hierarchical order is represented by the second dimension of the matrix, i.e., the rows called "Reification Transformations" (Zachman, 2008).

Zachman's Reification Transformations rows can be viewed in multiple ways from high level abstracts to low level instances (See Table 1). Each level contains artifacts that are relevant and appropriate for that level's audience or actors:

Table 1. A summary of Zachman's reification rows

Level of Decomposition	Degree of Reification	Audience Perspective	Artifact's Examples
Scope Level	Context	Executives as Planners	*What:* Business Type. *How:* Process Type.
Business Level	Concept	Business Managers as Owners	*Where:* Business Location and Connections. *Who:* Business Roles.
System Level	Logic	Architects as Designers	*When:* System Cycle. *Why:* System Purpose.
Technology Level	Physics	Engineers as Builders	*What:* Technology Specification. *How:* Technology Input/output.
Component Level	Assembles	Technicians as Implementers	*Where:* Tool Location. *Who:* Tool Roles and Responsibilities.
Operations Level	Instance Classes	Users & Workers as Participants	*When:* Operations Intervals. *Why:* Operations Ends and Means.

Another architecture framework, the US Department of Defense' Architecture Framework (DODAF), defines multiple levels for each of DOD's standard architecture views (US Department of Defense, 2010). Those views are integrated into the DODAF's Integrated Viewpoints, which include the following levels:

- **AV-1:** Overview and Summary Information
- **AV-2:** Integrated Dictionary
- **OV-1:** High Level Operational Concept Graphic
- **OV-5:** Operational Activity Model
- **OV-2:** Operational Node Connectivity Description
- **OV-3:** Operational Informational Exchange Matrix
- **SV-1:** System Interface Description
- **TV-1:** Technical Standards Profile

Distinguishing these reification levels allows identifying the scope and characteristics of the problems faced by the particular actors at each level, and developing applicable models and artifacts that address particular management concerns and focuses at each level.

3.2.3. The Lifecycle Dimension

Enterprises and their elements, like anything and everything in the universe, have lifecycles and life histories. The EA approach recognizes enterprise lifecycles and provides means to manage the different focuses and concerns of the enterprise at different lifecycle phases. Generalized Enterprise Reference Architecture and Methodology (GERAM) (IFIP/IFAC Task Force, 1999) establishes seven common lifecycle phases for any enterprise or entity and indicates that "the different life-cycle phases define types of activities that are pertinent during the life of the entity" (GERAM, 3.1.3.1).

The GERAM lifecycle phases for an enterprise entity are:

1. **Identification:** The set of activities that identifies the need to initiate a particular entity, its contents, its boundaries, and its relation to its internal and external environments.
2. **Concept:** The set of activities that are needed to develop the concepts of the underlying entity. These concepts include the definition of the entity's mission, vision, values, strategies, objectives, operational concepts, policies, business plans and so forth.
3. **Requirement:** The activities to develop descriptions of operational requirements of the enterprise entity, its relevant processes and the collection of all their functional, behavioral, informational and capability needs.
4. **Design:** The activities that support the specification of the entity with all of its components that satisfy the entity requirements. The Design phase is divided into two sub-phases: 1) Functional design for overall specifications and estimates; and 2) Detailed design for fabrication of the final physical system.
5. **Implementation:** The activities that define all those tasks that must be carried out to build or re-build the entity. This comprises implementation in the broadest sense, covering from purchasing, building or configuring, integrating, testing and validating, hiring and training, to releasing and evaluating.
6. **Operation:** The activities of the entity that are needed during its operation for producing the customer's product or service which is its special mission, along with all those tasks needed for monitoring, controlling, and evaluating the operation.
7. **Decommissioning:** The activities to re-mission, retrain, redesign, recycle, preserve, transfer, disband, disassemble, or dispose all or part of the entity at the end of its useful life in operation.

3.2.4. The Management Dimension

All enterprises, as well as their elements, perform similar internal management functions and face similar internal management challenges. They all need to manage their goals and directions; their particular business; their human, financial and material resources; their risks; their technology; and their management approaches. There are many EA frameworks and reference models that categorize the common management areas. For example, US government has defined many General Government functions (US OMB e-Government and Information Technology Office, 2012); Spewak's EA Planning defined Business, Data, Application, Technology areas (Spewak & Hill, 1993); Bernard's EA Cube defined Strategic, Business, Information, Systems & Services, Technology Infrastructure, Security (Bernard, 2012); and TeleManagement Forum's eTOM/NGOSS framework defined Strategy, Infrastructure, Product, Operation, and Enterprise Management (TM Forum).

Extracting the thinking from 20 or so different EA frameworks and reference models, and utilizing business administration theories, Luo defined a Generic Enterprise Management Architecture (Luo, 2006). This Generic Enterprise Management Architecture identified six common management areas, each of which contains several management domains that cover individual management functions. All of these management areas/domains/functions interact with each other by obtaining input from and producing output to all others (Figure 1).

Identifying common management areas enables developing common management processes, guiding principles, organization structures, information models, technology systems, and supporting services. Developing and implementing common, best practice approaches will, in turn, shorten the learning curve of management improvements. More importantly, connecting individual management areas into an interactive architecture enables managing explicitly the relationships and interactions among management

Figure 1. A generic enterprise management architecture

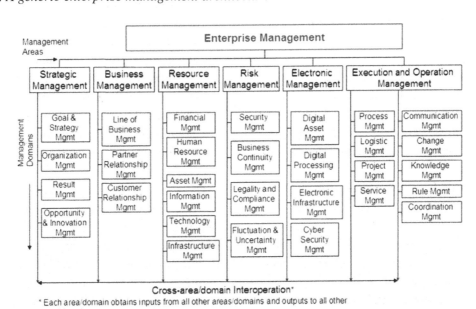

areas and gaining system synergy and enterprise optimizations that cannot come from silo operations.

3.2.5. The Business Dimension

One domain in the Generic Enterprise Management Architecture, the Line of Business Management domain, is itself a link to the biggest dimension of enterprise commonality, the Business Dimension. The Business Dimension is defined as the dimension that covers all possible lines of businesses in the world. The term "Business" is used here in its broadest sense, including all industries, all sectors, all governmental or inter-governmental functions, all academic and scientific activities, all social services, all sports and recreational activities, and so forth. Standard industry categorization, such as the North American Industry Classification System (NAICS), provides a solid foundation to codify and model standard lines of business by industry.

The Line of Business Management domain in the Management Dimension (i.e., the dimension described in subsection 3.2.4) can be further divided into these generic business functions according to the Value Chain developed by Porter (Porter, 1996):

1. **Inbound Logistics Management:** Materials handling, warehousing, inventory control, transportation.
2. **Operations Management:** Machine operating, assembly, packaging, testing, and maintenance.
3. **Outbound Logistics Management:** Order processing, warehousing, transportation, and distribution.
4. **Marketing and Sales Management:** Advertising, promotion, selling, pricing, channel management.
5. **Service Management:** Installation, servicing, spare part management.

Since the support activities (firm infrastructure, HR management, technological development, procurement) in Porter's Value Chain are covered by the other domains in the Management Dimension, they will not be repeated in the Line of Business Management domain.

The Business Dimension in this subsection, however, will further specify the value chain according to business specifications. For example, a research institute's line of business management may have these high level value chain specifications:

1. **Inbound Logistics Management:** Intake of information, knowledge, and inquiries; knowledge base management; contact and interaction tracking.
2. **Operations Management:** Research topic selection and prioritizing, research and analyses, research coordination, information and knowledge processing, result review and verification.
3. **Outbound Logistics Management:** Inquiry fulfillment, information and knowledge dissemination.
4. **Marketing and Sales Management:** Advertising, promotion, selling (for selling research products and services or for obtaining grants), pricing, channel management.
5. **Service Management:** Feedback handling; assisting application of research results; updating knowledge; renewing findings; providing supporting information, training, and/or consulting services.

There are almost infinite lines of business in the world. But the enterprises which conduct the same line of business would have common practice or patterns that can be defined and reused among that line of business. The US Federal Enterprise Architecture Business Reference Model (US OMB e-Government and Information Technology Office, 2012) is an example of standard business line categories that facilitates the development of common practice and patterns for each line of government businesses or services.

Identifying common best practices to manage individual lines of business saves organizations from reinventing the wheel or repeating known business mistakes. It also enables interoperation and coordination across organizations as well as the development of industry specific technologies to support or automate those common practices.

3.2.6. The Environment Dimension

An enterprise always exists in numerous contexts. All those contexts combined form the environment of the enterprise. An enterprise constantly interacts with its environment, both receiving influences, resources, and other impacts from the environment and producing influences, resources, and other impacts to the environment.

The environment of enterprises can be viewed from different perspectives:

1. **The Natural Environment:** This environment includes everything in the natural world that surrounds an enterprise.
2. **The Socio-Cultural Environment:** This environment includes social structures, behavior patterns, cultural norms, historical traditions, and other human and society expectations.
3. **The Economic-Political Environment:** This environment includes economic, political, legal, and other power, right, and rule formulation and execution contexts.
4. **The Knowledge-Technology Environment:** This environment includes science, technology, and other human knowledge and capabilities contexts.

The environment of enterprises constantly impacts all enterprises within it. The impacts from an environment to an enterprise may be viewed as:

- Resources, such as usable materials, energy, information, capability, knowledge;
- Drivers, such as incentives to encourage or threats to discourage certain behavior or actions;
- Signals, such as go-no-go signals, direction controls, feedbacks;
- Stimulants, such as cheers, shocks, irritants;
- Constraints, such as rules, limitations, boundaries, wastes; and
- Changes, i.e., the alteration of the state of anything in the environment.

On the other hand, every enterprise constantly produces these similar types of impacts to its environment. The interactions and interchanges between the enterprise and its environment constantly shape both the enterprise and the environment.

EA management helps enterprises establish holistic knowledge about its environment, develop reliable accountabilities and handling approaches to manage the interactions with its environment, and assure that the enterprise continuously survives and evolves in its environment.

3.2.7. Relationships and Interactions

Within and among the six dimensions identified above, a prevailing commonality is that everything and everyone has relationships. An entity is a "system" if it has parts that relate and interact with each other and with its environment. The EA approach has unique methods to investigate and manage relationships and interactions among enterprises' elements as well as the relationships and interactions between the enterprise (or its element) and its environment.

One of the EA methods to manage the relationships and interactions is to describe explicitly the relationships any element has. For example, below are just a few of the many relationships the

United Nations has (the phrase in the *italic font* describes a relationship):

- The United Nations *comprises* Member State;
- The UN *oversees* its Principal Organ;
- The UN *is subject to* International Law;
- The UN *possesses* International Legal Right.

Any enterprise entity has six common categories of relationships:

- Resource input from its environment
- Guidance and requirements from its environment
- Enabling services and supports from its environment
- Resource output to its environment
- Guidance and requirements to its environment
- Enabling services and supports to its environment

Figure 2 uses the Integrated Definition for Function Modeling (IDEF0) (US Airforce, 1990) diagram to show the interactive relationships

between two management areas described in subsection 3.2.4.

Each relationship presents the need and opportunity to align and optimize. Figure 3 illustrates how enterprise management areas take input from the external environment and other management areas and produce output to the external environment and other management areas (Luo, 2006). Each cell in the matrix is an IDEF0 diagram representing the interactions of the management area in the column with the management area in the row.

For example, the second row of the first column is the interaction between the Business Management Area and the Strategic Management Area. The Strategic Management Area provides guidance and requirements, allocates resources and enabling services to the Business Management Area. On the other hand, the Business Management Area sends requirements, produces resources, and provides enabling services back to the Strategic Management Area.

The cells in the top-left to down-right diagonal line represent the interactions between the individual management area with the enterprise's external environment and with itself. For example, Cell 3, 3 represents how the Resource Manage-

Figure 2. Interactions between two management areas

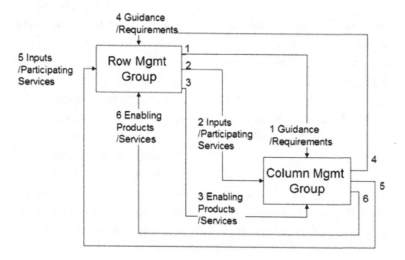

Figure 3. Interaction and alignment matrix among management areas and environment

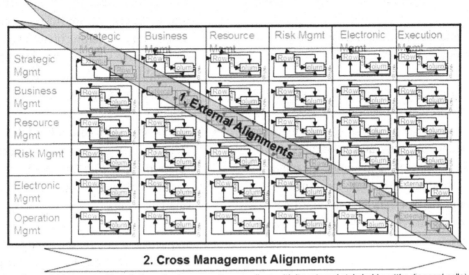

1. External Alignments: First of all, each management group aligns with its external stakeholders (the diagonal cells).
2. Cross Management Alignments: Each management group aligns with itself and every other management group.

ment Area interacts with the enterprise's external environment and itself. The Resource Management Area obtains resource input, customer requirements, guidance and regulations, and services from the external environment as well as from itself. It then produces resource output, guidance and requirements, and services to the external environment as well as to itself.

As the two large arrows in Figure 3 indicate, each of the interactions presents architecture alignment needs and opportunities. The diagonal cells represent the management areas' alignments with the environment and self, while the non-diagonal cells represent alignments with other management areas.

Explicitly and systematically documenting and managing relationships and interactions make holistic management and change coordination possible. This unique power of the EA approach can be seen more clearly in the next sub-section that discusses dynamic management.

3.3. Dynamics

Every enterprise entity constantly experiences changes within itself and from its environment. Enterprise managers must establish dynamic management capabilities to manage changes. Dynamic management capabilities include:

1. The abilities to respond to changes agilely and appropriately;
2. The abilities to identify early-on the change signals and prepare for changes in advance;
3. The abilities to initiate and lead desirable changes to advance the entity itself and its pursuits.

Of these three sets of abilities, the first set is reactive; the second set is proactive; while the third set is progressive. The first two sets of abilities define the adaptability of an enterprise. An enterprise needs adaptability to survive the vast, various, and ever-changing world. The third set of abilities goes beyond adaptability. It defines the progressiveness of an enterprise. Only with the abilities to progress can an enterprise evolve and thrive.

Dynamic management depends on three critical factors to succeed:

1. There are incentives for people to sense the change and seek for actions.
2. There are means, including information, knowledge, authority, and techniques, available for people to use to handle the change.
3. There exist coordination structures and mechanisms that can lead to coordinated, timely, and orderly responses and desirable changes.

The EA approach addresses these three factors and establishes foundations and mechanisms to build all three sets of dynamic management capabilities for enterprises. The EA approach to dynamic management is six-fold:

- **Know Who Should Do What:** A common problem in change management is that people are not clear who should be watching what changes and could take what actions about changes. This confusion results in gaps or overlaps on monitoring and acting on the changes. EA management implements the principle of "everything has an owner" and helps enterprises clearly define, document, and evaluate roles, responsibilities, processes, and accountabilities that support thorough change management.
- **Know all Changes, Both the Ones that Happened and the Coming Ones:** The ownership and accountability implemented through EA ensures that everything is watched by someone. EA also requires owners to document and maintain up-to-date current architecture. When changes are happening or showing signs of coming,

those changes and change signals could be quickly indicated by owners in their current architecture, and to be aggregated to an enterprise picture of all changes. Such an enterprise view of changes serves like a sand table in a war room, which facilitates the making of overall strategies to manage changes.

- **Know the Full Impacts of the Change:** Because EA documents connections and relationships with any element, the impact of a change of one element on the related elements can be assessed much more clearly and quickly, which helps manage impacts and handle the change.
- **Know the Options for Optimization:** The documented architecture allows enterprises to conduct "what if" analysis before deciding on actions to handle the change. For example, to respond to market changes, a company may create different designs of a new supply chain management process in the EA system to simulate the impact and results of the different designs. The results can be compared and measured against the goal, the requirements, and the constraints to make an informed decision on the most suitable design.
- **Know the Path to Coordination and Collaboration:** As the knowledge center that knows and connects strategic directions, stakeholders, policies, requirements, processes, technologies, and all other elements, the EA can help the enterprise identify and connect people who would be willing to collaborate on various changes; identify all applicable requirements and constraints; discover the least-costly and least-resistant path to coordinate changes; and design and govern orderly change courses.

- **Know the Opportunities and the Ways to Benefit from Them:** To gain competitive advantage or to achieve any mission, an enterprise cannot just react or adapt to changes. It must identify opportunities and develop strategies to create desirable changes. EA is a holistic tool that can help enterprises identify gaps, disconnections, wastes, and other less-than-optimum situations both within the enterprise and in the external environment. EA is also a change execution tool that can help enterprises set a target state and establish feasible transition plans to make desirable changes happen.

How EA enables dynamic management can also be illustrated from the OODA loop perspective. The Observe, Orient, Decide, and Act (OODA) loop represents a dynamic, recurring decision-making cycle (Boyd, 1976) that is widely applicable to military, business, academic, and other contexts. An entity that can process this cycle quicker than its opponent in unfolding circumstances would gain advantages.

EA management provides enterprises the tools and means to process the OODA loop quickly:

- **Observe:** EA ensures that everything is watched by someone and that everyone is watching the environment and the unfolding situations. EA provides a means for everyone to communicate the observations in standard forms to a central system that can generate holistic views of the current situation from all perspectives, enabling enterprises and their elements to see not only the "trees," but also the whole "forest."
- **Orient:** EA assembles scattered information and provides "all-things-considered" analysis tools to help the enterprise orient toward its goal.

- **Decide:** EA makes guidance and controls explicit and present in the relevant context. EA also identifies options to facilitate decision making.
- **Act:** EA helps plan coordinated actions as well as track and adjust dynamic executions.
- **Feedback:** EA provides the means to update the holistic information and to embody new knowledge and lessons learned to keep improving the decision-to-action process and results.

The EA approach to enabling dynamic management will be further elaborated in the Integration subsection below.

3.4. Integration

The six dimensions and the dynamic aspects of the EA approach may appear overwhelmingly complex by itself for any enterprise to undertake enterprise architecture management. Actually, the EA dimensions and dynamics just reflect the complex reality any enterprise encounters every day. EA reveals the inherent and implicit patterns in the chaos and introduces a systemic approach to tackle the complex reality. The EA approach includes integration mechanisms to condense all dimensions and dynamics into simple forms that are feasible for any enterprise to apply.

3.4.1. Consolidate Dimensions and Dynamics: The Enterprise Architecture Space

The dimensions and dynamics of the EA approach are inter-related. Figure 4 presents a structure to connect and consolidate all six enterprise dimensions into an *Enterprise Architecture Space. An Enterprise Architecture Space* is defined as *a collection of all architectural alignment needs an*

Figure 4. The enterprise architecture space and architecture alignments

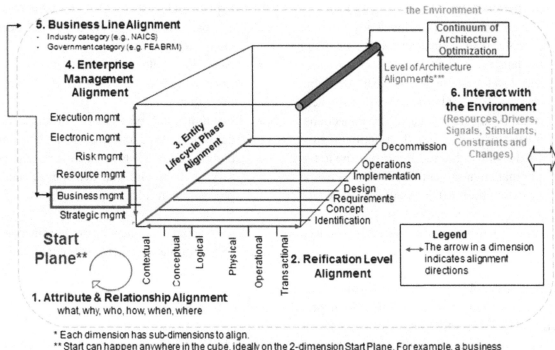

* Each dimension has sub-dimensions to align.
** Start can happen anywhere in the cube, ideally on the 2-dimension Start Plane. For example, a business transaction problem may trigger an architectural alignment process that starts at conceptual level, incorporates requirements from all management groups, then goes through the lifecycle of the change.
*** Level of Alignments is an average percentage that measures how requirements from all dimensions are met.

enterprise, or any of its elements, will encounter at any time of its existence.

This Enterprise Architecture Space reflects a fact that, in the real world, each enterprise or its element has to address, and is actually addressing, all those dimensions all the time. Similar like any physical item in the physical world that must always exist within the three-dimension physical space plus a time dimension, an enterprise entity cannot exist outside its Enterprise Architecture Space. The value of EA management is to make these EA dimensions explicit and help enterprises pursue architectural alignments holistically.

To illustrate how to achieve multi-dimensional and dynamic alignment using the enterprise architecture space, we will imagine a new Customer Relationship Management (CRM) System project as an example. We will walk this CRM example through the architecture alignments along the

lifecycle process in Figure 4. In the explanation below, the italics indicate how the context is linked to the Enterprise Architecture Space in Figure 4.

1. To initiate an entity, which could be an enterprise or any of its elements, the initiator first defines the proposed entity's basic attributes and relationships (this is to *align the Attribute and Interaction dimensions*) at the Identification lifecycle phase (*align the Lifecycle dimension*).

a. In our CRM project example, we need to identify business problems and justify proposed solutions at the identification phase. The high level attributes of the proposed solutions (what, why, who, how, when, where) and their major relationships to other elements should be determined and documented.

2. The attribute definitions should have different specifications to be communicated to audiences at the different reification levels (*align the Reification dimension*).

   a. Different groups of people would want to know different things about the CRM project. For example:

      i. Executives may want to know whether this investment will bring net returns or improvements to the organization. (*Contextual Level*)

      ii. Business managers may want to know how their current practice will be impacted. (*Conceptual Level*)

      iii. Existing business system owners may want to know how the proposed CRM system needs to interact with other business systems. (*Logical Level*)

      iv. Frontline customer representatives may want to know how their interaction with customers will be impacted. (*Transaction Level*)

3. The high-level requirements from all management groups to this entity, and from this entity to all management groups, are then identified and documented (*align the Management dimension*).

   a. The CRM project is a project in the business management area.

   b. The CRM needs to identify requirements FROM all management areas. For example: meeting strategic goals (*strategic management*); supporting business processes (*business management*); following acquisition processes (*resource management*), identifying risk and compliances associated with the project (*risk management*); identifying conformity with existing computing environment (*electronic management*), developing project plans (*execution management*).

   c. The CRM project also needs to identify its own requirements TO all management areas. For example: project goals and objectives require formal approval (*strategic management*); existing business processes should allow re-engineering to adapt to the new CRM practice and new system (*business management*); the total project funding should be approved and secured (*resource management*); accepted risks need explicit signed-off by the business sponsor (*risk management*); required IT infrastructure services should be provided (*electronic management*); project's execution is accepted as an integral part of enterprise execution (*execution management*).

4. The high-level business-specific requirements are also identified and documented (*align the Business dimension*).

   a. Assume our CRM is for a bank. The banking industry's common business processes and banking customer management requirements should be identified to develop the business requirements for the CRM. This bank's specific CRM requirements should also be identified.

5. The high-level roles, responsibilities, and processes for this entity to monitor and respond to the environment are defined and assigned (*align the Interaction dimension*).

   a. The CRM's project charter and plan should get agreement on the roles and responsibilities for the project and the future system. For example, the project manager should have the responsibility to monitor project risk status and the authority to take action to address risk changes.

6. All these high-level definitions provide the decision makers the needed information to

decide if this entity (e.g., the CRM project in our example) should be initiated.

7. Once the decision of initiating this particular entity is made, Steps 1-5 will be repeated at each lifecycle phase with more and more concrete contents appropriate to that lifecycle phase.

8. When change happens, the impacted contents will be updated and realigned to manage the change.

9. These continuously-maintained contents enable decisions being made on whether to advance the entity to its next lifecycle phase and on how this entity should interact, during any lifecycle phase, with all other entities in the enterprise and in the environment.

10. The quality of the multi-dimensional alignments along the CRM project lifecycle can be measured by the "Level of Architecture Alignments" as identified at the top right corner of Figure 4. This "Level of Architecture Alignments" will be explained in the next subsection (Subsection 3.4.2).

From the CRM project example we can see that normal project management and system development practices are addressing all EA dimensions and dynamics already. The advantage of EA management is not to reinvent wheels or create new reporting burdens in a business activity like this CRM project. Rather, EA brings a holistic perspective and an aggregation approach to connect individual efforts or entities (e.g., projects, systems, or business units) into an enterprise so the enterprise can manage both the "tree" and the "forest" based on dynamic information and collaboration.

The entity definition activities are important architecture alignment processes, because these definitions can only come from stakeholders' participation, clarification, negotiation and collaboration. As the entity grows through its lifecycle phases, the definitions of those dimensions are being reviewed and updated with more information,

more specifications, and continuous incorporation of changing situations.

The enterprise definitions are the foundation to guide continuous architecture alignments. The top-right line of the cube in Figure 4 represents the Continuum of Total Architecture Optimization when alignments on all dimensions have been achieved throughout the entity's lifecycle. Although it might be impossible to reach and stay in that perfect "Total Alignment Continuum," any effort to align the enterprise and move towards the optimum continuum will generate value to the enterprise.

Now we will revisit the term of "Enterprise Architecture Dimension." Enterprise Architecture Dimension is defined as *a problem field of an enterprise entity that contains all possible, known or unknown, problems or needs which can be addressed by a specific alignment effort.* Below is a summary of the EA dimensions and the EA alignments each dimension addresses:

1. The Attribute Dimension answers the "what it is" question (which covers all problems associated with this question) about an enterprise entity. Defining attributes aligns the entity with its purpose and quality requirements.

2. The Reification Dimension answers the "what matters to different audiences" question. Designing suitable artifacts for particular stakeholders aligns the entity with its stakeholders and its related entities at various levels.

3. The Lifecycle Dimension answers the "where we are in life" question. Evolving its focus through lifecycle aligns the entity with its own life phase and maturity levels.

4. The Management Dimension answers the "how we manage ourselves" question. Developing internal management strategy and approach aligns each and every management area within the entity.

5. The Business Dimension answers the "how we do our business" question. Optimizing

line of business management aligns the entity with its reason to exist and its source of resources.

6. The Environment Dimension answers the question of "how we deal with our environment." Identifying an entity's environment and developing proper interactions aligns the entity with its environment.

These six dimensions, including all elements and relationships within them, form the *Enterprise Architecture Space*. An enterprise's *Enterprise Architecture Space* is defined as the *collection of all architectural alignment needs an enterprise, or any of its elements, will encounter at any time of its existence.*

The EA Space reflects the "fractal" characteristics of enterprise entities. "Fractal" is a concept that describes anything that has self-similar patterns regardless of its scale (Benoit Mandelbrot, 1975). Enterprise entities are fractals because they face similar management categories and alignment needs regardless of the type of business they are in, the level of hierarchy they are at, and the environment they are in.

The EA Space provides the basic structure to capture enterprise fractal patterns. Any enterprise entity, from the international organizations like the United Nations, to a few-person team, or a one-person company, can use the same EA dimensions to document and align its activities and components.

The enterprises' fractal characteristics also allow the EA approach to use the same EA dimension structure to support aggregation and expansion. Like a set of Russian dolls, each enterprise entity has its direct EA space and each EA space is contained by one or more larger EA spaces. As long as all individual entities keep documenting and aligning their elements using the standard EA dimensions within their own EA spaces, the enterprise will have holistic views and

overall alignment status at any level, anywhere, and anytime.

Using the standard EA dimensions provides a structured way to tackle enterprise complexity. The EA space makes external complexity explicit and actionable within an enterprise's awareness range. The EA space also enables actions by individual entities being aggregated to higher level and being aware by other entities. Although the complexity will never reduce or go away, the EA approach provides holistic tools to equip enterprises for putting complexity into better control. Such enablement may be seen more clearly in later sub-sections and in the example in Section 4.

3.4.2. Measure Architecture Optimization: Level of Architecture Alignments

In Figure 4, the "Continuum of Architecture Optimization" and "Level of Architecture Alignments" still need explanation. These two concepts are not intrinsic parts of the EA dimensions. Rather, they are the mechanisms to measure how well an enterprise is achieving architecture alignments and optimization. Figure 5 is an illustration of how the alignment measurement chart may look like.

The horizontal axis in Figure 5 is *Time*. An enterprise entity's lifecycle phases are also marked along the Time axis. The vertical axis is *Percentage of Architecture Alignments*.

The *Percentage of Architecture Alignments* is defined as *a simple average percent that requirements at each architecture dimension are being satisfied:*

Percentage of Architecture Alignments = $\sum(A_t, R_t, M_t, B_t, L_t, E_t) / 6$

while

A_t is the average percent that the Attribute dimension's requirements are being met at time t;

R_t is the average percent that the Reification dimension's requirements are being met at time t;

Figure 5. Measuring EA alignments over an entity's lifecycle

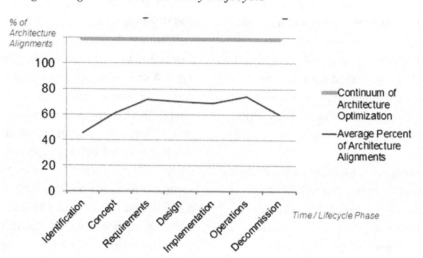

M_t is the average percent that the Management dimension's requirements are being met at time t;

B_t is the average percent that the Business dimension's requirements are being met at time t;

L_t is the average percent that the Lifecycle dimension's requirements are being met at time t;

E_t is the average percent that the Environment dimension's requirements are being met at time t; and

Constant 6 represents the six dimensions in the framework.

The requirements referred in the alignment measure include any and every requirement the enterprise or its element identify for itself or for others in each of the EA dimensions. Measuring how well the requirements are satisfied indicates if the entity is aligned within itself and with its external environment.

This composite alignment measure is set as a simple average across the 6 dimensions, because there seems no obvious good way to weight any dimension higher or lower. Although the indicator is simple, how to define requirements for each dimension and how to measure the percentage that a requirement is being met would require tremendous future research.

For the current illustration purpose, we will use a simple example to show how percentages of requirements being met can be established. Assume that we identified a few hundred requirements for the same Customer Relationship Management System project we used in the last subsection. Of these requirements, some came from the internal management dimension, some from the business dimension, some from the reification alignment dimension, and so on and so forth from each EA dimension. These requirements were applicable to different phases of the CRM project.

At the conclusion of each project phase, our quality inspection would verify the percentage that each applicable requirement was met. These percentages of requirements being met could then be aggregated into dimensional alignment percentage and enterprise alignment percentage. Table 2 provides fictional alignment percentages for EA dimensions at different lifecycle phases. The first data column, the Average % of Architecture Alignments, is the simple average of the dimensional alignment percentages. These average percentages of alignments are plotted in Figure 5 as the lower curve, which indicates how well the architecture alignment is at the each lifecycle phase of this CRM project.

Table 2. Average percentage of architecture alignments

Lifecycle Phase	Average % of Architecture Alignments	Attribute & Relationship Alignment%	Reification Level Alignment%	Enterprise Management Alignment%	Business Management Alignment%	Alignment% with the Environment
Identification	45.6	48	40	60	40	40
Concept	61.6	88	60	40	60	60
Requirements	72	60	80	60	80	80
Design	70.4	56	90	60	86	60
Implementation	68.8	80	68	66	64	66
Operations	74.4	60	80	56	90	86
Decommission	60	58	68	62	60	52

The top line in Figure 5, i.e., the Continuum of Architecture Optimization, represents the ultimate optimum of architectural alignments over the entity's lifecycle. This ultimate optimum's continuum is set above the 100% alignment level because of two reasons:

1. There are always unknown alignment requirements at any given time of the entity lifecycle. No enterprise can define, align, and measure results of the unknown.

2. There is a difference between the sum of individual alignments and the total optimum. The "100% alignment level" means that all individual requirements are met completely from any individual perspective. But from an enterprise perspective, an enterprise optimum may be higher than the sum of the individual alignments due to the system effect of "the whole can be more than the sum of the parts." By the same token, a higher level of optimum may be obtained even some individual requirements are only partially met or not met.

Generally, no enterprise can reach the ultimate architecture optimum due to existence of constraints and unknowns. Even though the optimum may not be reachable, EA management can help an enterprise move closer to the optimum and obtain the benefit of architecture alignments.

3.4.3. Connect the Dots: The EA Core Data Model

As indicated in Section 3.1, EA management is an information-based, holistic, and dynamic management discipline. The EA dimensions and dynamics are realized through the utilization of a central EA knowledge base to support architecting activities and alignments.

Holistic management starts with holistic information. The "holistic" capability of EA management comes from an architecture requirement that each and every element in an enterprise needs to provide and maintain its architecture definitions in standard EA forms throughout its lifecycle. All these individual definitions are assembled, related, and continuously maintained in the enterprise's central architecture knowledge base. This EA knowledge base can then provide holistic information and views for any enterprise decision circumstances.

This subsection will describe how the EA knowledge base is designed to capture architecture dimensions and to enable EA management. The next subsection will put the EA knowledge base into the overall EA execution picture to show how the different components of the EA approach work together to help the enterprise tackle complexity.

An EA knowledge base, generally called an "EA Repository," is a core component of the EA approach. The EA repository is a database system that stores and presents information and knowledge about the enterprise. The EA repository could store structured data, modeling diagrams, and unstructured documents; could present information in data reports, graphical views, modeling diagrams, and other presentation forms; should be centrally accessible by all elements of an enterprise; and should have the capabilities to support management decision making and architecture governance.

Unlike the majority of the traditional enterprise databases that store transaction-level data—such as sales data, customer activity records, or service records—the EA repository stores descriptive data about enterprise elements and their relationships. Therefore, the EA repository is also called a "Metadata Repository." Being able to document and present the relationships among elements is a unique feature of the EA repository system.

An EA repository system is structured by its data model, which is often referred as the repository's "Metamodel," due to the fact that the repository stores metadata. The EA metamodel embeds the EA dimensions and dynamics into the EA repository system. Figure 6 presents a core metamodel for the EA repository.

The core metamodel in Figure 6 connects the major data entity groups in an enterprise. The connections are based on the fact that an enterprise is an entity in which people get work done to achieve goals. Every element in an enterprise must contribute to getting work down. The enterprise core metamodel connects all entity categories through the process category in an IDEF0 model. This model sets the roles of all entities in the context of doing work and achieving the goal of the enterprise.

All data entities in the metamodel have a basic attribute and relationship structure which reflects the EA dimensions and dynamics. Figure 7 presents a base data entity that provides a core set of attributes and relationships most elements have. It serves as a starting template to create any specific data entity in the EA repository. Other attributes and relationships pertinent to each specific real world element

Figure 6. A core data model to document an enterprise

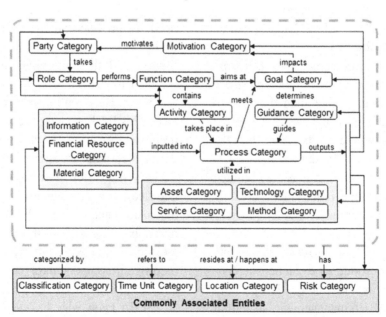

can be added to the copy of the base data entity to form a specific data entity. This specific data entity can then be used to document the real world enterprise element. Consider an example to see how the metamodel and base data entity are used to document enterprise elements in an EA repository.

Suppose we need to document policies. A data entity called "Policy" has been created in the EA repository database, copying the Base Data Entity to get the core attributes and relationships as in Figure 7. Referring to Figure 6, this Policy data entity belongs to the Guidance Category in the metamodel. As the metamodel indicates, the Policy entity is produced (outputted) by a policy making process and will guide other processes that fall into its jurisdiction.

Under this setting, we can start to document a policy instance in an EA repository as follows. The text in italic indicates the relevant EA dimensions and dynamics, as well as gives some explanations.

Name: Human Resource Training Policy 2010-10 *(Conceptual Level –What)*

Acronym: HRTP, P-2010-10 *(to facilitate searching and referring)*

Alias: HR Training Policy *(to facilitate searching)*

Description: This policy sets the scope, authorities, roles and responsibilities, processes, and rules for employee training development and management. *(Logical Level – What)*

Reification Level: Logical *(this is to say that this policy instance itself is at the Logical Level, i.e., it needs organizational specifics to be implemented to a particular unit at Physical Level.)*

Lifecycle Date: Initiation: 2010-5; Draft: 2010-5 -- 2010-6; Ratification and Approval: 2010-9; Issue: 2010-10; Effective: 2010-10; Review and renew: Each 3 years from 2010-10. *(Physical Level – When; lifecycle alignment)*

Last Updated Date: 2012-10-8 *(this is a "Transactional Level – When" for this data entry, rather than for the policy instance.)*

Owned by: Company HR Policy Office *(Physical Level – Who. All relationships support EA dynamics. In this instance the owner needs to*

Figure 7. Base data entity for element documentation

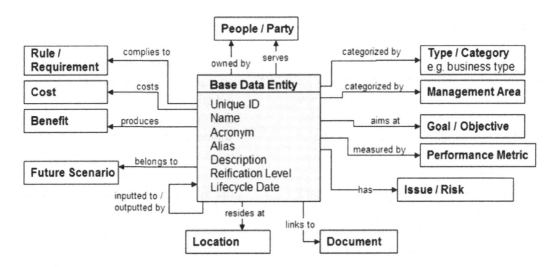

watch the environment impact (such as a regulation change) to this policy instance.)

Serves: Employee, Company *(Contextual Level – Who)*

Categorized by: Human Resource Management *(management alignment, business line alignment – Human Resource Line of Business)*

Complied to: Workforce Development Memo, Privacy Protection Act, Paperwork Reduction Act *(cross management alignment – Legality and Compliance Management)*

Aims at: Workforce Development Goal *(management alignment, Conceptual -Why)*

Measured by: Number of Employee Trained; Employee Retention Years; Performance Appraisal Average Score *(management alignment)*

Has: Risk of trained employee leaving to join competitors *(cross management alignment – Risk Management)*

Links to: the HRTP document *(Physical Level – What, Why, Who, How, When, Where)*

Costs: Creation cost - $2000, Enforcement cost - $3000/year. *(Physical Level – How)*

Produces: Capable workforce benefit, employee retention benefit *(Conceptual Level – Why)*

Outputted by: Policy making process

Complied by: Unit training plan *(management alignment. This relationship is an additional to the base entity's relationships. This relationship reflects a specific feature of this Policy element.)*

As illustrated in this example, simply documenting a single policy instance using the EA metamodel (including the base data entity) can cover each EA dimension and dynamic. EA management requires that every enterprise element be documented in the same manner in the central EA repository. The process of defining this information by its owner and stakeholders is the first step towards architecture alignment and tackling the enterprise complexity. The populated and maintained central EA repository can then provide the holistic information and knowledge that is critical for managing the complex enterprise in a systemic and dynamic way.

Although the repository data model may appear a too-detailed, too-technical topic in this context of presenting a general enterprise architecture approach, the significance of this core data model's design goes far beyond its technical implications:

- This data model translates the six EA dimensions into a standard, relatively simple core data entity that is suitable for documenting any kind of enterprise entities. The fractal character of the EA management is enabled and reflected by this data model.

- This data model relieves the burden of an enterprise entity from learning all the complexities beyond its border. This relief is achieved through using the data model to require each entity to document all of its inward and outward needs and requirements in a standard IDEF0 pattern. This standard documentation allows the assembling of all input, output, guidance, and enabling supports into the awareness of the entity. As long as the entity expresses all their outward requirements in the EA system, and properly handles all requirements brought to its awareness by the EA system, the entity is achieving enterprise coherence, without having to know the complexities behind those external requirements.

- This data model is the core mechanism to realize holistic management. To manage an enterprise in a holistic way, we need holistic information that is clear and actionable to enable decision making. The standard core data entity, the IDEF0-based relationship Web, and the multi-dimension EA concept in this data model enables the aggregation of individual information into holistic views for any level of enterprise management and any management perspective.

- This data model provides key capabilities to manage enterprise dynamics. As discussed in Section 3.3, the "*who, what, when, where, why, how*" and "*where we are*" for enterprise dynamic management can all be captured and presented by EA system through this data model. Without this knowledge, no enterprise can succeed in dynamic management.

In summary, the EA core data model is a critical bridge that helps enterprise tackle complexity and turns EA management concept into concrete EA operations. The multi-dimensional, dynamic EA management approach depends on the EA core data model to achieve integration and to reach realization.

3.4.4. Deliver EA Value: The EA Execution Triangle

The EA knowledge base is one of the core components in the EA approach arsenal. The other core components in the EA approach include:

- **EA Frameworks:** The EA frameworks define the basic structure and perspectives an EA management practice uses to identify and align the architecture. Widely-recognized EA frameworks include the *Zachman Enterprise Framework(* (Zachman, 2008), the US Federal Government's *Federal Enterprise Architecture Framework* (US OMB e-Government and Information Technology Office, 2012), the US Defense Department's *DOD Architecture Framework* (US Department of Defense, 2010), the ISO task force's GERAM (IFIP/IFAC Task Force, 1999), the *NATO Architecture Framework* (NATO, 2007), the teleManagement Forum's *eTOM/NGOSS* (TM Forum), Bernard's EA Cube (Bernard, 2012), and more. The integrated EA dimensions and dynamics presented in Subsection 3.4.1 is an extract of over 20 EA frameworks to provide a consolidated and simple method to cover the foundations.

- **EA Principles:** EA principles define the fundamental requirements to align the enterprise architecture. Examples of EA principles include: maintain individual ownership of responsibilities, avoid sole dependency, scrutinize each assumption, maintain a continuum of accountability, and unity of direction.

- **EA Processes:** EA management utilizes a Web of processes to manage architecting activities, including the processes to develop target architecture such as Spewak's Enterprise Architecture Planning (Spewak & Hill, 1993) and FEA's architecture transition (US Federal CIO Council); the processes to design architecture components such as TOGAF's architecting circle (The Open Group, 2011); the processes to govern architecture changes; the processes to update EA repository; and the processes to perform architecture analyses.

- **EA Plan:** An EA plan defines the target architecture that is aligned with enterprise's goals and lays out the transition roadmaps to lead the enterprise to realize the target architecture.

- **EA Governance:** EA governance establishes roles, responsibility, accountability, organization structure and processes to manage changes and maintain architecture alignments.

- **EA Tools:** EA tools are the information technology based systems that enable EA data management, processing, presentation, and automation of tasks.

The core components of the EA approach works together to deliver value to the enterprise. The unique values EA management can deliver to an enterprise include:

- **Reduce Waste caused by:**
  - Duplicates

- ◦ Disconnections and lack of coordination
- ◦ Un-optimized operations
- ◦ Insecure practices
- ◦ Local optimization at the cost of the enterprise
- ◦ Lost corporate knowledge and management continuity
- **Increase Opportunities and Capabilities by:**
  - ◦ Establishing readiness and responding agilely to ever-changing demand and environment
  - ◦ Applying a systematic approach to identifying and acting on opportunities to obtain benefits
- **Help Set Goals and Guide Dynamic Alignments by:**
  - ◦ Helping identify and agree on common goals
  - ◦ Guiding dynamic alignments across the enterprise towards achieving the goals.

The purpose of EA management is to optimize the enterprise for its goals. Figure 8 connects the components of the EA approach and links them with the values that EA delivers and with the ultimate goal of EA management.

The triangle in Figure 8 connects the EA Plan, EA Knowledge Base, and EA Governance with the full extent of EA value. This triangle is named the "Enterprise Architecture Execution Triangle." The strength of this execution triangle determines if and how much value EA management can deliver. All other EA components are realized through the EA Execution Triangle. If any side of the triangle is missing, the whole EA management cannot deliver value. If any side of the triangle is weak, the extent of the value EA management can deliver will be limited by the weakest side of the Execution Triangle.

The connection of the EA Approach and Value, especially the Enterprise Architecture Execution Triangle, is derived from EA's closest analogy, the discipline of City Planning. In city planning, the city planners and other participants follow city planning principles, apply various theories of city planning, take into consideration numerous perspectives, develop coherent city plans, establish control means and processes to govern the implementation and compliance of the plans, maintain and update city plan information in central data stores, and deliver the value of orderly developed, all-things-considered, harmonious city environments to their citizens (Keeble, 1951).

Figure 8. The connection of the EA approach and value

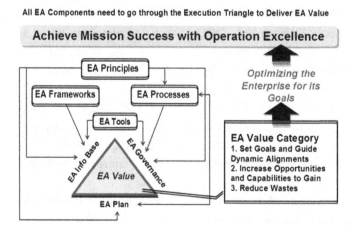

To turn the value of good city planning theory and principles as well as citizens' needs into a well-developed city, the city planners must have three sets of execution means. The first set of means is the city plan, or city design, which translates the principles and integrates the needs into the agreed-upon target design of the city. This plan/design provides specific direction and guidance on what the city will evolve into. The second set of means is the central knowledge base, or information collection. This knowledge base lets city planners, and all others involved, know where the city is now, where it wants to go, how changing one thing will impact others, and how to control the impact during changes. The third set of means is implementation governance—including zoning offices, building codes, quality guidelines, solar envelopes, and other controls—that assures all developments in the city conform to the city plan and comply with all requirements associated with the plan.

Needing these three execution means to get an entity from one state to a future state can also be seen in other contexts. A simple example could be that a person wants to drive from one place to another. This person would need: 1) a destination (the plan); 2) a map to know where he/she is and how to get to the destination (the knowledge base); and 3) the ability to steer his/her car toward the destination (the control). If any of the three execution means are missing, this person (or the city, or an enterprise) will not be able to get to the destination, i.e., will not be able to get the ultimate result / value.

In 2011, the US Government Accountability Office issued a report showing that the opportunities to reduce duplication in government programs, save tax dollars, and enhance revenue were widespread and significant (the US Government Accountability Office, 2011). Sample IT duplications indicated by the report include 622 human resources systems, 580 financial management systems, and 777 supply chain management systems in 2011. After implementing enterprise architecture programs across Federal government for over 10 years, the continuous existence of such widespread duplications caused the Federal executives to question the usefulness and value of enterprise architecture management.

Based on years of observation, architecting experience, and exchange with fellow enterprise architects across the US Federal government, the author would argue that lack of execution means and authority has been the real cause of the ineffectiveness of the EA program. Of the three execution means in the EA Execution Triangle in Figure 8, very few Federal agencies have all three in place and have given the EA program office sufficient authority to use these three means to execute EA management. Imagine a city government that does not allow its city planner to develop a plan that has the enforcing authority, does not allow the planner to collect and update infrastructure and other city information, and does not give the zoning office any authority to oversee the city developers. Then the city government would claim that the city planning program is useless in controlling ruthless city spreading. Many Federal enterprise architects are in exactly the same situation as the imaginary city planners. For the Federal government to receive the real benefit of EA management, strengthening the three EA execution means is a necessary and critical measure.

The discussion in this subsection is to emphasize that sound EA framework and methodology are not sufficient for helping enterprises manage complexity. The EA approach must include the execution means necessary to affect the decision making of the enterprise and to implement architecture principles. Only through effective execution of EA management can an enterprise evolve from an intuition-based, isolated, and chaotic management model into an information-based, holistic, systemic, and dynamic management approach. This transformation will significantly expand an enterprise's ability and freedom to tackle any complexity they may encounter.

4. A DISASTER RELIEF EXAMPLE

This section will demonstrate how to apply the EA approach to tackle real world complexity. A fictional disaster relief example is used to lay out the context and the challenges. At the end of each subsection that describes the relief operations, EA notes in italics will explain the EA approach applied in that subsection.

4.1. The Disaster

At the dawn of a rainy day in the hurricane season, millions of people in the Moonbay Region were woken up and devastated by a series of strong earthquakes. Severe storms followed and caused flash flood and landslides. This region of a highly populated, under-developed country had vast mountains at one side and crowded cities at the lower land. Most of the people in the region lived under poverty. The region's infrastructure was basic at best.

The earthquake, later measured at a magnitude of 8.5, caused visible damage to over 50% of the buildings and other structures in the region. The flood and landslides destroyed dozens of villages and many roads in the mountain area. Thousands of people were killed immediately, thousands were trapped in the rubble, and millions lost or were forced stay outside their homes. All power supply, water supply, telecommunications, and other infrastructure services went down after the shocks.

EA Notes:

The earthquake not only shocked the Moonbay Region physically but also shocked the "enterprise architecture" of the region. The daily life and business of the region were suddenly and totally interrupted; the urgency and scale of the need to save millions of people's lives became the top priority for the whole region in a split second; the scarcity of the resources

and infrastructure was immediately raised by the disaster to a crisis level; the aftershocks were looming dangers that could happen anytime. This shock from nature required the Moonbay Region enterprise to immediately adjust its priorities and architecture to handle the disaster and crises.

4.2. Forming of the Command Center

People started to show up at the city government compound at the central city of the region a short while after the first wave of earthquakes. Among the first group of people who came, there were the Deputy Mayor, the City Police Chief, some city emergency league members, some city government staff, some charity group volunteers, and some media reporters.

The Deputy Mayor assembled this first set of people in a wooden workshop structure on the compound. The main building of the compound sustained the initial shocks, but no one wanted to risk going into the building while the threat of aftershocks loomed. The Deputy Mayor thanked everyone for coming so quickly, asked briefly how their families were doing, and how was the situation in their neighborhood. Then the Deputy led people to assess the overall situations and to set the first priorities as below:

1. Form the City Disaster Command Center.
2. Restore power supply, telecommunications, fuel supply, and road throughput.
3. Coordinate rescue operations.
4. Coordinate emergency medical care operations.
5. Start feeding stations and establish supply networks to distribute disaster assistance supplies.

The Deputy appointed a Central Coordinator to manage the logistics of the Disaster Command Center and to assist the Deputy coordinate overall operations. The Deputy Mayor asked people to group into task teams according to their expertise as well as the needs to cover each priority area. She also asked the teams to elect a coordination lead for each team.

While the team forming and task assigning were going on, the Central Coordinator found some paper and started asking everyone present to register their names, mobile phone numbers, the neighborhood of their residence, their expertise, and the priority team they were participating in. The Central Coordinator asked a few people to put signs outside the workshop and around the compound to guide people to the Command Center location.

The Central Coordinator also asked everyone to keep some pieces of paper and pens with them all the time. These paper pieces would be used to record urgent needs, to register neighborhood coordinators, to log issues and problems, and to write down anything that should be kept a record or that would need attention later. The Central Coordinator asked everyone, especially the media, to spread widely the word about the City Disaster Command Center and how to contact it.

The task teams assessed the situations in their task areas and developed plans to take action. The plans utilized predefined emergency operation procedures from the Emergency League. Then the whole group re-gathered to share team plans, to establish the coordination and collaboration points and approach, and to address the immediate needs for their operations. The teams decided to have a daily status and coordination meeting at the Center to exchange status, to reassess the situation and to update the action plans. The Central Coordinator kept a copy of each team's structure, plan and contact information on his central planning board and in his central knowledge base.

The Police Chief was tasked to coordinate the emergency transportation fleet, comprising the police vehicles, the government official vehicles, and volunteering charity groups' vehicles. The fleet would help transport the task teams and supply materials to their destinations, and deliver messages before the telecommunication network was restored. During the team forming activities, the police had reached the Mayor's residence and found that he was injured by falling furniture and was being treated at an emergency room of a hospital. The Mayor asked the Deputy to continue leading the relief operations.

Before the teams jumped into action, the Deputy Mayor had a final word: Let's set up a high ethical code for ourselves and this whole operation – Love, Dedication, and Integrity. People looked at each other and nodded with deep thoughts. This country had been notorious about its government corruption. This reminder encouraged a different culture for the relief operation.

EA Notes:

The business priority for the Moonbay Region enterprise shifted to disaster relief operations at the moment of the first shock. A relief operation is highly dynamic and requires quick decisions and actions. The central city government initiated the enterprise's leadership and command center quickly and orderly. Operation priorities were clearly set by participants (strategic management); roles, responsibilities, and ethics were defined and agreed upon (organization management); the key actions were planned and coordinated (business management, coordination management); the execution logistics were assigned and worked out (execution management); and communication means were established (communication management).

The Central Coordinator actually played the role of an enterprise architect and had applied the EA approach. For example, he set up a central knowledge base (even it was a paper-based system) to assemble information and plans to support the coordination. This knowledge base would later prove to be a valuable asset to the whole relief operation.

4.3. Actions

The Infrastructure Team started the emergency infrastructure restoration procedures while the initial all-hands meeting was still in progress. Members were sent to the electricity and telecommunication companies to check their situation. Those members came back with the news that the power company experienced damages but expected to restore partial power supply later today. The telecommunications companies said they would be able to restore some phone services and cellular signals once the power was restored. The radio broadcast company also said they would be able to restore radio broadcasting once there was power supply.

Meanwhile, a military commander from the closest base had arrived. The military and the police had restored their emergency radio communication networks to communicate with their national headquarters and the national government. The national government notified the city that rescue teams and emergency supplies from around the country and other countries were on their way. The city asked them to please notify all rescue teams and supply fleets to register with the City Command Center and follow the central coordination command. The military commander took the responsibility to ensure that the major roads and bridges were clear for rescue traffic.

The Rescue Coordination Team first sent out several groups to the high density residence areas and major hospitals to assess the situations there. Those groups reported the damage and rescue needs back to the Command Center. They helped establish local coordination centers to coordinate local rescue operations in those areas. They recommended local centers to recruit residents to form street coordinator networks. They also helped hospitals establish emergency medical centers to treat the wounded.

As the day went on, more people were sent out to help establish local coordination centers. The rescue coordination networks kept expanding to cover more and more areas. All local centers and their contacts were registered with the Command Center. Based on the information provided by these networks, the first set of professional rescue teams were sent to areas where there were large amount of people found trapped alive under rubbles.

EA Notes:

The description in this subsection only touched a few aspects of the relief operations, but these actions all had important architecture impacts to this relief enterprise. Restoring communication capabilities is a first priority for any disaster relief operations (communication management). That capability had a dependency on power supply (resource management - infrastructure management). The commitment on restoring power supply very soon would help advance the whole relief operations.

Establishing a Web of local coordination networks with complete-coverage is critical to relief success. This network Web motivates full participation at all levels, enables coordination and collaboration, serves as the communication "nerve" system, and provides widely distributed "sensors" and response capabilities for the relief dynamics (organization management, communication management, coordination management, dynamic management).

While the relief operations was in full swing, it was critical that the Central Coordinator kept updating the central knowledge base to capture the highly fluid architecture and to provide a holistic, timely picture of everything going on by whom at where (informed enterprise management). This central knowledge base was critical to quickly identifying operation gaps and weaknesses to help adjust effort allocations. This knowledge base also preserved the contact networks to assure communication coverage across the city. Requiring all teams and fleets register with and follow the coordination command from the Command Center conforms to an EA governance principle that the whole operation must have one unified management and must maintain a central coordination.

4.4. Coordination and Innovation

Back at the city government compound, the Central Coordinator had been busy setting up the Relief Command Center. He got help from the military engineers to set up a communication center that was equipped with satellite and regular phones, media broadcasting connections, as well as a local computer network. The later restored partial power supply enabled the communications and recharge of devices and equipment at intervals. The Coordinator also assigned volunteers to set up and operate a Command Room, which was equipped with computers and maps of the city, the region, and the country.

The volunteers got a donation of a computer knowledge management system to store and present the central knowledge base. They kept updating the knowledge base when new information came in from the coordination networks and from other sources. They used the system's GIS capability to create maps that showed the damage extent and relief actions across the region. Another action the volunteers took was to create a relief coordination site under the city government's Web site. The relief site published the contact phone numbers for the coordination networks, the location of emergency medical centers, and other relief information. Since the local power supply was not stable, volunteers appealed to the international charity community to mirror the city site to ensure the relief operation information was always available. That appeal got immediate responses and multiple mirror sites went up right away.

The Relief Commander, i.e. the Deputy Mayor, and the leadership team examined the reports and maps generated by the knowledge base. The information indicated that several dense residential areas had reported large numbers of missing people

and requested more rescue crews and equipment. The rescue dispatch center, which also fed their information into the knowledge base, reported the expected date and time more external rescue teams would arrive with what kind of equipment. The leadership team reviewed and agreed on the plan to allocate the new crews. This information was passed back to the most needed areas so they knew how their requests would be fulfilled.

One of the requests emerged from the knowledge base was to find a proper way to utilize resources owned by private companies. This region's economy was characterized by large number of small vendors, craftsmen, and family stores. Many of them started donating as many resources to help the relief operation as they could afford, but the region needed as many resources as possible and as early as possible. The Deputy Mayor directed the Chief Resource Coordinator to establish mechanisms to borrow from local private companies their material supplies, services, facilities, and other capabilities on government IOUs or donation recognitions. The Resource Coordinator was also tasked to oversee the assembling and distribution of donations from external donators. The allocation of donations and supplies from all sources and in all forms was coordinated according to the needs identified by the relief networks in the central knowledge base.

The discipline to maintain up-to-date information in a central system to guide the operations enabled the leadership team to run a very effective and agile relief operation. For relief operations, timely information is life. For example, the published Web information brought real lifesaving results. While the city's emergency help lines were jammed after the quakes, many people trapped in rubble were able to contact their family, relatives, or friends after the wireless telecommunication was restored partially. When the receivers of the rescue calls were not local in the area, they were able to get information from the relief Web sites and contact local coordinators. There were volunteers at the local and central coordination centers that registered those relayed SOS calls into the central knowledge system, including the victim's name, location, situation, contact number, and so forth. These volunteers then contacted the rescue dispatch center to make sure that rescue was sent for those victims. They also contacted the victims back to help them keep hope.

EA Notes:

A disaster relief operation is always a distributed effort. Timely and effective coordination at all levels of the enterprise can help scattered efforts achieve best results. Establishing the communication and information processing capabilities of the Coordination Center strengthened the leaders' ability to address priorities and guide overall operations (coordination management). Assuring timely supplies for the rescue effort helped save lives (resource management). Communication relaying leveraged capabilities beyond the boundary of the enterprise to save lives (communication management).

The urgent needs that emerged from such a disaster also triggered people to find innovative solutions. The use of government IOUs and donation recognitions to utilize private supplies helped finance the supplies for the rescue operations (financial management, innovation management). The phone relay for victims was a crowd-sourcing effort to supplement the formal communication networks to help rescue victims (coordination management, communication management). Setting up computer knowledge base and Web sites helped support decision making and engage wider community to assist (knowledge management, information management). Plotting needs, relief actions, and other information into maps helped coordinate the relief operations and demonstrate progress (result management).

4.5. Conflicts and Crisis

While the inflow of the rescue crews coming from other regions and countries were continuing, one crew didn't arrive according to their scheduled arrival time. This crew came from a neighboring region on the other side of the mountain area. The communication with the crew was lost while the crew was passing the mountains.

The relief leadership team knew that the mountain area had been a base for rebels and suspected that the disappearing of the rescue crew and their supply cargo might be the work of the rebels. The leadership team sent an inquiry across the coordination networks to look for people who might be able to find the whereabouts of the rescue crew.

The inquiry got a response from a missionary group. The missionary group went to the rebel area before and was able to contact different rebel groups about the missing rescue crew. A rebel group told the missionary group that their base village had landslides and casualties, and that they were holding the rescue crew to help with the rescue effort and would keep the supply cargo. They were willing to release the rescue team if there could be a guarantee that more supplies and medical assistance would be transported to the rebels without threatening the safety of the rebels and the secrecy of the rebel base.

The missionary group mediated a negotiation between the central government and the rebel group. An agreement was reached that there would be a cease fire for a 6-month period to allow disaster relief operations. The missionary group would oversee the provision of humanitarian aids to the rebel base during this period, following rebels' secrecy protocols. The rebels would release the rescue crew after the initial life-saving rescue opportunity was over. The two sides would resume cease-fire negotiation before the end of the 6-month period. The information about this agreement and about the groups and people involved were recorded into the coordination knowledge system for future reference and accountability.

After two weeks of intensive rescue efforts amid many aftershocks and more rains, the chance to find people still buried alive became very slim. The Command Center announced that they were winding down the rescue operations and shifting the priority to providing better temporary housing to millions of people. During daily status briefings at the Center, reports showed a trend of increased diarrhea-type of flu and encephalitis cases at some crowed relief camps.

Since local hospitals were all only operating partially due to the earthquake damages, their ward had been filled with people wounded by the quakes. The ill people were mostly treated by mobile clinics and sent back to the camps to take medicine and rest. Several cases of death due to severe flu or acute encephalitis were reported. One of the relief camps had especially high number of infection cases.

A candidate from the opposite party, who was running for the Mayor of the central city while the earthquake hit, visited that camp and accused the current Mayor of ignorance. He promised the camp administrator that he would direct more medical assistance to the camp to prevent a pandemic outbreak. The candidate then used his influence and diverted some medical relief teams and supplies to the camp to provide treatments. Such diversion caused other camps to experience more shortage of medical assistance and increased disease infections.

Observing the disease cases spreading fast and far on the situation map, the leadership team called an urgent special meeting to develop a strategy and action plan. The Central Coordinator suggested the team to invite a wide range of parties, including the opponent candidates, to participate in this meeting.

The meeting was facilitated by a widely-respected local religious leader. The Mayor, relief leadership team, medical experts, charity organization leaders, and the opponent parties'

leaders all attended. The religious leader praised the participants for coming together during this devastating disaster and urged them to put aside their differences and address the urgent pandemic situation with sincere cooperation. The Central Coordinator briefed the attendees the outbreak status and the distribution of the medical resources and treatment efforts.

The participants debated on how to best allocate the limited medical resources. They finally agreed on taking multiple measures to get the outbreak under control. The measures included setting up infection control centers to isolate infected patients; distributing water treatment kits and mosquito nets; educating people to apply a hygienic and cautious approach to preparing food, keeping personal hygiene, and dealing with people with illness symptoms. The participants also agreed on forming a task force to carry out the measures and registering all measures and their owners into the coordination knowledge base to support continuous coordination and accountability. Although there were continuous disagreements along the course, this cooperation worked and the coordinated measures turned out to be very effective. The spread of the diseases was curbed in a few weeks while those who were ill got better treatment.

EA Notes:

Disaster relief operations are always highly dynamic. Many things happen at the same time with high urgency, many factors come into play, resources and information are always lacking, and the best and worst sides of people are often exposed. The two events in this subsection exemplify the importance of quickly finding key people, obtaining critical information, building coalitions, taking coordinated actions, and continuing to adapt to changing situations. The Command Center played a pivotal role in connecting the people and the dots effectively to achieve life-saving results under the fast changing and devastating situations. The central coordination knowledge base served its purpose of supporting informed management, enabling wide coordination, and preserving lasting accountability.

4.6. Transition

Several months after the initial earthquake shocked the Moonbay Region, the central city was still far away from returning to its pre-earthquake normal life. But the emergency relief organizations from around the country and around the world had to unwind their intensive emergency assistance operations. The Relief Command Center started a new run of coordination to lead the vast transition from emergency relief to long-term recovery.

The central coordination knowledge base, which had been kept up-to-date by many volunteers, proved to be extremely valuable for this transition effort. The Command Center was able to use the knowledge base to identify and contact all relief organizations. The Center asked each relief organization and local coordination center work together to identify operation successors and establish transition plans to transfer the operations. Such transition information and plans were documented in the knowledge base.

From the daily report of the knowledge base on transition status, the leadership team noticed that many relief organizations needed to leave but had difficulty finding local successors to continue necessary relief operations. If such situations were not addressed, the discontinuing of assistance and services might cause wide-spread devastation and unrest. The Command Center organized special meetings inviting relief organizations and local coordination center staff to analyze the situation, exchange ideas, and seek solutions.

At those meetings, participants identified major types of difficulties: lack of willing people, lack of reliable resources, and lack of trust on the government providing continuing support. The local centers which were able to transfer relief operations from external groups to local communities shared their experiences and lessons learned. Those centers motivated a wide range of community groups, from charity organizations, volunteer groups, religious organization, private companies, to neighborhood help groups, to share the relief responsibilities. The centers emphasized training residents to be more self-reliant. They also leveraged government resources and services to help the most vulnerable people.

Based on the analyses and on the transition success stories, the Command Center initiated several measures to assist the transition, including:

- Facilitating staff exchange between the local centers to bring the successful approach to those centers with transition difficulties;
- Adjusting relief resource allocation, filling avoidable gaps, and improving efficiency;
- Negotiating with the central government and international donors to secure continuous relief assistance; and
- Leveraging the Mayor's administrative power to provide tax breaks to encourage local business to hire more local people.

These measures reduced the transitional gaps caused by the withdrawal of the relief force. The measures also strengthened local communities to be more resilient and self-dependent. The strengthened local communities became the foundation for the long-term recovery.

The other part of the transition was to transform the temporary Relief Command Center to an on-going central program office that could coordinate long-term recovery. The change involved redefining the purpose of the Center and redesigning the structure, resources, processes, and other components of the central office. The change also involved transforming the coordination networks for the new purpose and priority. The central coordination knowledge base was one of the treasures the new central office inherited. The knowledge base helped ensure management and operation continuity, as well as provided the ready capability to architect the new organization and to support future coordination. The Deputy Mayor recognized the value of the central knowledge base and required establishing a similar knowledge networks for the whole city government.

EA Notes:

One of the strengths of EA management is to facilitate orderly changes. The Command Center successfully applied the EA approach to plan for the transition, coordinate the transition, address emerging problems, and transform the leadership structure for the new purpose. EA's capability on helping tackle the complexity brought by the disaster was recognized and would be further utilized at a wider context and scale.

4.7. Example Summary

Although "enterprise architecture management" was never mentioned by the disaster relief leadership or by anyone involved, the Moonbay earthquake relief operation clearly applied the EA approach pretty successfully. This "disaster relief enterprise" had all the dimensions any enterprise has – its core business was disaster relief; it had common internal management needs to manage strategic directions, businesses, resources, risks, electronic capabilities, and execution capabilities; it had attributes that were probed through the EA interrogatives; it had stakeholders that cared about various levels of reification; it passed through a life cycle; and it had to respond to the extreme environmental shocks and constraints agilely and orderly.

The relief operation also leveraged all components of the EA approach. For example:

- The operation stick to the architecture principle of "unified management" and had one central command center that coordinated a Web of local relief networks. This unified management structure maintained bilateral and multilateral communications and supported emergent dynamics at local levels. *(EA principles)*

- The dimensions of the operation reflected the EA frameworks. See more discussion on this in later paragraphs in this subsection. *(EA frameworks)*

- The Command Center utilized a central EA knowledge base built on EA knowledge tools. *(EA information base and tools)*

- The leadership team, operation teams, and other relief participants developed coordinated (i.e., architected) plans to guide relief operations. *(EA plans)*

- Processes were established to ensure local operations conform to the central coordination. *(EA processes and governance)*

The results of a successful relief operation that leveraged the EA approach should be more lives saved, less human suffering, faster recovery, and less resource waste.

Figure 9 illustrates a fictional assessment on the level of architecture optimization for the Moonbay relief operation, using the multi-dimensional, dynamic Architecture Space. The numbered explanations below refer to the circled numbers in Figure 9:

1. An extreme change from the environment, i.e., strong earthquakes, shocked the Moonbay enterprise. The shocks caused huge casualties, vast destruction, an acute shortage of resources, and a sharp rise in the urgency of saving lives and assisting millions of people.

2. Disaster relief suddenly became the core business of the whole region, setting priorities for all other businesses and activities.

3. The disaster relief priority changed dynamics of all other dimensions. It required the entire management activities focus on supporting the relief operations. It required the urgency at the transaction level, i.e., the level where actual life was being saved, determine the handling of activities at all other reification levels. It also required the relief operation

Figure 9. Assessing the architecture alignment level of the Moonbay relief operation

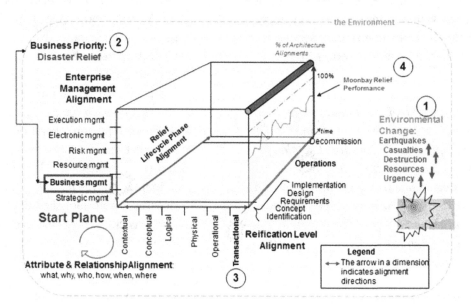

move quickly through its initial lifecycle phases and dive into the operation phase at the earliest possible point.

4. The "Moonbay Relief Performance curve" in Figure 9 illustrates the level of the architecture alignments along the Relief enterprise lifecycle. This fictional assessment curve indicates that this relief operation achieved various architecture alignments along its lifecycle. The ups and downs of the alignment curve illustrate the dynamics of the alignment activities. When a change happened, such as the hostage situation, the alignment level might drop. If realignment succeeded, the alignment level would improve.

As mentioned before, using the 6-dimension architecture alignments to analyze the relief operation may appear to be making the enterprise complexity worse, rather than simplifying it. But in reality, just like no single physical item can escape the 3 physical dimensions plus time dimensions, no enterprise entity or activity can escape the 6-dimension architectural combination. Each entity or each activity must have attributes,

relationships, different levels of reification, a lifecycle; and must handle requirements from management areas, from business lines, and from its environment.

The positive side of these inescapable six dimensions is that every action an enterprise takes automatically impacts all 6 dimensions simultaneously. Again, this is just like in the physical world where any of our moves is a change of our position in space and time simultaneously, even if we do not consciously know our exact longitude, latitude, elevation, and time before and after the move. In this relief example, the operation followed relief business patterns; addressed internal management needs; and managed relationships, interactions, and activity lifecycles. In another word, the relief operation addressed all six architecture dimensions simultaneously all the time, leveraged the basic EA management approach to tackle a highly dynamic and complex crisis, and achieved life-saving results.

The last thing to point out is that using this disaster relief example to illustrate the EA approach may appear to be only representing an atypical EA management case. During urgent circumstances such as in disasters, the stakeholders in a large enterprise, like the Moonbay region, may set aside temporarily their differences and disagreements to support centralized coordination and operation. Once the urgency fades, the temporary support may fade as well, leading to dissolution of central coordination.

It is true that in non-urgent situations, stakeholders may guard their own interests much more tightly and may be less willing to support central coordination activity such as EA management. But regardless the extent of willingness, the EA approach would still be applicable and could still help enterprise tackle complexity. The non-urgent situations will not change the six dimensions enterprises must address, although the emphases may shift; it will not eliminate the need to collect and aggregate enterprise information, although it may require a different approach to assure information feeding; it will not eliminate the need for cross-board governance, although it may require different incentives and authority. In short, regardless what circumstances an enterprise is in, the EA management approach will always be needed to manage the complexity an enterprise encounters.

5. FUTURE DIRECTIONS

The EA management discipline is still in its infancy. The EA approach is far from maturity; the understanding and recognition of EA's value is minimal; and the adoption of true EA management is very limited. Nevertheless, EA management is a highly needed discipline to address the core management challenge faced by all enterprises – how to tackle the interconnected complexity under resource limits and time constraints to achieve success.

Below are some future developments the EA field can pursue to advance the EA discipline as well as to provide more means to help enterprises tackle complexity with effectiveness and efficiency:

1. Raise EA Management from the CIO to the CEO level as the discipline to help execute strategies.

   EA management is considered an IT function by most organizations which run an EA program. Equating enterprise IT architecture with enterprise architecture is a mistake that prevents EA management from realizing its true value. EA management should be the approach any CEO Program Management Office (PMO) utilizes to manage the execution of the organization's strategy. Many government agencies have EA programs in the IT shop purely because of external mandates. They run the EA program as a paper-pushing game to satisfy those mandates. This is a complete waste of money and denial of the real value of EA management. The EA practitioners' community needs to continue advocating lifting EA management from the CIO to the CEO PMO level as a true strategy execution approach.

2. Develop and share standard best practice for management areas.

   The internal management areas categorized in the management dimension of the consolidated framework are common to all enterprises. There exist proven best practices and management patterns in each of those areas and sub-areas. The EA discipline can help enterprises manage the complexity in the management areas through codifying and standardizing the best practices, facilitating their implementations, and connecting the individual best practices into an interoperated management approach.

3. Develop and share standard best practice for industries.

   There also exists a vast knowledge pool of proven best practices and management patterns for every line of business. The EA discipline can help enterprises manage the complexity in business line management through codifying and standardizing the best practices, facilitating their implementations, and establishing interoperations across business lines, as well as interoperations between business line management and other internal management areas.

4. Evolve dynamic management methods. Dynamic management is the weakest section in the EA approach. The EA discipline needs to develop concepts, principles, methods, and tools to enable dynamic architecture management. The challenges are on how to maintain order in managing constant and simultaneous changes without introducing rigidity, sluggishness, and bureaucracy; and how to promote agility, innovation, and emergent adaptability without creating chaos.

Of these four future directions, the first one addresses the positioning of EA management, from an IT function to a true enterprise management function. Without this change, "EA" management under IT functions should be called IT architecture management.

Enterprise-wide IT architecture management has its value. It can help IT better align with an enterprise's mission, business and IT itself. But it is not EA management. IT architecture cannot make business lines align within themselves and with each other; cannot align internal management areas; cannot address the coherence issues that emerge along an enterprise's lifecycle; and cannot address the dynamics an enterprise experiences when interacting with its environment. Therefore, the value of IT architecture is limited to bringing partial coherence and partial optimization to IT.

Moving EA management to a CEO program office requires that the organization's top leadership understand the necessity and value of EA management. The major barrier to this understanding is that enterprise architecture has yet been accepted by the business community as a mainstream, mature management discipline. The EA discipline still needs to prove itself to the business community.

Due to this need of proving EA's business value, the other three future directions aim at strengthening the business and enterprise aspects of EA management. Direction 2 will strengthen the architecture for internal management; Direction 3 will strengthen the business line architecture management; and Direction 4 will strengthen EA management capability to help enterprise cope with the highly dynamic business and political environment. Advancing in these four future directions will help the EA management discipline evolve from the current IT-focused perspective and partial optimization practice to a truly holistic tool that enables enterprises to tackle enterprise complexity.

6. CONCLUSION

Complexity is intrinsic and inevitable for any enterprise. We cannot reduce complexity, but can look for better ways to handle, and benefit from, complexity. This chapter:

- Discussed the sources of enterprise complexity;
- Introduced an integrated EA management approach that identifies and leverages six dimensions of enterprise commonalities and dynamics;
- Presented means to assemble holistic information and support cross-board alignments;
- Provided methods to manage interconnected complexity and pursue architecture optimization; and
- Illustrated the application of the EA approach in a fictional disaster relief operation to help tackle complexity and dynamics.

Although the EA approach itself still has a long way to go to become a mature and widely accepted discipline, applying the holistic, systemic, and dynamic EA approach is a necessity for any enterprise to handle increasingly interconnected complexity and to gain competitive advantage. The integrated EA approach introduced in this chapter has been proven useful in real world EA management work, but more research is needed to evolve its capability.

REFERENCES

Airforce, U. S. (1990). *IDEF0 function modeling method*. Retrieved 10 28, 2012, from http://www.idef.com/IDEF0.htm

Argyris, C. (1982). *Reasoning, learning, and action: Individual and organizational*. San Francisco, CA: Jossey-Bass.

Bernard, S. (2012). *EA3: An introduction to enterprise architecture* (3rd ed.). Bloomington, IN: AuthorHouse.

Bertalanffy, L. V. (1969). *General system theory: Foundations, development, applications*. New York: George Braziller Inc..

Boulding, K. E. (1953). *The organizational revolution*. Harper & Brothers.

Boyd, J. (1976). *Destruction and creation*. U.S. Army Command and General Staff College.

Church, A. H. (1914). *The science and practice of management*. University of Michigan Library (reprint in 2009).

Commons, M. L., & Richards, F. A. (1984). A general model of stage theory. In Commons, M. L., Richards, F. A., & Armon, C. (Eds.), *Beyond Formal Operations: Late adolescent and adult cognitive development* (Vol. 1, pp. 120–140). New York: Praeger.

Cox, J., & Goldratt, E. M. (1986). *The goal: A process of ongoing improvement. Croton-on-Hudson*. NY: North River Press.

Fayol, H. (1918). *Administration industrielle et générale, prévoyance, organisation, commandement, coordination, controle*. Paris: H. Dunod et E. Pinat.

Fisher, R. A. (1925). *Statistical methods for research workers*. Cosmo Publications.

Follett, M. P. (1927). *Dynamic administration*. New York: Harper & Brothers Publishers (Reprint 1942).

Forum, T. M. (n.d.). *Business process framework (eTOM)*. Retrieved 10 28, 2012, from http://www.tmforum.org/BusinessProcessFramework/1647/home.html

Gantt, H. L. (1903). Aggraphical daily balance in manufacture. *Transactions of the American Society of Mechanical Engineers*, *24*, 1322–1336.

Gell-Mann, M. (1994). *The quark and the jaguar: Adventures in the simple and the complex*. San Francisco, CA: W.H. Freeman. doi:10.1063/1.2808634.

Hammer, M. (1990, July/August). Reengineering work: Don't automate, obliterate. *Harvard Business Review*, 104–112.

Holland, J. H. (1992). *Adaptation in natural and artificial systems: An introductory analysis with applications to biology, control, and artificial intelligence*. Cambridge, MA: MIT Press.

IFIP/IFAC Task Force. (1999). *GERAM: Generalised enterprise reference architecture and methodology*. Retrieved 10 28, 2012, from http://www.ict.griffith.edu.au/~bernus/taskforce/geram/versions/geram1-6-3/v1.6.3.html

Ishikawa, K. (1988). *What is total quality control? The Japanese way*. Prentice Hall.

Keeble, L. (1951). *Principles and practice of town and country planning*. London: Estates Gazette.

Kirby, M. W., & Rosenhead, J. (2011). Patrick Blackett: Profiles in operations research. In *International Series in Operations Research & Management Science. 147*, 1. Springer doi:10.1007/978-1-4419-6281-2_1.

Lewin, K. (1948). *Resolving social conflicts, selected papers on group dynamics* (Lewin, G. W., Ed.). New York: Harper & Row.

Likert, R. (1961). *New patterns of management.* New York: McGraw-Hill.

Luo, H. (2006). *Enterprise architecture alignment framework.* Retrieved 10 28, 2012, from http://www.aea-dc.org/resources/EA-Alignment-Framework-2009-6-28.ppt

Mayo, E. (1945). *The social problems of an industrial civilization.* Division of Research, Graduate School of Business Administration, Harvard University, Reprint Ed.

NATO. (2007). *NATO architecture framework v3.* Retrieved 10 28, 2012, from http://www.nhqc3s.nato.int/ARCHITECTURE/_docs/NAF_v3/ANNEX1.pdf

Porter, M. E. (1996). What is strategy? *Harvard Business Review*, 61–78. PMID:10158474.

Scott, W. D. (1911). *Increasing human efficiency in business - A contribution to the psychology of business.* The Macmillan Company.

Snowden, D. (2000). Cynefin: A sense of time and place: An ecological approach to sense making and learning in formal and informal communities. In *Proceedings of the Knowledge Management Annual Conference.* University of Aston.

Spewak, S., & Hill, S. (1993). *Enterprise architecture planning: Developing a blueprint for data, applications, and technology.* Wiley.

Taylor, F. W. (1911). *The principles of scientific management.* New York: Harper & Brothers.

Tead, O. (1916). Trade unions and efficiency. *American Journal of Sociology*, *22*(1), 30–37. doi:10.1086/212573.

The Open Group. (2011, Dec). *TOGAF version 9.1.* Retrieved 10 28, 2012, from http://www.opengroup.org/togaf/

US Department of Defense. (2010). *The DoD architecture framework, US department of defense.* Retrieved 10 28, 2012, from http://dodcio.defense.gov/dodaf20.aspx

US Federal CIO Council. (n.d.). *FEA practice guidance – Introducing segment architecture.* Retrieved 10 28, 2012, from http://www.cio.gov/index.cfm?function=specdoc&id=Practical%20Guide%20to%20Service%20Oriented%20Architecture%20(PGFSOA)%20v1.1&structure=Enterprise%20Architecture&category=Enterprise%20Architecture

US Government Accountability Office. (2011). *Opportunities to reduce potential duplication in government programs, save tax dollars, and enhance revenue.* Washingotn, DC: Author.

US OMB e-Government and Information Technology Office. (2012). *Federal enterprise architecture.* Retrieved 10 28, 2012, from http://www.whitehouse.gov/omb/e-gov/fea/

Weber, M. (1999). *Essays in economic sociology* (Swedberg, R., Ed.). Princeton University Press.

Wiener, N. (1948). *Cybernetics, or communication and control in the animal and the machine.* Cambridge, MA: MIT Press.

Zachman, J. (2008). *The Zachman framework™: The official concise definition.* Retrieved 10 28, 2012, from http://zachmaninternational.com/index.php/home-article/13

Zachman, J. A. (1987). A framework for information systems architecture. *IBM Systems Journal*, *26*(3). doi:10.1147/sj.263.0276.

ADDITIONAL READING

Appleby, R. C. (1994). *Modern business administration*. Financal Times Management.

Bossel, H. (2007). *Systems and models: Complexity, dynamics, evolution, sustainability*. Norderstedt, Germany: Books on Demand GmbH..

Briggs, J. (1992). *Fractals: The patterns of chaos: Discovering a new aesthetic of art, science, and nature*. Simon & Schuster.

Burlton, R. (2001). *Business process management: Profiting from process*. Sams Publishing.

Cheung, S. N. (1987). Economic organization and transaction costs. In *The New Palgrave: A Dictionary of Economics* (2nd ed., pp. 55–58). New York: Palgrave.

Doucet, G., Gøtze, J., Saha, P., & Bernard, S. (2009). *Coherency management: Architecting the enterprise for alignment, agility, and assurance*. Bloomington, IN: AuthorHouse.

Hay, D. C. (2011). Level 1 - The generic enterprise model. In Version, U. M. L. (Ed.), *Enterprise Model Patterns: Describing the World* (pp. 81–180). Bradly Beach, NJ: Technics Publications, LLC.

Herzum, P. (1999). *Business component factory: A comprehensive overview of component-based development for the enterprise*. Wiley.

Johnson, B. (1996). *Polarity management: Identifying and manage unsolvable problems*. HRD Press.

Johnson, N. (2009). Simply complexity: A clear guide to complexity theory (reprint 2009 ed.). Oneworld.

Kaplan, R. S., & Norton, D. P. (2004). *Strategy maps: Converting intangible assets into tangible outcomes*. Boston: Harvard Business Review Press.

Maurya, A. (2012). *Running lean: Iterate from plan a to a plan that works* (2nd ed.). Sebastopol, CA: O'Reilly Media.

Mitchell, M. (2009). What is complexity. In M. Mitchell (Ed.), Complexity: A Guided Tour (pp. 3-14). New York: Oxford.

Morgan, G. (1986). Images of organisation (Updated 2006 ed.). Sage Publications, Inc.

Osterwalder, A. (2010). *Business model generation: A handbook for visionaries, game changers, and challengers*. Wiley.

Reynolds, C. (2009). *Introduction to business architecture*. Course Technology PTR.

Ross, J. W., Weill, P., & Robertson, D. (2006). *Enterprise architecture as strategy: Creating a foundation for business execution*. Harvard Business Review Press.

Sessions, R. (2006). *A better path to enterprise architectures (model complexity)*. Retrieved 29 2012, 10, from http://msdn.microsoft.com/en-us/library/aa479371.aspx#sessionsfinal100_topic7

Sessions, R. (2007). *A comparison of the top four enterprise-architecture methodologies*. Retrieved 10 29, 2012, from http://msdn.microsoft.com/en-us/library/bb466232.aspx

Smith, J. M. (2012). *Elemental design patterns*. Addison-Wesley Professional.

Spewak, S. (1998). Enterprise architecture planning: Make IT all fit together. Washington, DC: Architecture Plus Seminars.

Teece, D. J. (2009). *Dynamic capabilities and strategic management: Organizing for innovation and growth (Reprint 2011 ed.)*. Oxford University Press.

von Halle, B., & Goldberg, L. (2009). *The decision model: A business logic framework linking business and technology (IT management)*. Auerbach Publications. doi:10.1201/9781420082821.

Waldrop, M. M. (1993). Visions of the whole. In Waldrop, M. M. (Ed.), *Complexity: The emerging science at the edge of order and chaos* (pp. 9–13). Simon & Schuster.

Zachman, J. (2006). Enterprise architecture: Managing complexity and change. In B. v. Halle, L. Goldberg, & J. Zachman (Eds.), Business Rule Revolution: Running Business the Right Way (pp. 43-57). Happy About.

KEY TERMS AND DEFINITIONS

Architecture Alignment: Is a dynamic process that establishes and maintains appropriate interoperability and fitting among related enterprise entities and components.

Complexity: Is defined as the number of factors and their connections that need to be considered by a decision maker.

Enterprise Architecture Dimension: Is defined as a problem field of an enterprise entity that contains all possible, know or unknown, problems or needs which can be addressed by a specific alignment effort. The Integrated EA framework introduced in this Chapter contains six EA dimensions, which address the following EA alignments: (1) The Attribute Dimension answers the "what it is" question (which covers all problems associated with this question) about an enterprise entity. Defining attributes aligns the entity with its purpose and quality requirements. (2) The Reification Dimension answers the "what matters to different audience" question. Designing suitable artifacts for particular stakeholders aligns the entity with its stakeholders and its related entities at various levels. (3) The Lifecycle Dimension answers the "where we are in life" question. Evolving its focus through lifecycle aligns the entity with its own life phase and maturity levels. (4) The Management Dimension answers the "how we manage ourselves" question. Developing internal management strategy and approach aligns each and every management area within the entity. (5) The Business Dimension answers the "how we do our business" question. Optimizing line of business management aligns the entity with its reason to exist and its source of resources. (6) The Interaction Dimension answers the question of "how we deal with neighbors and environment." Defining relationships and interactions aligns the entity with its related entities and its environment. These six dimensions, including all elements and relationships within them, form the Enterprise Architecture Space.

Enterprise Architecture Space: Is formed by the 6 enterprise architecture dimensions that encompasses all architectural alignment needs any enterprise encounters. Each enterprise entity has its direct EA space and each EA space is contained by one or more larger EA spaces.

Enterprise Entity: Is any enterprise or its element. An enterprise comprises elements that are connected by various relationships and mutual interactions. Any enterprise itself is almost always an element of a larger enterprise. The terms "enterprise," "enterprise element," and "enterprise entity" were used interchangeably in this chapter.

Enterprise: Is a set of people who are related by a common goal or goals formally or informally, permanently or temporarily, explicitly or implicitly.

Chapter 13
Enterprise Architecture's Identity Crisis:
New Approaches to Complexity for a Maturing Discipline

Paul R. Taylor
Monash University, Melbourne, Australia

ABSTRACT

This chapter outlines the rational foundations of the enterprise architecture discipline to date and describes ways and situations in which the traditional approaches of enterprise architecture fail to account for a number of contemporary market and economic situations and organizational behaviors. It characterizes new methods and approaches loosely based on systems thinking, with examples from the Australian e-government experience, and argues that the discipline must re-invent itself to incorporate a post-rational perspective to stay relevant. The chapter concludes with narratives of how the new enterprise architecture must engage with business to stay relevant over the next decade and beyond.

ENTERPRISE ARCHITECTURE AS A MATURING DISCIPLINE

Enterprise architecture has an identity crisis. Borne of an era of escalating software development and maintenance expenditure of U.S. military and government agencies, enterprise architecture has grown over three decades to encompass a disci-

pline of methods, tools and practices to manage information system complexity. The success of some of enterprise architecture's methods can be attributed to rational and objective analysis, classification and abstraction of selected features of complex and large-scale problems and systems. But over the last decade, paradigmatic market and business shifts such as the emergence of the

DOI: 10.4018/978-1-4666-4518-9.ch013

information and knowledge economies bought on by the Internet, personal and pervasive computing, and the digitisation of just about everything has put pressure on enterprise architecture's foundations. It is no longer enough to apply structural tools and problem decomposition to every kind of business problem, as may have been done successfully in the past – the complexity of today's business challenges is not always amenable to a 'divide-and conquer' approach.

As a consequence of this and other factors, enterprise architects need to look beyond its traditional foundations in a search for a new and more relevant identity. Like a teenager realising that the black and white world of childhood is in fact rendered in a thousand shades of grey, enterprise architecture must re-establish its identity before it can reach a new level of maturity for its next three decades. The discipline must re-evaluate its purpose, relationships, obligations and responsibilities to the organisations it serves. It must infuse new approaches and methods from outside its traditional domain of engineering to tackle the sorts of dynamic and ill-defined problems and systems rational analysis cannot solve.

To do this, enterprise architecture must embrace design as much as analysis, synthesis as much as simplification, with methods and tools drawn from systems thinking (Senge 1992), design and 'design thinking' (Brown 2008), perspective and problem negotiation, and facilitation. Enterprise architects must move closer to the business, and engage in the design of new businesses by brokering technology, vendor and product capabilities and services to meet rapidly changing business objectives. The new enterprise architecture will sit amidst the complexity and contradiction of the increasingly dynamic architecture of the organisation, serving the business' needs and being prepared to change, reconfigure or jettison established technologies and platforms without being bound by the chains of legacy or sunk cost. Not that the old methods will be abandoned – on the contrary, they continue to provide the foundation of the discipline and the main levers to understand

and manage complexity. But the new enterprise architecture will be integrative – able to hold rational *and* post-rational perspectives on problems and systems in creative tension (Martin 2007), drawing on both to design technology interventions that will be effective for today's dynamic, hyper-connected and loosely-coupled enterprises.

This chapter outlines the rational foundations of the enterprise architecture discipline and describes ways and situations in which the traditional approaches of enterprise architecture fail to account for a number of contemporary market and economic situations and organisational behaviours. It characterises new methods and approaches loosely based on design and systems thinking, with examples from e-government experience, and argues that the discipline must re-invent itself to incorporate a post-rational perspective to stay relevant. The chapter concludes with narratives of how the new enterprise architecture must engage with business to stay relevant over the next decade and beyond.

FORMATIVE YEARS

Enterprise architecture's formative years are well documented. The term 'enterprise architecture' was apparently coined by Steven H. Spewak, the Chief Architect at global logistics company DHL Systems (Spewak 1992). Spewak drew on the Zachman (1987) framework to propose an Enterprise Architecture Planning methodology (Spewak 1992). (Zachman originally referred to his framework as 'a framework for information system architecture'). Enterprise architecture gained legitimacy with the 1996 Clinger-Cohen Act which required US federal departments and agencies to establish and maintain enterprise architecture programs. Shortly after, a Chief Information Officer's Council was formed, which in 1998 established the Federal Enterprise Architecture Framework as a uniform planning and design structure. Under the Office of Management and Budget, compliance with agency Information Technology Architectures (based in turn on the Federal Enterprise Architecture Framework) became mandatory for all significant IT investments. In 2002, the Office of Management and Budget initiated the development of a Federal Enterprise Architecture with the objective of technology standardisation, unified planning, identification of opportunities to simplify business processes, and avoidance of redundant technology investments across the agencies. The parallel successes of enterprise architecture in the private sector are widely documented in the enterprise architecture and information systems literature (Hagan 2004; Ross, Weill et al. 2006; Chew and Gottschalk 2009).

Other national governments adopted and continue to invest in enterprise architecture for the management of large-scale information technology investments. The Australian Government Information Management Organisation (AGIMO) developed a focus on priority areas of government technology investment, including supporting information technology investment planning and decision-making, e-government and cross-agency services. In 2007, AGIMO released the first elements of the Australian Government Architecture, a business architecture adapted from the Federal Enterprise Architecture Framework and intended to improve the consistency and cohesion of government services to citizens and cost-effective delivery of information and communications technology services by government (AGIMO 2007; AGIMO 2011). The governments of the United Kingdom followed a similar path, investing in enterprise information and technology architecture to target specific outcomes.

Definitions

For the purposes of this discussion 'enterprise architecture' needs a definition. Enterprise architecture is the combination of the capabilities, resources and structures that an enterprise relies upon to deliver value. The purpose of the discipline of enterprise architecture is to optimise the often fragmented legacy of capabilities, resources and structures into an integrated environment that supports delivery of the business strategy, while at the same time being suitably responsive to change. Most definitions recognise that today's enterprise encompass end-to-end product, service and information flows that reach beyond acknowledged organisational boundaries to include partners, suppliers, and customers who play active roles in delivery of services and the creation of value.

Because of its all-encompassing scope, enterprise architecture is typically approached via frameworks that impose separation of domains or layers (this approach is discussed further below). One such domain is 'business architecture'. Business architecture is defined by the Object Management Group as 'a blueprint of the enterprise that provides a common understanding of the organisation and is used to align strategic objectives and tactical demands' (Object Management Group 2013). The business architecture 'blueprint' typically presents business level concerns such as services, processes and capabilities, deferring the detail of how these are realised, delivered or sustained to concerns within the application, technology and infrastructure domains or layers. This chapter challenges the relevance of enterprise and business architecture and its tools and agents (frameworks in the hands of enterprise architects) to the increasingly difficult task of tackling complexity in today's business environments.

Foundations

Enterprise architecture has always been considered a discipline based on the scientific principles of objective truth, rational analysis and repeatable processes. It is founded on the rational belief that complexity in a domain yields to the imposition of structured, objective methods. As such, it is typical of the products of the modern era, in which scientific rationalism was appropriated by planners and designers as a theory to underpin design and sweep away the informal and *ad hoc* practice of centuries of vernacularism. Until this point, much design was inseparable from making; design was a craft, exercised tacitly when a maker performed piecemeal assemblage, typically using locally available materials and resources (Alexander 1988; Lawson 1997). In pre-modern forms of designing, theory followed practice, not in the sense of being related to it or to owing its very existence to it, but as a kind of incidental by-product of making. In modern designing, theory in all its forms—from geometry to materials science to abstract representational forms—drove practice to the point of disembodying design from mind and action into inanimate, rational forms such as methodologies, processes and automata (Jones 1988). Enterprise architecture has strong ties to modernism, the primacy of theory and the pursuit of orderly frameworks and schemata.

Enterprise architecture owes some of its present-day identity on the fact that the activity of software making was first termed software *engineering*. Software creation has been profoundly shaped by the adoption of engineering as the metaphor of choice. There is no obvious point in the early history of software when the suitability of the engineering metaphor as a basis for the nascent discipline was openly debated. McIlroy (1968) demanded a hardware-like component-based software discipline to reduce risk in the mushrooming United States' Department of Defence software investment. Boehm (1976) first used the term in the context of his separation of a project into design and implementation phases, with a project management regime for each phase. McBreen (2002) claims that early systems development typically involved bespoke hardware development as well as software development, and as a result, conformance to an engineering project regime occupied the software team while the bespoke hardware was developed. Whatever the reasons, one thing is likely – the engineering metaphor was taken to imply a degree of formality and repeatability in software construction as is found in

other engineering disciplines. Software creation was widely perceived as hardware engineering's undisciplined sibling. In adopting the engineering metaphor, the emerging software industry revealed its desire to appropriate engineering's legitimacy and maturity. Enterprise architecture was borne at this time and directly from this lineage.

The appropriateness of the engineering metaphor to software creation has been widely debated. Eaves (1992) argued that the essential nature of software development is, and has always been, one of code-crafting as problem and requirements discovery happen in parallel. He concludes that the 'standard model of scientific research is not applicable in the domain' and 'we are (still) dealing with a craft' (p. 15). Eaves also refers to what he calls a 'rage for order' – the 'human instinct which forces the creation of illusory or aesthetic order out of chaos, if no other order is to be had' (p. 11). Others have explored alternative metaphors, including craft (McBreen 2002), theatre (Laurel 1993) and in philosophical terms, social construction and constructivism (Floyd 1992). The late-modern perspectives of enterprise architecture's founders help to explain its early emphasis on structure, planning and optimisation. But times have changed. The heat of the debates between Zachman, Finkelstein and Spewak and their ilk on framework structure and cell semantics has long since dissipated, and the foundations of modernism have been undermined by an increasingly socially constructed view of organisations and culture over the past two decades. It is time to take the same perspective on enterprise architecture, starting with its basic construct, the framework.

Frameworks

The framework is the fundamental structuring mechanism of enterprise architecture. The framework defines and separates concerns, leading to a logical sequence of discovery and discourse on concepts, business strategy, strategy, resources, and planning. As a vehicle for communication, the enterprise architecture framework provides a flattened view of the congruence of business and IT strategies and how, at a high level, IT will implement the strategies. Proponents claim that the benefits of the framework include business-IT alignment and agreement on the value and benefits of the enterprise architecture (Chew and Gottschalk 2009; TOGAF 2012).

A framework is a structural template that can be overlayed on top of the messiness of real world problems and systems to present a semblance of order. Frameworks have mechanisms that abstract and isolate the elements of business objectives, information, process, and technology as distinct layers. By separating these layers, frameworks make it possible to manage complexity by 'dividing and conquering'. The relationship between framework layers and abstraction is not necessarily one of increasing detail, as layering suggests. In Zachman's framework, for example, successive layers can imply further detail, but each successive layer represents a distinct concern, so the transition from one layer to the next is one of transformation, not decomposition. It is possible and acceptable to deal with information model detail in Zachman's information layer. Many enterprise architects, however, understand frameworks as dictating ordering and successive decomposition.

Frameworks as planning tools for the enterprise have served us well. They are well suited to the way people have tended to think about organisations over the past two decades. Framework 'thinking' worked well in conjunction with waterfall approaches to software engineering. So pervasive was framework thinking that the vendor and services marketplace organised itself around the boundaries – technology and platforms, products and services, for example – making for alignment between problem scoping and decomposition, program structure and procurement.

But the way we think about organisations is changing. Under the broad-based forces of globalisation and market deregulation, the ubiq-uity of Internet and pervasive access, and rapid advances in the technology and communications infrastructure, the economic and business context in which organisations operate is shifting. Much is being written on the major themes of these shifts, including digital disruption, organisational agility and the effects of technology-mediated social movements on media, marketing, collaboration and commerce, not to mention politics and culture itself. The enterprise architecture frameworks still in use today were conceived and established before these themes had emerged or had perceivable impact. Today's enterprise architects are dealing with business and organisational realities for which established enterprise architecture frameworks offer limited help. These limitations of frameworks fall broadly into three groups – organisational, structural and temporal changes.

Changing Organisational Paradigms

Changes to how organisations are viewed have been playing out over decades and can be summarised as the evolution from the Taylorian (1911) paradigm of organisation as hierarchical and deterministic machine, to contemporary views of the organisation as an open, socially constructed, multi-agent ecosystem (Heylighen, Cilliers et al. 2007). As in all evolutionary processes, paradigm shifts occur in response to contextual changes, and environmental selection ensures ever-increasing efficiency, viability and, in business terms, profitability (Kaplan 2000). How an organisation responds to change depends on its priorities and resources, and is subject to the organisation's strategies and the complexity of its systems. In many organisations, the overhead of governance (the means of decision-making, particularly determining priorities and making effective decisions) introduces decision-making latency that means its systems are always (to some degree) legacy systems. In strategic planning and enterprise architecture, change drives the need for almost continuous planning. The approach taken to planning is therefore an important determinant of an organisation's agility.

Changing organisational paradigms dictate how complexity manifests itself and is tackled. The way an architect chooses to deal with complexity says a lot about what they believe the problem to be. Complexity has traditionally been addressed using decomposition based on function. In civic planning, this leads to zoning; in software engineering, waterfall systems; in sociology, category dilemmas. Functionalist designers argued that classification and decomposition are effective design strategies that result in highly efficient designs, and for certain systems this is undoubtedly true. But behaviourist designers counter with the claim that functionalism works only for design problems of low complexity and in well-understood, stable, closed systems. Cities, like societies, organisations and cultures, need other kinds of thinking about design (Alexander 1988).

Business-IT Alignment

Secondly, the relationship between business and information technology has moved on from a customer-provider relationship to one of co-dependency. Technology has always been driven by business demand, and strategic planning methods hold that technology exists purely to serve business objectives. Business-technology alignment is a primary value proposition of enterprise architecture. Alignment occurs when technology investment supports business objectives and the business vision. Enterprise architecture teams often invest considerable efforts to develop and maintain models of an organisation's business, structure, processes, data and technology, as a basis for planning and management.

But increasingly, new business services are enabled and defined by new technology capabilities (pervasive, location-aware services, for example), and we have reached the point where it is no longer

sensible or even possible to perform strategic business planning without incorporating some kind of exploration of the capabilities of technologies to define new business services. Technology is now intrinsic to new business design. Orlov and Cameron (2007) were early observers of the dissolution of the business/technology boundary and 'business/IT alignment'. Recognising that technology touches every corner of business operations, from transaction automation, to mobile devices, to analytic insights, they argued that it investment in technology is not guaranteed to deliver business results or ensure maximized business benefits or use. Rather, technology and business are increasingly mutually-defining.

Timescales and Domain Stability

Thirdly, timescales for realising business-driven change and for delivering new technology-supported services are collapsing. Enterprise architecture grew out of the era of software development *in-the-large* when long (by today's standards) software development timescales were not invalidated by organisational shifts and a map of an organisation's technology could be assumed to be relatively stable over ten or more years. Enterprise architecture frameworks predate component and object-oriented development technologies, as well as (post-waterfall) rapid application development methods. Increasingly, the rate of business change outpaces the organisation's ability to respond.

Many factors have eroded the timeframes for business change. The Internet has introduced a new age of technology-mediated markets, trade and communication, the magnitude and extent of which rivals that of the printing press and electricity distribution. Globalisation of supply and labour markets has revolutionised how businesses create and distribute products. The option to dis-aggregate and distribute functional capabilities such as manufacturing and supply chain, and customer service through geographically independent services on a foundation of reliable global digital communications has revolutionised how companies resource operations. Escalating complexity is driven by other recently recognised forces including diversity, independence, ambiguity and emergence (Morowitz 2002). If it is to stay relevant, enterprise architecture must furnish tools and approaches that alleviate the problem.

Frameworks and Tools in Context

In 2004, the MITRE Group wrote that 'enterprise architecture is a discipline in its early years with the emphasis beginning to move from frameworks, modelling methods, and tools to compliance and performance issues'. The future of enterprise architecture is likely to 'focus on best practices, assessment and effective use of enterprise architecture to improve government management' (Hagan 2004). Beyond tools and frameworks, most assessments of enterprise architecture effectiveness point the finger at 'soft' factors, such as leadership and engagement style, communication, effective governance and continued commitment throughout the lifetime of systems initiatives. For the 2009 Enterprise Architecture Summit, Gartner analysts published the 'Ten Enterprise Architecture Pitfalls', headed up by 'selecting the wrong person as lead enterprise architect' and 'not engaging business people' (Gartner 2009). Their remaining traps can be summarized as follows: enterprise architecture must be business-driven, stakeholders at all levels must be engaged, the enterprise architect's efforts must be relevant, and outcomes must be promoted. Clearly, 'soft skills' are vitally important in the effective delivery of enterprise architecture (Frampton, Barrow et al. 2005).

Wrapping frameworks and tools with strong delivery skills will improve the perceived effectiveness of enterprise architecture, but as a solution to the multiple challenges facing the discipline, it is idiomatic and non-repeatable. It takes enterprise architecture into the space of performance art, the

very place from which the modernists dragged it some three decades ago. A more durable overlay is needed for enterprise architecture to find a lasting form of maturity.

ADOLESCENCE

As a discipline, enterprise architecture has established itself and a level of recognition but it is now experiencing a kind of adolescent awkwardness. Something more than frameworks, methods and analytical competency is needed for the discipline to 'grow up'. To navigate its adolescent years, enterprise architecture must resolve its relationship with the business it serves. The key to this is for enterprise architects to embrace design and to start practicing it beyond the information and technology domains. This section presents some accounts of design practice by business people in the domain of business, but using some of the tools, techniques and thinking of the enterprise architect. They describe architecture lifted to the level of the business, in which enterprise and technology concerns contribute but do not dictate. In each case, the people leading these initiatives did not call themselves enterprise architects, but they performed the business designer role in a fashion that signposts the way to maturity for the discipline of enterprise architecture.

An Architecture for Government Service Delivery

Despite all of the Western world's industrial and economic progress, substantial inequities in income and standard of living remain. The government in the State of Victoria, Australia, has been providing services to support the disadvantaged for over 150 years, particularly to children at risk through family violence, victims of drug or alcohol abuse, the disabled and the homeless. The scale of this 'social safety net' is noteworthy. In 2010-11, the department employed 11,700 staff in 57 offices who managed 55,000 child protection reports, 31,000 clients with disability needs, 26,000 families with child support, 39,000 homeless people and 83,000 in publicly-funded houses. The budget for 2011-12 was $3.4 billion, with over $1.3 billion going directly to community service organisations to deliver services.

The scale of the department's response motivates ongoing scrutiny, in terms of both financial accountability and measures of effectiveness. In recent years, research on people living in situations of social disadvantage has repeatedly shown that handing out relief to presenting problems temporarily alleviates need but often has limited impact on the cycle of poverty or disadvantage. The root causes of social problems are diffuse, and have motivated responses on many levels. Factors such as cultural diversity, social class, increasing complexity of need, and successive layers of legislation combine to limit the effectiveness of the human services sector in reducing entrenched disadvantage. With an aging and growing population base, governments have recognised the need to move on from traditional welfare approaches to new models of holistic and integrated care.

In late 2011, the Victorian government released a report (Wooldridge and Lovell 2011) that addressed some of these issues. The report recognised a fragmented and poorly coordinated support system where service providers focus on particular issues or groups of vulnerable people without a 'whole of system' view. The government's 'focus on programs rather than people', the report claims, has created a situation where individuals must make sense of services, navigate from door to door, and 'fit their particular problem to an existing program' to qualify for support. Effectiveness is also limited by failure to recognise the family circumstances of clients and the impact of relationships on their situation. The report acknowledges that the department has addressed 'solving problems after they occur rather than anticipating and intervening to prevent them'. This propensity to deliver crisis intervention rather than effecting lasting change drives dependency rather than independence. Recognising that disadvantage is not experienced in isolation but most often in families and communities by people with not one but multiple related needs, the report advocates moving from a 'problem and program' based model to one based on 'person and place'. By confronting all domains of disadvantage – personal, economic, and community – the goals of unlocking potential and enabling people to build better lives for themselves and their families can be achieved more consistently.

The antidote to crisis management, the authors argue, is to regard each individual as being on a path from dependency (with the attendant crises) through a self-realisation stage (in which workers help individuals to recognise their needs and the causes of crises) to maturity (when the individual self-manages with planned rather than unplanned assistance). The report recommends replacing the department's divisions and programs with a new structure that supports the delivery of coordinated personalised services. Case workers will form multi-specialty teams with processes and tools to respond more holistically to a client's individual circumstances.

The new model of operation recognises three categories of care delivery – 'managed', 'guided' and 'self-managed' support. 'Managed support' represents face-to-face intervention for families or individuals with high and/or multiple personal, social and economic needs over medium to long timeframes. In these cases, a client support worker will collaborate with the client (and their family wherever possible) to identify their goals and provide the comprehensive planning, support and coordination of services required to achieve their goals. 'Guided' support will be available to families and individuals requiring a moderate level of support to resolve the difficulties they are experiencing. In such situations, a case worker will support them to decide on their service and other needs so that they can progress to self-sufficiency. 'Self-managed' support will be available to the majority of clients who are capable of self-administering and managing their needs with minimal intervention, including finding and accessing information, referral options, or booking services.

There are several striking things about this proposal. The first is the way that analysis of service delivery practice and operating costs has informed a strategic plan based on a systemic perspective. At the core of the proposal is the recognition that the existing model of service delivery is broken – reactionary scheduling and delivery of services provides short-term relief but does not alter the cycle of disadvantage. This cycle is observed to be playing out regardless of the services, from youth justice to child support to disability. The recognition that disadvantage is experienced in multiple dimensions (personal, economic and community) and that individuals can be lifted through stages of self-awareness and capability to become self-sufficient is insightful. It is only by embedding this systemic model in the processes, services and work practices of the department and its agencies that the escalating demand can be met. Much detail in the new model remains to be ironed out. But the fact that the interdependent social and economic systems at work in the manifestation of disadvantage have been mapped lends credence to the proposed new model and the plan.

The second noteworthy characteristic is that the new operating model narrative paints an image of the business architecture of the new organisation, without explicitly calling out organisation, hierarchy or the mechanics of service delivery. It does this because it implies a new structure (replacement of program-focussed divisions with a services-centred cross-competency focus) and the essence of how the reconfigured business will operate. The kind of business architecture that an experienced enterprise architect would conceive of would, of course, consist of much more detail in the definitions than this – a view of organisation, capabilities, information and

operation to name the mainstays. But the essence of the business architecture can be seen to fall out of the operating model – cross-specialty case teams, prescriptive and managed care paths, a service-centric competency including service design and management, outcome monitoring, client-centricity and self-service, are some of the capabilities of the new business. The technology architecture layer of the enterprise architecture follows, and will include support for client identity, a services catalogue, a single and coordinated view of client, a common care plan, and a range of access channels. Most enterprise architects would be at home designing the identity, data, platform, security and integration architectures needed to support this new services-centric business model. But many would not be comfortable recognising and designing an intervention into the system of disadvantage.

An Architecture for Participation

In another department of the same government just across the street, a small team of business strategists was charged with up-skilling the State's workforce through increased participation in skills training. Vocational training in diverse skills such as apprenticeships, tourism services, hospitality and hairdressing is provided by a large sector of established technical institutes across the State. Skills training is widely acknowledged as being sensible and defensible government policy. A society with improved skills reduces the likelihood of skills shortages, lifts workforce participation, and stimulates employment and the economy. Government partially funds, accredits and administers the sector through its primary Skills Agency.

The strategists on the 'skills team' tackled a number of objectives, including alignment of supply with demand and policy, increased awareness and participation. The traditional way of achieving the objective of increased training participation would be to design a Website on a .gov domain and launch it with media fanfare and a ministerial press release. This typically results in a small spike in site visits but within a few months, the site is all but idle. Bureaucrats are then left with the problem of how to do better with next year's budget and the messy task of creatively interpreting Web analytics and other indicators to paint some kind of a picture of success.

The skills team recognised that for the online part of the campaign they needed to 'meet the people where they are'. First, the Skills Agency's Website was updated, but with minimal spend and only to make sure that content and links were correct and useable. Next, a marketing consultancy was engaged with the brief to identify the most effective places to engage the target audiences – males aged between 18 and 30 for building trade apprenticeships and males and females of similar age for hospitality industry training. For the prospective tradesmen, the consultancy identified a popular online football tipping competition run in partnership with one of the city's daily newspapers. For a small membership fee at the start of the season, football fans can pick and predict teams, winners and best and worst performers each week. The subscriber base is large, stable and homogeneous – sports-fanatics, average age 24, working/middle-class males. The Skills Agency placed selected trades apprenticeship advertisements on certain pages of the online tipping Website.

Recognising that the target demographic held a strong affinity with the brand and content of a long-standing metropolitan youth music FM station, and that this station cross-promoted the online football tipping game, the Skills Agency bought advertorial segments and placed skills and apprenticeship 'advocates' on the high-rating breakfast and drive shows. A few of these advocates (known by the agency as 'ambassadors') are high-profile sportsmen or personalities who supplement their on-air promotion with pre-edited tweets on twitter.com and status updates on Facebook.com. The station then launched a competition to offer a one-week placement with well-known employers.

The Skills Agency repeated the formula for the hospitality targets, this time using conventional television advertising during the current series of a hugely popular reality cooking show, celebrity chef ambassadors, and a week's work experience placement with one of the city's top restaurants. The campaign resulted in record awareness and take-up of the skills offerings, leading to a measurable increase in participation rates within the target demographics. The approach intelligently recognised and leveraged established communities, going with the flow rather than trying to divert the flow. As a result, no-one was required to change their routine and nothing was forced.

On the surface, there is not much of what we might think of as enterprise architecture in this story. If anything, enterprise architects might be excused for thinking that the chosen business solution minimised technology and architecture. But the approach to designing the most effective solution to the problem of skills participation with the available means is pure architecture, because it recognises and leverages existing systems in a way that minimises friction and investment and maximises immediate outcomes. The fact that the systems are social systems driven by human behaviours such as brand loyalty and the cult of personality should not exclude enterprise architecture. When the enterprise architect thinks in terms of systems, the means by which the system operates is mostly immaterial.

Architecting Clinical Space

The systems that influence or bound how people work exist in many forms. Architects of the built world have always been engaged in a discourse on how architecture and design meets human needs in the context of space and place. While architects have long been criticised for exhibiting a public preference for the ephemeral image over usefulness and the experience of longer-term habitation, they are increasingly being challenged to bring a human-centred approach to architecture and planning. 'Old design' has delivered deterministic outcomes based on discipline, particularly in visual communications, interior spaces, products, information design, architecture and planning. 'New design' pursues purposeful and holistic outcomes – design for experiencing, for emotion, for interacting, for sustainability, for service and for transforming.

Sanders and Westerlund (2011) describe developing and applying human-centred approaches to the design of a large scale hospital campus in post-Katrina New Orleans (NBBJ 2012). The tools they used (personas, timelines and journeys, participatory modelling, experience models) are user-centric participatory techniques that ensure a level of co-creation and ownership. They used puppets and scale models of patient rooms in the hands of nurses and clinicians to optimise the design of operating theatres and recovery rooms. They role-played clinical settings to challenge how and why nurses move between patient and other fixtures during routine care delivery. Sanders describes how the role-playing dissolved the distinction between professional architect/designer and client, delivering improved designs that represented user's specific needs without compromising the architect's professional design judgement.

Traditional architects and career nurses are 'on different planets' when it comes to what they think is important in the design of a theatre or ward, she argues. Architects often ignore or defer details that nurses think is of utmost importance – where the hand sanitation stations are positioned, for example. To an architect used to designing public buildings, this detail is tertiary. But when viewed from the perspective of meeting business objectives, it can be crucial. The placement of the sanitation stations can make or break the nurses' ability to meet infection control targets, and the placement of shelves is vital when you understand that the heavily unionised workforce is required to wear tunics or gowns without pockets for infection control and nurse safety. The architects were able to move beyond their preconceptions of hospital theatres and wards to consider the workflow systems at play. By using objectives to drive design, seemingly minor changes to a design can be hugely significant. The principle of driving design with business objectives to lay out physical spaces that support efficient workflow is equally applicable for the design of information systems.

Architecting Systems with Platforms

A final story illustrates that the business domain is not devoid of the kinds of archetypes and patterns from technology domains that architects are comfortable with. Some archetypes have important places in both business and system domains. When these can be deployed in the business architecture of a system, the alignment of the problem and solution spaces can powerfully dissolve complexity. The platform archetype is a good example, as the following story from the health informatics sector illustrates.

Information management in healthcare is undergoing a long-running transformation from paper-based records to paperless systems. Large investments in systems and infrastructure are being made in many public and private healthcare organisations to deliver a universal Electronic Medical Record (EMR). In Australia, the National E-Health Transition Authority has been governing the rollout of a national e-health infrastructure that will provide citizens with a personal electronic health record of every interaction with primary and allied health care providers, potentially over a lifetime. But the maturity and openness of the information infrastructures at the national and health provider levels have been moving at very different rates. The marketplace for health-care provider products has been, and continues to be dominated by ERP-styled offerings, some with proprietary, vendor-locked architectures and limited integration capabilities. Most of the vendors can deliver an integrated EMR but only if their proprietary modules are implemented across all of the hospital's clinical services. The experience of many healthcare providers is that ERP-class business systems provide comprehensive functionality and inter-module integration but in many cases are costly to customise or extend. Recognising this, the U.S. Health and Human Services Department awarded a research and development grant to a team at Harvard University to develop an open platform for health care applications (Mahidhar 2011).

The team from Harvard was tasked with liberating health data by designing an open and standards-based architecture so that vendors could build third-party applications capable of running on multiple platforms at low marginal cost. They recognised that a platform model was needed to deliver a health IT ecosystem, modelled on Apple's iStore or Amazon's platform services. Within a year the Harvard team developed 'Substitutable Medical Applications, Reusable Technologies' (SMART), an open-source architecture that offers a set of core services to facilitate substitutable health care applications, or plug-ins (Mandl, Mandel et al. 2012). The team published its application programming interfaces and initiated an open application development contest with a $5,000 prize. Fifteen different vendors or developer communities delivered 'apps' for use by clinicians and patients. The team also integrated the platform with Cerner APIs to deploy the SMART platform beside a leading healthcare vendor's ERP-class product.

The SMART environment, based on open standards and designed to support and encourage third-party light-weight application development, is an enabling technology platform with the potential to host a business ecosystem. The establishment of a viable ecosystem depends upon a number of much broader factors, including adoption by providers, integration support from vendors and community-based developers, and users (clinicians, allied healthcare professionals, administrators and patients and their carers). This remains SMART's biggest hurdle, but it is largely outside the influence of the Harvard team.

Enterprise architects will recognise the system archetypes underlying both NEHTA's e-health infrastructure and the SMART platform – the 'business ecosystem' built upon an enabling 'business platform'. The new business ecosystem, typified by Amazon and Apple, consists of capabilities and rules that organize and manage the commerce engine and maintain the independence and low or zero entry costs of users, authors and reviewer communities, as well as a marketplace of independent vendors who sell through the ecosystem's online stores. The platform provides and manages identity, authorisation, content, digital rights, inventory and supply chain, and publishing partners. The Amazon ecosystem facilitates a market in which the best authors and retailers do the most business and where micro-brands and reputations are made and lost. No single authority or group controls the others, and Amazon profits from each transaction on its platform. Ecosystems like these foster innovation through what has been called 'radical adjacency' – the ability for a participant to go beyond its normal business practice to seize an opportunity in widely adjacent markets. Spotting an opportunity to create a 'business ecosystem' by designing a platform rather than a point solution is a natural consequence of a systems-centric analysis.

TOWARDS MATURITY

The common theme through these stories is the application of a systems perspective to business architecture. By observing the primacy of business objectives, recognising the forces at play in the wider business and social context, and then designing and structuring interventions to most effectively meet these objectives whilst exploiting existing constraints and behaviours, the business architect can achieve the potential of enterprise architecture in a way that is not often realised. Maturity for enterprise architecture is down this kind of path, and it goes beyond the rational foundation of enterprise architecture to include business-centric architecture, design and 'systems thinking'.

'Systems thinking' (Checkland 1981; Senge 1992) is key. It is a holistic approach to understanding complex interactions and problems, or how things influence each other within a whole. 'Systems thinking' assumes that the component parts of a closed, open, social or natural system can best be understood in the context of relationships with each other and with other systems, rather than in isolation. The approach is most suited to open, socially constructed systems 'where having good participants produces better results than having good planners' (Shirky 2012). To further illustrate the kinds of new design approaches available to enterprise architects, some cameos of business-centric design and 'systems thinking' conclude the chapter.

Designing Systems that Exploit Human Behaviours

Governments have traditionally employed broad-brush mechanisms to influence citizen behaviour to achieve desired outcomes, including regulation, enforcement, taxation and subsidy. These devices, rooted in a rational and economic world-view, constitute the main macro-economic levers for controlling an economic system. At a micro-economic level, these controls impact in different ways depending on sector-based competitive, commercial and other forces. And at the level of individuals, the cause-and-effect relationship is diffuse at best.

Most government policy has been based on the theory that people rationally seek to maximise their welfare. But this model is increasingly swamped by the escalating complexity of choice. In their quests to identify alternative mechanisms for influence, psychologists and economists have started straying into each other's fields in their study of individual decision-making in a variety of social and everyday settings. In 'Nudge', Richard

Thaler and Cass Sunstein (2008) argue that people make many more decisions reactively and in-the-moment than analytically, drawing on arbitrary factors – product packaging, convenient access, simplicity or brand familiarity – as the means of choice. Their list of the fallacies of choice includes 'anchoring' (cognitive and perceptive bias based on personal experience), skewed perspectives of representativeness (for example, the perception that the probability of a coin toss outcome changes after a sequence), and 'status quo' (a person's inbuilt bias against change).

Other authors explore similar lines. In 'Predictably Irrational', Ariely (2008) explores the multitude of social and contextual influences that supplant rational thought in personal and collective decision-making. These include the influence of relationships and the effect that a decision will have on an important relationship, price anchoring (accepting the first price you see as the benchmark for all other offers), irrational attachment to a 'free' offer regardless of what other consequences come with that choice, and how decision-making behaviour changes during certain forms of stimulation, all with the slightly ironic twist that irrational behaviours are often observed repeatedly and are therefore predictable. In 'Freakonomics' Levitt and Dubner (2005) similarly claim that people often make predictable mistakes because they rely on heuristics, fallacies, and the influence of social interactions.

Recognising this human foible affords the insightful designer an opportunity to influence choices for common and individual good by architecting sensible defaults, so that human laziness is rewarded by better individual and collective outcomes. Examples include setting savings plan enrolment and risk profile defaults to 'on' and 'conservative', and placing healthy food options at eye-level. With its promises of quick wins for seemingly simple interventions, the theory has attracted followers, including UK Prime Minister Cameron, who established a 'Behavioural Insights Team' with the remit to 'find innovative ways of encouraging, enabling and supporting people to make better choices for themselves' (UK Cabinet Office 2010). The team initially tackled the application of behavioural insights to fraud (by designing changes that lead to higher compliance), energy efficiency (encouraging uptake of energy efficiency measures), consumer affairs (collective purchasing schemes) and health (organ donation and smoking cessation).

A subsequent review initiated by the House of Lords to determine the feasibility of using social and contextual cues to influence behaviour to complement laws and regulation, found that while 'nudging' worked at the individual level, behavioural change interventions appear to work best when they are part of a package of legislative, regulatory and fiscal measures. Useful behavioural change, the authors concluded, takes time – and typically much more than the allotted term of an elected politician. The review did little to dampen Prime Minister Cameron's support for his Behavioural Insights Team which continues down its path of designing behavioural interventions to shape social policy. For enterprise architects, behavioural insights and the ability to understand human choices has interesting implications for designing systems and interventions.

Designing Systems based on Co-Creation of Value

The building block of the services economy is the service. In economic terms, the service or 'tertiary' sector may be defined as whatever is not agriculture or manufacturing. A service is an activity or experience provided by one person or organisation to another for the recipient's benefit. Increasingly, products are sold with services, and the services contribute as much or more revenue than do the products. In information systems, a familiar example is that of 'systems integration' in which a vendor sells software product licenses but makes ten to one hundred times this revenue on the provision of professional services to configure,

customise, integrate and operationalize the resulting business system. In recent years, escalating competition fuelled by the availability of personal devices and online services has driven increasing focus on the design of customer interactions and the value added at each 'touch-point'. As well as the intensifying focus on the quality of the user experience, organisational designers now view the continuous design of services as an essential business capability.

The terms 'service science, management, and engineering' refer to the growing academic interest in the interdisciplinary field of getting the services (the value proposition from the customer's perspective and the touch-points) right. Enterprise architects are familiar with the notion of service and its application layer analogue (enterprise services in a Services-Oriented Architecture (Chew and Gottschalk 2009)) and the methods for designing enterprise services. But the 'services science' notion of service design is broader and is motivated by the creation of value as seen by the customer and enrichment of the customer relationship. The links between the services of enterprise architecture and those of 'services science' seem obvious but nevertheless involve a fundamental shift in mindset and problem orientation. Design theorists outside of information sciences have known for a long time about the importance of an organisation's ability to define design strategy and execute its design capability (Lockwood and Walton 2008). Service reform continues to be considered a central challenge in the UK (Demos 2012) and Australia (Australian Public Service Commission 2007; Parker and Bartlett 2008).

The social media revolution and its defining phenomena of participation such as 'crowdsourcing' (Howe 2009) has moved the discussion of the relevance of services from maximising the value provided by the service provider to the customer, to co-creation of value. A branch of 'services science' called Service-Dominant (S-D) logic has emerged that portrays value creation in conjunction with (rather than for) customers as a source of competitive advantage (Vargo and Lusch 2004; Vargo and Lusch 2008). According to Vargo and Lusch, S-D logic holds to ten premises of which four are foundational. The first foundation is that service (defined as 'the application of knowledge, skills and resources') is the fundamental basis of all exchange. The second holds that the customer is always a co-creator of value (value creation is therefore interactional). The third is that all social and economic actors are resource integrators – this implies that the context of value creation is networks (and networks of networks). The fourth foundational principle of Service-Dominant logic is that value is always uniquely and phenomenologically determined by the beneficiary – that is, value is a constructed (idiosyncratic, experiential, contextual, and meaning-laden) rather than objective thing.

The co-creation concept becomes relevant to enterprise architecture when the organisational capabilities needed to execute S-D logic in practice are considered. Karpen, Bove et al. (2012) looked at the question of what capabilities an organisation should develop to exploit co-creation. They proposed a portfolio of six capabilities for facilitating and enhancing interaction and resource integration, including the ability to understand individual customer's service contexts, service processes, and expected service outcomes ('individuated interaction capability'); the ability to enhance social and emotional links with customers in service processes ('relational interaction capability'); the ability to support fair and non-opportunistic customer service processes ('ethical interaction capability'); the ability to enable customers to shape the nature and content of service processes ('empowered interaction capability'); the ability to assist customer's own knowledge and competency development in service processes ('developmental interaction capability'); and the ability to facilitate coordinated and integrated service processes that include customers ('concerted interaction capability').

Examples of these principles and capabilities are not hard to find. Amazon's analysis of search and purchase patterns to better understand a visitor's interests is 'individuated interaction'. Old Spice's (or any of the thousands of other prominent consumer brands') YouTube channel which facilitates dialogue with the brand and among viewers is 'relational interaction'. 'Ethical interaction' is demonstrated by an organisation's corporate responsibility strategy which mandates supplier agreements and employee training for good interaction practices with customers. 'Empowered interaction' is demonstrated by Dell's famous online notebook configurator. The provision of customer training to boost product proficiency by publishing manuals and opening up the service department demonstrates 'developmental interaction'. And any supplier that federates or orchestrates the interactions between consumers and partners to deliver superior customer service demonstrates 'concerted interaction'. Collectively, these capabilities position an organisation for value co-creation at the point of service. Not every organisation will need to provide all capabilities, and investment will need to be guided by a form of strategic planning that places customer value at its centre. With some reorientation, enterprise architects are ideally placed to play a leading role in these kinds of service planning and design dialogues.

Designing Systems using "Design Thinking"

In recent years, the methods of designers have been appropriated by some business strategists under the moniker 'design thinking', an amalgam of design-based approaches packaged for a generalist audience, and populated by authors including Martin (2007) and Lockwood (2009), consultancies such as IDEO (Brown 2008) and commentators including Nussbaum (2012). 'Design thinking' is anything but a theory-driven movement, but it does tip its hat to a broad epistemological base including ethnography, wicked problems, systems theory, participatory design and iterative innovation models. Its adaptation of 'systems thinking' is particularly relevant to enterprise architects. Tim Brown's seminal example of 'design thinking' is Thomas Edison's ability to invent and at the same time, foresee how people would use the invention and design a context in which it would be successful. So while Edison is remembered for inventing the first electric light bulb, Brown argues that equal inventive genius can be seen in his design and construction of the generators and power distribution lines so that the electric light could be laid out to illuminate the gas-lit streets. Without this 'systemic' view, Brown argues, his invention might have remained little more than a 'parlour trick'.

'Design thinking' consists of a continuous iteration of three broad types of activity – inspiration, ideation and implementation. 'Inspiration' involves examination of the business problem through intense *in situ* observation, involving many disciplines to gain multiple perspectives, uncovering constraints, resources, changes, expert or skilled behaviours, and opportunities. 'Ideation' is a brainstorming activity in which participants and designers deconstruct observations and stories, often leading to roughly conceived or *ad hoc* prototypes. Ideation cycles rapidly to avoid burning energy on unproductive options. When an idea or option emerges, 'implementation' activities such as designing the user experience, engineering and improving the prototypes, and filling in the gaps in the context of the innovation to ensure its success completes the 'design thinking' process.

Brown's consultancy (IDEO) claims many successful examples of the application of the approach. One is a new product design for a neglected market segment that has parallels with the whole-system approach taken by Edison to invent his electric light scheme. Shimano, a Japanese manufacturer of bicycle components, worked with IDEO to conceive of a new product to appeal to

a large and cashed-up but widely disengaged cycling segment – Baby Boomers. Market research confirmed that although Boomers were put off by lycra-clad speedsters, modern cycle complexity and the dangers of road riding, they held fond memories of casual Sunday afternoon cycling on 'old fashioned' bikes with large mud-guarded wheels, wide seats, and upright handlebars. IDEO worked with Shimano to define a concept to reconnect American mid-age consumers with their joyous childhood experience of bikes and cycling. The multi-disciplinary design team came up with the concept of 'coasting', riding a minimalist bike built for pleasure rather than speed. The team prototyped the bikes, but went further to designate accessible cycling paths and popular, scenic precincts in many American cities, to address concerns of safety and to allow association between 'cruisers' and others engaged in causal recreation. The team worked with three leading cycle manufacturers to bring the bike to market. The launch campaign used laid back messages ('first one there's a rotten egg') and activated Websites with online and social media cross-promotion. After a successful launch in 2007, seven new cycle manufacturers signed up to produce Coasters within a year. This 'design thinking' story illustrates the focus on the designed artefact and its complete context of use. The designers created the object *and* a supportive ecosystem in which the product would succeed.

Towards Design Mastery

To grow beyond an adolescent stage of maturity, enterprise architects must engage with design outside of the technology domain. Although 'pure' business design may take the architect into foreign places, most of the design skills needed are not new. Architects have been practicing them as part of agile methodologies for a decade or more. To lead the kinds of design scenarios described in this chapter, enterprise architects could start by demonstrating some of the following kinds of designerly behaviours.

Observational Powers

Accounts of successful innovation and design projects consistently describe the power of observation. Tim Brown describes 'design thinking' as being powered by 'a thorough understanding, through direct observation, of what people want and need in their lives and what they like or dislike about the way particular products are made, packaged, marketed, sold and supported' (Brown 2008). Direct observation demands a range of techniques, from the kinds of observation and scenario-playing pioneered at Xerox ParcPlace to 'living with the tribe' as done by ethnographic researchers. The enterprise architect must become a keen and acute observer, able to step into the shoes of the people performing the tasks and using the tools at hand. This kind of observation balances impartiality and objective detachment with involved empathy, all the while seeing every detail and relating it to big-picture objectives and outcomes.

Centrality of Experience

A 'design ethos' cannot properly serve two masters. Making the user experience central may at times conflict with other business priorities – profits, return on investment, delivery timeframe, budget and quality to name a few. Design thinking incorporates iteration and failure-tolerance throughout the design process to deliver frequent and early feedback and allow constant revision in light of experience. 'Systems thinking' requires attention to the political, social and other systems that motivate behaviour. The process to perfect the human experience of a product or service is highly unpredictable, and innovation initiatives compete with other projects for resources and budget. To be motivated by user experience over profitability or other business contingencies, the enterprise architect must understand the place of the user experience amidst competing demands

throughout the designing, defending it where necessary, and only compromising it when the implications are understood.

Designing for Continuous Designing

New approaches to systems-centred design recognise that designing happens not at a point in time in the studio or behind a door labelled 'R&D Department' but in the full light of the business in all its situations, places and forms. Business architects must emancipate design and employ it, or facilitate collaborative designing in all phases and activities, from discovering and negotiating business objectives, researching the experience of participants and stakeholders, envisioning, conception and scenario-playing, prototyping and development, through to system development and operation. The mature business architect considers how their systems will cope amidst inevitable change and how their systems will support ongoing redesign.

Designing with a "Systems Thinking" Perspective

Systems theoretic models (Checkland 1981; Senge 1992) tackle large-scale 'soft' problems characterised by lack of structural clarity and complex interdependencies between the parts. 'Systems thinking' promotes taking an end-to-end view of systems in context and proposes a catalogue of generic system archetypes. In systems thinking, an intervention is considered successful if it results in an improved but ultimately stable system. A stable system is one that is dynamic and can support change, growth and contraction. Business architects must recognise the wider system in which their solutions exist, designing interventions or modifications where necessary so that their changes create or preserve the enclosing system's viability and stability under normal and exceptional conditions.

Dealing with Assumptions and Constraints

Hammer and Champy (1993) kicked off the business process reengineering movement in the 1990s with the call to 'slay the sacred cows'. 'Design thinking' also advocates opening up problems, reframing definitions and challenging assumptions. The business constraints and user expectations enshrined within existing systems are constantly evolving. By questioning and challenging assumptions, valuable problem insights can be found that allow new, alternate or novel solutions. Techniques such as ideation, prototyping, iteration, incremental refinement, collaborative design, synthesis, user-centric design, full lifecycle design, and service design all provide opportunities to uncover explicit and implicit assumptions. The business architect must go beyond questioning assumptions to understand the impacts and consequences of their interventions on the complete social and technological systems.

Designing the Delivery Path

Critics of 'design thinking' have observed its failure to deliver on innovation in many organisations, partly because of the emphasis placed on training, tools and techniques at the expense of facilitating the hard slog of innovation projects (Nussbaum 2012). Tim Brown, in a reflective moment, has agreed that 'design thinking' has largely been successful in making the big leaps that large organizations cannot make for themselves but less successful when the idea is handed off to the client organisation to deliver (Brown 2009). The 'design thinker' must look down the path of implementation to delivery and operation of the innovation, preparing the path in whatever ways can be foreseen and are possible at the time. The 'systems thinker' must articulate the system in its entire context, making changes if necessary to ensure that the system will operate as desired through all of the system's operating phases and under all conditions.

Facilitation, Not Heroics

From Le Corbusier to Frank Lloyd Wright, modern history is full of stories of heroic designers, typified by the creative genius who could single-handedly conceive a building uniquely responsive to the client's brief and the site and revolutionary in its statement in the architectural discourse at the same time. These larger-than-life characters may still be celebrated in architecture but they are the antithesis of today's systems designers. There is no doubt that design and systems thinking requires advanced design aptitude and skills but the abilities to co-design and facilitate other's designing are equally important as personal creativity and design ability. The enterprise architect must be capable of designing individually, jointly and collaboratively with others, facilitating the designing where it is most appropriate at the time, with the system or innovation project's overall goals and objectives always in mind.

Recognising Mature Practice

The established tools of enterprise architecture are still relevant to today's organisations. Modelling and proactively managing the technology environment using the frameworks, methods and tools of the established discipline is an essential practice for effective and efficient operations. But if enterprise architects do not aggressively engage in discussions, debates, analyses and executive level decision-making that forms new business services or evolves existing ones, others will in their place. Enterprise architects who stay in their technology comfort zone risk becoming marginalised as businesses adopt new networked, socially connected, open forms. If enterprise architects do not embrace these practices, they risk becoming marginalised in technology-centred corners, from where their influence diminishes. From here, the curse of irrelevance can quickly become real. As each new portion of the enterprise's information and communication technology services is modernised, outsourced or migrated to the cloud, the 'old' enterprise architecture loses a piece of its identity. Such erosion can only be countered by corresponding growth.

The future for enterprise architects is bright. But it is higher up the value chain that it has been in the past. Today's enterprise architects may increasingly use unfamiliar titles as they move primarily in business circles. Those who have practiced the discipline of enterprise architecture through their careers who are able to make this transition will know that they are doing many of the same things, thinking similar thoughts, and applying the same patterns and tools. The difference will be their demonstrated capacity to place themselves fairly and squarely in the business. Enterprise architects become business architects when they treat the objectives of the business as their number one priority and the organisation's information technology as a means to an end. With this focus, their architecting skills take on new relevance.

REFERENCES

AGIMO. (2007). *Australian government architecture: Principles. Australian Government Information Management Office.* AGIMO.

AGIMO. (2011). *Australian government architecture: Reference models. Australian Government Information Management Office.* AGIMO.

Alexander, C. (1988). *A city is not a tree.* London: Thames and Hudson.

Ariely, D. (2008). *Predictably irrational: The hidden forces that shape our decisions.* New York: HarperCollins.

Australian Public Service Commission. (2007). *Changing behaviour: A public policy perspective.* Retrieved from http://www.apsc.gov.au/__data/assets/pdf_file/0017/6821/changingbehaviour.pdf

Boehm, B. W. (1976). Software engineering. *IEEE Transactions on Computers, 25*(12), 1226–1241. doi:10.1109/TC.1976.1674590.

Brown, T. (2008). Design thinking. *Harvard Business Review.* PMID:18605031.

Brown, T. (2009). *Tim Brown urges designers to think big.* Retrieved from http://www.ted.com/talks/tim_brown_urges_designers_to_think_big.html

Checkland, P. (1981). *Systems thinking, systems practice.* Chichester, UK: Wiley.

Chew, E. K., & Gottschalk, P. (2009). *Information technology strategy and management: Best practices.* Hershey, PA: IGI Global. doi:10.4018/978-1-59904-802-4.

Demos. (2012). *Public services and welfare.* Retrieved 23 August, 2012, from http://www.demos.co.uk/publicservicesandwelfare

Eaves, D. (1992). *The prospects of a formal discipline of software engineering.* Monash University.

Floyd, C. (1992). Software development as reality construction. In Floyd, C., Budde, R., Zullighoven, H., & Keil-Slawik, R. (Eds.), *Software Development and Reality Construction.* Berlin: Springer-Verlag. doi:10.1007/978-3-642-76817-0_10.

Frampton, K. Barrow, et al. (2005). A study of the in-practice application of a commercial software architecture. In *Proceedings of the Australian Software Engineering Conference (ASWEC 2005).* Brisbane, Australia: IEEE Computer Society.

Gartner. (2009). *Gartner identifies ten enterprise architecture pitfalls.* Retrieved 13 August, 2012, from http://www.gartner.com/it/page.jsp?id=1159617

Hagan, P. J. (2004). *Guide to the (evolving) enterprise architecture body of knowledge.* The MITRE Corporation.

Hammer, M., & Champy. (1993). *Reengineering the corporation: A manifesto for business revolution.* New York: Harper.

Heylighen, F., & Cilliers, , et al. (2007). Complexity and philosophy. InBogg, J, & Geyer, R (Eds.), *Complexity, Science and Society.* Oxford, UK: Radcliffe Publishing.

Howe, J. (2009). *Crowdsourcing: Why the power of the crowd is driving the future of business.* New York: Three Rivers Press.

Jones, J. C. (1988). Softecnica. In Thackara, J. (Ed.), *Design after modernism.* London: Thames and Hudson.

Kaplan, S. M. (2000). Co-evolution in socio-technical systems. In *Proceedings of Computer Supported Cooperative Work (CSCW 2000).* Philadelphia: ACM Press.

Karpen, I. O., & Bove, , et al. (2012). Linking service-dominant logic and strategic business practice: A conceptual model of a service-dominant orientation. *Journal of Service Research, 15*(21).

Laurel, B. (1993). *Computers as theatre.* Reading, MA: Addison-Wesley.

Lawson, B. (1997). *How designers think.* Oxford, UK: Architectural Press.

Levitt, S., & Dubner. (2005). *Freakonomics: A rogue economist explores the hidden side of everything.* New York: William Morrow.

Lockwood, T., & Walton. (2008). *Building design strategy: Using design to achieve key business objectives.* New York: Allworth Press.

Lockwood, T. (2009). *Design thinking: Integrating innovation, customer experience, and brand value.* Allworth Press.

Mahidhar, V. (2011). Ecosystems for innovation: An interview with U.S. CTO Aneesh Chopra. *Deloitte Review,* 11. Retrieved 14 August, 2011, from http://www.deloitte.com/assets/Dcom-Australia/Local%20Assets/Documents/Industries/Government%20Services/Public%20Sector/Deloitte_review_issue_nine_2011.pdf

Mandl, K. D., & Mandel, , et al. (2012). The SMART platform: Early experience enabling substitutable applications for electronic health records. *Journal of American Medical Informatics, 19*(4).

Martin, R. L. (2007). *The opposable mind: How successful leaders win through integrative thinking.* Boston: Harvard Business School Publishing.

McBreen, P. (2002). *Software craftsmanship: The new imperative.* Boston: Addison-Wesley.

McIlroy, M. D. (1968). Mass produced software components. In *Proceedings of the First NATO Conference on Software Engineering.* Garmisch, Germany: IEEE.

Morowitz, H. (2002). *The emergence of everything: How The world became complex.* Oxford, UK: Oxford University Press.

NBBJ. (2012). *NBBJ architecture and design.* Retrieved 7 May, 2012, from http://www.nbbj.com

Nussbaum, B. (2012). Design thinking is a failed experiment: So what's next? *Co.DESIGN.* Retrieved 24 August, 2012, from http://www.fastcodesign.com/1663558/design-thinking-is-a-failed-experiment-so-whats-next

Object Management Group. (2013). *Business architecture working group.* Retrieved 18 March, 2013, from http://bawg.omg.org/

Orlov, L. M., & Cameron. (2007). *Business technology defined: Technology management is changing to deliver business results.* Forrester Research.

Parker, S., & Bartlett. (2008). *Towards agile government.* State Services Authority, Government of Victoria.

Ross, J. W., & Weill, , et al. (2006). *Enterprise architecture as strategy: Creating a foundation for business execution.* Boston, MA: Harvard Business School Press.

Sanders, E., & Westerlund. (2011). *Experiencing, exploring and experimenting in and with co-design spaces.* Paper presented at the Nordic Design Research Conference. Helsinki, Finland.

Senge, P. M. (1992). *The fifth discipline: The art and science of the learning organization.* Sydney, Australia: Random House.

Shirky, C. (2012). *Clay Shirky's internet writings.* Retrieved 14 August, 2012, from http://shirky.com/

Spewak, S. H. (1992). *Enterprise architecture planning: Developing a blueprint for data, application and technology.* QED Publishing Group.

Taylor, F. W. (1911). *The principles of scientific management.* New York: Harper and Row.

TOGAF. (2012). *The open group architecture framework (TOGAF).* Retrieved 27 July 2012, 2012, from http://www.opengroup.org/togaf/

UK Cabinet Office. (2010). *Behavioural insights team.* Retrieved 9 June 2012, from http://www.cabinetoffice.gov.uk/behavioural-insights-team

Vargo, S. L., & Lusch, . (2004). Evolving to a new dominant logic for marketing. *Journal of Marketing, 68*(1), 1–17. doi:10.1509/jmkg.68.1.1.24036.

Vargo, S. L., & Lusch, . (2008). From goods to service(s): Divergences and convergences of logics. *Industrial Marketing Management, 37*(3), 254–259. doi:10.1016/j.indmarman.2007.07.004.

Wooldridge, M., & Lovell. (2011). *Human services: The case for change.* Retrieved 7 August, 2012, from http://www.dhs.vic.gov.au/about-the-department/news-and-events/news/general-news/human-services-the-case-for-change

Zachman, J. A. (1987). A framework for information systems architecture. *IBM Systems Journal, 26*(3), 276–292. doi:10.1147/sj.263.0276.

Chapter 14
Growing Complexity and Transformations of the Power Sector:
India as an Example of Developing Regions using Enterprise Architecture and Smart Grids

Rahul Tongia
Carnegie Mellon University, USA & Smart Grid Task Force, Govt. of India, India

ABSTRACT

Enterprise Architecture (EA) can be thought of as a powerful tool to transform electricity (distribution) utilities into more service-oriented and also economically viable enterprises, if not sustainable enterprises (spanning the so-called triple-bottom-line, viz., profits, people, planet). Developing regions (such as India) face even greater challenges than global concerns about electricity. Developing regions' utilities are often loss making and have numerous operational challenges (including high theft and a weak/ unstable grid). They also face a populace with limited means to pay (putting pressures on pricing) but also a large swath of potential consumers whom they have not yet reached. The rise of Information and Communications Technology (ICT) offers the ability to know what (and how much) is going where, with high time and geographic precision, covering not merely flows of electricity but also money, information, control, manpower, etc. More than converting data into information, it can lead to improved decision-making ("knowledge" and "wisdom"). Ultimately, harnessing ICT not only speeds up processes, but also transforms the enterprise. The widest-reaching form of EA transformation has been called a Smart Grid, an ongoing transformation of utilities worldwide. EA done right is complex, but so is electricity distribution. Instead of hiding or ignoring complexities, EA internalizes them into the decision-making process. While decision-makers cannot ignore issues of political economy, an Enterprise Architecture lens focuses on incentives, operations, and planning important for all enterprises independent of public versus private ownership.

DOI: 10.4018/978-1-4666-4518-9.ch014

INTRODUCTION: ELECTRICITY AND ENTERPRISE ARCHITECTURE

Electricity is, in many ways, a century older than the modern high-tech IT industry (or ICT, Information and Communications Technology industry). People have regularly marveled that if Edison (rather Westinghouse or Tesla, who pushed for alternating current, or AC, for the power grid) were to visit a power grid today, they would find it rather similar. Admittedly, the distances are longer, voltages are higher, and, of course, consumption is vastly differently. But, the underlying system looks rather similar. On the other hand, Alexander Graham Bell would scarcely recognize modern communications, which have moved away from corded, analog phone lines (which are still important) to wireless, digital, and the Internet.

So what does Enterprise Architecture (EA) have to do with the power sector? To those applying a narrow engineering lens, it is a tool and perhaps an add-on to how to operate a power grid. However, there is evidence to show that EA is a core part of power systems, or at least should be.

Electricity faces enormous challenges, worldwide. It is on the order of only 3% percent of the global GDP, but a number of publications point to its disproportionate value, impacting not only the GDP (strongly correlated) but also quality of life.

The challenges vary by country and level of development, though all countries worry about security of supply, and, of course, economics. There is widespread and growing concern about environmental implications as well. While carbon emissions and global climate change have gathered much of the press, local pollution (land, air, and water) are also equally critical. Worries about radiation, e.g., have led to a slowdown if not reversal of nuclear power in a number of countries.

But in developing regions, the challenges are far greater, for several reasons. First, the price per kilowatt-hour (kWh) isn't much lower than in developed regions (or at least cost, if not price),

while incomes are much, much, lower. Thus, while in the US, the average household may spend 1.98% of their income on electricity,[1] in India, the *average* number might be slightly lower but doesn't factor in full costs, not to mention this is with very low per-capita consumption, some 20 times lower than the US.[2] In addition, a very substantial fraction of the population (1/3 of homes, likely more of the population given rural households are larger) doesn't have access to electricity (Census Commission, 2011). In India, Africa, and other regions with access difficulties, it is not just that the electricity doesn't reach the home (or, sometimes, the village) but even when there is a wire, it may not be carrying electricity – outages ("load-shedding") are common.

There are several other drivers for increased use of modern ICT and revamped Enterprise Architecture. Concerns and pressure for greener energy make IT not only an enabler but a driver for change (Bengtsson & Agerfalk, 2010). New services along the value chain (Wissner, 2011) including not just renewable power but home automation and control are increasingly being envisaged, especially for regions with an aging population and/or high labor costs.

The first portion of this chapter begins with an overview of the current electricity sector, and ongoing changes and reforms. The second portion brings in the concepts of Enterprise Architecture. We then examine some more detailed specifics and implications of EA, ending with a brief examination of Smart Grids, a term describing an ICT and control driven power system.

There are many sub-portions of each of these topics, many of which have their own books, e.g., Political Economy and Reform of power systems. There are also a number of books on IT for the Power Sector, and Smart Grids. This chapter aims to cross across domains and present an integrated view of EA for the power sector. Given the enormous scope of this, we choose India as a representative example of developing regions, both for data and ease reasons, and to keep the message concrete. At the same time, India itself is diverse, with over 75 different utilities, covering a population of 1.2 billion people. For reasons that will be expanded upon below, most of the chapter will focus on the distribution segment of the power sector.

BACKGROUND OF ELECTRICITY IN DEVELOPING REGIONS (ESPECIALLY INDIA)

Electricity Primer

The Institute for Electrical and Electronics Engineers (IEEE), the largest professional society in the world, has described the electric power grid as the largest controlled and most complex system in the world. The US National Academy of Engineering has also called the modern power grid the greatest technological achievement of the 20th century. While electricity may appear somewhat simple, flowing between two points based on a potential difference, the modern power grid is immensely complex with a very large number

of interconnected nodes, ranging from generation to transmission to distribution. For the most part, generation occurs in large if not centralized power plants, from where the transmission grid transports this electricity closer to points of end consumption. Long-distance transmission usually occurs at very high voltages, which reduces the technical losses of electricity through the wires. Distribution, which is often linked to retail delivery of services, is different not only because it occurs at a lower voltage, but also because distribution feeders are typically radial emanating from substations. In contrast, the transmission grid is more of a mesh (see Figure 1 for a simplified view of the chain).

Importantly, the electrical grid operates as Alternating Current (AC), which is very difficult to store. Thus, it requires continuous effort and rapidly varying balancing to maintain equilibrium between real-time supply and demand (factoring transmission and distribution losses). It is obvious that demand changes continuously, but even supply is not as predictable as might seem given technical limitations of generators in addition to variances in output from renewable sources of power. The traditional solution to managing this exceptionally complex dynamic process has been

Figure 1. Simplified power flow, North America (Source: FERC, US Dept. of Energy). This shows a linear flow (traditional) and not any complexities of meshes, alternate paths, etc. Transmission is high-voltage, while distribution is at so-called medium voltage; the exact voltages vary by country, e.g., India mostly uses 11kV for medium voltage distribution, and end-use voltage is 220V.

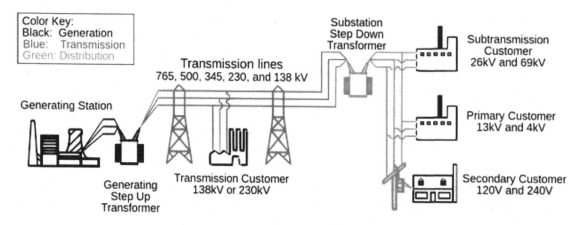

conservative engineering, which is expensive, and even this is beginning to reach its limits due to difficulties in many regions in adding new generation capacity or transmission lines.

While research is ongoing to physically control the flow of power using power electronics and solid-state devices, for the most part electricity flows like water based on physics. Another recent development has been the rise of decentralized generation closer to points of consumption. Far greater effort in the 1990s and 2000s was focused on the institutional aspects of the electricity sector, often dubbed reforms or deregulation.[3] What used to be a single vertically integrated utility handling all aspects of the power supply chain (generation, transmission, distribution, and retailing) has been broken up into different entities, sometimes in a competitive market structure.

Electricity in Developing Regions: Similar but yet Different

Developing countries also embraced this trend of reforms for a number of reasons, though the pace at which they reformed has varied significantly. In addition to seeking structural separation of responsibilities, developing regions typically had government owned or state owned enterprises operating as utilities. Thus, in addition to the dimensions of the de-integration, privatization was another focus of many reform efforts. There were a number of drivers for this ranging from lack of capital, the expectation of increased efficiency and competitiveness, and even a broader philosophical argument made towards reducing the role of government in areas where the private sector could operate well (Victor & Heller, 2006).

The Indian experience of reforms began in 1991, coinciding with broader economic liberalization. There have been several distinct phases of reforms (Tongia, 2006), the first focusing on increasing supply by inviting private (especially foreign) investment. Nearer the end of the decade, unbundling (and even privatization) was the key

thrust area, combined with the creation of independent regulators to help set "rational" tariffs outside political interference. The next (and ongoing) stages of restructuring in the Indian power sector have focused less on institutional aspects and more on competitive and operational aspects. This spans the Electricity Act of 2003 (liberalizing the market) to the mandate for bidding for power projects to ultra-mega power projects (very large size, offered specialized logistical/regulatory support), not to mention several flagship Central Government schemes related to rural electrification (The Rajiv Gandhi Grameen Vidyutikaran Yojana, or RGGYV) and overall improvements (APDP, the Accelerated Power Development Program), with newer iterations APDRP (adding "Reforms") and R-APDRP (Restructured–APDRP, which focuses on loss reduction).

While all these efforts have had some effect, underlying fundamentals have not changed as desired. The utilities are in severe financial loss (Table 1), and there is a drastic shortfall of power, measured in the 10s of percent in some utilities. This manifests itself in almost daily power cuts ("load shedding") in many areas, and the middle/upper class resorts to expensive and often polluting back-up power. Per kilowatt-hour (kWh) sold, utilities lose, on average, more than one rupee (~2 US cents) (Figure 2).

The central government has spent great effort to handle the losses of utilities after the fact through securitization of the debts, which might help at a liquidity level but not at a solvency level. Some experts believe this has relieved some of the pressure on utilities that would otherwise force quicker change.

If we revisit organizational structures, while some early efforts were made at privatization of distribution utilities, other than the states of Orissa (1999) and Delhi (2002), no other state has privatized its distribution utilities. Most have gone for corporatization, creating a public company instead of the erstwhile State Electricity Board (SEB). A very large fraction of states have unbundled and

Table 1. Indian public distribution utilities finances (source: Planning Commission, 2011). R.E. = Revised Estimate; AP = Annual Plan. "Surplus Other Sectors" comes from the higher tariff paid by sectors like Commercial and Industrial. Newer numbers indicate the actual (realized) losses might be higher for 2011 and 2012; the uncovered subsidy is on the order of 1% of the GDP. Subventions from the state might be promised but delayed or deferred (Assumes end of respective period [March 31st] exchange rate.).

$US Billion	Subsidy to Agricultural Consumers	Subsidy to Domestic Consumers	Subsidy on Interstate Sales	Gross Subsidy	Subvention Received from State	Net Subsidy	Surplus Other Sectors	Uncovered Subsidy
2007-08	8.36	3.95	-0.28	12.03	4.27	7.76	2.25	5.52
2008-09	7.61	4.23	-0.30	11.55	4.45	7.10	-0.71	7.81
2009-10	9.94	5.28	0.30	15.51	5.43	10.08	-0.62	10.70
2010-11 R.E.	9.85	5.32	0.13	15.30	4.02	11.28	0.01	11.27
2011-12 AP	8.79	4.82	0.09	13.70	3.41	10.29	0.92	9.37

Figure 2. Gap between cost and tariff in India (source: Planning Commission, 2011). R.E. = Revised Estimate; AP = Annual Plan. Cost are per official methodologies, and may understate true costs due to rising cost of fuel, insufficient capital investment by distribution utilities and limited statutory returns (Assumes end of respective period [March 31st] exchange rate).

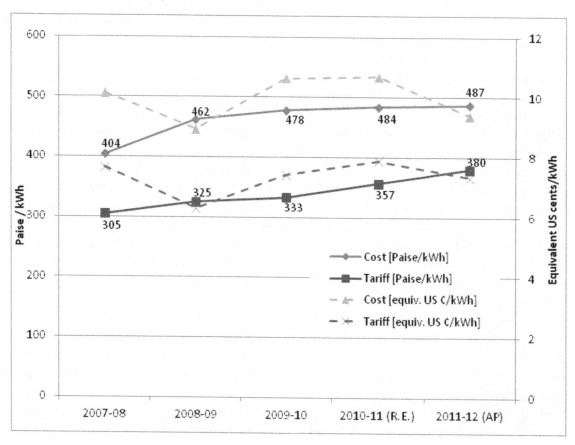

also split into geographic areas, e.g., the state of Karnataka has 5 ESCOMs (Electricity Supply COMpanies, or distribution companies). In all, there are approximately 75 distribution companies operating in India, almost all of them public. The exceptions (beyond Delhi and Orissa) are a few cities like Mumbai and Calcutta (renamed Kolkotta) which had private utilities from before independence whose licenses didn't lapse or weren't nationalized, and a handful of cities which privatized (or called in private operators as franchisees). This heterogeneity in Indian utilities, even the public ones, requires a strong caveat when making generalizations – there are some utilities that perform better, have lower losses, etc.

The entire theory and history of reforms (in India and elsewhere) have been dealt with in detail in Victor and Heller (2006). A few points are relevant for this chapter.

1. There is limited evidence that privatization inherently solves underlying difficulties. The experience of some privatization attempts was that there was a demand to increase tariffs to a level that met widespread resistance (Victor & Heller, 2006). Private players *might* be more nimble, efficient, and innovative (not to mention cash rich), but the covenants of privatization often limit their flexibility, e.g., the promise to retain employees. The fact that a number of countries such as the US (in parts), Singapore, etc. have successful public electric utilities indicates that public versus private might be a tangential issue. Instead, competition has been identified as a key driver for improved efficiency.

2. Regardless of public versus private, healthy regulation has been a hallmark of successful electricity service. This balances the needs for profitability (or at least viability) with consumer protections, quality, and service.

3. Tariffs are a fundamental issue for utilities, losing money per product (kWh) sold cannot continue indefinitely. Even if theft is curtailed, this will help to the tune of perhaps 10-12% – critical, but the gap in revenues is far higher (Figure 2).[4] At one level, every kWh sold has a cost, and a "simple" solution is to charge each consumer a price that covers not only the cost but a reasonable rate of return for the utility. There are a few issues with this. First, calculating the true cost per consumer is difficult, not only due to transaction costs of doing so but also because this number will vary based on grid conditions and supply options (with so-called network effects). Second, regulators (or decision-makers) typically don't want such complexity and variances in prices. They typically group consumers into categories, and charge the same per category across a particular geography if not the entire utility. In the US, the categories might be limited (residential, commercial, and industrial) while in India there is far more granularity. Ability to pay is a major concern for decision-makers, which is why India (and many developing regions) choose to charge less than the cost of supply to a number of consumers. In India, this is agricultural consumers (to keep the cost of food low, (Tongia, The political economy of Indian power sector reforms, 2006)) and residential consumers, on average. For some categories, there is a second layer of price differentiation by the creation of tiers or slabs, which increase in tariff with increasing consumption. Thus, lower consumption households pay far lower than higher consumption households. Similarly, so-called paying consumers (Commercial and Industrial, or C&I) pay higher than fully loaded costs, in effect cross-subsidizing other consumers. Even after such cross-subsidies,

there is still a shortfall. State Regulators in India have asked the state governments to pay for any net subsidies to keep the utilities whole (viable) but there are typically delays in getting such payments.[5]

4. Good data are important for successful enterprises, with not just accuracy but completeness, granularity, and interpretation. Uncertainty on data has hampered even the reforms/"deregulation" process – it is hard for enterprise valuation and operations to be accurately assessed. Such data are even used for equity calculations and equity returns (e.g., linked to loss reduction benchmarks), making accuracy doubly important.

For all the criticisms by free-market proponents of subsidies, they have a role to play for a developing country where affordability is demonstrably limited – the challenge is to make these efficient, appropriate (helping those who are intended) and diminishing over time. This policy choice on how to view electricity – as an essential public good versus a commodity ripe for pure market forces, is an underlying tension impacting the function of electricity utilities as viable enterprises. There is evidence that the notion of public good dominates in developing regions (Tongia, The political economy of Indian power sector reforms, 2006) beyond any distortions for political gain (e.g., vote banks via subsidies).

THE ELECTRICITY ENTERPRISE AND GROWING COMPLEXITIES OF SCALE, AND SCOPE[6]

A number of aspects of complexity of power systems have been mentioned already, including the need to balance supply and demand in real time, that too in a network of hundreds if not thousands of generators (even with centralized generation, before end-user distributed generation), hundreds of thousands of kilometers of transmission and distribution wires, and consumers numbering in the millions for large utilities. There is one additional underlying driver for EA and Smart Grids: time constants.

Many electrical assets not only last decades (generation plants, T&D wires, etc.) but can take multiple years to build out. On the other hand, consumer demand in developing regions is growing over 10%, and new changes like electric vehicles can wreak havoc on the existing system overnight (at a local level). For example, a single electric vehicle like the Nissan Leaf has 24 kWh of battery. While the US has more than 2 cars per household on average, even a single duty cycle is on the order of multiple weeks electricity consumption for a median *electrified* household in India.

Consider the act of adding a new consumer. In the West, turnover rates (people shifting residence) are high, as high as 30+% in some geographies, and a major expense for utilities. In India, first-time connections are common, due to urbanization, change in family structures, and simple electrification of previously non-electrified homes. In most states, unlike in the West, it is not as simple as just telephoning the company (or going online) and asking for service. Leaving aside issues of tariffs and connection costs (which vary as per the regulator and the distance to the nearest existing service point), the utility needs to know which distribution feeder and which distribution transformer they should connect to, and how the new load would affect these. A meter is required, and, for the most part, a licensed contractor is required for installing the meter. The first step is often filling out and submitting a form, with proofs of residence, photographs, revenue stamps (for Rs. 10), ID, etc., and deposits, to the nearest designated utility office.[7]

The activities in the utility checklist include (using the same utility in footnote 8 as an example):

*   Request Registration
*   Site Inspection
*   Dues Verification

- Demand Notice Generation
- Payment of Demand Notice
- Line Extension Advice
- Line Extension Completion Report
- Meter Issue and release of connection
- Meter Particulars Submission
- Update in billing system
- Issue of first bill

While the 10 page form is available online to download, each step requires physical signature on paper in "the file." Even the calculations for adding the load are complex. The utilities ask the consumer to list every appliance they intend to connect, and based on that they authorize a particular sized connection. The electrical questions at a distribution grid level include:

- Nearest Pole No.
- Distance from Pole (mts)
- Nearest Feeder Pillar No. for underground connection
- Distance from Feeder Pillar (mts)
- Length of Single Line Mains (mts)
- Distance from 11 or 0.4 kV transformer substation (mts)
- Capacity of Distribution Transformer [DT] (kVA)
- % Voltage Regulation in 11 kV
- % Voltage Regulation in LT (low voltage circuit)
- Connected load on DT (KW)

After their inspection (to answer the loading and location questions listed before), they then approve the connection "as is" or with a new line. The latter can take weeks if not months. Even the "as-is" process takes a very long time, in part due to lack of handy data or processes to streamline the procedure. If we imagine a well-designed IT system spanning GIS, assets, inventory, consumer indexing, billing, etc., then almost all the questions could be answered if not at the push of a button then with vastly quicker decision-making.

The bottom line is that business as usual (BAU) will not meet the needs for a modern power grid nor sustainability, let alone new (and even presently unknown) functionalities and business models. If we add more competition, then improved service and quick response become even more critical. This becomes the impetus for EA and Smart Grids, and this chapter. In addition to identifying the drivers, the current status, and architectures/frameworks for such solutions, this chapter brings a composite view of ongoing developments in India, instead of a case study which might be too utility-specific (and is premature, given the preliminary status of deployments thus far).

The Distribution Utility Enterprise

The AC grid handles the continuous flow of electricity, and Figure 1 showed a basic schematic. Whether it is a single integrated utility or a number of utilities handling different aspects of power flow is moot – the physics doesn't change. For simplicity sake, we structure most of the below arguments with separate generation, transmission, and distribution utilities.

For multiple reasons (part design, part legacy), the distribution sector is the one facing the greatest challenges, both financially and operationally. In India, generators would often be paid first, and similarly transmission companies would charge on a costs-plus mechanism (Tongia, The political economy of Indian power sector reforms, 2006). In theory, distribution companies would also be entitled to a regulated rate of return, but there were several difficulties with this. First, their returns were contingent on a reduction of losses. Financial losses were a combination of non-billing, non-collection, and theft (in addition to technical, or I^2R losses[8]). Second, Regulators asked the state governments to pay for any explicit subsidies desired, but they didn't always comply. Lastly, the enormous variance in tariffs, consumptions, etc. meant that in the absence of accurate consumption (and other) data, the utility could often get it wrong.

Other than the flow of electricity, there are several other flows of importance. First is money. In principle, and consumers of electricity would pay for everything, based on what and how much they consumed. The reality is a little more complicated. For starters, like every enterprise operating within the norms of government rules, there are financial implications relating to taxes, depreciation, etc. More importantly, given the public nature of electricity utilities, even if privately run and operated, there are often government subsidies or support mechanisms available impacting the flow of money. However, as our base case, we assume that the government wants the electric utility, regardless of public or private ownership, to be an economically viable enterprise.

The second flow is of manpower. Like all enterprises, a skilled and competitive labor force is very important. However, for government electricity utilities, there is a bit of a dichotomy regarding manpower. On one hand, analysts have accused the State Electricity Boards (SEBs) of being bloated, and certainly by some metrics, especially manpower per kilowatt hour delivered, they compare unfavorably with the rest of the world.[9] However, electricity consumption is relatively low in India, and this discrepancy diminishes if we consider employees per customer served. Drilling deeper, we find that many utilities actually face a shortfall of manpower, more so in rural areas. They also often lack specialized skill manpower including in information technology, accounting, etc. This limitation on skilled manpower has resulted in extensive outsourcing of tasks. We revisit this subsequently.

Even before utilities hire (or source) new skillsets, better oversight, incentives, and utilization of existing manpower will help productivity enormously. Linemen (field personnel) need basic tools to help them do their job better, e.g., rural linemen should be given a vehicle, given they could have feeders measuring tens of kilometers long.

While it may be unfair to generalize, the general perception of electric utilities in India is one of hierarchy, rigidity, and bureaucracy. Positions and seniority are often based predominantly if not entirely on number of years served, and the structure limits individual entrepreneurship or innovative characteristics. At the very top, the Managing Director (aka CEO) is more often than not a political appointee and a generalist bureaucrat, a member of the elite Indian Administrative Services (IAS). Often, they lack domain knowledge, and their tenure is typically slated to be three years or so; in practice, they can be transferred in six months or a year in a number of cases. While there are number of senior professionals who have voiced concerns over morale and specialist skills due to such systems (Rao, 2011) (Sreedharan, 2011), from an operational perspective, the lack of continuity and meaningful time frames for decision-making and implementing utility wide transformation processes is a major downside to the current system. There are numerous anecdotes about large projects being put on the back burner after a change in leadership not because of a systematic study but because of differences in priorities or even belief structures.[10]

The last and perhaps most important flow from an EA perspective is that of information and control, which jointly form the basis for the institutional organization of the enterprise. Unsurprisingly, a distribution utility is typically set up hierarchically, with smaller and smaller segments handling a limited geography. Figure 3 shows a typical utility hierarchy, starting with the corporate (head) office down to the section office farthest down. There may or may not be multiple zones or circles depending on the size of the utility, but there are invariably multiple divisions, and multiple sub-divisions per division. In some utilities, there can be over 100 section offices, if not more for large utilities spanning an entire state, e.g., Maharashtra.

Section offices may or may not handle finances (bills and collection), but do cover Operations and Maintenance (O&M). Subdivisions are where the finances are generally collated, but

Figure 3. Typical hierarchy of a distribution utility in India. For simplicity, not all the lower rung nodes are shown in the branching tree.

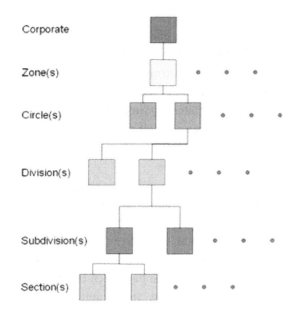

ultimately these are reconciled and audited at a division level. Oversight is generally at this level as well. This has implications for technology or process innovations. If one wants, e.g., to deploy a new technology on a single medium voltage (e.g., 11 kV) distribution feeder, while the operational impacts might be easy to determine, the financial implications are much harder to decompose since multiple feeders will be accounted for by common staff – something as nuanced as manpower efficiency and productivity will be difficult to pinpoint unless the right scale of deployment is chosen.

Information Flows

Figure 1 might suggest a simple network, but the reality of the grid is one that is immensely complex, demanding real-time balancing. Supply can vary due to power plant outages, not to mention an increasing use of variable and unpredictable renewables, and even load itself varies by time of day, day of week, season, etc. As soon as sup-

ply dips below demand, either the grid starts to become unstable, or some consumers must be disconnected ("load-shed" in Indian parlance). The only alternative is to make sure one always has at least enough supply – but such over-engineering is expensive. It is for improved operations and optimization that utilities seek more and better information, with many unknowns as distributed generation, unbundling, merchant power, large-scale renewables, etc. lead to much greater and newer directions for power flows than the traditional grid was engineered for (Ilic, 2010).

Like all enterprises, utilities must use information for both operational and planning perspectives. First and foremost, the power must flow to end-users, and given the real-time balancing required between supply and demand, accurate load prediction is a key need, regardless of whether the utility owns its own generation assets or procures power from outside (either via long-term contracts or a market mechanism, or both). This is complicated by the fact that power demand in developing regions is growing rapidly, both due to organic growth and because of the addition of previously un-electrified households. Thus, planning covers load as well as physical grid topology planning for safety and cost-effectiveness.

Operationally, one of the most important information flows a distribution utility handles is measuring and accordingly billing for the flow of power. Power entering a distribution substation is accurately measured for the most part – there may even be a financial transaction if the utility is not vertically integrated. It is from this point onwards that there are challenges in the math. Electricity can be delivered without measurement, if consumers are unmetered (e.g., the bulk of agricultural consumers in India, who pay flat rates or capacity-based payments). There will be some amount of technical (I^2R) losses, and there may be theft. Thus, there are 3 unknowns, with one equation! Inevitably, official statistics must rely on assumptions such as how much power a pumpset consumes, or fraction pilfered, etc.

Figure 4 shows a prototypical Indian distribution utility IT flow from a short period back; it is based on an actual utility (2010) but the basics are similar across many utilities.

A few of the highlights of this system include:

1. Different data are created at different layers – it is unclear how well data flows up and down the layers. There are a number of "monthly reports" and similar created, but deeper analytics are limited.
2. Some technologies have been put in place top down, but the operational need is in the field.
3. Some information is not yet digitized, especially at the field level
4. There is strong reliance on vendors to operate a number of systems, even business critical systems.

Meter reading is a vital component of the system – that's how utilities bill and get paid. In many utilities, for smaller consumers, utilities don't read meters themselves, but outsource this to an agency. That agency gets paid a few rupees per read. In many cases, their staff use a handheld metering reading instrument (MRI) where they manually punch in the readings, and the MRI is synced to the database at the end of the day.[11] For smaller consumers, digital meters are not yet the norm, and so automated or even semi-automated systems aren't available.

In the era before computerization (which is limited in its deployment even today, especially in remote areas), this involved ledgers that handled all the relevant data, e.g., consumer information, billing information, materials inventory, purchase orders, etc. For the most part, each functionality existed in a silo, e.g., "works" (capital works).

Figure 4. Generic Indian utility information flows (as-is). Not every utility would have each component shown, e.g., geographic information systems (GIS). B&C = Billing and Collection; MIS = Management Information System. Note that "store" is the term for the in-house warehouse. The symbols chosen are merely for illustration purposes and meant to be generic, e.g., Web-based vs. email.

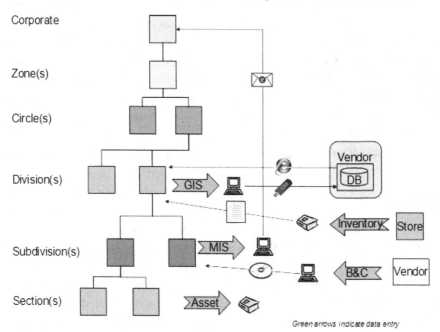

Simple computerization began a few years back, and this has sped up many processes (Figure 4). However, at least until recently, there hasn't been sufficient engagement across departments or functional roles, let alone any significant improvement in data sharing, let alone analytics. One utility invested millions of dollars in remote meter reading for distribution transformers. Given limited budgets, they could not deploy this on all the distribution transformers. To gain widespread visibility, they scattered these across the utility, rural and urban, big and small. However, they didn't deploy these on 100% of the distribution transformers of a given feeder – without this, one cannot audit the power flow! When asked for characteristics of "bad" transformers (high failure rates), were these more rural, or large, or

old, the response was simply to let me look at the "Monthly Report." This exemplifies the lack of clarity on who needs what data where, when, why.

Figure 5 shows a generic schema for how a unified utility information system (dubbed UIS) would interact with the different operational modules and functionalities such that information would be shared instead of re-created, improving accuracy and efficiency.

If we consider functionalities for the utility with EA in mind, there is an obvious overlap between data and modules. Location, which might be captured in a Geographic Information Systems (GIS) platform, is of immense importance to both network operations and to grid planning. Consumer information is important for a number of domains, not least of which is billing and collec-

Figure 5. Integrated (future) information and domain framework (generic – unified utility information systems, aka UIS). The modules shown are not claimed to be universal – only shown for representativeness.

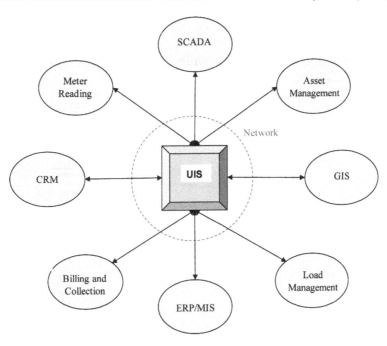

CRM = Customer Relationship Management
ERP = Enterprise Resource Planning
MIS= Management of Information Systems
GIS = Geographic Information Systems
SCADA = Supervisory Control and Data Acquisition (system)

tion. The question becomes how do these interact? Is there one data set? Correct data set? It is in the advantage of the system (accuracy, efficiency, audit, etc.) if databases are re-used instead of separate or disparate. The first implication of this is that different systems need to be interconnected, i.e., a strong network is required. The second is that now the system architects have a number of choices and options. The generic schema in Figure 6 shows that one can interconnect different nodes with different technologies. Not all make sense from a security, business case, or operational perspective. It requires further planning to choose appropriate enterprise architectures. We delve deeper into some of the globally mooted EA models subsequently.

Presently, the government program R-APDRP aims to improve this by standardizing IT flows. The main goal of R-APDRP is to reduce "AT&C" (aggregate technical and commercial) losses, which are only at the distribution level, to below

15% in urban and semi-urban areas. To this end, the first part, Part A, with 20% of the funding (or Rs. 10,000 crore, approximately US$2 billion), focuses on IT for proper measurements (and operations). The main limitations of the program, other than the *enormously* ambitious scope in a very compressed timeframe, include:

1. Not deploying this across the utility (ostensibly for financial reasons, and to start with lower hanging fruit
2. Centralized (committee-driven) technology specification[12]
3. Lack of clarity on how well this system will be internalized bottom-up by the utilities; there are limits to how much and for how long an outside vendor can do.
4. Limited feedback loops in system design of how technologies and business processes are linked, especially if we want learning and iteration.

Figure 6. Improved information flows across the utility (generic and simplified). DSS = Decision Support System; DB = database.

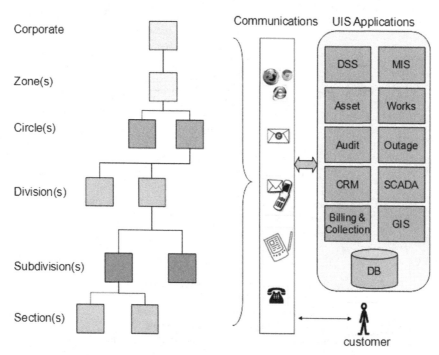

As a simple example of this, the Automated Meter Reading (AMR) system for distribution transformers (not end-consumers) has 15 minute readings for parameters like voltage, current, etc. But, the modem is specified up to upload the data only at the end of the month. If we consider the spectrum of increasing smarts (or functionality) of IT for power (Figure 7), R-APDRP only takes us to auditing (that too, in a limited manner, reconciling month-end energy flows at a distribution transformer level, for urban and semi-urban areas). Given the importance of stemming losses, this is immensely valuable, but with a simple redesign, the system could easily provide outage detection/notification, etc. If one truly wanted to find out

about theft (identified as a discrepancy) then one would rather know about this in (near) real time instead of at the end of the month.

The only modest changes that would be required would be that the modem should be data centric (always on), there should be a small battery (to transmit even during power outages) and some change in the logic.

This lack of linkage between technologies, desired functionalities, and business case is a significant hurdle to optimal design of any enterprise architecture, whether one is going all the way to a Smart Grid or not. Restated, *design* becomes the key challenge (Figure 8), though one cannot ignore execution of designs as a bottleneck as well.[13]

Figure 7. Increasing "smarts" in harnessing ICT for electricity

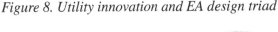

Accounting → Auditing → Monitoring → Control

Figure 8. Utility innovation and EA design triad

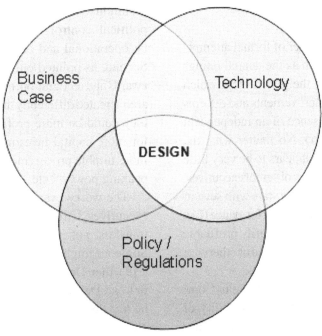

BUSINESS PROCESSES, INDICATORS, AND TRANSFORMATION

There are many metrics a utility can follow to measure its performance. An investor-owned utility, common in the United States, can easily see its stock price as one measure of its performance. Of course, stock price valuations should have an underlying basis, perhaps linked to the fundamentals. Profit maximization is not the mantra of a regulated utility as envisaged in the current environment in most developing regions – there is a stipulated rate of return that the enterprise can enjoy after meeting certain performance expectations. The performance expectations can be targets, even aspirational targets, captured as Key Performance Indicators (KPIs), which can include things like:

- Electrification rate
- Losses
- Outages
- Equipment failure rates (especially transformers)[14]
- Viability if not profitability
- etc.

There have been a number of formal attempts at rating state utilities such as the annual ratings report commissioned by the government which factors in institutional improvements and reforms at a state level (e.g., presence of an independent state electricity regulator). No matter what the rating of the utility, there appears to be very little impact on the career trajectory of senior executives. A single distribution utility in a state with several may have very good operational performance (low losses) but yet they are not necessarily profitable and certainly the staff isn't higher paid or otherwise incentivized compared to their peers.

The government appointed Shunglu Committee examining the finances and viability of distribution utilities also pointed out that a major challenge was and remains the accuracy of numbers (Shunglu, 2011). Information is demanded for periodical reports and it is produced – but (almost) no one digs deeper into the accuracy of the data, let alone the assumptions, methodology, etc.

Improved quality of data is something the government is working hard towards. There was an IT Task Force Report in 2002 for the power sector, which talked about harnessing the power of information technology to improve auditing and reduce losses. These were not deployed in large scale, and one of the anecdotal criticisms came that areas under scrutiny seem to improve while adjoining regions seemed to decrease their performance in an almost mirror fashion! It is for this reason that R-APDRP's first part, $2 billion out of an approximate $10 billion, was slated for IT for precise measurements, including setting up boundary meters so that the areas under coverage will be precisely measured.

At a workshop, off the record, a discussant asked what is the KPI of a utility Managing Director? After people proposed highly visible things like utility loss reduction (the objective of the entire R-APDRP), he said, only half in jest, "not getting transferred the next day." This highlights two major challenges. First, there is political control over what should otherwise be operational and enterprise decision making. Second, as pointed out before, other than token awards and recognition, better performing utilities aren't treated differently than their peers. In theory, they could be more profitable, have permission for more capital investments, be able to follow more nimble procurement processes,[15] buy more peaking power,[16] etc.

The worry over transfers isn't just for senior executives. Utility staff at all levels face periodic transfers, not just geographic but also domain. Someone might be in charge of Human Resources (HR), then Demand Side Management, then work in Load Despatch. In some states, one could also be transferred between state utilities. Thus, very deep and cutting edge skills and experience are difficult to maintain. Even training and education (termed capacity building) is paid lip service – national level or international courses are often available only to very senior officers, instead of mid-professionals who might benefit the most.

How do we fix this? While we examine the use of advanced technology (including Smart Grids) subsequently, there are a few suggestions that have been suggested and even begun implementation (in parts). Most deal with responsibility and accountability, with or without institutional change. One proposal has been to create a new level of accounting that matches operations, i.e., the substation. Each one would have to operate as a business unit, and be, if not profitable (due to consumer mix, say), then transparent about its inputs, costs, revenues, etc. A slightly larger version of this is the use of Franchisees who take over operations across a particular geography. These entities, mostly from the private sector but they could be other public sector enterprises, would follow the same norms as the utility (who would remain the licensee), but be willing to inject the required capital for improved operations. Their earnings would be based on improved KPIs, especially loss reduction.

The latter has mostly been done at a city level, and has been mooted by the Shunglu Committee amongst others. However, this type of pseudo-privatization has a few pitfalls. First, external players are most likely to undertake areas that are inherently viable, i.e., urban areas. This cherry-picking carries longer-term utility viability implications (Tongia, The political economy of Indian power sector reforms, 2006). Second, if the business model is sharing benefits such as loss reduction, then the worse off a particular area is, the more potential money is on the table. This argument could be a justification for any intervention (even "gold-plated technology") since the Return on Investment (RoI) would appear positive. Third, it is unclear if there are enough skilled operators with the expertise, time, patience, and finances to do this in a scalable manner – some critics have worried about business houses (conglomerates) entering this space on a quick-returns financial and not long-term operational calculation.

2008 IT for Power Task Force Update

Recognizing the limits of the 2002 IT Task Force Report on IT for the Power Sector, the Ministry of Power asked Infosys and CSTEP[17] to create an update, focused on revamping distribution utilities, ultimately leading to a Smart Grid.

The fundamental driver for the change was a convergence underway between different enablers of a modern, digitally enhanced power system (Figure 9).

The roadmap for transforming the distribution utility is shown in Figure 10.

Figure 9. Digital convergence (source: "Technology: Enabling the Transformation of Power Distribution", 2008)

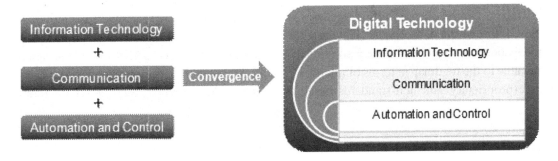

Figure 10. Distribution technology trajectory (DTT). This is India-specific in terms of programs (and shows one of multiple options and pathways) (source: "Technology: Enabling the Transformation of Power Distribution", 2008)

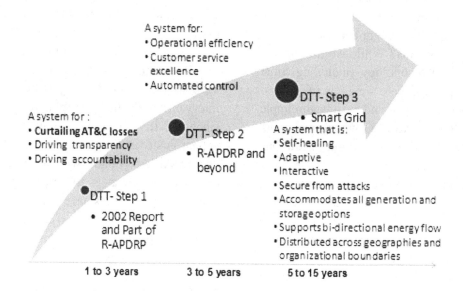

How this is to be achieved is spelled out in more detail in the 2008 Report (see Figures 11-13).

We can see that in just a few years, the details of the Trajectory might need updating given changes in technology. More importantly, which functionalities are enabled and when would need to depend on the specifics of the utility and business case (see Figure 8). E.g., net metering might come sooner if consumers want rooftop solar panels. The utility might enable demand response (load reduction in response to a signal) if peak load management is their priority. In addition, a utility might enable some solutions only for selected consumers (by size and/or geography).

Examining the DTT roadmap, Figure 14 shows an illustrative Digital Technology Trajectory Roadmap. Some of the components shown may exist today, but it is not clear if present solutions are amenable to the roadmap in terms of interoperability (proprietary and non-standards-based

solutions can always be made to interoperate but only after significant effort, that too with the full cooperation of the technology provider).

From an EA perspective, the same report suggests an Information Systems Reference Model (Figure 15).

Full implementation of the 2008 proposals (with or without updates/modifications) would effectively lead one to a Smart Grid.

Enterprise Architecture for the Power Sector Revisited

There are formal methodologies for Enterprise Architecture, and the power utility domain has several, including a popular one called The Open Group Architecture Framework (TOGAF) (http://www.opengroup.org/togaf), which has widespread industry support. TOGAF 9.1, available online, has an Architecture Development Model (The Open Group, 2012), which focuses on Requirements

Figure 11: Step 1 of the distribution technology trajectory. This is per the report "Technology: Enabling the Transformation of Power Distribution" (2008) and step 1 from Figure 10. The IT portrayed is very "standard" in most world-class utilities. (DT = Distribution Transformer; HT = High Tension (aka High Voltage); BW = Bandwidth; IS = Information System; SS = Substation)

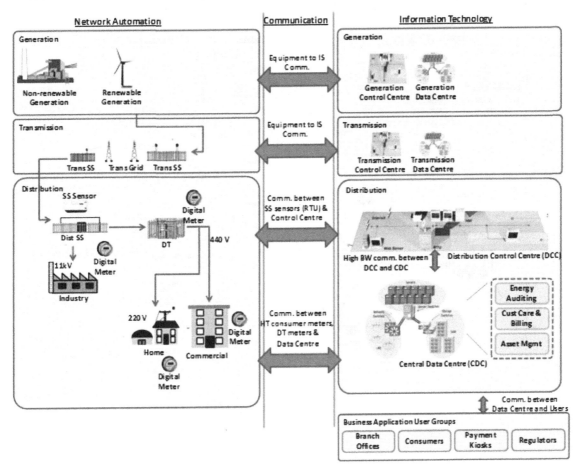

Management through an iterative cycle starting with the baseline ("Preliminary") going through:

1. Architecture Vision
2. Business Architecture
3. Information Systems Architecture
4. Technology Architecture
5. Opportunities and Solutions
6. Migration Planning
7. Implementation Governance
8. Architecture Change Management
   … (back to) …
1. Architecture Vision

This chapter does not focus on as deep specifics on any explicit or particular architecture, but we draw from them as appropriate.

Based on such processes, there are a number of models for EA that have been proposed. An early Architecture is Intelligrid, with backing from the Electric Power Research Institute (EPRI). Note that some companies do not release their Smart Grid Reference Architecture, while a number of them have released these publicly in an attempt to build an ecosystem around these, e.g., Microsoft's Smart Energy Reference Architecture (SERA), or IBM/ Southern California Edison/Cisco's Smart Grid

Figure 12. Step 2 of the distribution technology trajectory. This is per the Report "Technology: Enabling the Transformation of Power Distribution" (2008) and step 2 from Figure 10. The enhanced IT portrayed enables distributed generation, innovative billing options, and improved outage management/recovery. SCADA = Supervisory Control and Data Acquisition (system); SW = software; FFA = Field Force Automation

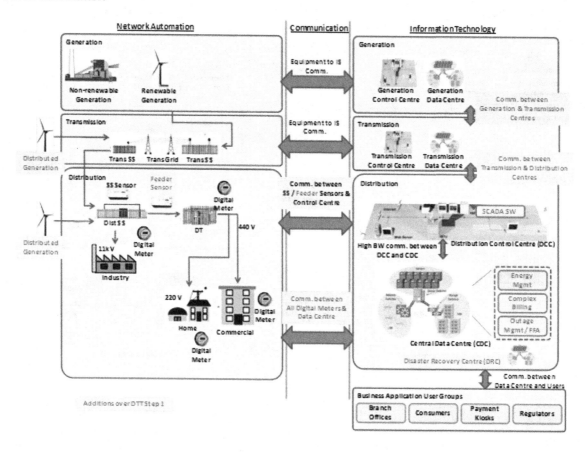

Reference Architecture (SGRA). A representative EA for power systems is shown in Figure 16.

A significant takeaway from Figure 16 is the fact that of the multiple modules, there are some that exist (or need only minimal changes), and some that will be brand new, while there will be some in-between, that will need measurable effort for enhancement. Importantly, for many geographies, utilities already exist and one cannot apply clean-slate EA design. This adds change-management as a layer above and beyond any desired EA trajectory.

SMART GRIDS

A broad transformation of the electricity enterprise and electricity system under different stages of implementation worldwide is the use of digital information, communications, and control technologies for making the grid "smarter." While nebulous, a Smart Grid covers not only the utility but the entire ecosystem of the power grid including the physical infrastructure, regulatory framework, consumer participation, etc.

Figure 13. Step 3 of the distribution technology trajectory. This is per the report "Technology: Enabling the Transformation of Power Distribution" (2008) and step 3 from Figure 10. The enhanced IT portrayed enables far greater consumer participation via options like net-metering, smart loads, and demand response. ETRM = Energy Trading and Risk Management

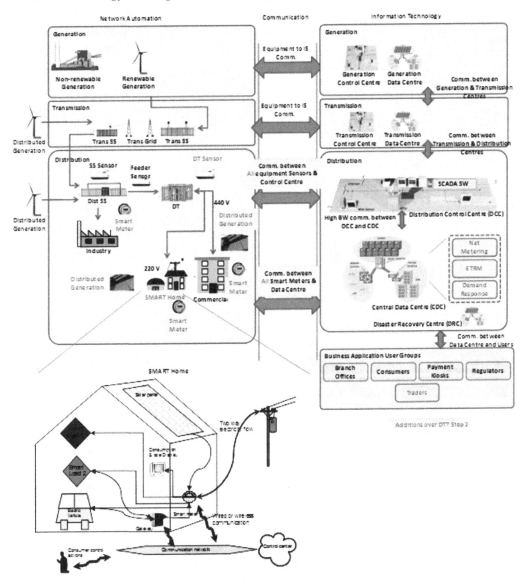

Overview and Drivers

Much has been written about Smart Grids in many publications and online media. What is generally agreed upon is that a Smart Grid is not a single technology or design, but a catch-all phrase for a power system transformed by the use of digital communications and control technology to be more efficient, resilient, renewables friendly, and nimble.

Most definitions, e.g., the US Dept. of Energy's, are based on functionality; a Smart Grid shall be designed for and have functionality towards (US Dept. of Energy, 2009):

Figure 14. Illustrative digital technology trajectory roadmap. This is per the Report "Technology: Enabling the Transformation of Power Distribution" (2008).

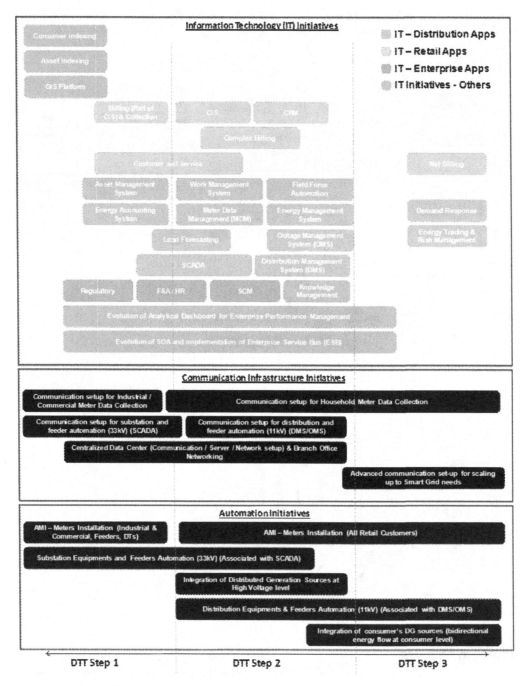

AMI = Advanced Metering Infrastructure; DT = Distribution Transformer; kV = kiloVolt; DMS = Distribution Management System; OMS = Outage Management System; DG = Distributed Generation; SCM = Supply Chain Management; F&A = Finance & Accounting; CIS = Customer Information System; CRM = Customer Relationship Management

Figure 15. Information systems reference model. This is per the report "Technology: Enabling the Transformation of Power Distribution" (2008).

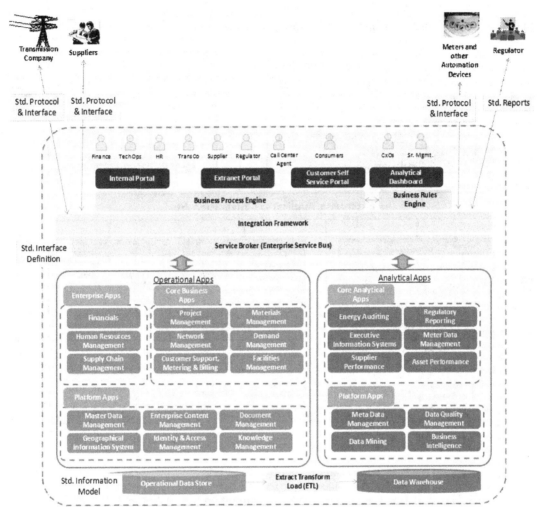

1. "Enabling Informed Participation by Customers
2. Accommodating All Generation and Storage Options
3. Enabling New Products, Services, and Markets
4. Providing the Power Quality for the Range of Needs
5. Optimizing Asset Utilization and Operating Efficiently
6. Operating Resiliently: Disturbances, Attacks, and Natural Disasters"[18]

Coming up with a pithy definition of a Smart Grid might be a Sisyphean task – it may also be inaccurate. There could be more than one definition, with each utility choosing different aspects as their Smart Grid, not to mention many deployments will come in stages. One can draw several analogies from the Internet. Just like use of TCP/IP and other communications protocols in an Internetworking system doesn't make the Internet (capital I – the global system for interoperable communications), deploying a smart meter doesn't necessarily give us a Smart Grid (maybe that can

Figure 16. (One possible) target application architecture (adapted from: Karanam, Nambiar, Srivastava, Shukla, & Chandramouli, 2011, used with permission). Not all utilities have all the modules shown already in operation, and some "new" applications might already be in service. ISO/RTO = Independent System Operator/Regional Transmission Operation.

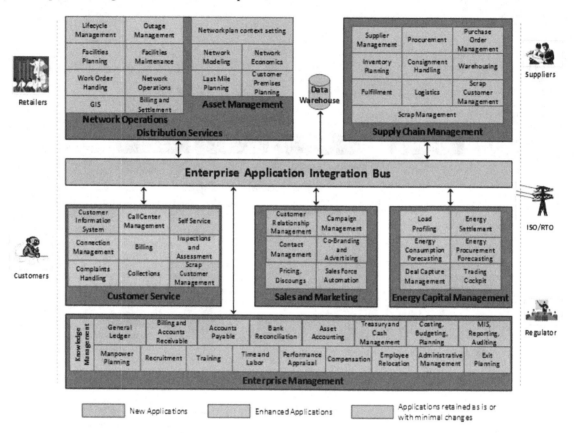

be a smart grid). However one might choose to define the details of a Smart Grid, there are aspects of functionality, modularity, and interoperability that one would need to demonstrate before making the smart grid a Smart Grid. Without a threshold or other criteria, even self-defined, a Smart Grid would always be subjective.[19]

At a fundamental architectural level, there are several changes to the grid of 100+ years. First, power flows are measured and monitored with very high precision and granularity (both spatial and temporal). This can allow precision in not only billing but even control. In the short run, such control would be by traditional equipment (such as

circuit breakers), but in the future, new technologies such as solid-state power flow devices could offer online control. Second, consumers could also become producers, using distributed and renewable generation (and storage, e.g., plug-in electric vehicles) to change the direction of power flows in the so-called last mile. There would be a number of additional possible changes including enhanced market competition. Indeed, the Smart Grid is not any particular option or design, it is an *enabling infrastructure* for any chosen option. Of course, who chooses (consumers, utilities, regulators, technology providers, etc.) is an ongoing discussion, let alone why or how.

The drivers for developing and developed regions are different (Table 2). Formally, the US DoE's goals are identified in the functionalities listed above, and the European Technology Platform (ETP) states the main drivers are (EU ETP WG-3, 2010):

1. Competitiveness
2. Sustainable development
3. Security of supply

The US promulgated Smart Grids through the 2007 Energy Independence and Security Act (EISA), while a number of countries (especially in Europe) and provinces of Canada pushed for if not mandated aspects of Smart Grids such as smart metering instead of a Smart Grid overall. Sometimes, the mandate wasn't even for smart meters per se, but functionality like differential tariffs and net metering (for consumer renewable) that effectively call for smart meters.

India has embraced Smart Grids relatively recently,[20] creating a Smart Grid Task Force in 2010 as an Inter-governmental body (similar to the US) and a Smart Grid Forum, a Public-Private-Partnership (PPP) voluntary body bringing multiple stakeholders together for advancing smart grids.[21] Of course, many of the activities underway, e.g., R-APDRP, aren't labeled Smart Grid, but are part of it, if not directly then the precursors to a Smart Grid. This extends to many SCADA and automation projects underway as well. The main difference or question is whether these are being envisaged as part of a broader transformation, or in a standalone mode.

While the potential for Smart Grids is high, there are a number of challenges, which include high up-front costs, evolving technology, etc. In addition to such global concerns, there are some India (or developing region) specific concerns. These include a much poorer/weaker grid that may need strengthening before the full benefits of a smart grid can be unleashed.

A SWOT analysis of Smart Grids for India is given in Table 3.

EA for Smart Grids

The power of Smart Grids isn't its technology—it is a broader transformation of the power system. A number of authors and presenters term it a journey instead of a destination—from a developing country vantage point, it may be important to think of it as a process, and not a product. Thus, one cannot (should not) just try and find the cheapest "widget" – that is a flawed endeavor.

If we examine the technical/functional domains of a smart grid and the business implications or improvements for the utility, we can see that the potential is vast (PA Consulting, 2010) (see Table 4).

Directed by the 2007 Energy Independence and Security Act (EISA), the US National Institute of Standards and Technology (NIST) has created several reference frameworks for the Smart Grid, with version 2.0 released in February 2012 (NIST, 2012).

The EA fundamentals for a Smart Grid as endorsed or cited by a number of organizations (including NIST) are based on a layered approach,

Table 2. Different drivers for smart grids in developed vs. developing regions

Developed (EU or US)	Developing (e.g., India)
1. Push towards greener (sustainable) grids (esp. Europe's mandated 20/20/20 plan – 20% less carbon, 20% more efficiency, and 20% renewable by 2020). 2. Need to handle a large number of electric vehicles 3. Need for grid modernization and improved security/resiliency 4. Reduce manpower costs (including automated meter readings) 5. Promote competition	1. Immense shortfall of power 2. Losses, both technical and financial (including theft) 3. Huge projected growth in the coming years 4. Manpower issues (skills, connivance/interference), etc. (The above are the ones that contrast with developed regions, whose drivers may still apply but not in the short run)

Table 3. SWOT analysis for smart grids for India

Strengths	Weaknesses
• Valuable tool in a portfolio for improving sustainability; impacts other aspects as well (finances, renewables, etc.) • Increasing government support for change • Availability of sizeable funding (more so from the Center than State) • Low labor costs • Strong IT and professional capabilities in-country	• The costs are still very high. In an absolute sense, Indian costs should be lower (with homegrown IT, lower labor costs, etc.), but the per-consumer monthly spend is also very low. • Any change creates winners and losers – the latter will resist • Evolving standards – global solutions are especially expensive • Lack of appropriate data (baseline) • Weak grid that will need strengthening • Limited IT deployments (consumer indexing, asset indexing, GIS, etc.)[22] • Limited Smart Grid skilled manpower within utilities
Opportunities • Can be synergized with broader reforms and process improvements in utilities. • Things are so bad right now that perhaps decision-makers are willing to embrace changes (general recognition that Business As Usual cannot go on) • An India-centric smart grid can be chosen and designed which can focus on different functionalities (at least in the short run) compared to other global deployments. • Can help identify system losses precisely, helping utility financials.[23] • Limited legacy deployment • Modularity can allow utilities to focus on their pressing needs first • India, more so than most developing countries, can create globally attractive solutions for export.	**Threats** • Vested interests (1) – beneficiaries of today's system with high losses, subsidies, and cross-subsidies • Vested interests (2) – technology providers who benefit from proprietary solutions • Regulatory uncertainty (1) – what costs will be allowed into the rate base, how, etc. • Regulatory uncertainty (2) – lack of clarity on variable tariffs and improved pricing (already a contentious topic)

Table 4. Smart grid functionalities/domains and the business process implications (adapted from USAID, 2010)

	Availability	Reliability	Reduce Operating Costs	Reduce Commercial Losses (esp. Theft)	Increase Electricity Supply	CRM Applicable
Automated meter reading			•	•	•	•
Remote disconnection and reconnection			•	•		•
Outage monitoring and evaluation	•	•		•		
Mini-SCADA	•	•	•		•	
DSM and Load Management		•	•		•	•
Renewable energy					•	•
Distributed, standby and off-grid generation		•			•	•
Time-of-use tariffs[24]			•		•	•
Islanding	•	•	•		•	•
Capacitor control		•	•			
Demand response			•	•	•	•
Phasor Measurement Unit[25]	•	•	•			

such that the Technical, Information, and Organizational aspects interface properly, i.e., data can be recognized properly as information, in the context of operations and incentives. Such a layered approach allows modularity of solutions and interoperability, and has been the hallmark of the global Internet with a 7 Layer OSI stack. E.g., the top layer of the Internet, the Application layer, can use any solution as a Web browser, independent of the lowest (Physical) Layer solution, which could be wireless, optical fiber, etc. (see Figure 17).

The NIST framework (simplified) has 7 domains as shown in Table 5 (NIST, 2010).

These actors interconnect as shown in Figure 18.

As per a synopsis of NIST's Framework (Tuite, 2010):

The Smart Grid is divided into seven linked domains, each comprising organizations, buildings, individuals, systems, devices, or other "actors" that use "applications." Domains may include sub-domains. They may also have overlapping

Figure 17. GridWise architecture council (GWAC)'s 8 layer stack for interoperability and information exchange

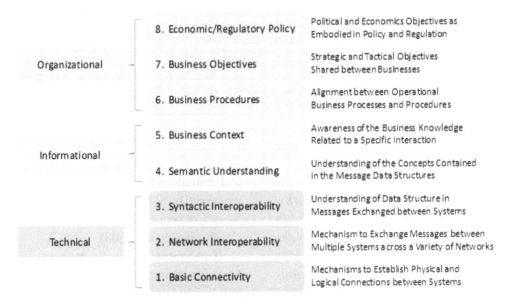

Table 5. Simplified NIST framework (NIST, 2010)

	Domain	Actors in the Domain
1	Customer	The end users of electricity. May also generate, store, and manage the use of energy. Traditionally, three customer types are discussed, each with its own domain: residential, commercial, and industrial.
2	Markets	The operators and participants in electricity markets.
3	Service Provider	The organizations providing services to electrical customers and to utilities.
4	Operations	The managers of the movement of electricity.
5	Bulk Generation	The generators of electricity in bulk quantities. May also store energy for later distribution.
6	Transmission	The carriers of bulk electricity over long distances. May also store and generate electricity.
7	Distribution	The distributors of electricity to and from customers. May also store and generate electricity.

Figure 18. 7 domains of smart grid from NIST's smart grid framework 1.0 (redrawn from NIST framework by electronicdesign.com)

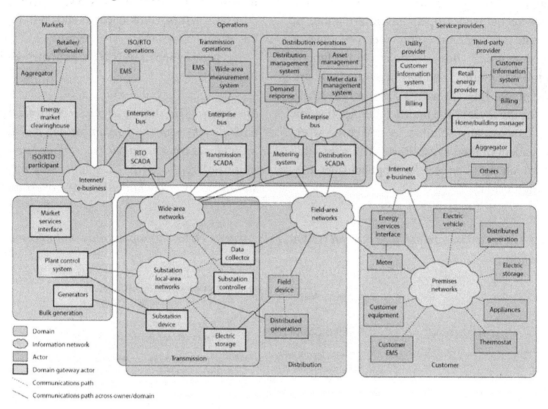

functionality. Note that the transmission and distribution domains often share networks, which is why they are shown overlapping. Within the domains, the actors are devices, computer systems, software programs, people, or whole organizations. Any actor may make decisions and exchange information with other actors. Organizations may have actors in more than one domain.

What are the relationships between actors? A unified view from the NIST framework is shown in Figure 19. This very full diagram hints at the enormous complexity of EA for Smart Grids. Even this is not complete, and there can be further interactions and sub-modules within this.

How does one make sense of such an architecture? Rather, how does one build one up? Building up Use Cases has been mooted as a powerful tool to focus on specific functionalities

and examine its flows. Smart Grid Use Cases were pioneered by Southern California Edison for their SmartConnect (Smart Grid) program (Southern California Edison, 2008).

If we consider a significant use case, Advanced Metering Infrastructure (which many consider a building block for additional functionalities), its slice is shown in Figure 20.

We can tie the logical flows back to the actors and their domains (Figure 21). NIST makes available the logical flows for several important Use Cases online.[26]

Technical Options for Smart Grid EA

How exactly are the nodes (actors) linked? This is where many utility decision-makers have longed for a "simple" solution ("Tell us what to do"). If there is a smart meter and a smart appliance, how exactly are they to be interconnected?

Figure 19. NIST smart grid unified logical diagram (source: NIST smart grid interoperability panel, 2012)

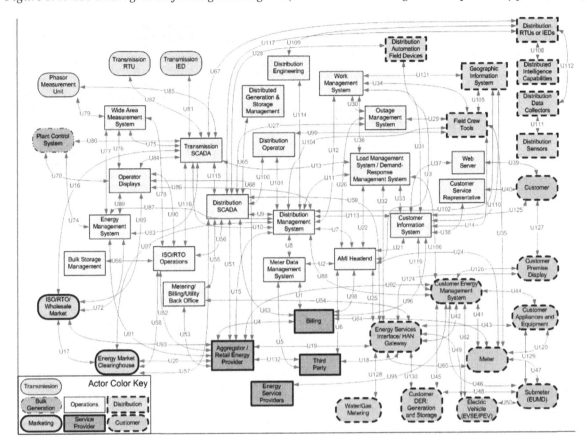

One of the lessons most Smart Grid designers have harped upon is the need for standards, that too ones that foster interoperability. But the devil is in the details – there are often multiple standards to choose from. NIST itself identifies a portfolio of standards that can be used for different functionalities. To illustrate such options, consider using a cellular modem for interconnection (also dubbed M2M = machine to machine communications). One could use either of two popular standards (each finding different favor in different countries, with the US the exception, split almost evenly): GSM and CDMA. Both are standards, just have slightly different implications (more market than technical, except when considering migration pathways to 3G if not 4G).

The sources of standards vary – some are national bodies, some are multi-lateral, some are professional bodies, and some are industry driven

consortia. Given the range of technology spaces (Information, Communications, and Electrical/Automation), it is inevitable there will be a large suite to consider.

The Institute for Electrical and Electronics Engineers (IEEE) is a major stakeholder in Smart Grid standards, working on the P2030 project for Smart Grid interoperability (not to mention working closely with NIST) (http://smartgrid.ieee.org/standards). They already have a number of standards for communications and electricity even pre-Smart Grid. Electricity meters, as they evolve to smart meters, will need national certification. In the US, this is ANSI (American National Standards Institute), while in India has the Bureau of Indian Standards (BIS). BIS follows IEC (International Electrotechnical Commission) standards, which are used (directly or indirectly) in most countries.

Figure 20. AMI use case logical flow (source: NIST smart grid interoperability panel, 2012)

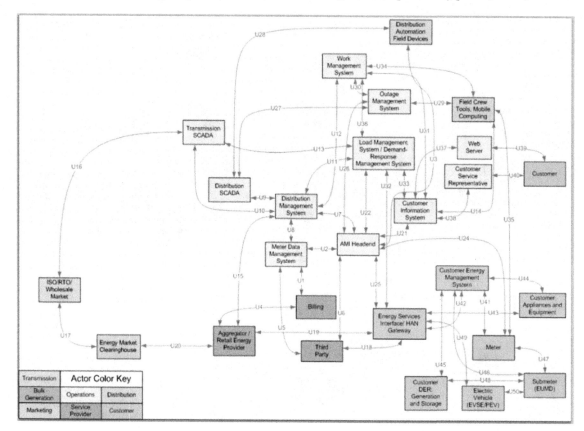

For Smart Meters, as an example of a Smart Grid Component, India is coalescing towards the use of IEC 62056 (DLMS/COSEM) as a standard, offering interoperability and other benefits. There are, similarly, a range of standards for things like sub-station automation, SCADA, Common Information Model (CIM), etc. (http://www.iec.ch/smartgrid/standards/) Many of the standards specify data formats/structures, meta-data, etc. allowing interoperability across nodes and devices (actors).

Most countries want to piggyback or build upon global standards, instead of re-inventing the wheel. The Smart Grid Task Force of India has publicly stated so, but at the same time has called for Indian innovation, to solve Indian needs. More than anything else, a lack of existing homegrown standards makes global standards all the more relevant, if nothing else than as a starting point.

If we think back to the traditional power system (Figure 1), a Smart Grid is a profound change, not merely for the flow of power but also money, information, and control. A European Technology Platform (ETP) vision for the future is shown in Figure 22.

LESSONS LEARNED AND DISCUSSION

There are a number of lessons for utilities in developing regions, many of which are "obvious" and relate to proper project management and change management. These include establishing metrics, baseline data, performance indicators, etc. However, there are a few domain and developing country lessons learned from other IT for power projects, which are listed below (in no particular order):

Figure 21. AMI systems use cases: actors, logical interfaces, and networks (Source: Sisley, 2010) WMS = Work Management System ; DRMS = Demand Response Management System; MDMS = Meter Data Management System; EMS = Energy Management System; LMS = Load Management System; DER = Distributed Energy Resources; RTO/ISO = Regional Transmission Organization/Independent System Operator; DA = Distribution Automation

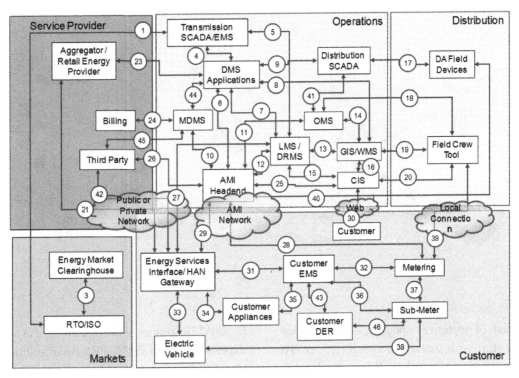

1. Planning, Planning, Planning (AKA Good Design)

Not only are utility needs evolving, so is the regulatory and policy landscape. On top of this, technology is evolving, and nowhere is it changing faster than in ICT. The only way to handle such change is to:

a. Understand What (and Why) You Need

From an Indian perspective, the two most-cited "killer apps" are loss reduction and load management/control. While reducing theft is very important financially, there is also the case that one doesn't need a Smart Grid to do so. More importantly, the savings from theft control might only be on the order of 10-15% in most cases, at best (see Footnote 5). In contrast, over the next 20 years, the expected growth in load is going to be 100-150%. It is the peak which is the biggest challenge for India, and fixing this will involve not only more supply per se but different types of generators (peakers) and also broader transformations including tariff changes.

b. Figure out Options for Meeting the Needs, Then Make Informed Choices

Solutions should be standards-based, ideally open standards, and modular. Not everything possible is appropriate, at least for now, but "good enough" should not be designed to preclude future changes.

Figure 22. The new EU energy world depicted (source: Figure 14 of Energy Retailers' Perspective on the Deployment of Smart Grids in Europe [EU ETP WG-3, 2010]). "Retailer = Thin Retailer (Balance Supplier, Billing Agent, Customer Service)/ Sourcing Responsible = Balance Responsible + Trade Responsible Party / VPP = Virtual Power Plant / μg = Microgrid. Third Parties are new entrants to the market like pure Demand Response service providers, or data services companies."

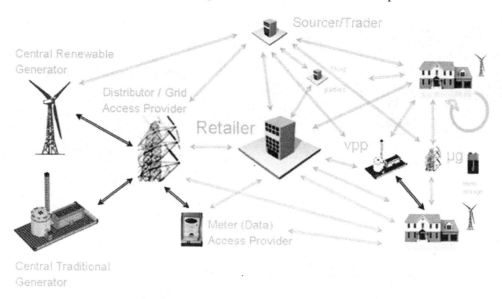

Instead of technical specifications, utilities can first start with *functional specifications*. To illustrate, one could ask that all fire-proof doors be made of material X and be Y inches thick. Instead, one could just require that any fire-proof door be certified to withstand a flame temperate of M degrees for N period of time, leaving solution providers the space to innovate solutions. Of course, given network effects and the need for interoperability, some coordination and standards are required.

c. Keep in Mind the Evolution of Technology

This will prevent technology obsolescence. If electrical hardware is meant to last 15-20 years, how can this sync with IT hardware which has a much shorter life? A modular, layered approach is the only option.[27] Instead of just backwards compatibility, so-called "forward compatibility" may also be important (anticipating and enabling future solutions). The challenges aren't just money

(a 3G AMR solution is not that much, if at all, more expensive than a GSM/GPRS AMR solution), but also figuring out the right timeframe(s).[28]

d. Have a Long-Term Roadmap

Technology for technology's sake is expensive. A small deployment may not cost much, but it won't lead to enterprise-wide transformation either. Even if a pilot deployment is successful (however that might be defined), then what? A road-map helps plan and sequence efforts, including iterations which are often overlooked. One *tool* for planning for Smart Grids is the Smart Grid Maturity Model, administered by Carnegie Mellon's Software Engineering Institute.

Decision-makers face an enormous array of choices, but if they focus only on technology choices, they may not reap all the benefits. Most technologies operate in an ecosystem – earlier use of computers in enterprises did not result in major productivity gains since these sometimes ended up being "glorified typewriters." It was only with complementary investments in software, training, and networking did computerization lead to greater productivity. Similarly, a utility will not see the full benefits of a smart meter unless they are also willing to put in "smart" (improved) tariffs. That said, if a utility is anyways undertaking an end-of-life type decision on upgrading meters, the incremental costs of a smart (or at least smart-ready) meter are not likely to be that high.

e. Utilize a Cost Benefit Analysis (CBA) for Improving Decision-Making

A CBA differs from typical Return on Investment (RoI) calculations done by investors in that it captures societal costs and benefits. Avoiding diesel saves consumers money, but unless the utility is compensated for it, and RoI will miss this value. Another significant difference is that costs and benefits need not be monetary only – things like time, pollution, choice, convenience, etc. are also quantified, but they may ultimately need to be converted to a common metric (usually money) for comparison. This is where we see the first challenge, which is the assumption(s) needed for making conversions. E.g., if avoiding diesel saves also consumers time, what is the value of saving an hour per week? Clearly, everyone will have a different value, so the choices ahead of modelers are to either use a standard (perhaps "typical") value, or to use distributions to capture the underlying variance (better but much harder).

CBAs are also difficult because the benefits accrue over time, and this thus necessitates the use of a discount rate (again, it could be contentious – financial discount rates and social discount rates aren't always similar). Benefits are also unlikely to be known *a priori*. This is highlighted when we have fundamentally unknowable quantities such as what will be the consumer responsiveness to a pricing signal.

A societal CBA also examines overall net benefits – increased benefits to some while decreased for others (e.g., a peak surcharge helps utilities but hurts consumers equally) becomes a wash. In theory, a regulated utility should be revenue neutral, so any peak surcharge should be equally offset by an off-peak discount. There are two wrinkles to this. First is that there will be some winners and some losers – how do we balance these? Just a net positive (analogous to the Kaldor-Hicks criteria in economics) might not be enough – one may want mechanisms to cap the losses or risks to some consumers (e.g., a formula that even with variable pricing one's bill will not go up more than "x"%). Second, there are transaction costs (especially the infrastructure) – how are those to be handled? To what extent can and should these be included in the rate base?

2. Recognize What One Knows and What One Does Not

The ingredients of a Smart Grid may exist, and even work, but they are not yet proven to work with the following needs: India-level price-performance, open standards, modularity, etc.

a. Learn the Differences for Each Utility's Needs

Every utility is different in terms of legacy, topology, manpower, consumer mix, and maybe even regulations. What works in one technology might or might not work in another. As a simple example, the European distribution grid is closer to India's with hundreds of consumers per Distribution Transformer (DT). In contrast, the US has 4-7 consumers per DT, typically (and fewer in rural areas). This has enormous implications for communications technologies.

At a business case level, each region will have different regulations and policies in place. As just one example, the lack of market mechanisms with mark-to-market pricing for power transactions in India reduces the value of load curtail via demand response schemes.

Fundamentally, the preparedness of a utility for a Smart Grid will be much lower in developing regions, especially when we consider capacity building, grid preparedness, etc.

b. Utilize Meaningful Pilots

When considering smart grids or other large transfer made of projects, especially ones dealing with technology, a number of utilities are keen to move ahead with pilot projects. However, it is unclear if they understand the exact role of pilot projects in the broader roadmap for enterprise wide deployment. Pilots can be considered of two types: learning pilots and deployment pilots (Table 6).

So why do utilities jump into pilot projects perhaps prematurely, that too sometimes at a larger scale than ideal?[29] A large pilot project becomes quite visible and represents action - it also involves real money, which is always exciting for the stakeholders. It also appears cheaper on a per-consumer basis than a small pilot, but that is inherent and not an appropriate criteria.

c. Undertake R&D and Foster Innovation

The electric power industry is notorious for low levels of R&D, with the US R&D spend as fraction of sales widely reported as being lower than the share spent by the dog food industry.[30] While many of the tools and solutions for a Smart Grid

are available today, a good amount of R&D is required, not only for improved solutions (e.g., in energy storage) but also for understanding *systems levels changes* as one transforms the power sector.

Since the Indian grid and topology (especially long rural runs) may be more of an issue than in developed regions, it may require local R&D. As an example, one of the technology bottlenecks the Indian Smart Grid Forum has identified is cost-effective but robust communications (especially for smart metering). This may necessitate not just pilots but innovation and testbeds.

While it is premature for this to emerge just yet (and there are competing visions of this), ultimately, equipment in the Smart Grid should be plug-and-play interoperable. This might require a neutral testing facility for certification – but the exact standard(s) is yet to be chosen.[31]

Many experts state the government shouldn't be picking technology winners directly – but it can nudge innovation along. One of the techniques available to foster innovation is the use of challenge grants, such as the X-Prize and DARPA's prizes. Such grants aren't new. One of the most successful uses of such grants was actually combined with *functionality specification* (performance) in the 1970s for making refrigerators much approximately 4x more energy efficient (over several decades). Industry was offered a challenge grant to push innovation to figure out how it could be done, that too at a lower price (in real terms).

Table 6. Comparing learning and deployment pilots. One could choose to worry about things like standards in a learning pilot, if the goal is to check if the standards-based solution works. However, if a learning pilot wants to first understand how much scope there is for the benefit side of any solution, then one could black box the technology.

Learning Pilots	Deployment Pilots
• Focus on functionality ("does it work?") • Solution need not be the same as eventually desired • Relatively small-scale chosen (smallest appropriate scale to provably learn from the pilot) • Costs will be high	• Factor in scalability • Focus on price-performance • Factor in all other desired criteria such as modularity, standards, etc. • Issues of competition, market power, etc. also come in to the picture • Best undertaken within the context of a wider deployment roadmap

d. Learn from Complementary Domains such as ICT for Development (ICTD)

There is rich literature and lessons learned from the interdisciplinary domain called ICTD, which includes e-health, e-learning/e-education, e-governance, etc. One of the frameworks for the Digital Divide (Tongia, Subrahmanian, & Arunachalam, 2005) encompasses:

- Awareness
- Availability
- Accessibility
- Affordability

Much of the effort in Smart Grids and EA has been on Availability (creating solutions) and Affordability (bringing the costs down). Much less has been spent on raising awareness (of possibilities and options) and accessibility (cognitive and institutional more than physical).

e. Capacity Building

This enormously important aspect of learning and skills enhancement is constrained by more than funding and availability of materials (though those are important). It actually starts with bridging the *awareness gap* (point 2.d above), which can help identify new areas for capacity building. Lack of skilled manpower has been identified as a major bottleneck for utilities overall by the government (Ministry of Power, 2012), even before we consider EA and Smart Grids. While this report identifies a shortfall of material, institutions, and funding, it doesn't capture the challenge of domains and disciplines, viz., the need for not only training utility staff in domains outside power systems such as finance, management, etc., but also that key decision-makers would need inter-disciplinary skills and training.

3. Improve how Technologies are Chosen

a. Reconsider the Procurement Process

Much has been debated if not written about the limitations and challenges with procurement and bidding ("tendering") in India. Fundamentally, the actors buying, specifying, installing, and using any solution for the most part aren't the same, and there aren't sufficient feedback loops to improve the process. From an EA perspective the process has issues including:

- Lowest Cost becomes the overwhelming criteria (so-termed L1, L2, etc.)
- Technological differentiation, even in a hybrid scoring bid (technical plus financial), diminishes
- The time for understanding differences in proposed solutions is often too short.[32]

Some projects are driven by outsiders, which many have called inevitable given limited skills within utilities – in India, the Central Government also has the money, given states are facing enormous deficits and most utilities are (severely) loss-making (Table 1 and Figure 2). Nonetheless, any technology guidelines or specifications should be considered a starting place, and changes should be encouraged as long as the utility can demonstrate it has thought through the process and has a good reason – these should not be called "deviations" as today.

While it is beyond the scope of this chapter to examine procurement issues at a level of detail required to fully understand the challenges and possible improvements, it is worth pointing out that a fundamental limitation is not just the process but mindset ("just tell me what to do" a.k.a. looking for an easy solution) – this relates to human capacity issues (see point 3.b below). We examine other aspects of procurement when looking at specifications in point 5.f below).

b. Capacity Building

Capacity building for utilities is a well-documented overall need (mentioned in point 2.e above). Less understood is the impact on technology decision-making. Utilities mostly rely on outsiders ("consultants") to undertake technology projects. While one school of thought is to outsource what is not a core competency, one still needs minimum skills to engage with the outsiders. Outsiders even play a prominent role at the specifications and bidding level (a different consultant than the implementing one, mostly). Thus, if a utility is not able to understand what it needs, or what the options are and their trade-offs, it is unlikely to understand what the best option is. More cynically, how does a utility know it isn't being taken for a ride? One phrase that can describe the current situation is where utilities are being "educated by vendors." Even if utilities lack niche skills, they must find trusted, neutral, and yet skilled experts on their side.

Lack of skilled people is an enormous challenge (in a nation of 1.2 billion people!), and fixing that will take more than money (and good salaries). It is worth emphasizing that the challenge of manpower is most prominent in rural areas, and outsourcing doesn't always fix that, especially for skilled professionals.

4. Understand Criticalities and Nuances of Time, Location

a. Understanding Time Constants and Actor Constraints requires Domain Expertise

Domains that need to work together span electrical, IT, communications, etc. If one is doing sophisticated ("smart") metering, where should

that information go? If one designs it such that it goes all the way to the central data server (or cloud), that may take too long for actions that require prompt local action, e.g., disconnection due to overload (which needs central policy control but local actuation).

Some data come instantaneously and regularly – others, especially load profiling, can take years to build up and create reliable analytics.

One of the challenges of timeframes is that many bids are BO (build, operate). R-APDRP has 5 year timeframes for vendors – while IT equipment may be ripe for upgrades in 5 years, the electrical portion should last several times longer. How is this optimized in the design and the contracting?

b. The "Who" (or "What") and "Where" of Data Creation and Data use are Critical

Updating data to keep it current is a major challenge that many projects fail to do. No matter how good a particular solution is ("drop in"), if the people in the field don't use it properly, e.g., updating new connections or assets, the databases will fall into disarray (no pun intended).

Keeping in mind the human capacity challenges and also the fact that field (especially rural) staff are overworked, what utility professionals need is not even information (which comes from data) but knowledge/wisdom, i.e., something that helps them make better decisions, in short, a Decision Support System (DSS).

c. Any Transformation will take Time

Unrealistic expectations help no one, and "failures" of this nature will unnecessarily give the technology or EA itself a bad name. The planning, design and prototyping portion of a Smart Grid deployment can take many years (exemplified by testbeds and deployments in Europe and the US). This is even before we add the precursor work that needs to be done in developing regions (see footnote 23). We also need to consider the physical state of some distribution segments in India (see Figure 23).

This is even before we consider the sheer scale of the grid in many developing regions; India has roughly as many people lacking electricity as Sub-Saharan Africa.

However, as daunting as such efforts must be, utilities should not lose sight of the *transformation* that EA revamps and ICT can offer. Otherwise, adding digital technologies might simply be doing things like before, albeit slightly faster (and at some cost). There is significant experience with e-Governance projects worldwide to highlight the cost and complexities of doing it right (Figure 24).

Figure 23. Reality check (date unknown, Source: Marcus Forrell)

Figure 24. Gartner's stages of e-governance

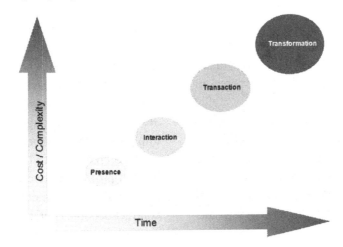

5. Beware of False Dichotomies (and other Misconceptions)

A number of issues aren't either-or, but rather somewhere in between. Stated another way, one should understand the pluses and minuses of each end, and try and form a hybrid solution if possible.

a. "A Smart Grid can Wait: Let's First Give People Power"

This false dichotomy assumes a linear progression of electricity utilities. Certainly one has to be cautious when deploying a technology intensive solution that might not work in the existing environment, but these are not mutually exclusive options. EA driven solutions can actually help with short-term needs such as managing shortfalls of power and reduce losses. More importantly, the long term process and planning need to align. A lot of equipment has a very long life span. If one is anyways buying new meters, and moving towards digital meters, then such meters should be if not smart then at least smart ready (standards-compliant, communications ports that can be interfaced with down the road, etc.)

b. "Gradualism Works better than Big Bang" (or even vice versa)

This is also false dichotomy related somewhat to the previous point. We actually need one to lead into the other, for example, as part of a well-planned roadmap. Many of the actions that utilities are contemplating or even taking today are actually steps towards a smart grid, such as the increased use of automation and SCADA.

Any advanced and technology intensive solution needs to be considered holistically. While on one hand one doesn't inherently need such a smart solution for every need, such a solution may have increased chances of working because it's operations and findings may be hard to refute. E.g., this is perhaps one of the better arguments that can be made for the Indian government scheme to have a biometrics-based Universal ID (UID) for improved delivery of government services. The use of mobile technologies has exploded in just over a decade, and many people predict similarly disruptive technologies to emerge for the electricity sector as well.

c. Top Down vs. Bottom Up

As discussed previously, top-down has found favor in India and many developing regions because of funding and control reasons. Bottom-up by end-users is critical because ultimately the users of any system must want to use the system, or it will fall into disuse or disarray. One can actually combine both options through proper planning (e.g., guidance and funding top-down, with deeper design, execution, and utilization driven bottom-up).

d. "Electricity is a Public Good, and Hence the Money is Less Relevant"

The debate between electricity's social contract and a view that it is a commodity best managed by well functioning markets is an old one. There are number of utility professionals who have a disdain for finance and economics, treating these as a distraction from their core obligation of safe delivery of power to the citizens.

Electricity has enormous public value, and policy makers are free to choose progressive policies and cross subsidies as appropriate. However, the utility delivering the service should be kept whole and outside such issues. To this end, the regulators have asked state governments to pay any desired subsidies, though the details and practical implementation leave a lot to be desired. Without a viable enterprise (which requires a minimum level of profits for covering both costs of capital as well as reinvestment), the long-term social contract becomes untenable.

In reality, it is not electricity per se but the service (lighting, cooling, lifting water, etc.) that consumers and citizens want. Such a framing has already been embraced by progressive utilities such as DONG energy, Denmark, and will help us think of new means to incentivize service. Instead of more money for more power delivered, if a utility can deliver the same service with less power, they should be equally compensated. Thus, a utility investment in end-use energy efficiency should be allowed similar returns to capital investments (such frameworks have been dubbed "negawatts").

e. Public vs. Private

This unresolved debate has been discussed elsewhere in the chapter. From an EA perspective, it is mostly irrelevant; ownership shouldn't affect viable operations. Even an entirely private operator functioning in a competitive market space is still subject to oversight and regulation.

Of course, theory and practice are only the same in theory, and not in practice. There is evidence (limited to only a few utilities) in India that privatization helps operations (most notably in Delhi), not for any theoretical reason but because a private player is more likely to be subject to hard fiscal constraints unlike their public counterparts.

f. "The Tighter the Specification, the Better"

Critics of the current procurement process state that specifications is where a number of bids can be gamed. Leaving aside such possibilities, or even outright graft in procurement, many specifications are overly specified, perhaps in part to make evaluation easier but also because of the misconception that tighter or higher specification is always better. This ignores the fact that there are often trade-offs, and this also hampers innovation and alternative solutions. We have already discussed how functional specifications can be better than pure technical specifications, especially

for fast evolving and complex technologies. More specifically, we are discussing process integrated technologies and not a widget.

The current system's limitations were highlighted during R–APDRP, with specifications that stated a minimum clock speed for server processors (MHz). During one state's pre-bid clarification conference, technology providers pointed out that the technology was moving towards slightly slower speed but higher performing multicore processors which would also save energy. The official clarification was that technology providers were free to provide higher functionality and even speeds, they would have to adhere to the minimum clock speed specification.

Over specification is easy to understand – it makes evaluation much simpler. If one left too much flexibility and options for big respondents, this would require much greater time, effort, and skills on the part of the utilities to make proper comparisons. What is less well appreciated is that so-called "better" (tighter) specifications can actually be counterproductive as well. This extends to not only specifics of any technology but also prequalification (termed "empanelment"). Often, the requirements in India and elsewhere ask for things like a minimum bank balance and track record of several (3-5) years. While the goal may be understandable, to ensure that only serious players respond to the bid, this does nothing to ensure that the proposed solution itself is proven. This also limits new entrants, startups, etc., who naturally bring risks but also value; there can be alternative mechanisms to reduce risks than strict age-of-company-based qualification norms.

As an example, a little while back, an Indian utility was seeking service providers to build and operate their billing system, and they specified as a minimum requirement the vendor should be CMM (Capability Maturity Model) Level 3 certified. Discussions with utility brought out that the current billing systems were scattered among several service providers who had disparate and non-integrable (proprietary) solutions covering portions of the utility's geography. They wanted to consolidate. One of their several providers was actually doing a very good job and had spent considerable effort building up the solution, working bottom-up to understand the utility's needs. That provider was also not the most expensive of their several, which prompted my question why don't they consider simply extending his contract, with the requirement that he follow industry standards allowing for interoperability. Other than a few responses about due process, one reaction was "But he's only Level 2 certified." This reflects a complete lack of understanding of what certification processes like CMM (or ISO) offer, which is insight into the processes and predictability of an entity, telling us nothing about the actual output itself. A picture (Figure 25) reminds us of the limitations of such certifications. While process certifications can certainly be useful as additional information when comparing options, it is restrictive to make these mandatory minimum requirements, especially for certifications with multiple levels such as CMM.

Figure 25. A reminder of the limits of certifications as predictors of output (Photo: A. Thatte, used with permission)

g. "Automation Costs Jobs"

While it is true that some amount of jobs can be made redundant through automation and mechanization, workforce actually needs to be retrained and their skill sets updated so that they can provide alternative and newer services. When the Indian Railways was proposing computerization over two decades back, there was a lot of resistance. Ultimately, staff embraced computerization since now multiple reservations offices could be opened up around a city, not to mention the improved service they could provide passengers.

Transformed enterprise architectures and a Smart Grid can also unleash innovation for new services and products, leading to greater employment overall. This is beyond the view that the human factor is actually the source of many of the problems, including connivance if not outright manipulation, for example, with meter reading.

6. Geographies (Jurisdictions) Must Align

If we look back to the various flows that occur across a utility, one of the major difficulties becomes when finances, control, oversight, planning, etc. do not align geographically. A physical substation, today, might cover more than one section office or even subdivision. This makes it difficult to reconcile technical with financial with strategic decision-making.

The process of reform and deregulation brings this aspect into even more stark focus, since now we are dealing with different entities across boundaries. In some states in India, the final substation, from where the distribution feeders emanate, is owned not by the distribution utility but by the state transmission utility. Such things are an artifact of how reforms were undertaken, and perhaps even a fallout of a design that over-emphasizes and over empowers transmission over distribution (Tongia, 2006).

Issues of non-optimal geographic boundaries are not limited to the electricity sector. Numerous studies have shown how hierarchical and localized jurisdictions for voting and democracy do not always align. Thus, neighboring houses might share a city level elected official, but not share local ward jurisdictions (below) or state representatives (above). The reasons for such non-overlaps can include attempts to gerrymander resources and political power. In the electricity world, more than any single specific driver might be simply the effect of legacy and inertia.

Geographies also become important when we try and examine real data. A very large geography might average out a lot of underlying trends and patterns. Urban areas are not only likely to look and behave differently than rural ones, they may also require different solutions, both technologically and policy wise.

If we summarize, some of the real challenges for EA solutions (including Smart Grids) include:

1. **Complexity:**
    The electric power sector is enormously complex. Ignoring or not fully appreciating the complexities and operating in silos that don't factor in broader interconnectivities does not make the complexity go away. Enterprise architecture offers a formal methodology for understanding and working with such complexities.
    Even before we get to the level of a Smart Grid, market and regulatory changes electricity are pushing enormous complexity onto an already complex system. Opening up markets for generation has resulted in utilities buying power from further and further away, which places new burdens on the transmission network. Increasing renewables, with their variability and uncertainty, similarly places new burdens upon the grid. Another major shift is that of granularity – new services and options are demanded not just by handful of

bulk consumers but expected by smaller and smaller sizes of consumers.

In many cases, regulators and policymakers did not ask for EA or a Smart Grid, they only ask for certain functionalities such as differential tariffs consumers that would automatically imply such changes. For developing regions, we have the added challenges of a much weaker starting base, both technologically and institutionally, not to mention the sheer size and scale involved. Anyone dismissing such complexities and challenges ("we know the answer") either doesn't quite understand the challenges, or, quite possibly, they're trying to sell something.

A sub-set of complexity is often termed *big data*. Creating, storing, analyzing, and harnessing enormous volumes of data is a relatively new challenge, and one utilities haven't thought about much yet. 15 minute meter readings are over 35,000 readings per consumer per year, and there are proponents who state that for peak periods, one may want even higher-resolution data.

2. **Change Management:**

Any transition is difficult, let alone transformation. Not only do people resist change due to fears of the unknown, it is rational for the beneficiaries of today's status quo to resist such change. Not only do we have differences in where stakeholders think we should go, there is even less agreement on how we should get there. Utilities have thus far shown limited appetite and/or ability to deal with the complexities, nuances, trade-offs, and long-term effort needed to make EA and Smart Grids a success.

3. **Lack of Alignment of Stakeholders, Incentives, and Feedback Loops:**

Consumers are the linchpin of any sustainable electricity system. However, other than oversimplified platitudes about prices in tariffs, they have till date been very limited participants in the process, especially when we consider other metrics and factors such as electricity quality, availability, choice, service responsiveness, etc.

While utilities have to grapple with a number of stakeholders outside the system, they also need to recognize the very large number of stakeholders within their enterprise. When Southern California Edison was planning their smart grid initiatives, they undertook approximately 140 internal workshops to solicit feedback and secure buy-in from employees.

Ultimately, no matter what the exact specifics of the enterprise and its architecture, feedback loops, both positive and negative, and the only way to improve decision-making. However, this represents a shift from today's mostly command-and-control system with centralized and top-down authority. The present system results in asking questions of a strategic nature being viewed as confrontational (or even insubordination).

Related to the above change in organizational hierarchy is the tendency for risk aversion. Utilities worldwide are considered conservative, and this is magnified in developing regions where it is easier not to try new or risky endeavors (especially given the compressed timeframes for many leadership positions).

ICT correlates with transparency, which is also something selected stakeholders might resist. Whether it is incomplete, missing, or sheer bad (incorrect – through omission or commission) data, the end-result is mostly the same. Non-optimal policies may continue, and one always keeps bogeymen alive to shoulder the blame (non-paying consumers, theft, agriculture, etc.)

4. **Design Challenges (Technology, Policy/ Regulation, and Business Case):**

There are still a lot of challenges in choosing the best architectures and designs for the utility enterprise or a Smart Grid. While many of the challenges are universal or global, a few are more pertinent to developing regions. In particular, rural areas represent a significant challenge for utilities. The distances are large and the density low, and consumer willingness/ability to pay is one to two orders of magnitude lower than in developed regions. This impacts everything from technology choices (for example, communications options) to political economy (rural areas have entrenched systems of cross subsidy, some appropriate and some less so).

Many proponents are optimistic given the continued improvements in technology. They point out that the volumes are so large that eventually the costs will come down on a per consumer basis, just like today mobile telephony is the cheapest in India. The unanswered question remains how do we cross the chasm from today's low-volume high-cost world to the future that should be high-volume low-cost?

Initial deployments of any technology are more expensive compared to high-volume periods. If we treat the initial additional costs as a societal burden, it would not be wrong to treat going down the learning curve as a public good, worthy of public funding (Figure 26).

If the low-cost future commoditizes solutions, then why would technology providers innovate? However, this might also be another false dichotomy since there is value to be harnessed in value-added and specialized services instead of the commodity (hardware), just like we have seen for Wi-Fi.

Discussion

It is beyond the scope of the chapter to be prescriptive let alone offer a model EA. It is also somewhat premature, since many of the deployments are works in progress. The process is more important

Figure 26. Learning curve costs (generic). Any initial deployments help all subsequent deployments by going down the learning curve, and hence public support for these (e.g., pilots) can be justified. One could consider such a cost equivalent to a dead-weight loss.

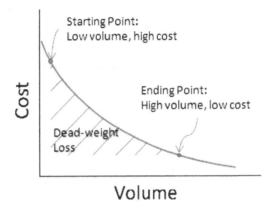

than the exact details of the solution. However, we can proclaim that technological determinism is dangerous – we don't know the "right" solution yet. No solution, not EA improvements or even a Smart Grid, is a panacea for the challenges facing the electricity sector. There are always tradeoffs that require not only multi-domain skills but multi-stakeholder interaction. As the adage in IT reminds us, "Cheaper, faster, better – pick any two." A Smart Grid (or even other similar EA) requires not just innovative solutions (products) but innovative realization (processes).

Enterprise architecture isn't about technology per se. Technology is but a means to an end. EA relates to the various flows of the enterprise, and the fundamental design of the institution. In many ways, an EA lens sharpens the picture on the entire spectrum of thinking of utilities: operations, planning, interactions, incentives, metrics, etc. It has relatively little to do with ownership (public versus private becomes a red herring), and everything to do with the creation of a viable enterprise. While political economy isn't ignored, even governmental institutions *can* be run professionally, delivering quality electricity to their constituency. The fact that several government utilities in India actually have managed low losses, improved service, etc. shows that while ownership may be a bottleneck, it is not an insurmountable constraint. More than anything, there needs to be political consensus and political will for change. If utilities do not plan for a transformation, not only will they limp along, business as usual, at some point, will precipitate into a sudden and possibly chaotic failure. EA gives them a means to transform proactively.

REFERENCES

Bengtsson, F., & Agerfalk, P. J. (2010). Information technology as a change actant in sustainability innovation. *The Journal of Strategic Information Systems*, *20*(1), 96–112. doi:10.1016/j.jsis.2010.09.007.

Census Commission. (2011). *Census of India*. Govt. of India.

Consulting, P. A. (2010). *The smart grid vision for India's power sector*. New Delhi: USAID.

CSTEP, Infosys. (2008). *Technology: Enabling the transformation of power distribution - Roadmap & reforms*. New Delhi: Ministry of Power, Govt. of India.

Dept, U. S. of Energy. (2009). *Smart grid system report*. Washington, DC: US Dept. of Energy.

EU ETP WG-3. (2010). *Energy retailers' perspective on the deployment of smart grids in Europe*. Flanders: EU.

Ilic, M. (2010). Transforming SCADA into dynamic monitoring and decision systems: The missing link in smart grids. In *Proceedings of the IEEE Power and Energy Society General Meeting 2010*. IEEE.

Karanam, R., Nambiar, A., Srivastava, M., Shukla, B. K., & Chandramouli, A. (2011). *Enterprise architecture for utilities*. Bangalore: Infosys.

Ministry of Power. (2012). *Report of the working group on power for twelfth plan (2012-17)*. New Delhi: Ministry of Power, Govt. of India.

NIST. (2010). *NIST framework and roadmap for smart grid interoperability standards, release 1.0*. Washington, DC: NIST.

NIST. (2012). *NIST framework and roadmap for smart grid interoperability standards, release 2.0*. Washington, DC: NIST.

NIST Smart Grid Interoperability Panel. (2012). *NIST smart grid interoperability panel wiki*. Washington, DC: NIST. Retrieved from http://collaborate.nist.gov/twiki-sggrid/bin/view/SmartGrid/WebHome

Planning Commission. (2011). *Annual report 2011-12 on the working of state power utilities and electricity departments*. Govt. of India.

Rao, S. L. (2011). Keynote address, sustainability of indian electricity. In *Proceedings of the IEEE Workshop on Sustainable Energy: Economics, Environment and Equity*. Bangalore, India: IEEE.

Shunglu, V. K. (2011). *High level panel on financial position of distribution utilities*. New Delhi: Govt. of India.

Sisley, E. (2010). *Enterprise architecture for the smart grid: A status update*. Pittsburgh, PA: Software Engineering Institute.

Sisley, E. (n.d.). *Review of NIST's unified logical architecture* (Feb 2010 draft). Pittsburgh, PA. *NIST*.

Southern California Edison. (2008). *Use cases*. Retrieved from http://www.sce.com/info/smartconnect/facts/resource-center/use-cases.htm?from=usecases

The Open Group. (2012). *TOGAF 9.1*. Retrieved October 16, 2012, from http://www.opengroup.org/togaf

Tongia, R. (2006). The political economy of Indian power sector reforms. In Victor, D., & Heller, T. (Eds.), *The Political Economy of Power Sector Reforms: The Experiences of Five Major Developing Countries*. Cambridge, UK: Cambridge University Press.

Tongia, R., Subrahmanian, E., & Arunachalam, V. S. (2005). *ICT for sustainable development - Defining a global research agenda*. Bangalore: Allied Press.

Tuite, D. (2010). *Smart grid design opportunities extend from the meter to the mercantile exchange*.

US Energy Information Administration. (2012). *Electricity*. Retrieved October 21, 2012, from www.eia.doe.gov

Victor, D., & Heller, T. (2006). *The political economy of power sector reform* (Victor, D., & Heller, T., Eds.). Cambridge, UK: Cambridge University Press.

Wissner, M. (2011). The smart grid – A saucerful of secrets? *Applied Energy*, *88*, 2509–2518. doi:10.1016/j.apenergy.2011.01.042.

ENDNOTES

[1] Per the US Dept. of Energy, the 2010 average residential electricity bill was $1,335 (US Energy Information Administration, 2012), while the average *household* earnings were approximately $67,530 (per the US Census bureau).

[2] Per the Planning Commission's 2012-12 Annual Report on Workings of the State Power Utilities and Electricity Departments, the average residential tariff in India was Rs. 3.20/kWh for households, and the total residential consumption was 149,628 MkWh. Assuming 67% electrification, and 244.5 million occupied census residences (both from the 2011 Census, excludes residences used for commercial purposes), average expenditure would come to approximately (with averages of averages used, which can be wrong given a skew), about US$55/household. Up to date numbers on household incomes in India are harder to find. Interpolating the National Council on Applied Economic Research (NCAER)'s data gives what appears to be a high number of Rs. 175,000 average household income in 2011. A GDP based estimate would imply markedly lower household earnings. Even with what appears to be a high income level, this translates to 1.67% of income spent on electricity. However, this is highly misleading since the median and mean vary far more in India (with lots of households at the lower end lacking electricity), and also because the Rs. 3.20/kWh itself doesn't cover the full *average* delivered costs, estimated at Rs. 4.87/kWh (with costs likely higher for households) (Planning Commission, 2011). On top of this, low consumption is heavily cross subsidized, and increases in consumption lead to higher tariffs (on a tiered basis), likely at higher escalation rates than growth of income.

[3] "Deregulation" is a misnomer, since newer systems invariably call for an independent Regulator. The term stems from a shift away from centralized planning to market-based systems.

[4] The technical losses in India are higher than many other countries based on topology and legacy, with long feeder runs leading

to relatively lower voltages. Thus, if total losses are estimated at 28%, theft and non-collection might be only ~half of this.

5   Utilities are forced to rollover such receivables, and themselves delay payments to their suppliers.

6   Portions of this section draw upon author's prior (unpublished) work for utilities in India.

7   A sample, purely for illustration purposes, is from the Jaipur Discom: http://www.jaipurdiscom.in/forms/newcon.pdf

8   Square of the current times the resistance. Since current is inversely proportional to voltage for a constant power level, the lower the voltage, the higher the current (and physical losses). This is one reason the low-voltage distribution segment has the greatest losses of power.

9   The late Prime Minister Rajiv Gandhi had jokingly referred to the SEBs as State Employment Boards.

10 This chapter will need to refer to anecdotes more than desired due to both lack of systematic studies and the unwillingness of some stakeholders to publicly make statements that they have made in private or semi-private forums.

11 Critics contend that this manual step is a source of immense manipulation of data.

12 The System Requirements Specification (SRS) document has very tightly specified what is to be designed, deployed, etc. While there is benefit to this for meeting a minimum common platform/performance (given some utilities are technologically behind others), the specifications have been written as technical specifications, and not functional specifications. Thus, the AMR (automated meter reading) module didn't write 3G for the wireless modem, it says GSM/GPRS.

Few, if any, service providers have asked for the exception to allow 3G, which should not be expensive and also would be backwards compatible in case 3G services aren't available in select areas.

13 Proper design should factor in on-ground realities and incentive structures, making poor execution less likely. The two need not be thought of as separate.

14 Distribution transformers are a major asset of utilities, and a high failure rate is both expensive and disruptive to consumers. While in the West, these may last 40 years, in India the failure rate can range from several percent to well over 10% per annum! One of the reasons cited is overloading, which improved monitoring and measurements can help with. However, there are possibly other factors such as poor quality procurement.

15 A small number of profitable public sector enterprises are recognized by the government of India as *Navaratnas* ("9 gems"), and given increased autonomy and financial powers – no distribution utility figures in this list.

16 Most states lump all utilities together when considering bulk supply power purchase tariffs – thus, an individual utility has even lower incentives to comply with the dispatch schedule or reduce demand at the peak.

17 The Infosys then Chairman, Nandan Nilekani, was the chair of the previous IT Task Force Report (2002), also chairing this Report, and CSTEP was chosen as a niche non-profit Think Tank with specialized skills in this domain. DISCLAIMER: the author of this chapter was a co-author of the 2008 report, *Technology: Enabling the Transformation of Power Distribution*.

18 This Report in 2009 merged two points from the *NETL Modern Grid Initiative* of 2008 list

of smart-grid attributes in "Characteristics of the Modern Grid" related to "self-heals" and "resists attacks."

19 Subjectivity would always be in the eye of the beholder. When the US courts were ruling on obscenity in a pornography case in 1964, Justice Stewart famously stated that while he couldn't define it, "I know it when I see it."

20 "Late" may be relative to developed countries, but India is ahead of many developing countries, except China.

21 Disclaimer: The author was involved in the creation of these entities, and is presently Advisor to both the bodies.

22 The Central Government flagship program R-APDRP aims to change this, at least for urban areas.

23 The flip argument is one doesn't need a Smart Grid to cut down theft – in and of itself, a Smart Grid can only identify problems, solving them will require process improvements (e.g., enforcement).

24 One doesn't need a smart meter to have time of use tariffs, but one needs an upgraded digital meter at the least; most consumer meters are older, analog meters, incapable of differential tariffs.

25 Phasor Measurement Units (PMUs) are applicable at the transmission level, and help improve system (state) visibility.

26 http://collaborate.nist.gov/twiki-sggrid/bin/view/SmartGrid/CsCTGArchi-Usecase-AMI-Diagram http://collaborate.nist.gov/twiki-sggrid/bin/view/SmartGrid/CsCTGArchi-Usecase-Distribution-Diagram http://collaborate.nist.gov/twiki-sggrid/bin/view/SmartGrid/CsCTGArchi-Usecase-Electric-Storage-Diagram http://collaborate.nist.gov/twiki-sggrid/bin/view/SmartGrid/CsCTGArchi-Usecase-Electric-Transportation-Diagram http://collaborate.nist.gov/twiki-sggrid/bin/view/SmartGrid/CsCTGArchi-Usecase-HAN-BAN-Diagram http://collaborate.nist.gov/twiki-sggrid/bin/view/SmartGrid/CsCTGArchi-Usecase-WASA-Diagram

27 While not yet commercially ready, flexible chips such as software-defined-radios (for communications) might help with this challenge – they can adapt to different protocols and modulation schemes.

28 Some decades back, India suffered when it did not wait for digital telephone exchanges (which were just around the corner) and went ahead with older crossbar technology. The digital solutions were not only smaller but also more robust, and, of course, on a lifecycle basis, became vastly cheaper.

29 For R-APDRP, the pilot city for the utility BESCOM was Bangalore (some 6 million people!)

30 Indian and developing country R&D in the electricity sector is far lower than the US (and at the public distribution utility level close to zero).

31 It is possible that there will not be a single standard but multiple competing standards that meet similar functionality, e.g., GSM and CDMA are somewhat comparable from an end-user perspective.

32 In R-APDRP, a state-level bid (on the order of US$100 million), with submissions of hundreds of pages, was evaluated in just over a day(!).

APPENDIX

Table 7. Acronyms

3G	3rd Generation (mobile communications)
AC	Alternating Current
AMI	Advanced Metering Infrastructure
AMR	Automated Meter Reading
ANSI	American National Standards Institute
AT&C	Aggregate Technical and Commercial (losses)
B&C	Billing and Collection
BIS	Bureau of Indian Standards
BW	Bandwidth
C&I	Commercial and Industrial
CBA	Cost-Benefit Analysis
CDC	Central Data Center
CIM	Common Information Model
CMM	Capability Maturity Model
COSEM	COmpanion Specification for Energy Metering
CRM	Customer Relationship Management
crore	10^7 (i.e., 10 million)
DA	Distribution Automation
DB	Database
DCC	Distribution Control Center
DER	Distributed Energy Resources
DLMS	Device Language Message Specification
DMS	Distribution Management System
DoE	Dept. of Energy (US)
DR	Demand Response
DRMS	Demand Response Management System
DSS	Decision Support System
DT	Distribution Transformer
DTT	Distribution Transformation Trajectory
EA	Enterprise Architecture
EPRI	Electric Power Research Institute
EISA	Energy Independence and Security (Act, 2007)
EMS	Energy Management System
ERP	Enterprise Resource Planning
ESCOM	Electricity Supply Company (aka Distribution Company, or DISCOM)
ETP	European Technology Platform
ETRM	Energy Trading and Risk Management

continued on following page

Table 7. Continued

EU	European Union
F&A	Finance and Accounting
FERC	Federal Energy Regulatory Commission
FFA	Field Force Automation
GIS	Geographic Information Systems
GPRS	General Packet Radio Service (data standard for GSM)
GSM	Global System for Mobile Communications (2nd Generation mobile communications)
HAN	Home Area Network
HT	High Tension (high voltage)
ICT	Information and Communications Technology (or Technologies)
ICTD	ICT for Development
IEC	International Electrotechnical Commission
IEEE	Institute for Electrical and Electronics Engineers
IS	Information System
ISO	International Organization for Standardization
ISO / RTO	Independent System Operator / Regional Transmission Operator
IT	Information Technology
KPI	Key Performance Indicator
kV	kiloVolt
kWh	kilowatt-hours
lakh	10^5 (i.e., hundred thousand)
LMS	Load Management System
MDMS	Meter Data Management System
MIS	Management Information System
MRI	Meter Reading Instrument
NIST	National Institute of Standards and Technology
OMS	Outage Management System
OSI	Open Systems Interconnection
R-APDRP	Restructured-Accelerated Power Development and Reforms Program
RoI	Return on Investment
SCADA	Supervisory Control and Data Acquisition
SCM	Supply Chain Management
SEB	State Electricity Board
SGMM	Smart Grid Maturity Model
SS	Substation
SW	Software
SWOT	Strengths, Weaknesses, Opportunities, Threats
USAID	US Agency for International Development
VPP	Virtual Power Plant
WMS	Work Management System

502

Compilation of References

Aalesina, A., & Spolaore, E. (1997). On the number and size of nations. *The Quarterly Journal of Economics, 112*(4), 1027–1056. doi:10.1162/003355300555411.

Abcouwer, A., Maes, R., & Truijens, J. (1997). *Contouren van een generiek model voor informatiemanagement.* Amsterdam: Universiteit van Amsterdam.

Abegunde, D., & Stanciole, A. (2006). *An estimation of the economic impact of chronic noncommunicable diseases in selected countries.* Geneva, Switzerland: World Health Organization.

Abraham, R. (2002). *The genesis of complexity.* Retrieved from www.ralph-abraham.org

Ackoff, R. (1999). *Russell Ackoff: A lifetime of systems thinking.* Retrieved August 7, 2012 from http://www. pegasuscom.com/levpoints/ackoff_a-lifetime-of-systems-thinking.html

Ackoff, R. L. (1994). *The democratic corporation: A radical prescription for recreating corporate America and rediscovering success.* New York: Oxford University Press.

Ackoff, R., & Emery, F. (1972). *On purposeful systems: An interdisciplinary analysis of individual and social behavior as a system of purposeful events.* Chicago: Aldine-Atherton.

Adger, W. N. (2000). Social and ecological resilience: Are they related? *Progress in Human Geography.* doi:1 0.1191/030913200701540465.

Adler, N., & Hashai, N. (2007). Knowledge flows and the modeling of the multinational enterprise. *Journal of International Business Studies, 38*(4), 639–657. doi:10.1057/palgrave.jibs.8400284.

Afshani, J., Harounabadi, A., & Dezfouli, M. A. (2012). A new model for designing uncertain enterprise architecture. *Management Science Letters, 2,* 689–696. doi:10.5267/j.msl.2012.01.005.

Agarwal, R., & Sambamurthy, V. (2002). Principles and models for organizing the IT function. *MIS Quarterly Executive, 1*(1), 1–16.

Ağca, V., & Uğurlu, Ö.Y. (2008). Türk imalat işletmelerinde stratejik eğilimin strateji oluşturma yeteneği ve performans ilişkisine etkisi. *İktisat İşletme ve Finans, 23*(273), 79-103.

AGIMO. (2007). *Australian government architecture: Principles. Australian Government Information Management Office.* AGIMO.

AGIMO. (2011). *Australian government architecture: Reference models. Australian Government Information Management Office.* AGIMO.

Ahaus, C. T. B. (1998). Balanced scorecard & model nederlandse kwaliteit. Projectgroep bedrijfskunde TNO BV. ISBN 90 267 2477 2

Airforce, U. S. (1990). *IDEF0 function modeling method.* Retrieved 10 28, 2012, from http://www.idef.com/IDEF0.htm

Akbaba, A. (2006). Measuring service quality in the hotel industry: A study in a business hotel in Turkey. *Hospital Management, 25,* 170–192. doi:10.1016/j.ijhm.2005.08.006.

Aldrich, M. (2008). *Innovative information systems 1980-1990.* Retrieved from http://www.aldricharchive.com/innovative_information.html

Alexander, J. (2007). *The value of enterprise architecture.* Retrieved from http://www.statcan.gc.ca/conferences/it-ti2007/pdf/alexander04a-eng.pdf

Alexander, C. (1988). *A city is not a tree.* London: Thames and Hudson.

Allega, P. (2009). *Defining the span of control for enterprise architecture. No. G00172267.* Gartner.

Alpkan, L., Bulut, C., Gunday, G., Ulusoy, G., & Kilic, K. (2010). Organizational support for intrapreneurship and its interaction with human capital to enhance innovative performance. *Management Decision, 48*(5), 732–755.

Alter, S. (2008). Service system fundamentals: Work system, value chain, and life cycle. *IBM Systems Journal, 47*(1), 71–85. doi:10.1147/sj.471.0071.

Alt, R., Abramowicz, W., & Demirkan, H. (2010). Service-orientation in electronic markets. *Electronic Markets, 20,* 177–180. doi:10.1007/s12525-010-0047-6.

Andersson, U., Forsgren, M., & Holm, U. (2007). Balancing subsidiary influence in the federative MNC: A business network view. *Journal of International Business Studies, 38*(5), 802–818. doi:10.1057/palgrave.jibs.8400292.

Anonymous. (1999). Finance and economics: Economics focus: Man of the hour. *The Economist, 353,* 82.

Ansoff, H. I. (1965). *Corporate strategy.* New York: McGraw-Hill.

Anupindi, N. V., & Coady, G. A. (2011). *Enterprise architecture turnaround.* Trafford Publishing.

Aral, S., & Weill, P. (2007). IT assets, organizational capabilities, and firm performance: How resource allocations and organizational differences explain performance variation. *Organization Science, 18*(5), 763–780. doi:10.1287/orsc.1070.0306.

Argyris, C. (1982). *Reasoning, learning, and action: Individual and organizational.* San Francisco, CA: Jossey-Bass.

Ariely, D. (2008). *Predictably irrational: The hidden forces that shape our decisions.* New York: HarperCollins.

Ariely, D. (2009). *Predictably irrational.* London: Harper Collins Publishers.

Ariño, A., & Reuer, J. J. (2004). Designing and renegotiating strategic alliance contracts. *The Academy of Management Executive, 18*(3), 37–48. doi:10.5465/AME.2004.14776166.

Ariyachandra, T., & Watson, H. J. (2006). Which data warehouse architecture is most successful? *Business Intelligence Journal, 11*(1), 4–6.

Armson, R. (2011). *Growing wings on the way – Systems thinking for messy situations.* Devon, UK: Triarchy Press.

Arnould, E. J. (2008). Service-dominant logic and resource theory. *Journal of the Academy of Marketing Science, 36,* 21–24. doi:10.1007/s11747-007-0072-y.

Arthur, W. B. (1999). Complexity and the economy. *Science, 284*(5411), 107–109. doi:10.1126/science.284.5411.107 PMID:10103172.

Ashby, W. R. (1957). *An introduction to cybernetics.* London: Chapman & Hall.

Ashby, W. R. (1958). Requisite variety and its implications for the control of complex systems. *Cybernetica, 1*(2), 83–99.

Ashford, N., & Hall, R. (2011). *Technology, globalization and sustainable development: Transforming the industrial state.* Cambridge, MA: MIT Press.

Asia and Pacific Centre for Information and Communication Technology (APCICT). (2011). *E-government capability maturity model.* Incheon City, South Korea: United Nations and Asia Development Bank.

Asian Development Bank. (2012). Green urbanization in Asia. In *Key Indicators for Asia and the Pacific 2012.* Retrieved from http://www.adb.org/sites/default/files/pub/2012/ki2012-special-chapter.pdf

Asia-Pacific Development Information Program (APDIP). (2007). *E-government interoperability: A review of government interoperability frameworks in selected countries.* Bangkok, Thailand: United Nations Development Program Regional Center.

Asia-Pacific Development Information Program (APDIP). (2007). *E-government interoperability guide.* Bangkok, Thailand: United Nations Development Program Regional Center.

Atilgan, T. (2006). The effects of the textile and clothing sector on the economy of Turkey. *Fibres & Textiles in Eastern Europe, 14*(4), 16–20.

Atkinson, R. D., & McKay, A. S. (2007). *Digital prosperity – Understanding the economic benefits of information technology revolution*. Washington, DC: The Information Technology & Innovation Foundation. doi:10.2139/ssrn.1004516.

Auer, A. (2005). The constitutional scheme of federalism. *Journal of European Public Policy, 12*(3), 419–431. doi:10.1080/13501760500091166.

Australian Government Information Management Office (AGIMO). (2010). *Engage: Getting on with government 2.0: Report of the government 2.0 taskforce*. Canberra, Australia: Department of Finance and Deregulation, Government of Australia.

Australian Public Service Commission. (2007). *Changing behaviour: A public policy perspective*. Retrieved from http://www.apsc.gov.au/__data/assets/pdf_file/0017/6821/changingbehaviour.pdf

Aziz, Obitz, Modi, & Sarkar. (2005). *Enterprise architecture: A governance framework -- Part I: Embedding architecture into the organization*. Technical report. Infosys Technologies Ltd.

Bachus, C. (2005). Governance for sustainable development and civil society participation. In L. Hens & B. Nath (Eds.), *The World Summit on Sustainable Development: The Johannesburg Conference*. Retrieved from http://link.springer.com/book/10.1007/1-4020-3653-1/page/1

Bækgaard, L. (2005). *From use cases to activity cases*. Paper presented at ALOIS'2005 - Action in Language, Organisation and Information Systems. Limerick, Ireland.

Bækgaard, L. (2009). Service scenarios - A socio-technical approach to business service modeling. In *Proceedings of ECIS'2009 - European Conference of Information Systems 2009*. Verona, Italy: ECIS.

Baldwin, A., Mont, M. C., Beres, Y., & Shiu, S. (2010). Assurance for federated identity management. *Journal of Computer Security, 18*(4), 519–550.

Balogun, J., & Hope Hailey, V. (2004). *Exploring strategic change*. Upper Saddle River, NJ: Prentice Hall.

Barber, J. (2005). Production, consumption and the world summit on sustainable development. In L. Hens & B. Nath (Eds.), *The World Summit on Sustainable Development: The Johannesburg Conference*. Retrieved from http://link.springer.com/book/10.1007/1-4020-3653-1/page/1

Barber, J. (2007). Mapping the movement to achieve sustainable production and consumption in North America. *Journal of Cleaner Production*. doi:10.1016/j.jclepro.2006.05.010.

Bardhan, I. R. et al. (2010). Information system in services. *Journal of Management Information Systems, 26*(4), 5–12. doi:10.2753/MIS0742-1222260401.

Barros, A., & Dumas, M. (2005). *Service interaction patterns: Towards a reference framework for service-based business process interconnection*. Queensland University of Technology.

Bartlett, C. A., & Ghoshal, S. (1993). Beyond the m-form: Toward a managerial theory of the firm. *Strategic Management Journal, 14*, 23–46. doi:10.1002/smj.4250141005.

Bar-Yam, Y. (2003). When systems engineering fails – Toward complex systems engineering. In *Proceedings of the International Conference on Systems, Man, & Cybernetics*, (Vol. 2, pp. 2021-2028). Piscataway, NJ: IEEE.

Bar-Yam, Y. (2002). *Large scale engineering and evolutionary change: Useful concepts for implementation of FORCEnet*. Cambridge, UK: NECSI.

Bar-Yam, Y. (2003). Unifying principles in complex systems. In Roco, M. C., & Bainbridge, W. S. (Eds.), *Converging Technology for Improving Human Performance* (pp. 380–409). Boston: Kluwer.

Bar-Yam, Y., & Kuras, M. L. (2003). *Complex systems and evolutionary engineering*. Cambridge, UK: NECSI.

Baskerville, R., & Pries-Heje, J. (2008). The design theory nexus. *Management Information Systems Quarterly, 32*(4), 731–755.

Bates-Eamer, N., Carin, B., Lee, M. H., Lim, W., & Kapila, M. (2012). *Post-2015 development agenda: Goals, targets and indicators*. Retrieved from http://www.cigionline.org/sites/default/files/MDG_Post_2015v3.pdf

Bayraktar, E., & Tatoglu, E. (2010). Assessing the link between strategy choice and operational performance of Turkish companies. In *Proceedings of the 14th International Research/Expert Conference in Trends in the Development of Machinery and Associated Technology TMT 2010*, (pp. 805-808). Mediterranean Cruise.

Bean, S. (2011). *Rethinking enterprise architecture using systems and complexity approaches*. Retrieved August 10, 2012 from http://www.irmuk.co.uk

Bednyagin, D., & Gnansounou, E. (n.d.). *Real options valuation of fusion energy R&D programme*. Lausanne, France. *Ecole Polytechnique Fédérale*..

Beer, S. (1979). *The heart of enterprise*. New York: John Wiley.

Beer, S. (1981). *Brain of the firm* (2nd ed.). New York: John Wiley.

Beer, S. (1985). *Diagnosing the system for organizations*. New York: John Wiley.

Begossi, A., & de Avila-Pírez, F. D. (2005). World summit on sustainable development 2002: Latin America and Brazil, biodiversity and indigenous people. In L. Hens & B. Nath (Eds.), *The World Summit on Sustainable Development: The Johannesburg Conference*. Retrieved from http://link.springer.com/book/10.1007/1-4020-3653-1/page/1

Bellman, B. (2012). *Managing organizational complexity: Enterprise architecture and architecture frameworks with an overview of their products, artifacts and models*. Retrieved from http://ertekprojects.com/url/4

Bengtsson, F., & Agerfalk, P. J. (2010). Information technology as a change actant in sustainability innovation. *The Journal of Strategic Information Systems*, *20*(1), 96–112. doi:10.1016/j.jsis.2010.09.007.

Bennett, E. M., Peterson, G. D., & Gordon, L. J. (2009). Understanding relationships among multiple ecosystem services. *Ecology Letters*. Retrieved from http://onlinelibrary.wiley.com/doi/10.1111/j.1461-0248.2009.01387.x/full?goback=%2Egde_788017_member_181915703

Bergeron, B. (2003). *Essentials of shared services*. Hoboken, NJ: John Wiley & Sons.

Berkes, F., Colding, J., & Folke, C. (Eds.). (2003). *Navigating social–ecological systems: Building resilience for complexity and change*. Cambridge, UK: Cambridge University Press.

Bermann, G. A. (1994). Taking subsidiarity seriously: Federalism in the European community and the United States. *Columbia Law Review*, *94*(2), 331–457. doi:10.2307/1123200.

Bernard, H. (1976). *Totale oorlog en revolutionaire oorlog* (*Vol. I*). Brussels: Royal Military Academy. [course].

Bernard, S. (2005). *Enterprise architecture*. Bloomington, IN: AuthorsHouse.

Bernard, S. (2012). *EA3: An introduction to enterprise architecture* (3rd ed.). Bloomington, IN: AuthorHouse.

Bernard, S. A. (2004). *An introduction to enterprise architecture* (1st ed.). Bloomington, IN: Authorhouse.

Bernus, P., Baltrusch, R., Tølle, M., & Vesterager, J. (2002). Better Models for agile virtual enterprises – The enterprise and its constituents as hybrid agents. In Karvoinen, I. et al. (Eds.), *Global Engineering and Manufacturing in Enterprise Networks* (pp. 91–103). Helsinki, Finland: VTT.

Bernus, P., Nemes, L., & Smith, G. (Eds.). (2003). *Handbook on enterprise architecture*. Berlin: Springer. doi:10.1007/978-3-540-24744-9.

Bernus, P., Nemes, L., & Williams, T. J. (Eds.). (1996). *Architectures for enterprise integration*. London: Chapman and Hall. doi:10.1007/978-0-387-34941-1.

Berryman, J. M. (2007). Judgments during information seeking: A naturalistic approach to understanding of enough information. *Journal of Information Science*, 1–11.

Bertalanffy, L. V. (1969). *General system theory: Foundations, development, applications*. New York: George Braziller Inc..

Besen, S. M., & Farrell, J. (1994). Choosing how to compete: Strategies and tactics in standardization. *The Journal of Economic Perspectives*, *8*(2), 117–131. doi:10.1257/jep.8.2.117.

Birkinshaw, J., & Heywood, S. (2010, May). Putting organizational complexity in its place. *The McKinsey Quarterly*.

Birkmeier, D., et al. (2012). The role of services in governmental enterprise architecture: The case of the German federal government. In Saha (Ed.), Enterprise Architecture for Connected E-Government – Practices and Innovations. Hershey, PA: IGI Global.

Bizz Design. (n.d.). Retrieved from http://www.bizzdesign.nl/tools/architect

Bloomberg, J. (2011). *Why nobody is doing enterprise architecture.* Retrieved August 11, 2012 from http://www.zapthink.com/2011/04/05/why-nobody-is-doing-enterprise-architecture/

Boehm, B. W. (1976). Software engineering. *IEEE Transactions on Computers, 25*(12), 1226–1241. doi:10.1109/TC.1976.1674590.

Boglind, A., Hällstén, F., & Thilander, P. (2011). HR transformation and shared services: Adoption and adaptation in Swedish organizations. *Personnel Review, 40*(5), 570–588. doi:10.1108/00483481111154441.

Boh, W. F., & Yellin, D. (2006). Using enterprise architecture standards in managing information technology. *Journal of Management Information Systems, 23*(3), 163. doi:10.2753/MIS0742-1222230307.

Booch, G. (2010, March/April). Enterprise architecture and technical architecture. *IEEE Software*, 95–96.

Borman, M. (2010). Characteristics of a successful shared services centre in the Australian public sector. *Transforming Government: People. Process and Policy, 4*(3), 220–231.

Boucharas, V., Van Steenbergen, M. E., Jansen, R. L., & Brinkkemper, S. (2010). *The contribution of enterprise architecture to the achievement of organizational goals: Establishing the enterprise architecture benefits framework.* No. Technical Report UU-CS-2010-014. Utrecht, The Netherlands: Department of Information and Computing Sciences, Utrecht University.

Boukhedouma, S., et al. (2012). Adaptability of service based workflow models: The chained execution architecture. *BIS*, 96-107

Boulanger, P.-M. (2010). Three strategies for sustainable consumption. *Sapiens.* Retrieved from http://sapiens.revues.org/1022

Boulding, K. E. (1953). *The organizational revolution.* Harper & Brothers.

Bouwman, H., van Houtum, H., Janssen, M., & Versteeg, G. (2011). Business architecture in the public sector: Experiences from practice. *Communications of the Association for Information Systems, 29*(1), 411–426.

Bower, J. L. (2000). The purpose of change: A commentary on Jensen and Senge. In Beer, M., & Nohria, N. (Eds.), *Breaking the Code of Change* (pp. 83–95). Boston: Harvard Business school Press.

Bowser, M., Cantle, N., & Allan, N. (2011). *Unraveling the complexity of risk.* Paper presented at Open Forum of The Actuarial Profession. London, UK.

Boyd, J. (1976). *Destruction and creation.* U.S. Army Command and General Staff College.

Brach, M. (2003). *Real options in practice.* Hoboken, NJ: John Wiley & Sons.

Breton, A. (2000). Federalism and decentralization: Ownership rights and the superiority of federalism. *Publius, 30*(2), 1–16. doi:10.1093/oxfordjournals.pubjof.a030076.

Britton, G. A., & Parker, J. (1993). An explication of the viable system model for project management. *Systems Practice, 6*(1), 21–51. doi:10.1007/BF01059678.

Brocklesby, J., & Cummings, S. (1996). Designing a viable organization structure. *Long Range Planning, 29*(1), 49–57. doi:10.1016/0024-6301(95)00065-8.

Brooks, B. (2007). The pulley model: A descriptive model of risky decision-making. *Safety Science Monitor, 11*(1), 1–14.

Brooks, F. Jr. (1982). *The mythical man month.* Reading, MA: Addison-Wesley.

Brown, T. (2009). *Tim Brown urges designers to think big.* Retrieved from http://www.ted.com/talks/tim_brown_urges_designers_to_think_big.html

Brown, C. V. (1999). Horizontal mechanisms under differing IS organization contexts. *Management Information Systems Quarterly, 23*(3), 421–454. doi:10.2307/249470.

Brown, C. V., & Magill, S. L. (1994). Alignment of the IS functions with the enterprise: Toward a model of antecedents. *Management Information Systems Quarterly, 18*(4), 371–403. doi:10.2307/249521.

Brown, C. V., & Magill, S. L. (1998). Reconceptualizing the context-design issue for the information systems function. *Organization Science, 9*(2), 176–194. doi:10.1287/orsc.9.2.176.

Brown, T. (2008). Design thinking. *Harvard Business Review*. PMID:18605031.

Buckl, S. (2011). *Developing organization-specific enterprise architecture management functions using a method base*. (PhD Thesis). Technische Universität München, Munich, Germany.

Buckl, S., Matthes, F., & Schweda, C. M. (2010). A situated approach to enterprise architecture management. In *Proceedings of the IEEE International Conference on Systems, Man, and Cybernetics*, (pp. 587-592). Istanbul, Turkey: IEEE.

Buckl, S., Matthes, F., & Schweda, C. M. (2011). A method base for EA management. In *Proceedings fo the IFIP Working Conference on Method Engineering (ME 2011)*. Paris, France: IFIP.

Buckl, S., Dierl, T., Matthes, F., & Schweda, C. M. (2010). A modeling language for describing EA management methods. In *Proceedings of Modellierung betrieblicher Informationssysteme (MobIS2010)*. Dresden, Germany: MobIS.

Burke, B. (2011). *Is a federated architecture the right approach? No. G00219399*. Gartner.

Burke, B., & Burton, B. (2011). *What is the right approach to developing an enterprise architecture? No. G00219400*. Gartner.

Burke, B., & Tuft, B. (2012). *Federated architecture diagnostic: Understanding the four levels of enterprise architecture consolidation. No. G00234790*. Gartner.

Burke, L. A., & Miller, M. K. (1999). Taking the mystery out of intuitive decision making. *The Academy of Management Executive, 13*(4), 91–99.

Burton, B., & Allega, P. (2010). Hype cycle for enterprise architecture 2010. *Gartner Industry Research ID Number: G00201646.*

Burton, B., & Allega, P. (2011). Hype cycle for enterprise architecture. *Gartner Research ID Number: G00214756.*

Burton, B. (2010). *Survey results: Which EA approach are organizations using? No. G00174847*. Gartner.

Butland, B., Jebb, S., Kopelman, P., McPherson, K., Thomas, S., Mardell, J., & Parry, V. (2007). *Tackling obesities – Future choices*. London: Department of Business, Innovation and Skills, Government Office for Science.

Cakanyildirim, M., & Haksöz, C. (2012). *CSCMP global perspectives – Turkey*. Council of Supply Chain Management Professionals.

Camazine, S. (2001). *Self-organization in biological systems*. Princeton, NJ: Princeton University Press.

Cambell, C. D. (2011). *Systems thinking in personalized medicines*. Paper presented in 2011 MIT SDM Conference on Systems Thinking for Contemporary Challenges. Retrieved on July 30, 2012 from http://sdm.mit.edu/systemsthinkingconference/2011/docs/Campbell_2011-Systems-Thinking-Conference.pdf

Canadian Environmental Assessment Agency. (2004). *Cabinet directive on the environmental assessment of policy, plan and program proposals*. Ottawa, Canada: Author.

Canter, J. (2000). *An agility based OODA model for the e-commerce / e-business enterprise*. Retrieved June 28, 2012 from http://www.iohai.com/iohai-resources/agility-based-ooda-model.html

Capar, N., & Kotabe, M. (2003). The relationship between international diversification and performance in service firms. *Journal of International Business Studies, 34*, 345–355. doi:10.1057/palgrave.jibs.8400036.

Capital. (2008, February). Dünya devi P&G B&G ile büyüyor. [World giant P&G grows with B&G]. *Capital*, 114-124.

Capital. (2008, February). Lüks devi çift haneli nasıl büyüyor?. [How does the luxury giant show two-digit growth?]. *Capital*, 140-144.

Capital. (2008, May). Hesaplar yeniden yapılıyor. [Recounts being made]. *Capital*, 136-144.

Carlton, D. W., & Klamer, J. M. (1983). The need for coordination among firms, with special reference to network industries. *The University of Chicago Law Review. University of Chicago. Law School, 50*(2), 446–466. doi:10.2307/1599497.

Cassidy, L. D. (2005). Basic concepts of statistical analysis for surgical research. *The Journal of Surgical Research, 128*(2), 199–206. doi:10.1016/j.jss.2005.07.005 PMID:16140341.

Castellani, B. (2009). *Complexity map*. Retrieved from http://www.art-sciencefactory.com/complexity-map_feb09.html

Census Commission. (2011). *Census of India*. Govt. of India.

Chaitin, G. J. (1966). On the length of programs for computing finite binary sequences. *Journal of the ACM, 13*, 547–569. doi:10.1145/321356.321363.

Chandler, A. D. (1962). *Strategy and structure*. Cambridge, MA: MIT Press.

Chandler, A. D. (1969). *Strategy and structure: Chapters in the history of the American industrial enterprise*. Cambridge, MA: The MIT Press.

Chandler, A. D. (1991). The functions of the HQ unit in the multibusiness firm. *Strategic Management Journal, 12*, 31–50. doi:10.1002/smj.4250121004.

Chandler, A. D., & Mazlish, B. (2005). *Leviathans: Multinational corporations and the new global history*. Cambridge, UK: Cambridge. doi:10.1017/CBO9780511512025.

Chandrasekaran, N., & Ensing, G. (2004). ODC: A global IT services delivery model. *Communications of the ACM, 47*(5), 47–49. doi:10.1145/986213.986237.

Chang, C. M. (2010). *Service systems management and engineering – Creating strategic differentiation and operational excellence*. Hoboken, NJ: Wiley. doi:10.1002/9780470900208.

Chapman, J. (2004). *System failure – Why governments must learn to think differently* (2nd ed.). London: DEMOS.

Charette, N. R. (2005). Why software fails. IEEE Spectrum. Retrieved from http://spectrum.ieee.org/computing/software/why-software-fails/0

Checkland, P. (1981). *Systems thinking, systems practice*. Chichester, UK: Wiley.

Cherbakov, L., & Galambos, G. et al. (2005). Impact of service orientation at the business level. *IBM Systems Journal, 44*(4), 653–668. doi:10.1147/sj.444.0653.

Cherns, A. B. (1976). Principles of socio-technical design. *Human Relations, 29*, 783–792. doi:10.1177/001872677602900806.

Chesbrough, H., & Spohrer, J. (2006). A research manifesto for services science. *Communications of the ACM, 49*(7), 35–40. doi:10.1145/1139922.1139945.

Chew, E. K., & Gottschalk, P. (2009). *Information technology strategy and management: Best practices*. Hershey, PA: IGI Global. doi:10.4018/978-1-59904-802-4.

Chichilnisky, G. (1998). *A radical shift in managing risks: Practical applications of complexity theory*. Retrieved from http://ssrn.com/abstract=1375437 or http://dx.doi.org/10.2139/ssrn.1375437

Christensen, C. R., Andrews, K. R., Bower, J. L., Hamermesh, G., & Porter, M. E. (1982). *Business policy: Text and cases* (5th ed.). Homewood, IL: Irwin.

Christopoulos, S., Horvath, B., & Kull, M. (2012). Advancing the governance of cross-sectoral policies for sustainable development: A metagovernance perspective. *Public Administration and Development*. Retrieved from http://onlinelibrary.wiley.com/doi/10.1002/pad.1629/pdf

Church, A. H. (1914). *The science and practice of management*. University of Michigan Library (reprint in 2009).

Cilliers, P. (2004). A framework for understanding complex systems. In Proceedings of the Workshop on Organisational Networks as Distributed Systems of Knowledge. London: World Scientific Publishing.

Cisco Internet Business Solutions Group (IBSG). (2004). *Connected government: Essays from innovators*. London: Premium Publishing.

Cisco Internet Business Solutions Group (IBSG). (2009). *Realizing the potential of the connected republic: Web 2.0 opportunities in the public sector* (Cisco Systems Incorporated White Paper). Cisco.

CNBC-e Business. (2008, May). Kişisel bakım dünyasının kralı. [The king of the personal care world]. *CNBC-e Business*, 110-112.

CNBC-e Business. (2008, May). Butik olsun benim olsun. [Let it be boutique, but let it me mine. *CNBC-e Business*, 128-130. CNBC-e Business. (2008, August). Türk hazır giyimini zirveye taşıyanlar. [Those who crown the Turkish apparel industry]. *CNBC-e Business*, 42-52.

CNBC-e Business. (2008, August). Tuborg'un havasının kaçış öyküsü. [The story of how the air went off Tuborg]. *CNBC-e Business*, 54-56.

CNBC-e Business. (2008, August). Kozmetikte ikinci yatırım dalgası. [Second wave of investment in cosmetics]. *CNBC-e Business*, 70-72.

CNBC-e Business. (2008, August). 10 metrekarede büyük yarış. [Big race on the 10 meter-square]. *CNBC-e Business*, 74-76.

CNBC-e Business. (2008, August). Gripin al bir şeyin kalmaz. [Take a Gripin pill and you will be all right]. *CNBC -e Business*, 108-110.

CNBC-e Business. (2008, August). Taklitle uğraşmak düşman başına. [Fighting imitation? I wouldn't wish it on my worst enemy]. *CNBC-e Business*, 110-111.

Cobb, B., & Charnes, J. (2007). Real options valuation. In *Proceedings of the 2007 Winter Simulation Conference,* (pp. 173-182). IEEE.

Cobb, C., & Bean, K. B. (2006). Unitary: A concept for analysis. *Journal of Theory Construction & Testing*, *10*(2), 54–57.

Collan, M. (2008). *A new method for real option valuation using fuzzy numbers*. Retrieved April 12, 2011 from http://ideas.repec.org/p/amr/wpaper/466.html

Collan, M., Fullér, R., & Mezei, J. (2009). A fuzzy pay-off method for real option valuation. *Journal of Applied Mathematics and Decision Sciences*, (1): 1–14. doi:10.1155/2009/238196.

Collins, J., & Porras, J. (1996). Building your company's vision. *Harvard Business Review*.

Commission on Growth and Development. (2008). *The growth report: Strategies for sustained growth and inclusive development*. Retrieved from http://cgd.s3.amazonaws.com/GrowthReportComplete.pdf

Commissioner of the Environment and Sustainable Development Canada. (2009). *Managing sustainable development*. Retrieved from http://www.oag-bvg.gc.ca/Internet/English/sds_fs_e_33574.html

Common Wealth Fund. (2010). *US ranks last among 7 countries on health system performance*. Retrieved from http://www.eurekalert.org/pub_releases/2010-06/cf-url062210.php

Commons, M. L., & Richards, F. A. (1984). A general model of stage theory. In Commons, M. L., Richards, F. A., & Armon, C. (Eds.), *Beyond Formal Operations: Late adolescent and adult cognitive development* (*Vol. 1*, pp. 120–140). New York: Praeger.

Conover, W. J. (1998). *Practical nonparametric statistics*. New York: John Wiley & Sons.

Consulting, P. A. (2010). *The smart grid vision for India's power sector*. New Delhi: USAID.

Cook, M. A. (1996). *Building enterprise information architectures: Reengineering information systems*. Upper Saddle River, NJ: Prentice Hall.

Corporation, I. B. M. (2009). *The new voice of the CIO – Insights from the global chief information officer study*. Somers, NY: IBM Institute for Business Value, IBM Corporation.

Corporation, I. B. M. (2010). *Capitalizing on complexity – Insights from the global chief executive officer study*. Somers, NY: IBM Institute for Business Value, IBM Corporation.

Corporation, I. B. M. (2010). *The world's 4 trillion dollar challenge – Using a system-of-system approach to build a smarter planet*. Somers, NY: IBM Institute for Business Value, IBM Corporation.

Cover, T. M., & Thomas, J. A. (2006). *Elements of information theory* (2nd ed.). Hoboken, NJ: Wiley.

Cox, J., & Goldratt, E. M. (1986). *The goal: A process of ongoing improvement. Croton-on-Hudson*. NY: North River Press.

Cram, F. (2011). Whānau Or & action research. Paper prepared for Te Puni Kōkiri. Wellington, New Zealand.

Crutchfield, J. P. (2009). The hidden fragility of complex systems—Consequences of change, changing consequences. In Ascione, G., Massip, C., & Perello, J. (Eds.), *Cultures of change: Social atoms and electronic lives* (pp. 98–111). Barcelona, Spain: ACTAR D Publishers.

CSTEP, Infosys. (2008). *Technology: Enabling the transformation of power distribution - Roadmap & reforms*. New Delhi: Ministry of Power, Govt. of India.

Currie, W., & Parikh, M. (2004). Exploring the supply-side of web services: The need for market positioning. In *Proceedings of ICIS*, (pp. 339-350). ICIS.

Curtis, B., Hefley, W. E., & Miller, S. (2001). *People capability maturity model*. Pittsburgh, PA: Carnegie Mellon University, Software Engineering Institute.

Dandapani, K. (2004). Success and failure in web-based financial services. *Communications of the ACM*, *47*(5), 31–33. doi:10.1145/986213.986233.

Davenport, T. H. (2005). The coming commoditization of processes. *Harvard Business Review*, *83*(6), 100–108. PMID:15942994.

David, I.T. (2005). Financial management shared services: A guide for federal users. *Journal of Government Financial Management*, 55-60.

Davis, E. W., & Spekman, E. R. (2003). *The extended enterprise: Gaining competitive advantage through collaborative supply chains*. FT Press.

De Caluwé, L., & Vermaak, H. (2003). *Learning to change: A guide for organization change agents*. London: Sage Publications.

de Geus, A. (2002). *The living company*. Boston: Harvard Business Press.

de Guerre, D., Noon, M., & Salter, S. (1997). *Syncrude Canada limited: A Canadian success story*. Paper presented at the Association for Quality and Participation Annual Spring Conference. Clevland, OH.

de Guerre, D. (2000). The codetermination of cultural change over time. *Systemic Practice and Action Research*, *13*(5), 645–663. doi:10.1023/A:1009529626810.

De Leeuw, A.C.J. (1982). *Organisaties: Management, analyse, ontwerp en veranderin*. Assen, Germany: van Gorcum.

de Oliveira, P., & Antonio (Eds.). (2012). *Green economy and good governance for sustainable development: Opportunities, promises and concerns*. United Nations University.

de Savigny, D., & Taghreed, A. (Eds.). (2009). Systems thinking for health systems strengthening. Geneva: Alliance for Health Policy and Systems Research, WHO.

Deel, B. (2008). *De algemene rekenkamer: Lessen uit ICT-projecten bij de overhead*.

DeGennaro, T. (2010). *The profile of corporately supported EA groups: Tactics for improving corporate management's support for EA in large firms*. Forrester.

Deloitte. (2011). *2011 global shared services survey*. Retrieved from http://www.deloitte.com/assets/Dcom-UnitedStates/Local%20Assets/Documents/IMOs/Shared%20Services/us_sdt_2011GlobalSharedServicesSurveyExecutiveSummary.pdf

Deming, E. W. (1982). *Out of the crisis*. Cambridge, MA: MIT Press.

Demos. (2012). *Public services and welfare*. Retrieved 23 August, 2012, from http://www.demos.co.uk/public-servicesandwelfare

Denning, P. J., & Hayes-Roth, R. (2006). Decision making in very large networks. *Communications of the ACM*, *49*(11), 19–23. doi:10.1145/1167838.1167852.

Denyer, S., & Lakshmi, R. (2012, August 1). In India, although power is restored, doubts remain. *Washington Post*.

Department of Commerce. (2003). *IT architecture capability maturity model*. Washington, DC: Department of Commerce, Government of the USA.

Department of Environment, Food and Rural Affairs, United Kingdom. (2012). *Adapting to climate change: Helping key sectors to adapt to climate change*. Retrieved from http://www.defra.gov.uk/publications/files/pb13740gov-summary-adapt-reports.pdf

Department of Environment, Food and Rural Development, United Kingdom. (2012). *Adapting to climate change: Evidence-based plan 2011/12*. Retrieved from http://www.defra.gov.uk/publications/files/pb13486-ep-adapting-climate-change.pdf

Dept, U. S. of Energy. (2009). *Smart grid system report*. Washington, DC: US Dept. of Energy.

Dettmer, H. W. (2011). *Systems thinking and the Cynefin framework: A strategic approach to managing complex systems*. Retrieved August 1, 2012 from http://engine-for-change.com/Weblog/2012/04/link-fuel-3/

DeVol, R., Bedroussian, A., Charuworn, A., Chatterjee, A., Kim, I., Kim, S., & Klowden, K. (2007). *An unhealthy America – The economic burden of chronic disease*. Santa Monica, CA: Milken Institute.

Dico, A. S. (2012). Towards whole-of-government EA with TOGAF and SOA. In Saha (Ed.), Enterprise Architecture for Connected E-Government – Practices and Innovations. Hershey, PA: IGI Global.

Dikmen, I., & Birgonul, M. T. (2003). Strategic perspective of Turkish construction companies. *Journal of Management Engineering*, *19*(1), 33–40. doi:10.1061/(ASCE)0742-597X(2003)19:1(33).

Dikshit, R. D. (1975). *The political geography of federalism: An inquiry into origins and stability*. New York: Wiley.

Dod, C. I. O. (2007). *Global information grid (GIG), architecture federation strategy, version 1.2*. Department Of Defense.

Dollery, B., Hallam, G., & Wallis, J. (2009). Shared services in Australian local government: A case study of the Queensland local government association model. *Economic Papers*, *27*(4), 343–354. doi:10.1111/j.1759-3441.2008.tb01048.x.

Dooley, K. (2002). Organizational complexity. In Warner, M. (Ed.), *International Encyclopedia of Business and Management* (pp. 5013–5022). London: Thompson Learning.

Dornbusch, R., Fischer, S., & Startz, R. (2010). *Macroeconomics*. New York: McGraw-Hill/Irwin.

Doucet, G., Gotze, J., Saha, P., & Bernard, S. A. (2009). *Coherency management: Architecting the enterprise for alignment, agility and assurance*. Bloomington, IN: AuthorHouse.

Doucet, G., Gtze, J., Bernard, S., & Saha, P. (2009). *Architecting the enterprise for alignment, agility and assurance*. International Enterprise Architecture Institute.

Drecun, V. (2003). *Federated enterprise offers a breakthrough for supply chain collaboration*. D.H. Brown Associates, Inc..

Dromey, R. G. (2006). Formalizing the transition from requirements to design. In Liu, Z., & He, J. (Eds.), *Mathematical Frameworks for Component Software, Models for Analysis and Synthesis* (pp. 173–206). London: World Scientific. doi:10.1142/9789812772831_0006.

Drucker, P. (1999). *Management challenges for the 21st century*. New York: Harper Business Press.

Drucker, P. F. (1954). Building the structure. In *The Practice of Management*. New York: Harper & Row.

Drucker, P. F. (1957). *Management in de praktijk*. G.J.A. Ruys Uitgeversmaatschappij N.V..

Dryzek, J. S., Downes, , Hunold, , & Schlosberg,. (2003). *Green states and social movements: Environmentalism in the United States, United Kingdom, Germany and Norway*. Oxford, UK: Oxford University Press. doi:10.1093/0199249024.001.0001.

Dutta, S., & Mia, I. (2010). *Global information technology report 2009-2010 – ICT for sustainability*. Geneva, Switzerland: INSEAD and World Economic Forum.

Dutta, S., & Mia, I. (2011). *Global information technology report 2010-2011: ICT for sustainability*. Geneva, Switzerland: INSEAD and World Economic Forum.

Dye, T. R. (1990). *American federalism: Competition among governments*. Lexington, MA: Lexington Books.

EARF. (n.d.). Retrieved July 15, 2012, from http://earf.meraka.org.za/earfhome/our-projects-1/completed-projects/?

Eaves, D. (1992). *The prospects of a formal discipline of software engineering*. Monash University.

Edwards Deming, W. (n.d.). *Wikipedia.* Retrieved August 1, 2012, from http://en.wikipedia.org/wiki/W._Edwards_Deming

Egelhoff, W. G. (1982). Strategy and structure in multinational corporations: An information-processing approach. *Administrative Science Quarterly, 27*(3), 435–458. doi:10.2307/2392321.

Eisenhardt, K., & Sull, D. (2001, January). Strategy as simple rules. *Harvard Business Review*, 106–116. PMID:11189455.

EIU. (2011). *The complexity challenge – How businesses are bearing up.* London: Economist Intelligence Unit.

Elazar, D. J., & Merkaz Ha-Yerushalmi Le-'Inyene Tsibur U-Medinah. (1991). *Federal systems of the world: A handbook of federal, confederal, and autonomy arrangements.* Harlow, UK: Longman Current Affairs.

Elazar, D. J. (1973). Curse by bigness or toward a post-technocratic federalism. *Publius, 3*(1), 239–298.

Elazar, D. J. (1997). Contrasting unitary and federal systems. *International Political Science Review, 18*(3), 237–251. doi:10.1177/019251297018003002.

Emery, F. E. (1959). *Characteristics of socio-technical systems: The emergence of a new paradigm of work.* Canberra, Australia: ANU/CCE.

Emery, F. E. (1972). Characteristics of socio-technical systems. In Davis, L. E., & Taylor, J. C. (Eds.), *Design of Jobs* (pp. 157–186). Harmondsworth, UK: Penguin Books.

Emery, F. E. (1976). *In pursuit of ideals.* Canberra, Australia: ANU/CCE.

Emery, F. E., & Thorsrud, E. (1969). *Form and content in industrial democracy.* London: Tavistock.

Emery, F., & Trist, E. (1965). The causal texture of organizational environments. *Human Relations, 18*, 21–32. doi:10.1177/001872676501800103.

Emery, M. (1993). *Participative design for participative democracy.* Canberra, Australia: ANU/CCE.

Emery, M. (2000). The current version of Emery's open systems theory. *Systemic Practice and Action Research, 13*(5), 685–703. doi:10.1023/A:1009577509972.

Erbil, Y., Acar, E., & Akinciturk, N. (2010). Evidence on innovation as a competitive strategy in a developing market: Turkish building material suppliers' point of view. In *Proceedings of the Second International Conference on Construction in Developing Countries (ICCIDC-II).* Retrieved from http://acare2.tripod.com/academic/Erbil_et_al_2010.pdf

Erl, T. (2005). *Service-oriented architecture: concepts, technology, and design.* Hoboken, NJ: Prentice Hall.

Ernst, A. (2008). Enterprise architecture management patterns. In *Proceedings of the Pattern Languages of Programs Conference 2008.* Nashville, TN: PLoP.

Ernst, A. (2010). *Pattern-based approach to enterprise architecture management.* (PhD thesis). Technische Universität München, München, Germany.

Espejo, R., & Harnden, R. (1989). *The viable system model: Interpretations and applications of stafford beer's VSM.* Chichester, UK: John Wiley.

EU ETP WG-3. (2010). *Energy retailers' perspective on the deployment of smart grids in Europe.* Flanders: EU.

European Union. (2012). *Redesigning health for Europe for 2020.* Luxembourg: European Union.

Eurostat. (2007). Measuring progress towards a more sustainable europe: 2007 monitoring report of the EU sustainable development strategy. Eurostat.

Evans, C. (2007). Modelling service. *Business Strategy Review*, 53–59.

Eveleens, J. L., & Verhoef, C. (2010). The rise and fall of the chaos report figures. *IEEE Software Journal, 27*, 30–36. doi:10.1109/MS.2009.154.

Evers, M. (2004). *Mechanisms to support organizational learning: The integration of action learning tools into multidisciplinary design team practice.* Breukelen: University Nyenrode.

Fajnzylber, P., Lederman, D., & Loayza, N. (2002). Inequality and violent crime. *Journal of Law and Economics.* Retrieved form http://siteresources.worldbank.org/DEC/Resources/Crime&Inequality.pdf

Falshaw, J. R., & Glaister, K. W. (2006). Evidence on formal strategic planning and company performance. *Management Decision*, *44*(1), 9–30. doi:10.1108/00251740610641436.

Farndale, E., Paauwe, J., & Hoeksema, L. (2009). Insourcing HR: Shared service centres in the Netherlands. *International Journal of Human Resource Management*, *20*(3), 544–561. doi:10.1080/09585190802707300.

Fayol, H. (1918). *Administration industrielle et générale, prévoyance, organisation, commandement, coordination, controle*. Paris: H. Dunod et E. Pinat.

FDA. (2011). Building the infrastructure to drive and support personalized medicine. Retrieved on July 30, 2012 from http://www.fda.gov/AboutFDA/ReportsManualsForms/Reports/ucm274440.htm

Federalist. (1966). *The federalist papers, a collection of essays written in support of the constitution of the United States*. Garden City, NY: Anchor Books.

Fenton, E. M., & Pettigrew, A. M. (2000). Theoretical perspectives on new forms of organizing. In Pettigrew, A. M., & Fenton, E. M. (Eds.), *The Innovating Organization* (pp. 1–46). Thousand Oaks, CA: Sage. doi:10.4135/9781446219379.n1.

Fereira, N., Kar, J., & Trigeorgis, L. (2009, March). Option games: The key to competing in capital-intensive industries. *Harvard Business Review*.

Fernandez, G., Zhao, L., & Wijegunaratne, I. (2003). Patterns of federated architecture. *Journal of Object Technology*, *2*(3), 135–149. doi:10.5381/jot.2003.2.3.a4.

Fichman, R. (2004). Real options and IT platform adoption: Implications for theory and practice. *Information Systems Research*, *15*(2), 132–154. doi:10.1287/isre.1040.0021.

Filippov, M., Ordeshook, P. C., & Shvetsova, O. (2003). *Designing federalism: A theory of self-sustainable federal institutions*. New York: Cambridge University Press.

Fishenden, J., Johnson, M., Nelson, K., Polin, G., Rijpma, G., & Stolz, P. (2006). The new world of government work: Transforming the business of government with the power of information technology. *Microsoft Public Services and e-Government Strategy Discussion Paper*.

Fisher, R. A. (1925). *Statistical methods for research workers*. Cosmo Publications.

Flood, L. R. (1999). *Rethinking the fifth discipline – Learning within the unknowable*. London: Routledge.

Floyd, C. (1992). Software development as reality construction. In Floyd, C., Budde, R., Zullighoven, H., & Keil-Slawik, R. (Eds.), *Software Development and Reality Construction*. Berlin: Springer-Verlag. doi:10.1007/978-3-642-76817-0_10.

Folke, C. Carpenter, Elmqvist, Gunderson, Holling, & Walker. (2002). *Resilience and sustainable development: Building adaptive capacity in a world of transformations*. Retrieved from http://era-mx.org/biblio/Resilience.pdf

Folke, C. Colding, & Berkes (2002). Building resilience for adaptive capacity in social-ecological systems. In F. Berkes, J. Colding, & C. Folke (Eds.), Navigating Social-Ecological Systems: Building Resilience for Complexity and Change. Cambridge, UK: Cambridge University Press.

Follett, M. P. (1927). *Dynamic administration*. New York: Harper & Brothers Publishers (Reprint 1942).

Forst, L. I. (1997, January). Febraury). Fulfilling the promises of shared services. *Strategy and Leadership*. doi:10.1108/eb054578.

Forum, T. M. (n.d.). *Business process framework (eTOM)*. Retrieved 10 28, 2012, from http://www.tmforum.org/BusinessProcessFramework/1647/home.html

Foster, J. L. (1978). Regionalism and innovation in the American states. *The Journal of Politics*, *40*(1), 179–187. doi:10.2307/2129981.

Frampton, K. Barrow, et al. (2005). A study of the in-practice application of a commercial software architecture. In *Proceedings of the Australian Software Engineering Conference (ASWEC 2005)*. Brisbane, Australia: IEEE Computer Society.

Friedman, M. (1937). The use of ranks to avoid the assumption of normality implicit in the analysis of variance. *Journal of the American Statistical Association*, *32*(200), 675–701. doi:10.1080/01621459.1937.10503522.

Friedman, M. (1939). A correction: The use of ranks to avoid the assumption of normality implicit in the analysis of variance. *Journal of the American Statistical Association, 34*(205), 109.

Friedman, T. L. (2005). *The world is flat: A brief history of the twenty-first century*. New York: Farrar, Straus and Giroux.

Funston, F., & Wagner, S. (2010). *Surviving and thriving in uncertainty: Creating the risk intelligent enterprise*. Hoboken, NJ: John Wiley & Sons.

Fuzzy Pay-Off Method for Real Option Valuation. (n.d.). *Wikipedia*. Retrieved April 10, 2011, from http://en.wikipedia.org/wiki/Fuzzy_Pay-Off_Method_for_Real_Option_Valuation

Gaballah, A. D., & Tondeur. (2002). Education, employment and sustainable development in the European Union. *Jounal of Materials*. Retrieved from http://iWeb.tms.org/ED/JOM-0211-24.pdf

Galbraith, J. R. (1973). *Designing complex organizations*. Reading, MA: Addison-Wesley Pub. Co..

Galbraith, J. R. (1995). *Designing organizations: An executive briefing on strategy, structure, and process*. San Francisco: Jossey-Bass Publishers.

Galbraith, J. R. (2000). *Designing the global corporation*. San Francisco, CA: Jossey-Bass.

Gall, N. (2010). From hierarchy to panarchy – Hybrid thinking's resilient network of renewal. *Gartner Research ID Number: G00209754*.

Galliers, R., & Currie, W. (Eds.). (2011). The Oxford handbook of management information systems. Oxford, UK: Oxford.

Gallopín, G. (2003). *A systems approach to sustainability and sustainable development*. Retrieved from http://www.eclac.org/publicaciones/xml/8/12288/lcl1864i.pdf

Gantt, H. L. (1903). Aggraphical daily balance in manufacture. *Transactions of the American Society of Mechanical Engineers, 24*, 1322–1336.

GAO. (2010). *Organizational transformation - A framework for assessing and improving enterprise architecture management (version 2.0)*. Washington, DC: United States Government Accountability Office.

Garcia, L. (1993). A new role for government in standard setting? *StandardView, 1*(2), 2–10. doi:10.1145/174690.174691.

Garcia-Lorenzo, L., Mitleton-Kelly, E., & Galliers, R.D. (2003). Organizational complexity – Organizing through the generation and sharing of knowledge. *International Journal of Knowledge, Culture and Change Management*.

Gartner. (2009). *Gartner identifies ten enterprise architecture pitfalls*. Retrieved 13 August, 2012, from http://www.gartner.com/it/page.jsp?id=1159617

Gartner. (2012). *Garter identifies ten enterprise architecture pitfalls*. Retrieved from http://www.gartner.com/it/page.jsp?id=1159617

Gaziulusoy, İ. (2011). *Complexity and co-evolution*. Retrieved August 10, 2012 from http://systeminnovationforsustainability.com/tag/complex-system/

GEA Groeiplatform. (n.d.). Retrieved from www.groeiplatformgea.nl

Gell-Mann, M. (1994). Complex adaptive systems. In Cowan, G. A., Pines, D., & Meltzer, D. (Eds.), *Complexity: Metaphors, models, and reality* (pp. 17–45). Reading, MA: Addison-Wesley.

Gell-Mann, M. (1994). *The quark and the jaguar: Adventures in the simple and the complex*. San Francisco, CA: W.H. Freeman. doi:10.1063/1.2808634.

Gershenson, C. (2002). Complex philosophy. In *Proceedings of the 1st Biennial Seminar on Philosophical, Methodological & Epistemological Implications of Complexity Theory*. La Habana, Cuba: Academic Press.

Gershenson, C. (2004). Introduction to random Boolean networks. In M. Bedau, P. Husbands, T. Hutton, S. Kumar, & H. Suzuki (Eds.), *Proceedings of the 9th International Conference on the Simulation and Synthesis of Living Systems,* (pp. 160-173). Retrieved from http://arxiv.org/abs/nlin/0408006

Gershenson, C. (2007). *Design and control of self-organizing systems*. Mexico City: CopIt ArXives.

Gharajedaghi, J. (2004). *Systems methodology: A holistic language of interaction and design - Seeing through chaos and understanding complexities*. Retrieved August 9, 2012 from http://www.interactdesign.com/JGsystems.htm

Gharajedaghi, J. (2011). *Systems thinking: Managing chaos and complexity – A platform for designing business architecture*. Amsterdam: Morgan Kaufmann.

Ghoshal, S., & Bartlett, C. A. (1990). The multinational corporation as an interorganizational network. *Academy of Management Review, 15*(4), 625–626.

Gibbins, R. (2001). Local governance and federal political systems. *International Social Science Journal, 53*(167), 163–170. doi:10.1111/1468-2451.00305.

Glaister, K. W., Dincer, O., Tatoglu, E., Demirbag, M., & Zaim, S. (2008). A causal analysis of formal strategic planning and firm performance: Evidence from an emerging country. *Management Decision, 46*(3), 365–391. doi:10.1108/00251740810863843.

Glemarec, J., & de Olivera. (2012). The role of the visible hand of public institutions in creating a sustainable future. *Public Administration and Development*. Retrieved from http://onlinelibrary.wiley.com/doi/10.1002/pad.1631/pdf

Glenn, E. J. (1996). *Chaos theory: The essentials for military applications*. Newport, RI: Naval War College.

Glissman, S., & Sanz, J. (2009). *A comparative review of business architecture: IBM research report*. San Jose, CA: IBM.

Goldenfeld, N., & Kadanoff, L. P. (1999). Simple lessons from complexity. *Science, 284*(5411), 87–89. doi:10.1126/science.284.5411.87 PMID:10102823.

Goldkuhl, G. (2006). Action and media in interorganizational interaction. *Communications of the ACM, 49*(5), 53–57. doi:10.1145/1125944.1125975.

Gooderham, P. N., & Ulset, S. (2002). 'Beyond the m-form': Towards a critical test of the new form. *International Journal of the Economics of Business, 9*(1), 117–138. doi:10.1080/13571510110103010.

Gore, J. (1996). *Chaos, complexity, and the military*. National Defense University.

Graham, A. (2012). *The enterprise data model – A framework for enterprise data architecture* (2nd ed.). Koios Associates.

Grant, G., McKnight, S., Uruthirapathy, A., & Brown, A. (2007). Designing governance for shared services organizations in the public service. *Government Information Quarterly, 24*, 522–538. doi:10.1016/j.giq.2006.09.005.

Graves, T. (2012). *The enterprise as story*. Essex, UK: Tetradian Books.

Gray, V. (1973). Innovation in the states: A diffusion study. *The American Political Science Review, 67*(4), 1174–1185. doi:10.2307/1956539.

Greefhorst, D., & Proper, H. A. (2011). *Architecture principles – The cornerstones of enterprise architecture*. Berlin: Springer. doi:10.1007/978-3-642-20279-7.

Grefen, P., Ludwig, H., Dan, A., & Angelov, S. (2006). An analysis of web services support for dynamic business process outsourcing. *Information and Software Technology, 48*(11), 1115–1134. doi:10.1016/j.infsof.2006.03.010.

Gregor, S., Hart, D., & Martin, N. (2007). Enterprise architectures: Enablers of business strategy and IS/IT alignment in government. *Information Technology & People, 20*(2), 96–120. doi:10.1108/09593840710758031.

Grenadier, S. (2000). Option exercise games: The intersection of real options and game theory. *Journal of Applied Corporate Finance, 13*(2), 99–107. doi:10.1111/j.1745-6622.2000.tb00057.x.

Grimm, M. Klasen, & McKay (Eds.). (2007). Determinants of pro-poor growth: Analytical issues and findings from country studies. New York: Palgrave Macmillan.

Guida, G., & Tasso, C. (1994). *Design and development of knowledge-based systems: From life cycle to development methodology*. Chichester, UK: John Wiley & Sons.

Güleş, H. K., Türkmen, M., & Özilhan, D. (2011). Tekstil ve otomotiv yan sanayi küçük ve orta ölçekli işletmelerinde üretim ve işletme performansı. *İktisat İşletme ve Finans, 26*(304), 79-112.

Gulev, R. E. (2009). Cultural repercussions. *Industrial Management & Data Systems*, *109*(6), 793–808. doi:10.1108/02635570910968045.

Gunday, G., Ulusoy, G., Kilic, K., & Alpkan, L. (2011). Effects of innovation types on firm performance. *International Journal of Production Economics*, *133*(2), 662–676. doi:10.1016/j.ijpe.2011.05.014.

Gupta, A. K., & Govindarajan, V. (2000). Knowledge flows within multinational corporations. *Strategic Management Journal*, *21*(4), 473–496. doi:10.1002/(SICI)1097-0266(200004)21:4<473::AID-SMJ84>3.0.CO;2-I.

Haas, L. M., Lin, E. T., & Roth, M. A. (2002). Data integration Through database federation. *IBM Systems Journal*, *41*(4), 578–596. doi:10.1147/sj.414.0578.

Hagan, P. J. (2004). *Guide to the (evolving) enterprise architecture body of knowledge*. The MITRE Corporation.

Halstead, D., Somerville, N., Straker, B., & Ward, C. (2009). The way to gov 2.0: An enterprise approach to web 2.0 in government. *Microsoft US Public Sector White Paper*.

Hamel, G. (2007). *The future of management*. Boston: Harvard Business School Press.

Hammer, M., & Champy. (1993). *Reengineering the corporation: A manifesto for business revolution*. New York: Harper.

Hammer, M. (1990, July/August). Reengineering work: Don't automate, obliterate. *Harvard Business Review*, 104–112.

Hammer, M. (2007). The process audit. *Harvard Business Review*, *85*(4), 111–123. PMID:17432158.

Hammer, M., & Stanton, S. (1999). How process enterprises really work. *Harvard Business Review*, *77*(6), 108–118. PMID:10662000.

Handy, C. (1992). Balancing corporate power: A new federalist paper. *Harvard Business Review*, *70*(6), 59–72. PMID:10122692.

Handy, C. B. (1989). *The age of unreason*. Boston, MA: Harvard Business School Press.

Handy, C. B. (1994). *The age of paradox*. Boston, MA: Harvard Business School Press.

Handy, C. B. (1999). Subsidiarity is the word for it. *Across the Board*, *36*(6), 7–8.

Han, K., Oh, W., Im, K. S., Oh, H., Pinsonneault, A., & Chang, R. M. (2012). Value cocreation and wealth spillover in open innovation alliances. *Management Information Systems Quarterly*, *36*(1), 291–316.

Harrison, H. (2009). Togaf™ 9 certified study guide. The Open Group, Van Haren Publishing. ISBN 9 789087 535704

Hasselbring, W. (1997). Federated integration of replicated information within hospitals: System design and architecture. *International Journal on Digital Libraries*, *1*(3), 192–208. doi:10.1007/s007990050016.

Hausmann, K. (2011). *Sustainable enterprise architecture*. Boca Raton, FL: CRC Press. doi:10.1201/b10793.

Hawawini, G., Subramanian, V., & Verdin, P. (2003). Is performance driven by industry- Or firm-specific factors? A new look at the evidence. *Strategic Management Journal*, *24*, 1–16. doi:10.1002/smj.278.

Hayek, F. A. (1945). The use of knowledge in society. *The American Economic Review*, *35*(4), 519–530.

Henderson, J. C., & Venkatraman, N. (1993). Strategic alignment: Leveraging information technology for transforming organizations. *IBM Systems Journal*, *32*(1), 4–16. doi:10.1147/sj.382.0472.

Herlands, D., & Brown, K. (2005). *Strategies for chronic disease management*. Washington, DC: The Advisory Board Company.

Herring, H., & Sorrell (Eds.). (2009). *Energy efficiency and sustainable consumption: The rebound effect*. New York: Palgrave McMillan.

Herzberg, F. (1966). *Work and the nature of man*. Ohio.

Herzog, S. (n.d.). *Gharajedaghi*. Retrieved June 28, 2012 from http://www.aleph.at/books/gharajedaghi.html

Hevner, A. R., March, S. T., Park, J., & Ram, S. (2004). Design science in information systems research. *Management Information Systems Quarterly*, *28*, 75–106.

Heylighen, F., & Cilliers, , et al. (2007). Complexity and philosophy. In Bogg, J, & Geyer, R (Eds.), *Complexity, Science and Society*. Oxford, UK: Radcliffe Publishing.

Heywood, S., Spungin, J., & Turnbull, D. (2007). Cracking the complexity code. *The McKinsey Quarterly,* (2): 85–95.

Hill, T. P. (1977). On goods and services. *The Review of Income and Wealth, 23*(4), 315–338. doi:10.1111/j.1475-4991.1977.tb00021.x.

Himmelstein, D. U., Thorne, D., Warren, E., & Woolhandler, S. (2009). Medical bankruptcy in the United States, 2007 – Results of a national study. *The American Journal of Medicine, 122*(8), 741–746. doi:10.1016/j.amjmed.2009.04.012 PMID:19501347.

Hjort-Madsen, K. (2009). *Architecting government understanding enterprise architecture adoption in the public sector. (PhD-Thesis).* Copenhagen, Denmark: The IT University.

Hodgkinson, S. L. (1998). The role of the corporate IT function in the federal IT organization. In Earl, M. J. (Ed.), *Information Management: The Organizational Dimension* (pp. 247–269). New York: Oxford University Press.

Holden, L. M. (2005). Complex adaptive systems: Concept analysis. *Journal of Advanced Nursing, 52*(6), 651–657. doi:10.1111/j.1365-2648.2005.03638.x PMID:16313378.

Holland, J. H. (1992). *Adaptation in natural and artificial systems: An introductory analysis with applications to biology, control, and artificial intelligence.* Cambridge, MA: MIT Press.

Holland, J. H. (1992). Complex adaptive systems. *Daedalus, 121*(1), 17–30.

Holt, J., & Perry, S. (2010). *Modelling enterprise architectures.* The Institution of Engineering and Technology.

Homer, J. B., & Hirsch, G. B. (2006). System dynamics modeling for public health – Background and opportunities. *American Journal of Public Health, 96*(3). doi:10.2105/AJPH.2005.062059 PMID:16449591.

Hoogervorst, J. (2011). A framework for enterprise engineering. *International Journal of Internet & Enterprise Management, 7*(1), 5–40. doi:10.1504/IJIEM.2011.038381.

Hoogervorst, J. A. P. (2004). Enterprise architecture: Enabling integration, agility and change. *International Journal of Cooperative Information Systems, 13*(3), 213–233. doi:10.1142/S021884300400095X.

Hoogerworst, J. A. P. (2009). *Enterprise governance and enterprise engineering.* Diemen, The Netherlands: Springer. doi:10.1007/978-3-540-92671-9.

Hovhannisian, K. (2001). *Exploring on the technology landscapes: Real options thinking in the context of the complexity theory.* Paper presented at the DRUID Winter Conference. Aalborg, Denmark.

Howcroft, D., & Richardson, H. (2012). The back office goes global: Exploring connections and contradictions in shared service centres. *Work, Employment and Society, 26*(1), 111–127. doi:10.1177/0950017011426309.

Howe, J. (2009). *Crowdsourcing: Why the power of the crowd is driving the future of business.* New York: Three Rivers Press.

Hsiao, D. K. (1992). Federated databases and systems: Part 1 - A tutorial on their data sharing. *The VLDB Journal, 1*(1), 127–179. doi:10.1007/BF01228709.

Huang, C., Kao, H., & Li, H. (2007). Decision on enterprise computing solutions for an international tourism. *International Journal of Information Technology & Decision Making, 6*(4), 687–700. doi:10.1142/S0219622007002666.

Huijboom, N., & Van Den Broek, T. (2011, March/April). Open data – An international comparison of strategies. *European Journal of ePractice,* (12), 4 – 16.

Iacob, M.-E., Jonkers, H., Lankhorst, M. M., & Proper, H. A. (2009). *ArchiMate 1.0 specification.* The Open Group.

IDS. (n.d.). Retrieved from http://www.ids-scheer.nl/nl/ARIS/ARIS_ARIS_Platform/28569.html

IFIP-IFAC Task Force. (1999). GERAM - The generalised enterprise reference architecture and methodology. In Bernus, P., Nemes, L., & Schmidt, G. (Eds.), *Handbook on Enterprise Architecture* (pp. 22–64). Berlin: Springer.

Ilic, M. (2010). Transforming SCADA into dynamic monitoring and decision systems: The missing link in smart grids. In *Proceedings of the IEEE Power and Energy Society General Meeting 2010.* IEEE.

Independence Partners. (2013). *Complex adaptive systems theory elements.* Retrieved January 3, 2013 from http://www.dspmatch.com/

Infomag. (2008, October). Devremülke alternatif geliyor!. [Alternative arriving to timeshared residences!. *Infomag*, 32-34.

Infomag. (2008, October). TOKİ'nin gelmesi gereken noktayı hayal eden başkaları var. [There are others who imagine where TOKİ should reach]. *Infomag*, 115-118.

Infosys. (2011). *Infosys partners with Philips in the journey to transform their shared service centers (SSC)*. Bangalore, India: Infosys.

INSEE & OECD. (2008). *Survey of existing approaches to measuring socio-economic progress*. Commission on Measurement of Economic Performance and Social Progress. Retrieved from http://www.stiglitz-sen-fitoussi.fr/documents/

International Labor Organization (ILO). (2007). *Decent work for sustainable development*. Retrieved from http://www.ilo.org/public/english/standards/relm/ilc/ilc96/pdf/rep-i-a.pdf

Irdesel, I., Ertek, G., & Demirelli, A. (2012). *A graph-based methodology for constructing expert systems and its application in the strategic management domain* (Working Paper).

Ishikawa, K. (1988). *What is total quality control? The Japanese way*. Prentice Hall.

ISO15288. (2000). *Systems and software engineering – System life cycle processes*. Geneva: ISO.

ISO15704. (2000). *Industrial automation systems – Requirements for enterprise reference architectures and methodologies*. Geneva: ISO TC184.SC5.WG1.

Jackson, M. (2011). *Practical foresight guide*. Retrieved from www.shapingtomorrow.com

Jackson, T. (2005). *Motivating sustainable consumption: A review of evidence on consumer behavior and behavioural change*. Retrieved from http://www.c2p2online.com/documents/MotivatingSC.pdf

Jahani, B., Javadein, S., & Jafari, H. (2010). Measurement of enterprise architecture readiness within organizations. *Business Strategy Series*, *11*(3), 177–191. doi:10.1108/17515631011043840.

Janssen, M., & Hjort-Madsen, K. (2007). Analyzing enterprise architecture in national governments: The cases of Denmark and Netherlands. In *Proceedings of the 40th Annual Hawaii International Conference on Systems Sciences (HICSS'07)*. IEEE.

Janssen, M., & Kuk, G. (2006). *A complex adaptive system perspective of enterprise architecture in electronic government*. Paper presented at the 39th Hawaii International Conference on System Sciences. Hawaii, HI.

Janssen, M., & Wagenaar, R. (2004). An analysis of a shared services centre in e-government. In *Proceedings of the 37th Annual Hawaii International Conference on System Sciences (HICSS'04)*. IEEE.

Janssen, M., & Joha, A. (2006). Motives for establishing shared service centers in public administrations. *International Journal of Information Management*, *26*, 102–115. doi:10.1016/j.ijinfomgt.2005.11.006.

Janssen, M., Joha, A., & Zuurmond, A. (2009). Simulation and animation for adopting shared services: Evaluating and comparing alternative arrangements. *Government Information Quarterly*, *26*, 15–24. doi:10.1016/j.giq.2008.08.004.

Jennings, N. R., & Wooldridge, M. (1995). Applying agent technology. *Journal of Applied AI*, *9*(4), 351–361.

Jensen, A. Ø. (2010). *Government enterprise architecture adoption: A systemic-discursive critique and reconceptualisation*. (MSc Thesis). IT University, Copenhagen, Denmark.

Joffe, M., & Mindell, J. (2006). Complex causal process diagrams for analyzing the health impacts of policy interventions. *American Journal of Public Health*, *96*(3). doi:10.2105/AJPH.2005.063693 PMID:16449586.

Joha, A., & Janssen, M. (2010). Public-private partnerships, outsourcing or shared service centres? Motives and intents for selecting sourcing configurations. *Transforming Government: People. Process and Policy*, *4*(3), 232–248.

Johnson, M. W. (2010). *Seizing the white space – Business model innovation for growth and renewal*. Boston: Harvard Business Press.

Johnston, A. (2005). *Masters of order and unorder*. Retrieved August 10, 2012 from http://www.agilearchitect. org/agile/articles/order%20and%20unorder.asp

Johnston, S., & Menguc, B. (2007). Subsidiary size and the level of subsidiary autonomy in multinational corporations: A quadratic model investigation of Australian subsidiaries. *Journal of International Business Studies*, *38*(5), 787–801. doi:10.1057/palgrave.jibs.8400294.

Jones, J. C. (1988). Softecnica. In Thackara, J. (Ed.), *Design after modernism*. London: Thames and Hudson.

Jonkers, H., van Burren, R., Arbab, F., de Boer, F., Bonsangue, M. M., Bosma, H., & ter Doest, H. (2003). Towards a language for coherent enterprise architecture descriptions. In *Proceedings of the 7th IEEE International EDOC Conference (EDOC 2003)*. Brisbane, Australia: IEEE Computer Society.

Josey, A. et al. (2009). *TOGAF version 9 – A pocket guide* (2nd ed.). Amsterdam: Van Haren Publishing.

Joyce, D. (2011). *We don't need no frickin architects*. Retrieved August 6, 2012 from http://leanandkanban. wordpress.com/2011/05/18/we-dont-need-no-frickin-architects/

Jreisat, J. E. (2002). *Comparative public administration*. Westview Press.

Kagerman, H., Osterle, H., & Jordan, J. M. (2011). *IT driven business models – Global case studies in transformation*. Hoboken, NJ: John Wiley & Sons.

Kandjani, H., & Bernus, P. (2011). Engineering self-designing enterprises as complex systems using extended axiomatic design theory. *IFAC Papers OnLine*, *18*(1), 11943–11948.

Kaner, M., & Karni, R. (2007). Engineering design of a service system: An empirical study. *Information Knowledge Systems Management*, *6*, 235–263.

Kanie, N. Betsil, Zondervan, Biermann, & Young. (2012). A charter moment: Restructuring governance for sustainability. *Public Administration and Development*. Retrieved from http://onlinelibrary.wiley.com/doi/10.1002/pad.1625/pdf

Kaplan, S. M. (2000). Co-evolution in socio-technical systems. In *Proceedings of Computer Supported Cooperative Work (CSCW 2000)*. Philadelphia: ACM Press.

Kaplan, R. S., Norton, D. P., & Barrows, E. A. (2008). *Developing the strategy: Vision, value gaps, and analysis*. Boston: Harvard Business School Publishing Corporation.

Kaplan, R. S., & Porter, M. E. (2011, September). How to solve the cost crisis in healthcare. *Harvard Business Review*. PMID:21939127.

Kappelman, L., Mcginnis, T., Pettite, A., & Sidorova, A. (2008). Enterprise architecture: Charting the territory for academic research. In *Proceedings of the Fourteenth Americas Conference on Information Systems*. Toronto, Canada: IEEE.

Karanam, R., Nambiar, A., Srivastava, M., Shukla, B. K., & Chandramouli, A. (2011). *Enterprise architecture for utilities*. Bangalore: Infosys.

Karimi, J., & Konsynski, B. R. (1991). Globalization and information management strategies. *Journal of Management Information Systems*, *7*(4), 7–26.

Karmis, D., & Norman, W. J. (2005). *Theories of federalism: A reader*. New York, NY: Palgrave Macmillan.

Karokola, G., & Yngström, L. (2009). Discussing e-government maturity models for the developing world - Security view. *ISSA*, 81-98.

Karpen, I. O., & Bove, , et al. (2012). Linking service-dominant logic and strategic business practice: A conceptual model of a service-dominant orientation. *Journal of Service Research*, *15*(21).

Kauffman, S. A. (1993). *The origins of order: Self-organization and selection in evolution*. New York: Oxford University Press.

Kearns, G. S., & Sabherwal, R. (2006). Strategic alignment between business and information technology: A knowledge-based view of behaviors, outcome, and consequences. *Journal of Management Information Systems*, *23*(3), 129–162. doi:10.2753/MIS0742-1222230306.

Keeble, L. (1951). *Principles and practice of town and country planning*. London: Estates Gazette.

Kemp, R. Parto, & Gibson. (2005). Governance for sustainable development: Moving from theory to practice. *International Journal of Sustainable Development*. Retrieved from http://kemp.unu-merit.nl/pdf/IJSD%20 8(1)%2002%20Kemp%20et%20al.pdf

Kemp, R., & Martens. (2007). Sustainable development: How to manage something that is subjective and never can be achieved? *Sustainability: Science, Policy and Practice*. Retrieved from http://sspp.proquest.com/archives/vol3iss2/0703-007.kemp.html

Kickert, W. J. M., & Van Gigch, J. P. (1979). A metasystem approach to organizational decision making. *Management Science, 25*(12). doi:10.1287/mnsc.25.12.1217.

Kim, W., Choi, B. J., Hong, E. K., Kim, S. K., & Lee, D. (2003). A taxonomy of dirty data. *Data Mining and Knowledge Discovery, 7*(1), 81–99. doi:10.1023/A:1021564703268.

Kincaid, J. (2001). Economic policy-making: Advantages and disadvantages of the federal model. *International Social Science Journal, 53*(167).

King, P. T. (1982). *Federalism and federation*. Baltimore, MD: Johns Hopkins University Press.

Kirby, M. W., & Rosenhead, J. (2011). Patrick Blackett: Profiles in operations research. In *International Series in Operations Research & Management Science. 147*, 1. Springer doi:10.1007/978-1-4419-6281-2_1.

KL. (2012). Work instructions, form-based application, housing support, first-time application. *Association of Danish Local Governments*. Retrieved August 20, 2012 from http://www.kl.dk/ImageVault/Images/id_53025/scope_0/ImageVaultHandler.aspx

Kogut, B., & Zander, U. (1993). Knowledge of the firm and the evolutionary theory of the multinational corporation. *Journal of International Business Studies, 24*(4), 625–645. doi:10.1057/palgrave.jibs.8490248.

Kogut, B., & Zander, U. (2003). A memoir and reflection: Knowledge and an evolutionary theory of the multinational firm 10 years later. *Journal of International Business Studies, 34*(6), 505–515. doi:10.1057/palgrave.jibs.8400066.

Koh, L., Demirbag, M., Bayraktar, E., Tatoglu, E., & Zaim, S. (2007). The impact of supply chain management practices on performance of SMEs. *Industrial Management & Data Systems, 107*(1), 103–124. doi:10.1108/02635570710719089.

Kolmogorov, A. N. (1969). On the logical foundations of information theory and probability theory. *Problems of Information Transmission, 5*(3), 1–4.

Kombit. (2012). *Fælleskommunal rammearkitektur – Konkurrence, digitalisering og sikker drift*. Retrieved June 1, 2012, from http://www.kombit.dk/rammearkitektur

Kombit. (2012). *Fælleskommunal rammearkitektur – Godkendelse af centrale elementer*. Retrieved June 1, 2012, from http://www.kombit.dk/rammearkitektur

Komiyama, H. Takeuchi, Shiroyama, & Mino (Eds.). (2011). Sustainability science: A multidisciplinary approach. United Nations University Press.

Korhonen, J. J. (2012). *Out-of-box requires lesser mind*. Retrieved August 9, 2012 from http://www.ebizq.net/blogs/agile_enterprise/2012/05/out-of-box-requires-lesser-mind.php

KPMG. (2011). *Confronting complexity – Research findings and insights*. KPMG International. Publication Number 110307.

KPMG. (2012). *Expect the unexpected – Building business value in a changing world*. KPMG International.

KPMG. (2012). *Transforming healthcare – From volume to value*. KPMG International.

Krafzig, D., Banke, K., & Slama, D. (2004). *Enterprise SOA: Service-oriented architecture best practices*. Upper Saddle River, NJ: Prentice Hall.

Kreklow, S. R., & Kinney, A. S. (2007). The effective organization of administration functions through shared services. *Government Finance Review, 23*(3), 61–62.

Krugman, P., & Wells. (2012). *Microeconomics*. World Publishers.

Kruskal, W. H., & Wallis, W. A. (1952). Use of ranks in one-criterion variance analysis. *Journal of the American Statistical Association, 47*(260), 583–621. doi:10.1080/0 1621459.1952.10483441.

Kudryavtsev, D., & Grigoriev, L. (2011). Systemic approach towards enterprise functional decomposition. In *Proceedings of the 2011 IEEE Conference on Commerce and Enterprise Computing*, (pp. 310-317). IEEE.

Kumar, K., & Hillegersberg, J. V. (2004). New architectures for financial services. *Communications of the ACM, 47*(5), 27–30.

Kurtz, C. F., & Snowden, D. J. (2003, Fall). The new dynamics of strategy sense-making in a complex-complicated world. *IBM Systems Journal*, 1–23.

Kwaliteitscirkel van Deming. (n.d.). *Wikipedia*. Retrieved from http://nl.wikipedia.org/wiki/Kwaliteitscirkel_van_Deming

La Trobe University. (2008). *System reform and development for chronic disease management*. Victoria, Australia: Australian Institute for Primary Care.

Lai, V. S. (2008). The information system strategies of MNC affiliates: A technology-organization-environment analysis. *Journal of Global Information Management, 16*(3), 74–96. doi:10.4018/jgim.2008070104.

Lai, V. S., & Wong, B. K. (2003). The moderating effect of local environment on a foreign affiliate's global is strategy-effectiveness relationship. *IEEE Transactions on Engineering Management, 50*(3), 352–361. doi:10.1109/TEM.2003.817290.

Land, M., Proper, E., Waage, M., Cloo, J., & Steghuis, C. (2008). *Enterprise architecture: Creating value by informed governance*. Berlin: Springer Publishing Company, Incorporated.

Láng, I. (2005). Sustainable development: A new challenge for the countries in Central and Eastern Europe. In Hens & Nath (Eds.), *The World Summit on Sustainable Development: The Johannesburg Conference*. Retrieved from http://link.springer.com/book/10.1007/1-4020-3653-1/page/1

Langenberg, K., & Wegmann, A. (2004). *Enterprise architecture: What aspect is current research targeting? (Technical report)*. Lausanne, Switzerland: Laboratory of Systemic Modeling, Ecole Polytechnique Fédérale de Lausanne.

Langford, M. (2012). *Measurement choices and the post-2015 development agenda*. Retrieved from http://post2015.files.wordpress.com/2013/01/art-of-the-impossible-langford-final.pdf

Lankhorst, M. M. et al. (2005). *Enterprise architecture at work: Modelling, communication and analysis*. Berlin: Springer.

Lankhorst, M. M. (2009). *Enterprise architecture at work: Modelling, communication and analysis* (2nd ed.). Berlin: Springer. doi:10.1007/978-3-642-01310-2.

Lankhorst, M. M., van Buuren, R., van Leeuwen, D., Jonkers, H., & ter Doest, H. (2004). Enterprise architecture modelling-The issue of integration. *Advanced Engineering Informatics, 18*(4), 205–216. doi:10.1016/j.aei.2005.01.005.

Lankhorst, M. et al. (Eds.). (2009). *Enterprise architecture at work*. Berlin: Springer Verlag. doi:10.1007/978-3-642-01310-2.

Lapalme, J. (2012). Three schools of thought on enterprise architecture. *IT Professional, 14*(6), 37–43. doi:10.1109/MITP.2011.109.

Latham, R. (2002). Information technology and social transformation. *International Studies Review, 4*, 101–115. doi:10.1111/1521-9488.t01-1-00254.

Laurel, B. (1993). *Computers as theatre*. Reading, MA: Addison-Wesley.

Lawson, B. (1997). *How designers think*. Oxford, UK: Architectural Press.

Le, L.-S., & Wegmann, A. (2005). Definition of an object-oriented modeling language for enterprise architecture. In *Proceedings of the 38th Annual Hawaii International Conference on System Sciences*. IEEE.

Lebel, L., Anderies, Campbell, Folke, Hatfield-Dodds, Hughes, & Wilson. (2006). Governance and the capacity to manage resilience in regional social-ecological systems. *Ecology and Society*.

Leechul, B. (2010). *Building an enterprise architecture for statistics Korea*. Paper presented at Management of Statistical Information Systems (MSIS 2010). Daejeon, Republic of Korea.

Lee, Y., & Lee, S. (2011). The valuation of RFID investment using fuzzy real option. *Expert Systems with Applications, 38*, 12195–12201. doi:10.1016/j.eswa.2011.03.076.

Leischow, S. J., Best, A., Trochim, W. M., Clark, P. I., Gallagher, R. S., Marcus, S. E., & Matthews, E. (2008). Systems thinking to improve the public's health. *American Journal of Preventive Medicine, 35*(2S). doi:10.1016/j.amepre.2008.05.014 PMID:18619400.

Levin, S.A., Barrett, Aniyar, Baumol, Bliss, Bolin, ... Sheshinsky. (1998). Resilience in natural and socioeconomic systems. *Environment and Development Economics.* doi:10.1017/S1355770X98240125.

Levitt, S., & Dubner. (2005). *Freakonomics: A rogue economist explores the hidden side of everything.* New York: William Morrow.

Lewin, K. (1948). *Resolving social conflicts, selected papers on group dynamics* (Lewin, G. W., Ed.). New York: Harper & Row.

Libet, B. (2011). Do we have free will? In Sinnott-Armstrong, W., & Nadel, L. (Eds.), *Conscious Will and Responsibility* (pp. 1–10). Oxford, UK: Oxford Press.

Li, H., & Williams, T. J. (1994). *A formalization and extension of the Purdue enterprise reference architecture and the Purdue methodology. TR 158 Purdue Lab. of Applied Industrial Control.* West Lafayette, IN: Purdue University.

Liimatainen, K., Hoffman, M., & Heikkilä, J. (2007). *Overview of enterprise architecture work in 15 countries.* Helsinki, Finland: Ministry of Finance, Government of Finland.

Likert, R. (1961). *New patterns of management.* New York: McGraw-Hill.

Li, M., & Vitányi, P. (2008). *An introduction to Kolmogorov complexity and its applications* (3rd ed.). Berlin: Springer. doi:10.1007/978-0-387-49820-1.

Lindgardt, Z., Reeves, M., Stalk, G., & Deimler, M. S. (2009). *Business model innovation – When the game gets tough, change the game.* Boston: Boston Consulting Group.

Lloyd, S. (2001). Measures of complexity: A nonexhaustive list. *IEEE Control Systems Magazine, 21*(4), 7–8. doi:10.1109/MCS.2001.939938.

Lockwood, T., & Walton. (2008). *Building design strategy: Using design to achieve key business objectives.* New York: Allworth Press.

Lockwood, T. (2009). *Design thinking: Integrating innovation, customer experience, and brand value.* Allworth Press.

Longepe, C. (2007). *The enterprise architecture IT project – The urbanisation paradigm.* London: Kogan Page.

Lorek, S., & Fuchs. (2011). Strong sustainable consumption governance: Precondition for a de-growth path? *Journal of Cleaner Production.* Retrieved from http://www.academia.edu/1573624/Strong_sustainable_consumption_governance_-_precondition_for_a_degrowth_path

Lowe, D., & Ng, S. (2006). *The implications of complex adaptive systems thinking for future command and control.* Paper presented at 11th International Command and Control Research and Technology Symposium. Cambridge, UK.

Lugtigheid, R. B. (2007). *Architectuur bij PGGM, een praktijkvoorbeeld. Technical report.* Ordina.

Lu, J., & Callan, J. (2006). Full-text federated search of text-based digital libraries in peer-to-peer networks. *Information Retrieval, 9*(4), 477–498. doi:10.1007/s10791-006-6388-2.

Luken, J.P. (2004). Zijn competenties meetbaar? Dilemma en uitweg bij het werkbaar maken van het competentiebegrip. *Tijdschrift voor Hoger Onderwijs, 22*.

Luo, H. (2006). *Enterprise architecture alignment framework.* Retrieved 10 28, 2012, from http://www.aea-dc.org/resources/EA-Alignment-Framework-2009-6-28.ppt

Lusch, R. F., & Vargo, S. L. et al. (2008). Toward a conceptual foundation for service science: Contributions from service-dominant logic. *IBM Systems Journal, 47*(1). doi:10.1147/sj.471.0005.

Macmillan. (2010). *English dictionary for advanced learners* (2nd ed). Hueber.

Maddison, A. (2001). *The world economy: A millennial perspective.* Paris: OECD Development Centre. doi:10.1787/9789264189980-en.

Madhavaram, S., & Hunt, S. D. (2008). The service-dominant logic and a hierarchy of operant resources: Developing masterful operant resources and implications for marketing strategy. *Journal of the Academy of Marketing Science, 36,* 67–82. doi:10.1007/s11747-007-0063-z.

Maglio, P. P., & Spohrer, J. (2008). Fundamentals of service science. *Journal of the Academy of Marketing Science, 36,* 18–20. doi:10.1007/s11747-007-0058-9.

Maglio, P. P., & Srinivasan, S. et al. (2006). Service systems, service scientists, SSME, and innovation. *Communications of the ACM, 49*(7), 81–85. doi:10.1145/1139922.1139955.

Mahidhar, V. (2011). Ecosystems for innovation: An interview with U.S. CTO Aneesh Chopra. *Deloitte Review, 11.* Retrieved 14 August, 2011, from http://www.deloitte.com/assets/Dcom-Australia/Local%20Assets/Documents/Industries/Government%20Services/Public%20Sector/Deloitte_review_issue_nine_2011.pdf

Mallat, N., & Rossi, M. et al. (2004). Mobile banking services. *Communications of the ACM, 47*(5), 42–46. doi:10.1145/986213.986236.

Malnight, T. W. (2001). Emerging structural patterns within multinational corporations: Toward process-based structures. *Academy of Management Journal, 44*(6), 1187–1210. doi:10.2307/3069396.

Mandl, K. D., & Mandel, , et al. (2012). The SMART platform: Early experience enabling substitutable applications for electronic health records. *Journal of American Medical Informatics, 19*(4).

Mann, H. B., & Whitney, D. R. (1947). On a test of whether one of two random variables is stochastically larger than the other. *Annals of Mathematical Statistics, 18*(1), 50–60. doi:10.1214/aoms/1177730491.

Manning, R. (2009). *Using indicators to encourage development: Lessons from the millennium development goals.* Danish Institute of International Studies, Report 2009/1. Retrieved from http://www.diis.dk/graphics/Publications/Reports2009/DIIS_Report_2009-

Manor, J. (1998). Making federalism work: India defies the odds. *Journal of Democracy, 9*(3), 21–36. doi:10.1353/jod.1998.0048.

Markus, M. L., Kien Sia, S., & Soh, C. (2012). Mnes And information management: Structuring and governing IT resources in the global enterprise. *Journal of Global Information Management, 20*(1), 1–17. doi:10.4018/jgim.2012010101.

Martin, A. (2012). Enterprise IT architecture in large federated organizations: The art of the possible. *Information Systems Management, 29*(2), 137–147. doi:10.1080/10580530.2012.662103.

Martin, J. (1989). *Information engineering: Introduction (book I).* Englewood Cliffs, NJ: Prentice-Hall.

Martin, J. (1990). *Information engineering: Planning & analysis (book iI).* Englewood Cliffs, NJ: Prentice-Hall.

Martin, R. L. (2007). *The opposable mind: How successful leaders win through integrative thinking.* Boston: Harvard Business School Publishing.

Masika, R., & Joekes. (1997). *Environmentally sustainable development and poverty: A gender analysis.* Report for the Swedish International Development Agency. Retrieved from http://www.bridge.ids.ac.uk/reports/re52.pdf

Matthes, F., Buckl, S., Leitel, J., & Schweda, C. M. (2008). *Enterprise architecture management tool survey 2008.* Munich, Germany: Technische Universität München.

Matthews, A. (2012). *Enterprise architecture & systems thinking.* Retrieved August 7, 2012 from http://www.enterprise-advocate.com/2012/07/enterprise-architecture-systems-thinking/

Matthews, A. (2012). *Enterprise architecture & complexity theory.* Retrieved August 7, 2012 from http://www.enterprise-advocate.com/2012/07/enterprise-architecture-complexity-theory/

Mauboussin, M. (2011, September). Embracing complexity. *Harvard Business Review,* 89–92.

Maxwell School of Citizenship and Public Affairs. (2003). *Evolving federalisms: The intergovernmental balance of power in America and Europe.* Syracuse, NY: Maxwell School of Syracuse University.

Mayo, E. (1945). *The social problems of an industrial civilization.* Division of Research, Graduate School of Business Administration, Harvard University, Reprint Ed.

Maznevski, M., Steger, U., & Amann, W. (2007). *Perspectives for managers* (white paper). Lausanne, Switzerland: IMD.

McBreen, P. (2002). *Software craftsmanship: The new imperative*. Boston: Addison-Wesley.

McGarvey, B., & Hannon, B. (2004). *Dynamic modeling for business management – An introduction*. New York: Springer-Verlag. doi:10.1007/b97269.

McGregor, D. (1960). *The human side of enterprise*. New York: McGraw-Hill.

McGuire, C. (2012). Public policy frameworks in environmental settings: An argument for new policy frameworks to support new policy directions. *Environmental Management and Sustainable Development*. Retrieved from http://www.macrothink.org/journal/index.php/emsd/article/view/1537

McHugh, P., Merli, G., & Wheeler, W. A. III. (1995). *Beyond business process reengineering: Towards the holonic enterprise*. Chichester, UK: John Wiley & Sons.

McIlroy, M. D. (1968). Mass produced software components. In *Proceedings of the First NATO Conference on Software Engineering*. Garmisch, Germany: IEEE.

McIvor, R., McCracken, M., & McHugh, M. (2011). Creating outsourced shared services arrangements: Lessons from the public sector. *European Management Journal*. doi:10.1016/j.emj.2011.06.001.

Mckay, D. H. (1996). *Rush to union: Understanding the European federal bargain*. New York: Clarendon Press, Oxford University Press. doi:10.1093/acprof:oso/9780198280583.001.0001.

McLuhan, M. (1962). *The Gutenberg galaxy: The making of typographic man*. Toronto, Canada: University of Toronto Press.

Meadows, D. Meadows, Randers, & Behrends. (1972). The limits of growth. Universe Books.

Meadows, D. (1999). *Leverage points: Places to intervene in a system*. Hartland, VT: The Sustainability Institute.

Mega. (n.d.). Retrieved from http://www.mega.com/en/c/product

Meier, G., & Stiglitz. (2001). *Frontiers of development economics: The future in perspective*. World Bank and Oxford University Press.

Melvin, J. (2003). *Axiomatic system design: Chemical mechanical polishing machine case study*. (PhD Thesis in Mechanical Engineering). MIT, Cambridge, MA.

Menzel, D. C., & Feller, I. (1977). Leadership and interaction patterns in the diffusion of innovations among the American states. *The Western Political Quarterly*, *30*(4), 528–536. doi:10.2307/447654.

Mercer Consulting. (n.d.). Retrieved from http://www.mercer.com

Mercer, M. (2011). Shared services & cost saving collaboration deserve respect. *Public Management*, 8–12.

Merritt, A., & Stubbs. (2012). Complementing the local and global: Promoting sustainability action through linked local-level and formal sustainability funding mechanisms. *Public Administration and Development*. Retrieved from http://onlinelibrary.wiley.com/doi/10.1002/pad.1630/pdf

Mestrum, F. (2005). Poverty reduction and sustainable development. In Hens & Nath (Eds.), *The World Summit on Sustainable Development: The Johannesburg Conference*. Retrieved from http://link.springer.com/book/10.1007/1-4020-3653-1/page/1

Meyer, B. (1988). *Object-oriented software construction*. Englewood Cliffs, NJ: Prentice Hall.

Microsoft Corporation. (2009). *Connected health framework* (2nd ed.). Microsoft Corporation.

Microsoft Corporation. (2010). *Connected government framework – Strategies to transform government in the 2.0 world* (White Paper). Microsoft Corporation.

Microsoft Corporation. (2012). *Connected government framework reference architecture version 1.0*. Microsoft Corporation.

Miles, R. E., Snow, C. C., Meyer, A. D., & Coleman, H. J. (1978). Organizational strategy, structure and process. *Academy of Management Review*, *3*(3), 546–562. PMID:10238389.

Mill, J. S. (2005). Of federal representative governments. In Karmis, D., & Norman, W. J. (Eds.), *Theories of Federalism: A Reader* (pp. 165–172). New York, NY: Palgrave Macmillan.

Ministry of Information and Communications Technology. (2006). *E-government strategy.* Jordan E-Government Program. Retrieved October 14, 2012 from http://www.thieswittig.eu/docs/mpc_strategies/jordan/jordan_e-governmenstrategy.pdf

Ministry of Power. (2012). *Report of the working group on power for twelfth plan (2012-17).* New Delhi: Ministry of Power, Govt. of India.

Mintzberg, H. (1979). *The structuring of organizations: A synthesis of the research.* Englewood Cliffs, NJ: Prentice-Hall.

Mintzberg, H., Lampel, J., & Ahlstrand, B. (1998). *Strategy safari: A guided tour through the wilds of strategic management.* New York: Free Press.

Misra, S., & Mondal, A. (2011). Identification of a company's suitability for the adoption of cloud computing and modelling its corresponding return on investment. *Mathematical and Computer Modelling, 53,* 504–521. doi:10.1016/j.mcm.2010.03.037.

Moghaddam, M. R. S., Sharifi, A., & Merati, E. (2008). Using axiomatic design in the process of enterprise architecting. In *Proceedings of the 3rd International Conference on Convergence and Hybrid Information Technology,* (pp. 279-284). ICCT.

Mohan, S. (2006). Making the case for shared services in the public sector. *Accountancy Ireland, 38*(4), 14–15.

Montier, J. (2010). *The little book of behavioral investing.* Hoboken, NJ: John Wiley & Sons.

Morecroft, J. (2007). *Strategic modelling and business dynamics – A feedback systems approach.* West Sussex, UK: John Wiley and Sons.

Morita, S., & Zaelke. (2005). *Rule of law, good governance and sustainable development.* Paper presented at the Seventh International Conference on Environmental Compliance and Enforcement. Retrieved from http://www.inece.org/conference/7/vol1/05_Sachiko_Zaelke.pdf

Morowitz, H. (2002). *The emergence of everything: How The world became complex.* Oxford, UK: Oxford University Press.

Morrison, T., & Lane. (2005). What 'whole of government' means for environmental policy management: An analysis of the 'connecting government' initiative. *Australasian Journal of Environmental Management.* Retrieved from http://www.tandfonline.com/doi/abs/10.1080/14486563.2005.9725071

Mudacumura, G. Mebratu, & Hague. (2005). Sustainable development policy and administration (public administration and public policy). New York: Taylor and Francis.

Muehlfeit, J. (2006). *The connected government framework for local and regional government* (White Paper). Microsoft Corporation.

Mumford, E. (1995). *Effective systems design and requirements analysis: The ETHICS approach.* London: Macmillan.

Mumford, E. (2006). The story of socio-technical design: Reflections on its successes, failures and potential. *Information Systems Journal, 16,* 317–342. doi:10.1111/j.1365-2575.2006.00221.x.

Mun, J. (2006). *Real options analysis versus traditional DCF valuation in layman's terms.* Retrieved April 09, 2011, from http://www.realoptionsvaluation.com/download.html#CASESTUDIES

Mundell, R. A. (1961). A theory of optimum currency areas. *The American Economic Review, 51*(4), 657–665.

Murray, J. G., Rentell, P. G., & Geere, D. (2008). Procurement as a shared service in English local government. *International Journal of Public Sector Management, 21*(5), 540–555. doi:10.1108/09513550810885822.

Mwanza, D. (2005). Water for sustainable development in Africa. In Hens & Nath (Eds.), *The World Summit on Sustainable Development: The Johannesburg Conference.* Retrieved from http://link.springer.com/book/10.1007/1-4020-3653-1/page/1

Mykhashchuk, M., Buckl, S., Dierl, T., & Schweda, C. M. (2011). *Charting the landscape of enterprise architecture management – An extensive literature analysis.* Paper presented at Wirtschaftsinformatik. Zürich, Switzerland.

Najam, A., & Cleveland. (2005). Energy and sustainable development at global environmental summits: An evolving agenda. In Hens & Nath (Eds.), *The World Summit on Sustainable Development: The Johannesburg Conference.* Retrieved from http://link.springer.com/book/10.1007/1-4020-3653-1/page/1

Nannen, V. A. (2010). *Short introduction to model selection, Kolmogorov complexity and minimum description length (MDL).* Retrieved from http://arxiv.org/abs/1005.2364

NASCIO. (2003). Enterprise architecture maturity model version 1.3. Technical Report. Washington, DC: National Association of State Chief Information Officers (NASCIO).

Nath, B. (2005). Education for sustainable development: The Johannesburg summit and beyond. In Hens & Nath (Eds.), *The World Summit on Sustainable Development: The Johannesburg Conference.* Retrieved from http://link.springer.com/book/10.1007/1-4020-3653-1/page/1

National Information Society Agency (NIA). (2008). *2008 informatization white paper.* Ministry of Public Administration and Security, Government of Republic of Korea.

NATO. (2007). *NATO architecture framework v3.* Retrieved 10 28, 2012, from http://www.nhqc3s.nato.int/ARCHITECTURE/_docs/NAF_v3/ANNEX1.pdf

NBBJ. (2012). *NBBJ architecture and design.* Retrieved 7 May, 2012, from http://www.nbbj.com

Neumayer, E. (2011). *Sustainability and inequality in human development.* Human Development Research Paper, United Nations Development Program. Retrieved from http://hdr.undp.org/en/reports/global/hdr2011/papers/HDRP_2011_04.pdf

Niehaves, B., & Krause, A. (2010). Shared service strategies in local government - A multiple case study exploration. *Transforming Government: People. Process and Policy, 4*(3), 266–279.

Nielsen, F. (1996). Human behavior: Another dimension of standards setting. *StandardView, 4*(1), 36–41. doi:10.1145/230871.230878.

Nierstrasz, O., Gibbs, S., & Tsichritzis, D. (1992). Component-oriented software development. *Communications of the ACM, 35*(9), 160–164. doi:10.1145/130994.131005.

NIST Smart Grid Interoperability Panel. (2012). *NIST smart grid interoperability panel wiki.* Washington, DC: NIST. Retrieved from http://collaborate.nist.gov/twiki-sggrid/bin/view/SmartGrid/WebHome

NIST. (2010). *NIST framework and roadmap for smart grid interoperability standards, release 1.0.* Washington, DC: NIST.

NIST. (2012). *NIST framework and roadmap for smart grid interoperability standards, release 2.0.* Washington, DC: NIST.

Nordfors, L., Ericson, B., Lindell, H., & Lapidus, J. (2009). eGovernment of tomorrow – Future scenarios for 2020. *Gullers Group. Vinnova Report VR, 2009,* 28.

Nunan, F. Campbell, & Foster. (2012). Environmental mainstreaming: The organizational challenge of policy integration. *Public Administration and Development.* Retrieved from http://onlinelibrary.wiley.com/doi/10.1002/pad.1624/pdf

Nussbaum, B. (2012). Design thinking is a failed experiment: So what's next? *Co.DESIGN.* Retrieved 24 August, 2012, from http://www.fastcodesign.com/1663558/design-thinking-is-a-failed-experiment-so-whats-next

O'Neill, T., Denford, M., Leaney, J., & Dunsire, K. (2007). Managing enterprise architecture change. In Saha, P. (Ed.), *Handbooks of Enterprise Systems Architecture in Practice.* Hershey, PA: IGI Global. doi:10.4018/978-1-59904-189-6.ch011.

O'Sullivan, J. et al. (2002). What's in a service? Towards accurate description of non-functional service properties. *Distributed and Parallel Databases, 12,* 117–133. doi:10.1023/A:1016547000822.

Oates, W. E. (1999). An easy on fiscal federalism. *Journal of Economic Literature, 37*(3), 1120–1149. doi:10.1257/jel.37.3.1120.

Object Management Group. (2013). *Business architecture working group.* Retrieved 18 March, 2013, from http://bawg.omg.org/

O'Donnell, A. (2009). The big picture. *Insurance & Technology*, *34*(8), 34–35.

Office of Management and Budget. (2007). *Federal enterprise architecture consolidated reference model version 2.3*. Washington, DC: The White House.

Office of Management and Budget. (2012). *Digital government: Building a 21ˢᵗ century platform to better serve the American people*. Washington, DC: The White House.

Office of the Chief Information Officer. (2013). *Stay connected – South Australian government ICT strategy*. Adelaide, Australia: Government of South Australia.

Okumus, F. (2003). A framework to implement strategies in organizations. *Management Decision*, *41*(9), 871–882. doi:10.1108/00251740310499555.

Olken, B. Dell, & Jones. (2012). Temperature shocks and economic growth: Evidence from the last half century. *American Economic Journal: Macroeconomics*. Retrieved from http://economics.mit.edu/files/7642

Olson, L. (2005). Management of chemicals for sustainable development, menutextcount, class_name, data_text = 1556, asharticle. In Hens & Nath (Eds.), *The World Summit on Sustainable Development: The Johannesburg Conference*. Retrieved from http://link.springer.com/book/10.1007/1-4020-3653-1/page/1

Olson, E. E., & Eoyang, H. G. (2001). *Facilitating organization change: Lessons from complexity science*. Hoboken, NJ: John Wiley & Sons.

On, P., Vanborre, F., Stanick, K., & Williams, J. (2006). Experts' perspective. *Business Intelligence Journal*, *11*, 25–29.

Op't Land, M., Proper, H. A., Waage, M., Cloo, J., & Steghuis, C. (2008). *Enterprise architecture – Creating value by informed governance*. Berlin: Springer.

Open Epolicy Group Harvard Law School, & Berkman Center For Internet And Society. (2005). *Roadmap for open ICT ecosystems*. Cambridge, MA: Berkman Center For Internet & Society at Harvard Law School.

Open Group. (2011). *TOGAF version 9.1*. Open Group. Retrieved December 12, 2012 from http://www.opengroup.org/architecture/togaf91/downloads.htm

Open Group. (2012). *Architecture governance*. Retrieved from http://pubs.opengroup.org/architecture/togaf8-doc/arch/chap26.html#tagfcjh_32

Organization for Economic Cooperation and Development. (2002). *Governance for sustainable development: Five OECD case studies*. Retrieved from http://www.ulb.ac.be/ceese/nouveau%20site%20ceese/documents/oecd%20governance%20for%20sustainable%20development%205%20case%20studies.pdf

Organization for Economic Cooperation and Development. (2003). *Policy coherence: Vital for global development*. Paris: OECD.

Organization for Economic Cooperation and Development. (2008). *Gender and sustainable development: Maximizing the economic, social and environmental role of women*. Paris: OECD.

Organization for Economic Cooperation and Development. (2010). *Perspectives on global development, 2010*. Retrieved from http://www.oecd.org

Organization for Economic Cooperation and Development. (2010). *Environmental performance review of japan 2010*. Retrieved from http://www.oecd-library.org/docserver/download/fulltext/971012e.pdf

Orlov, L. M., & Cameron. (2007). *Business technology defined: Technology management is changing to deliver business results*. Forrester Research.

Osinga, F. B. (2007). *Science, strategy and war: The strategic theory of John Boyd (strategy and history)*. Abington, UK: Routledge.

Osterweil, L. (1987). Software processes are software too. In *Proceedings of the 9th International Conference on Software Engineering*, (pp. 2-13). Los Alamitos, CA: IEEE.

Ostroff, F. (1999). *The horizontal organization: What the organization of the future looks like and how it delivers value to customers*. New York: Oxford University Press.

Overseas Development Institute. (2013). *Tracking proposals on future development goals*. Retrieved from http://post2015.org/2013/01/08/tracking-proposals-on-future-development-goals/

Pan, A., & Vina, A. (2004). An alternative architecture for financial data integration. *Communications of the ACM, 47*(5), 37–40. doi:10.1145/986213.986235.

Pardo, T. A., & Burke, G. B. (2008). *Improving government interoperability: A capability framework for government managers*. Albany, NY: Center for Technology in Government, University at Albany.

Parker, S., & Bartlett. (2008). *Towards agile government*. State Services Authority, Government of Victoria.

Parsons, T. (1951). *The social system*. London: Routledge and Kegan Paul.

participatory approach.

Paulson, L. D. (2006). Services science: A new field for today's economy. *IEEE Computer, 39*(8), 18–21. doi:10.1109/MC.2006.277.

Pautz, M., & Rinftet. (2012). *The Lilliputians of environmental regulation: The perspective of state regulators*. London: Routledge.

Pava, C. H. P. (1983). *Managing new office technology: An organizational strategy*. New York: The Free Press.

Pearson, K. (1904). *On the theory of contingency and its relation to association and normal correlation*. Cambridge, UK: Cambridge University Press.

Peeters, H. (2005). Sustainable development and the role of the financial world. In Hens & Nath (Eds.), *The World Summit on Sustainable Development: The Johannesburg Conference*. Retrieved from http://link.springer.com/book/10.1007/1-4020-3653-1/page/1

Peng, Y., Iiu, H., Tao, H., & Ming, F. (2009). A study on the value network of telecom service and the organization change of Chinese telecom operator. In *Proceedings of the 6th International Conference on Service Systems and Service Management (ICSSSM '09),* (pp. 493-497). Xiamen, China: ICSSSM.

Peppard, J. (1999). Information management in the global enterprise: An organizing framework. *European Journal of Information Systems, 8*(2), 77–94. doi:10.1057/palgrave.ejis.3000321.

Pepper, S. (1961). *World hypotheses: A study in evidence*. Los Angeles, CA: University of California Press.

Perdicoulis, A. (2010). *Systems thinking and decision making in urban and environmental planning*. Northampton, MA: Edward Elgar.

Perrow, C. (1999). *Normal accidents: Living with high-risk technologies*. Princeton, NJ: Princeton University Press.

Peterson, P. E. (2003). The changing politics of federalism. In Maxwell School Of Citizenship And Public Affairs (Ed.), *Evolving Federalisms: The Intergovernmental Balance of Power in America and Europe* (pp. 25-42). Syracuse, NY: Maxwell School of Syracuse University.

Pettigrew, A. M., & Fenton, E. M. (2000). *The innovating organization. London*. Thousand Oaks, CA: Sage.

Pettigrew, A., Thomas, H., & Whittington, R. (2001). *Handbook of strategy & management*. Thousand Oaks, CA: Sage Publications.

Petzinger, T. Jr. (1999). *The new pioneers: The men and women who are transforming the workplace and marketplace*. New York: Simon & Schuster.

Pisano, U. (2012). *Resilience and sustainable development: Theory of resilience, systems thinking and adaptive governance*. Retrieved from http://www.sd-network.eu/quarterly%20reports/report%20files/pdf/2012-September-Resilience_and_Sustainable_Development.pdf

Planning Commission. (2011). *Annual report 2011-12 on the working of state power utilities and electricity departments*. Govt. of India.

Popper, K. (1959). *The logic of scientific discovery*. London: Hutchington & Co..

Porter, M. E. (1980). *Competitive strategy: Techniques for analysing industries and competitors*. New York: Free Press.

Porter, M. E. (1985). *Competitive advantage: Creating and sustaining superior performance*. New York: Free Press, Collier Macmillan.

Porter, M. E. (1996). What is strategy? *Harvard Business Review*, 61–78. PMID:10158474.

Porter, M. E., & Teisberg, E. O. (2006). *Redefining health care – Creating value-based competition on results*. Boston: Harvard Business School Press.

Prabhupada, S. (1997). *Bhagavad gita as it is*. Bhaktivedanta Book Trust.

Prahalad, C. K., & Doz, Y. L. (1981). An approach to strategic control in MNCS. *Sloan Management Review*, *22*(4), 5–13.

Prahalad, C. K., & Doz, Y. L. (1987). *The multinational mission: Balancing local demands and global vision*. New York: Free Press, Collier Macmillan.

Prajogo, D. I. (2007). The relationship between competitive strategies and product quality. *Industrial Management & Data Systems*, *107*(1), 69–83. doi:10.1108/02635570710719061.

Princen, T. Maniates, & Conca. (2002). Confronting consumption. Cambridge, MA: MIT Press.

Proudhon, P. (2005). The principle of federation. In Karmis, D., & Norman, W. J. (Eds.), *Theories of Federalism: A Reader* (pp. 173–188). New York, NY: Palgrave Macmillan.

Provan, K. G. (1983). The federation as an interorganizational linkage network. *Academy of Management Review*, *8*(1), 79–90.

Pucket, S., & Purdy, S. C. (2011). Are voluntary movements initiated preconsciously? The relationships between readiness potentials, urges, and decisions. In Sinnott-Armstrong, W., & Nadel, L. (Eds.), *Conscious Will and Responsibility* (pp. 1–10). Oxford, UK: Oxford Press.

Pulkkinen, M. (2006). Systemic management of architectural decisions in enterprise architecture planning: Four dimensions and three abstraction levels. In *Proceedings of the 39th Hawaii International Conference on System Sciences – 2006*. IEEE.

Purdue University. (2011). *New approach needed to prevent major 'systemic failures'*. Retrieved on July 30, 2012 from http://www.purdue.edu/newsroom/research/2011/110131VenkatasubramanianF.html

PWC. (2008). *Point of view shared service center 2nd generation: Taking the next step to reach a more efficient level of evolution*. PriceWaterhouseCoopers.

Qian, Y., & Weingast, B. R. (1997). Federalism as a commitment to preserving market incentives. *The Journal of Economic Perspectives*, *11*(4), 83–92. doi:10.1257/jep.11.4.83.

Quartel, D. A. C., & Steen, M. W. A. et al. (2007). COSMO: A conceptual framework for service modelling and refinement. *Information Systems Frontiers*, *9*, 225–244. doi:10.1007/s10796-007-9034-7.

Raadt van der, B., Slot, R., & Van Vliet, H. (2007). *Experience report: Assessing a global financial services company on its enterprise architecture effectiveness using NAOMI*.

Rabaey, M. (2011). *Game theoretic real option approach of the procurement of department of defense: Competition or collaboration*. Paper presented at the 8th Annual Acquisition Research Symposium. Monterey, CA.

Rabaey, M., Hoffman, G., & Vandenborre, K. (2004). *Aligning business- and resource-strategy: An interdisciplinary forum*. Paper presented at the 13th International Conference on Management Technology (IAMOT 2004). Washington, DC.

Rabaey, M., Vandijck, E., & Tromp, H. (2003). Business intelligent agents for enterprise application integration. In *Proceedings of the 16th International Conference on Software & Systems Engineering and their Applications*. CMSL/CNAM.

Rabaey, M. (2012). A public economics approach to enabling enterprise architecture with the government cloud in Belgium. In Saha, P. (Ed.), *Enterprise Architecture for Connected E-Government: Practices and Innovations*. Hershey, PA: IGI Global. doi:10.4018/978-1-4666-1824-4.ch020.

Rabaey, M. (2012). Holistic investment framework for cloud computing: A management-philosophical approach based on complex adaptive systems. In Bento, A., & Aggarwal, A. (Eds.), *Cloud Computing Service and Deployment Models: Layers and Management*. Hershey, PA: IGI Global. doi:10.4018/978-1-4666-2187-9.ch005.

Rabaey, M. (2012). A complex adaptive system thinking approach of government e-procurement in a cloud computing environment. In Ordóñez de Pablos, P. (Ed.), *E-Procurement Management for Successful Electronic Government Systems*. Hershey, PA: IGI Global. doi:10.4018/978-1-4666-2119-0.ch013.

Rabaey, M., & Mercken, R. (2012). Framework of knowledge and intelligence base: From intelligence to service. In Ordoñez de Pablos, P., & Lytras, M. D. (Eds.), *Knowledge Management and Drivers of Innovation in Services Industries*. Hershey, PA: IGI Global. doi:10.4018/978-1-4666-0948-8.ch017.

Rabaey, M., & Mercken, R. (forthcoming). Complex adaptive systems thinking approach for intelligence base in support of intellectual capital management. In Ordoñez de Pablos, P. (Ed.), *Intellectual Capital Strategy Management for Knowledge-Based Organizations*. Hershey, PA: IGI Global. doi:10.4018/978-1-4666-3655-2.ch007.

Rabaey, M., Tromp, H., & Vandenborre, K. (2007). Holistic approach to align ICT capabilities with business integration. In Cunha, M., Cortes, B., & Putnik, G. (Eds.), *Adaptive Technologies and Business Integration: Social, Managerial, and Organizational Dimensions* (pp. 160–173). Hershey, PA: Idea Group Publishing.

Rabaey, M., Vandenborre, K., Vandijck, E., Timmerman, M., & Tromp, H. (2007). Semantic web services and BPEL: Semantic service oriented architecture - Economical and philosophical issues. In Salam, A., & Stevens, J. (Eds.), *Semantic Web Technologies and eBusiness: Toward the Integrated Virtual Organization and Business Process Automation* (pp. 127–153). Hershey, PA: Idea Group Publishing. doi:10.4018/978-1-59904-192-6.ch005.

Rabhi, F.A., Yu, H., Dabous, F.T., & Wu, S. (2007). A service-oriented architecture for financial business processes. *Information Systems and e-Business Management, 5*(2), 185-200.

Ranis, G. (2004). *The evolution of development thinking: Theory and policy*. Paper delivered at the Annual World Bank Conference on Development Economics. Washington, DC. Retrieved from http://siteresources.worldbank.org/DEC/Resources/84797-1251813753820/6415739-1251814066992/Gustav_Ranis_Evolutiion_of_Thinking_formattd.pdf

Rao, S. L. (2011). Keynote address, sustainability of indian electricity. In *Proceedings of the IEEE Workshop on Sustainable Energy: Economics, Environment and Equity*. Bangalore, India: IEEE.

Raymond, L., & Croteau, A. (2006). Enabling the strategic development of SMEs through advanced manufacturing systems. *Industrial Management & Data Systems, 106*(7), 1012–1032. doi:10.1108/02635570610688904.

Reed, G.E. (2006, May-June). Leadership and systems thinking. *Defense AT & L.*

Reisner, R. A. F. (2011). *A leader's guide to transformation – Developing a playbook for successful change initiatives*. IBM Center for the Business of Government Report.

Reitsma, E., Jansen, P., Van der Werf, E., & Van den Steenhoven, H. (2004). *Wat is de beste veranderaanpak*. Management Executive.

Reitz, J. G. Breton, Dion, Dion, Phan, & Banerjee. (2009). Multiculturalism and social cohesion: Potentials and challenges of diversity. Berlin: Springer.

Requejo, F. (2004). Value pluralism and multinational federalism. *The Australian Journal of Politics and History, 50*(1), 23–40. doi:10.1111/j.1467-8497.2004.00318.x.

Reuer, J. J., & Ariño, A. (2007). Strategic alliance contracts: Dimensions and determinants of contractual complexity. *Strategic Management Journal, 28*(3), 313–330. doi:10.1002/smj.581.

Richardson, K.A. (2008). Managing complex organizations – Complexity thinking and the science and art of management. *E:CO Issuen, 10*(2), 13 – 26.

Riker, W. H. (1964). *Federalism: Origin, operation, significance*. Boston: Little Brown.

Riker, W. H. (1969). Six books in search of a subject or does federalism exist and does it matter? *Comparative Politics, 2*, 135–146. doi:10.2307/421485.

Riker, W. H. (1975). Federalism. In Greenstein, F. I., & Polsby, N. W. (Eds.), *Handbook of Political Science, Governmental Institutions and Processes* (pp. 93–172). Reading, MA: Addison-Wesley.

Rind, D. (1999). Complexity and climate. *Science, 284*(5411), 105–107. doi:10.1126/science.284.5411.105 PMID:10102804.

Ritchley, T. (1991). Analysis and synthesis – On scientific method based on a study by Bernhard Riemann. *Systems Research*, *8*(4), 21–41. doi:10.1002/sres.3850080402.

Rival, L. (2012). *Sustainable development through policy integration in Latin America: A comparative approach*. Retrieved from http://www.unrisd.org/80256B3C005BCCF9/httpNetITFramePDF?ReadForm&parentunid=DA1744ED6C1FFD03C12579F3002A5769&parentdoctype=paper&netitpath=80256B3C005BCCF9/(httpAuxPages)/DA1744ED6C1FFD03C12579F3002A5769/$file/7%20Rival-Web.pdf

Roberts-Schweitzer, E. Greaney, & Duer (Eds.). (2006). *Promoting social cohesion through education: Case studies and tools for using textbooks and curricula*. World Bank Institute. Retrieved from http://www.iiep.unesco.org/fileadmin/user_upload/Cap_Dev_Technical_Assistance/pdf/2010/Promoting_Social_Cohesion_through_Education.pdf

Rochart, J. F. (1979). Chief executive define their own data needs. *Harvard Business Review*.

Rockart, J. F., Earl, M. J., & Ross, J. W. (1996). Eight imperatives for the new IT organization. *Sloan Management Review*, *38*(1), 43–55.

Rodden, J. (2004). Comparative federalism and decentralization: On meaning and measurement. *Comparative Politics*, *36*(4), 481–500. doi:10.2307/4150172.

Rodrigues, L. C., Lancellotti, M., & Riscarolli, V. (2006). ATM technology as Brazilian banks strategy. In *Proceedings of the 15th International Conference on Management of Technology (IAMOT 2006)*. Beijing, China: IAMOT.

Roman, D. et al. (2005). Web service modeling ontology. *Applied Ontology*, *1*(1), 77–106.

Romme, A., Georges, L., & van Witteloostuijn, A. (1999). Circular organizing and triple loop learning. *Journal of Organizational Change Management*, *12*(5), 439–453. doi:10.1108/09534819910289110.

Ross, J. (2003). *Creating a strategic IT architecture competency: Learning in stages*. Cambridge, MA: MIT Sloan School of Management. doi:10.2139/ssrn.416180.

Ross, J. W., & Beath, C. (2005). *The federated broker model at the DOW chemical company: Blending world class internal and external capabilities. No. CISR WP No. 355 And Sloan WP No. 4559-05*. Cambridge, MA: Center For Information Systems Research, Sloan School of Management.

Ross, J. W., & Weill, , et al. (2006). *Enterprise architecture as strategy: Creating a foundation for business execution*. Boston, MA: Harvard Business School Press.

Ross, J. W., Weill, P., & Robertson, D. C. (2006). *Enterprise architecture as strategy: Creating a foundation for business execution*. Boston: Harvard Business School Press.

Ross, J. W., Weill, P., & Robertson, D. C. (2008). *Enterprise architecture as strategy*. Boston: Harvard Business School Press.

Rothboeck, S. (2010). *Skills for green and decent jobs and sustainable development: The ILO perspective*. Retrieved from http://iveta2010.cpsctech.org/downloads/materials/full%20papers/2.%20Skills%20for%20Green%20and%20Decent%20Jobs%20and%20Sustainable%20Development.pdf.

Rothwell, A. T., Herbert, I. P., & Seal, W. (2011). Shared service centers and professional employability. *Journal of Vocational Behavior*, *79*, 241–252. doi:10.1016/j.jvb.2011.01.001.

Rouse, W. B. (2000). Managing complexity – Disease control as a complex adaptive system. *Information Systems Management*, *2*(2), 143–165.

Rouse, W. B. (2007). Complex engineered, organizational and natural systems – Issues underlying the complexity of systems and fundamental research needed to address these issues. *Systems Engineering*, *10*(3), 260–271. doi:10.1002/sys.20076.

Rouse, W. B. (2008). Healthcare as a complex adaptive systems – Implications for design and management. *The BRIDGE: Linking Engineering and Society*, *38*(1), 17–25.

Rousseau, J. (2005). A lasting peace through the federation of Europe: Exposition and critique of St. Pierre's project. In Karmis, D., & Norman, W. J. (Eds.), *Theories of Federalism: A Reader* (pp. 59–85). New York, NY: Palgrave Macmillan.

Roy, J. (2006). E-government and local governance in Canada: An examination of front line challenges and federal tensions. *Public Administration and Management*, *11*(4), 306–350.

Ruigrok, W., Achtenhagen, L., Wagner, M., & Rüegg-Stürm, J. (2000). ABB: Beyond the global matrix towards the network multidivisional organization. In Pettigrew, A. M., & Fenton, E. M. (Eds.), *The Innovating Organization* (pp. 117–143). Thousand Oaks, CA: Sage. doi:10.4135/9781446219379.n4.

Rust, R. T., & Miu, C. (2006). What academic research tells us about service. *Communications of the ACM*, *49*(7), 49–54. doi:10.1145/1139922.1139948.

Rwangoga, N. T., & Baryayetunga, A. P. (2007). E-government for Uganda: Challenges and opportunities. *International Journal of Computing and ICT Research*, *1*(1), 36–46.

Saaty, T. L. (1980). *The analytic hierarchy process*. New York: McGraw-Hill.

Sachs, J. (2012). From millennium development goals to sustainable development goals. *The Lancet*. Retrieved from http://www.thelancet.com/journals/lancet/article/PIIS0140-6736(12)60685-0/fulltext#article_upsell

Saha, P. (2006). A real options perspective to enterprise architecture as an investment activity. *Journal of Enterprise Architecture*, *2*(3), 50.

Saha, P. (2007). A synergistic assessment of the federal enterprise architecture framework against GERAM (ISO15704:2000). In Saha, P. (Ed.), *Handbook of Enterprise Systems Architecture in Practice*. Hershey, PA: IGI Global. doi:10.4018/978-1-59904-189-6.ch001.

Saha, P. (2007). *Handbook of enterprise systems architecture in practice*. Hershey, PA: IGI Global. doi:10.4018/978-1-59904-189-6.

Saha, P. (2008). *Advances in government enterprise architecture*. Hershey, PA: IGI Global. doi:10.4018/978-1-60566-068-4.

Saha, P. (2012). *Enterprise architecture and connected e-government – Practices and innovations*. Hershey, PA: IGI Global. doi:10.4018/978-1-4666-1824-4.

Sambamurthy, V., & Zmud, R. W. (1999). Arrangement for information technology governance: A theory of multiple contingencies. *Management Information Systems Quarterly*, *23*(2), 261–290. doi:10.2307/249754.

Sampson, S. E., & Froehle, C. M. (2006). Foundations and implications of a proposed unified services theory. *Production and Operations Management*, *15*(2), 329–343. doi:10.1111/j.1937-5956.2006.tb00248.x.

Sanchez, R., & Heene, A. (2000). A competence perspective on strategic learning and knowledge management. In Rob, C., & Sam, I. (Eds.), *Strategic Learning in a Knowledge Economy*. Boston: Butterworth Heinemann. doi:10.1016/B978-0-7506-7223-8.50004-6.

Sanders, E., & Westerlund. (2011). *Experiencing, exploring and experimenting in and with co-design spaces*. Paper presented at the Nordic Design Research Conference. Helsinki, Finland.

Sargut, G., & McGrath, R. G. (2011, September). Learning to live with complexity – How to make sense of the unpredictable and the undefinable in today's hyperconnected business world. *Harvard Business Review*, , 68–76. PMID:21939129.

Savigny, D., & Adam, T. (2009). *Systems thinking for health systems strengthening*. Geneva, Switzerland: World Health Organization.

Schekkerman, J. (2006). *How to survive in the jungle of enterprise architecture frameworks: Creating or choosing an enterprise architecture framework*. Victoria, Australia: Trafford Publishing.

Schendel, R. et al. (2011). *ICT project guidebook: E-government capability maturity model*. Manila: Asian Development Bank.

Schnelle, E. (1978). *Neue wege der kommunikation*. Spielregeln, Arbeitstechniken und Anwendungsfälle der Metaplan-Methode. Number Heft 10. Hanstein, K¨onigstein/Taunus.

Schulz, V., & Brenner, W. (2010). Characteristics of shared service centers. *Transforming Government: People. Process and Policy*, *4*(3), 210–219.

Schwaninger, M. (2006). *Intelligent organizations – Powerful models for systemic management*. Berlin: Springer.

Scott, W. D. (1911). *Increasing human efficiency in business - A contribution to the psychology of business*. The Macmillan Company.

Seal, W., & Herbert, I. (2009, Spring). The role of shared services. *Management Services*, 43-47.

Seitjs, G., Crossman, M., & Billou, N. (2010). Coping with complexity. *Ivey Business Journal*. Retrieved from http://www.iveybusinessjournal.com/topics/leadership/coping-with-complexity

Selden, S. C., & Wooters, R. (2011). Structures in public human resource management: Shared services in state governments. *Review of Public Personnel Administration*, *31*(4), 349–368. doi:10.1177/0734371X11408698.

Seligmann, P.S., Wijers, G.M., & Sol H.G. (1989). *Analyzing the structure of I.S. methodologies, an alternative approach*.

Senge, P. (1990). *The fifth discipline*. New York: Doubleday Currency.

Senge, P. M. (1990). *The fifth discipline*. New York: Currency.

Senge, P. M. (1990). *The Fifth Discipline: The Art and Practice of the Learning Organization*. New York: Currency Doubleday.

Senge, P. M. (1992). *The fifth discipline: The art and science of the learning organization*. Sydney, Australia: Random House.

Senge, P. M. (2006). *The fifth discipline*. London: Random House.

Sessions, R. (2006). *A better path to enterprise architecture*. Retrieved from http://msdn.microsoft.com/en-us/library/aa479371.aspx#sessionsfinal100_topic3

Shapiro, C., & Varian, H. R. (1999). The art of standards wars. *California Management Review*, *41*(2), 8–32. doi:10.2307/41165984.

Shapiro, S. S., & Wilk, M. B. (1965). An analysis of variance test for normality (complete samples). *Biometrika*, *52*(3/4), 591–611. doi:10.2307/2333709.

Shattuck, L., & Miller, N. (2006). Naturalistic decision making in complex systems: A dynamic model of situated cognition combining technological and human agents. *Organizational Behavior*, *27*(7), 989–1009.

Shen, C. (2009). A Bayesian networks approach to modeling financial risks of e-logistics investments. *International Journal of Information Technology & Decision Making*, *8*(4), 711–726. doi:10.1142/S0219622009003594.

Sheth, A. P., & Larson, J. A. (1990). Federated database systems for managing distributed, heterogeneous, and autonomous databases. *ACM Computing Surveys*, *22*(3), 183–236. doi:10.1145/96602.96604.

Sheth, A., & Verna, K. et al. (2006). Semantics to energize the full services spectrum. *Communications of the ACM*, *49*(7), 55–61. doi:10.1145/1139922.1139949.

Shewart, W. A. (1986). *Statistical method from the viewpoint of quality control*. New York: Dover Publication.

Shirky, C. (2012). *Clay Shirky's internet writings*. Retrieved 14 August, 2012, from http://shirky.com/

Shpilberg, D., Berez, S., Puryear, R., & Shah, S. (2007). Avoiding the alignment trap in IT. *MIT Sloan Management Review*, *49*(1), 51–58.

Shunglu, V. K. (2011). *High level panel on financial position of distribution utilities*. New Delhi: Govt. of India.

Siew Kien, S. I. A., Soh, C., & Weil, P. (2010). Global IT management: structuring for scale, responsiveness, and innovation. *Communications of the ACM*, *53*(3), 59–64. doi:10.1145/1666420.1666449.

Simon, H. (1978). Rationality as a product and a process of thought. *American Economic Review*. Retrieved from http://www.jstor.org/discover/10.2307/1816653?uid=3739832&uid=2129&uid=2&uid=70&uid=4&uid=3739256&sid=21101715134507

Simons, R. (1995). *Levers of control: How managers use innovative control systems to drive strategic renewal*. Boston: Harvard College.

Sisley, E. (2010). *Enterprise architecture for the smart grid: A status update*. Pittsburgh, PA: Software Engineering Institute.

Sisley, E. (n.d.). *Review of NIST's unified logical architecture* (Feb 2010 draft). Pittsburgh, PA. *NIST*.

Slot, R. G. (2010). *A method for valuing architecture-based business transformation and measuring the value of solutions architecture*. (PhD thesis). Universiteit van Amsterdam, Amsterdam, The Netherlands.

Slowinski, G., & Sagal, M. W. (2003). *The strongest link: Forging a profitable and enduring corporate alliance*. New York: American Management Association.

Slywotzky, A. J., Morrison, D. J., Moser, T., Mundt, K. A., & Quella, J. A. (1999). *Profit patterns: 30 ways to anticipate and profit from strategic forces reshaping your business*. New York: John Wiley & Sons Ltd..

Slywotzky, A. J., Mundt, K. A., & Quella, J. A. (1999, June). Pattern thinking. *Management Review*, 32–37.

Slywotzky, A., & Morrison, D. (2001). Becoming a digital business: It's not about technology. *Strategy and Leadership*, *29*(2), 4–9. doi:10.1108/10878570110387671.

Smarr, L. (1985). An approach to complexity: Numerical computations. *Science*, *228*, 403–403. doi:10.1126/science.228.4698.403 PMID:17746870.

Smit, R. (2007, February 23). Manieren om strategie te verknallen. *Financieel Dagblad*.

Smith, K. L. (2011). *An introduction to PEAF – Pragmatic enterprise architecture framework*. Great Notley: Pragmatic EA.

Smith, L. B., & Thelen (Eds.). (1993). *A dynamic systems approach to development: Applications*. Cambridge, MA: MIT Press.

Smit, H., & Trigeorgis, L. (2009). Valuing infrastructure investment: An option game approach. *California Management Review*, *51*(2), 79–100. doi:10.2307/41166481.

Smith, C., Henschel, E., & Lefeber, R. (2008). Consolidation and shared service. *Government Finance Review*, *24*(5), 14–20.

Snowden, D. (2000). Cynefin: A sense of time and place: An ecological approach to sense making and learning in formal and informal communities. In *Proceedings of the Knowledge Management Annual Conference*. University of Aston.

Snowden, D. J., & Boone, M. E. (2007, November). A leader's framework for decision making. *Harvard Business Review*. PMID:18159787.

Snowden, D., & Boone, M. (2007, November). A leader's framework for decision making: Wise executives tailor their approach to fit the complexity of the circumstances they face. *Harvard Business Review*, 68–76. PMID:18159787.

Snyder, A. (1986). Encapsulation and inheritance in object-oriented programming languages. *ACM SIGPLAN Notices*, *21*(11), 38–45. doi:10.1145/960112.28702.

Sol, H. G. (1988). Information systems development: A problem solving approach. In *Proceedings of 1988 INTEC Symposium Systems Analysis and Design: A Research Strategy*. Atlanta, GA: INTEC.

Southern California Edison. (2008). *Use cases*. Retrieved from http://www.sce.com/info/smartconnect/facts/resource-center/use-cases.htm?from=usecases

Sowa, J. F., & Zachman, J. A. (1992). Extending and formalizing the framework for information systems architecture. *IBM Systems Journal*, *31*(3), 590–616. doi:10.1147/sj.313.0590.

Spanos, Y. E. (2004). Strategy and industry effects on profitability: Evidence from Greece. *Strategic Management Journal*, *25*, 139–165. doi:10.1002/smj.369.

Spewak, S. H. (1992). *Enterprise architecture planning: Developing a blueprint for data, application and technology*. QED Publishing Group.

Spewak, S. H., & Hill, S. C. (1993). *Enterprise architecture planning: Developing a blueprint for data, applications, and technology*. New York: John Wiley-QED Pub..

Spohrer, J., & Riecken, D. (2006). Service science. *Communications of the ACM*, *49*(7), 31–34.

Srivastan, R. (2012). *History of development thought: A critical anthology*. Routledge India.

Stepan, A. (1999). Federalism and democracy: Beyond the U.S. model. *Journal of Democracy*, *10*(4), 19–34. doi:10.1353/jod.1999.0072.

Stepan, A. C. (2001). Towards a new comparative politics of federalism, (multi)nationalism, and democracy: Beyond Rikerian federalism. In *Arguing Comparative Politics* (pp. 1–369). Oxford, UK: Oxford University Press.

Sterman, J. D. (2000). *Business dynamics – Systems thinking and modeling for a complex world*. Boston: Irwin McGraw-Hill.

Sterman, J. D. (2010). *Business dynamics – Systems thinking and modeling for a complex world*. Tata McGraw-Hill.

Stern, N. (2006). *The economics of climate change: The stern review*. Cambridge, MA: Cambridge University Press.

Stewart, A., & Wilkison. (2005). Health: A necessity for sustainable development. In Hens & Nath (Eds.), *The World Summit on Sustainable Development: The Johannesburg Conference*. Retrieved from http://link.springer.com/book/10.1007/1-4020-3653-1/page/1

Stewart, A. T. (1998). *Intellectual capital: The new wealth of organizations*. Crown Publishing Group. doi:10.1002/pfi.4140370713.

Stewart, T. A., & Raman, A. P. (2008). Finding a higher gear. *Harvard Business Review*, *86*(7), 68–76. PMID:18543809.

Stiglitz, J. Sen, & Fitoussi. (2009). *Report by the commission on the measurement of economic performance and social progress*. Retrieved from http://www.stiglitz-sen-fitoussi.fr/documents/rapport_anglais.pdf

Stringl. (2005). Science, research, knowledge and capacity building. In Hens & Nath (Eds.), *The World Summit on Sustainable Development: The Johannesburg Conference*. Retrieved from http://link.springer.com/book/10.1007/1-4020-3653-1/page/1

Stroh, P. D. (2000). Leveraging change: The power of systems thinking in action. *Reflections: The SoL Journal*, *2*(2). doi:10.1162/15241730051092019.

Suh, N. P. (1990). *The principles of design*. New York: Oxford University Press.

Suh, N. P. (1999). A theory of complexity, periodicity and the design axioms. *Research in Engineering Design*, *11*, 116–133. doi:10.1007/PL00003883.

Suh, N. P. (2001). *Axiomatic design: Advances and applications*. New York: Oxford University Press.

Suh, N. P. (2003). *Complexity: Theory and applications*. New York: Oxford University Press.

Suh, N. P. (2005). Complexity in engineering. *CIRP Annals-Manufacturing Technology*, *54*(2), 46–63. doi:10.1016/S0007-8506(07)60019-5.

Suh, N. P., & Do, S. (2000). Axiomatic design of software systems. *CIRP Annals-Manuf Technology*, *49*(1), 95–100. doi:10.1016/S0007-8506(07)62904-7.

Su, N., Akkiraju, R., Nayak, N., & Goodwin, R. (2009). Shared services transformation: Conceptualization and valuation from the perspective of real options. *Decision Sciences*, *40*(3), 381–402. doi:10.1111/j.1540-5915.2009.00243.x.

Swanson, E. B. (2012). The managers guide to IT innovation waves. *MIT Sloan Management Review*, *53*(2), 75–83.

Swedish Environmental Protection Agency. (2008). *Sweden's environmental objectives in brief*. Author.

Swedish International Development Agency (SIDA). (1995). *Promoting sustainable development likelihoods: A report from the taskforce on poverty*. Author.

Sykes, A. O. (1995). *Product standards for internationally integrated goods markets*. Washington, DC: Brookings Institution.

Systems-thinking. (n.d.). *Knowledge management—Emerging perspectives*. Retrieved August 7, 2012 from http://www.systems-thinking.org/kmgmt/kmgmt.htm/

Systems-wiki. (n.d.). *Viable systems model*. Retrieved January 4, 2013 from http://www.systemswiki.org

Tanriverdi, H. (2006). Performance effects of information technology synergies in multibusiness firms. *Management Information Systems Quarterly*, *30*(1), 57–77.

Tao, C., Jinlong, Z., Benhai, Y., & Shan, L. (2007). *A fuzzy group decision approach to real option valuation*. Wuhan, China: Huazhong University of Science and Technology. doi:10.1007/978-3-540-72530-5_12.

Tarr, G. A. (2001). Laboratories of democracy? Brandeis, federalism, and scientific management. *Publius*, *31*(1), 1–37. doi:10.1093/oxfordjournals.pubjof.a004880.

Taslak, S. (2004). Factors restricting success of strategic decisions: Evidence from the Turkish textile industry. *European Business Review, 16*(2), 152–164. doi:10.1108/09555340410524256.

Taylor, F. W. (1911). *The principles of scientific management.* New York: Harper & Brothers.

Taylor, J. C., & Felten, D. F. (1993). *Performance by design: Socio-technical systems in North America.* Englewood Cliffs, NJ: Prentice Hall.

Taylor, W. (1991). The logic of global business: An interview with ABB's Percy Barnevik. *Harvard Business Review, 69*(2), 90–105.

Tead, O. (1916). Trade unions and efficiency. *American Journal of Sociology, 22*(1), 30–37. doi:10.1086/212573.

Teece, D., Pisano, G., & Shuen, A. (1997). Dynamic capabilities and strategic management. *Strategic Management Journal, 18*(7), 509–533. doi:10.1002/(SICI)1097-0266(199708)18:7<509::AID-SMJ882>3.0.CO;2-Z.

Tester, Drake, Driscoll, Golay, & Peters. (2005). *Sustainable energy: Choosing among options.* Cambridge, MA: MIT Press.

Tester, J. W. Drake, Driscoll, Golay, & Peters. (2012). *Sustainable energy.* Retrieved from http://mitpress.mit.edu/sites/default/files/titles/content/9780262201537_sch_0001.pdf

The Institute of Systematic Leadership. (2012). T*he historical link between systems thinking and leadership.* Retrieved from http://www.systemicleadershipinstitute.org/systemic-leadership/theories/the-historic-link-between-systems-thinking-and-leadership/

The Open Group. (2009). The open group architecture framework (TOGAF) enterprise Ed. version 9. San Diego, CA: The Open Group.

The Open Group. (2011, Dec). *TOGAF version 9.1.* Retrieved 10 28, 2012, from http://www.opengroup.org/togaf/

The Open Group. (2012). *TOGAF 9.1.* Retrieved October 16, 2012, from http://www.opengroup.org/togaf

Thenmozhi, M. (2012). *Module 9 - Strategic management.* Lecture Notes, Department of Management Studies, IIT Madras.

Theuerkorn, F. (2004). *Lightweight enterprise architectures.* Boca Raton, FL: Auerbach Publications. doi:10.1201/9780203505311.

Tiebout, C. M. (1956). A pure theory of local expenditures. *The Journal of Political Economy, 64*(5), 416–424. doi:10.1086/257839.

Tocqueville, A. D. (2005). Federal theory in democracy in America. In Karmis, D., & Norman, W. J. (Eds.), *Theories Of Federalism: A Reader* (pp. 147–163). New York, NY: Palgrave Macmillan.

TOGAF. (2012). *The open group architecture framework (TOGAF).* Retrieved 27 July 2012, 2012, from http://www.opengroup.org/togaf/

TOGAF. (n.d.). *TOGAF 9.1.* Retrieved August 10, 2012 from http://pubs.opengroup.org/architecture/togaf9-doc/arch/

Tolga, A., & Kahraman, C. (2008). Fuzzy multiattribute evaluation of R&D projects using a real options valuation model. *International Journal of Intelligent Systems, 23,* 1153–1176. doi:10.1002/int.20312.

Tongia, R. (2006). The political economy of Indian power sector reforms. In Victor, D., & Heller, T. (Eds.), *The Political Economy of Power Sector Reforms: The Experiences of Five Major Developing Countries.* Cambridge, UK: Cambridge University Press.

Tongia, R., Subrahmanian, E., & Arunachalam, V. S. (2005). *ICT for sustainable development - Defining a global research agenda.* Bangalore: Allied Press.

Trigeorgis, L. (2002). *Real options and investment under uncertainty: What do we know?* Brussels, Belgium: Nationale Bank van België. doi:10.2139/ssrn.1692691.

Trist, E. (1981). *The evolution of socio-technical systems: A conceptual framework and an action research program.* Issues in the Ontario Quality of Working Life Center Occasional Paper No. 2. Toronto, Canada: Ontario Ministry of Labour.

Trochim, W. M., Cabrera, D. A., Milstein, B., Gallagher, R. S., & Leischow, S. J. (2006). Practical challenges of systems thinking and modeling in public health. *American Journal of Public Health, 96*(3). doi:10.2105/AJPH.2005.066001 PMID:16449581.

Truex, D. P., Baskerville, R., & Kelin, H. (1999). Growing systems in emergent organizations. *Communications of the ACM, 42*(8), 117–123. doi:10.1145/310930.310984.

Tuite, D. (2010). *Smart grid design opportunities extend from the meter to the mercantile exchange.*

Tukker, A. Emmert, Charter, Vezzoli, Sto, Andersen, … Lahlou. (2008). Fostering change to sustainable production and consumption: An evidence-based view. *Journal of Cleaner Production.* Retrieved from http://www2.lse.ac.uk/socialPsychology/research_activities/publications/saadi_lahlou/fosteringchange.pdf

Turkishtime. (2009, April). Pepsi'nin yüzü hep gülecek mi?. [Will Pepsi always smile?]. *Turkishtime*, 92-95.

Turkishtime. (2009, April). Yeni yatırımlar için ısınıyor. [He is warming up for new investments]. *Turkishtime*, 110-111.

Türkiye (2009, January). Sıfır sermaye ile yola çıkan Orhan Turan, bugün 40 milyon dolarlık yatırım yapabilen ODE Yalıtım'ı yarattı: En büyük sermayesi, büyük düşünebilmesi…. [Orhan Turan started with zero capital, and he created ODE Insulation, which can make an investment of 40 million dollars: His biggest capital is thinking big….]. *Türkiye*, 52-55.

Türkiye. (2008, December). Ses kafanızın derinliklerinde titreşerek gözlerinizden dışarı akar. [The sound blinks in the depth of your head and flows out of your eyes.]. *Türkiye*, 123.

Türkiye. (2009, April). Dünya krizle çalkalansa bile ilaç sektörü kendine güveniyor: Hem de haklı sebeplerle. [The pharmaceutical industry trusts itself: Due to valid reasons]. *Türkiye*, 84-92.

Türkiye. (2009, February). Bedavalar da yetmiyor, 'İndirim' yeniden tanımlanacak. [Even the free giveaways are not enough, 'Sale' will be redefined]. *Türkiye*, 21-23.

Türkiye. (2009, April). Yolunuzu bulmak için tüketicinin sesini dinleyin. [Listen to the consumer to find your way]. *Türkiye*, 53-67.

Turle, M. (2010). Shared services: An outline of key contractual issues. *Computer Law & Security Report, 2*(6), 178–184. doi:10.1016/j.clsr.2010.01.009.

Turquality. (2012). Retrieved from http://www.turquality.com

Uhl-Bien, M., Marion, & McKelvey. (2007). Complexity leadership theory: Shifting leadership from the industrial age to the knowledge era. *The Leadership Quarterly, 18*, 298–318. doi:10.1016/j.leaqua.2007.04.002.

UK Cabinet Office. (2010). *Behavioural insights team.* Retrieved 9 June 2012, from http://www.cabinetoffice.gov.uk/behavioural-insights-team

Ulanowicz, R. E. (2009). *A third window: Natural life beyond Newton and Darwin.* West Conshohocken, PA: Templeton Foundation Press.

Ulbrich, F. (2006). Improving shared service implementation: Adopting lessons from the BPR movement. *Business Process Management Journal, 12*(2), 191–205. doi:10.1108/14637150610657530.

Ulbrich, F. (2010). Adopting shared services in a public-sector organization. *Transforming Government: People. Process and Policy, 4*(3), 249–265.

Ulrich, D. (1995). Shared services: From vogue to value. *Human Resource Planning, 18*(3), 12–23.

Ulrich, D., & Grochowski, J. (2012). From shared services to professional services. *Strategic HR Review, 11*(3), 136–142. doi:10.1108/14754391211216850.

Ulusoy, G., & Yegenoglu, H. (2007). Innovation performance and competitive strategies in the Turkish manufacturing industry. In *Proceedings of the 8th International Research Conference on Quality, Innovation and Knowledge Management,* (pp. 907-915). New Delhi, India: IEEE.

Ulusoy, G., Çetindamar, D., Yegenoglu, H., & Bulut, Ç. (2007). An empirical study on the competitiveness and innovation in four sectors of the Turkish manufacturing industry. In *Proceedings of the 14th International Annual EurOMA Conference,* (pp. 438-447). Ankara, Turkey: EurOMA.

Ulusoy, G. (2003). An assessment of supply chain and innovation management practices in the manufacturing industries in Turkey. *International Journal of Production Economics, 86*, 251–270. doi:10.1016/S0925-5273(03)00064-1.

Ulusoy, G., & İkiz, İ. (2001). Benchmarking best manufacturing practices: A study into four sectors of Turkish industry. *International Journal of Operations & Production Management, 21*(7), 1021–1043. doi:10.1108/01443570110393478.

Umapathy, K., & Purao, S. (2007). A theoretical investigation of emerging standards for web services. *Information Systems Frontiers, 9*(1), 119–134. doi:10.1007/s10796-006-9021-4.

United Nations Conference on Sustainable Development Rio+20. (2012). *The future we want – Outcome document of the conference.* Retrieved from http://daccess-dds-ny.un.org/doc/UNDOC/GEN/N12/381/64/PDF/N1238164.pdf?OpenElement

United Nations Conference on the Environment and Development. (1992). *Rio declaration.* Retrieved from http://daccess-dds-ny.un.org/doc/UNDOC/GEN/N92/836/55/PDF/N9283655.pdf?OpenElement

United Nations Conference on the Environment and Development. (1992). *Conference report.* Retrieved from http://daccess-dds-ny.un.org/doc/UNDOC/GEN/N92/836/55/PDF/N9283655.pdf?OpenElement

United Nations Department of Economic and Social Affairs (UNDESA). (2008). *United Nations e-government survey 2008: From e-government to connected governance.* New York: United Nations.

United Nations Department of Economic and Social Affairs (UNDESA). (2010). *United Nations e-government survey 2010: Leveraging e-government at a time of financial and economic crises.* New York: United Nations.

United Nations Department of Economic and Social Affairs (UNDESA). (2012). *United Nations e-government survey 2012: E-government for the people.* New York: United Nations.

United Nations Department of Economic and Social Affairs. UNDESA. (2010). *Trends in sustainable development: Chemicals, mining, transport, waste management.* Division for Sustainable Development, UNDESA. Retrieved from http://www.uncsd2012.org/content/documents/205Trends_chem_mining_transp_waste.pdf

United Nations Department of Economic and Social Affairs. UNDESA. (2010). *Trends in sustainable development: Sustainable production and consumption.* Division for Sustainable Development, UNDESA. Retrieved from http://www.uncsd2012.org/content/documents/15Trends_in_sustainable_consumption_and_production.pdf

United Nations Department of Economic and Social Affairs. UNDESA. (2012). *A guidebook to the green economy, issue 1: Green economy, green growth, and low-carbon development, history, definitions and a guide to recent publications.* Division for Sustainable Development, UNDESA. Retrieved from http://www.uncsd2012.org/content/documents/528Green%20Economy%20Guidebook_100912_FINAL.pdf

United Nations Development Program. (2011). *Human development report 2011: Sustainability and equity: A better future for all.* Retrieved from http://hdr.undp.org/en/reports/global/hdr2011/download/

United Nations Development Program. (2012). *Triple wins for sustainable development: Case studies of sustainable development in practice.* Retrieved from http://www.undp.org/content/dam/undp/library/Cross-Practice%20generic%20theme/Triple-Wins-for-Sustainable-Development-Web.pdf

United Nations Development Program. (2012). *Governance for peace: Securing the social contract.* Retrieved from http://www.beta.undp.org /content/undp/en/home/librarypage/crisis-prevention -and-recovery

United Nations Development Program. (2009). *Fighting climate change: Human solidarity in a divided world. Human Development Report 2007/2008.* UNDP.

United Nations Economic Commission for Europe. Organization for Economic Cooperation and Development, & Eurostat. (2008). *Measuring sustainable development: Report of the joint UNECE/OECD/Eurostat working group on statistics for sustainable development.* Retrieved from http://www.oecd.org/dataoecd/30/20/41414440.pdf

United Nations Environmental Program, UNEP. (1995). *Poverty and the environment: Reconciling short-term needs with long-term sustainability goals.* UNEP.

United Nations Environmental Program. UNEP. (2011). *Towards a green economy: Pathways to sustainable development and poverty eradication.* Retrieved from http://www.unep.org/greeneconomy/Portals/88/documents/ger/ger_final_dec_2011/Green%20EconomyReport_Final_Dec2011.pdf

United Nations General Assembly. (1987). *Our common future.* Retrieved from http://www.un.org/documents/ga/res/42/ares42-187.htm

United Nations General Assembly. (1992). *Resolution on the report of the United Nations conference on environment and development.* Retrieved from http://www.un.org/documents/resga.htm

United Nations General Assembly. (1992). *Rio declaration on environment and development.* Retrieved from http://www.un.org/documents/ga/conf151/aconf15126-1annex1.htm

United Nations General Assembly. (2012). *Resolution adopted by the general assembly endorsing the outcome document of the United Nations conference on sustainable development entitled the future we want.* Retrieved from http://daccess-dds-ny.un.org/doc/UNDOC/GEN/N11/476/10/PDF/N1147610.pdf?OpenElement

United Nations General Assembly. (2012). *Note of the secretary general on submitting the report resilient people, resilient planet: A future worth choosing.* Retrieved from http://www.un.org/ga/search/view_doc.asp?symbol=A/66/700&referer=/english/&Lang=E

United Nations Secretary General's High Level Panel on Global Sustainability. (2012). *Resilient people, resilient planet: A future worth choosing.* Retrieved from http://www.un.org/gsp/sites/default/files/attachments/GSPReport_unformatted_30Jan.pdf

United Nations. (2002). *Global challenge, global opportunity: Trends in sustainable development.* United Nations Johannesburg Summit. Retrieved from http://www.un.org/esa/sustdev/publications/critical_trends_report_2002.pdf

United States Department of Defense. (2012). *DoD architecture framework version 2.02.* Retrieved January 8, 2013, from http://dodcio.defense.gov/dodaf20.aspx

United States General Accounting Office. (2003). *Enterprise architecture: Leadership remains key to establishing and leveraging architectures for organizational transformation.* No. GAO-04-40. Washington, DC: U.S. General Accounting Office.

United States Government Accountability Office. (2010). *Organizational transformation: A framework for assessing and improving enterprise architecture management (version 2.0).* No. GAO-10-846G. Washington, DC: Government Accountability Office.

United States. (2008). *Budget of the U.S. government: fiscal year 2009.* Office of Management and Budget. Retrieved October 15, 2012, from http://www.whitehouse.gov/omb/budget/fy2009/pdf/budget.pdf

United States. (2010). *HHS enterprise architecture — framework version 16.0.* U.S. Department of Health and Human Services. Retrieved October 8, 2012, from http://www.hhs.gov/ocio/ea/documents/hhseaframeworkpdf.pdf

United States. (2012,). *The common approach to federal enterprise architecture.* Executive Office of the President. Retrieved January 10, 2013, from https://cio.gov/wp-content/uploads/downloads/2012/09/common_approach_to_federal_ea.pdf

Urban, F., & Nordensvard. (2013). *Low carbon development.* London: Routledge.

US Department of Defense. (2010). *The DoD architecture framework, US department of defense.* Retrieved 10 28, 2012, from http://dodcio.defense.gov/dodaf20.aspx

US Energy Information Administration. (2012). *Electricity.* Retrieved October 21, 2012, from www.eia.doe.gov

US Federal CIO Council. (n.d.). *FEA practice guidance – Introducing segment architecture.* Retrieved 10 28, 2012, from http://www.cio.gov/index.cfm?function=specdoc&id=Practical%20Guide%20to%20Service%20Oriented%20Architecture%20(PGFSOA)%20v1.1&structure=Enterprise%20Architecture&category=Enterprise%20Architecture

US Government Accountability Office. (2011). *Opportunities to reduce potential duplication in government programs, save tax dollars, and enhance revenue.* Washingotn, DC: Author.

US OMB e-Government and Information Technology Office. (2012). *Federal enterprise architecture.* Retrieved 10 28, 2012, from http://www.whitehouse.gov/omb/e-gov/fea/

Vale, R., & Vale. (2013). *Living with a fair share ecological footprint.* London: Routledge.

Van Dale Groot woordenboek van de Nederlandse taal. (2010). *Van dale* (14th ed.). Martinus Nijhoff, Den Haag, The Netherlands.

van den Berg, M., & van Steenbergen, M. (2006). *Building an enterprise architecture practice – Tools, tips, best practices, ready-to-use insights.* Dordrecht, The Netherlands: Springer.

Van den Berg, M., & van Steenbergen, M. (2010). *Building an enterprise architecture practice.* Berlin: Springer.

Van Hillegersberg, J., Boeke, R., & Van den Heuvel, W. J. (2004). Potential of webservices to enable smart business networks. *Journal of Information Technology, 19*(4), 281–287. doi:10.1057/palgrave.jit.2000027.

Van Zeijl-Rozema, A. Corvers, Kemp, & Martens. (2008). Governance for sustainable development: A framework. *Sustainable Development.* Retrieved from http://www.onlinelibrary.wiley.com/doi/10.1002/sd.367/abstract

Van't Wout, J., Waage, M., Hartman, H., Stahlecker, M., & Hofman, A. (2010). *The integrated architecture framework explained.* Berlin: Springer. doi:10.1007/978-3-642-11518-9.

Vargo, S. L., & Lusch,. (2008). From goods to service(s): Divergences and convergences of logics. *Industrial Marketing Management, 37*(3), 254–259. doi:10.1016/j.indmarman.2007.07.004.

Vargo, S. L., & Lusch, R. F. (2004). Evolving to a new dominant logic for marketing. *Journal of Marketing, 68,* 1–17. doi:10.1509/jmkg.68.1.1.24036.

Vargo, S. L., & Lusch, R. F. (2008). Service-dominant logic: Continuing the evolution. *Journal of the Academy of Marketing Science, 36,* 1–10. doi:10.1007/s11747-007-0069-6.

Vargo, S. L., & Lusch, R. F. (2008). Why service? *Journal of the Academy of Marketing Science, 36,* 25–38. doi:10.1007/s11747-007-0068-7.

Venkatraman, N., & Henderson, J. C. (1993). Strategic alignment. *IBM Systems Journal, 32*(1), 4–16.

Venkatraman, N., Henderson, J. C., & Oldach, S. (1993). Continuous strategic alignment: Exploiting information technology capabilities for competitive success. *European Management Journal, 11*(2), 139–149. doi:10.1016/0263-2373(93)90037-I.

Victor, D., & Heller, T. (2006). *The political economy of power sector reform* (Victor, D., & Heller, T., Eds.). Cambridge, UK: Cambridge University Press.

Villarreal, R. (2012). *Regulatory quality improvements for preventing corruption in public administration: A capacity building perspective.* Retrieved from http://unpan1.un.org/intradoc/groups/public/documents/undpadm/unpan049594.pdf

Villarreal, R. (2012). *Countering corruption from one or two sides? Opportunities and Challenges in cooperation between government and civil society.* Retrieved from http://www.surrey.ac.uk/sbs/events/COUNTERING%20CORRUPTION%20FROM%20ONE%20OR%20TWO%20SIDES%20-%20GOVERNMENT%20AND%20CIVIL%20SOCIETY%20Roberto%20Villarreal.pdf

Vitányi, P. (2007). Analysis of sorting algorithms by Kolmogorov complexity (a survey). *Entropy, Search, Complexity. Bolyai Society Mathematical Studies, 16,* 209–232. doi:10.1007/978-3-540-32777-6_9.

von Bertalanffy, L. (1968). *General system theory: Foundations, development, applications.* New York: George Braziller.

von Helfenstein, S. (2009). *Real options 'in' economic systems and the demise of modern portfolio theory.* Paper presented at the 13th Annual International Real Options Conference. Braga, Portugal.

Von Simson, E. M. (1990). The 'centrally decentralized' IS organization. *Harvard Business Review, 68*(4), 158–162. PMID:10107960.

Wagenaar, R. (2006). Governance of shared service centers in public administration: Dilemma's and trade-offs. In *Proceedings of ICEC'06.* ICEC.

Wagter, R. (2009). Sturen op samenhang op basis van GEA – Permanent en event driven. Van Haren Publishing, Zaltbommel.

Wagter, R., Nijkamp, G., & Proper, H. A. (2007). *Overview 1th phase - General enterprise architecturing*. White Paper GEA-1, Ordina, Utrecht, The Netherlands.

Wagter, R., Proper, H. A., & Witte, D. (2007). *White paper GEA-7*. De GEA Architectuurfunctie: Strategisch specialisme, Ordina, Nieuwegein, The Netherlands.

Wagter, R., Proper, H. A., & Witte, D. (2011). Enterprise coherence-governance assessment. In *Proceedings of the 2nd Working Conference on Practice-driven Research on Enterprise Transformation*. Berlin: Springer.

Wagter, R., Proper, H. A., & Witte, D. (2012). Enterprise coherence in the Dutch ministry of social affairs and employment. In *Proceedings of the 7th International Workshop on Business/IT-Alignment and Interoperability (BUSITAL2012)*. Berlin: Springer.

Wagter, R., Proper, H. A., & Witte, D. (2012). Enterprise architecture: A strategic specialism. In *Proceedings of 2012 IEEE 14th International Conference on Commerce and Enterprise Computing (CEC 2012)*. Hangzhou, China: IEEE.

Wagter, R., Proper, H. A., & Witte, D. (2012). *A practice-based framework for enterprise coherence*. Berlin: Springer-Verlag.

Wagter, R., van den Berg, M., Luijpers, J., & van Steenbergen, M. (2005). *Dynamic enterprise architecture: How to make IT work*. Hoboken, NJ: John Wiley.

Walker, B., & Salt. (2006). *Resilience thinking: Sustaining ecosystems and people in a changing world*. Island Press.

Walker, B., Carpenter, Anderies, Abel, Cumming, Janssen, Lebel, … Pritchard. (2002). *Resilience management in social-ecological systems: A working hypothesis for a*

Walker, J. I. (1969). The diffusion of innovations among the American states. *The American Political Science Review, 63*, 880–889. doi:10.2307/1954434.

Wang, S., & Lee, C. (2010). A fuzzy real option valuation approach to capital budgeting under uncertainty environment. *International Journal of Information Technology & Decision Making, 9*(5), 695–713. doi:10.1142/S0219622010004056.

Watkins, M. E. (2012, June). How managers become leaders – The seven seismic shifts of perspective and responsibility. *Harvard Business Review*, 65–72. PMID:22741419.

Watts, R. (2001). Models of federal power sharing. *International Social Science Journal, 53*(1), 23–32.

Watts, R. L. (1999). *Comparing federal systems* (2nd ed.). Montreal, Canada: McGill-Queen's University Press.

Watts, R. L. (2005). Comparing forms of federal partnerships. In Karmis, D., & Norman, W. J. (Eds.), *Theories of Federalism: A Reader* (pp. 233–253). New York, NY: Palgrave Macmillan.

Weber, E. (2003). *Bringing society back in grassroots ecosystem management, accountability and sustainable communities*. Cambridge, MA: Massachusetts Institute of Technology Press.

Weber, M. (1999). *Essays in economic sociology* (Swedberg, R., Ed.). Princeton University Press.

Wegmann, A. (2003). Alain Wegmann: On the systemic enterprise architecture methodology (seam). *ICEIS Conference Proceedings, 3*, 483-490.

Wegmann, A. (2003). On the systemic enterprise architecture methodology (SEAM). In *Proceedings of the International Conference on Enterprise Information Systems 2003 (ICEIS 2003)*, (pp. 483–490). ICEIS.

Wegmann, A. (2003). *The systemic enterprise architecture methodology, business and IT alignment for competitveness*.

Wegmann, A., Kotsalainen, A., Matthey, L., Regev, G., & Giannattasio, A. (2008). Augmenting the Zachman enterprise architecture framework with a systemic conceptualization. In *Proceedings of the 12th IEEE International EDOC Conference (EDOC 2008)*, (pp. 3–13). EDOC.

Weick, K. E., & Sutcliffe, K. M. (2007). *Managing the unexpected: Resilient performance in an age of uncertainty* (2nd ed.). San Francisco, CA: Jossey-Bass.

Weill, P., Malone, T. W., D'Urso, V. T., Herman, G., & Woerner, S. (2005). *Do some business models perform better than others? A study of the 1000 largest US firms.* Cambridge, MA: MIT Press.

Weill, P., & Ross, J. W. (2004). *IT governance: How top performers manage IT decision rights for superior results.* Boston: Harvard Business School Press.

Weill, P., & Ross, J. W. (2005). A matrixed approach to designing IT governance. *MIT Sloan Management Review, 46*(2), 26–34.

Wen, L., & Dromey, R. G. (2009). A hierarchical architecture for modeling complex software intensive systems using behavior trees. In *Proceedings of the 9th Asia-Pacific Complex Systems Conference,* (pp. 292-299). IEEE.

Weng, G., Bhalla, U. S., & Iyengar, R. (1999). Complexity in biological signaling systems. *Science, 284*(5411), 92–96. doi:10.1126/science.284.5411.92 PMID:10102825.

Wen, L., & Dromey, R. G. (2006). Architecture normalization for component-based systems. *Electronic Notes in Theoretical Computer Science, 160,* 335–348. doi:10.1016/j.entcs.2006.05.032.

Weske, M. (2012). *Business process management – Concepts, languages, architectures.* Berlin: Springer. doi:10.1007/978-3-642-28616-2.

West, M. D. (2011). *Enabling personalized medicine through health information technology: Advancing the integration of information.* Retrieved on July 30, 2012 from http://www.brookings.edu/research/papers/2011/01/28-personalized-medicine-west

Whitehouse. (1996). *Management of federal information resources.* Retrieved August 9, 2012 from http://www.whitehouse.gov/omb/circulars_a130

Whitesides, G., & Ismagilov, R. F. (1999). Complexity in chemistry. *Science, 284*(5411), 89–92. doi:10.1126/science.284.5411.89 PMID:10102824.

Wibbels, E. (2000). Federalism and the politics of macroeconomic policy and performance. *American Journal of Political Science, 44*(4), 687. doi:10.2307/2669275.

Wibbels, E. (2001). Federal politics and market reform in the developing world. *Studies in Comparative International Development, 36*(2), 27–53. doi:10.1007/BF02686208.

Wiener, N. (1948). *Cybernetics, or communication and control in the animal and the machine.* Cambridge, MA: MIT Press.

Wilkinson, R., & Pickett. (2010). *The impact of incomes inequalities on sustainable development in London.* Report for the London Sustainable Development Commission. Retrieved from http://www.londonsdc.org/documents/The%20impact%20of%20income%20inequalities%20on%20sustainable%20development%20in%20London.pdf

Wilkins, R. B. (2004). Federalism: Distance and devolution. *The Australian Journal of Politics and History, 50*(1), 95–101. doi:10.1111/j.1467-8497.2004.00323.x.

Williams, B., & Hummelbrunner, R. (2009). *Systems concepts in action – A practitioner's toolkit.* Palo Alto, CA: Stanford University Press.

Williamson, O. (1994). The institutions and governance of economic development and reform. In *Proceedings of the World Bank Annual Conference on Development Economics.* Washington, DC: World Bank.

Williamson, O. (1994). Visible and invisible governance. *The American Economic Review.* PMID:10134748.

Williams, T. J. (1994). *Purdue guide for master planning & implementation programs.* West-Lafayette, IN: Purdue University.

Willson, P., & Pollard, C. (2009). Exploring IT governance in theory and practice in a large multi-national organisation in Australia. *Information Systems Management, 26*(2), 98–109. doi:10.1080/10580530902794760.

Wilson, J. A. (2012). *Evaluating the effectiveness of reference models in federating enterprise architectures.* (Dissertation). The George Washington University, Washington, DC.

Wilson, J., Mazzuchi, T., & Sarkani, S. (2010). Federating enterprises architectures using reference models. In *Proceedings International Conference on Information Warfare and Security* (pp. 481-488). IEEE.

Wilson, B. (1990). *Systems – Concepts, methodologies and applications*. Chichester, UK: Wiley.

Wilson, D. A. (2004). Shared services: A strategy for reinventing government. *Government Finance Review, 20*(4), 37–44.

Wilson, K., & Doz, Y. L. (2011). Agile innovation: A footprint balancing distance and immersion. *California Management Review, 53*(2), 6–26. doi:10.1525/cmr.2011.53.2.6.

Windley, P. (2002). *eGovernment maturity*. Retrieved June 1, 2012, from http://www.windley.com/

Winter, K., Buckl, S., Matthes, F., & Schweda, C. M. (2010). Investigating the state-of-the-art in enterprise architecture management methods in literature and practice. In *Proceedings of MCIS*. Retrieved from http://aisel.aisnet.org/mcis2010/90

Wissner, M. (2011). The smart grid – A saucerful of secrets? *Applied Energy, 88*, 2509–2518. doi:10.1016/j.apenergy.2011.01.042.

Wooldridge, M., & Lovell. (2011). *Human services: The case for change*. Retrieved 7 August, 2012, from http://www.dhs.vic.gov.au/about-the-department/news-and-events/news/general-news/human-services-the-case-for-change

World Bank. (2003). *Sustainable development in a dynamic world. World Development Report 2003*. Washington, DC: World Bank.

World Bank. (2010). *Development and climate change. World Development Report 2010*. Washington, DC: World Bank.

World Commission on Environment and Development (Brundtland Commission). (1987). *Our common future*. Report of the Brundtland Commission. Retrieved from http://www.un-documents.net/our-common-future.pdf and http://www.un.org/documents/ga/res/42/ares42-187.htm

World Economic Forum. (WEF). (2011). *The future of government – Lessons learned from around the world*. Geneva, Switzerland: World Economic Forum.

World Economic Forum. (WEF). (2011). *The global information technology report 2010/2011 – Transformations 2.0*. Geneva, Switzerland: World Economic Forum.

World Economic Forum. (WEF). (2012). *Global risks 2012*. Geneva, Switzerland: World Economic Forum.

World Economic Forum. (WEF). (2012). *Young global leaders – Guide to influencing complex systems*. Geneva, Switzerland: World Economic Forum.

World Economic Forum. (WEF). (2013). *Sustainable health systems – Visions, strategies, critical uncertainties and scenarios*. Geneva, Switzerland: World Economic Forum.

World Health Organization. (2005). *Preventing chronic diseases – A vital investment*. Geneva, Switzerland: Department of Chronic Diseases and Health Promotion, World Health Organization.

World Summit on Sustainable Development. (2002). *Report of the world summit on sustainable development: Political declaration*. Retrieved from http://www.un.org/esa/sustdev/documents/WSSD_POI_PD/English/POI_PD.htm

World Summit on Sustainable Development. (2002). *Report of the world summit on sustainable development: Plan of implementation*. Retrieved from http://www.un.org/esa/sustdev/documents/WSSD_POI_PD/English/POIToc.htm

Yamin, M., & Forsgren, M. (2006). Hymer's analysis of the multinational organization: Power retention and the demise of the federative MNE. *International Business Review, 15*(2), 166–179. doi:10.1016/j.ibusrev.2005.07.006.

Yin, R. K. (2009). *Case study research – Design and methods* (4th ed.). Thousand Oaks, CA: Sage Publications.

Yusuf, S. Deaton, Derviş, Easterly, Ito, & Stiglitz. (2009). *Development economics through the decades: A critical look at 30 years of the world development report*. World Bank. Retrieved from http://www-wds.worldbank.org/external/default/WDSContentServer/WDSP/IB/2009/01/14/000334955_20090114045203/Rendered/PDF/47108 0PUB0Deve101OFFICIAL0USE0ONLY1.pdf

Zachman, J. (2008). *The Zachman framework™: The official concise definition.* Retrieved 10 28, 2012, from http://zachmaninternational.com/index.php/home-article/13

Zachman, J. A. (2006). *Federated enterprise architecture.* Retrieved August 3, 2011 http://www.intervista-institute.com/zachman-fa.php

Zachman, J. A. (1987). A framework for information systems architecture. *IBM Systems Journal, 26*(3), 276–292. doi:10.1147/sj.263.0276.

Zenghelis, D. (2010). *The economics of network powered growth* (White Paper). CISCO Internet Business Solutions Group (IBSG).

Zokaei, K., Seddon, J., & O'Donovan, B. (2011). *Systems thinking – From heresy to practice.* Hampshire, UK: Palgrave Macmillan.

About the Contributors

Pallab Saha is with the National University of Singapore, Institute of Systems Science. His current research and consulting interests include Enterprise Architecture (EA) and Governance. Dr. Saha has published four books, *Handbook of Enterprise Systems Architecture in Practice; Advances in Government Enterprise Architecture; Coherency Management: Architecting the Enterprise for Alignment, Agility, and Assurance;* and *Enterprise Architecture for Connected E-Government: Practices and Innovations*. His books are widely referred, making it to the *Top Seller* list in 2008 and 2009. His papers have been translated and published in Arabic, Korean, Russian, and Polish. Identified as a Technology Thought Leader by Forrester, Dr. Saha is the primary author of the *Methodology for AGency ENTerprise Architecture (MAGENTA)* and *Government EA Guidebook* for the Government of Singapore and has led them to international prominence. They are available in IDS Scheer's ARIS Toolset. He is a two-time recipient of the Microsoft research grant in EA supported by UN and World Bank. He has provided advisory services to the MINDEF, DSTA, IDA, IHIS, IPOS, CPF Board, SingHealth, Governments of Oman and Kazakhstan, Great Eastern Life Assurance, and delivered executive programs to Governments of Bhutan, China, Taiwan, and Panama. He has been invited as a distinguished speaker to the World Bank, Carnegie Mellon University, UN University, The Open Group, Microsoft, SAP Labs, Denmark IT Society, Korea Institute for IT Architecture, IEEE, SGGovCamp, Nanyang Business School, George Mason University, IIM Bangalore, Governments of South Australia, Jordan, UAE, Macau, Korea, Kazakhstan, Colombia, Nepal, Bangladesh, and several Singapore government agencies. His work has been cited by the UN, WHO, US DOD, Carlsberg, and The Open Group, and has contributed to the World Bank's EA Guidelines for Vietnam and Bangladesh. Featured as an Architect in the Spotlight by the *Journal of EA*, he has been an examiner for research degree to the University of NSW, a Visiting Researcher to the UN University, an expert reviewer to the *ACM Enterprise Architecture Tech Pack*, an invited guest faculty to the LKY School of Public Policy, and an expert member to DSTA's Technical Competency Accreditation Panel. Earlier, as Head of Development he has managed Baxter's offshore centre in Bangalore. He has had engagements in Fortune 100 organizations in various capacities. Dr. Saha holds a Ph.D in Management (Information Systems) from the Indian Institute of Science, Bangalore, and has received the best research design and best thesis awards. He is an alumnus of the MIT Sloan Executive Program.

* * *

Lars Bækgaard holds a Ph.D. in Computer Science from Aalborg University, Denmark. He is an associate professor at Aarhus University, Denmark, where he supervises students who engage in problem-based projects. He teaches business information systems, technology management, and research methodology. His research interests include business information systems, service innovation, enterprise architecture, and conceptual modeling. He is a member of the Association of Information Systems, and he has published papers in and serves as a referee for international journals.

Peter Bernus has worked internationally on various aspects of enterprise integration as researcher, consultant, project leader, and trainer for Industry, Government, and Defence (ADF) in projects for petrochemical engineering, shipbuilding, and defense logistics. He is also the series co-editor for Springer Verlag, managing editor of the *Handbook on Enterprise Architecture*, the *Handbook on Architectures of Information Systems*, and member of editorial boards of several international journals. Bernus is past chair of the IFIP-IFAC Task Force for Architectures for Enterprise Integration, which developed GERAM, an international standard for the requirements of enterprise architecture frameworks (ISO 15704:2000), foundation chair of IFIP WG5.12 on Architectures for Enterprise Integration. He is currently an Associate Professor at Griffith University teaching enterprise architecture and director of the IIIS Centre for Enterprise Architecture Research and Management Program. Bernus's interests include engineering design methodologies in the broadest sense of engineering, Enterprise Architecture Frameworks and standards, Virtual enterprises and Enterprise Networks, Enterprise Architecture Practice, Governance and Management and Complex Systems Engineering.

Özcan Bilgin is a 2011 graduate of Manufacturing Systems Engineering Program at Sabancı University. Since his graduation, he has been managing his own logistics company, Bilgin Logistics. His specializations include logistic management, supply-chain management, strategic management, and statistical data analysis.

Sabine Buckl is a senior researcher at the chair for Software Engineering of Business Information Systems at the Technische Universität München (TUM). She received her diploma degree in Informatics (Minor, electrical engineering) and her PhD in Computer Science from Technische Universität München. Sabine's research interests center around methods, models, and tools for the management of enterprise architectures and application landscapes as part thereof. Putting emphasis on enterprises as socio-technical systems, she is especially interested in the organization specific-design of the enterprise architecture management function. Findings from her research have been published as books, e.g. the *Enterprise Architecture Management Tool Survey, Enterprise Architecture Management Pattern Catalog*, and presented at international scientific conferences such as ICIS, ECIS, and practice-oriented conferences such as the Open Group Conference.

Donald W. de Guerre is an associate professor at Concordia University in Montreal. He received a Ph.D. in Human and Organization Systems from the Fielding Graduate University in California. He has a distinguished international career as a consultant and manager. His major area of interest is the development of participative governance and organization and the further development of open systems theory.

Gürdal Ertek is an Assistant Professor at Sabancı University, Istanbul, Turkey. He received his B.S. from Industrial Engineering Department of Boğaziçi University, Istanbul, Turkey, in 1994, and his Ph.D. from School of Industrial and Systems Engineering at Georgia Institute of Technology, Atlanta, GA, in 2001. His research areas include warehousing and material handling, and data visualization and mining. He has been awarded with Boğaziçi University Alumni Scholarship, Hacı Ömer Sabancı Scholarship, and Fulbright Scholarship. Dr. Ertek has taught more than 2000 students in lecture-styled courses and has supervised more than 500 students in project courses, such as PROJ 102 (Project Course) and ENS 491 (Senior Project). He has also extensively served as a reviewer for R&D projects submitted to TÜBİTAK (Turkish National Science Foundation).

Mert İnanoğlu is a 2011 graduate of Manufacturing Systems Engineering Program at Sabancı University. His specializations include strategic management and statistical data analysis. He is a production planning engineer for a company that manufactures earthmoving and industrial machines.

Hadi Kandjani is a researcher and lecturer in the Centre for Enterprise Architecture Research and Management (CEARM) at Griffith University. He completed his Bachelor degree in Management Science and received his Masters degree in Information Technology Management specializing on Information Resources Management from Allameh Tabatabaee University. He has worked as a system designer and an enterprise architect for several years in industry. During his PhD in Enterprise Architecture at Griffith University with Peter Bernus, he introduced and published in the new field of *Enterprise Architecture Cybernetics* aiming at extending the theory and application of Enterprise Architecture in the design, creation, and management of enterprises as complex systems, with the intention to harmonize, formalize, synthesize, and systematize results of multiple disciplines. His research interests are: Enterprise Architecture Frameworks and Standards; Enterprise Architecture Practice, Governance, Management and Interoperability; Enterprise Modeling; Complex Systems Engineering; Systems Thinking and Cybernetics; Strategic Management and Strategic Thinking; Virtual enterprises and Enterprise Networks; and Engineering Self-evolving Systems.

Nihat Kasap has been serving as an assistant professor at Sabancı University, Istanbul, Turkey, following his Ph.D. from Warrington College of Business Administration at University of Florida, Gainesville, FL, USA, in 2004. His research areas include telecommunication pricing and QoS strategies, mobile government, data mining, heuristics, and optimization.

Raghuraman Krishnamurthy is a Chief Architect in Cognizant's Life Sciences Business Unit's Technology Consulting Group. His current interest areas include enterprise architectures, innovation, mobile applications and big data. He has worked with several major pharmaceuticals in envisioning and leading transformational initiatives. He has presented papers at conferences and was named a senior member of the prestigious Association of Computing Machinery (ACM). He enjoys solving complex business technical challenges and is an advocate of systems thinking. He likes to spend time with academia in sharing knowledge and learning. He was invited as a guest lecturer in the Indian Institute of Technology, Chennai. Raghuraman Krishnamurthy holds a master's degree from the Indian Institute of Technology, Mumbai, and is a TOGAF-certified enterprise architect.

James Lapalme is an assistant professor of software and IT engineering at l'École de Technologie Supérieure (ETS) in Montréal, Canada. He is also an enterprise architecture consultant. His major areas of interest are enterprise architecture and the design of sustainable and innovative organisations that offer quality of work life. Dr. Lapalme holds a PhD in computer science from l'Université de Montréal.

Haiping Luo is the Chief Enterprise Architect at International Trade Administration (ITA), US Department of Commerce. Before joining ITA in 2008, Ms. Luo was a senior data and enterprise architect at the Department of Veterans Affairs and Government Printing Office. Ms. Luo founded the Washington DC Metro Area Chapter, Association of Enterprise Architects, and led its activities for over seven years. Ms. Luo also initiated the International Standards Committee for Enterprise Architecture in the Association of Enterprise Architects and serves as its first chairperson. Ms. Luo obtained her Ph.D on agriculture economics from the University of Kentucky, USA, and had over 17 years of economic policy research experience for various government agencies and research institutes. Ms. Luo has over 25 years of computer programming and application development experience in a wide range of research, business, and healthcare contexts and has certificates on enterprise architecture, project management, and information system security.

Edward Newman leads the Enterprise Architecture (EA) Certificate Program in the iCollege at the National Defense University. Prior to the University position, as a practitioner, Professor Newman has over 20 years in consulting experience primarily focused on USA federal government, both defense and civilian and is experienced in a variety of EA methodologies such as EAP, ISP, FSAM, TOGAF, Federated EA, as well as EA governance. In supporting large federal organizations is where the federated EA approach was developed as traditional EA methodologies demonstrated limitations. His research interests are in enterprise architecture, ICT Governance and Strategy, and supporting analytics.

Henderik A. Proper, Erik to friends, is a senior research manager at the Public Research Centre - Henri Tudor in Luxembourg. He also holds a chair in Information Systems at the Radboud University Nijmegen. Erik currently leads the Enterprise Engineering research team involving researchers from these two institutions. His Luxembourg based team works on three large FNR (Luxembourgish research funding agency) funded research projects. Erik is driven by the desire to create theories that work. Therefore, he has always mixed his work in academia with work in industry, by working for consultancy firms. He co-authored two books on enterprise architecture, and provided substantial contributions to two other books about this topic. Erik is one of the co-initiators of the development of the ArchiMate language for Enterprise Architecture. He is also an editor in chief of a book series on Enterprise Engineering, published by Springer.

Marc Rabaey was a senior officer in the Belgian Ministry of Defense (MOD) where he fulfilled different functions: IT-manager Medical Service, IT-procurement manager Medical Service, System Manager of the Assistant Chief of Staff Evaluation, System Manager Education of MOD, and Technical Director Royal Military Academy. His main projects were the migration of the applications of the Belgian Medical Service from Mainframe to Client/Server architecture, the implementation of an imaging, workflow and document management in the Medical Administration and the conceptualization of the information system of Evaluation and Education of MOD. He is now Business IT consultant in

Open-Raxit. He holds the degrees of Commercial Engineer (IT) and Master in Social and Military Science. He has a PhD Applied Economics in progress at the University of Hasselt, Belgium. The main subject is the Complex Adaptive Systems Thinking approach to investment of IT, more specifically in the domain of Cloud Computing.

Christian M. Schweda is head of Enterprise Architecture (EA) Research at iteratec GmbH, Munich. He received his diploma in Computer Science and a Ph.D. in Computer Science from Technische Universität München. Christian continues his practice-driven research within the field of EA management at the IT consulting company, iteratec. A main topic of his research is the design and evolution of organization-specific EA meta-models, which address the concerns of the EA management stakeholders. Findings of his research have been presented at international conferences like the ICIS and ECIS—and practice-oriented—for example, The Open Group Conference.

Torben Tambo is M.Sc., GDBA and associate professor at AU Herning, Aarhus University, where he is programme coordinator for M.Sc. in Technology-based Business Development. Previous to this, he served 17 years in IT, management and consultant roles within manufacturing and trading companies. Research interests include information systems, enterprise architecture, retailing, and supply-chain management. Torben has previously published with *International Public Policy Review, Journal of Economic Dynamics and Control, Journal of Enterprise Architecture,* and contributed to several books published by IGI Global.

Paul R. Taylor is an enterprise architect and business systems consultant based in Melbourne, Australia. He has over twenty years' experience in a variety of industry roles, including architect, project manager, software engineer, and writer for Deloitte, Logica, Unisys, HP, Simsion Bowles, and Agentis. He has tackled many complex system design challenges and understands the elements of successful systems design in business contexts. It is from this base of experience that he writes on the behavior of business systems thinkers and designers. He has published over 30 papers on information system design and is interested in documenting system design ethnographies, case studies, and the intersection of business system design and other categories of design theory. Paul holds honours and master's degrees in computer science and a Ph.D. in information systems design from Monash University.

Selin Tokman is a 2011 graduate of Manufacturing Systems Engineering Program at Sabancı University. She currently studies MBA at Golden Gate University, San Francisco, USA. Her specializations include strategic management, statistical data analysis and digital marketing.

Rahul Tongia is a scholar, researcher, and advisor in areas of technology and policy, and was recently Principal Research Scientist/Program Director, CSTEP (Center for Study of Science, Technology, and Policy [CSTEP], a Bangalore-based not-for-profit research center, of which he was a co-founder). He is Technical Advisor, India Smart Grid Task Force, and led CSTEP efforts as Advisor & Knowledge

Partner, India Smart Grid Forum, both of which he was instrumental in setting up. His areas of research are broad and interdisciplinary, spanning technology and policy, with domain expertise in energy/power and IT/telecom. He has been a faculty member at Carnegie Mellon University for a dozen years with appointments in the Dept. of Engineering & Public Policy and the School of Computer Science (going on leave in 2009 to come to India). In addition to extensive work in the ICT domain, including ICT for human development, and the digital divide (having been Vice-Chair of the UN ICT Task Force Working Group on Low-Cost Connectivity Access), his energy work has spanned seminal studies on India's nuclear power program, importing natural gas, and on power pricing, and his current area of focus is on Smart Grids, harnessing ICT to improve the power grid. He was on the Technology Advisory Board for Southern California Edison's project on advanced metering ("Smart Connect"). At CSTEP, he has worked on a major report on IT for the Power Sector for the Min. of Power (2008), and has advised state power utilities, the state government, and the Ministry of Power on IT roadmaps and smart grid deployments, including pioneering smart grid demo. He and his colleagues have also worked on a number of Smart Grid roadmaps and pilot projects in India. Dr. Tongia has a Ph.D. in Engineering & Public Policy from Carnegie Mellon University and a Sc.B. in Electrical Engineering from Brown University.

Roberto Villarreal has over 25 years of professional experience in development policy making, implementation, and reform. He has served in the departments of the economy, finance, and social development, and the executive office of the President, as in inter-departmental commissions and state-owned enterprises in the government of Mexico, where he has been involved in poverty alleviation, social protection, gender equality, vulnerable populations, housing, urban and rural development, regional planning, infrastructure, public investment, competitiveness, technology, intellectual property, policy coordination, public administration, and public governance. He has also worked in the Organization for Economic Cooperation and Development (OECD) and the United Nations Department of Economic and Social Affairs (UNDESA). He holds a doctorate in economics from the Massachusetts Institute of Technology (MIT), master studies in economics at El Colegio de México (COLMEX), and a college degree in industrial and systems engineering from the Instituto Tecnológico y de Estudios Superiores de Monterrey (ITESM).

Roel Wagter is a management consultant, Partner at PMtD, and Ph.D. student at Radboud University Nijmegen in the field of Enterprise Architecture. He has held numerous managerial positions in which he gained more than thirty years of experience in the field of business and IT alignment. This experience is the foundation for his ideas on enterprise architecture. He is the founder of the internationally recognised method Dya® (Dynamic Enterprise Architecture). In early 2006, he both initiated and became responsible for the innovation programme "General Enterprise Architecting" (GEA). Within the scope of this innovation programme he founded an open innovation alliance. Twenty large organisations in the field of government institutions, private enterprises and the science community take part in this alliance. In the period 2001 until present, he published three books, eight white papers, seven industrial papers, and seven scientific papers in this field.

Lian Wen (Larry) is a lecturer in the School of ICT in Griffith University. He completed a Bachelor degree in Mathematics from Peking University and then a Master degree in EE from Chinese Academy of Space Technology. Afterward, he has worked as a software engineering and a project manager for different IT companies. He received his PhD in software engineering in 2007 from Griffith University, and then worked as a research fellow in the Software Quality Institute, Griffith University. His research interest includes: Software Engineering (in particular, software change and behavior engineering), Complex Systems, Scale-Free Networks, Enterprise Architecture, and logic programming.

Dirk Witte is currently working as a Principal Business Consultant at CGI and experienced in solving business issues in an integral manner and hence improving the quality of decision-making. His academic interest is focused on the reciprocal relationship between organizational structures and its corresponding performance to find effective patterns for intervention. These patterns are subsequently used in his practice as a management consultant. For the past six years, Dirk has explored the philosophy of solving business issues by analyzing and applying the causal relationships between statements that make up the directional framework of an organization. In addition, Dirk tries to explain the unfolding manifestation of organisations from the angle of complexity theory.

Index